Wang Kai

INFOGRAPHIC DESIGN IN MEDIA

images
Publishing

INTRODUCTION

Today's era has been labelled "Big Data Times". This, in a broad sense, is massive amounts of data with a wide range and number well beyond peoples' imagination. However, now this concept is now called "mass data".

The data here have not been the simple traditional digit concept, and they have already evolved into the full sample information repository of the large scale, type of variety, splitting update rate. Their explosive growth has dramatic changed era of our life and work. All transactions of the actual world can be quantified and data-mated, and what the large data collection contains has heightened necessarily to use only a new technology system to extract, manage, analyze, dispose and apply. Therefore, the data infographic has to become a necessary part that is taken seriously by the public, along with the carrier of visual information that is just the media, and the infographic world emerged as the times required, innovation, advertisement presentation of this new times media is responsible for the transmission of information, monitoring of environment, and meanwhile attempts to enhance the aesthetic standards of the whole society. In all, the creative and informative method to convey information in this new era has made key contribution to how the global media react to the transformation happened in the times which characterizes mass data and nurtures modern people.

Contemporary designers have realized the challenge. They begin to constantly update their concept and adapt the infographic and big data era media development to satisfying the requirement of global readers after they have adapted to the transmission of the complicated information in simple manner of graph or chart. Information graphics of media is a special subject which is not only a well-designed infographic chart but also quickly deliver the information by using vision stimuli for the purpose that the reader simultaneously is corresponded with the social status of media and establishes a brand image.

These requirements have far exceeded initial business data statistics, and present in the company annual report, business or sales and are display methods frequently used for the article of magazine or newspaper; it also mixes which people to read the media of information to who wants to obtain double expectation of rational sense and perceptual sense. It must not only satisfy with people's focus on key current events, hot spots or personal interests in theme of contents and concepts but also coordinate with main body of this information in the text by the readability factor of words and pictures. Contemporarily it also accords with media of self-brand and professional characteristics and ingeniously welds the art and technology into media, which brings design trends new thoughts and creative pattern into.

CONTENTS

A Information, Data - Infographic Era in Transformation

Data is an extremely special social consciousness, which is seen as one part of modern science and is the infographic reflection of new media times to objective information and regular pattern. As a kind of knowledge form it is always in the process of physical form of ongoing transformation. Contemporary it is a kind of culture, moreover is a special enormous physical strength and become by conversion into productivity, which happen the whole society revolutionary changes. The data of infographic may make the abstract or boring concept and information satisfy with the requirements of effective transmission content and simultaneously reach the formal aesthetic by the means of art and design, which also not only contemporary gains more attention from reader but only is settled to get real understanding. Therefore to master the data visual representation is fully prepared for display methods of media visualization.

Data infographic design contains elements of rational and perceptual sense of these two categories of design. Rational sense includes font, the dotted line, drafting, columns and etc, in where the font is the most important visual element. Therefore the individuality and creative ideas of different media can be felt from font reading factor and the aspect of specific use; and perceptual sense includes graphics, color, spatial layout and etc, which is grasped by relying on designer' acuity for the emotion and in which the graphical and picture selection is the most important element of perceptual visual sense, also the core part of whole newspaper pages. Color is "expression language" of newspaper and is visual media design elements of reflection of the media inner spirit; blank is flavoring agents in space, just right blank is the key means of compelling and enhancing the brand effect.

For example Figure 1-1 and Figure 1-2, this series of chart is about discussion of surrogacy in India. When the researchers launch the first round of discussion in the way of survey on internet they find the great controversy on this subject. Thus the designer uses a unique Indian heavily saturated green and red rose color on behalf of the women and designer himself neutral attitude towards this event; the red rose cover designs portfolio made together with round, triangular, square or prismatic to reflect traditional geometric pattern of Islamic culture in India, they are not only supporting the green lines in chart but also expressing the author's love for Indian beauty; the author also considers a lot on designing graphic of dark green shading, and he does not adopt garish colors but only a classic white with points, lines, polygons of varieties of graphic design elements and attempts to calmly, rationally and profoundly discuss the theme, striving reader not to generate it biased understanding and as it were racking minds.

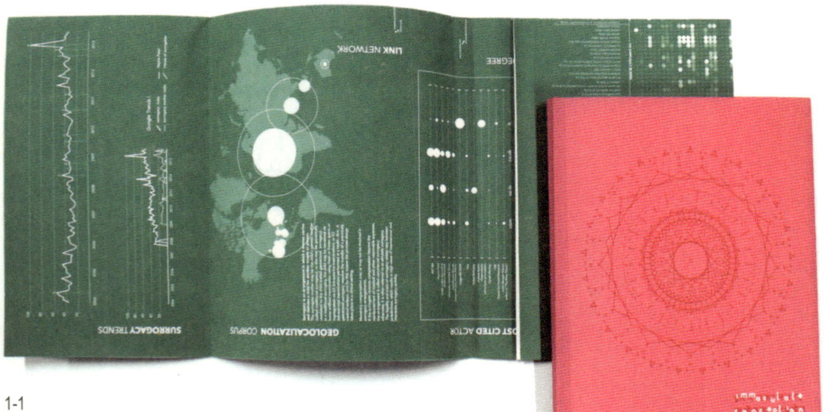

1-1

The perfect combination of data and design elements is the two important elements of media reacting information and the variety of changes between them can clearly see the movement difference and status of society to help eliminate uncertainty on which society groups understand some scene. In the process of creation, sometimes, the choice of colors can even produce some special visual effects and achieve certain goals. For example this chart shows the comparison with LED lamps and conventional bulbs. As Figure 2 the author chooses the blue series to describe all information of LED lamps to express that the people select LED lamps as the rational consumer attitudes. Contemporary, when the specific data is compared the gray-purple is represented the ordinary lamp life which make us associated directly with the dark moments of incandescent ultimately scrapped before, and a bright red is selected to represent the brightness of bulbs makes reader to consider the doubts whether a high level brightness is necessary or not, also the gray-orange has been used to represent common energy-saving lamps, showing moderate brightness but power consumption being still high, even it is better choice but still a gap on concept where it compared with LED. The author also attempts to use the cute little icons in the page and dashed boxed in the table to make the original boring preaching become a slightly fresh visual and graphic soft text so that the viewers in a relaxed state mind to gradually understand the advantage of LED and shakes their sense of dependence on the traditional bulbs, also produces gracious feel for the LED.

1. Infographic, Wisdom Gene of Media World

It is 5 to 6 years ago, the major methods of media for conveying data information in beautiful ways relies on plug-speak, simply speaking which converts the text message into image symbols, to guide people attention and consideration for information by means of visualization. This kind of visual information

1-2

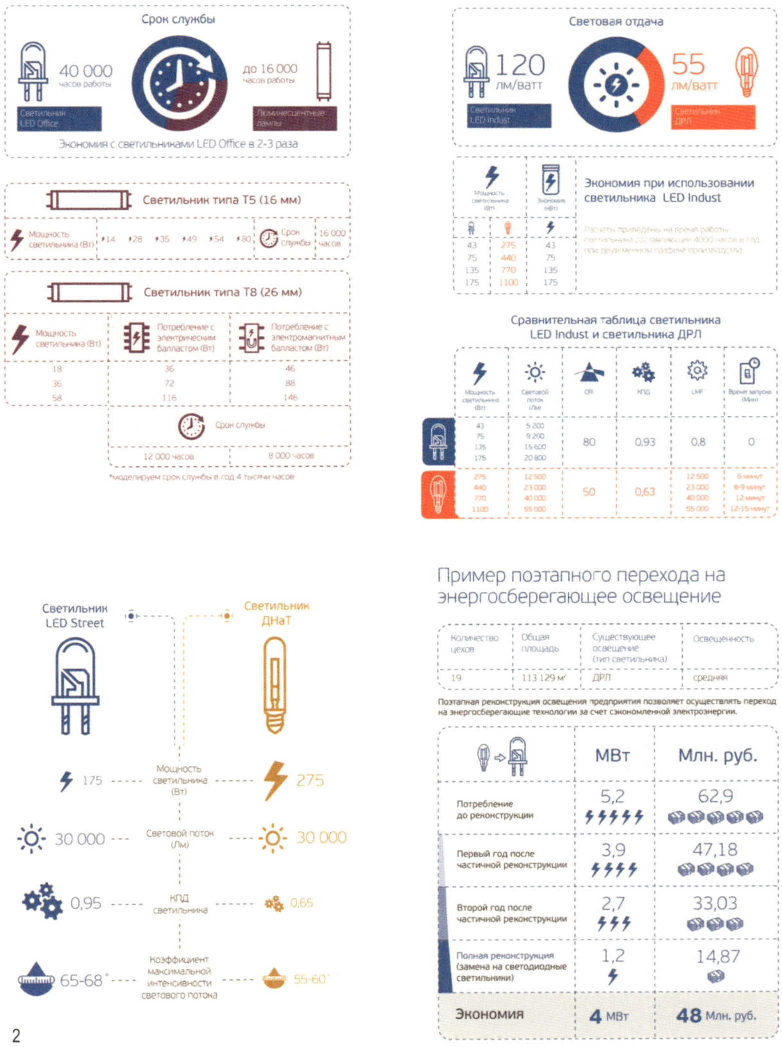

2

3

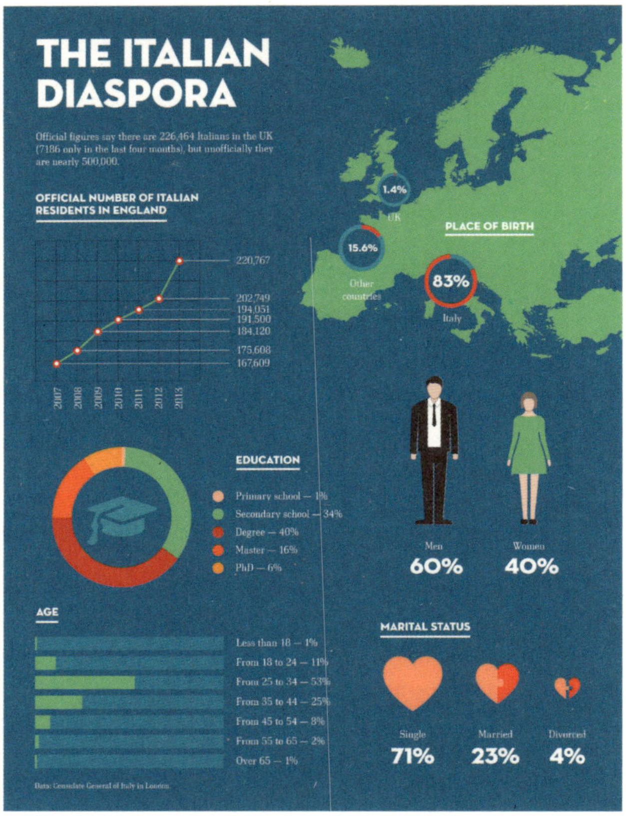

4

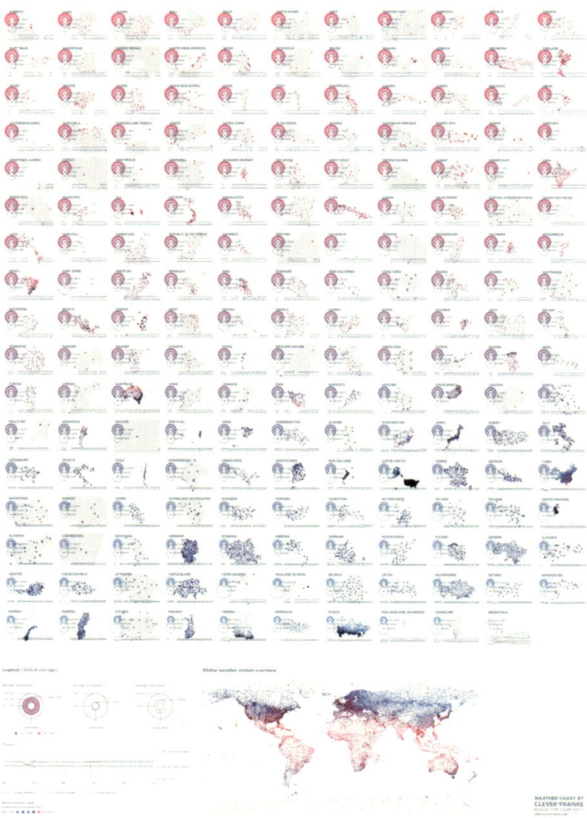

processing approach surly helps concentrate the main point and express the elements of core information. When the big data era abruptly arrives and large amounts of data spews out dazzles people, even rapid response can not be done in time, so this infographic way has been impossible to satisfy with the requirements of spread, and media has to transform the think way to analysis, processing with new technology approach and demonstrate the infographic works complies with times demands.

In fact the media has successfully applied infographic design to quantity of data for long time. For example Figure 3 shown, this is a report about the distribution of Italian population living in the UK. According to the old conventional methods to do the statistical data of these trivial amounts is very time-consuming. However, in today's big data, media can quickly do the statistic and analyze of all the data directly through bank accounts and capital flows and draw the general conclusion. At this moment we have to admit that the big data era media infographic development is not only facing the technical problems but also facing the problem of the reconstruction strategy and it will have a profound impact on the future of media ecology and development pattern.

In the traditional media era the media are largely fragmented whose survival mainly repends on advertisement and market competition with homogeneous media so there is not enough innovation contents and simple profit models. The arrival of the big data era has challenged the organizational and operational capacity of media, in the environment of competitive critical analysis and management capabilities and how to have the best decisions and insights on topics selection infers the operation conditions, in which the key point is to integrate traditional business data with new type data, comprehensive analysis of the customer to further improve the user experience and sales. And all the fundamental starting, the capacity of analysis and management on critical data depends on the understanding of big data and how big the data model mastered. Only at the beginning to collect the full sample data, contemporary using the mathematical algorithm to analyze and model, accumulation of information and integration of data make the final data more targeted, statistical and analysis of the underlying relations by which media can display certain status at last or predict the probability of an even occurring more accurate and more convincing. For example Figure 4, it is a ranked list of annual average temperature of counties around world in 1962-2012. According to the temperature level designer gives each country a color value point and distributes all these points as per their geographic location in the global map. The effect of big data is straightforward and perfectly displayed in the final chart, shocking and convincing.

Another example Figure 5 describes travel. Designer use five full-editions in magazine to describe in detail the global various travelers of different target, patterns, destinations selection, habits differences and favorite activities varieties in the destination etc, which completely describes travelers of various options, numerous and eloquent. The designs couple with a slightly sweet and without losing individuality graphic illustration scene creates a humorous and relaxed atmosphere for reading so that the readers will unconsciously learn a lot of information.

Currently the media has been increasingly recognised that scientific, economic and social value implicates behind the big data and tries more applications to public business and social service to reflect its social care and awe. For example Figure 06 may see, the designer tries to use a drop of water i.e. the concept of one earth to promote people to pay more attention to the water issues in India, in which it specially describes storage capacity and demand capacity of water in Delhi and leads

5

6

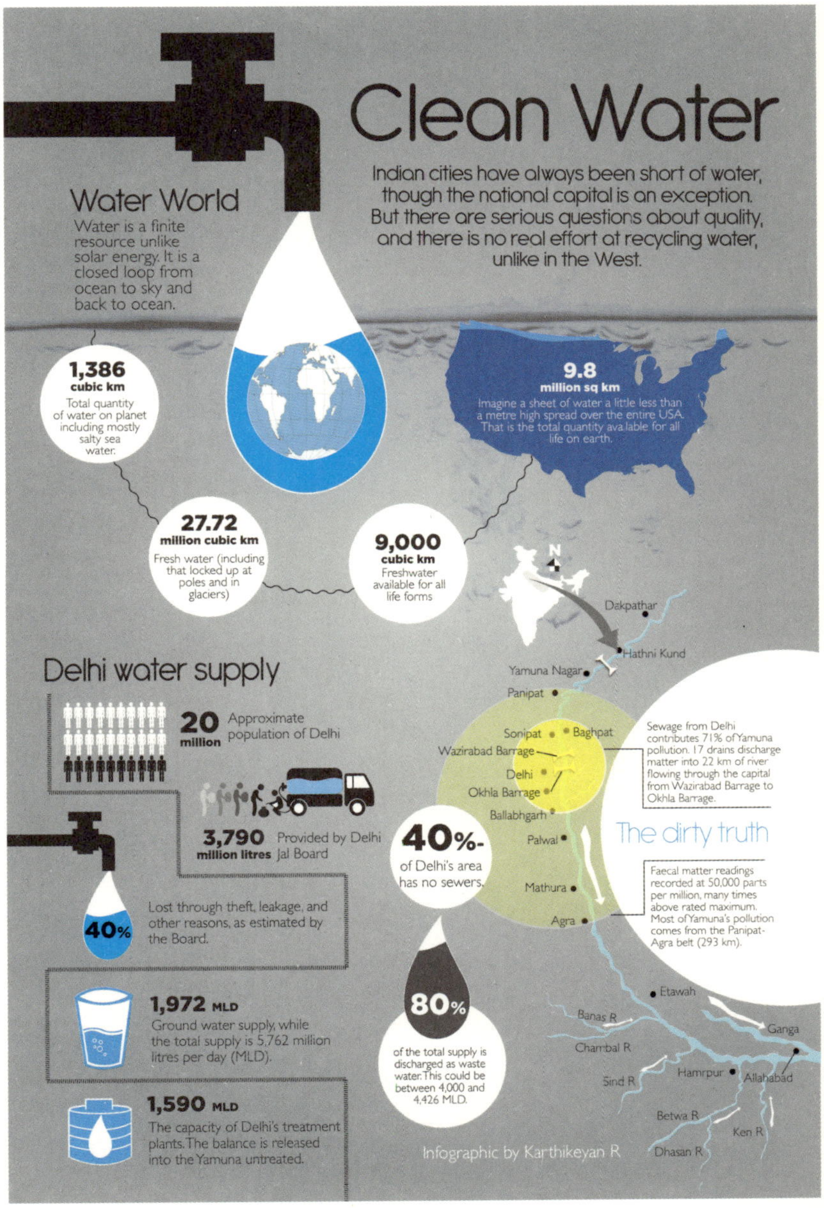

7-1

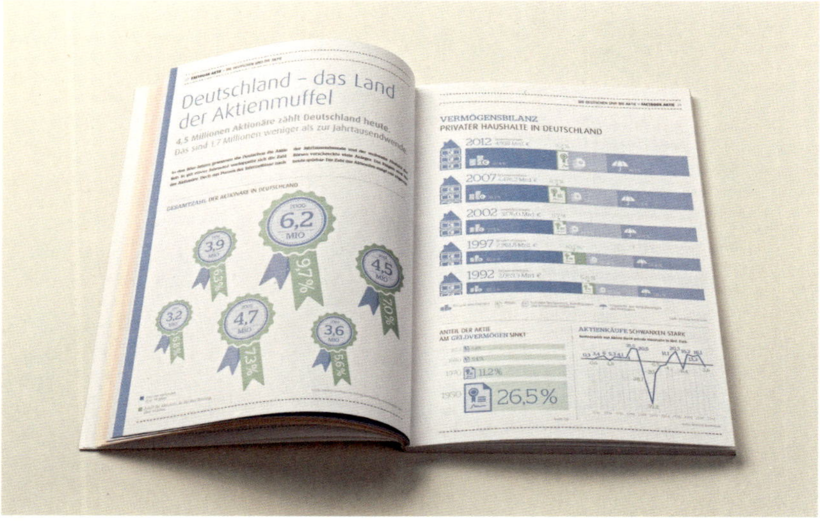

7-2

to the reason of water shortage. This data reflect completely the relations and status between energy users and environment to urge people to consider more sustainable development between society and public living environment. In Figure 7-1 and Figure 7-2 we find, this magazine sponsored by the bank cooperating much with research institutions forms some type of newspaper media of an independent and in-depth analysis of social financial environment. They mainly speak their own visual concentrates on many financial investment programs of German such as the stock market indices, investment strategy, stock equity culture etc and try to use visual expression of the usual and attractive approach to show the original complex and lengthy analysis report to make sure final data more affine and humane.

2. Media Convergence Era

The first time concept of "media convergence era" is presened by professor Rampur at the University of Massachusetts of Technology. It original means that a variety of media show the tendency of compound integrate. The media convergence not only a new kind of media form which includes public platform, blogs, Weibo and etc but also "in an unprecedented way, through the analysis of huge amounts of data obtain huge value products and services, or profound insight", make people conform to the trend in the era of big data, self-renewal in thoughts, ideas, and through the data processing and analysis within a reasonable time and space to capture, management, processing, and finishing. It is the key point to help information acquisition and decision makers to reach a new understanding of the target. In the era of big data the media show us a new kind of innovation ability that is the new concept of data analysis. So for the media workers we should pay attention to the data not to the data products. And focus on how to master them and let them become the force for revolution.

In media era background, the media function breaks through the traditional restrictions and has digital, mobile, Internet, interactive features base on the development of new media, the fusion of terminal equipment, innovation of multimedia technology, etc. At the same time people's life style also changed following the changes of the society, science and culture. As timeliness, information intensified fragmentation, audience share more information during information transmission. So infographic design is widely used in the financial media and seems all the problems have been a better solution, then it became popular in public.

Media convergence is an inevitable trend of new media development, and infographic design will no doubt become the core focus of its creation. In the background of the media convergence, the development of new media, integration of various mobile end terminal equipment, innovation and application of multimedia technology, the whole social environment of digital, mobile, and interactive features that allow people to have the new requirements about the timely and effective data and information. Meanwhile information has become more fragmented, interaction between readers is becoming stronger and these changes in the function of the media are breaking the traditional limitations. And it leads the future direction of the development of visual media, and has a tremendous impact on creation and dissemination.

The most obvious example for infographic design in media convergence era is able to adjust the format of responsive designed. As Figure 8-1 and Figure 8-2 series, from figure we can see in order to let public obtain uniform but various visual information by different media that the designer provides corresponding layout and graphic size for light box, posters, magazines, mobile phone platform and other applications of different media.

Figure 9 is a more complete and more representative example. This is a newspaper in 2020 send to KTG group from the designer in which describe the living environment and survival challenge in the future. Obviously, the propaganda media make themselves in the new media era ahead, it directly launchesmore than newspapers, magazines, PAD, mobile phone platform and media information to release media, make its brand directly under the environment of weave a more complete

8-1

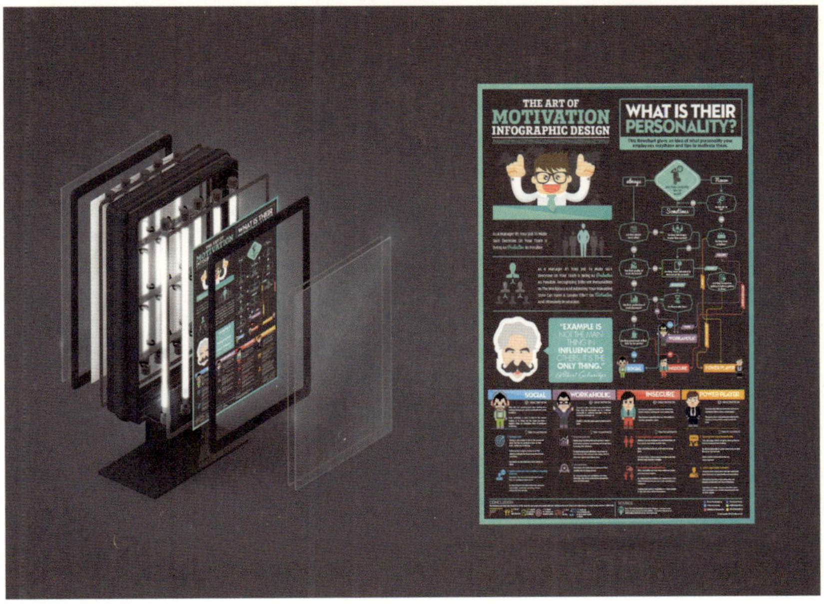

8-2

9

information to the public network in big data era , show their own professional and characteristic comprehensive and completely, and expect this design draft show its foresight mentality and make them comfortably in the leading status of this new era.

3. Revolution of Expression

The global visual practices prove that the new media era is changing the expression of everything in the media. First it uses chart instead of boring test to transmit information as people can get information much more quickly by chart than characters; Second, it develops the variety of media which mixes expression of multimedia in new media era, and satisfies the requirement of people who demands the transmissible method in the new media era. Finally, the most important thing is the interactions between it and the thinking way in big data era, making the visual focus on the aesthetic concept which abides by the law of human thinking again. Change the meaning of the traditional media (Information just need transmit quickly), try to use public visual way to provide more support to the traditional media transfer in order to make the resonance in public.

Figure 10-1 and Figure 10-2 is a magazine which researches the culture in Russia. We can see Matryoshka doll is the mainline of the figure. The designer puts the most important element such as: Red square culture, currency, traffic speed, population and sex structure, territory, language, national emblem, type of television signal in symmetric vector graphics accompany with the colour red and blue from national flag just in one proper layout. The graphical expression of core idea of the text content and the method of key words, to make it for the next long text bring a relaxed and enjoyable reading experience, and with the theme of traditional culture, make the readers feel the Russian contemporary art design of The Times, and it is a close connection between the markets, making people have a new understanding of contemporary culture to Russia.

From the era of reading to the era of view then to the media era; From costar to the full graphical layout, graphic concept has become more and more popular even as the protagonist in many big media's the important pages. Infographic readability, fast information transmission effectiveness, audience's feelings and favorite have gradually become the tendency that each media to keep their charm and mien in the whole media era

10-1

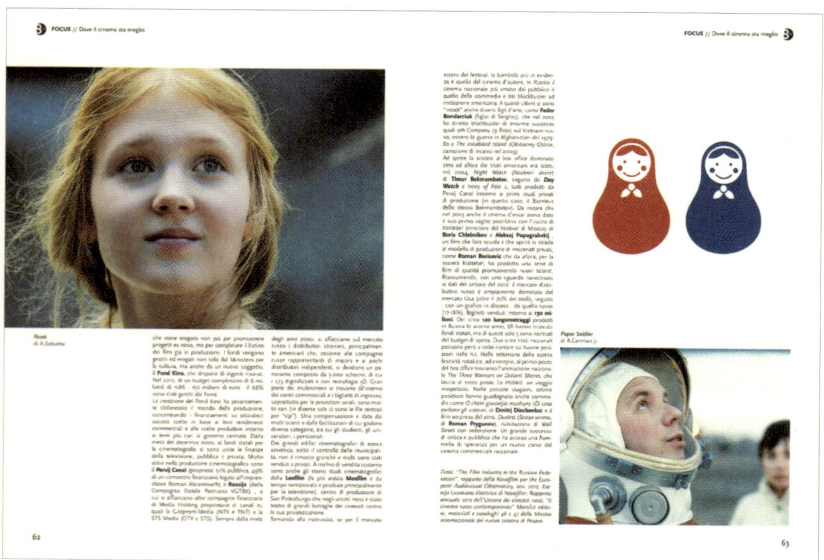

10-2

and become most important advantages to expand marketing opportunities. Each media keeps their specialty skill such as information figurization, news images to maintain their own location and position and effort to earn more market shares.

At figure 11, variation and integration involved with multiple formats, colours, and models show the following processes, such as core manipulation of military power, enactment and implementation of policies, allocation of budget, legal determination of unfair treatment, supervision of the court system and government hierarchy, normal approval of laws and regulations. Also, the visual graphics here demonstrates how to handle the deviation from normal procedure, to lobby the federal government to enact domestic or foreign policies, to nominate president candidates, to procure reliable information by expansion of sensitive resources, to understand the three elements in a balanced federal system, among others. As a result, the adoption of visual graphics with rule-like embodiment makes serious political issues, assertions, and social discussions, vivid and lively. At the meantime, the slightly gray style in colour is adopted to highlight the theme of the entire picture, which is serious but vital.

After compare these two infographic designs, we can see it clearly that in the era of big data, infographic is not a simple chart, but must be matched higher aesthetic and design standard, with advertising visual language and thinking concept improve the original visual ideas, from visuals, human care, advertising perspective to enhance the value and advertising perspective, highlight personality and characteristics of different media, and make effort to own much market share.

11

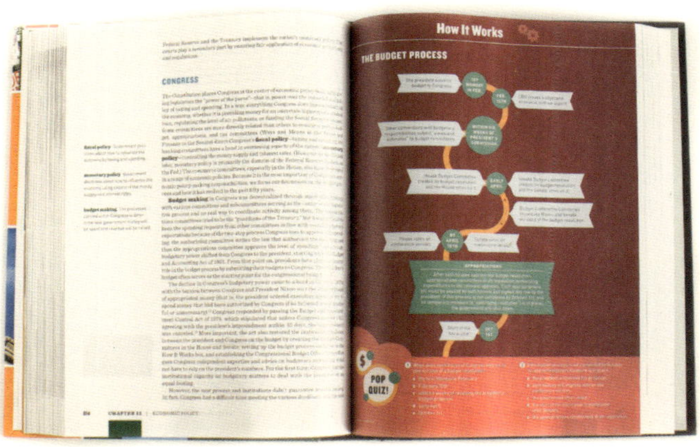

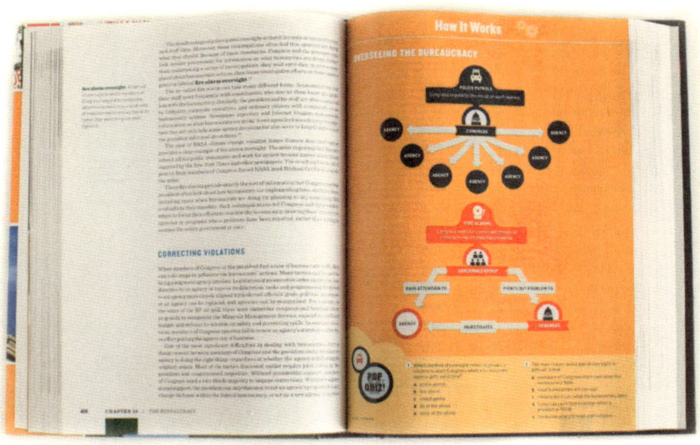

B Infographic in Media

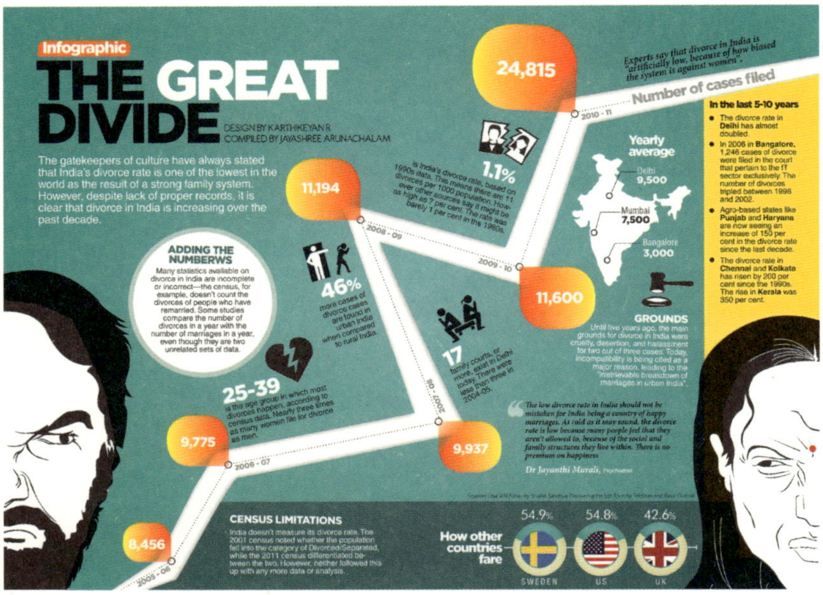

12

The particularity of the big data era is providing the tremendous development space for the accuracy and predictability of the information from media. Media need not to waste time to collect and analyze data, when the simulation data into a computer can read the digital information, data storage and processing becomes quite convenient and easy. If supported by the corresponding program, then need few months to complete data collection before can finish in just a few days. And what media professionals need to do is in mass issued news, clear its authenticity and value, and choose proper infographic language, to explore, research and display of the concept of an event or social all relevant information, and improve the readability of the work.

1. Visual of the Infographic

The creation and design of infographic is a kind of discipline which satisfies modern society development's require about diversification, multi-level and more framework, and it also conforms to the demands of the rapid pace of life of people. In the high-pressure social environment people often tend to be in a happy way and entertainment spirit to treat daily information without direct contact with the work. So in order to meet the demand of spiritual hierarchy the design of infographic should take emotional way. Just like human factors specialists and designers Patrick Jordan (Patrick Jordan) who had done design according to the institute said: The mainly emotional experience of people are the security, self-confidence, proud and excited, freedom and satisfaction, entertainment, nostalgia and so on. And these emotional experiences are corresponded to the functions of the product such as "characteristics, practical, aesthetic, reliable, convenient and fancy". There are also emotional characteristics in the expression of infographic information. Designers can make the information with these characteristics much more interesting and reliable. Let people easy to accept the color on the vision, exquisite by touch and all kinds of close breath smell to stimulate human senses, thereby the information will straight touch people's heart by emotion.

As Figure12 the outsiders always think the reason of low divorce rate in India is their family life-style. However the fact is that India prejudice against women is not eliminated, the official didn't record the the number of divorced women at the time of the census official statistics. But in the recently 5 to 10 years the divorce rate in New Delhi is doubled and the divorce events Qty in India are three times in 2010 than in 2005. In order to express the views of the author on this event and resonance the public, first, author uses the relatively gentle blue-green to show the positive attitude towards marriage, at the same time complementary with orange circle diagram and the existence of the giant screamed waveform curve to show the conflict and its dynamics that can not ignore; moreover the author also made a portrait of couple of glare male and female, intuitive show the marriage dissatisfaction with each other, witty and objectively shows the real social status.

2. Existence of Infographic

In the era of new media, we do not need to focus on the causal relationship between issues but need to find and use infographic language to show the correlation between such issues, and deduce the truth of the event as soon as possible base on the all sample data. Even if the relationship can't accurately informed why this issue happened, but it can also remind the public the issue is happening. The infographic expression of information, makes the media show their fair and neutral standpoint in the social environment. So all information can be found in the most simple way to convey the most logical inference, it makes the comprehensive understanding of social dynamics and the attention points more convenient. As Figure 13-1 and Figure 13-2, designer lists the data of the surgery quantity and its success rate related data, and show them as a graphs; then complementary with mixture of yellow and pink as color version, plus white text and lines, makes the public to look at this chart dispassionately, and understand its status in social development. Compare with its uncertainty and a variety of speculation in a few years ago this kind of expression is more intuitive and persuasive, and the information obtained is more completely.

3. Directionality of the Infographic

Yesterday we were not in big data era when we creat infographic chart entirely depend on the traditional sample design sampling survey in the scientific, representativeness, the validity of the analysis, etc, which made us have to repeatedly consideration the sampling standard, try to quantitative data precisely in infographic expression. In big data era of new media, we faced amounts of data, by controlling the resources we can do multi-dimensional analysis

13-1

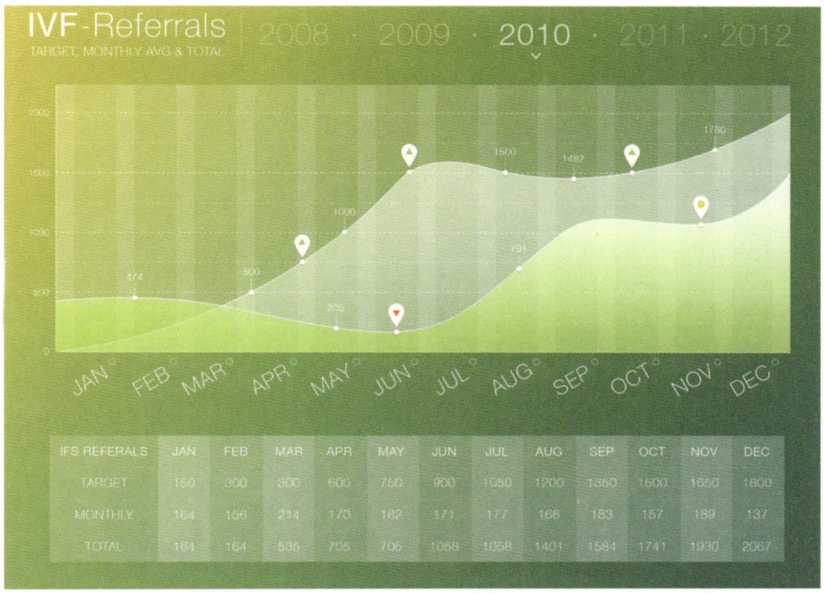

13-2

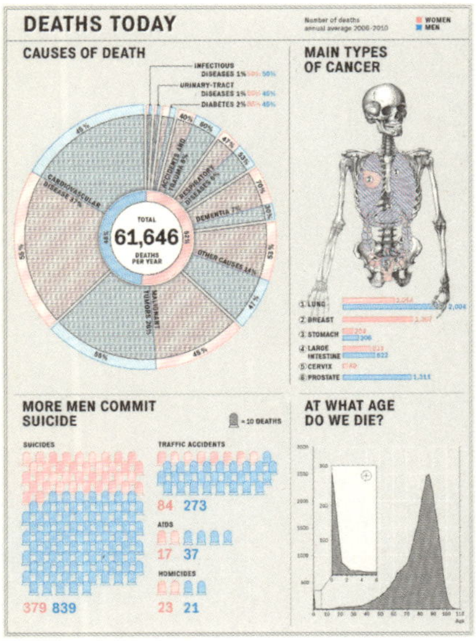

14

15

depend on our willingness to show "all" data related to our goals. Infographic analysis may cause more macro significance base on the clear expression of the big data direction. As Figure14, this chart shows the modern manner of death in Swiss. It compares the data of 1910 with 2010 by chart which includes the children birth rate, average life expectancy in the elderly population, population of death due to infection. And the main types death such as cancer, suicide, etc. To expresses neutral attitude of the designer by multilayer gray and blue & pink single line in this chart. In Figure15 it shows the present situation of the Indian wedding completely. Designer uses the brick red to represent the festival and the traditional Indian culture, the cute doll with tradition wedding dress in the middle to represent bride and groom. Then Using white roundness as backdrop and describe the related events in concise diagram according to which the readers have a comprehensive understanding about "the cost of the wedding is getting more expensive, the basic expenses may cost 1/5 of the wealth in people's life", increase the reliability base on the integrity analysis to the data.

C The Infographic Brings Media Variation

1. The News More "Cute"

The infographic has undoubtedly become a part of our lives. When people's requirements on basic consultant are satisfied, the requirement of user experience on the feelings such as all the feelings prior to, during and afterwards reading or using a infographic works / products including physical, psychological reactions, behavior comfort, emotion accordance degree and every aspect of requirements to become media designer have to currently challenge problems. Jobs said that the success or failure depends on the user experience. No matter how complex the information or product is the user experience of infographic design need to solve out two core contents, one of which to satisfy with people's heart talks i.e. the emotional communication, the other of which is the media of display technology that gets a breakthrough to continuously improving contents so as to reach the media infographic to a new height.

Figure 16 the author first use wood veins as a background of infographic chart which renders a true and natural ambience for the whole works and second use a variety of graphics related wine to straightly describe the various drinking culture of Hungary including their favorite brands, drinking amount, drinking ways, wine-producing districts, etc. contemporary the yellow, orange and red being adopted for stimulating appetite, according to which people read and get the intuitive, cordial and warm, then the consumer desires happens.

Figure 17 is a Middle East Economic Weekly. The design idea of publication layout is to use visual language to express the theme of the connotation of the article and keep reading more fluid. Therefore the adoption of graphics or pattern is the characteristic of expressing core concepts, for example using the graphics in the layout designer straightly describes the core concepts with an extremely exaggerated close-up scene, naked saying money, treasure and stock market ups-downs, its straightforward and bold seem to mark the reader booster to stimulate them to read further and to improve the magazine sale targets.

17

2. The Emotion Requirements with Satisfaction

"Data news" is key change that media deal with the big data era in which the infographic ways that converts these data into a graphics are the fundamental core technology. The modern people who live in vortex of information read everyday, pass a lot of dazzling information and constantly mechanically copy them again and gain. So repeatedly people naturally generate anxiety and even antipathy to an excessive amount of information, while the interesting, strange, concise, smart visual language improves people's psychological predicament, and generates them the trust and closeness feelings. Therefore what designers do is to interpret and analyze a large amount of data, further explore and completely grasp the complex layered relationship between the data and the society, to attempt the more vivid media presentation forms and means as much as possible, not necessary to extremely worry about the audience's acceptance. The reader of this generation growing up along with the internet is always full of expectation and curiosity with the fresh and unknown, the user experience in their hearts is what themselves do emotional reaction on things is the objective reality they concerned most. They never neglect the mind that share to be respected and loved, and put other spiritual requirements on the top position.

Hiring employees is a headache for all companies. As a senior professional job-hunter company uses this set of brochures, as Figure 18 breaks the conventional way of narrative graphics design to deal the entire human resource atmosphere with tree-dimensional and cartoon gamification ways and also to display this set of system complex and changeable with virtual communities of visual language, reader knows that the professional headhunter company serves for this item of overall situations understanding from the by-side. The saturated rose color is supplemented emphasis that they hold optimism, positive and

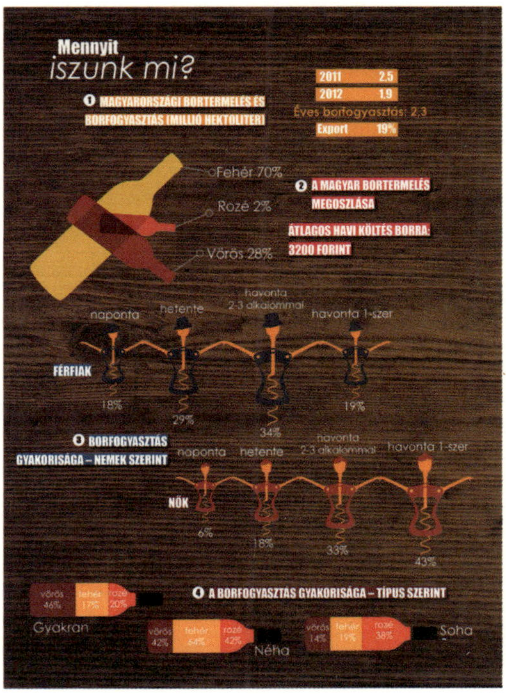

16

18

19-1

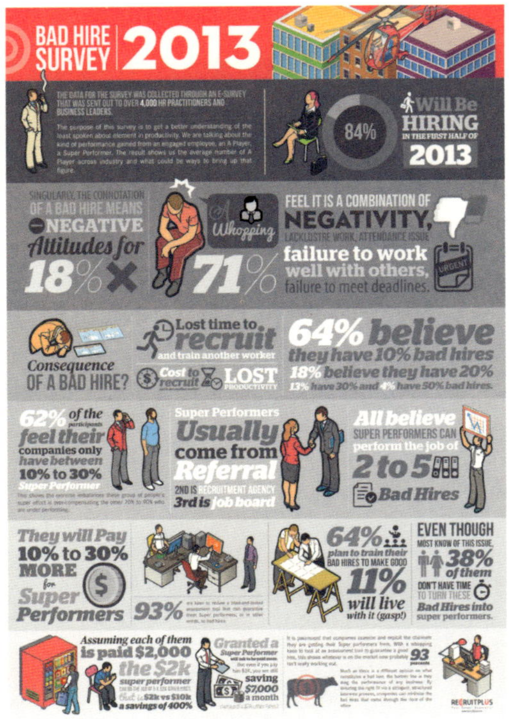

19-2

"process from the big to small" assist text "the entire process from problem raised to resolve", which cause the reader's mind change from dignified to easier along with the variety of the colour tone and ultimately come to the conclusion that the company is extremely professional and credible.

profession spirit.

Figure 19-1 and Figure 19-2, headhunter company designs a chart for describing the "wrong employment result investigation", this design continues the concepts of gamification and scenification, and make patchwork arrangement, streamlined text and conceptualization digital particularly lists all the unqualified employees' shortcomings and accordingly, the various effects to the enterprise, which not only gives the warnings to the enterprise but also passes on the professional and responsible manner. That selection of the color and size of the text work in designing this chart appears a degree of relaxation. Designers select the main color of gray to cover the entire menu, then the red rose color is adopted on the title echoing with the company's main color, and the gray "gradient from deep to shallow" and words

3. Innovations on Carrier Technology

As the cost of infographic tools and methods continue to lower more and more data including text, position, contents of infographic. The new technology allows the possibility of data analysis and transformation applying, coupled with application of multimedia methods, according to which interactive infographic has gradually become one of the new media channels for information dissemination. Specially the arrival of 4G times promotes the traditional media to really express its core assets—value of data, they attempts more and more to launch the "cloud" technology so that readers can realize original high-definition presentation of traditional paper medium in computer, mobile client, tablet PCs with touch screen and other outdoor terminals to provide the watchable, listenable, applicable and various kind of information and advertisements in which infographic is the representative of all the visual forms. The emergence of new technology materials such as the glass feasible bent 45 degrees, or 90% transparency maintained, low resistance, high bending, high corrosion, flexibility of "Nano-silver ink printed transparent conductive thin film" supplies the infographic more exhibition possibility. The development of mobile new media and technology blur the boundaries of traditional media and internet media, and the traditional printing equipment and materials also began a new round of reshuffle in the process of development of infographic so infographic design has occupied the integrated multi-service platform which is created by what the media cross-border merge, the requirement in line with which has become the inevitable choice of various media.

Using a mobile phone to deal with the financial management and query is that the bank must do the application development for satisfying the mobile media requirements of customers, and is the inevitable tendency of digital age. Therefore this launch of two types of phones and tablet applications as Figure 20 and Figure 21, shows the attitude of banks adapting to the infographic trend, and the final successful communication between the designer and bank. Financial management and control, specially application loans from the banks is what people want to do but it is too cumbersome and complicated, the mail list bank always gives swell and dizzy people so designer uses more relaxed and concise geometric shapes in Figure 20, straightforward and clear bold, gentle blue, and slightly three-dimensional effects, tries to create a more comfortable, natural and rather than a strong sense of design reading environment; and use the interface of clear layout and segmentation not only to understand reader to quickly understand the process and methods of loan but also to improve this loan of embarrassing things into natural and amiable. And another bank APP, Fugure 21 more heavier rose color, dark blue, clear solid body graphics are adopted to make concise of long-winded exaggerated

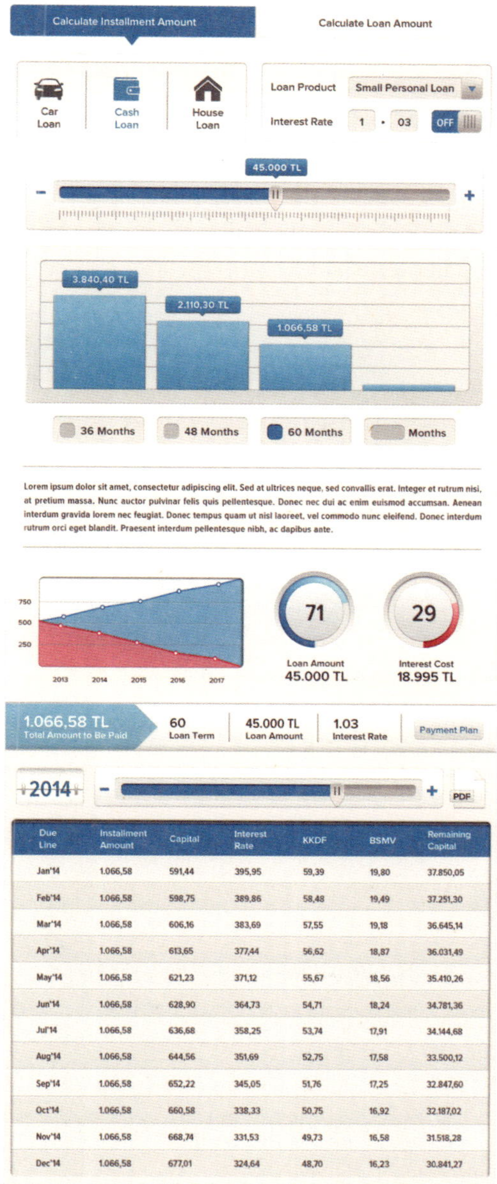

20

21

financial statement to present in front of customers, which help customer remember and is easy for bank to manage and operate under work.

Figure 22-1 and Figure 22-2, it is the website of using the infographic language to display and specializing in statistical analysis of data. Their core research is to identify the key words of all the comments about an institution on the internet, to show and connect these words with dots and lines and then objectively analyzes with visual language the recognition and likeability of these institutions on the internet of this wide open platform. The designer makes the interface minimalist and full of spirituality. A huge blank shape is more prominent and also is easier for the requirements of varieties of media responsiveness layout. This is a more specific infographic design and leaves readers more impression.

22-1

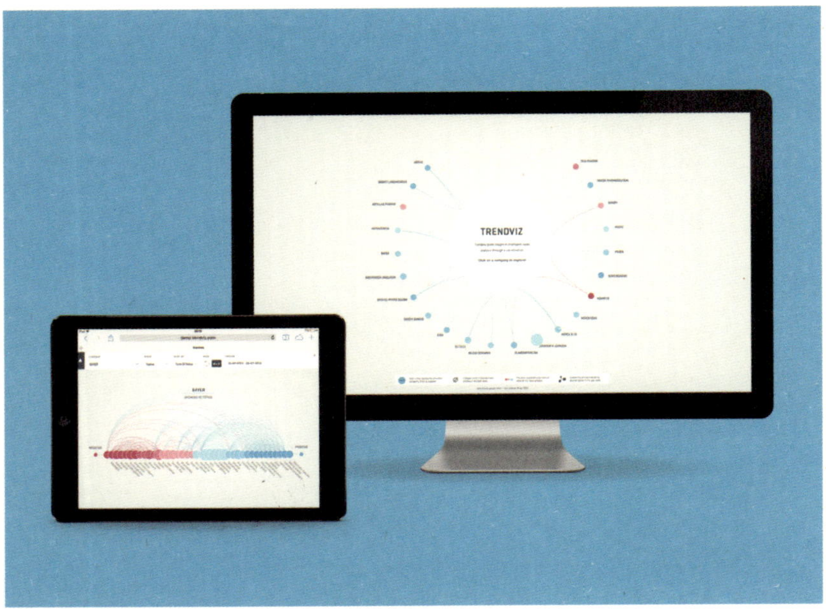

22-2

4. The Story More Splendid

The effective infographic solution is the core principles of expressing accurately media information and can express completely the main idea of media information with innovative forms i.e. when and where and what happened is said with the best storytelling method, accurately understanding and appropriate visual representation to be refined and restructured, also the accurate, innovative and aesthetic of these three elements to be considered and reaches people pleasing visual effect.

In the media the story is the content, infographic is form and emotion is the main line. The form and content should be understood as a symbiotic whole and emotion is the original starting of media reflecting the human care in the context of information visualization. In the other words the content and form does not exist clear boundaries, both toward working together for the purposes of information communication, but emotion, is the invariant axis between information and them. If "Emotion" can not be accompanied by the "Form" to generate information as "Easy to perceive" of visual elements then how different between the expression & existence of information and other information are. Data is gotten through scientific experiments, testing and statistics. Compared with data, number is only an abstract symbol, which also can not be divorced from this fundamental concept in the media. Otherwise, the rhetoric can become the boring or strange things concrete, vivid and easy to get. Therefore, when we use rhetoric to describe the data, it will be able to play the effect of "abstract being concrete, profound being plain", which interests readers in reading and even extends the memory period. Rational use of rhetoric is not only to materialize the abstract numbers but also to infographic the vague language, which increases the attractiveness and attention of information reported. However, when readers read an information infographic process that they understand an analogy or metaphor replies on their lives experience and background. To select which variables as visual contents and how to utilize people's thinking habits to inspire their perception and think the material and spiritual words beyond language words is the important part of infographic design improving self-worth. Especially when the infographic has become an integral part of media how to properly use analogy or metaphor etc such visual rhetoric methods in this whole wide open and transparent platform to help reader thinking, not only improves the perception of visual works but also completely express the core contents of information is a very arduous creative activities.

Figure 23 series, infographic chart states the shooting position, numbers and accuracy rate of Miami Heat Team confronting the different opponents. This is the works of a relatively simple data but the author uses a combination of reality and virtue, combination of basketball court plan and colorful parabola, which brings the reader a fantastic visual effect and creates a fireworks-like bright colorful night scene, dazzling and colorful.

Hurricane Festival in Germany is quite famous music festival as Figure 24-1 and Figure 24-2, which has four stages, more than 100 performances, approximately 73,000 audiences. The purpose of this series of chart is used to display the music festival of history, development process, environment and location variation, the amount of equipments supplies, the frequency and overall status about the utilization of bathroom, transportation of audience, participation methods and means, the source of honored guest and quantity of performance in which it sums up dozens of data statistics. Although the contents are various, when the author makes the design and layout happen variations in the foreground and background, modernist wave point in application, harmonization in primary colors which adopts the maroon colors of symbolizing the rock and land and secondary colors, variation repeated of irregular geometric shapes and organic shapes, which does not show reader a trace of tedious feeling and instead in which the readers are gradually stimulated by the model and color, excites and cheers time after time for the amazing data. It full meet the designer's original intention of which attracts more music-loved people concerning about this music festivals.

23

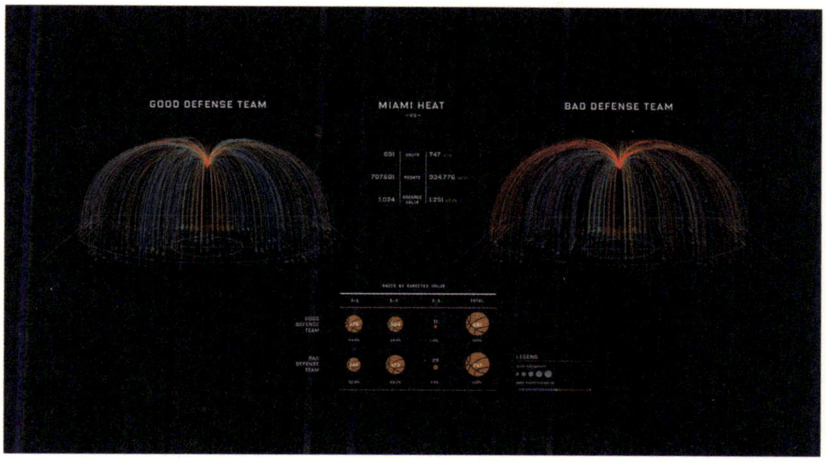

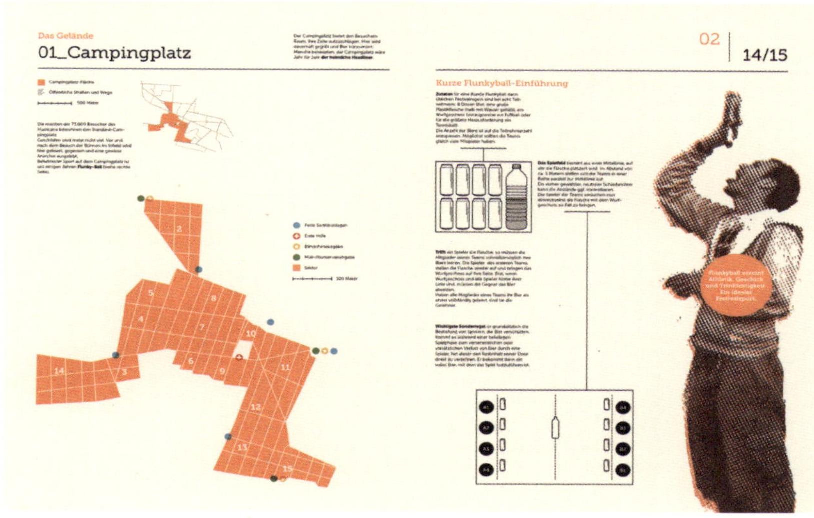

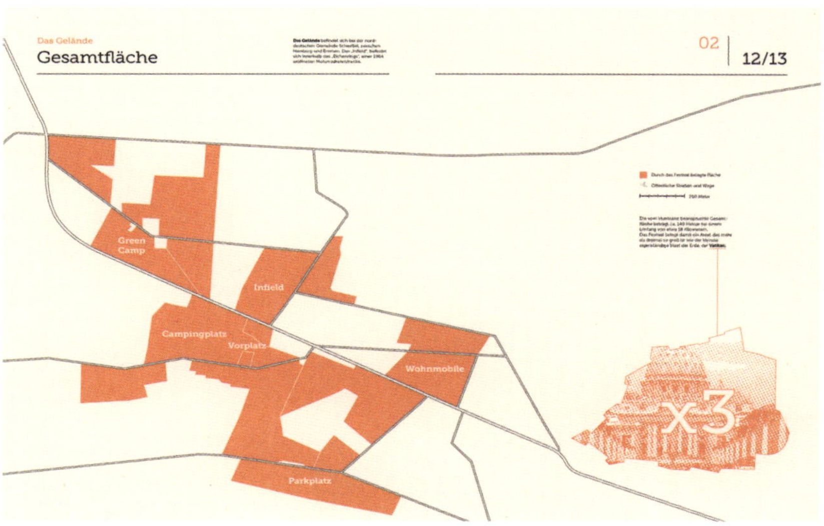

24-1 / 24-2

D Infographic Design Method of Media

1. Graphical Comparison

People need the press in both qualitative and quantitative aspects of higher demand when exposed to the whole community of network data. On one hand, the different media organizations rely on the development of data technology have more convenient means of reports, data content is also more abundant; On the other hand, the emergence of new media age, people have more sources of information, it is easier to suspect to the views similar or even contrary views of the information; So more and more comprehensive grasp of the whole sample data, objective facts and subjective analysis requirements are also higher. In this case, the fact large amounts of data for a comparative analysis would be a better approach. This "relative" form appears that there will be two or more indicators associated unfolded ratio, the contrast between the reaction phenomenon and their interrelated.

As shown in Figure 25, the designer put the chairs of 150 years with a single line graphic outline, first put them on a timeline comparison, then, turn their front and side aspect respectively, and marked where these chairs produced, clear and focused display all the data associated with the chair, so that readers can take the initiative and actively participate in the discussion of this topic chair, and with the necessities of life in a number of the characteristics listed in the chart to compare different levels of so that the final complete information is also more convincing.

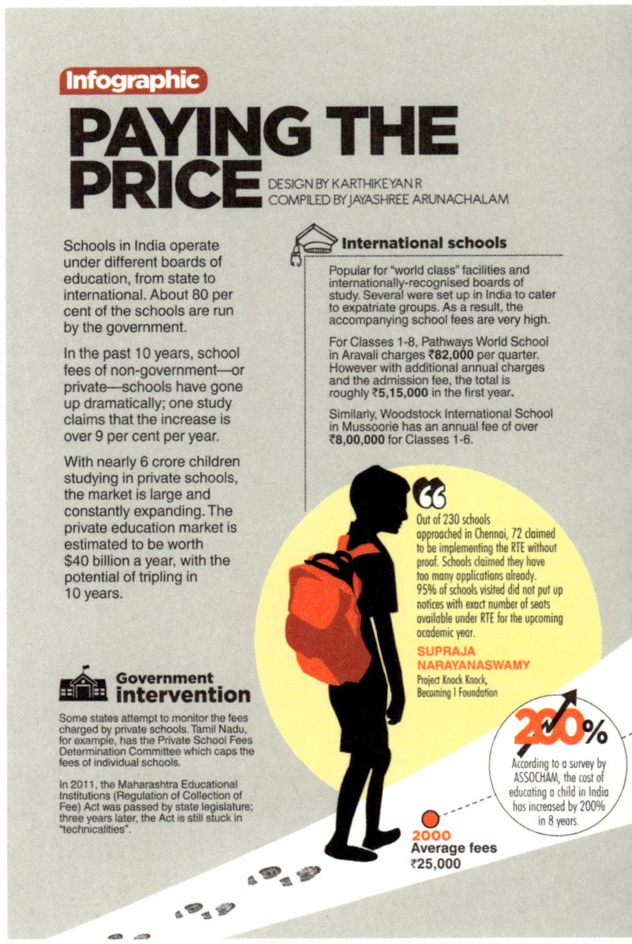

26

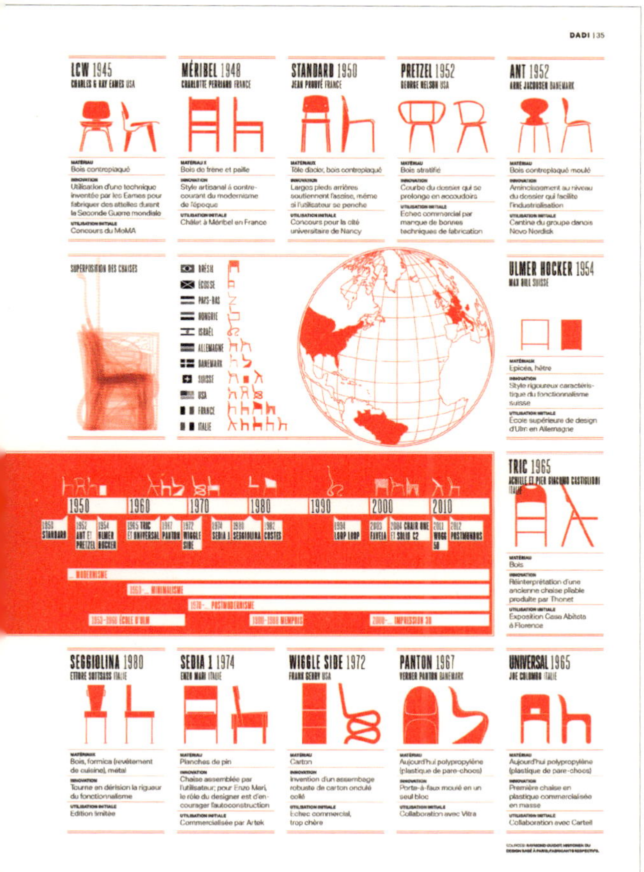

25

2. More Straightforward

Media information, such as news are not the Bureau's annual summary reports, but more direct facts of the show, including the reasons for the relevant event occurred, the results of the entire development process, leading to the various aspects of the effect produced, and future and so on. The specific data did not have any real meaning for reader, it will be too obvious professional and seem cold, lack of humane care, giving readers psychological resistance. Therefore, the data obfuscate parts into a whole, although slightly lower accuracy of data, but the accuracy of the information delivered by the fact that the whole was not affected in any way, the reader will be more willing to accept.

For example, Figure 26 shows the growth trend of tuition works year after year for Indian children, it is handled this way: the percentage of data which, in the molecule with the integers, such as 60 or 200; and some of the more specific values, such as 2000-2015 the average tuition per year value, which throw away all the hundreds digit zero start, and the use of 25,000 or 300,000 of such values. The effect is that the reader can see the differences between them more straightforward, and complete data will be able to maximize the difference. After such a treatment works do not need to bother too much unwanted memories, not only easy to read, but also easy to play variability features graphic designers, giving the works for more design elements

27

3. Information Association

Life is full of figures, and the era of big data let it more frequently moved in front of us, but also to create a large space for infographic development. It constantly repeated data visualization, forcing us to see it every day, and accept it appears in every second of our existence, the attendant, it makes people love and hate figures, love it, because can not without it, hate it, because it is too boring, and makes life without passion. The same situation also appears in the communication process of infographic information in the major media, indeed, figures can help the reader create the trust to the information they got, but when the data infographic graphs in the same period of time spews out, they will be reduced cortical activity, after three seconds of memory, if can not remember them, the data has become tasteless. For the publisher of the media three seconds is so short, therefore, excellent infographic program become a pillar for the dissemination of information, it plays a good role in the swap: When the designer given a lengthy similar concepts to each group of complex data , such as when certain things for imagining, imagine those associated with the reader will inspire intimacy of their hearts, to take the initiative in reading a message, remember that data quickly and efficiently on behalf of related things, and take the initiative on data generated by the association memory.

Figure 27 is an excellent design to demonstrate the association of water with a chart. People often confused with the volume of water in the relationship between the data, in general, it often comes from the most intuitive notion that a water meter digital copy of each month , but this chart designer has broken the conventional understanding of the water more than the other common things in daily life and its consumption in the production process closely together, such as the amount of water to wash clothes and spent a bathtub full of water, an apple in the birth process of water consumed, the amount of water required for the production of a glass of beer, making a piece of whole wheat bread, and it takes similar things compared in the same time, tell the reader how to save water in the best way by compared to the relevant data. For example, planting coffee beans take more water than tea, so if drinking tea more than coffee that is indirectly done to conserve water. Design of the entire chart in the unexpected, but reasonable. The numbers in designer's pen fresh up which let both authors and readers enjoy themselves.

Figure 28-1 and Figure 28-2 is an anti-narrative normal web design methods, simile a huge key to web design methods base on the word we often say, "Open the door to the design." This sentence manifested visual way, and sensationalized let readers mind fit visual experience; then visual the third design method by intensity and strength of the rocket, metaphor the technology advances fast after learning, achieve readers' expectations. Although the layout of this chart of step one, step two, step three are arranged somewhat violated the visual reading from left to right, in descending order, the visual center of the design is a bit confusing and scattered, but its metaphor design approach is worth learning and thinking.

28-1

28-2

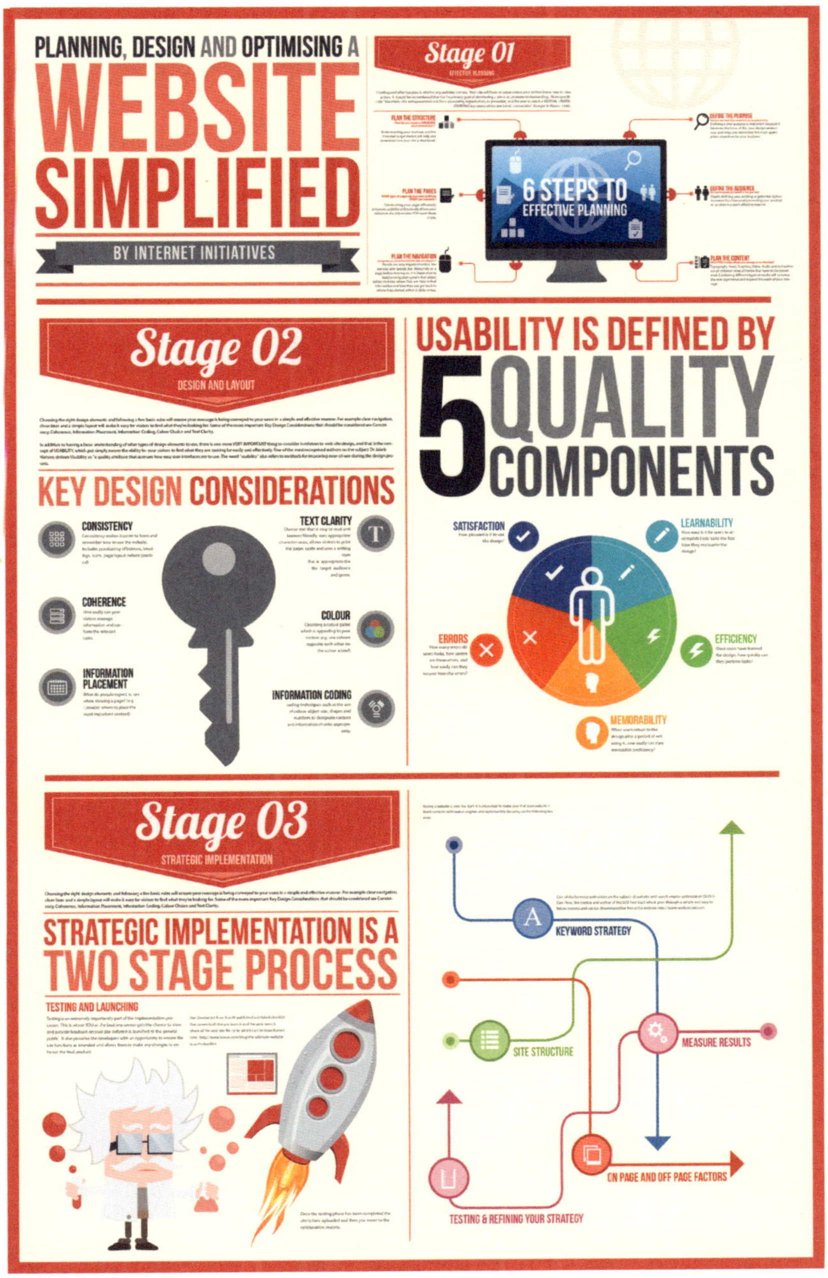

Travel Infographics

- Completion Year: 2013
- Designer: Bárdos Barbara
- Client: Ash and Diamond Culture Magazine

- Work Introduction

The aim of this infographic is to visualize the major trends of the rapidly increasing worldwide tourism. We used the baseball cap as a major symbol, this represents the worldwide tourist. Our tourist (cap) goes through on the regular way of the tourist trips, such as various travel style, destinations, spending habits, activities and so on.

Az utazás célja
(az összes utazás százalékában)

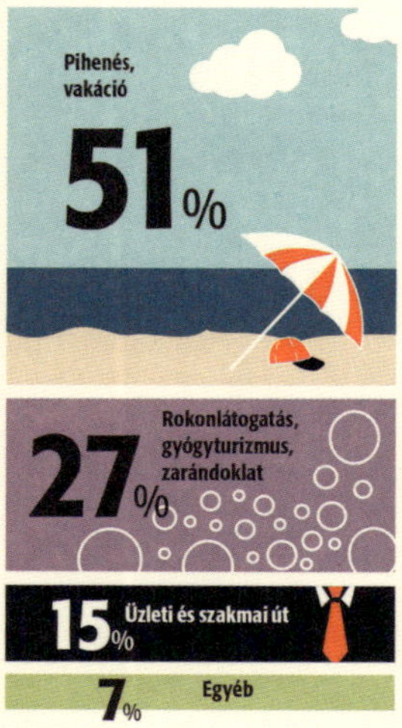

5. Tate Modern, London 4 802 287
6. National Gallery of Art, Washington 4 392 252
7. National Palace Museum, Tajpej 3,849,577
8. Centre Pompidou, Párizs 3,613,076
9. National Museum of Korea, Szöul 3,239,549
10. Musee d'Orsay, Párizs (n. a.)

A jelenség nem korlátozódik kizárólag Európára: hasonló bevásárlóparadicsommá nőtte ki magát az elmúlt években az Arab-félsziget is. Bahreinben például a kiskereskedők árbevétele tavalyelőtt 12, tavaly 14 százalékkal nőtt, az 1996 óta megrendezett Dubai Shopping Festivalon pedig 2012-ben közel 3 millió látogató költötte a pénzét akciós ruhákra, ékszerekre és hasonlókra. Az utazási irodák bevásárlócsomagjai itt is ismertek, számos szállodát pedig egybeépítenek egy-egy bevásárlóközponttal, ezért a vendégek fele el sem hagyja az épületet, csak a medence, a szoba és az üzletek között ingázik.

BUSINESS AS USUAL

Az elmúlt tizenöt évben meghatározó erővé vált az idegenforgalmon belül az üzleti turizmus is, amit az UNWTO adatai is igazolnak: a felmérések szerint az utazók 16 százaléka valamilyen munkaügyben veszi a nyakába a világot. Ez a piaci szegmens nemcsak hatalmas, hanem meglehetősen színes is – az értekezletek, jutalomutak, konferenciák és kiállítások apropóján zajló idegenforgalmat is magában foglalja. Az üzleti utasok általában business classon vagy első osztályon repülnek, drága szállodákban laknak. Érdekesebb azonban az üzleti utak tovagyűrűző hatása. Tavaly például a munkaügyben utazók 40 százaléka tért vissza a családjával vagy baráti társasággal oda, ahová előtte hivatalból kirendelték, és magáncélból hosszabb időt töltött az adott országban.

MOBILFORRADALOM

A XXI. századi turizmus kapcsán a többségnek már nem a szervezett turistaút, az utazási irodákban húzott sorszámok és prospektusok jutnak eszébe, hanem leginkább a TripAdvisor.com, a Booking.com vagy egy-egy népszerű utazási blog. Ez nem véletlen: a XIX. századi vasúti fejlesztések, majd a XX. században kialakult légi közlekedés után a XX. században az internet és a közösségi média az a forradalom, amely gyökerestül megváltoztatja az utazási szokásainkat. Ahogyan azt a statisztikák is jelzik, az utazástervezésben a fő tanácsadó szerepét a weboldalak vették át: az útikönyvek eladásai az elmúlt öt évben 40 százalékkal csökkentek, miközben az utazók 40 százaléka azt mondja, hogy valamilyen formában használja a tervezés során a közösségi médiát, és minden második ember számol be arról, hogy mások – például bloggerek vagy a weboldalakon szállásokat, éttermeket értékelő idegen utazók – véleményére hagyatkozva dönti el, merre induljon útnak. Ez a szállásadóknak és a vendéglátóipar szereplőinek dolgát egyfelől megkönnyíti, másfelől viszont új kihívások elé állítja őket. Reagálniuk kell az észrevételekre, és az alaptalan vádakat is meg kell tanulniuk jól kezelni. Az alkalmazkodás tétje hatalmas: 2011-ben csak az Egyesült Királyságban 1,7 milliárd font értékű szállásfoglalást lehetett közvetlenül visszavezetni a TripAdvisorig.

A net nem is csak a tervezés fázisában van jelen: az utazók 54 százaléka a foglalást online intézi, méghozzá egyre gyakrabban mobileszközről. A közeljövőben valószínűleg az okostévékre is nagy szerep hárul, ezért egyes piaci szereplők, mint a Teletext Holidays vagy akár a szerb turisztikai hivatal, már be is indították saját csatornáikat. Az okostelefonok, tabletek, laptopok, a Facebook és az Instagram nem hiányzik útközben sem (hacsak nem kifejezetten „digitális elvonókúrára" megy az ember, mert már ilyesmire is lehet jelentkezni), segítségükkel akár élő egyenesben is közvetíthető egy nyaralás, és a lehetőséggel sokan élnek is.

EXTRÉM „SZAKÁGAK"

Az ily módon „öntudatra ébredt" és önállósult turisták tömegei gyökeres változásokat idéznek elő az idegenforgalomban.

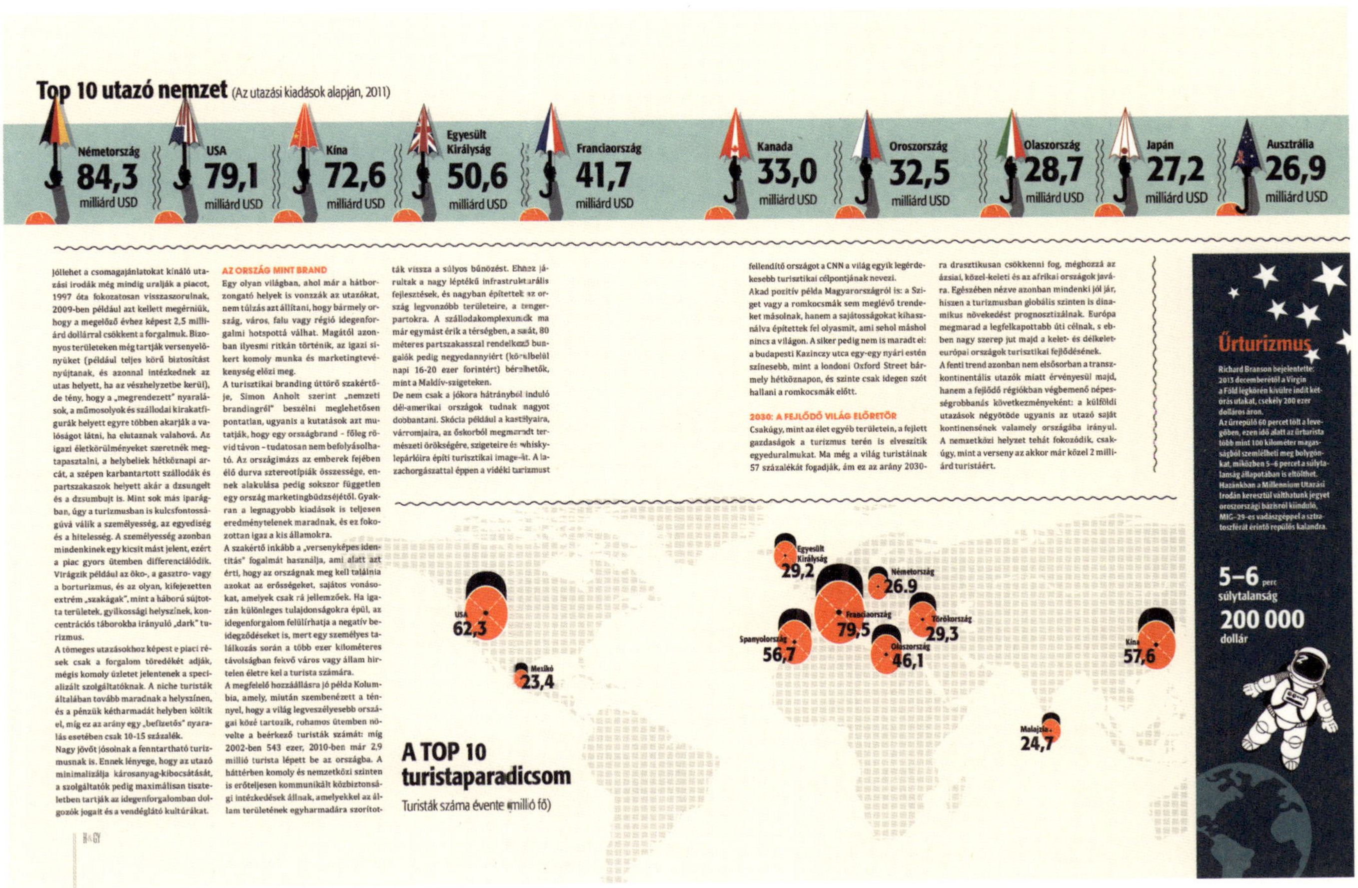

Top 10 utazó nemzet (Az utazási kiadások alapján, 2011)

Németország	84,3 milliárd USD
USA	79,1 milliárd USD
Kína	72,6 milliárd USD
Egyesült Királyság	50,6 milliárd USD
Franciaország	41,7 milliárd USD
Kanada	33,0 milliárd USD
Oroszország	32,5 milliárd USD
Olaszország	28,7 milliárd USD
Japán	27,2 milliárd USD
Ausztrália	26,9 milliárd USD

Jóllehet a csomagajánlatokat kínáló utazási irodák még mindig uralják a piacot, 1997 óta fokozatosan visszaszorulnak, 2009-ben például azt kellett megérniük, hogy a megelőző évhez képest 2,5 milliárd dollárral csökkent a forgalmuk. Bizonyos területeken még tartják versenyelőnyüket (például teljes körű biztosítást nyújtanak, és azonnal intézkednek az utas helyett, ha az vészhelyzetbe kerül), de tény, hogy a „megrendezett" nyaralások, a műmosolyok és szállodai kirakatfigurák helyett egyre többen akarják a valóságot látni, ha elutaznak valahová. Az igazi életkörülményeket szeretnék megtapasztalni, a helybeliek hétköznapi arcát, a szépen karbantartott szállodák és partszakaszok helyett akár a dzsungelt és a dzsumbujt is. Mint sok más iparágban, úgy a turizmusban is kulcsfontosságúvá válik a személyesség, az egyediség és a hitelesség. A személyesség azonban mindenkinek egy kicsit mást jelent, ezért a piac gyors ütemben differenciálódik. Virágzik például az öko-, a gasztro- vagy a borturizmus, és az olyan, kifejezetten extrém „szakágak", mint a háború sújtotta területek, gyilkossági helyszínek, koncentrációs táborokba irányuló „dark" turizmus.

A tömeges utazásokhoz képest e piaci rések csak a forgalom töredékét adják, mégis komoly üzletet jelentenek a specializált szolgáltatóknak. A niche turisták általában tovább maradnak a helyszínen, és a pénzük kétharmadát helyben költik el, míg ez az arány egy „befizetős" nyaralás esetében csak 10-15 százalék.

Nagy jövőt jósolnak a fenntartható turizmusnak is. Ennek lényege, hogy az utazó minimalizálja károsanyag-kibocsátását, a szolgáltatók pedig maximálisan tiszteletben tartják az idegenforgalomban dolgozók jogait és a vendéglátó kultúrákat.

AZ ORSZÁG MINT BRAND

Egy olyan világban, ahol már a hátborzongató helyek is vonzzák az utazókat, nem túlzás azt állítani, hogy bármely ország, város, falu vagy régió idegenforgalmi hotspottá válhat. Magától azonban ilyesmi ritkán történik, az igazi sikert komoly munka és marketingtevékenység előzi meg.

A turisztikai branding úttörő szakértője, Simon Anholt szerint „nemzeti brandingről" beszélni meglehetősen pontatlan, ugyanis a kutatások azt mutatják, hogy egy országbrand – főleg rövid távon – tudatosan nem befolyásolható. Az országimázs az emberek fejében élő durva sztereotípiák összessége, ennek alakulása pedig sokszor független egy ország marketingbüdzséjétől. Gyakran a legnagyobb kiadások is teljesen eredménytelenek maradnak, és ez fokozottan igaz a kis államokra.

A szakértő inkább a „versenyképes identitás" fogalmát használja, ami alatt azt érti, hogy az országnak meg kell találnia azokat az erősségeket, sajátos vonásokat, amelyek csak rá jellemzőek. Ha igazán különleges tulajdonságokra épül, az idegenforgalom felülírhatja a negatív beidegződéseket is, mert egy személyes találkozás során a több ezer kilométeres távolságban fekvő város vagy állam hirtelen életre kel a turista számára.

A megfelelő hozzáállásra jó példa Kolumbia, amely, miután szembenézett a ténnyel, hogy a világ legveszélyesebb országai közé tartozik, rohamos ütemben növelte a beérkező turisták számát: míg 2002-ben 543 ezer, 2010-ben már 2,9 millió turista lépett be az országba. A háttérben komoly és nemzetközi szinten is erőteljesen kommunikált közbiztonsági intézkedések állnak, amelyekkel az állam területének egyharmadára szorították vissza a súlyos bűnözést. Ehhez járultak a nagy léptékű infrastrukturális fejlesztések, és nagyban építettek az ország legvonzóbb területeire, a tengerpartokra. A szállodakomplexumok ma már egymást érik a térségben, a saját, 80 méteres partszakasszal rendelkező bungalók pedig negyedannyiért (körülbelül napi 16-20 ezer forintért) bérelhetők, mint a Maldív-szigeteken.

De nem csak a jókora hátrányból induló dél-amerikai országok tudnak nagyot dobbantani. Skócia például a kastélyaira, várromjaira, az őskorból megmaradt természeti örökségére, szigeteire és whiskylepárlóira építi turisztikai image-át. A lazachorgászattal éppen a vidéki turizmust fellendítő országot a CNN a világ egyik legérdekesebb turisztikai célpontjának nevezi.

Akad pozitív példa Magyarországról is: a Sziget vagy a romkocsmák sem meglévő trendeket másolnak, hanem a sajátosságokat kihasználva építettek fel olyasmit, ami sehol máshol nincs a világon. A siker pedig nem is maradt el: a budapesti Kazinczy utca egy-egy nyári estén színesebb, mint a londoni Oxford Street bármely hétköznapon, és szinte csak idegen szót hallani a romkocsmák előtt.

2030: A FEJLŐDŐ VILÁG ELŐRETÖR

Csakúgy, mint az élet egyéb területein, a fejlett gazdaságok a turizmus terén is elveszítik egyeduralmukat. Ma még a világ turistáinak 57 százalékát fogadják, ám ez az arány 2030-ra drasztikusan csökkenni fog, méghozzá az ázsiai, közel-keleti és az afrikai országok javára. Egészében nézve azonban mindenki jól jár, hiszen a turizmusban globális szinten is dinamikus növekedést prognosztizálnak. Európa megmarad a legfelkapottabb úti célnak, s ebben nagy szerep jut majd a kelet- és délkelet-európai országok turisztikai fejlődésének.

A fenti trend azonban nem elsősorban a transzkontinentális utazók miatt érvényesül majd, hanem a fejlődő régiókban végbemenő népességrobbanás következményeként: a külföldi utazások négyötöde ugyanis az utazó saját kontinensének valamely országába irányul. A nemzetközi helyzet tehát fokozódik, csakúgy, mint a verseny az akkor már közel 2 milliárd turistáért.

A TOP 10 turistaparadicsom

Turisták száma évente (millió fő)

USA	62,3
Mexikó	23,4
Egyesült Királyság	29,2
Franciaország	79,5
Németország	26,9
Törökország	29,3
Spanyolország	56,7
Olaszország	46,1
Kína	57,6
Malajzia	24,7

Űrturizmus

Richard Branson bejelentette: 2013 decemberétől a Virgin a Föld legkörén kívülre indít kétórás utakat, csekély 200 ezer dolláros áron.

Az űrrepülő 60 percet tölt a levegőben, ezen idő alatt az űrturista több mint 100 kilométer magasságból szemlélheti meg bolygónkat, miközben 5–6 percet a súlytalanság állapotában is eltölthet.

Hazánkban a Millennium Utazási Irodán keresztül válthatunk jegyet oroszországi bázisról kiinduló, MIG–29-es vadászgéppel a sztratoszférát érintő repülős kalandra.

5–6 perc súlytalanság

200 000 dollár

H&GY

Banjo

- Completion Year: 2012
- Designer: Andras Dancsak
- Client: Aller DK youth magazine (Denmark)

• Work Introduction

It's a giant wall chart infographic explains how the banjo works. Andras Dancsak is an amateur musician and plays many instruments. He didn't find any diagram like this and decided to create some. Many musicians are interested in the secrets of their instruments. He thinks it's very useful for beginners when they start to play the instrument.

• Magazine Introduction

Aller Media is magazine publisher in the Nordic countries, headquartered in Copenhagen, Denmark. It publishes Elle, Café, Femina, Allers and Se & Hør. It publishes 34 magazines every month which are read by over 4 million people.

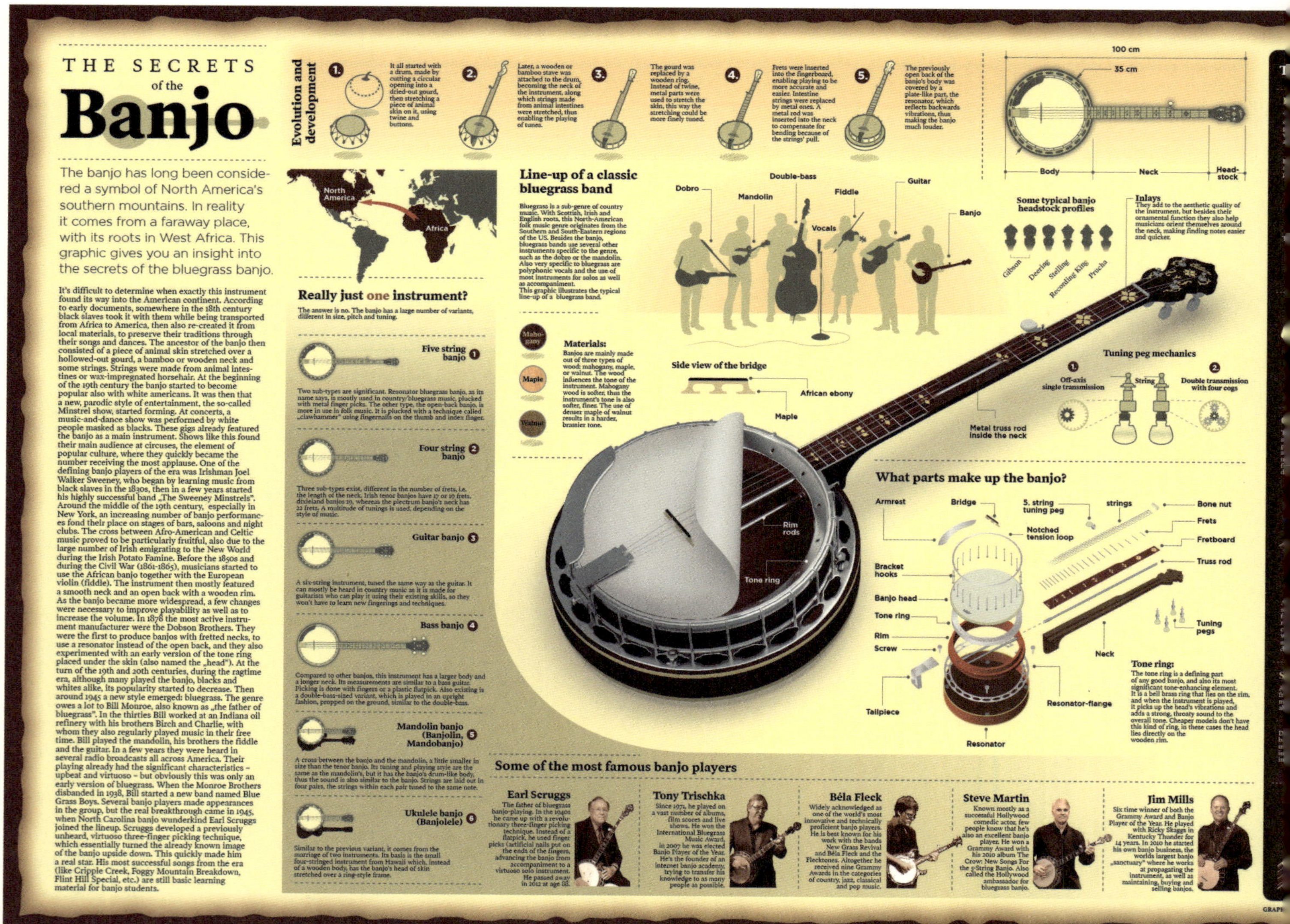

Monthly Bulletin for Central Asia and Mongolia "Çapar. CA & M"

- Completion Year: 2013
- Designer: Anton Egorov
- Client: Japan Tobacco International

- Work Introduction

The upper infographic is about historical connections between countries of Central Asia and Mongolia, while the lower infographic displays ratio of area & population for countries of Central Asia and Mongolia.

The Chair, from One Form to Another

- Completion Year: 2012
- Designer: Thibaud Tissot, Benjamin Bollmann
- Client: DADI Magazine

• Work Introduction

The infographic gives information about famous designer chairs and the innovations that made them, such as new materials and construction techniques. Each chair is drawn at scale, based on dimensions provided by the manufacturer. The timeline at the center of the infographic retraces the main design movements of the 20th century and shows the release date of each 24 chairs. This allows the reader to understand the chairs' historical context.

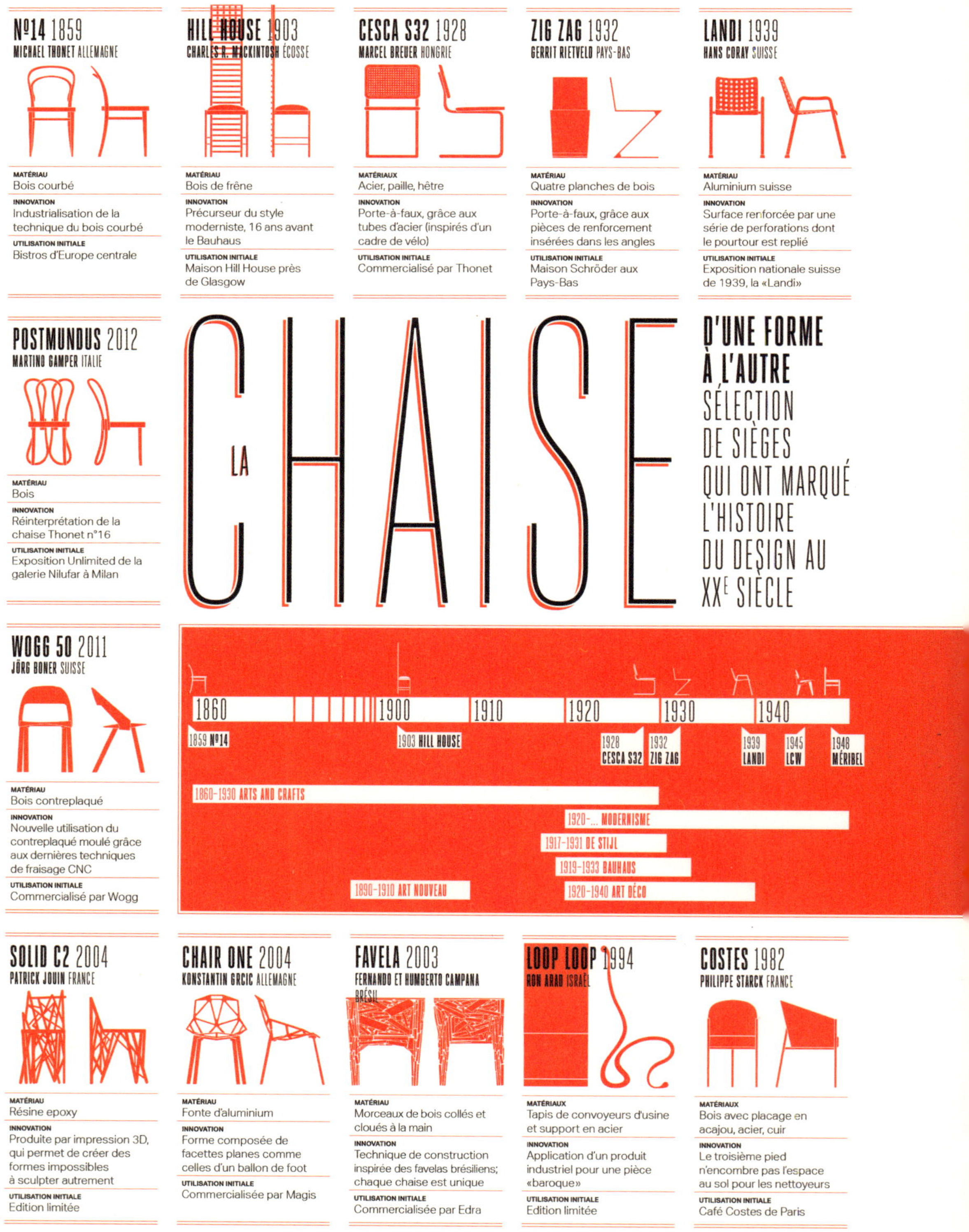

• Magazine Introduction

DADI is a Swiss magazine covering design, architecture and contemporary art. It used to run a print edition in French and German throughout Switzerland and has become entirely web-based in 2013.

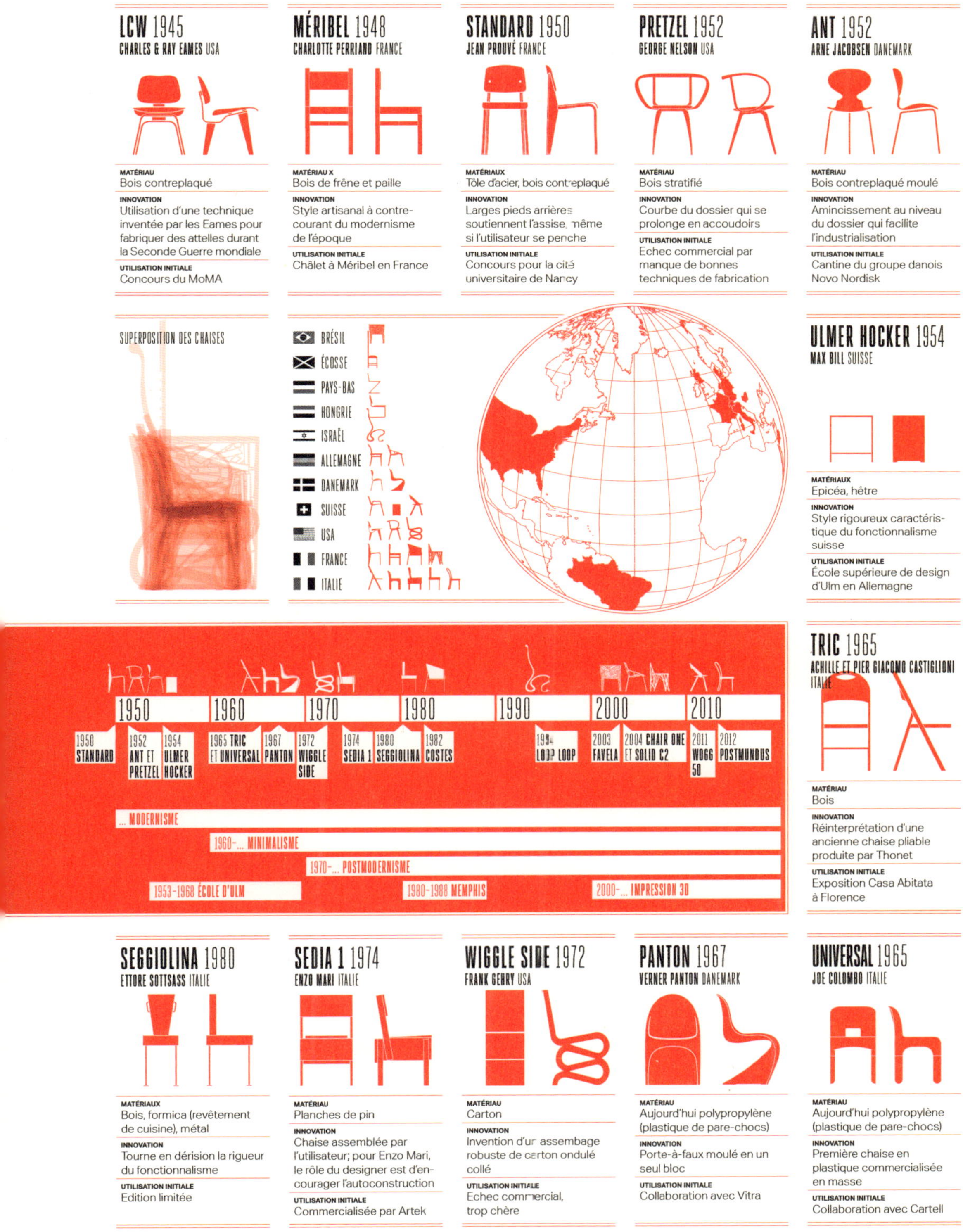

How the Swiss Die

- Completion Year: 2012
- Designer: Thibaud Tissot, Benjamin Bollmann
- Client: Reflex Magazine

• Work Introduction

The infographic presents Swiss death statistics today and compares them with those from 100 years ago. It shows the causes of death and the main types of cancer, as well as the suicide and murder rates. It also highlights historical decline in infectious diseases due to advances in the fields of vaccination, antibiotics and hygiene. The production of "How The Swiss Die" involved extensive research into the archives of the Swiss Federal Statistical Office in order to find, extract ad filter relevant historical data. For the design, an emphasis was put on clarity and functionality, the hallmarks of 20th-century Swiss graphic design.

• Magazine Introduction

Reflex was a Swiss science magazine published in French and English by the Ecole polytechnique fédérale de Lausanne (EPFL) and entirely produced by the Geneva-based press agency LargeNetwork. It has now been replaced by European science magazine Technologist.

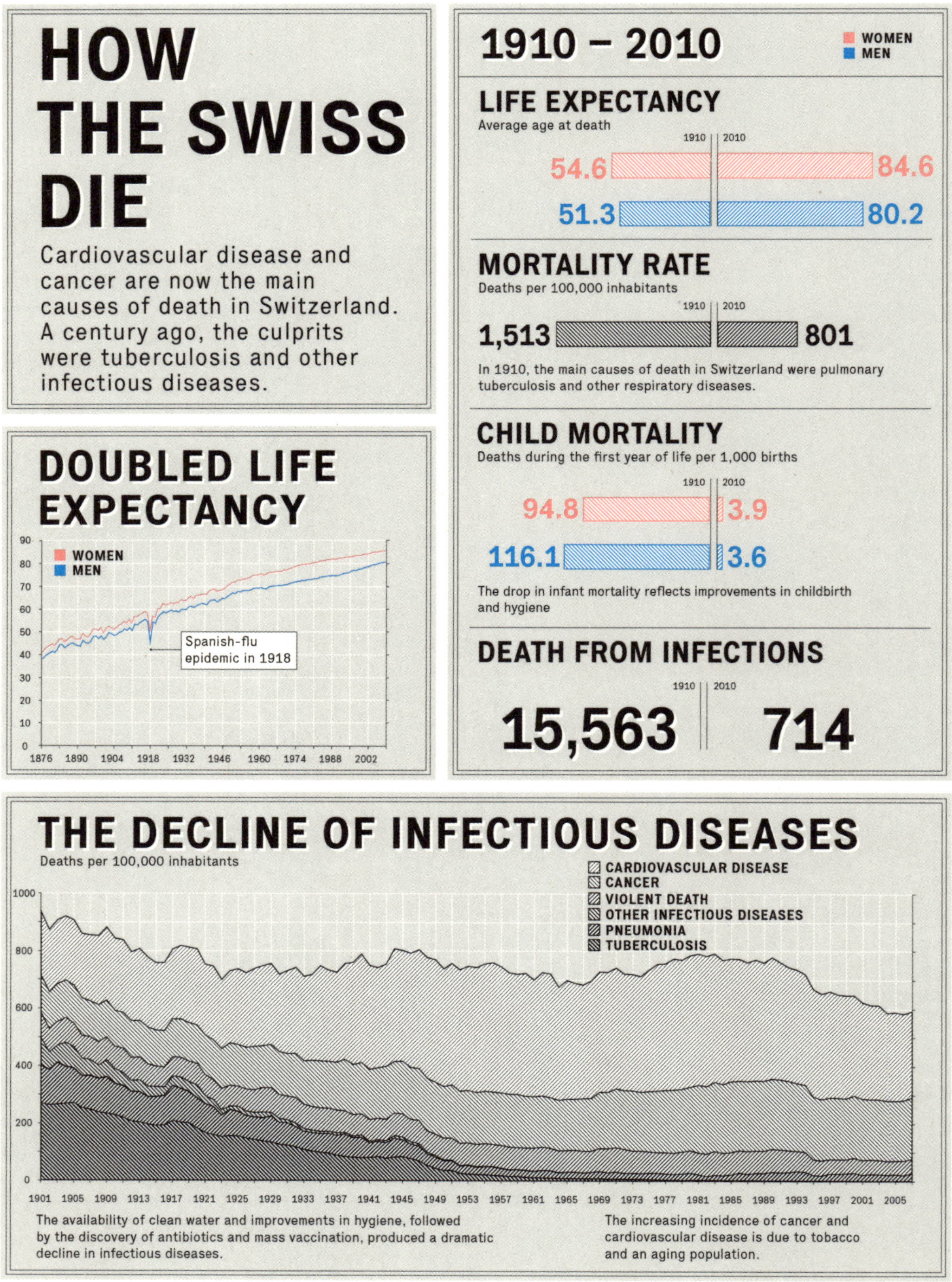

DEATHS TODAY

Number of deaths
annual average 2006-2010

WOMEN
MEN

CAUSES OF DEATH

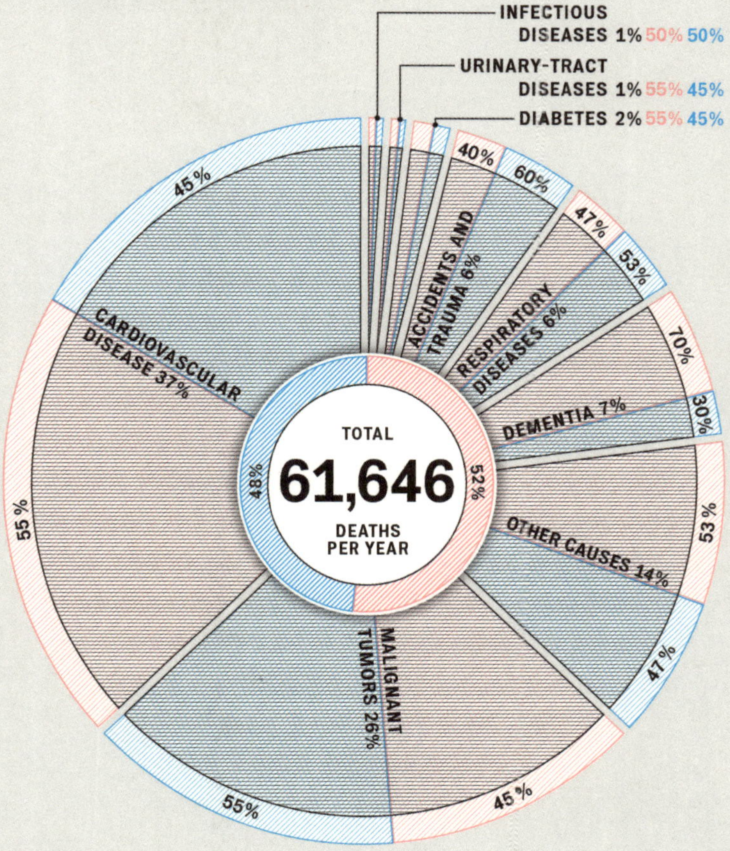

MAIN TYPES OF CANCER

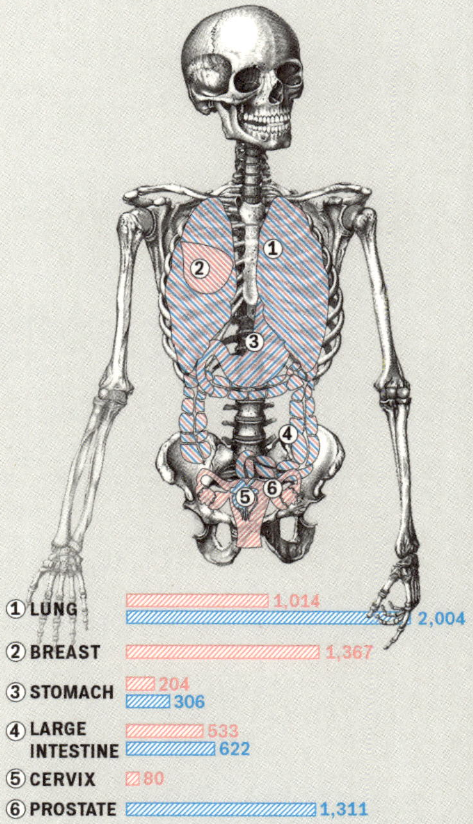

MORE MEN COMMIT SUICIDE

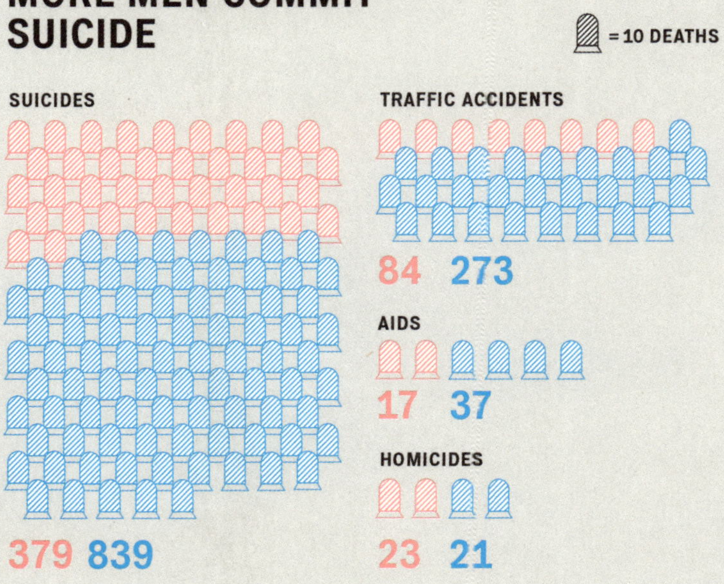

AT WHAT AGE DO WE DIE?

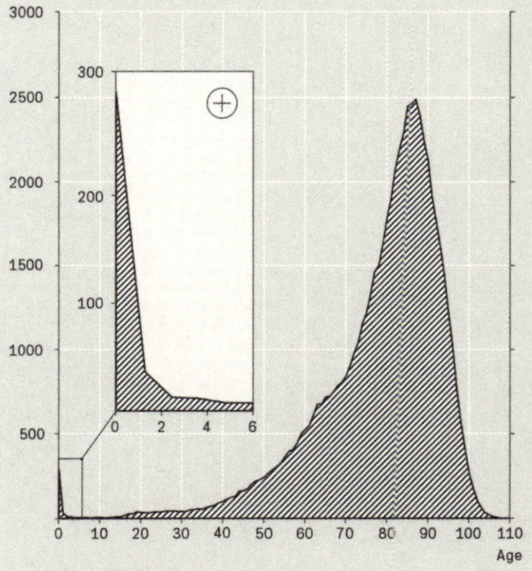

Focus Russia Article

- Completion Year: 2013
- Designer: Di Rese Lorenzo Mauro (drlm.it)
- Client: Istituto Luce-Cinecittà

• Work Introduction

Focus Russia is one of the rubric on the 8½ Magazine. The all cross-media project is designed by 19novanta agency, Rome. In russian culture there are so many historical aspects to be represented, the designer chooses some of these, trying to rework all of these features in a modern way. The article can be opened by an infographic about Russia and its cinemas. The illustrations are created to express each data in a better way.

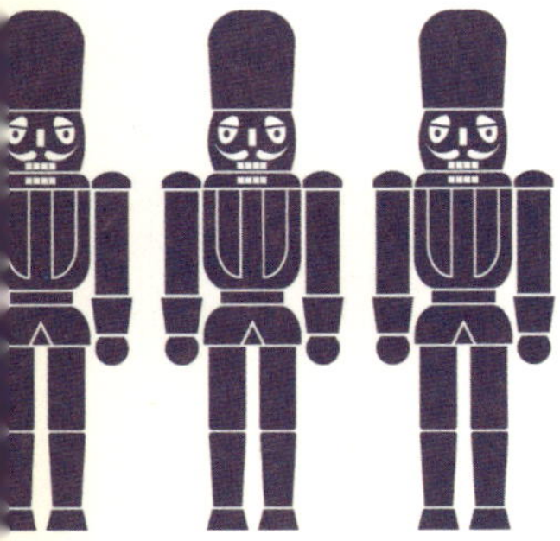

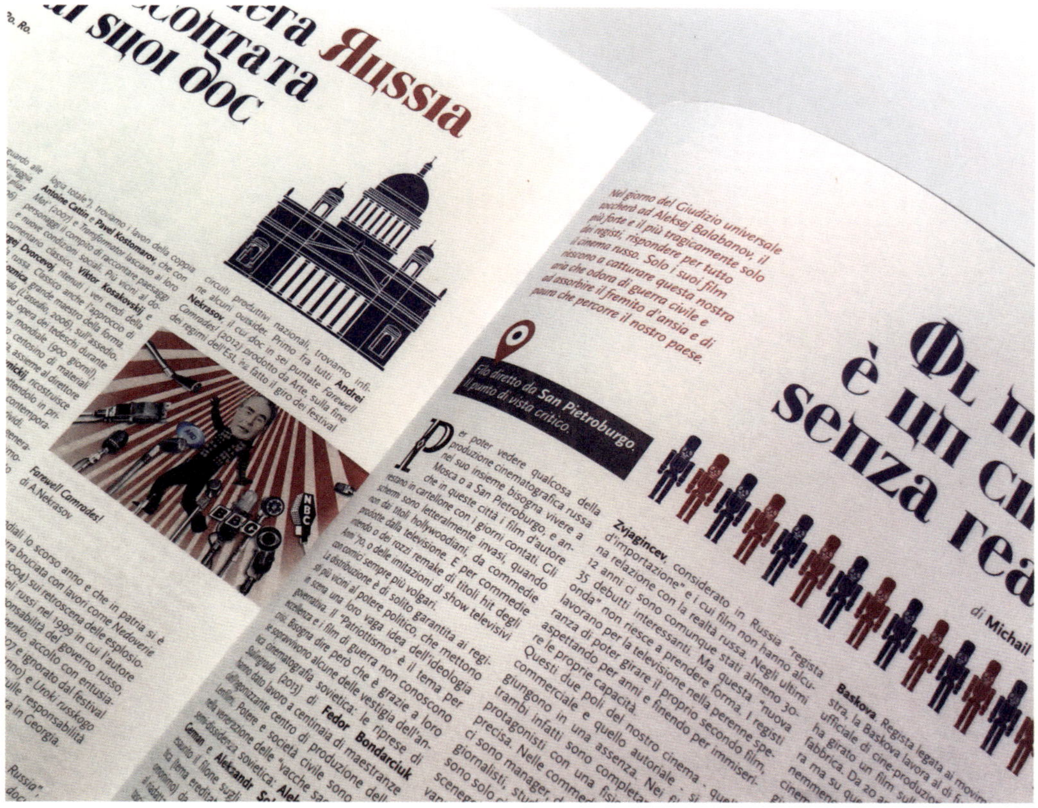
Russia
Filo diretto da San Pietroburgo.
Il punto di vista critico.
è un ci
senza rea

Lingua ufficiale
17.075.400 km²
Presidente
Forma di governo
Densità
Moneta
9
fusi orari
Capitale
IL CASO
RUSSIA
FOCUS
schermi cinematografici
2000
digitali
1000
analogici
190
etnie

Fountain Ink Magazine

- Completion Year: 2013-2014
- Designer: KARTHIKEYAN R

- Work Introduction

The "essay" section is a platform for lively debate and plays host to opinions from all sides. The "Photo Story" section produces the best of photo-journalism in India, and is the only visual storytelling medium of its kind in Indian media. The interview section of the magazine has featured some of the biggest names in Indian and world literature. Our readers are from primarily from the upper middle class and the upper class, as well as intellectuals and academicians.

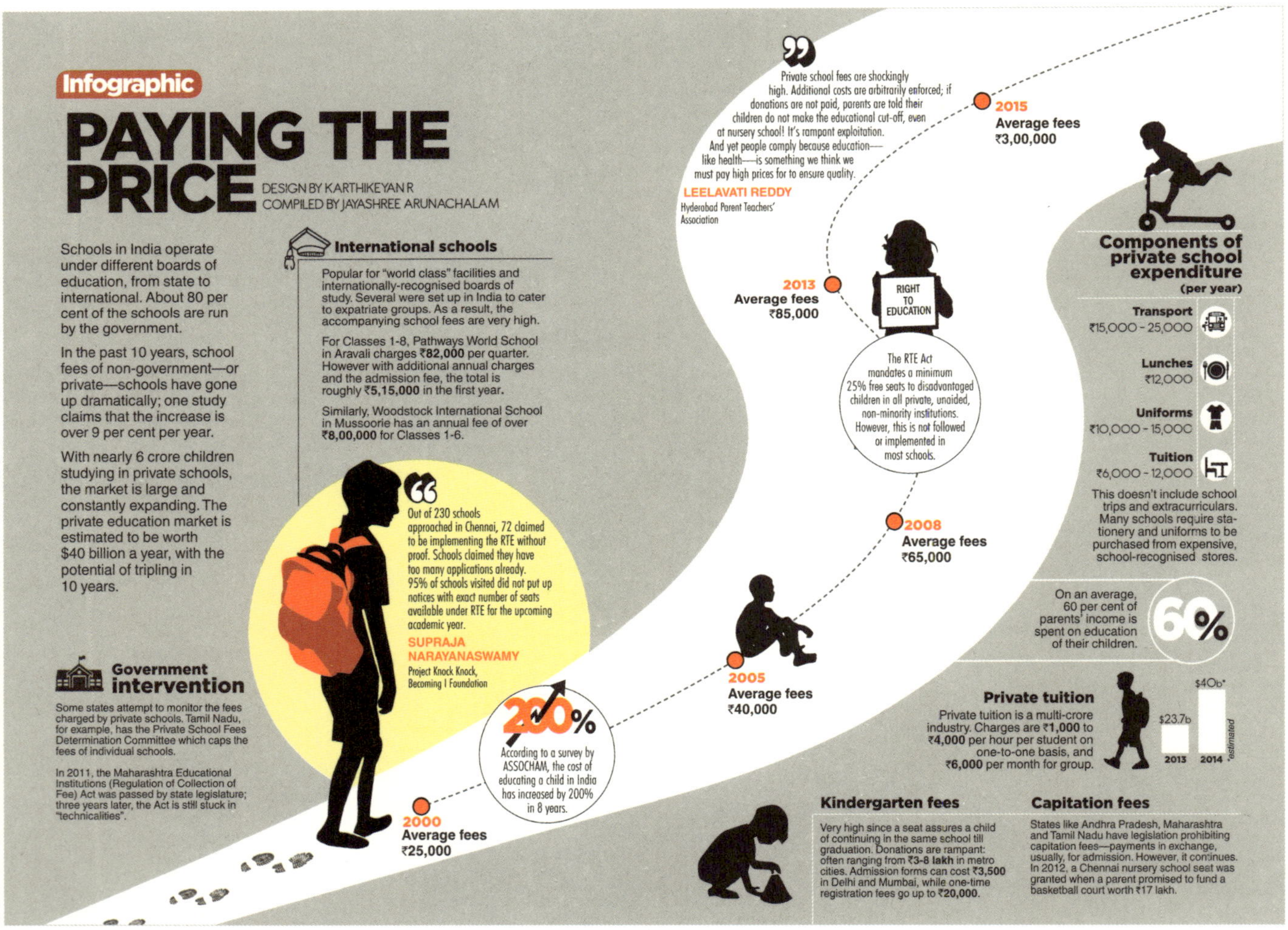

Infographic

DESIGN BY KARTHIKEYAN R
COMPILED BY JAYASHREE ARUNACHALAM

TIED UP IN KNOTS

While the rest of the industry world battled recession, one industry in India grew, and continues to grow, by leaps and bounds—the wedding industry. Paychecks might get smaller, but the amount that people are willing to spend on weddings is only going up. The average Indian spends one-fifth of total wealth accumulated in a lifetime on an offspring's wedding.

DECORATION
₹60,000 upward

FOOD
₹700 - ₹2,000 plate per person

INVITE
₹300 - ₹1,500 per card

FLOWERS
₹50,000 upward

VENUE
₹2,00,000 upward

SIZE OF THE INDUSTRY

One crore weddings happen every year in India, and the wedding market in India is estimated to be over ₹1,10,000 crore.

BRIDAL MEHNDI
Between ₹1,000 - ₹5,000

VENUE

Large marriage halls with a capacity of 1,000 in metropolitan cities start at ₹3,50,000, which does not include additional electricity/water charges of ₹1,00,000. Many venues insist on payment of 50% of the total in cash without receipt, so they pay no tax on it.

SUIT / SHERWANI
₹15,000 - ₹1,00,000

PLANNING

A wedding planner helps with venue, decoration, catering, makeup artist and clothing, and other details. Large wedding planning firms charge at least 10% of the total wedding budget for consultation.

TAKE-HOME GIFTS
₹1,00,000 upward

SANGEET

have a series of choreographed dances, audio-visual presentations, and music. A dance choreographer starts at ₹5,000 and a DJ at ₹10,000, depending on the number of hours.

THE EASY WAY

For a court wedding under the Special Marriage Act, 1954, a fee of between ₹100-200 (depending on the state) is charged and the marriage certificate is received in 30 days.

SARI/ LEHENGA
Between ₹10,000 - 1,50,000

PANDAL
₹10,000

EXPANDING CEREMONIES

Large weddings now include mehndis, sangeets, the wedding ceremony, a reception, and often a post-wedding party, with or without alcohol. Some families also include morning-after lunches and breakfasts.

PHOTO / VIDEO
₹30,000 to ₹1,50,000 per day

BRIDAL MAKEUP
Between ₹5,000 - 50,000

> "The assumption is that Hindu weddings are the most lavish, but Christian and Muslim weddings today often incorporate the same sangeet-party-reception structure. Weddings are also like hospital services in India—you're willing to pay any amount. It's uncommon for people to scrimp when it comes to weddings
>
> **Diyashree Banerjee,**
> wedding planner

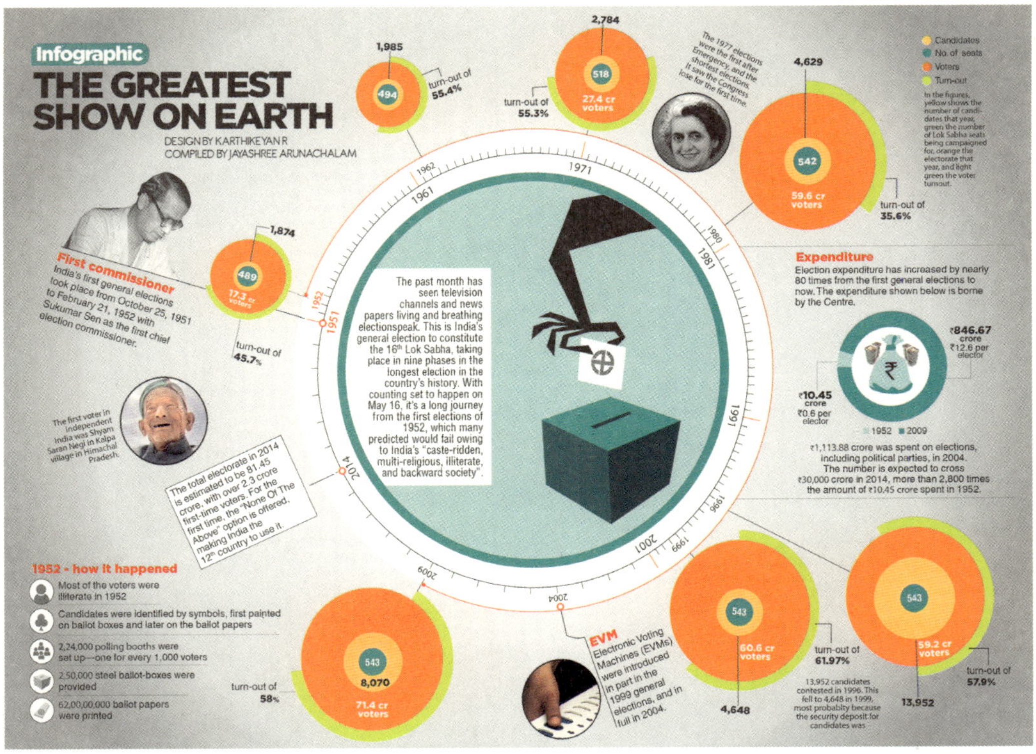

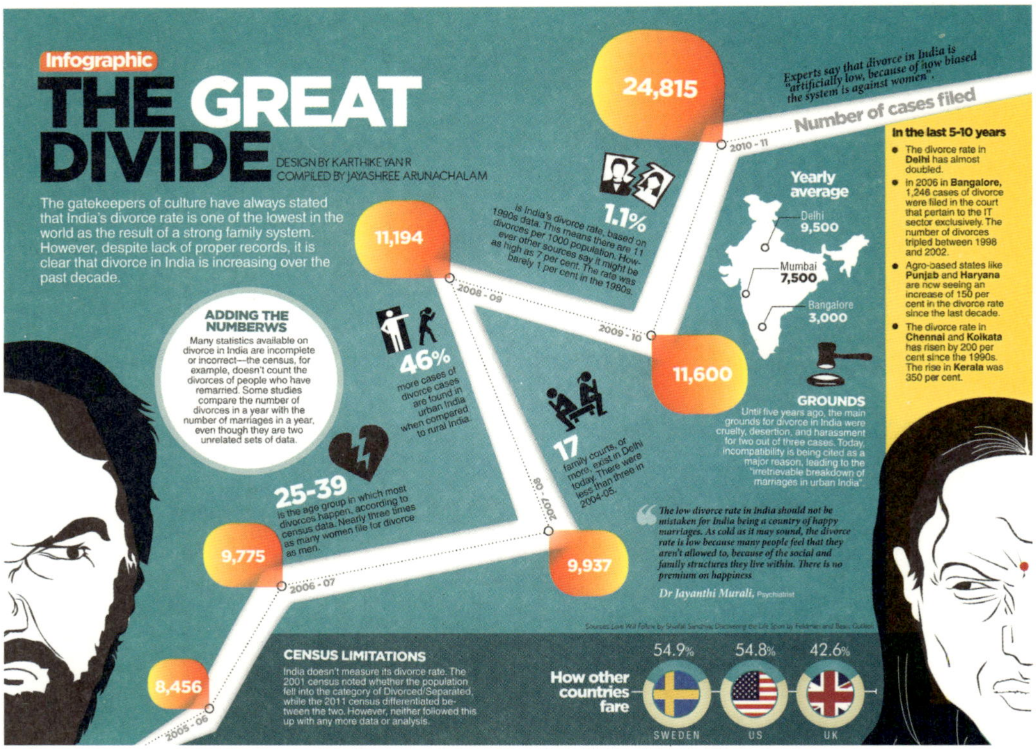

• Magazine Introduction

Fountain Ink, an award-winning monthly magazine of narrative journalism, launched in November 2011, is now in its fourth year of publication. The circulation has steadily risen during this period, both print and digital, as has our profile on social media. They have a news-stand circulation of 40,000 copies per month, in addition to 20,000 paid subscribers. The magazine is distributed in the four metros and in over 70 Tier I, II, III cities and towns.

Southern Innovator Magazine

- Completion Year: 2014
- Designer: Sólveig Rolfsdóttir, Eva Hrönn Guðnadóttir, David South
- Client: United Nations Office for South-South Cooperation/UNDP

- Work Introduction

Southern Innovator's fifth issue tackles the theme of waste and recycling. Like all editions of the magazine, it offers readers a snapshot of an area of challenge and change facing the global South, infused with the latest data, while providing practical, inspiring solutions to stimulate ideas and action.

- Magazine Introduction

Southern Innovator magazine has been published by the United Nations Office for South-South Cooperation since 2011. The creative team who developed Southern Innovator is consisted of graphic designer and illustrator Sólveig Rolfsdóttir, graphic designer Eva Hrönn Guðnadóttir, editor and writer David South, and editor-in-chief Cosmas Gitta. It celebrates the global South's rising innovator culture.

Infographics and News Pages

- Completion Year: 2014
- Designer: Adrian Luca
- Client: ITP Publishing

• Work Introduction

All submitted pages are regular news pages and double page spread opening pages for the main features. The idea of new design is to add more visual elements and make all pages more fluent and easy to read. The design draw the eyes to key elements highlighting essential information.The result shows how the design came out following the story, not an infographic on purpose.

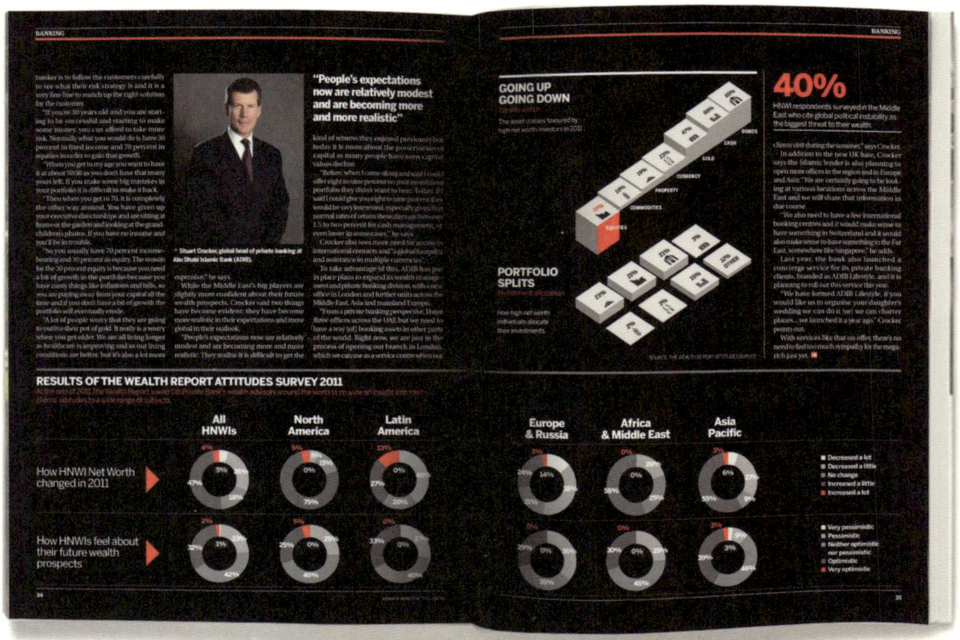

85
Lebanon
67
Saudi Arabia
58
Egypt
16
Morocco
17
Iraq
14
Kuwait
25

20%
MEDIA
8%
Transport
Finance
SECTORS
8%
Property
Number of British visitors to Dubai in 2012.
150
Number of direct flights between Dubai and the UK every week.
£500m
Sum already invested in the UK by Masdar
Automotive 6%
Energy 6%
Advisory 6%
Arts 4%
Construction 4%
Law 4%
Retail 4%
Culture & Society 2%
Education 2%
Telecoms 2%
Science 2%
Sport 2%

Retail 6%
Science 6%
Sport 4%
Telecoms 4%
Transport 3%
Education 2%
Banking & Finance 19%
Culture & Society 18%
Construction & Industry
Arts &

SPECIAL POLITICS

POLITICS SPECIAL

Does Iran really have the ability to shut down the Strait of Hormuz?

Alternative routes map

page 38

In dire straits

BY ED ATTWOOD

On the morning of 12 October 2000, a small 35-foot skiff approached the US Navy destroyer USS *Cole*, which was busy refuelling in the Yemeni port of Aden. The craft was spotted by a few members of the *Cole's* crew, who assumed that the approaching boat was carrying rubbish. The two men on the skiff even waved to crew members topside of the vessel.

Seconds later, the boat rammed the *Cole* amidships, with as much as 300kg of explosives tearing a 40-foot-by-40-foot gash in the side of the vessel. Alongside the two suicide bombers, seventeen American sailors were killed, with 39 wounded. Although the *Cole* was later repaired and is still in active commission, the attack had huge ramifications for the US Navy. How could the *Cole* have left itself open to such an attack? Why did the then-rules of engagement not allow Navy crewmen to fire upon potential aggressors without the express permission of the captain or senior officers? And lastly, how could such a basic assault — with boat

30

31

GCC MAP

MAP GCC

SAUDI

Saudia jet crash lands in Madinah

Twenty nine people were injured when a Saudi Arabian Airlines (Saudia) Boeing aircraft made an emergency landing at Madinah Airport in the west of the country early last Sunday, the General Authority of Civil Aviation said. It said 18 of the injured were treated at the airport while 11 were taken to hospital. A spokesman for Saudi Arabian Airlines, who did not give his name, said three people were seriously injured. The flight, arriving from Mashhad in Iran before dawn, was carrying 315 passengers and suffered a technical malfunction, the authority said. It said the pilot had reported a problem with a rear wheel. The Saudia spokesman said the plane was leased from another company.

SAUDI ARABIA

29

Number of passengers injured during Saudi Arabian Airlines' emergency landing at Madinah Airport last week.

KUWAIT

Budget surplus narrows as spending soars

STATS

$37.9bn

Kuwait's budget surplus for April to September.

Kuwait's budget surplus narrowed in the first six months of its fiscal year as spending soared over 50 percent, partly thanks to increased outlays on public sector wages, while oil revenues fell, figures from the Finance Ministry showed. The budget surplus for April to September was KD10.72bn ($37.9bn), a Reuters calculation based on official data showed. That was down 15 percent from KD12.65bn during the same period a year earlier. Although Kuwait's fiscal position is still strong because of its oil wealth, the IMF has told the government that it will need to invest in infrastructure projects and control public wage growth.

Kuwaiti finance minister Sheikh Salem Abdulaziz Al Sabah.

BAHRAIN

Alba reports production milestone

Aluminium Bahrain achieved a production record of 912,700 metric tonnes per annum (mtpa) in 2013. The owner of the world's fourth-largest aluminium smelter posted a jump of 22,483 mtpa from the 890,217 mtpa produced in 2012. A ceremony to mark this milestone was held last Sunday and was attended by Alba's CEO, Tim Murray, other top executives and members of Alba's labour union, management staff and company employees. Murray said: "Alba was able to exceed 900,000 mtpa for the first time in its 40-year history, which is the result of the dedication of its hard working and loyal employees. We feel this increase in productivity is directly linked to the improvement in safety performance."

Aluminium Bahrain achieved a production record of 912,700 metric tonnes per annum in 2013.

Alba is the world's fourth-largest aluminium smelter.

SAUDI ARABIA

111

Number of aircraft in Saudi Arabian Airlines' fleet, including 35 Airbus A320s.

The Mall of Qatar will comprise 400 shops, including 50 luxury brands and four department stores.

QATAR/DOHA

$820m

Value of the Mall of Qatar shopping complex.

"THE PROPOSED CENTRE WILL UNDERTAKE REQUIRED TESTS FOR HALAL FOOD AND OTHER PRODUCTS TO ENSURE THAT ALL SUCH PRODUCTS ARE FREE FROM ANY CHEMICAL OR ARTIFICIAL ADDITIONS WHICH ARE NOT COMPLYING WITH THE ISLAMIC LAW"

Hussain Nasser Lootah, director general of Dubai Municipality.

The Central Bank of Oman.

OMAN/MUSCAT

$4.68bn

Oman's total projected deficit in its 2014 budget.

QATAR

More global brands heading for Doha

Attracting luxury brands to Qatar will be key to making the country a shopping hotspot in the GCC, according to an industry professional. Donald Weir, general manager of the Mall of Qatar, told ITP publication *Construction Week*: "We are currently in discussion with a number of retailers who will not only be present in Qatar for the first time, but also completely new to the region and we are extremely excited about the role these brands will play in changing the retail space in Qatar and across the region. Here, at the Mall of Qatar, we see the potential in the market for luxury retail."

UAE

Halal accreditation centre planned

Dubai will soon launch an international accreditation centre for halal food as part of the emirate's drive to become the world's capital for the Islamic economy. Hussain Nasser Lootah, director general of Dubai Municipality, announced that an action team has been appointed to set up the centre and will be led by Salem Bin Mesmar, assistant director general, Health, Safety & Environment Monitoring Sector. Mesmar said: "The move is expected to boost the business activities of Dubai as it comes in the most wanted context in both local and global levels."

OMAN

$520m worth of sukuk issuance planned for 2014

The Oman government is planning to float OMR200m ($520m) worth of sovereign sukuk in the domestic market this year partly to meet the projected budget deficit, it was reported. The total projected deficit in 2014 budget is OMR1.8bn ($4.68bn), which will be met by way of OMR200m foreign borrowing, OMR200m sukuk, a surplus of OMR1bn from 2012 and another OMR400m financial reserve, the *Times of Oman* said.

16

Vol. 15/02, January 2014

17

• Magazine Introduction

Arabian Business magazine is the Middle East region's premier weekly magazine, focusing on the English speaking and Arabic speaking business community. The magazine provides weekly in-depth analysis of the latest regional and international news and its influence on business in the Gulf.

FFF, Firenze Fast Forward

- Completion Year: 2011
- Designer: Gianni Sinni, Donatello D'Angelo, Fupete
- Client: FFF

• Work Introduction

The infographics covered many topics related to the city of Florence: the areas of the city closed to traffic with iron chains, the flood of water and tourists and a map of cultural events. By taking advantage of the variety of graphic, the designer adds more design elements to the work.

• Magazine Introduction

FFF, Firenze Fast Forward, is a magazine, published since 2009 to 2011, that aims to make visible people and projects that promote the idea of an alternative vision of the future of the city. A future that can be drawn not only by administrators and politicians by profession, but by all those who, in different disciplines, make daily exercise of creativity. A section of the magazine is devoted to analyzing specific themes through infographics.

| EVENTO AUTOCONVOCATO

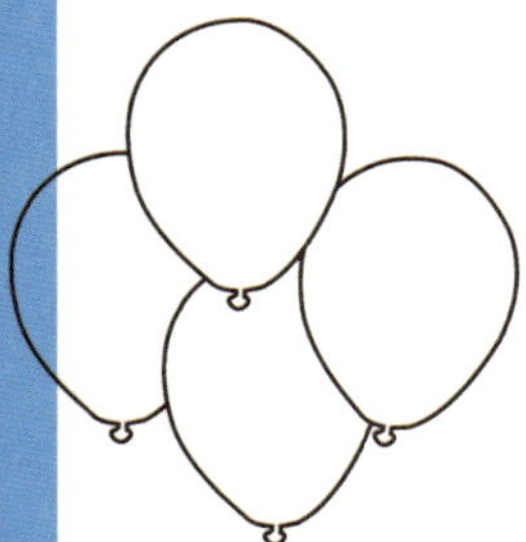

WWW.FIRENZEFASTFORWARD.IT/URBANFRUITS/IDA/

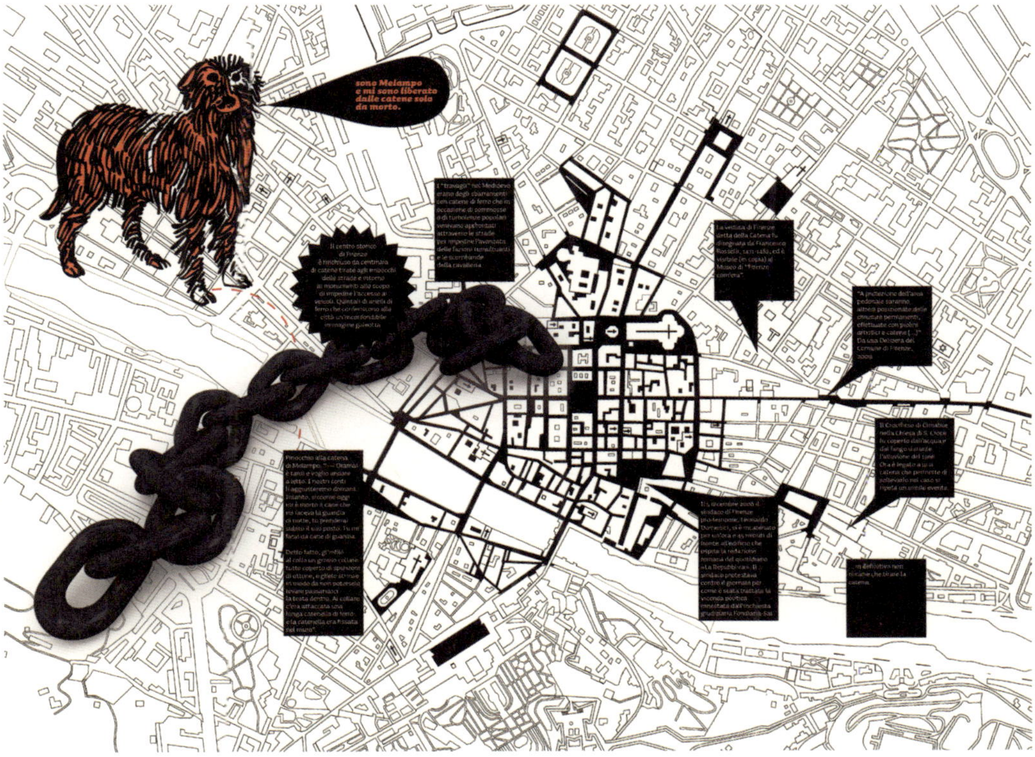

DESIGN ACTIVISM LEVEL

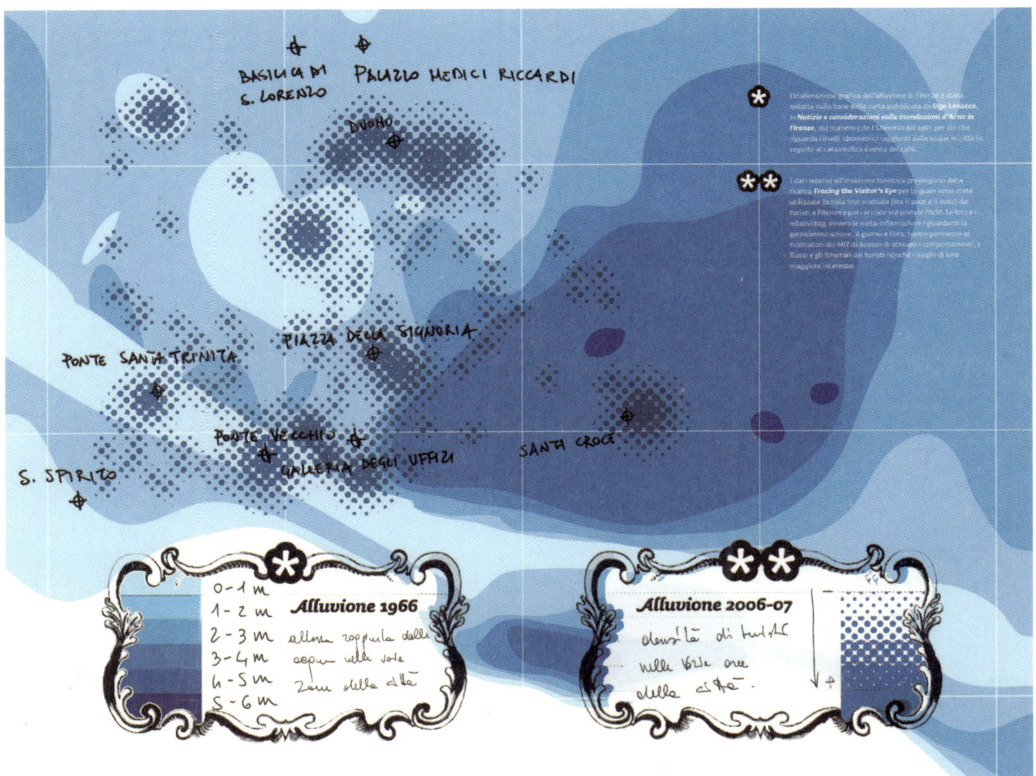

Rap

- Completion Year: 2013
- Designer: Uve Portillo
- Client: Gauss Multimedia

• Work Introduction

The designer was told to elaborate an infographic design based on Yorokobu's magazine style. The topic she had to analyze was urban tribes, and among all of the urban tribes that exist nowadays she decided to analyze Hip Hop culture. Not all the information is real, part of it is there just to make people laugh.

• Magazine Introduction

The infographic presented here is a classwork and was designed to fit into a popular Spanish magazine named Yorokobu. The magazine focus in culture, curiosities and presenting a deeper knowledge of daylife issues. The topic that had to be analyzed were urban tribes. This infographic is focused on Hip-Hop culture.

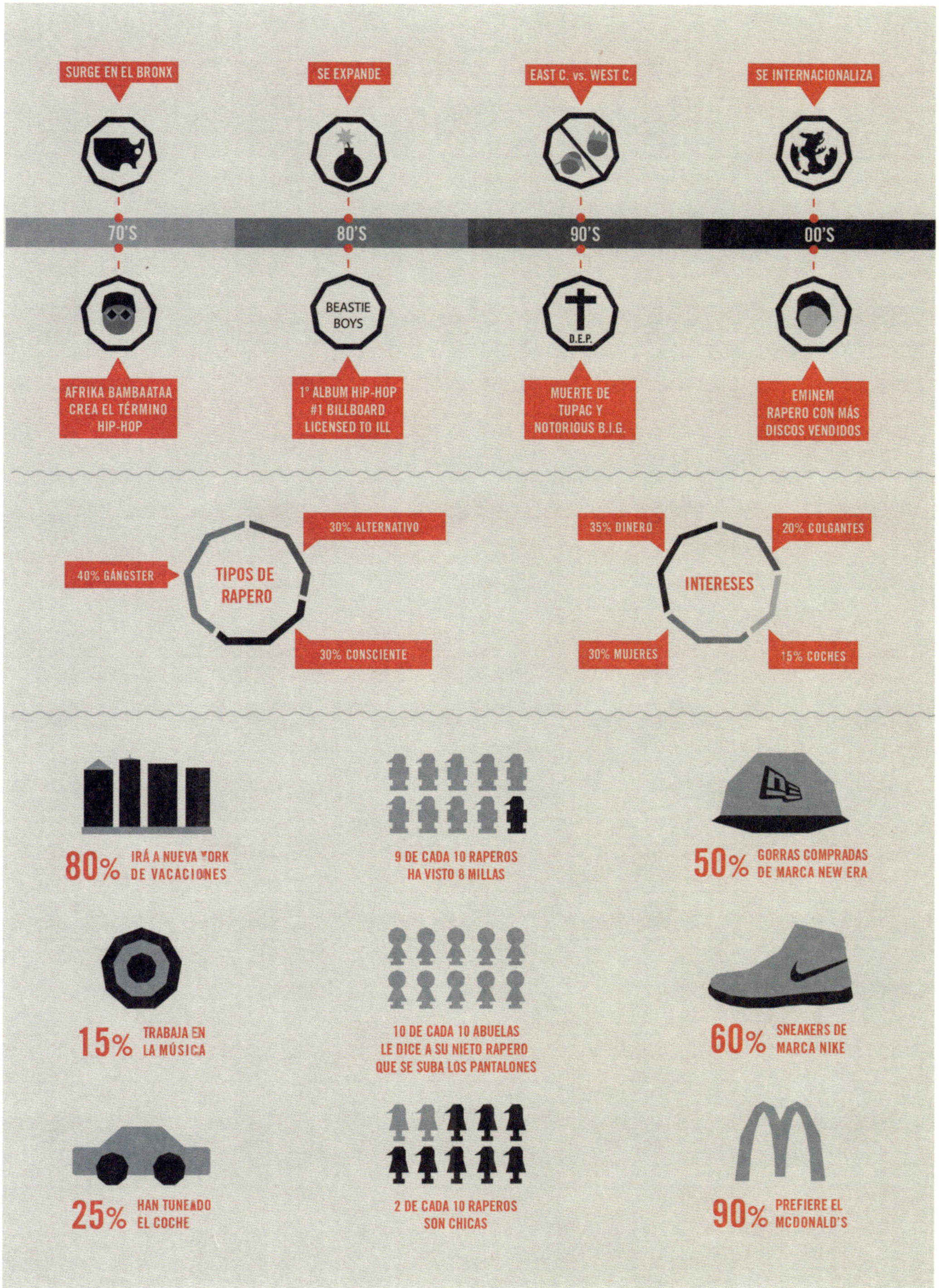

- Completion Year: 2013
- Designer: Uve Portillo
- Client: Gauss Multimedia

• Work Introduction

The infograph starts with a timeline of wine production and is followed by consumption data by genre and the frequency of that consumption. Under that we can see the parts of a wine bottle and the label structure. The last two columns of the infograph are filled with curiosities about wine around the world. The information is in Spanish & all the data is real.

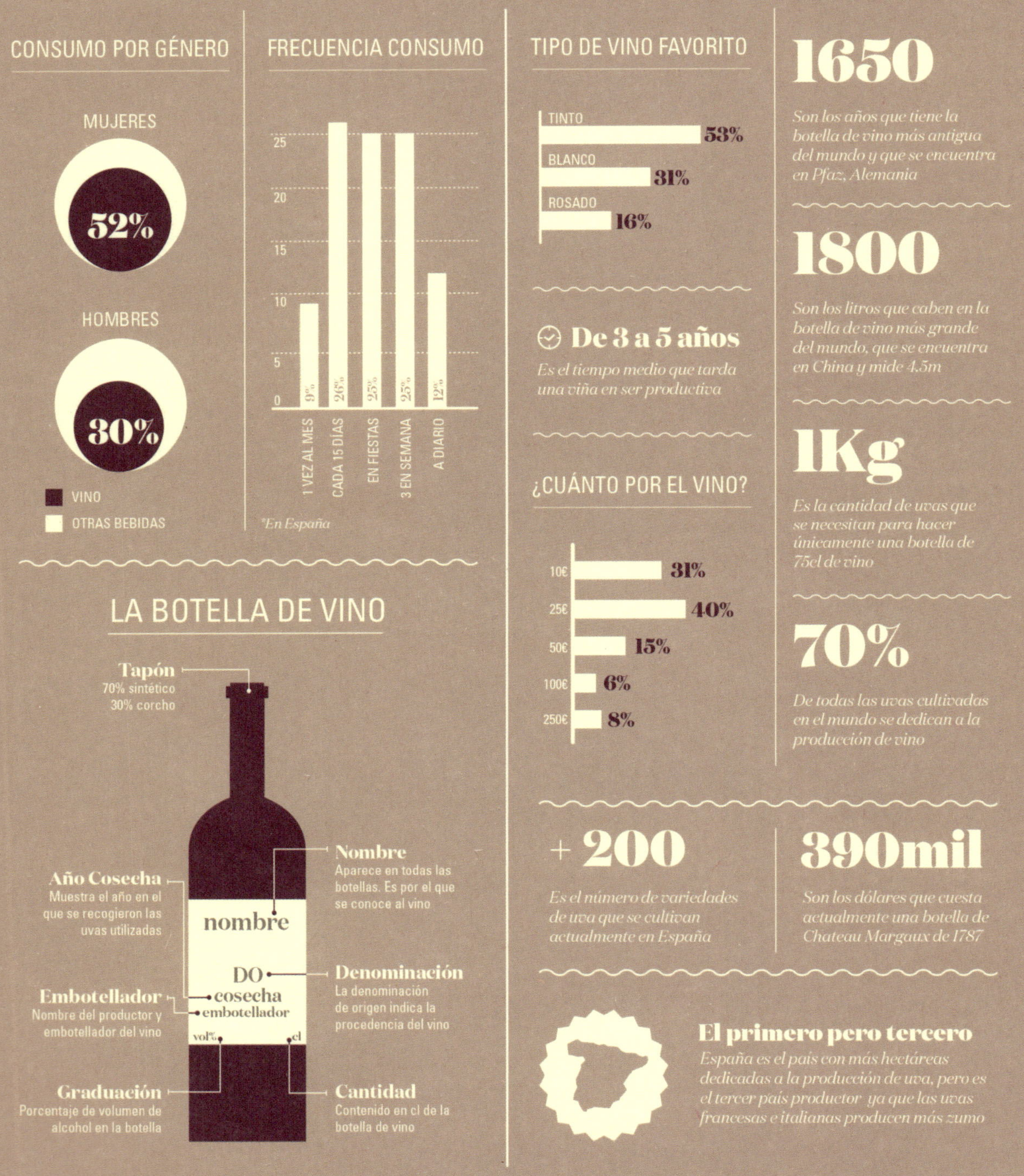

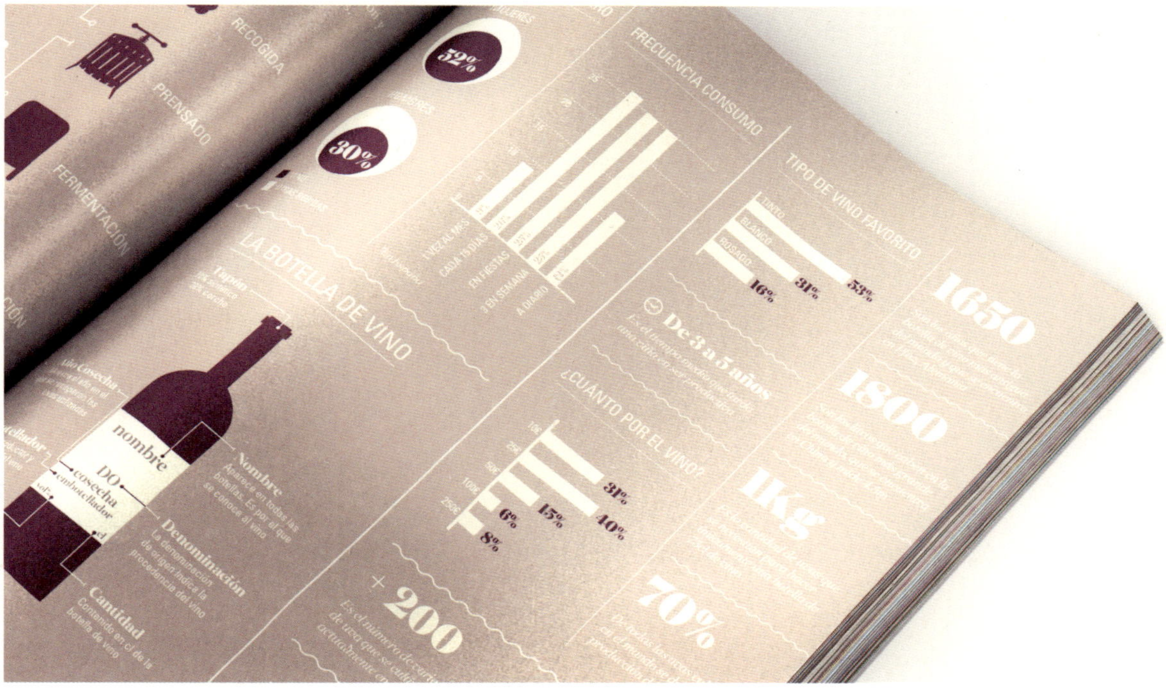

• Magazine Introduction

The infographic presented here is a classwork andwas designed to fit into a fictional magazine that the students had to create. The magazine wanted to engage with a masculine and wealthy target interested in culture, food, beverages and modern life. All of it sourrounded by an elegance halo.

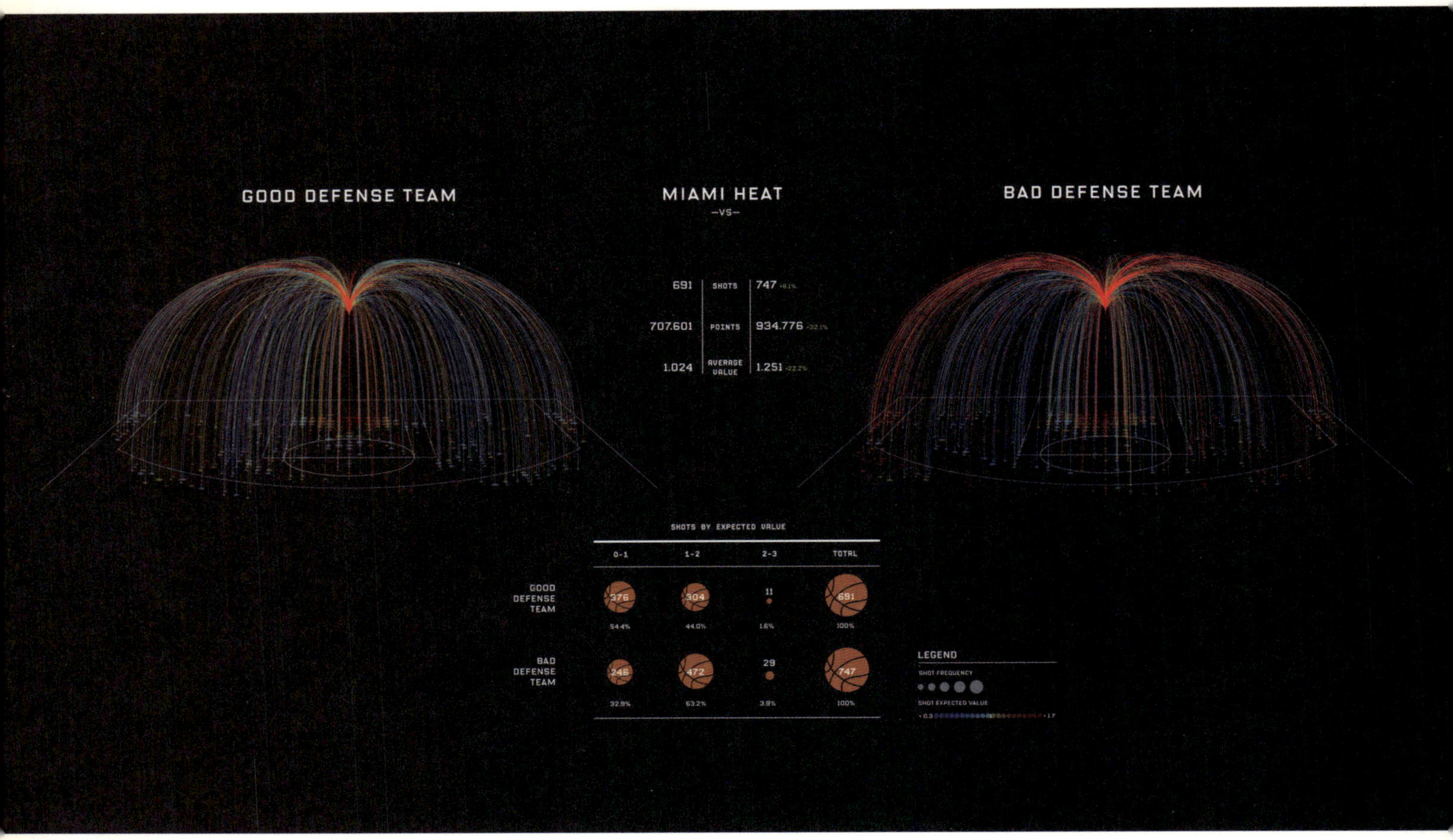

WIRED

- Completion Year: 2013
- Designer: Gert Franke, Thomas Clever, Jonas Groot Kormelink, Wouter van Dijk
- Client: WIRED

• Work Introduction

The visualization shows how often the players, of the basketball team Miami Heat, shoot from each position on the court, and how many points those shots deliver. The result shows that while the number of shots doesn't differ much, Miami Heat players are more efficient in taking their 3-point shots. This visualization was created using a dataset from Accenture.

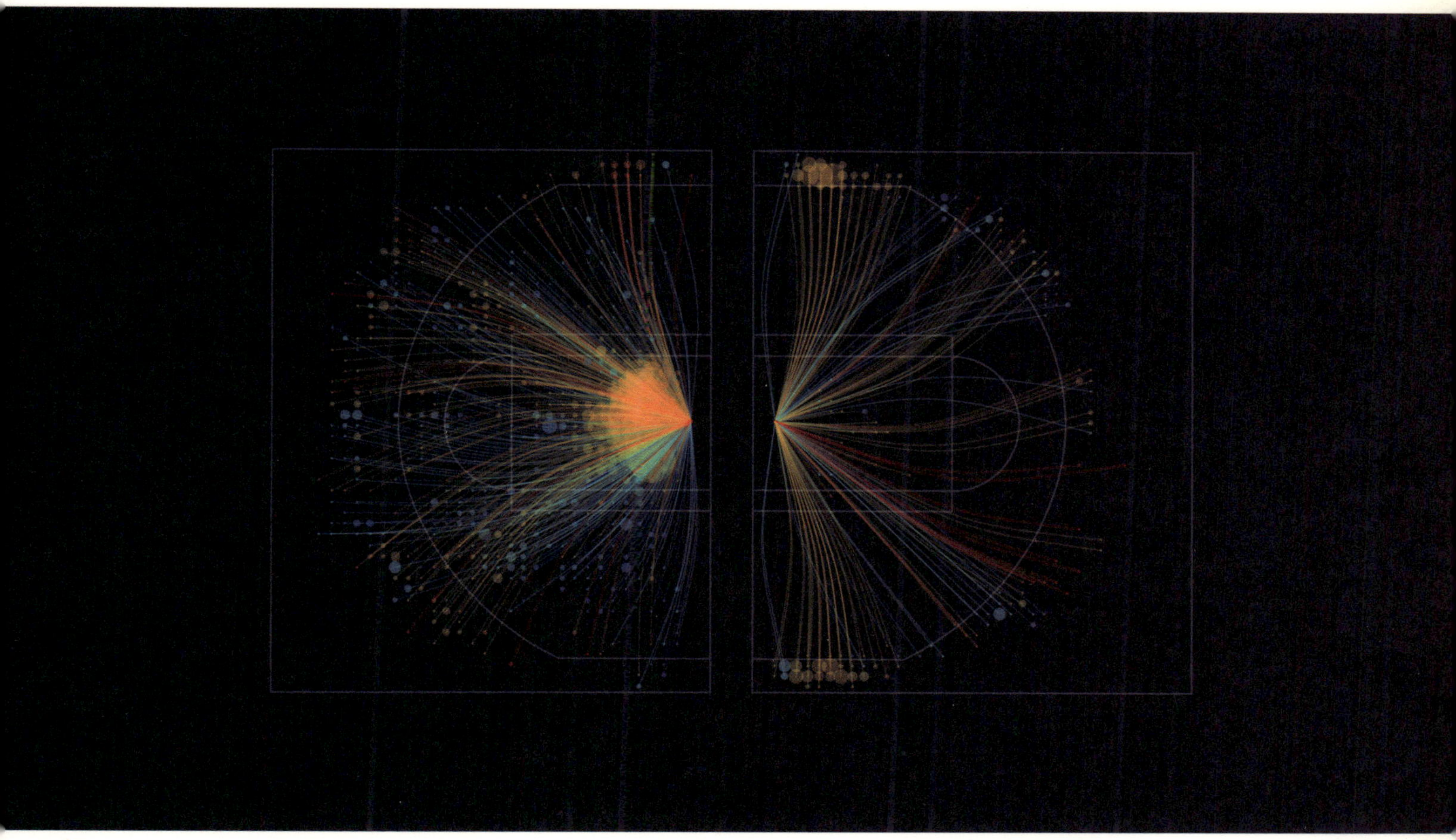

• Magazine Introduction

WIRED is a full-color monthly American magazine, published in both print and online editions, that reports on how emerging technologies affect culture, the economy and politics.

Veltins – Arena

- Completion Year: 2010
- Designer: Alex Novichkov
- Client: "Football Kak Delo" Magazine

- Work Introduction

Infographic about Veltins-Arena, Germany.
Infographic provides statistical data and illustrations

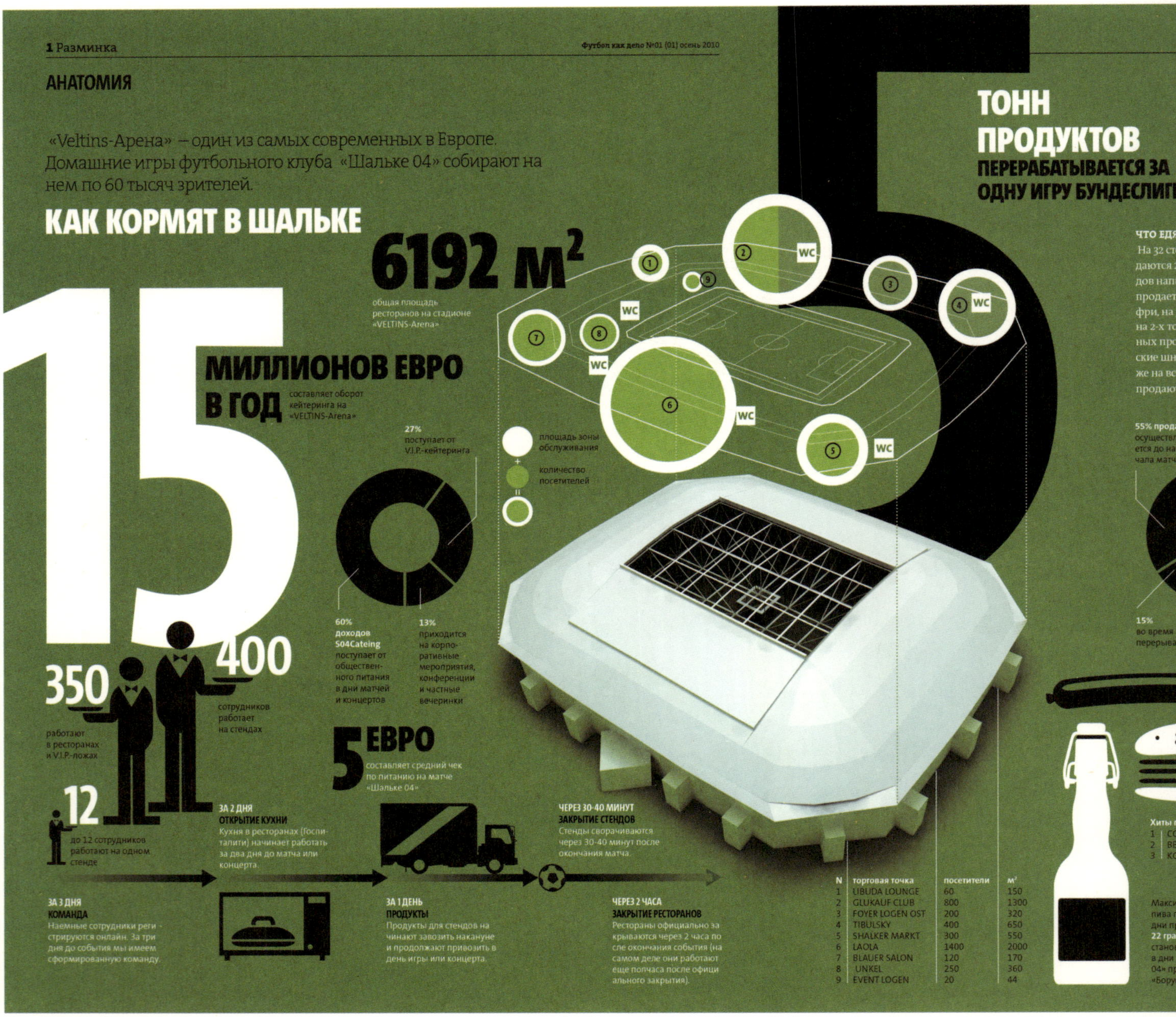

N	торговая точка	посетители	м²
1	LIBUDA LOUNGE	60	150
2	GLUKAUF CLUB	800	1300
3	FOYER LOGEN OST	200	320
4	TIBULSKY	400	650
5	SHALKER MARKT	300	550
6	LAOLA	1400	2000
7	BLAUER SALON	120	170
8	UNKEL	250	360
9	EVENT LOGEN	20	44

Video of Football Matches

- Completion Year: 2010
- Designer: Alex Novichkov
- Client: "Football Kak Delo" Magazine

- Work Introduction

The infographic is about football matches video recording. It provides video recording process visualization.

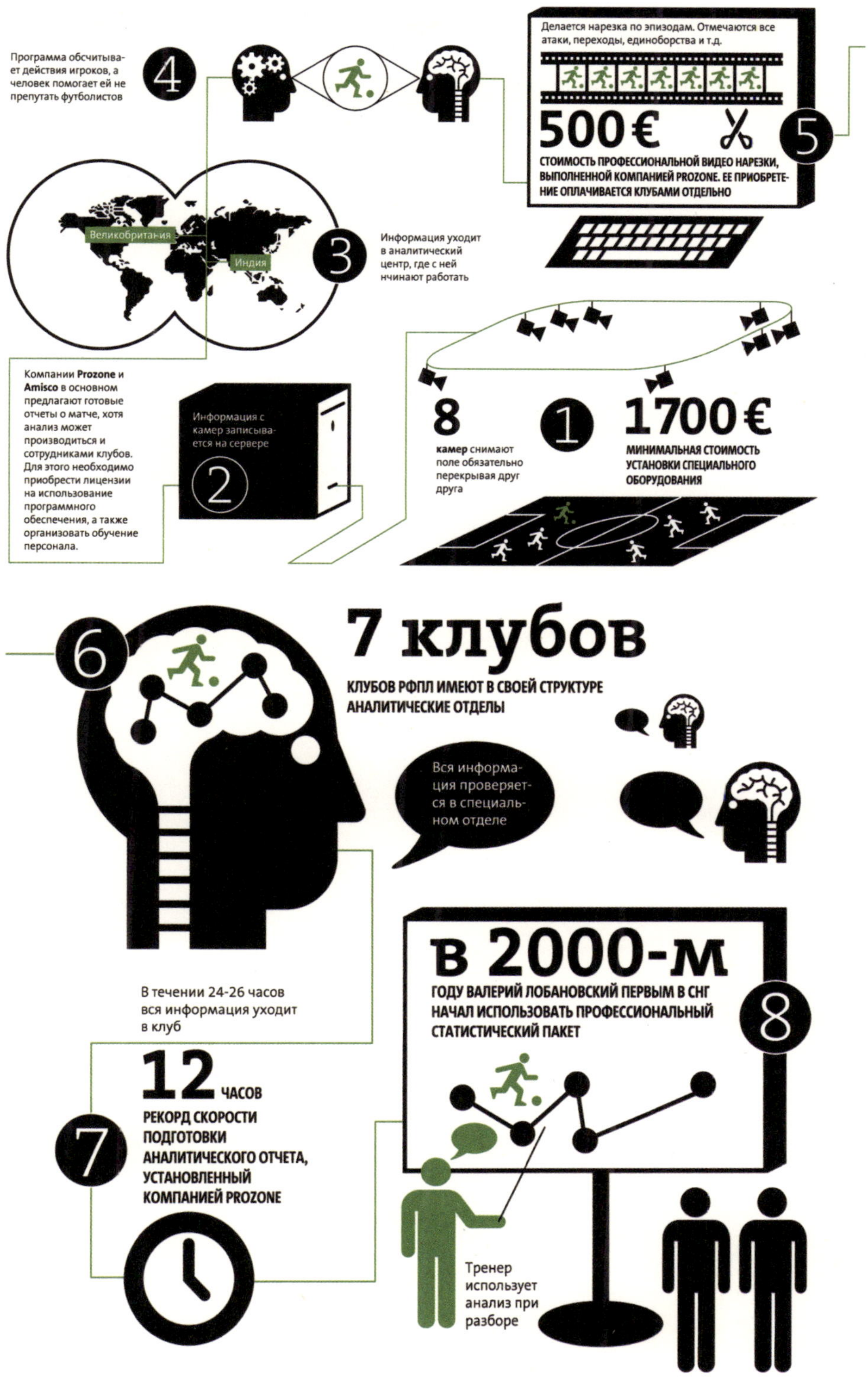

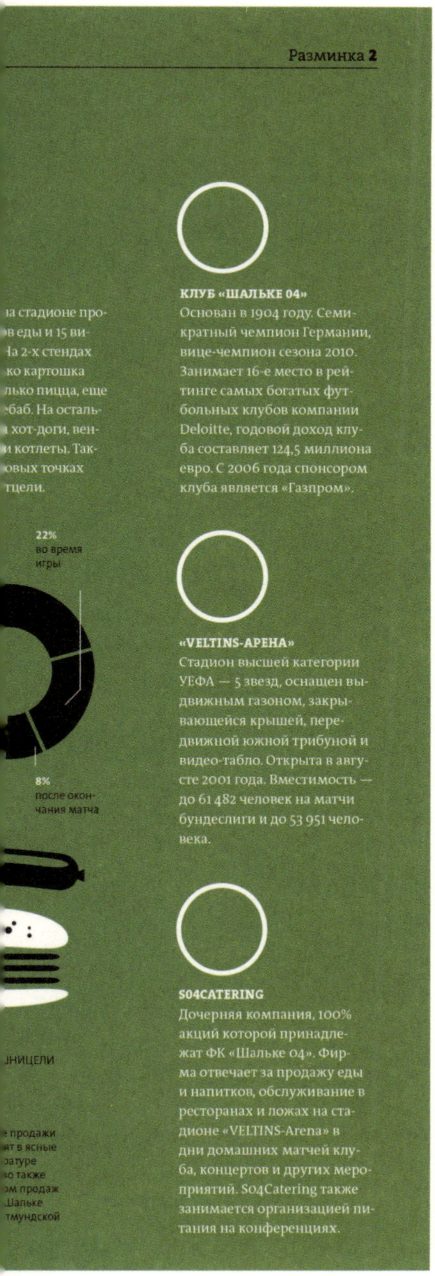

- Magazine Introduction

"Football kak delo" (Russian: Футбол как дело, literally: "Football as a Business ") — a publication for professionals in the football business, accumulating Russian and foreign experience in sports management. The magazine contains interviews with leading experts, exclusive materials of its own correspondents, analytical reviews, useful business information.

LASER History Timeline

- Completion Year: 2011
- Designer: Alex Novichkov, Anton Fedorov
- Client: "Vokrug Sveta" Magazine

- Work Introduction

The project 'LASER history timeline' provided a visualization which is about the creator's information.

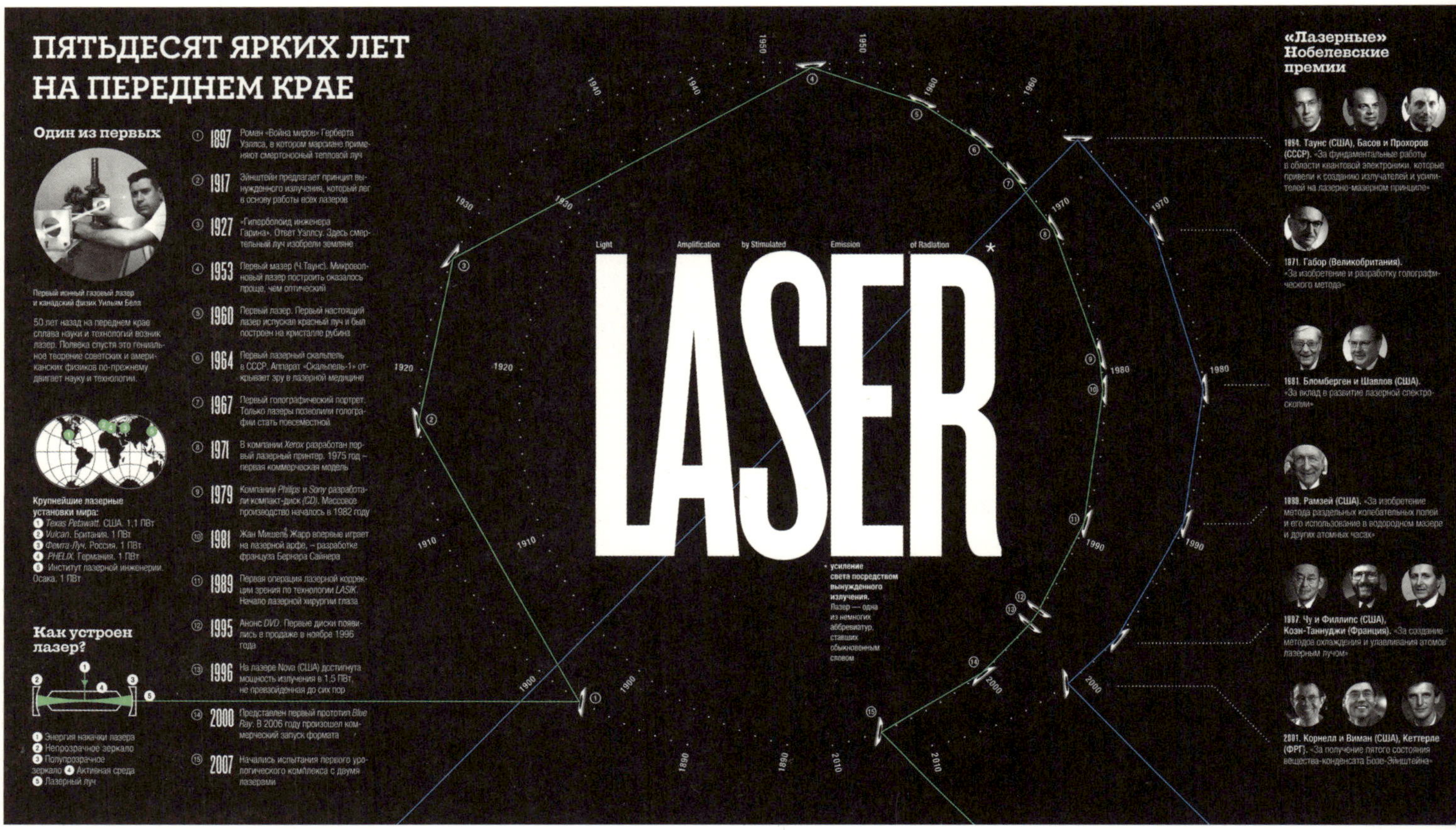

Lamps History Timeline

- Completion Year: 2010
- Designer: Alex Novichkov, Anton Fedorov
- Client: "Vokrug Sveta" Magazine

- Work Introduction

The project 'Lamps history timeline' provided lamps schematic illustration and the creator's information.

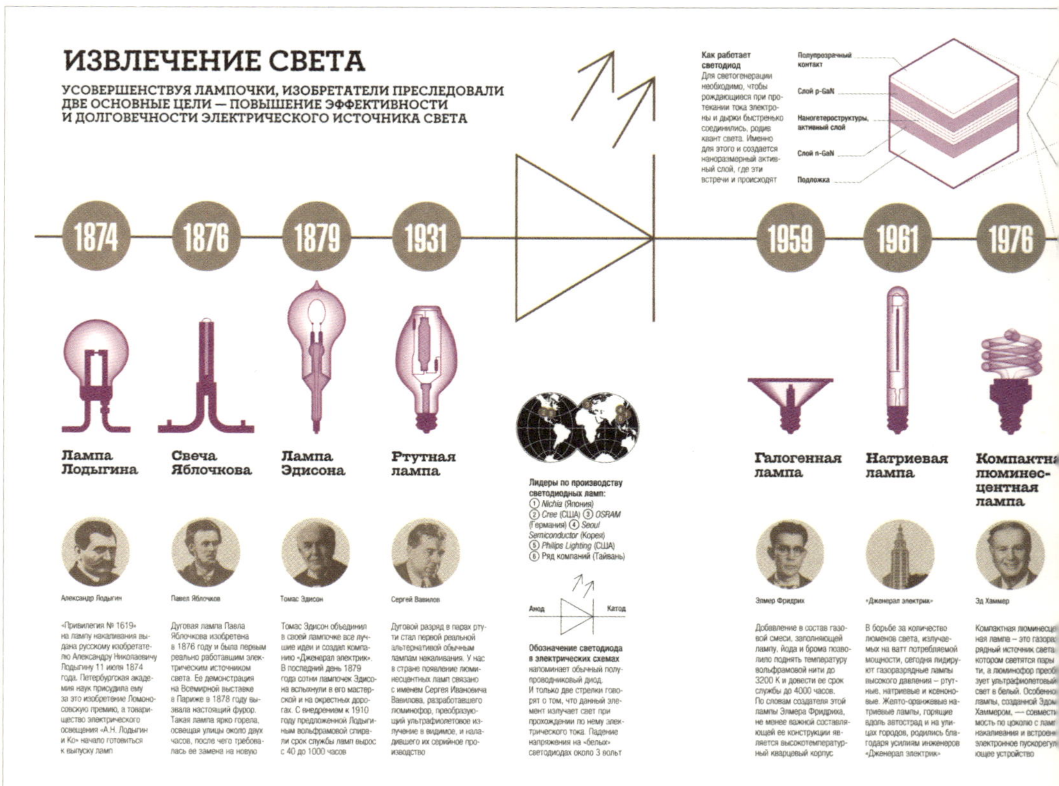

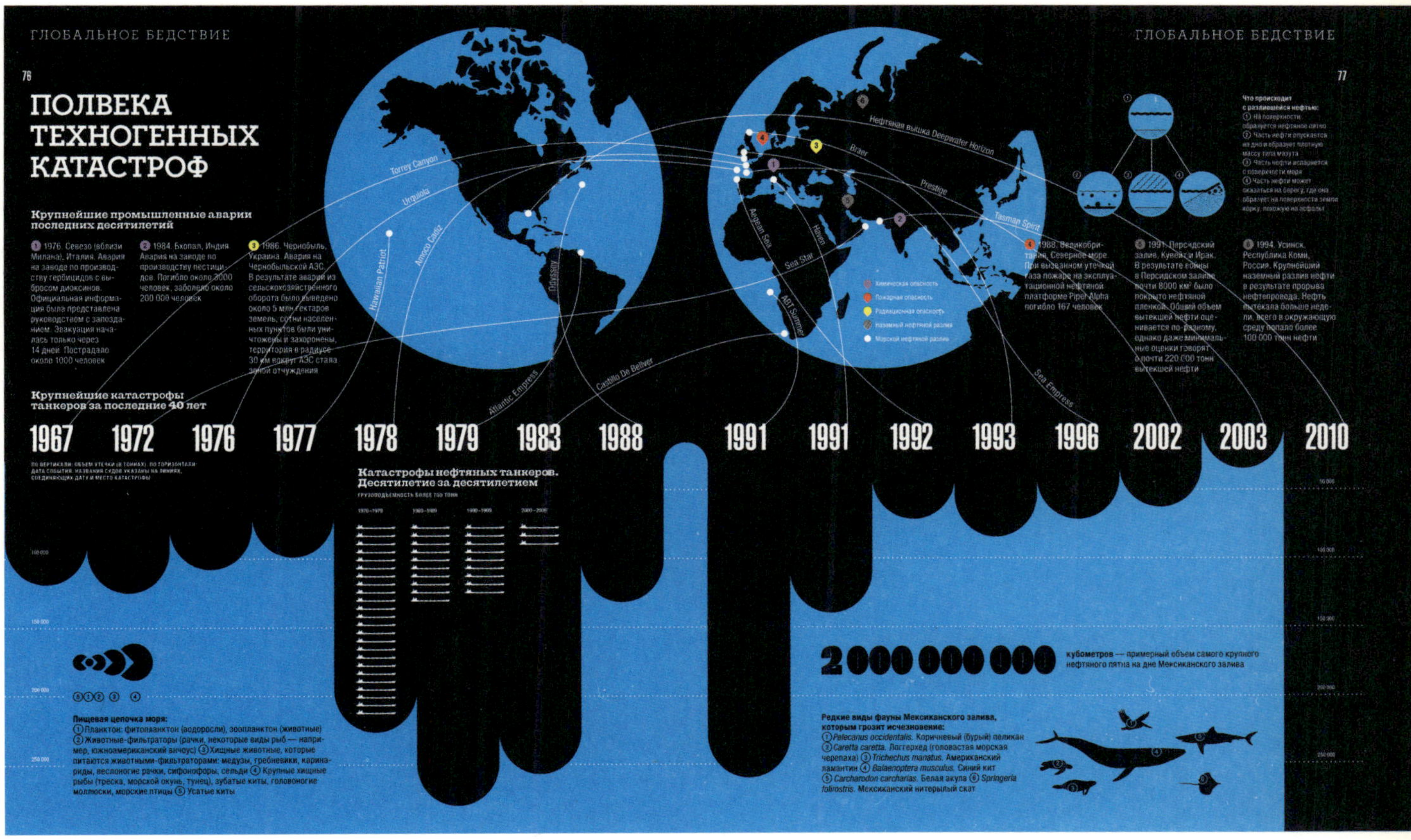

The Greatest Man – Made Disasters

- Completion Year: 2010
- Designer: Alex Novichkov, Anton Fedorov, Dima Barbanel
- Client: "Vokrug Sveta" Magazine

- Work Introduction

Infographic provides oil spills timeline and greatest man-made disasters location. Oil spill in Mexican Golf visualization have not final view because it was not stopped. The histogram that marks the oil spill messages of different years bases on the colours of blue and black, making the visual effect easy to understand.

Before Civil War USA Population

- Completion Year: 2011
- Designer: Alex Novichkov
- Client: "Vokrug Sveta" Magazine

• Work Introduction

Demography statistic visualization with map. Visualization includes data on the size and composition of the population in the U.S. states.

The creative and unique infographic shows the stereo feeling of the 3D effect, which makes the discrepancies among cities visualized.

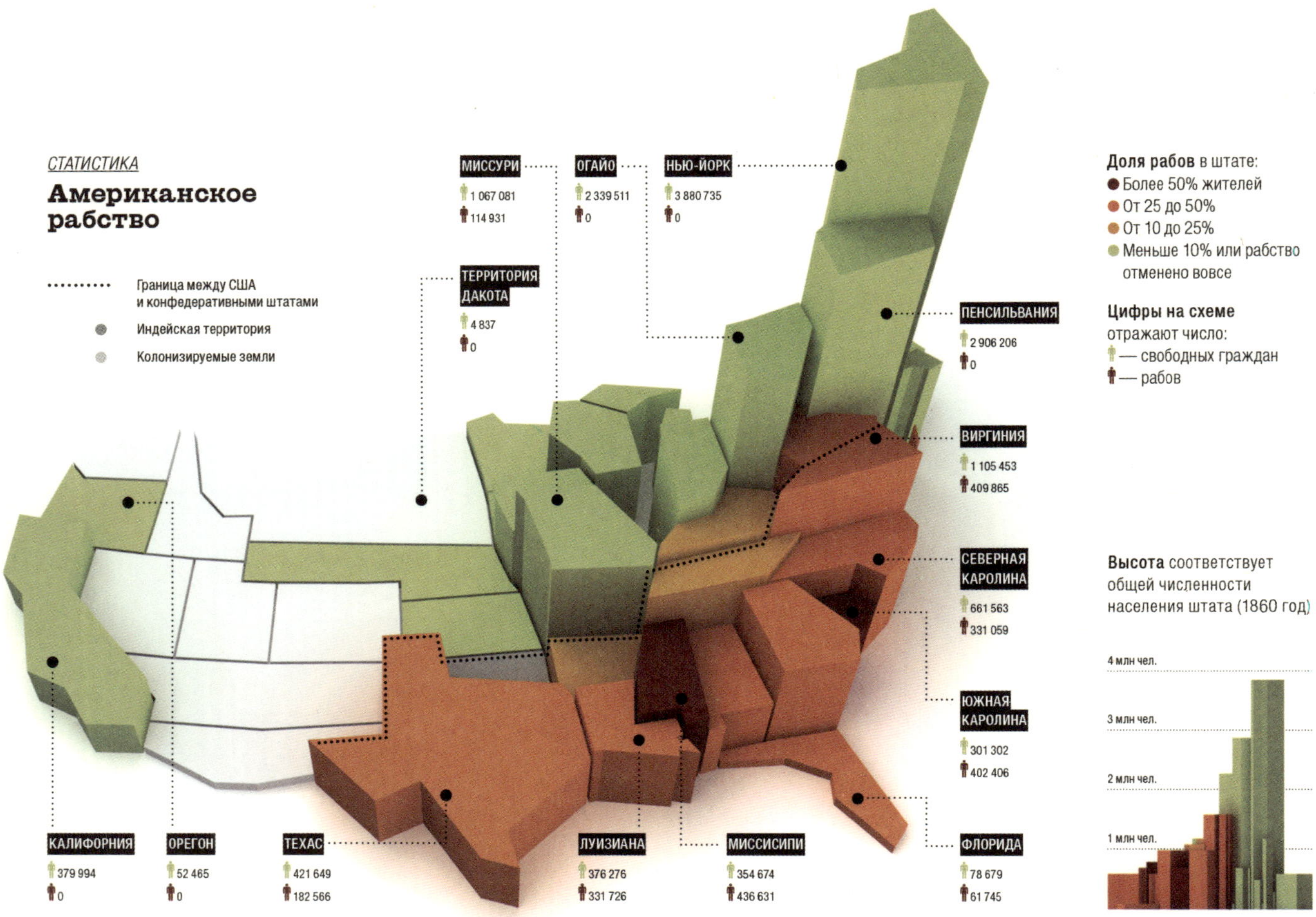

• Magazine Introduction

"Vokrug sveta" (Russian: "Вокруг света", literally: "Around the World") is a Russian geographic magazine. It is the longest running magazine in the Russian language. The first issue was printed in Saint Petersburg, in December 1861, almost thirty years before the establishment of the National Geographic Magazine. Thus, it is one of the oldest popular science magazines in the world. Release of Vokrug sveta was suspended twice: from 1918 to 1927, during the Russian Revolution, and from 1941 to 1945, during World War II. Nevertheless, the magazine always resumed and continues to be published to this day.

Illustrations for Simple Wine News Magazine-85

- Completion Year: 2014
- Designer: Ruslan Valikhanov
- Client: SWN

- Work Introduction

The illustrations show the process of making white wine, from collection the grapes to assemblage.

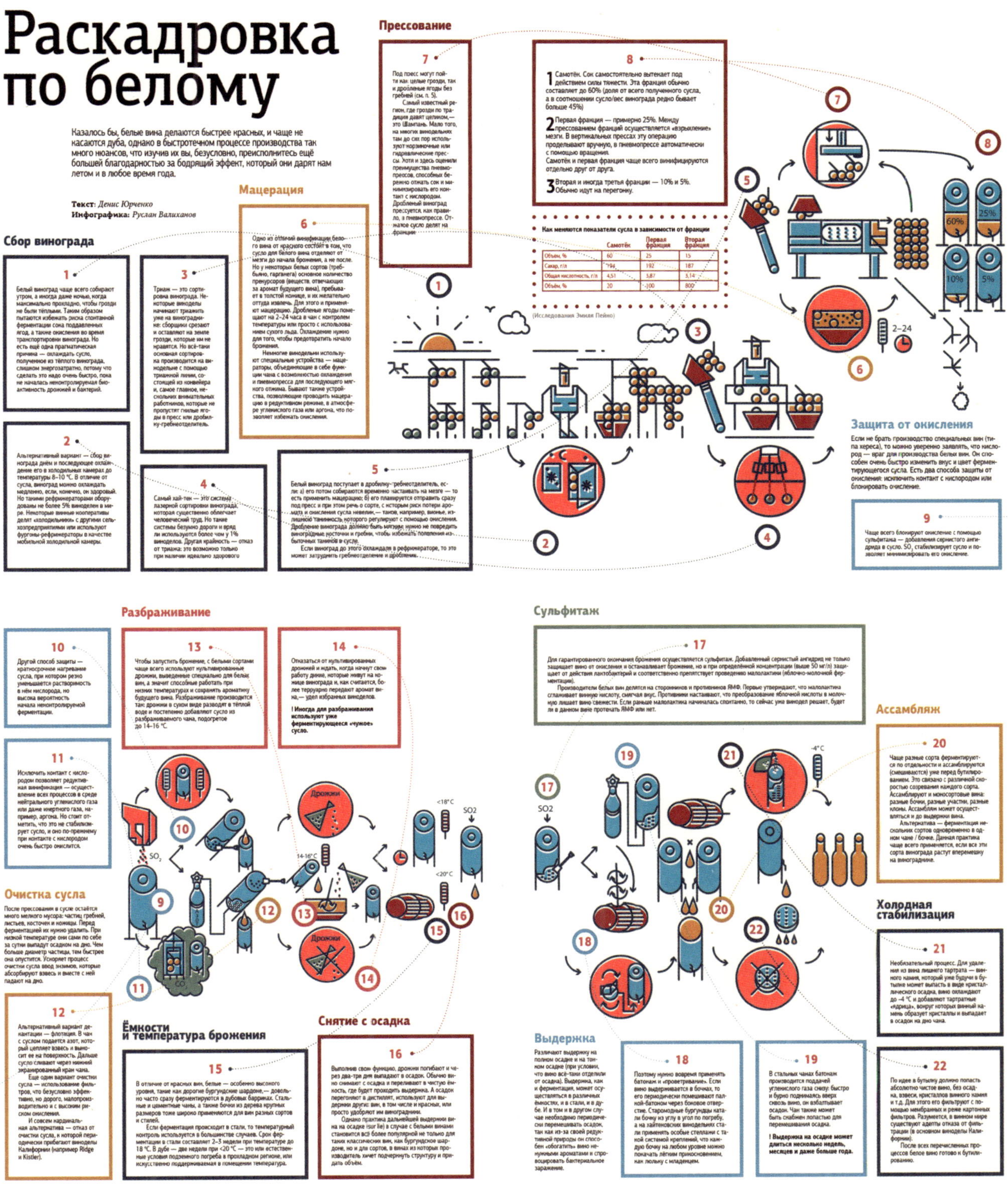

Illustrations for Simple Wine News Magazine-84

- Completion Year: 2014
- Designer: Ruslan Valikhanov
- Client: SWN

- Work Introduction

This picture presents the biodynamic winery as a microcosm. The tree levels of involvement in biodynamic practices are shown. All the biodynamic preparations and treatments are described.

- Magazine Introduction

Simple Wine News is a monthly magazine. It is distributed in the biggest cities of Russia. Edition is devoted to all aspects of winemaking, wine selling, culture of drinking wine, gastronomy and restaurant business. It has a strong reputation as the leading enogastronomy edition in Russia. Edition is devoted to all wine professionals and people who interested in wine culture.

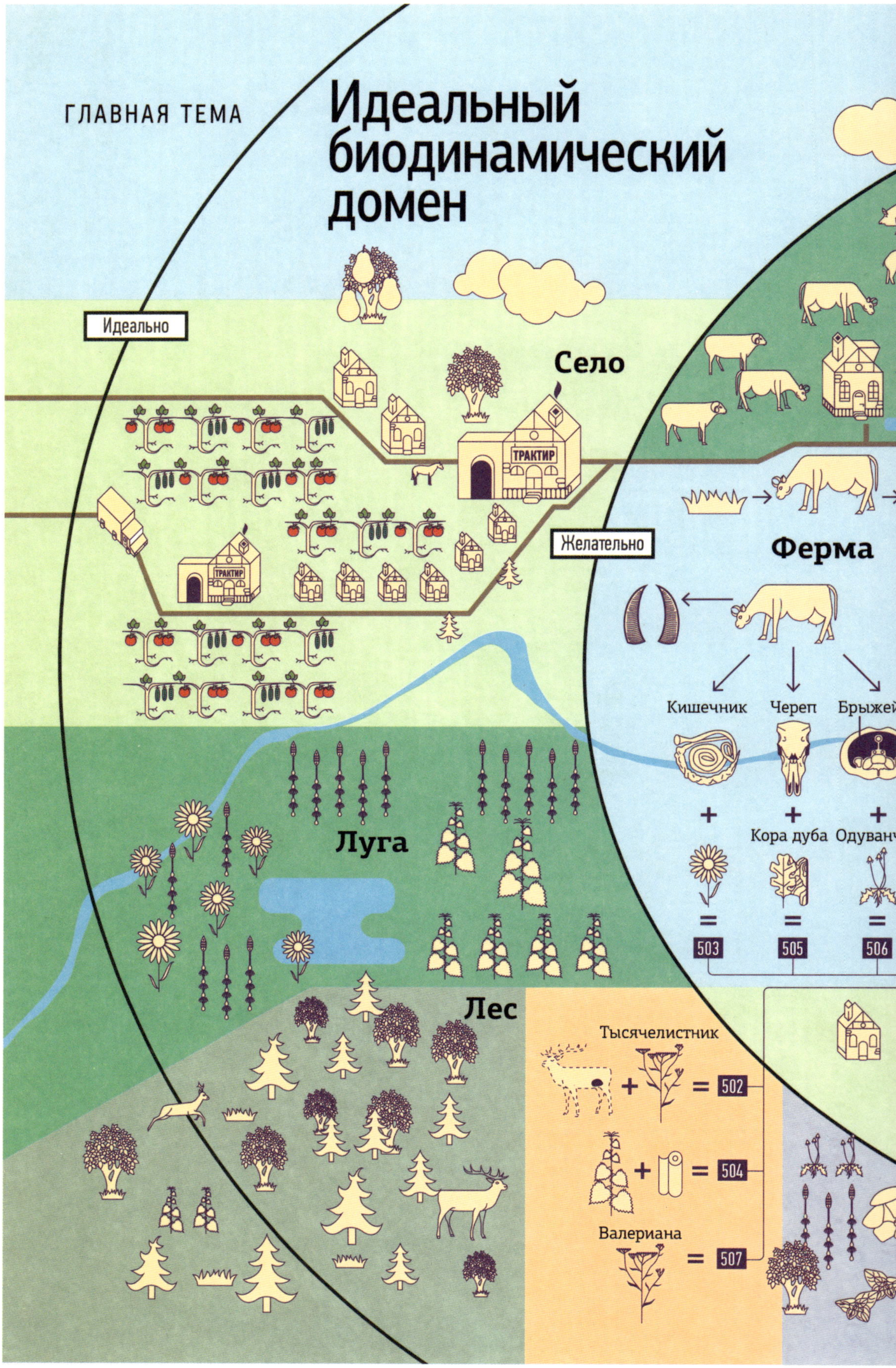

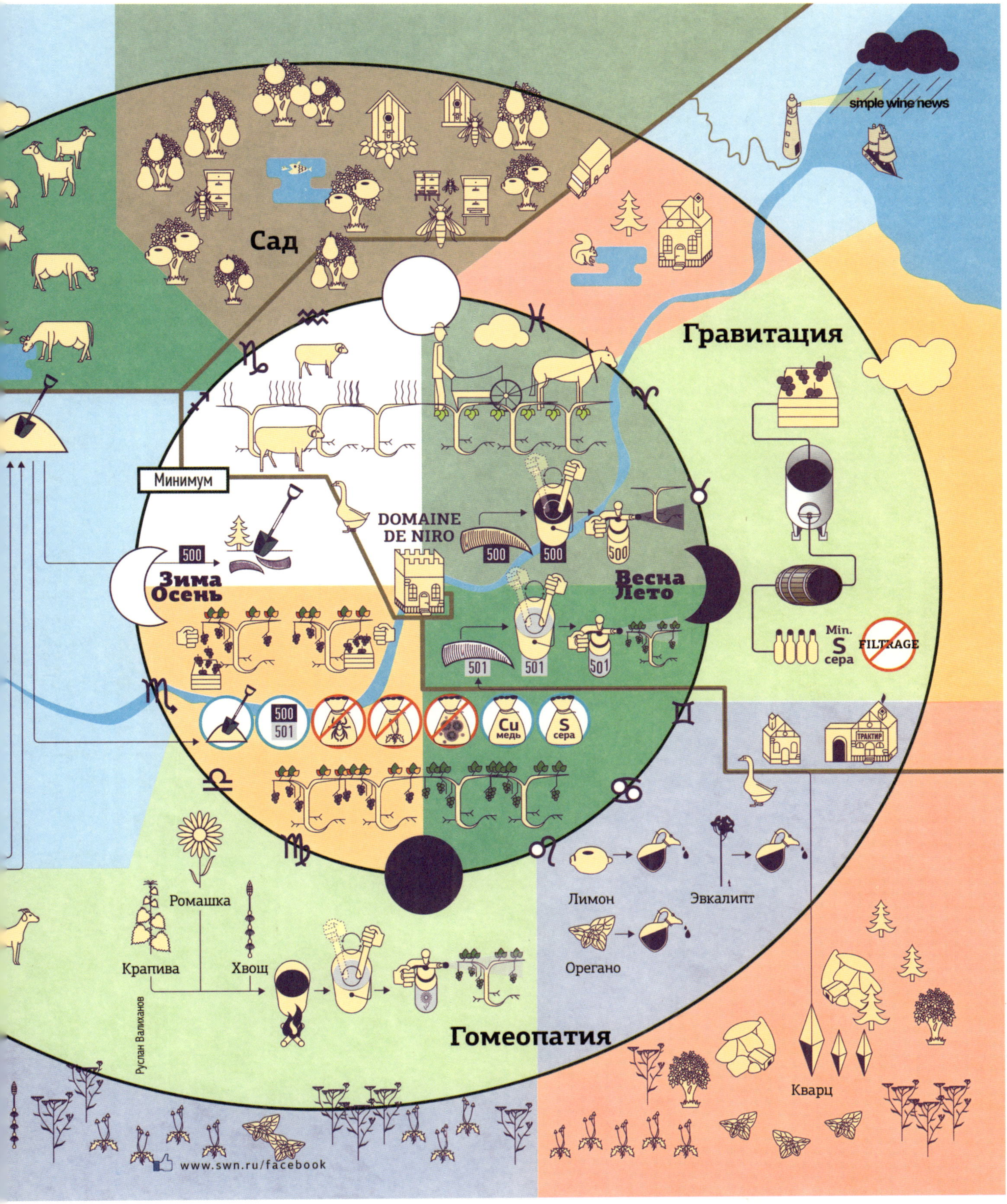
simple wine news
Сад
Гравитация
Минимум
DOMAINE DE NIRO
500
Зима Осень
Весна Лето
500
500
501
501
501
Min. S сера
FILTRAGE
ТРАКТИР
500 501
Cu медь
S сера
Ромашка
Крапива
Хвощ
Лимон
Эвкалипт
Орегано
Гомеопатия
Кварц
Руслан Валиханов
www.swn.ru/facebook

Light Technologies

- Completion Year: 2014
- Designer: Anton Ermolenko
- Client: Rustes

• Work Introduction

Company "Rustes" is a manufacturer of professional solutions in the field of LED lighting. Here, the designer adopts blue and purple color respectively to represent the lifespan of LED light, and by designing tabulation with lively icons and dotted line, the designer makes the benefit from LED lighting technologies visualized.

Светильник LED Street		Светильник ДНаТ
175	Мощность светильника (Вт)	275
30 000	Световой поток (Лм)	30 000
0,95	КПД светильника	0,65
65-68°	Коэффициент максимальной интенсивности светового потока	55-60°

Пример поэтапного перехода на энергосберегающее освещение

Количество цехов	Общая площадь	Существующее освещение (тип светильника)	Освещенность
19	113 129 м²	ДРЛ	средняя

Поэтапная реконструкция освещения предприятия позволяет осуществлять переход на энергосберегающие технологии за счет сэкономленной электроэнергии.

	МВт	Млн. руб.
Потребление до реконструкции	5,2	62,9
Первый год после частичной реконструкции	3,9	47,18
Второй год после частичной реконструкции	2,7	33,03
Полная реконструкция (замена на светодиодные светильники)	1,2	14,87
Экономия	**4** МВт	**48** Млн. руб.

Срок службы

40 000 часов работы — Светильник LED Office

до 16 000 часов работы — Люминесцентные лампы

Экономия с светильниками LED Office в 2-3 раза

Световая отдача

120 лм/ватт — Светильник LED Indust

55 лм/ватт — Светильник ДРЛ

Светильник типа T5 (16 мм)

Мощность светильника (Вт)	14	28	35	49	54	80	Срок службы	16 000 часов

Светильник типа T8 (26 мм)

Мощность светильника (Вт)	Потребление с электрическим балластом (Вт)	Потребление с электромагнитным балластом (Вт)
18	36	46
36	72	88
58	116	146
Срок службы	12 000 часов	8 000 часов

*моделируем срок службы в год 4 тысячи часов

Экономия при использовании светильника LED Indust

Мощность светильника (Вт): LED	Мощность светильника (Вт): ДРЛ	Экономия (кВт)
43	275	43
75	440	75
135	770	135
175	1100	175

Расчеты приведены на время работы светильника составляющее 4000 часов в год при двухсменном графике производства

Сравнительная таблица светильника LED Indust и светильника ДРЛ

	Мощность светильника (Вт)	Световой поток (Лм)	CRI	КПД	LMF	Время запуска (Мин)
LED Indust	43 75 135 175	5 200 9 200 15 600 20 800	80	0,93	0,8	0
ДРЛ	275 440 770 1100	12 500 23 000 40 000 55 000	50	0,63	12 500 23 000 40 000 55 000	6 минут 8-9 минут 12 минут 12-15 минут

L'A-Bici, European & Italian Bike Industry

- Completion Year: 2014
- Designer: Emanuele Ercoli, Federica Ricci
- Client: Accademia delle Arti e Nuove Tecnologie (AANT)

• Work Introduction

The target was to design an infographic tri-fold about the bycicle market share in Europe from 2,000 to 2012 with a focus on Italian situation and bicycles uses in all the continent. Futura is the choosen font.

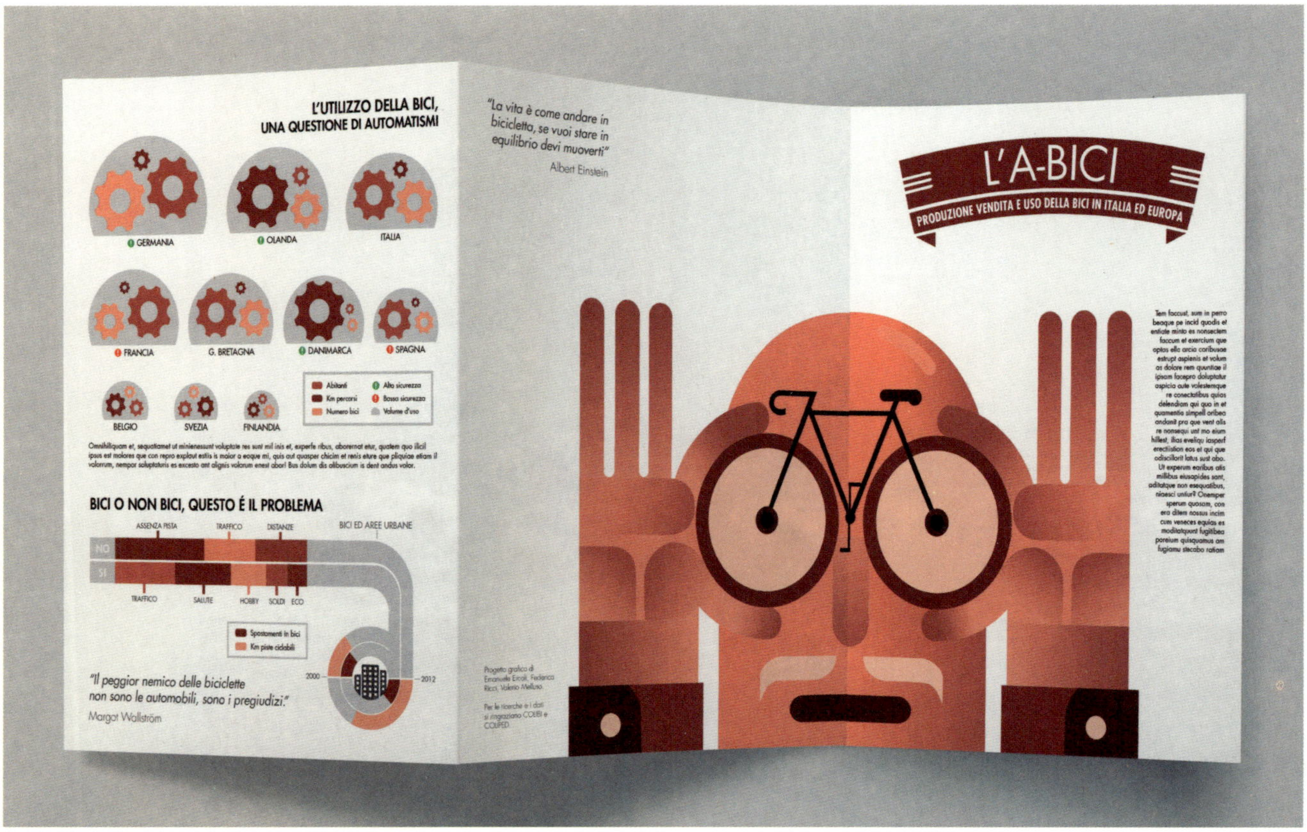

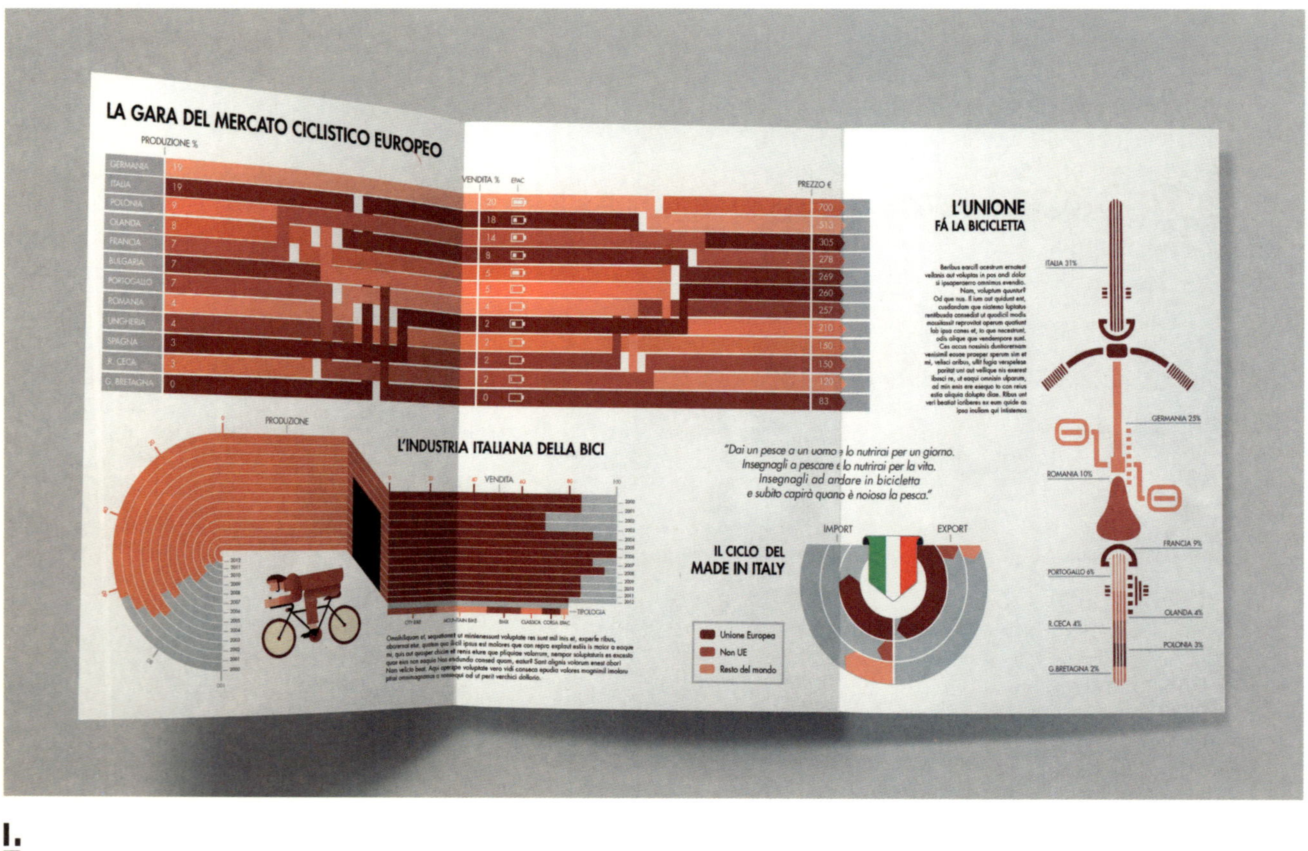

Quaff & Co.s Best Little Wine Guide

• Completion Year: 2014
• Designer: Emily Parker

• Work Introduction

The concept for this piece was to provide a complete, single source of wine information in a simplistic, imaginative, visually appealing and exciting way thus enticing the end user to absorb the information as easily as possible.

Integrated Public Report 2012

- Completion Year: 2013
- Designer: Artonica Branding and Creative Agency
- Client: Financial Corporation URALSIB

• Work Introduction

The major visual theme in the report is an active informative graphics. They are designed in a such way, so you can read them as a table data and infographics in the same time. The feature of this report is a bookjacket, which is a A1 poster with most important parts of visual information on it.

Текучесть персонала по возрастным группам, %
31,5%
27,3%
14,2%
12,7%
До 25 лет
25–34 года
35–54 года
Старше 55 лет
Текучесть персонала в разбивке по регионам, %
39,1%
31,5%
26,3%
26,3%
20,3%
23,5%
25,2%
Центральная дирекция
Северо-Западная дирекция
Сибирско-Дальне-восточная дирекция
Московская дирекция
Приволжская дирекция
Южная дирекция
Уральская дирекция
Текучесть персонала по кварталам, %
22,2%
Программа «Социальная потребительская корзина»

Распределение новых сотрудников по регионам, %
4 114 чел.
33,1%
18,8%
10,0%
9,4%
8,8%
8,2%
7,0%
5,5%
Центральные офисы
Приволжская дирекция
Южная дирекция
Уральская дирекция
Московская дирекция
Коэффициент потерянных дней (абсентеизм), %
8,6%
3,7%
2,6%
3,4%
2,4%
2,5%
0,6%
Северо-Западная дирекция
Уральская дирекция
Центральные офисы (Москва, Уфа)
Центральная дирекция
Московская дирекция
Гендерный баланс, %
67,4
23,8
64,3
27,8
86,3
16,3
83,3
Всего по Корпорации
Руководящие органы
Новые сотрудники Центральных офисов (Москва, Уфа)
Новые сотрудники Региональной сети
Дни нетрудоспособности
Текучесть персонала
Женщины
Мужчины
Минимальный размер оплаты труда

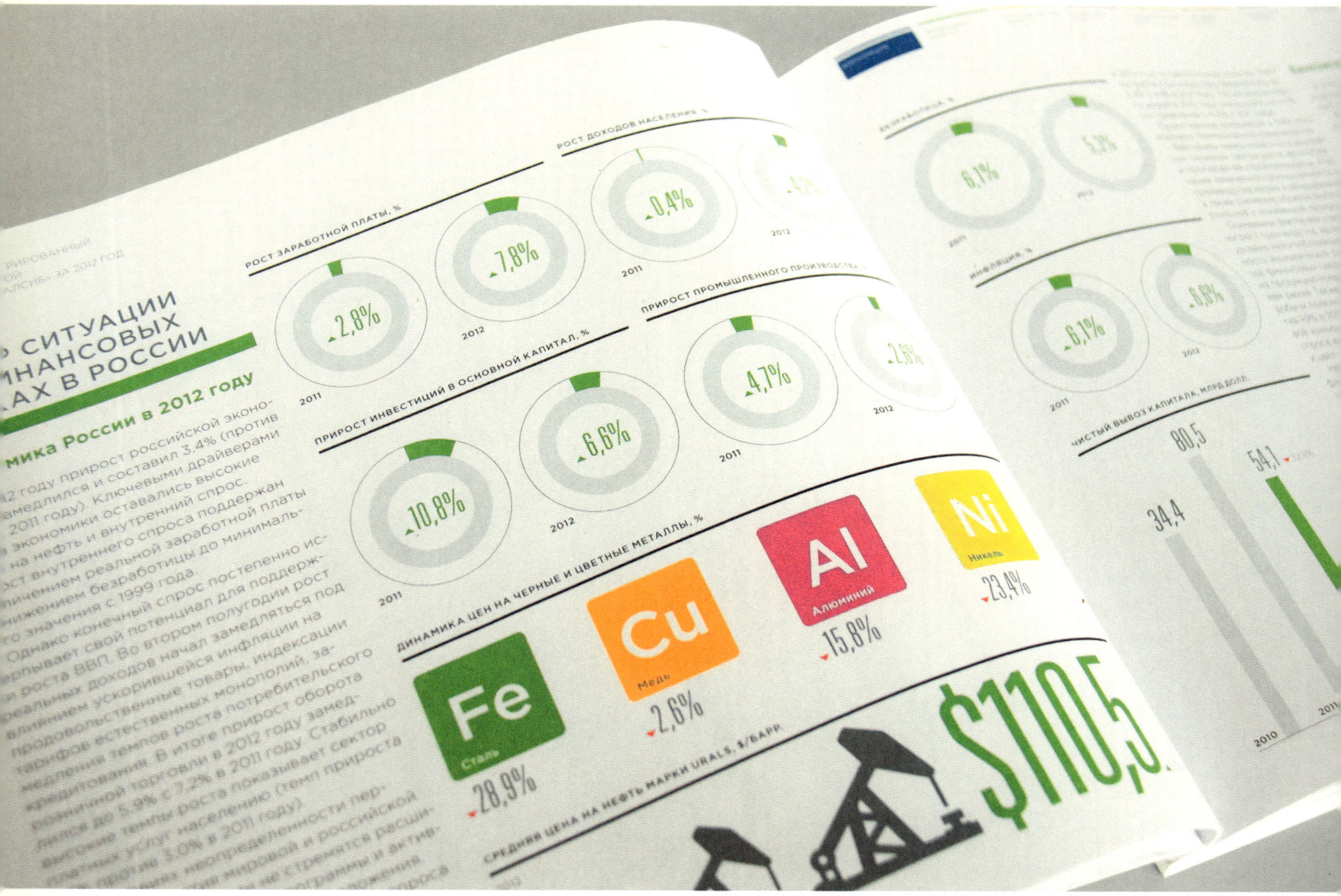
РОСТ ЗАРАБОТНОЙ ПЛАТЫ, %
2,8%
7,8%
РОСТ ДОХОДОВ НАСЕЛЕНИЯ, %
0,4%
ПРИРОСТ ИНВЕСТИЦИЙ В ОСНОВНОЙ КАПИТАЛ, %
10,8%
6,6%
ПРИРОСТ ПРОМЫШЛЕННОГО ПРОИЗВОДСТВА, %
4,7%
ИНФЛЯЦИЯ, %
6,1%
ДИНАМИКА ЦЕН НА ЧЕРНЫЕ И ЦВЕТНЫЕ МЕТАЛЛЫ, %
Fe
Сталь
28,9%
Cu
Медь
2,6%
Al
Алюминий
15,8%
Ni
Никель
23,4%
СРЕДНЯЯ ЦЕНА НА НЕФТЬ МАРКИ URALS, $/БАРР.
$110,5
ЧИСТЫЙ ВЫВОЗ КАПИТАЛА, МЛРД ДОЛЛ.
80,5
54,1
34,4
2010
2011

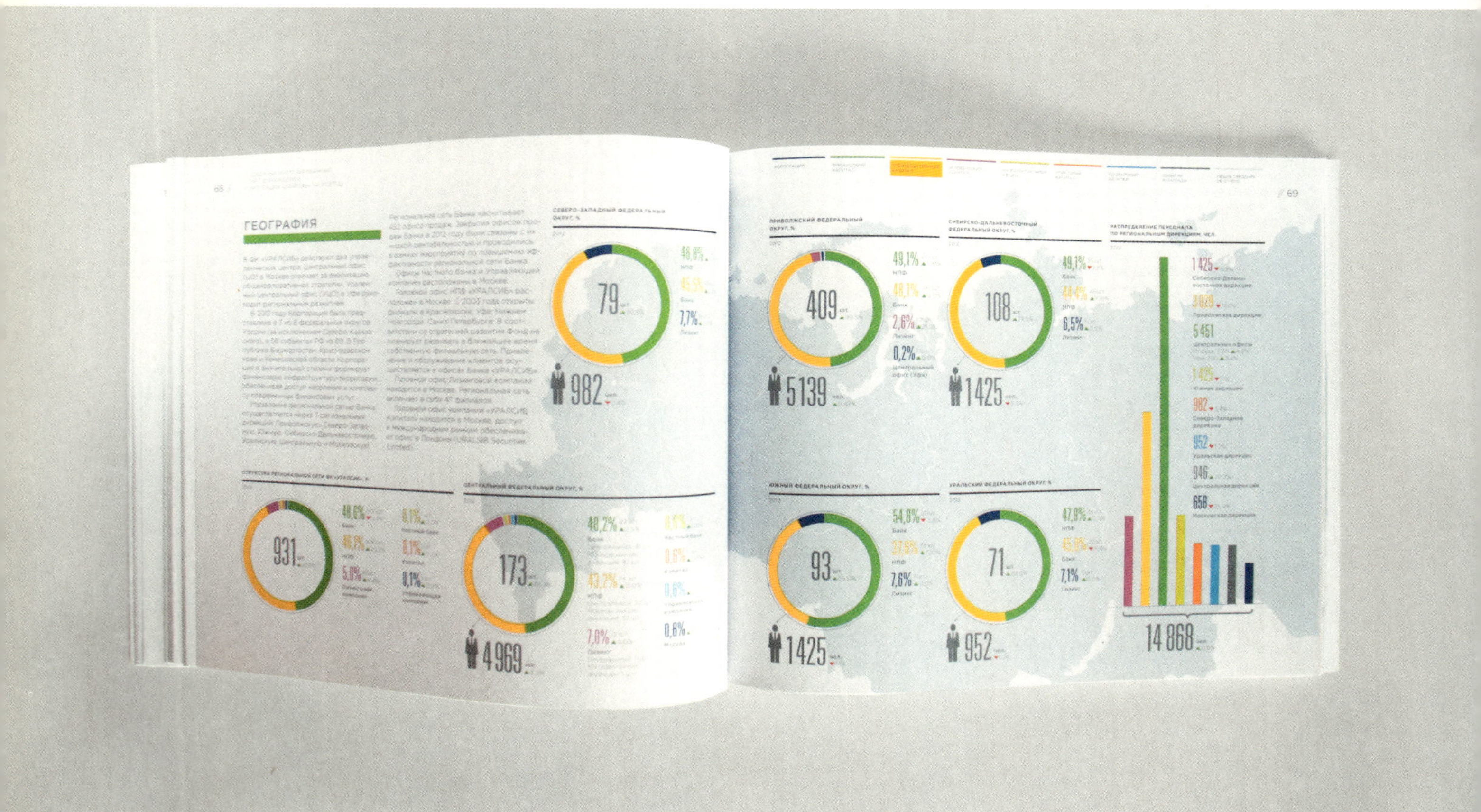
ГЕОГРАФИЯ
79
982
409
5139
108
1425
931
173
4969
93
1425
71
952
14 868

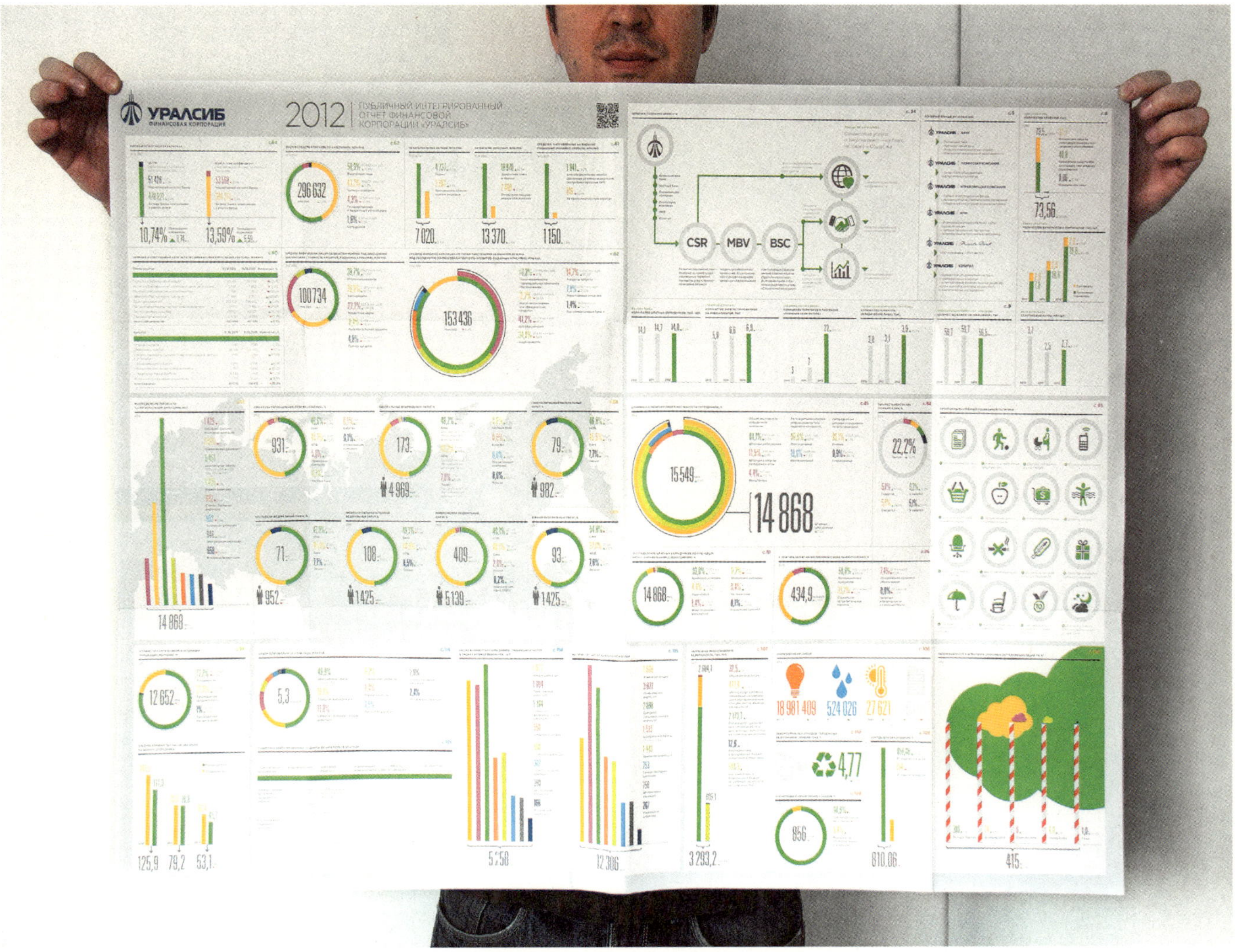
УРАЛСИБ
ФИНАНСОВАЯ КОРПОРАЦИЯ
2012
ПУБЛИЧНЫЙ ИНТЕГРИРОВАННЫЙ
ОТЧЕТ ФИНАНСОВОЙ
КОРПОРАЦИИ «УРАЛСИБ»
CSR
MBV
BSC
14 868
15 549
296 632
153 436
4,77

СТРУКТУРА
ПЕРСОНАЛА
15 549
14 868
14 868
14 868
509

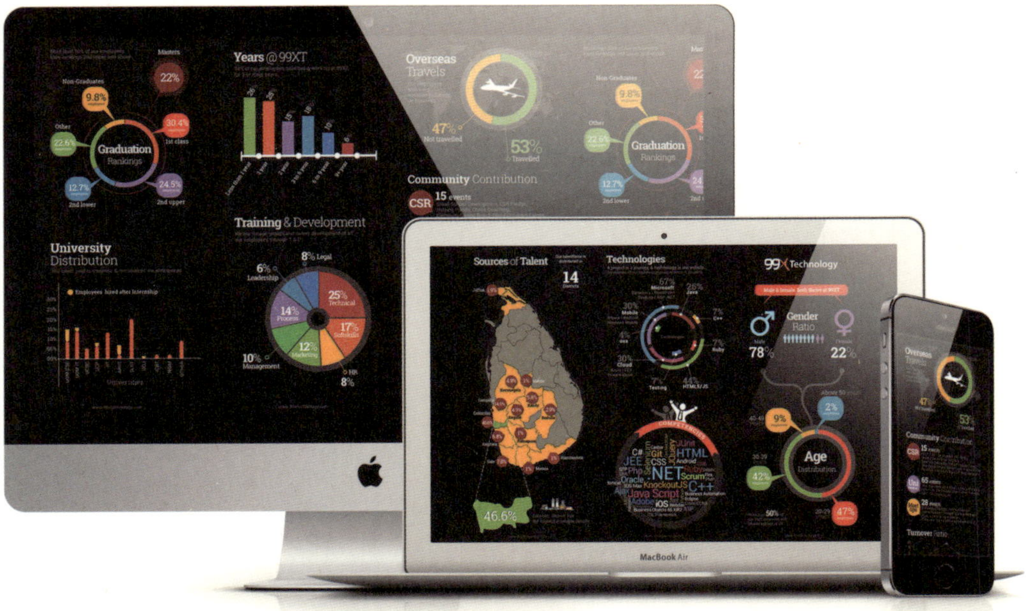

99X Technology HR Summery – 2013

- Completion Year: 2014
- Designer: Nishad Nadeeke Rupasinghe
- Client: 99X Technology

- Work Introduction

Main idea of the project was to organize the HR details in graphical a manner that is enjoyable to read instead of traditional annual report. The design was done using flat colours on a dark theme according to the corporate colours. Design elements are created using Photoshop and Illustrator.

99X Technology

Male & female, both thrive at 99XT

Gender Ratio

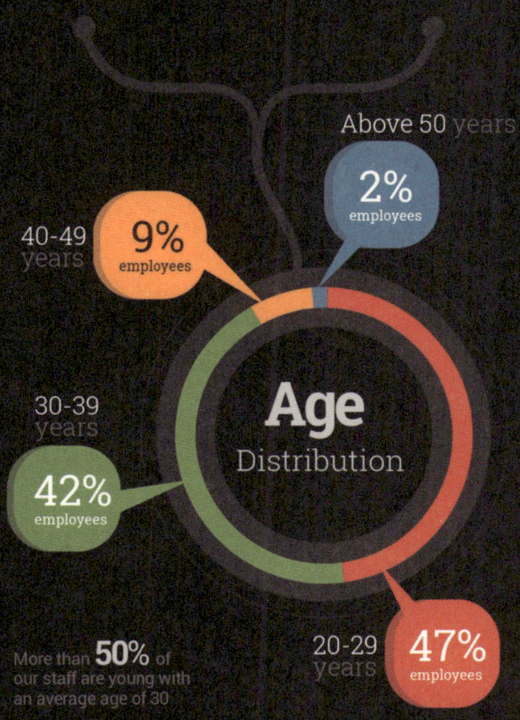

More than **50%** of our staff are young with an average age of 30

Overseas Travels

Our employees who have travelled to Europe on business

Community Contribution

CSR 15 events
Small School Development, CSR Pledge, Helping Hands, Chess Coaching, Electricity Saving Board, Blood Donation Camps, Blind School Project, Kandy Cancer Treatment Fund, So Others May See, eVillage, CSR Piggy Banks etc.

Uni Relations 65 events
Mock Interviews, Workshops, Lecturing, Mentoring, Career Day, Intern Summit, Conferences, Trainings, Self Driven Internship etc.

Meet ups 28 events
Architecture Meetups, Perf Test Meetups, Mobile Developer Meetups, Selenium Meetups, Agile Conference, Agile Meetups, Software Product Engineering Conference etc.

Sources of Talent

Our talentforce is distributed in **14** Districts

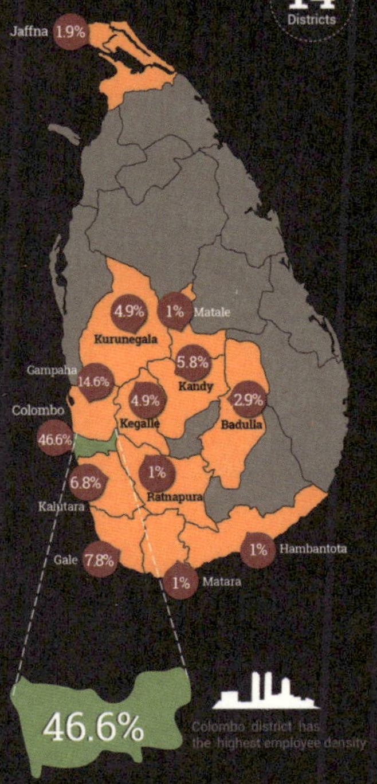

Colombo district has the highest employee density

University Distribution

The talent pool is immense & our sources are widespread

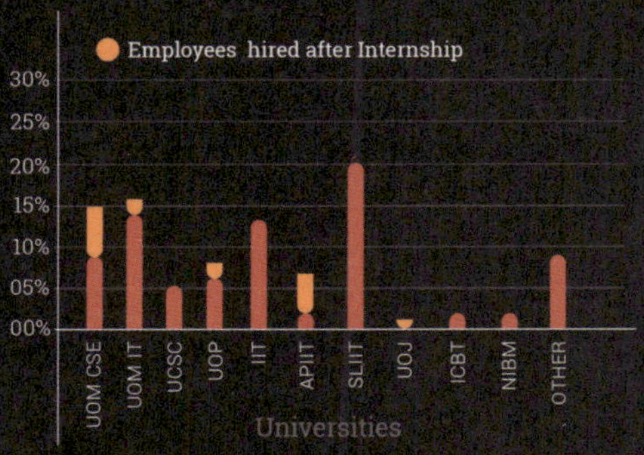

Training & Development

We encourage growth and career development of all our employees through T & D

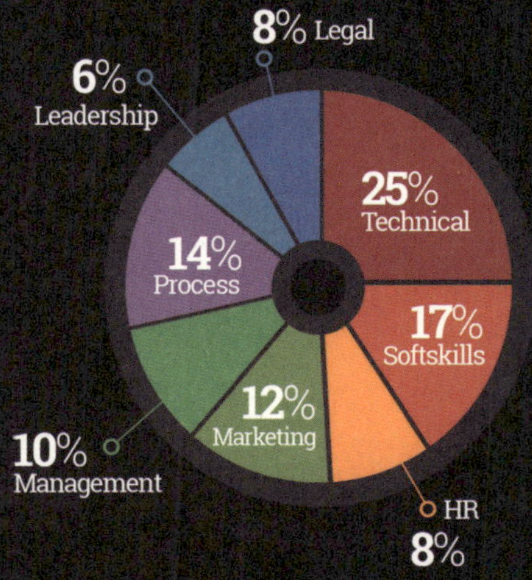

RecruitPlus Corporate Profile Brochure Design

- Completion Year: 2013
- Designer: Rayz Ong
- Client: Recruitplus

- Work Introduction

A corporate profile brochure design for RecruitPlus Consulting. RecruitPlus Consulting is an award-winning mid-career professional placement and recruitment agency based in Singapore. Since 2004, we have been experts in recruiting the best and brightest talents for organizations that truly understand the key to success is investing for the right people.

Vision
We aim to be the first choice market leader in human resource enabling services. We desire a well-respected reputation by all in the market.
Values
Service Excellence
Resilience
Unity
Collaborate and Create
Professionalism
Pride and Integrity in what we do
Leadership by Example
"Walk the Talk"
$3,000,000
345
$5,000,000
450
2012
Managed Services
Work Pass Application
Payroll
Income Tax
Onboarding/Offboarding
Preparation of LOA
Learning
What's so different about our seminars?
100%

Lifting your business to new heights
Vision
We aim to be the first choice market leader in human resource enabling services.

Services
Consultancy
Learning
RECRUITPLUS
Talent Specialist

Hurricane-Visualized Information

- Completion Year: 2013
- Designer: Stefan Große Halbuer

- Work Introduction

The Hurricane festival is one of Germany's biggest music festivals with four stages, 100 acts and about 73,000 visitors each year. This work was made for the class "Designing Information" at Muenster UAS, Germany, and comprehensively displays facts and infographics about the Festival. Our aim was to create some kind of newspaper for not only the festival visitors, but also all people that are interested in what a festival is all about.

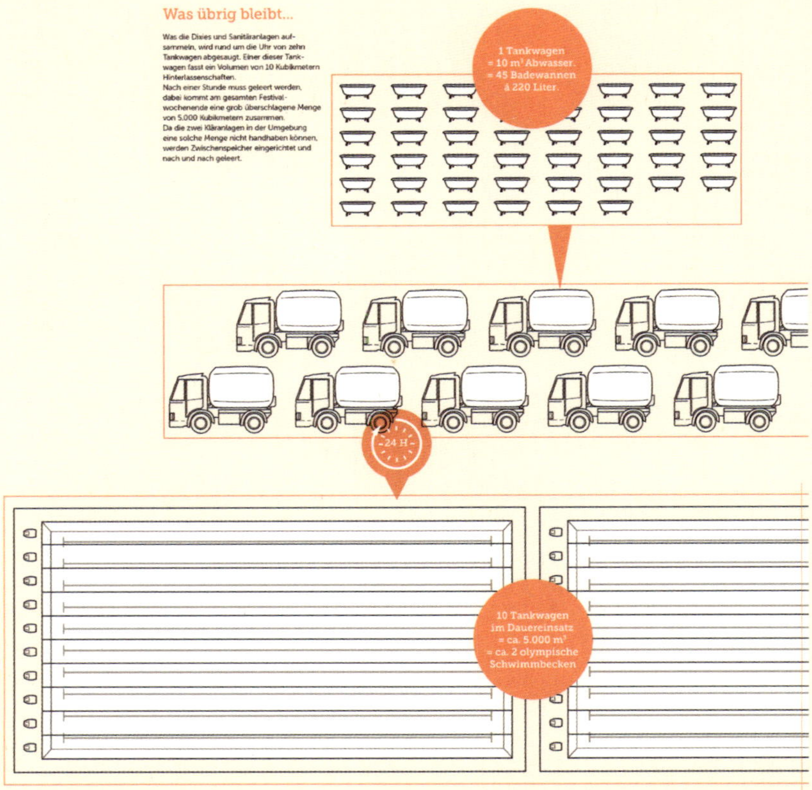

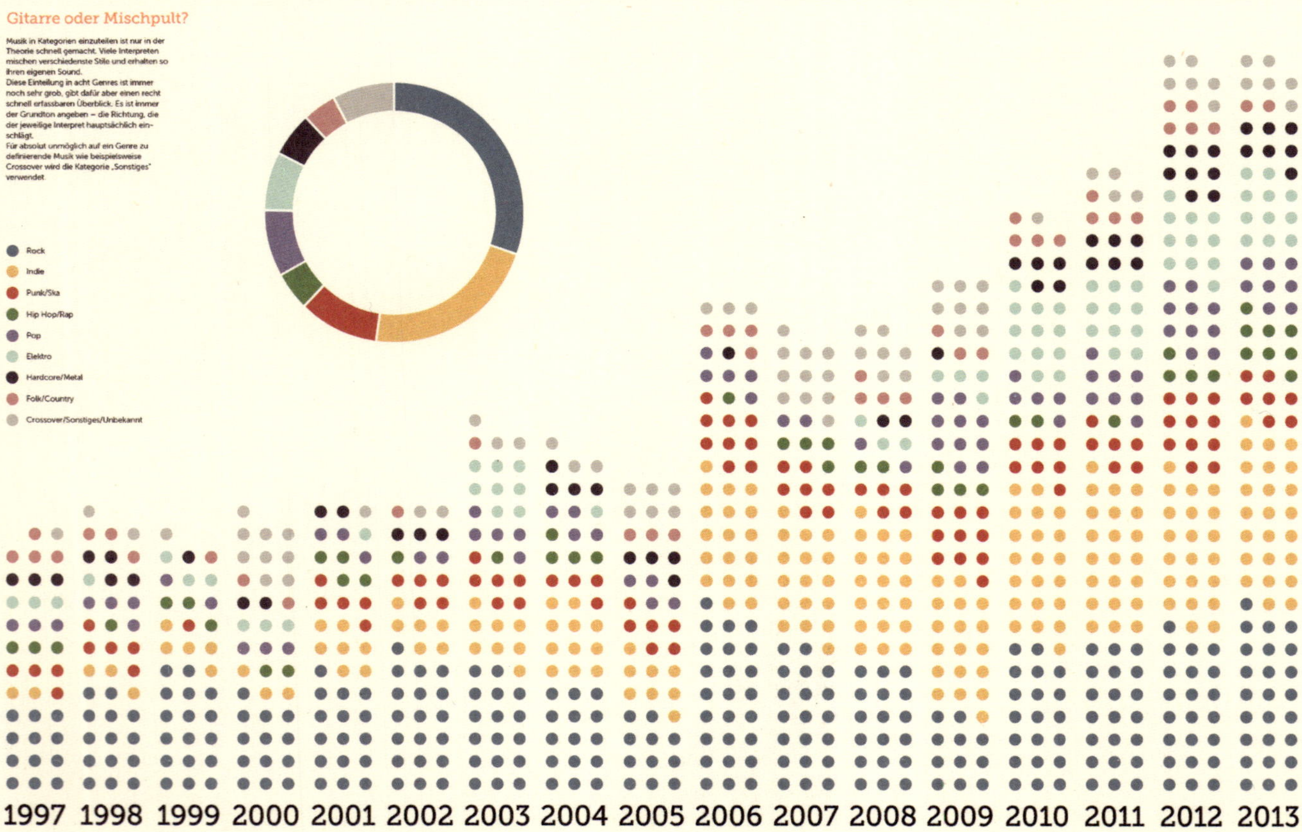

Fleißiger Bühnenbau

An der Timeline lässt sich parallel zur Entwicklung der Besucherzahlen (S.4) und der Anzahl der auftretenden Acts (S. 34) gut ablesen, wie sich das Festival immer weiter vergrößert hat: Alle paar Jahre gab es entweder eine neue Bühne oder die Erweiterung/Vergrößerung einer bereits Bestehenden.
Auch Ereignisse, die neben dem ganz normalen Festival-Wahnsinn sonst noch hängen geblieben sind, werden kurz angerissen.

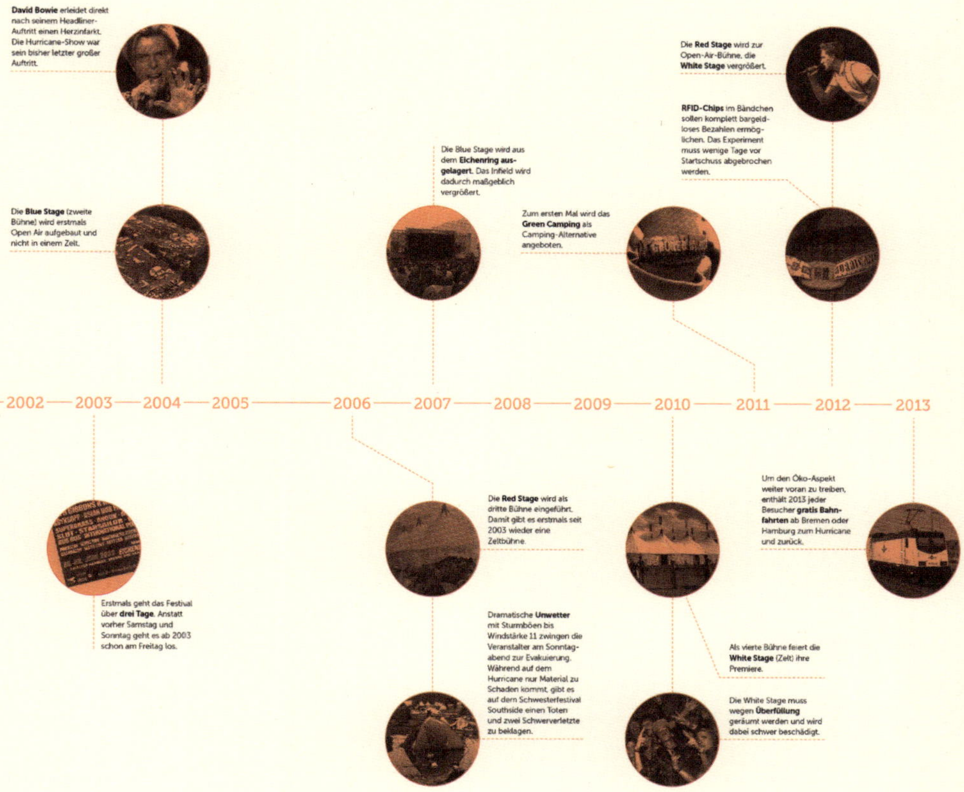

Frühe Vergangenheit

Im September 1973 fand erstmals ein musikalisches Ereignis in Scheeßel statt. Unter dem Titel „Es rockt in der Heide" wurde ein zweitägiges Festival veranstaltet.
Anfang September 1977 wurde wieder ein Festival angesetzt, dieses Mal unter dem Titel „First Rider Open Air". Nachdem allerdings einige angekündigte Bands nicht erschienen, weil sie aufgrund von Misswirtschaft nicht bezahlt werden konnten, protestierten viele Besucher und setzten die Bühne in Brand. Bei den darauf folgenden Krawallen gab es mehrere Verletzte, es entstand ein Sachschaden von ca. 1,5 Millionen Deutsche Mark.
20 Jahre später wagte man mit dem Hurricane Festival einen erneuten Versuch – dieses Mal mit großem Erfolg.

Besucherzahlen

Insgesamt zugelassen sind bei der derzeitigen Größe des Geländes **maximal 78.000 Menschen** – inklusive Hilfskräfte. Über diese Zahl hinaus wäre das Festival nicht versichert. Wie begehrt die Tickets sind und ob das Festival überhaupt ausverkauft wird, richtet sich stark nach dem Line-Up. In den letzten Jahren haben Festivals im Allgemeinen aber so an Beliebtheit gewonnen, dass schon früh vor Bekanntgabe aller Auftritte alle Karten vergriffen waren.
2006 wurde das Kontingent nach massivem Platzmangel in 2005 künstlich zurück gefahren.

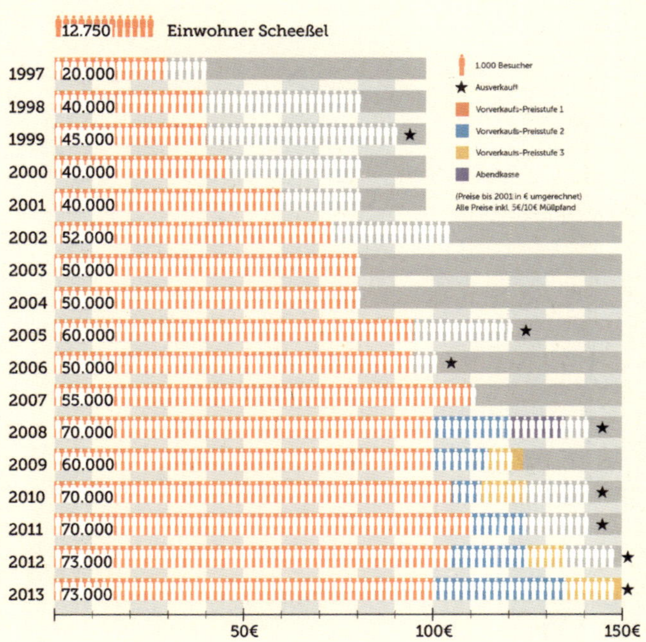

Ticketpreis

Auf allen europäischen Festivals sind die Ticketpreise während der letzten Jahre stark angestiegen. Das liegt vor allem an den Gagen der Musiker. Laut Hurricane-Veranstalter Folkert Koopmans fließen bis zu **50% des Ticketpreises ins Booking**. Honorare im hohen 6-stelligen Bereich sind bei Headlinern normal.
Der Ticketpreis wird traditionell in mehrere Preisstufen aufgeteilt. Jedes Jahr gibt es eine begrenzte Anzahl günstiger „Wildcard-Tickets". Mit dem Kauf weiß man allerdings nicht, wer auftreten wird – echte Fans vertrauen den Bookern.
Die Einnahmen decken insgesamt 60–70% der Gesamtausgaben, der Rest wird durch Sponsoring und Gastronomie erwirtschaftet.

Sonstiges

Unter sonstige Ausgaben fallen Posten wie etwa Versicherungen, Reinigungskosten, Wasser/Strom, Beschilderung und Marketing.

Geländemiete

Die Miete des Geländes ca. 140 Hektar großen Geländes kann mit 2-4% veranschlagt werden (Festival-Durchschnittswert).

GEZ/KSK

Auch die GEZ kassiert bei Festivals ab: Ein festgelegter Prozentsatz (Festival-Durchschnitt sind 3-5%) muss für die Aufführungsrechte abgeführt werden. Auch die Künster-Sozialkasse bekommt einen Anteil für die Dienstleistungen, die von Grafikern und Künstlern erbracht werden.

Örtliche Kosten

Ein weiterer großer Anteil geht in die Aufwände, die vor Ort entstehen. Dabei handelt es sich um verschiedene Kostenstellen im infrastrukturellen Bereich (Bühne, Ton, Licht, Zäune, Dixies, Fahrzeuge,...) sowie beispielsweise Personalkosten und Catering.

Gagen

40-50% der Einnahmen gehen an die Musiker. Je größer der Name und je bombastischer die Show, desto mehr wird verlangt. Am meisten nehmen selbstverständlich die Headliner. Kleinere Bands, die tagsüber auf der Red oder White Stage spielen, freuen sich dagegen über den Bekanntheitszuwachs, den ein Auftritt auf einem großen Festival verspricht. Sie geben sich mit kleinen Gagen und dem Werbeeffekt zufrieden.

ca.

25.000 Fahrzeuge

stehen während des Wochenendes auf dem Parkplatz. Abzüglich z.B. der ca. 14.000 Bahnanreisenden kommen so durchschnittlich etwa **2,3 Besucher** auf ein Auto.

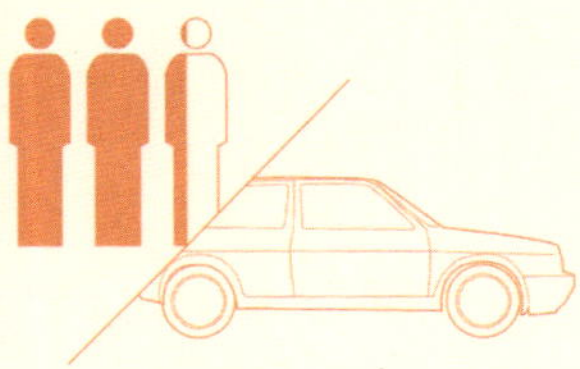

Viel mehr Leute passen in ein durchschnittliches Gefährt auch nicht herein, wenn man sich für ein Festival mit professioneller **Ausstattung** eingedeckt hat.

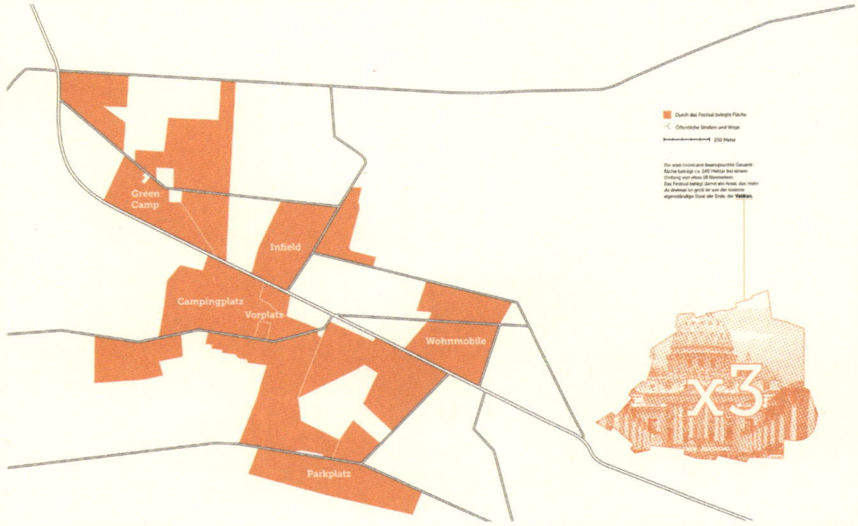

5.000

Hilfskräfte verdienen am Hurricane-Wochenende ihr Geld auf dem Gelände – vom Rettungssanitäter bis zum Bierstandpersonal.

Davon:

550 Sicherheitskräfte
500 Sanitäter und Ärzte
350 Polizisten

Diese drei Berufsgruppen haben die wohl schwierigsten Einsätze. Der **Polizeibericht 2012** hat neben 2.750 Versorgungs- und Hilfeleistungen folgende 480 Einsätze erfasst:

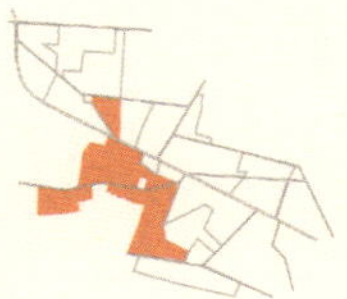

Die meisten der 73.000 Besucher des Hurricane bewohnen den Standard-Campingplatz.
Geschlafen wird meist nicht viel. Vor und nach dem Besuch der Bühnen im Infield wird hier gefeiert, gegessen und eine gewisse Anarchie ausgelebt.
Beliebtester Sport auf dem Campingplatz ist seit einigen Jahren **Flunky-Ball** (siehe rechte Seite).

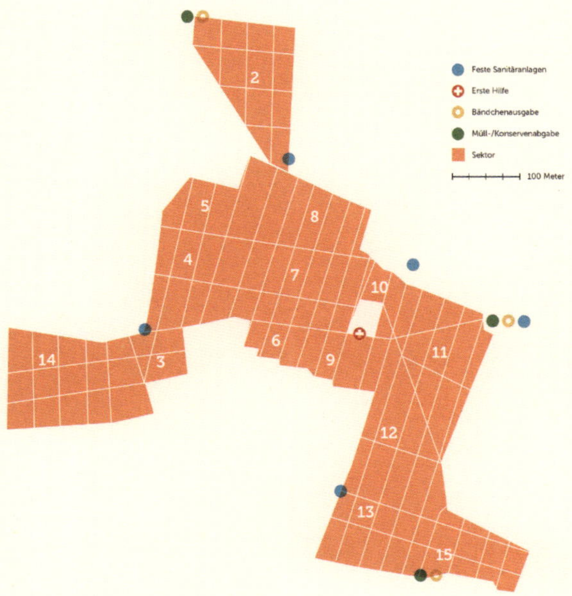

Kurze Flunkyball-Einführung

Zutaten für eine Runde Flunkyball nach üblichen Festivalregeln sind bei acht Teilnehmern: 8 Dosen Bier, eine große Plastikflasche (halb mit Wasser gefüllt), ein Wurfgeschoss (vorzugsweise ein Fußball oder für die größere Herausforderung ein Tennisball).
Die Anzahl der Biere ist auf die Teilnehmerzahl anzupassen. Möglichst sollten die Teams gleich viele Mitspieler haben.

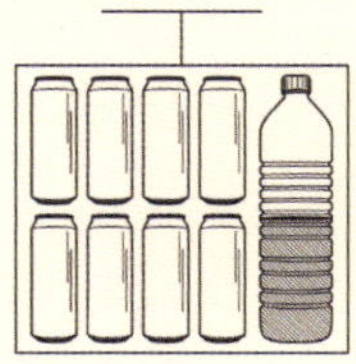

Das Spielfeld besteht aus einer Mittellinie, auf der die Flasche platziert wird. Im Abstand von ca. 5 Metern stellen sich die Teams in einer Reihe parallel zur Mittellinie auf.
Ein vorher gewählter, neutraler Schiedsrichter kann die Abstände ggf. kontrollieren.
Die Spieler der Teams versuchen nun abwechselnd die Flasche mit dem Wurfgeschoss zu Fall zu bringen.

Trifft ein Spieler die Flasche, so müssen die Mitglieder seines Teams schnellstmöglich ihre Biere leeren. Die Spieler des anderen Teams stellen die Flasche wieder auf und bringen das Wurfgeschoss auf ihre Seite. Erst, wenn Wurfgeschoss und alle Spieler hinter ihrer Linie sind, müssen die Gegner das Bier absetzen.
Haben alle Mitglieder eines Teams ihr Bier als erstes vollständig geleert, sind sie die Gewinner.

Wichtigste Sonderregel ist grundsätzlich die Bestrafung von Spielern, die Bier verschütten. Kommt es während einer beliebigen Spielphase zum versehentlichen oder vorsätzlichen Verlust von Bier durch eine Spieler, hat dieser den Restinhalt seiner Dose direkt zu verzehren. Er bekommt dann ein volles Bier, mit dem das Spiel fortzuführen ist.

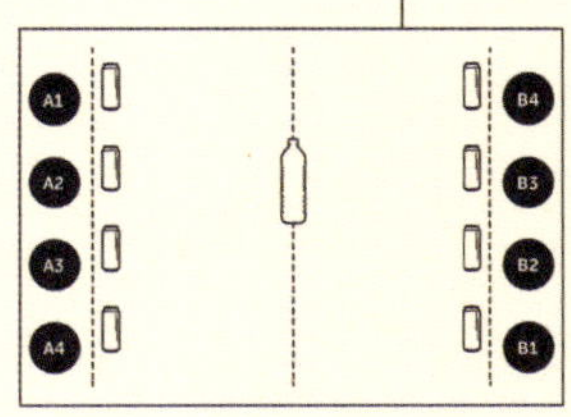

Die Ausrüstung

für ein Festival will perfekt abgestimmt sein. So einige Gegenstände, die man sonst für absolut nutzlos hält, können auf einem Festival-Campingplatz zum Beinahe-Lebensretter werden.
Es geht insbesondere auch darum, möglichst Platz sparend zu packen. Der Raum in Rucksack und Auto ist meist extrem begrenzt, außerdem muss das Ganze teilweise mehrere Kilometer weit vom Park- zum Campingplatz geschleppt werden.

Diese Seite gibt Aufschluss darüber, was unbedingt mit muss und was man im Idealfall dabei haben sollte.

Essenzielles

Ohne diese Gegenstände kann man gleich zu Hause bleiben:

Very nice to have

Ohne geht man nicht unter, aber diese Dinge sollte man zum Großteil dabei haben. Vieles ist auch in den Shops auf dem Hurricane erhältlich oder von den Camp-Nachbarn ausleihbar.

Civic Education

- Completion Year: 2013
- Designer: Stinne Marie Wilhelmsen

- Work Introduction

To improve the danish basic knowledge about government systems and functions, the designer curated, authored, designed and produced a book about 1. The Monarchy, 2. The Democracy, 3. The Parliament, 4. The Government and 5. about The Courts — in Denmark. All design elements has roots in something Danish.

The typeface is a digitalised re-drawing of the original number plate typeface by Nauer Klint, 1976. Colours are gold for the monarchy and royal red to represent the Danish flag, Dannebrog.

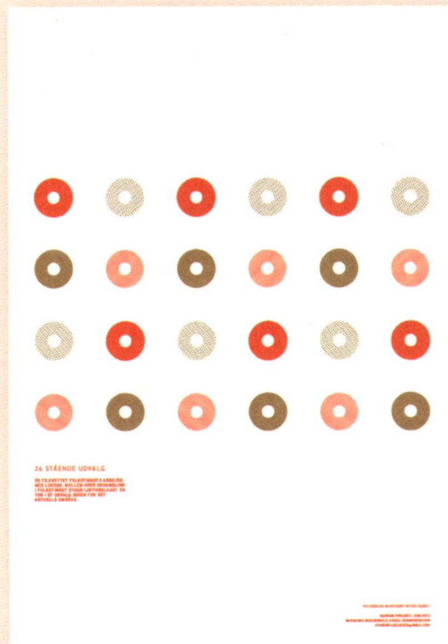

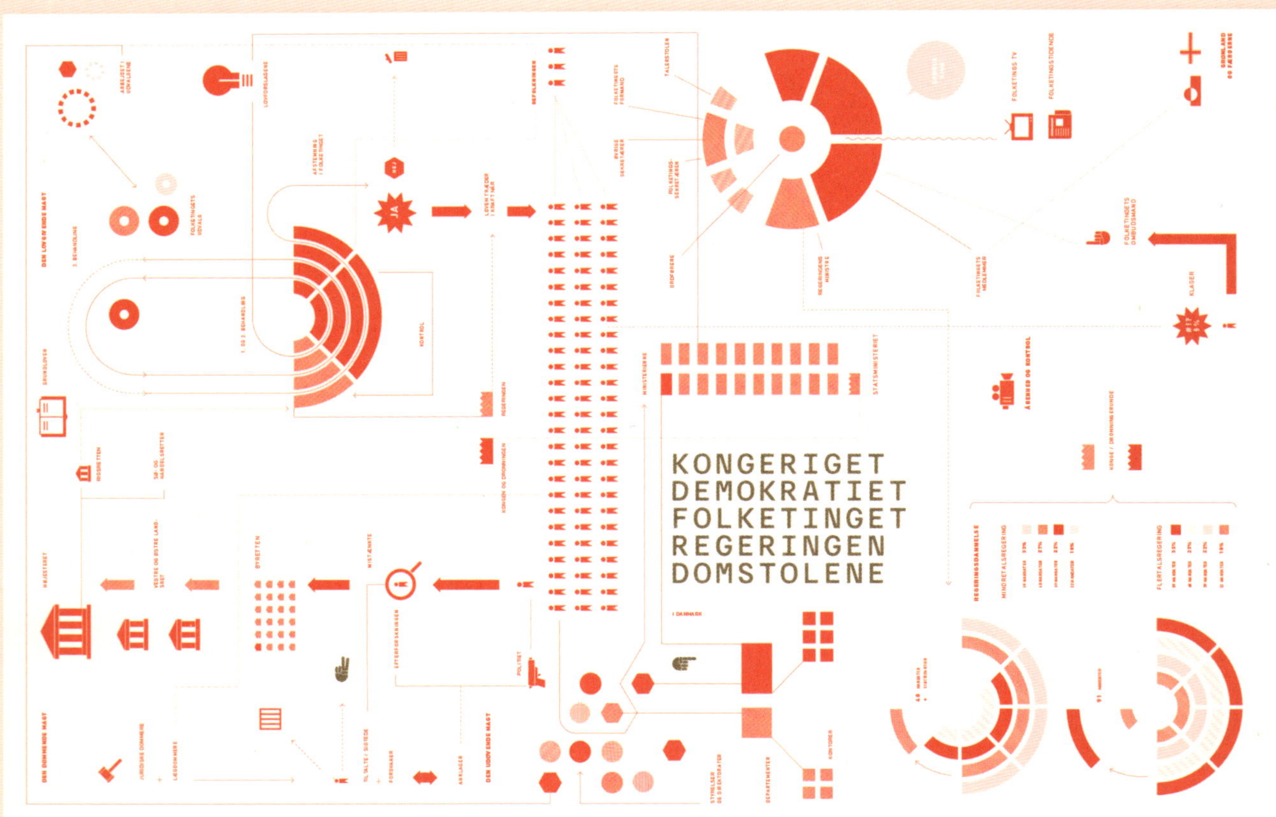

0%
#12
28
×34
11

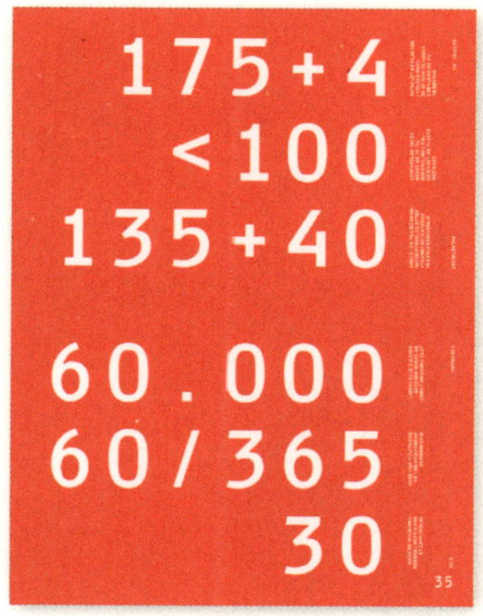
175+4
<100
135+40
60.000
60/365
30
35

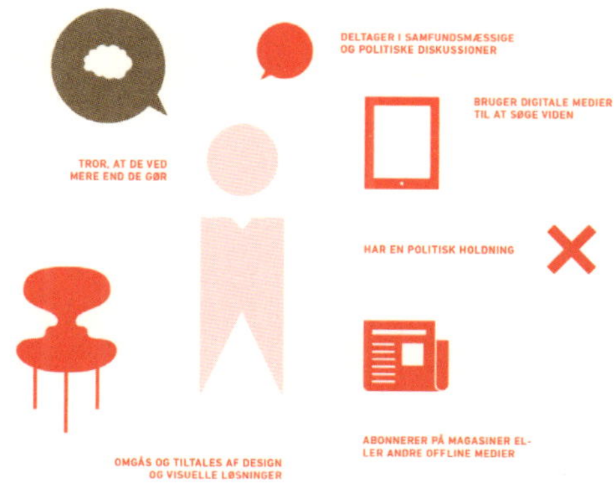
DELTAGER I SAMFUNDSMÆSSIGE OG POLITISKE DISKUSSIONER
BRUGER DIGITALE MEDIER TIL AT SØGE VIDEN
TROR, AT DE VED MERE END DE GØR
HAR EN POLITISK HOLDNING
ABONNERER PÅ MAGASINER ELLER ANDRE OFFLINE MEDIER
OMGÅS OG TILTALES AF DESIGN OG VISUELLE LØSNINGER

175+4
<100
135+40
60.000
60/365

34
SPØRGSMÅL DER ALLE FØLGES OP AF EN VURDERING AF SIKKERHEDEN PÅ DET RIGTIGE SVAR.
250
DELTAGERE I UNDERSØGELSEN
50%
ER UTILFREDSE MED DERES EGEN PARATVIDEN OM DANMARK

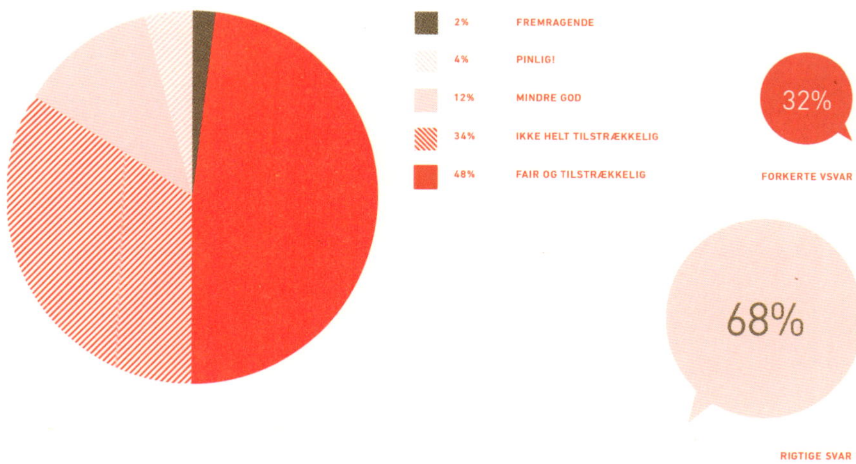
2% FREMRAGENDE
4% PINLIG!
12% MINDRE GOD
34% IKKE HELT TILSTRÆKKELIG
48% FAIR OG TILSTRÆKKELIG
32%
FORKERTE VSVAR
68%
RIGTIGE SVAR

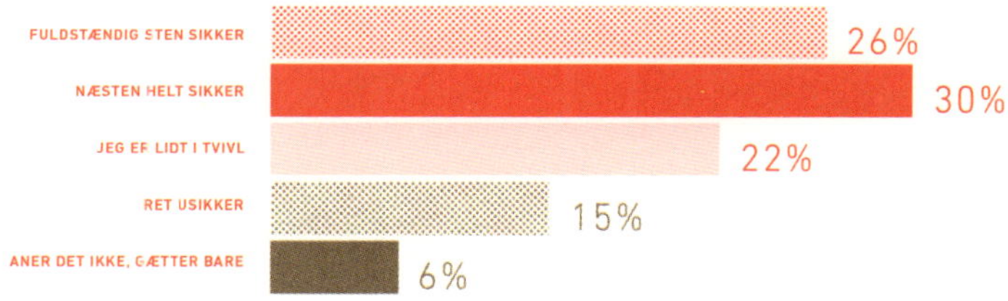
FULDSTÆNDIG STEN SIKKER 26%
NÆSTEN HELT SIKKER 30%
JEG ER LIDT I TVIVL 22%
RET USIKKER 15%
ANER DET IKKE, GÆTTER BARE 6%

81% AF SPØRGSMÅLENE I UNDERSØGELSEN HØRER I STØRRE ELLER MINDRE GRAD TIL ALMINDELIG PARATVIDEN.
4% NEJ, BESTEMT IKKE
16% NEJ
33% JA, TIL DELS
34% JA
14% JA BESTEMT

.2
15

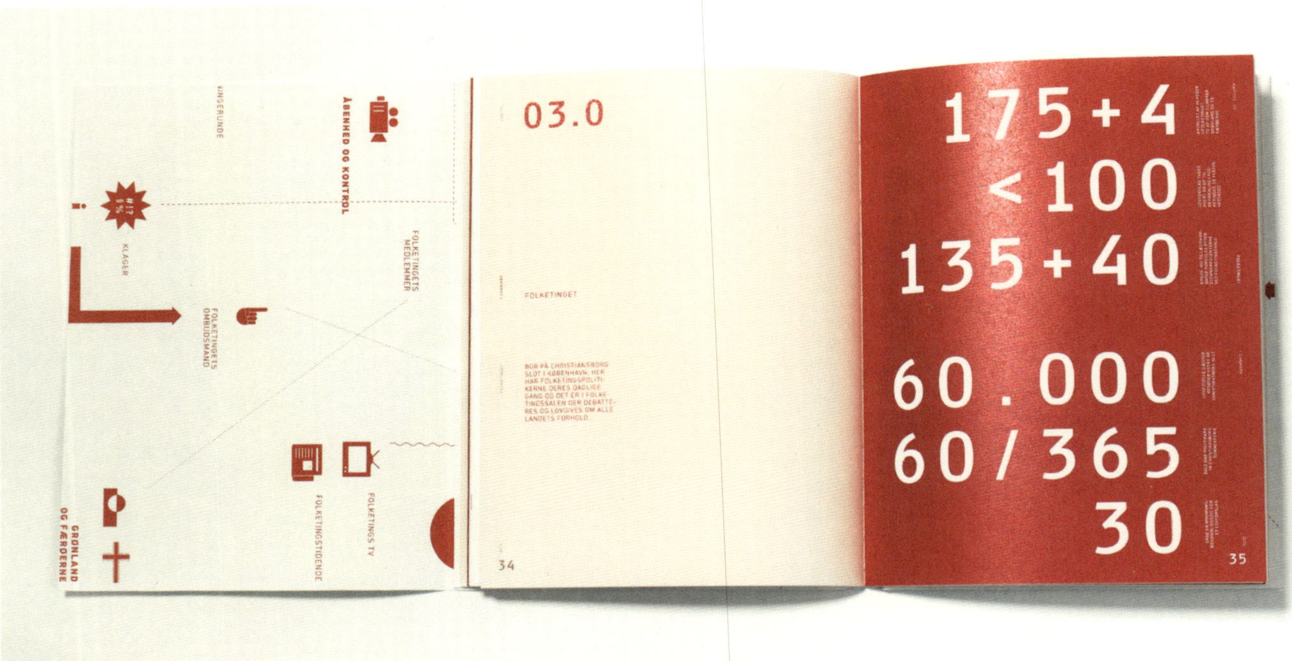
ÅBENHED OG KONTROL
KLAGER
FOLKETINGETS MEDLEMMER
FOLKETINGETS OMBUDSMAND
FOLKETINGS TV
FOLKETINGSTIDENDE
GRØNLAND OG FÆRØERNE
03.0
FOLKETINGET
34
175+4
<100
135+40
60.000
60/365
30
35

KONGERIGET
DEMOKRATIET
FOLKETINGET
REGERINGEN
DOMSTOLENE
ÅBENHED OG KONTROL
GRØNLAND OG FÆRØERNE
DEN LOVGIVENDE MAGT
BEFOLKNINGEN

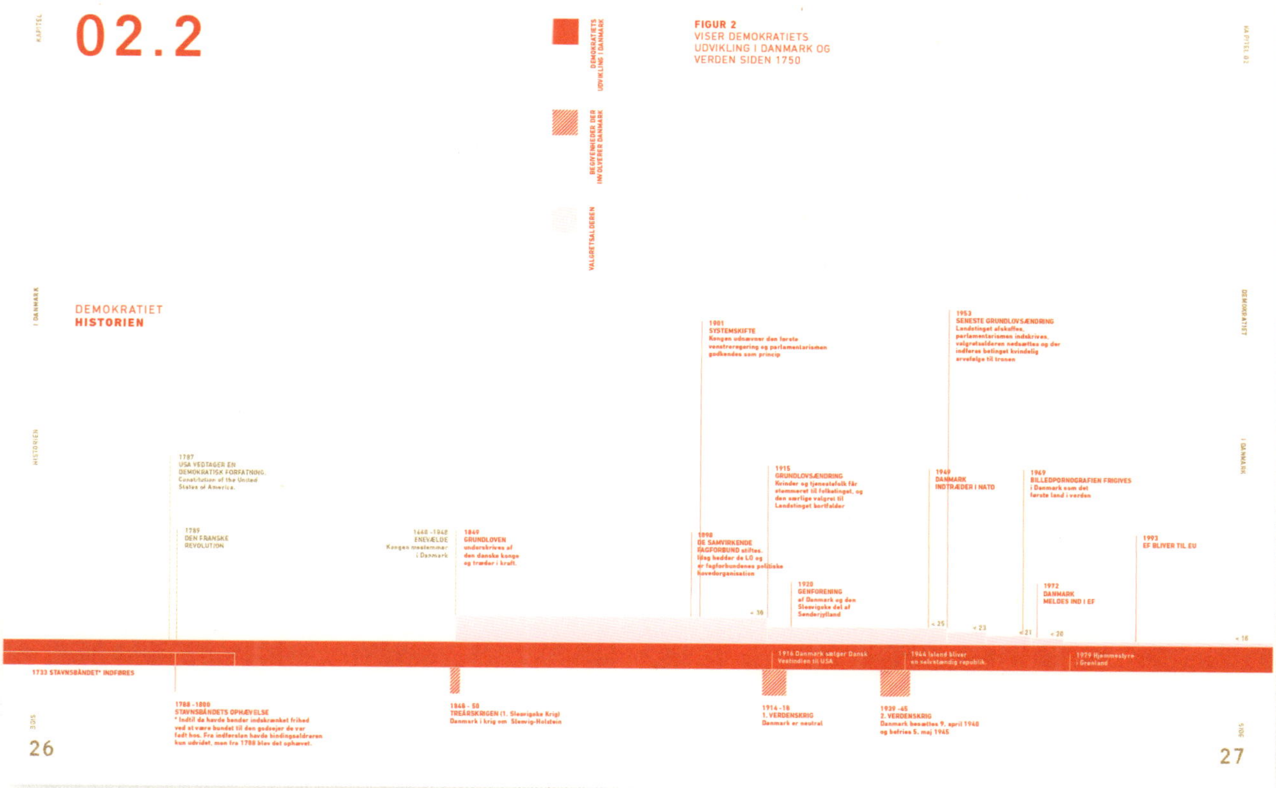
02.2
FIGUR 2
VISER DEMOKRATIETS
UDVIKLING I DANMARK OG
VERDEN SIDEN 1750
DEMOKRATIET
HISTORIEN
26
27

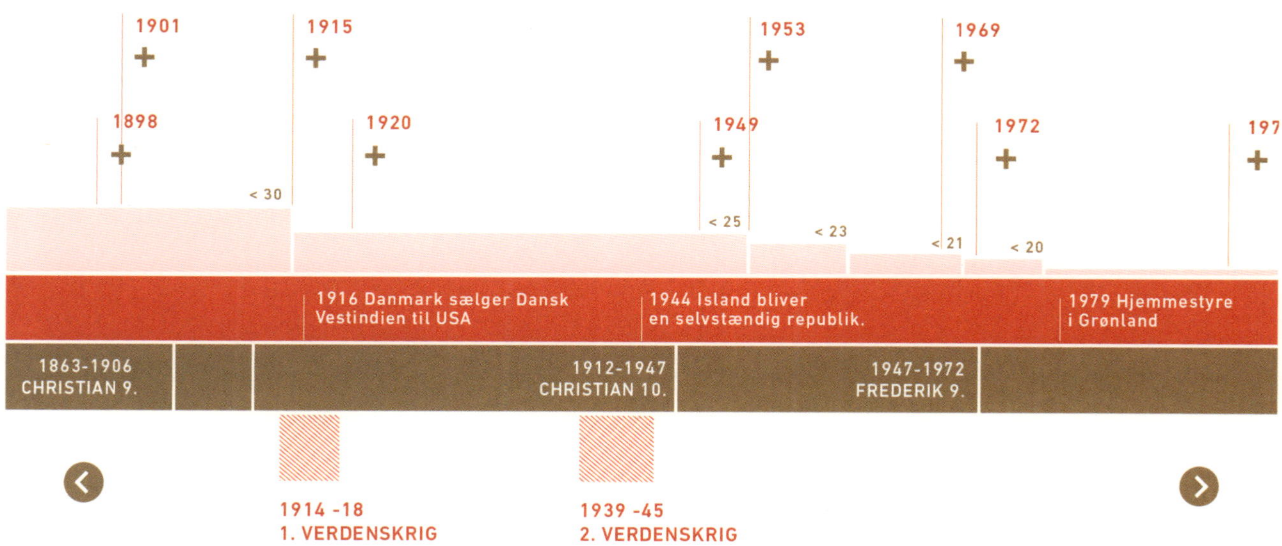
1901
1915
1953
1969
1898
1920
1949
1972
197
< 30
< 25
< 23
< 21
< 20
1916 Danmark sælger Dansk
Vestindien til USA
1944 Island bliver
en selvstændig republik.
1979 Hjemmestyre
i Grønland
1863-1906
CHRISTIAN 9.
1912-1947
CHRISTIAN 10.
1947-1972
FREDERIK 9.
1914 -18
1. VERDENSKRIG
1939 -45
2. VERDENSKRIG

Gender Wage Gap

- Completion Year: 2013
- Designer: Valentina D'Efilippo
- Client: Harper Collins

- Work Introduction

The data compares median, low and high earners across different countries showing how much less women earn than men. The artwork is included in *The Infographic History of the World*, published by Harper Collins.

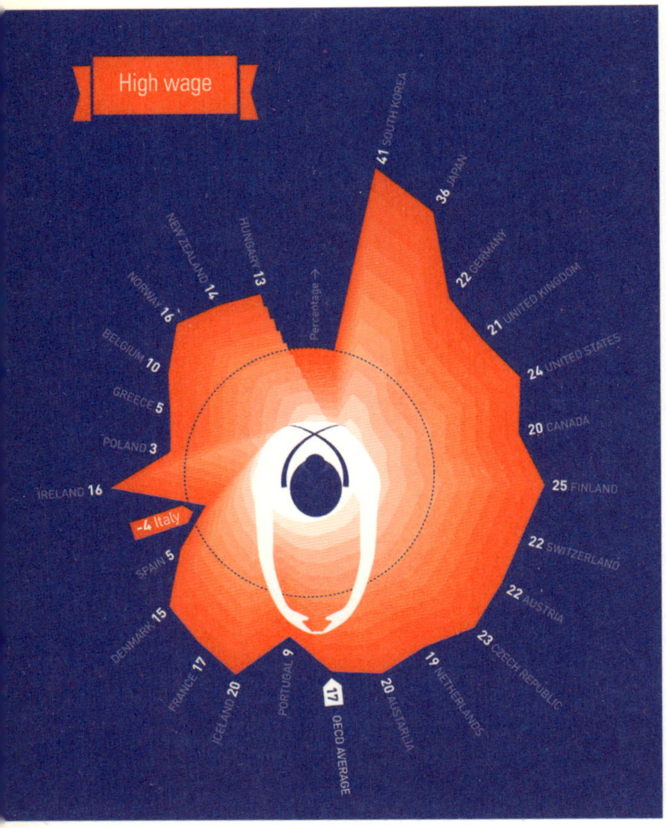

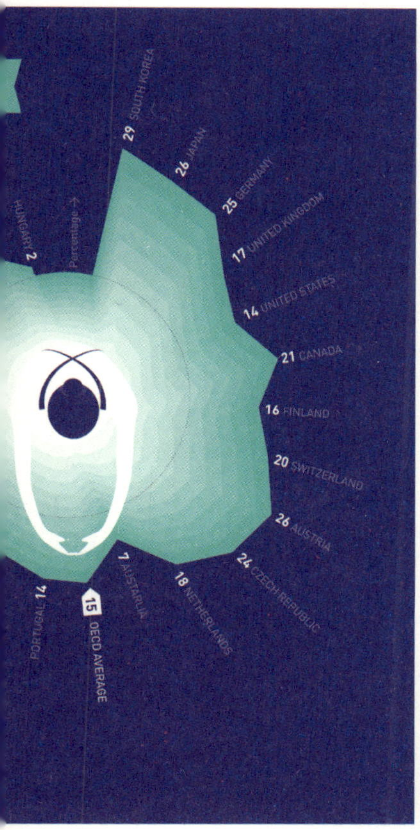
29 SOUTH KOREA
26 JAPAN
25 GERMANY
17 UNITED KINGDOM
14 UNITED STATES
21 CANADA
16 FINLAND
20 SWITZERLAND
26 AUSTRIA
24 CZECH REPUBLIC
18 NETHERLANDS
7 AUSTRALIA
15 OECD AVERAGE
PORTUGAL 14
HUNGARY 2
Percentage →

SOUTH KOREA
JAPAN
GERMANY
UNITED KINGDOM
UNITED STATES
CANADA
FINLAND
SWITZERLAND
AUSTRIA
CZECH REPUBLIC
NETHERLANDS
AUSTRALIA
OECD AVERAGE
PORTUGAL
ICELAND
FRANCE
DENMARK
SPAIN
ITALY
IRELAND
POLAND
GREECE
BELGIUM
NORWAY
NEW ZEALAND
HUNGARY
HIGH WAGE
MEDIUM WAGE
LOW WAGE
DATA SOURCE:
OECD EMPLOYMENT OUTLOOK 2013
DESIGN BY VALENTINA D'EFILIPPO
THE INFOGRAPHIC HISTORY OF THE WORLD, HARPER COLLINS 2013

Factbook

- Completion Year: 2013
- Designer: Stefan Weyer, Karsten Täuber, Ali Tercan, Isabel Herzbach
- Client: comdirect bank AG

• Work Introduction

This publication by the comdirect bank AG in collaboration with Handelsblatt Research Institute – an independent centre of excellence belonging to the financial newspaper Handelsblatt—aims to teach anyone who associates terms like "DAX" or "investment strategies" with dull theory a fascinating lesson. It contains the results of a comprehensive study, complemented by a range of interesting facts about equity culture. All of this is attractively presented, resulting in an entertaining read and an equally inviting reference book.

WERTPAPIERE
18-29

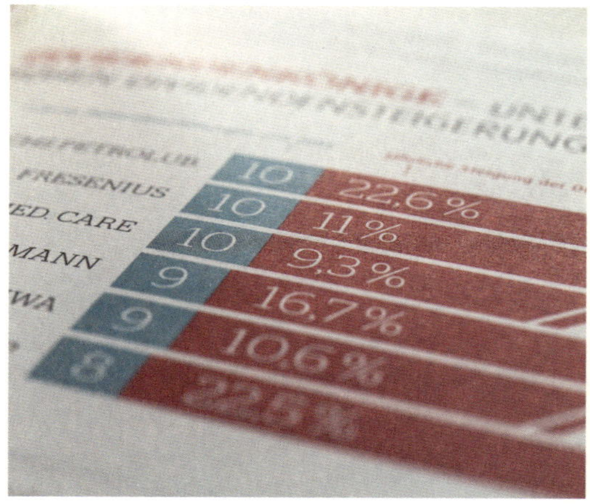
FRESENIUS
10
22,6 %
MED. CARE
10
11 %
MANN
10
9,3 %
9
16,7 %
9
10,6 %
8
22,5 %

FACTBOOK AKTIE > DIE DEUTSCHEN UND DIE AKTIE
Deutschland – das Land der Aktienmuffel
4,5 Millionen Aktionäre zählt Deutschland heute.
Das sind 1,7 Millionen weniger als zur Jahrtausendwende.
GESAMTZAHL DER AKTIONÄRE IN DEUTSCHLAND
2000
6,2 MIO
9,7%
3,9 MIO
6,3%
4,5 MIO
7,0%
3,2 MIO
6,8%
4,7 MIO
7,3%
3,6 MIO
5,6%
DIE DEUTSCHEN UND DIE AKTIE > FACTBOOK AKTIE 21
VERMÖGENSBILANZ
PRIVATER HAUSHALTE IN DEUTSCHLAND
2012
4.939 Mrd. €
2007
4.476,2 Mrd. €
2002
3576,0 Mrd. €
1997
2.961,8 Mrd. €
1992
2.059,3 Mrd. €
ANTEIL DER AKTIE
AM GELDVERMÖGEN SINKT
1970
11,2%
1950
26,5 %
AKTIENKÄUFE SCHWANKEN STARK

Coca-Cola
AN DER BÖRSE SEIT
1919
GESCHÄTZTER WERT
77,8 MRD
US-DOLLAR
WERTVOLLSTE
MARKE
DER WELT
Google
AN DER BÖRSE SEIT
18.8.2004
BAUTE SEINE ERSTEN
SERVER
PROTOTYPEN
AUS LEGOBAUSTEINEN
sky
AN DER BÖRSE SEIT
2005
70 SENDER
DAVON 20 EIGENE
Apple
AN DER BÖRSE SEIT
12.12.1980
GESCHÄTZTER WERT
76.5 MRD
US-DOLLAR
H&M
AN DER BÖRSE SEIT
1974
HAT ÜBER
2.800
GESCHÄFTE
IN 40 LÄNDERN
DIE AKTI
IM ALLTAG
McDonald's
AN DER BÖRSE SEIT
21.4.1965
VERTRETEN IN
119 LÄNDERN
DER ERDE
ExxonMo
AN DER BÖRSE SEIT
1911
SCHÜTTET SEIT
125 JAHREN
DIVIDENDEN AUS
BDF
Beiersdorf
AN DER BÖRSE SEIT
1929
GEGRÜNDET
1882
VOM APOTHEKER
PAUL C. BEIERSDORF

RSE SEIT
74
NN VON
MRD. €
2012
KORD DER
TSCHEN
HICHTE

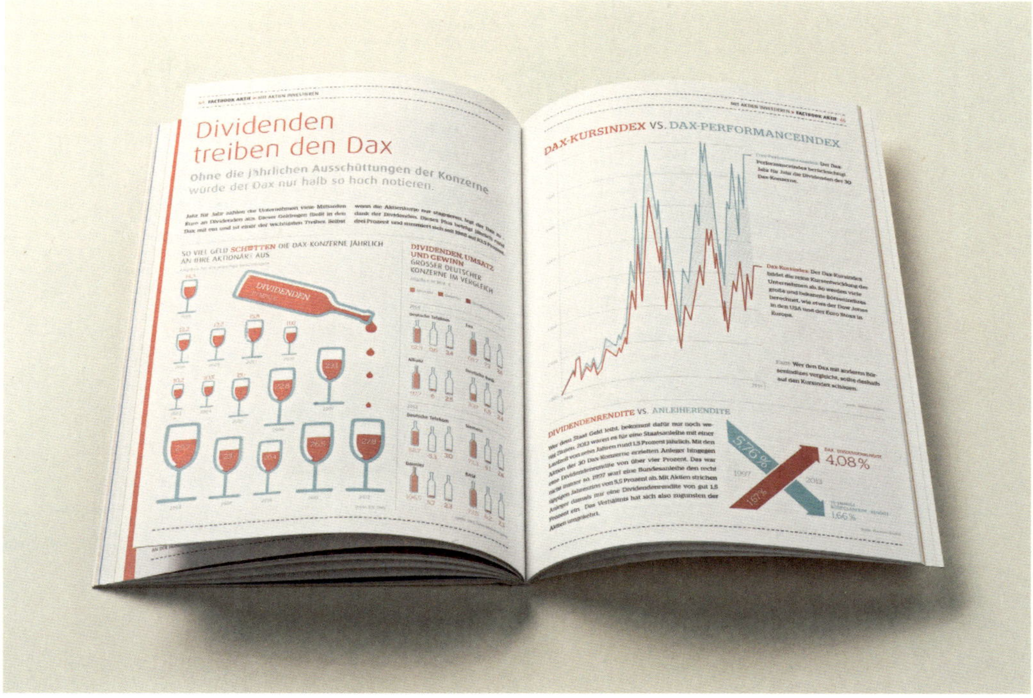
Dividenden
treiben den Dax
Ohne die jährlichen Ausschüttungen der Konzerne würde der Dax nur halb so hoch notieren.
DAX-KURSINDEX VS. DAX-PERFORMANCEINDEX
DIVIDENDENRENDITE VS. ANLEIHERENDITE
4,08 %

WELTWEITER ETF-MARKT
NEUE REKORDE BEI GELDZUFLÜSSEN IN ETPS
260
263
DAS MEISTE GELD KOMMT AUS DEN USA

- Completion Year: 2012
- Designer: Di Rese Lorenzo Mauro (drlm.it)

- Work Introduction

The aim of this book is to make the graphic designer think over his/her active role in society so as not to limit his/her work to the communication of fair and supportive messages but also to become a promoter of those messages.

The purpose of this book it is not to give solutions but to highlight a real problem and to offer tools to understand how to improve this job. It is up to each single individual to be aware of the situation and act to improve it.

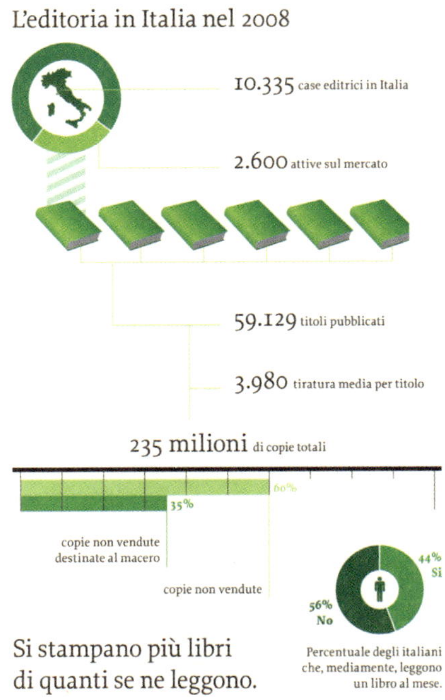

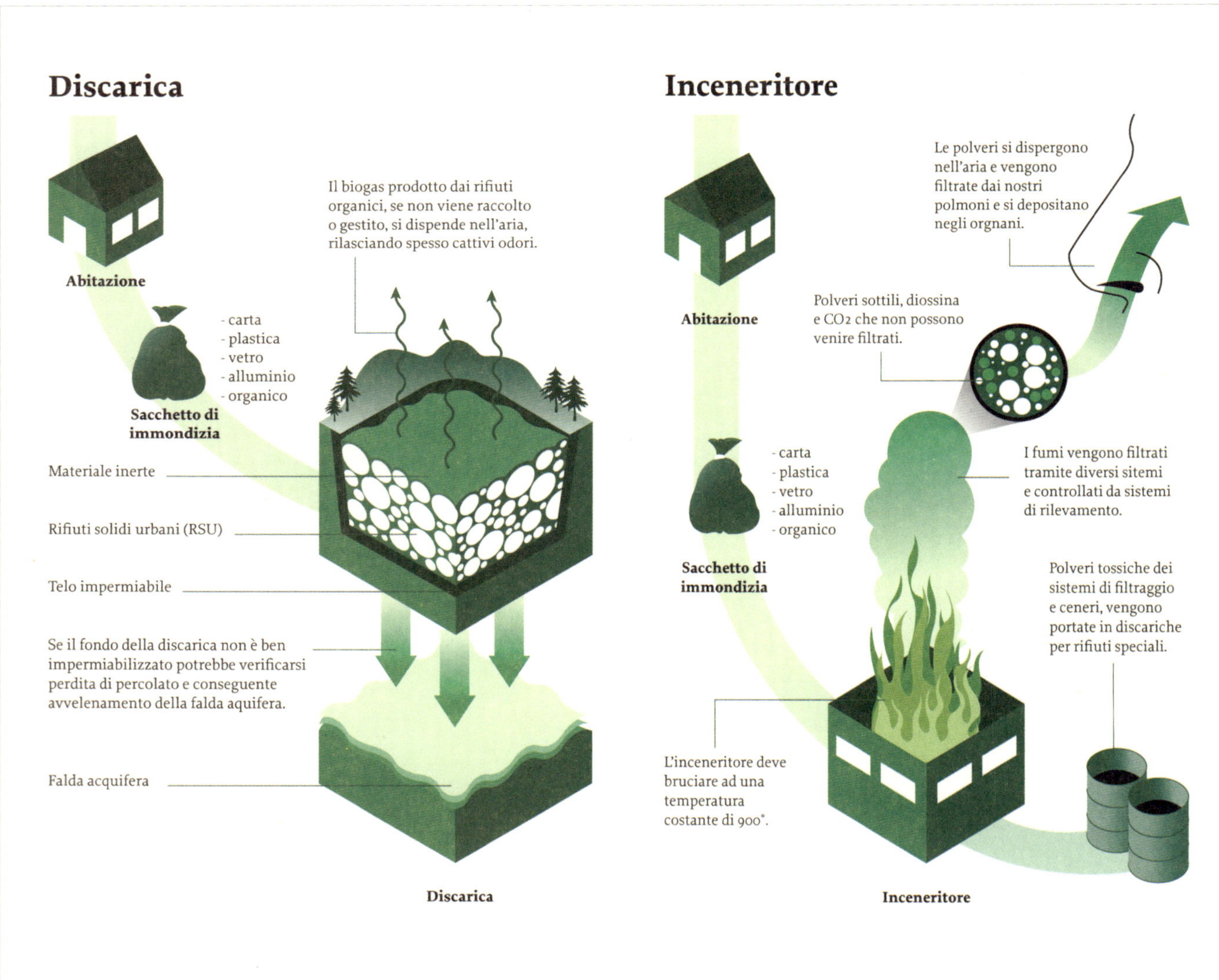

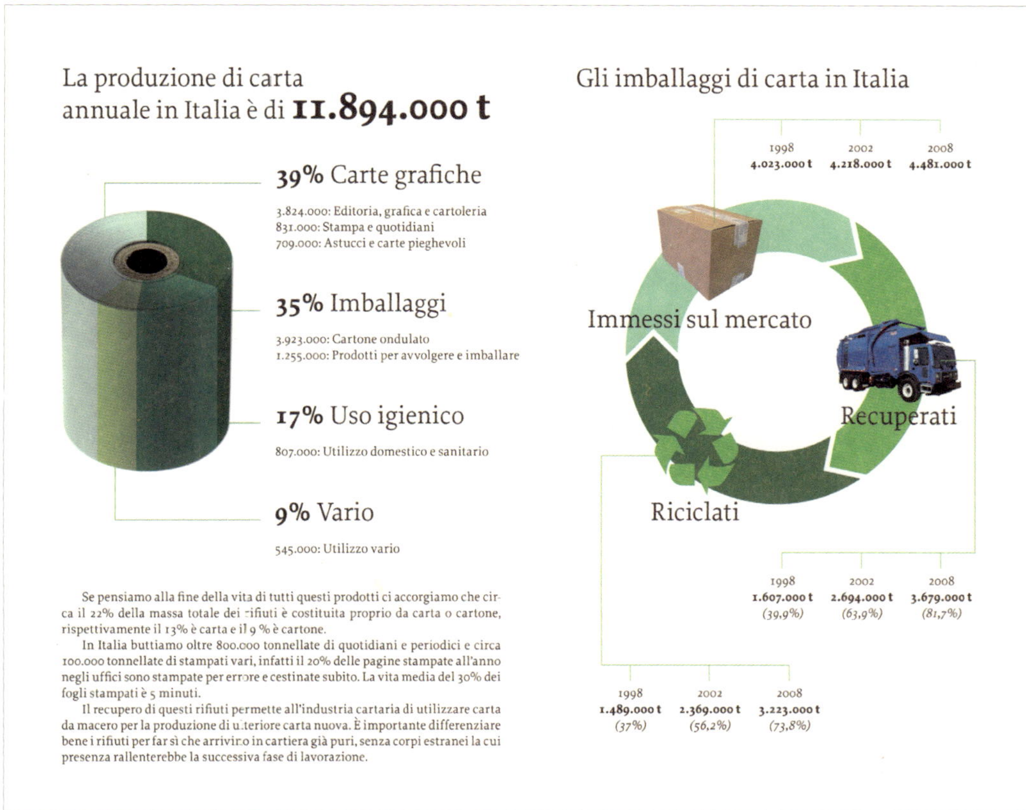
La produzione di carta annuale in Italia è di **11.894.000 t**
39% Carte grafiche
3.824.000: Editoria, grafica e cartoleria
831.000: Stampa e quotidiani
709.000: Astucci e carte pieghevoli
35% Imballaggi
3.923.000: Cartone ondulato
1.255.000: Prodotti per avvolgere e imballare
17% Uso igienico
807.000: Utilizzo domestico e sanitario
9% Vario
545.000: Utilizzo vario
Se pensiamo alla fine della vita di tutti questi prodotti ci accorgiamo che circa il 22% della massa totale dei rifiuti è costituita proprio da carta o cartone, rispettivamente il 13% è carta e il 9 % è cartone.
In Italia buttiamo oltre 800.000 tonnellate di quotidiani e periodici e circa 100.000 tonnellate di stampati vari, infatti il 20% delle pagine stampate all'anno negli uffici sono stampate per errore e cestinate subito. La vita media del 30% dei fogli stampati è 5 minuti.
Il recupero di questi rifiuti permette all'industria cartaria di utilizzare carta da macero per la produzione di ulteriore carta nuova. È importante differenziare bene i rifiuti per far sì che arrivino in cartiera già puri, senza corpi estranei la cui presenza rallenterebbe la successiva fase di lavorazione.
Gli imballaggi di carta in Italia
1998 **4.023.000 t**
2002 **4.218.000 t**
2008 **4.481.000 t**
Immessi sul mercato
Recuperati
Riciclati
1998 **1.607.000 t** (39,9%)
2002 **2.694.000 t** (63,9%)
2008 **3.679.000 t** (81,7%)
1998 **1.489.000 t** (37%)
2002 **2.369.000 t** (56,2%)
2008 **3.223.000 t** (73,8%)

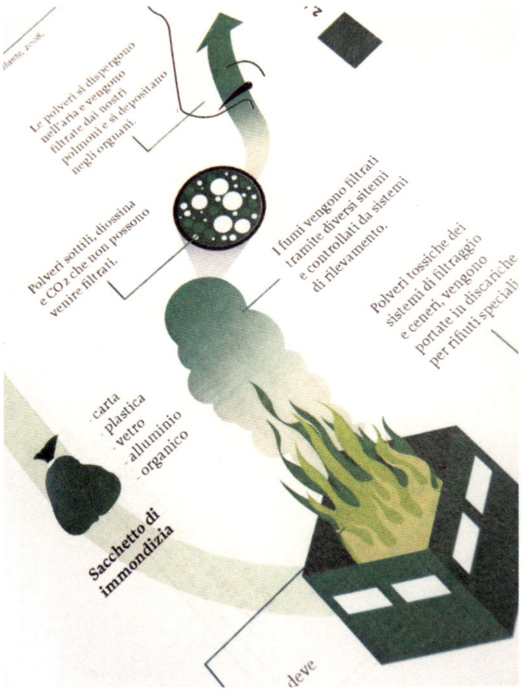
carta
plastica
vetro
alluminio
organico
Sacchetto di immondizia

39% Carte grafic
35% Imballaggi
3.923.000: Cartone ondulato
1.255.000: Prodotti per avvolgere e imballare
17% Uso igienico
807.000: Utilizzo domestico e sanitario
9% Vario

Dal Nido Alla Scuola Superiore 2014

- Completion Year: 2014
- Designers: Gianni Sinni, Silvia Basso, Alberto Bolzonetti, Lorella Chiavacci
- Client: Regione Toscana

• Work Introduction

From nursery to high school is the 2014 edition of the annual report book published by the Region of Tuscany to make public the database of information that is supporting planning and investment in education in Tuscany. The usage of bright colours, contrasting pie charts, attractive icons make the report vivid and simple.

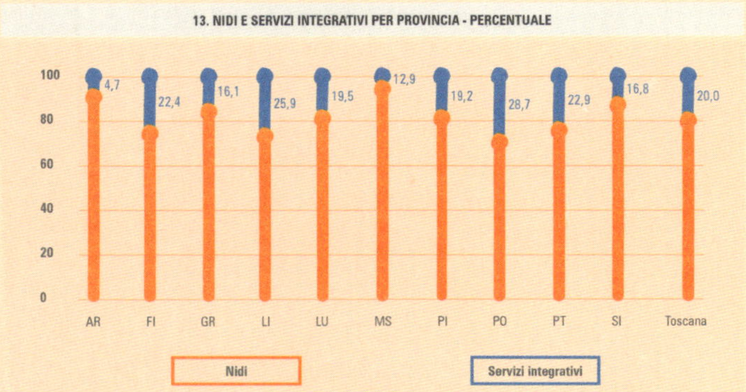

INFANZIA

POPOLAZIONE 3-36 MESI **3.425**
RICETTIVITÀ SERVIZI **1.242**
DOMANDE AL 1/09 **1.405**
LISTA D'ATTESA AL 1/09 **444**
ISCRITTI AL 31/12 **1.64**
PERCENTUALE DI COPERTURA **85,7%**

PEZ

287.574,06 €

TOTALE RISORSE INFANZIA

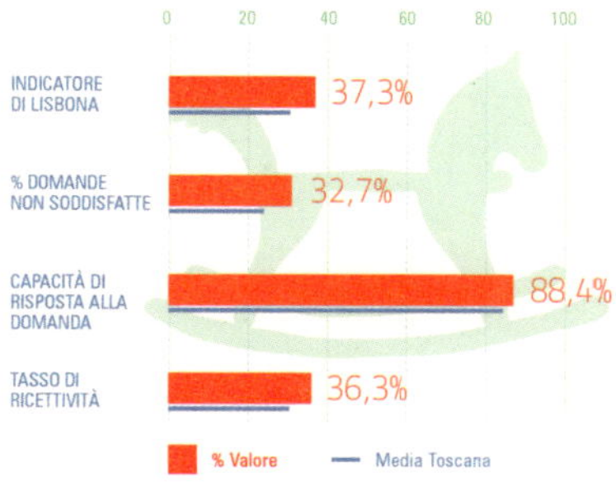

SOSTENERE E SVILUPPARE IL SISTEMA DEI SERVIZI **78,0%**

PROMUOVERE LA CONTINUITÀ EDUCATIVA **6,8%**

RAFFORZARE IL SISTEMA CON COORDINAMENTO E FORMAZIONE **15,0%** — Vincolo del 15%

RISORSE VINCOLATE

COORDINAMENTO ZONALE **76,1%**	
Servizi coinvolti	33
Incontri previsti	15
Ore previste	45
Coordinatori	2

FORMAZIONE CONGIUNTA **23,9%**		
Educatori	Pubblici	210
Educatori	Privati	30
Educatori	Totale	240
	Incontri	20
	Ore	40
Insegnanti	Pubblici	120
Insegnanti	Privati	-
Insegnanti	Totale	120
	Incontri	20
	Ore	40

FORMAZIONE EDUCATORI **0,0%**		
Educatori	Pubblici	-
Educatori	Privati	-
Educatori	Totale	-
	Incontri	-
	Ore	-

SERVIZI EDUCATIVI 39

SERVIZI PUBBLICI **20**
- 21 NIDI
- 6 SERVIZI INTEGRATIVI

SERVIZI PRIVATI **18**
- 10 NIDI
- 2 SERVIZI INTEGRATIVI

ISTRUZIONE

POPOLAZIONE 6-18 ANNI **17.456**
VOTO MEDIO LICENZA MEDIA **7,3**
VOTO MEDIO MATURITÀ **74,8**

PEZ

174.308,35 €

TOTALE RISORSE ETÀ SCOLARE

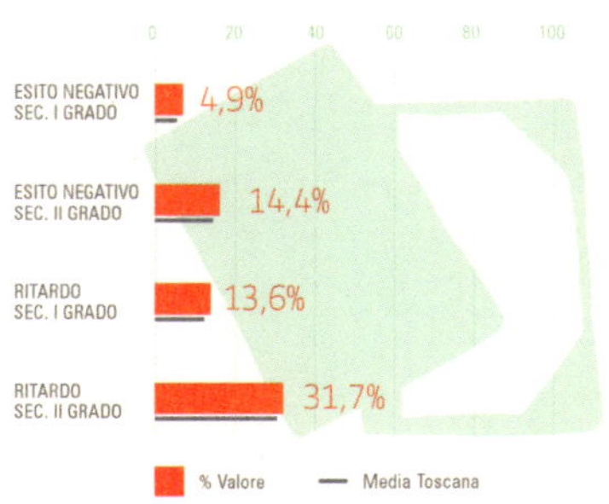

PROMUOVERE INCLUSIONE DISABILI **28,2** — Vincolo del 25%

PROMUOVERE INCLUSIONE STRANIERI **26,4** — Vincolo del 15%

PROMUOVERE CONTRASTO AL DISAGIO **1,1%**

PROMUOVERE ESPERIENZE EDUCATIVE SOCIALIZZANTI **44,3%**

RISORSE VINCOLATE

ALUNNI 16.681

	PRIMARIA	SEC. I GRADO	SEC. II GRADO
	39,2%	25,6%	35,1%
STRANIERI %	7,5%	8,0%	5,2%
DISABILI %	2,8%	4,2%	2,3%

		INCLUSIONE DISABILI					INCLUSIONE STRANIERI				
		Infanzia	Primaria	Sec. I Grado	Sec. II Grado	Totale	Infanzia	Primaria	Sec. I Grado	Sec. II Grado	Totale
Laboratori	Allievi	400	1.562	420	160	2.542	325	1.500	30	180	2.035
Didattica in compresenza	Docenti/ esperti	4	48	290	20	362		36	90	-	126
	Allievi	44	350	400	50	844		450	225	-	675
Supporto e recupero	Docenti/ esperti	-	-	-	-	-		-	-	-	-
	Allievi	-	-	-	-	-		-	-	-	-
Predisposizione e documentazione	Docenti/ esperti	-	-	-	-	-	-	-	-	-	-
Supporto genitorialità	Docenti/ esperti	-	-	-	-	-	-	-	-	-	-
	Famiglie	-	-	-	-	-	-	-	-	-	-
Formazione aggiornamento	Destinatari	25	25	-	-	50	5	5	10	10	30

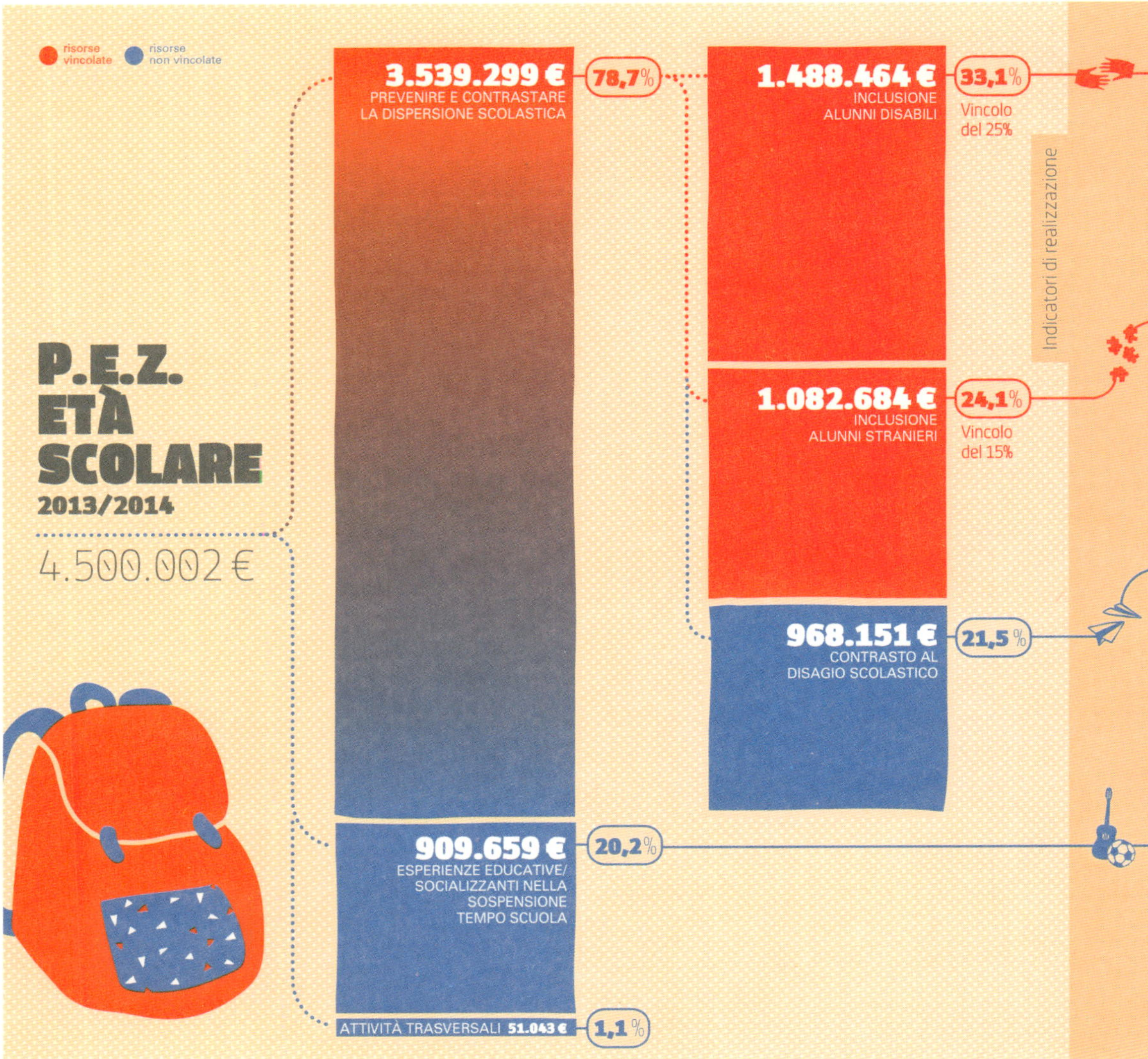

Inclusione alunni disabili	
55.309 allievi	Laboratori
16.390 allievi	Didattica in compresenza
6.338 allievi	Supporto e recupero disciplinare
220 docenti totali 8 esperti	Predisposizione progetti e documentazione
3.715 famiglie	Supporto genitorialità
1.044 destinatari	Formazione/aggiornamento/tutoraggio/consulenza

Inclusione alunni stranieri	
41.279 allievi	Laboratori
6.924 allievi	Didattica in compresenza
8.714 allievi	Supporto e recupero disciplinare
124 docenti totali 1 esperti	Predisposizione progetti e documentazione
5.719 famiglie	Supporto genitorialità
537 destinatari	Formazione/aggiornamento/tutoraggio/consulenza

Contrasto al disagio scolastico	
30.801 allievi	Laboratori
5.355 allievi	Didattica in compresenza
14.152 allievi	Supporto e recupero disciplinare
102 docenti totali 9 esperti	Predisposizione progetti e documentazione
7.328 famiglie	Supporto genitorialità
2.575 destinatari	Formazione/aggiornamento/tutoraggio/consulenza

ESPERIENZE EDUCATIVE/ SOCIALIZZANTI NELLA SOSPENSIONE TEMPO SCUOLA	
423.311 destinatari	Attività nei periodi di sospensione estiva (centri estivi)
24 destinatari	Soggiorni estivi
49.068 destinatari	Att. extrascolastiche educative/ludico/ricreative

IL PROCESSO DI ACCOGLIENZA

RISPETTO ALLA POPOLAZIONE 3-36 MESI

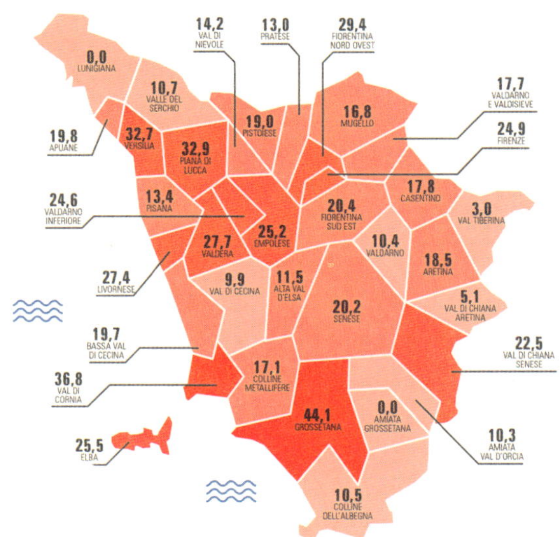

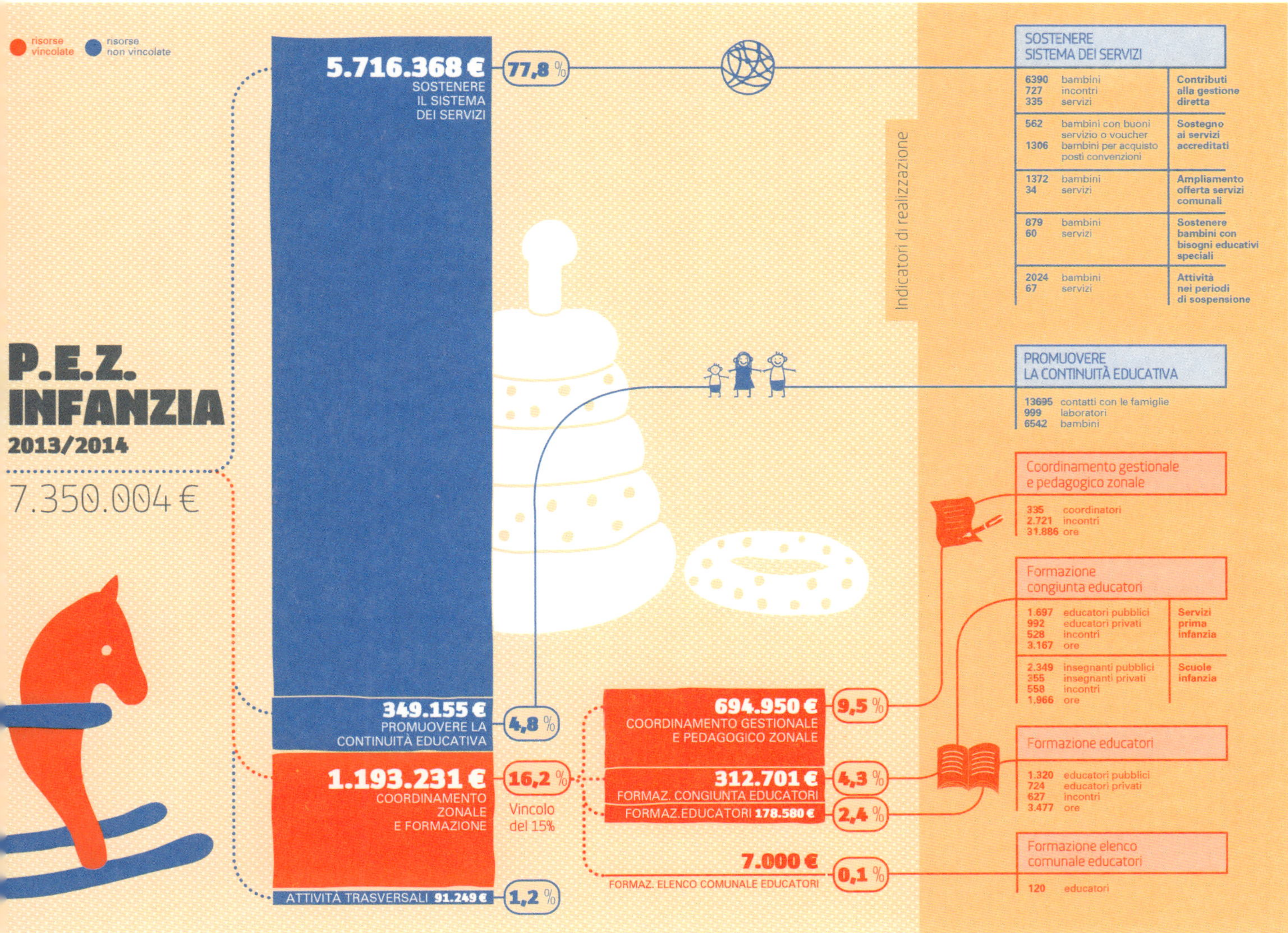

127. STRANIERI DI PRIMA E SECONDA GENERAZIONE PER SCUOLA SECONDARIA DI SECONDO GRADO E PROVINCIA – AS 2012/2013

	Liceale		Professionale		Tecnica		Totale	
	Nati estero	Nati Italia	Nati estero	Nati Italia	Nati estero	Nati Italia	Nati estero	Nati Italia
AR	419	76	592	45	536	56	1.547	177
FI	870	213	1.822	246	1.114	177	3.806	636
GR	190	15	299	10	255	12	744	37
LI	163	29	350	22	354	40	867	91
LU	239	38	421	69	291	49	951	156
MS	141	32	204	19	107	14	452	65
PI	325	62	422	38	347	47	1.094	147
PO	291	121	294	45	435	168	1.020	334
PT	233	40	503	88	271	37	1.007	165
SI	304	80	545	62	504	94	1.353	236
Toscana	3.175	706	5.452	644	4.214	694	12.841	2.044

Fonte: Elaborazioni su dati SISR

128. PERCENTUALE ALUNNI STRANIERI DI SECONDA GENERAZIONE E RAPPORTO DI COESISTENZA PER TIPOLOGIA DI SECONDARIA DI SECONDO GRADO – AS 2012/2013

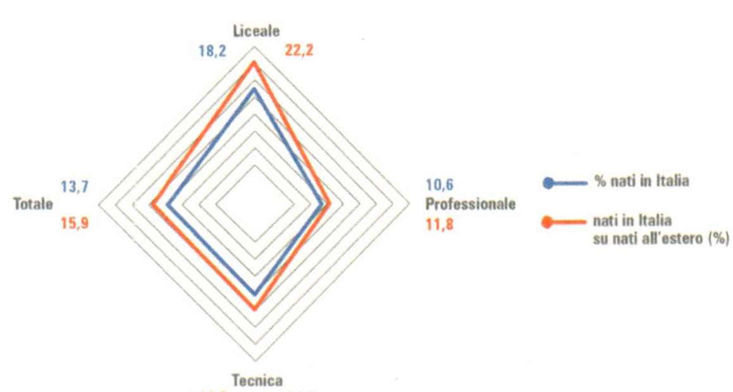

26. ALUNNI PER ORDINE E TASSO DI CRESCITA TOTALE - TOSCANA

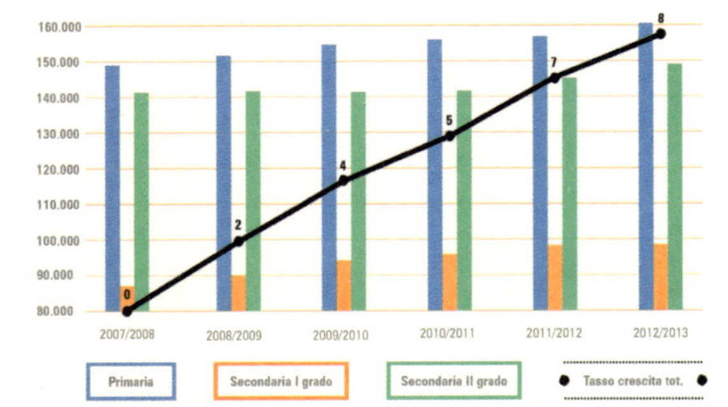

Fonte: Elaborazione su dati SISR

27. ALUNNI PER ORDINE - NUMERI INDICE 2007/2008

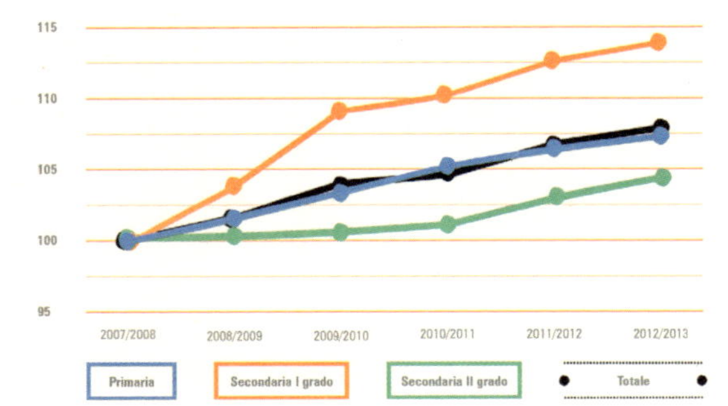

88. IMPORTO MEDIO, MASSIMO E MINIMO DELLA RETTA MASSIMA APPLICABILE PER TIPOLOGIA DI SERVIZIO EDUCATIVO (EURO) - SERVIZI NON COMUNALI

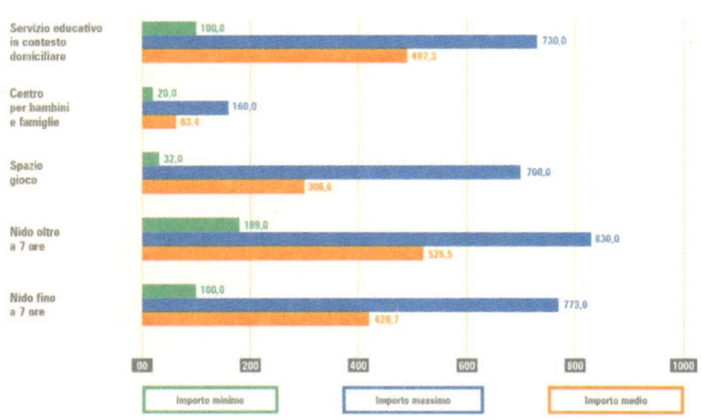

Fonte: Elaborazione su dati SIRIA

89. IMPORTO MEDIO, MASSIMO E MINIMO DELLA RETTA MASSIMA APPLICABILE PER TIPOLOGIA DI SERVIZIO EDUCATIVO (EURO) - SERVIZI COMUNALI

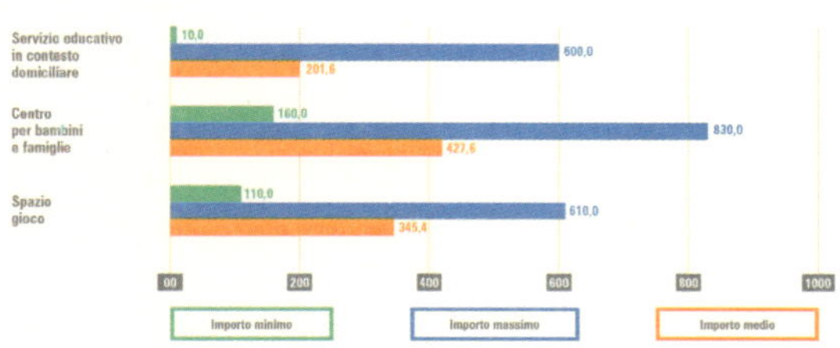

Fonte: Elaborazione su dati SIRIA

NIDI PER CLASSI DI RETTE MASSIME

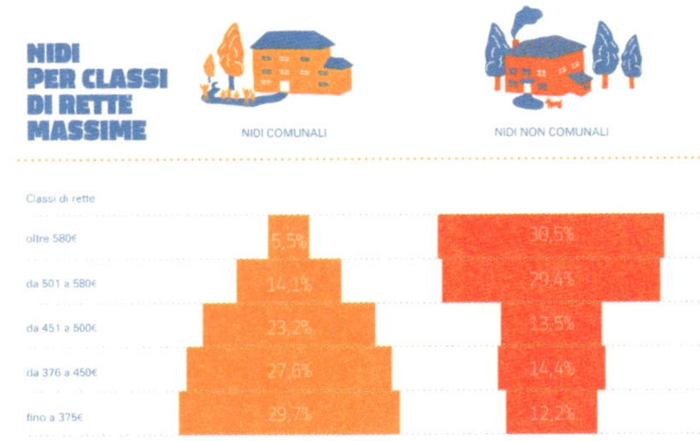

31. ALUNNI PER ORDINE E GENERE - AS 2012/2013

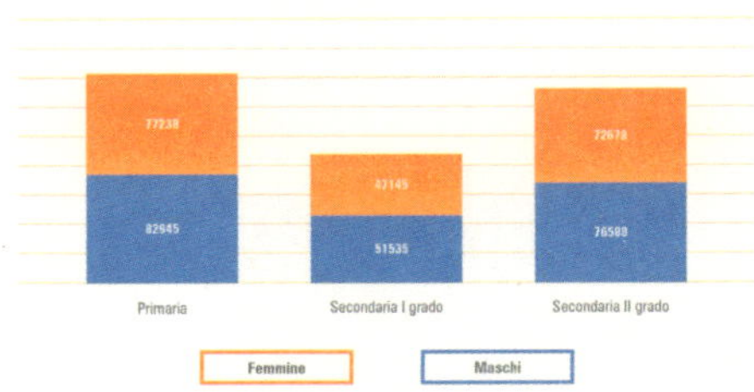

Fonte: Elaborazione su dati SISR

32. ALUNNI PER TIPOLOGIA DI SCUOLA SECONDARIA DI II GRADO, ANNI 2007-2012 - NUMERO INDICE

A livello provinciale, a Prato, Firenze e Siena l'importo della retta massima per la frequenza di un nido è superiore alla media regionale, sia tra i nidi comunali che tra quelli non comunali. L'importo massimo applicabile in termini assoluti si registra nell'Unione Valdera per i nidi non comunali e nel Valdarno e Valdisieve per quelli comunali e in entrambi i casi ammonta ad 830 euro mensili.

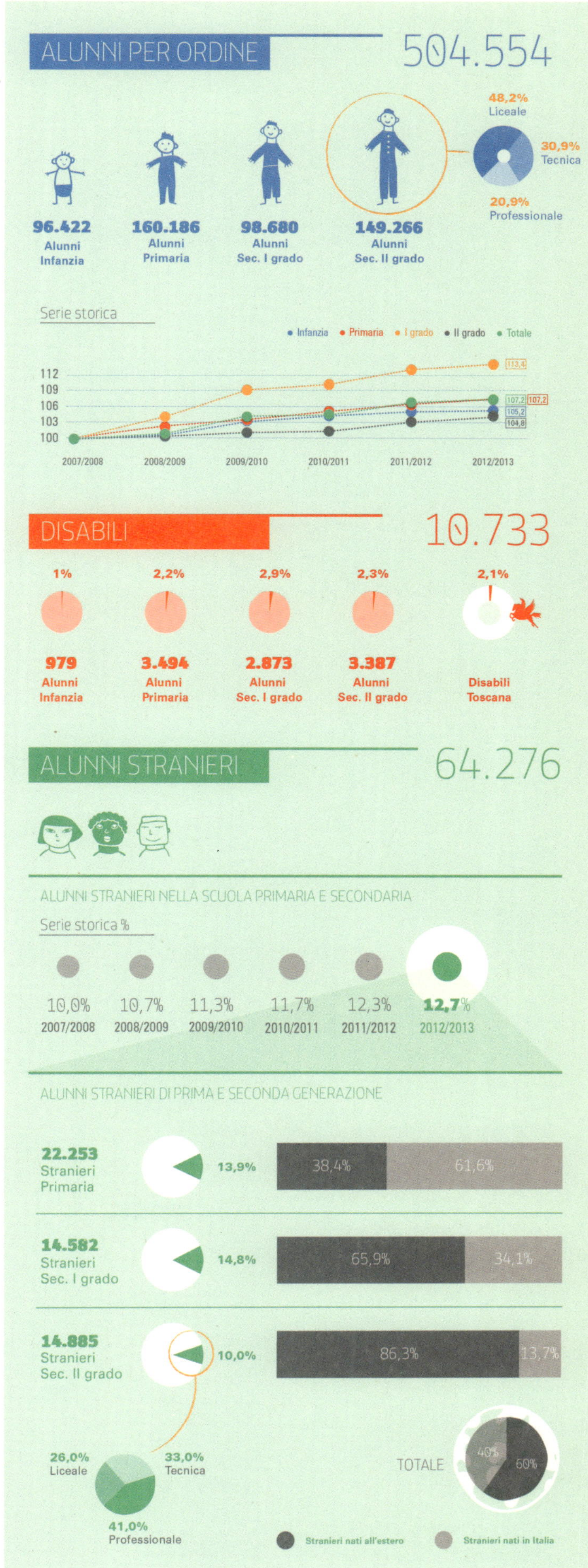
ALUNNI PER ORDINE
504.554
96.422
Alunni
Infanzia
160.186
Alunni
Primaria
98.680
Alunni
Sec. I grado
149.266
Alunni
Sec. II grado
48,2%
Liceale
30,9%
Tecnica
20,9%
Professionale
Serie storica
Infanzia
Primaria
I grado
II grado
Totale
112
109
106
103
100
113,4
107,2
107,2
105,2
104,8
2007/2008
2008/2009
2009/2010
2010/2011
2011/2012
2012/2013
DISABILI
10.733
1%
2,2%
2,9%
2,3%
2,1%
979
Alunni
Infanzia
3.494
Alunni
Primaria
2.873
Alunni
Sec. I grado
3.387
Alunni
Sec. II grado
Disabili
Toscana
ALUNNI STRANIERI
64.276
ALUNNI STRANIERI NELLA SCUOLA PRIMARIA E SECONDARIA
Serie storica %
10,0%
2007/2008
10,7%
2008/2009
11,3%
2009/2010
11,7%
2010/2011
12,3%
2011/2012
12,7%
2012/2013
ALUNNI STRANIERI DI PRIMA E SECONDA GENERAZIONE
22.253
Stranieri
Primaria
13,9%
38,4%
61,6%
14.582
Stranieri
Sec. I grado
14,8%
65,9%
34,1%
14.885
Stranieri
Sec. II grado
10,0%
86,3%
13,7%
26,0%
Liceale
33,0%
Tecnica
41,0%
Professionale
TOTALE
40%
60%
Stranieri nati all'estero
Stranieri nati in Italia

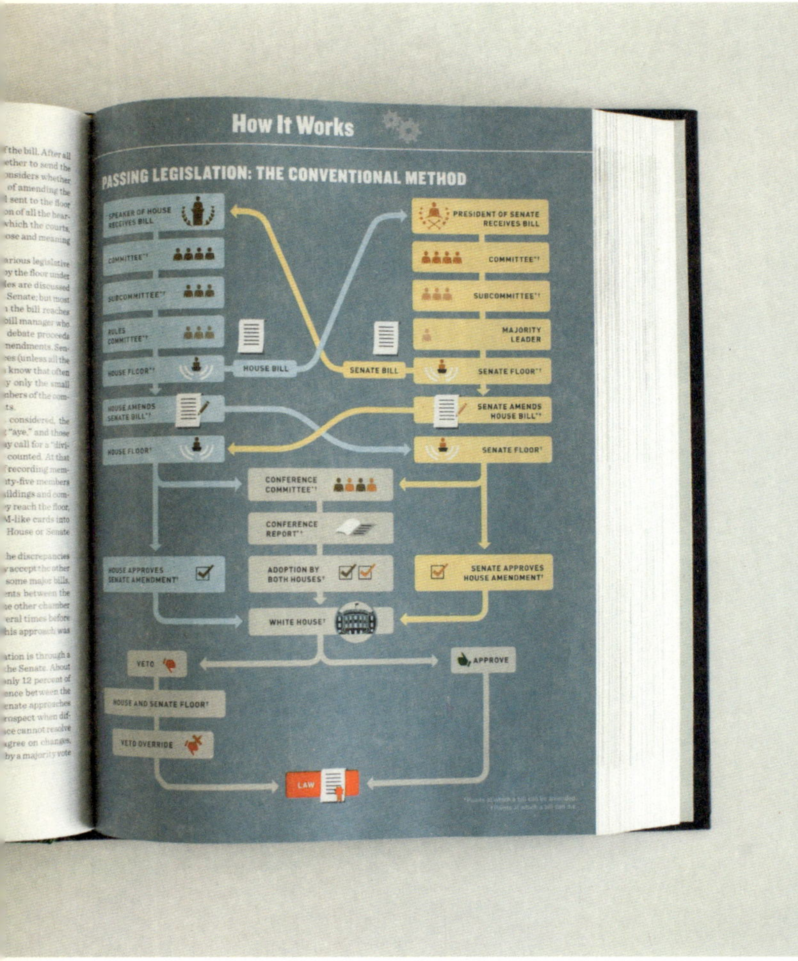

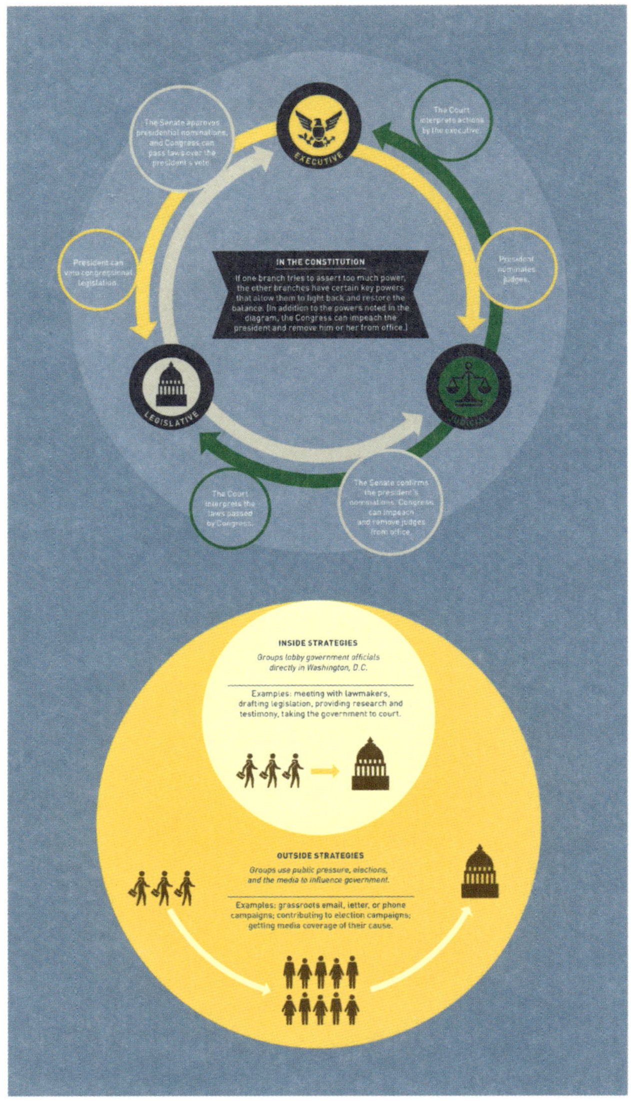

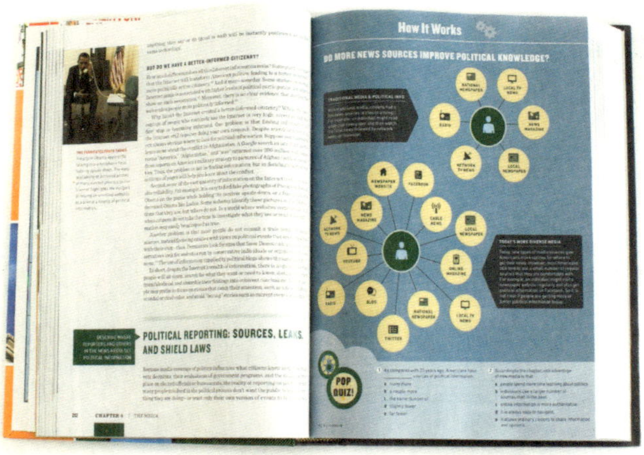

Learn the Essentials of American Politics

- Completion Year: 2014
- Designer: Julia Zeltser (Principal + Creative Director), Jason Lynch (Art Director), Wen Ping Huang (Designer)
- Client: W.W. Norton

• Work Introduction

Hyperakt developed a series of infographics in collaboration with the book's authors to introduce students to various systems, hierarchies and balances in US governance. Each graphic is designed as a flowchart to present information in as simple and accessible a way as possible. Hyperakt interpreted complex legal and social concepts with custom icons, intuitive diagrams and cheerful colors. Hyperakt's ambition was to make civics inviting and engaging, and inspire a new generation to invest their hopes in America.

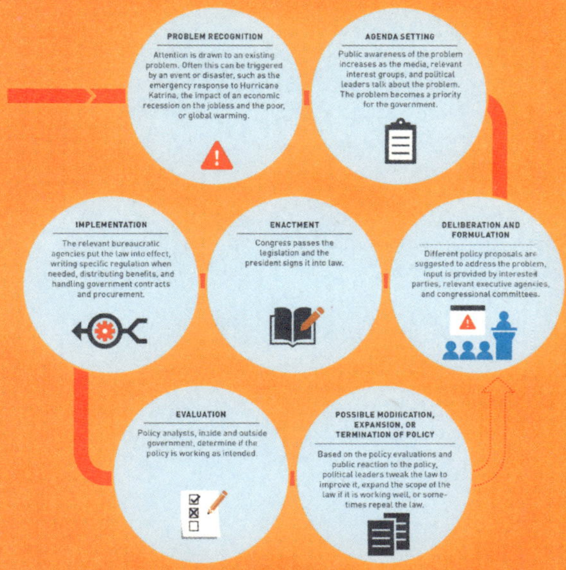
PROBLEM RECOGNITION
Attention is drawn to an existing problem. Often this can be triggered by an event or disaster, such as the emergency response to Hurricane Katrina, the impact of an economic recession on the jobless and the poor, or global warming.
AGENDA SETTING
Public awareness of the problem increases as the media, relevant interest groups, and political leaders talk about the problem. The problem becomes a priority for the government.
DELIBERATION AND FORMULATION
Different policy proposals are suggested to address the problem, input is provided by interested parties, relevant executive agencies, and congressional committees.
ENACTMENT
Congress passes the legislation and the president signs it into law.
IMPLEMENTATION
The relevant bureaucratic agencies put the law into effect, writing specific regulation when needed, distributing benefits, and handling government contracts and procurement.
EVALUATION
Policy analysts, inside and outside government, determine if the policy is working as intended.
POSSIBLE MODIFICATION, EXPANSION, OR TERMINATION OF POLICY
Based on the policy evaluations and public reaction to the policy, political leaders tweak the law to improve it, expand the scope of the law if it is working well, or sometimes repeal the law.

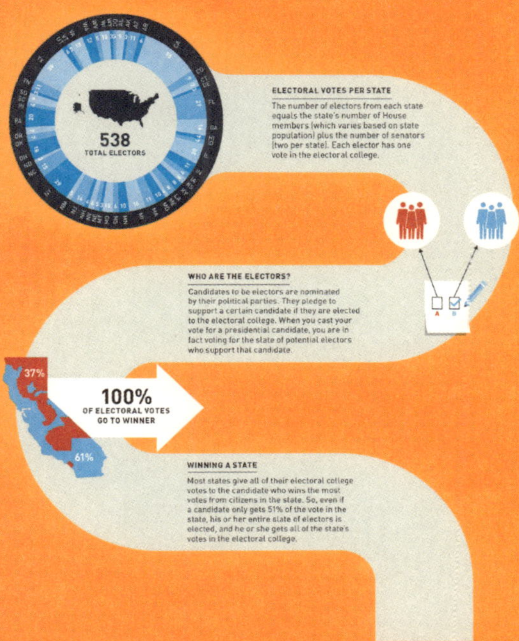
538
TOTAL ELECTORS
ELECTORAL VOTES PER STATE
The number of electors from each state equals the state's number of House members (which varies based on state population) plus the number of senators (two per state). Each elector has one vote in the electoral college.
WHO ARE THE ELECTORS?
Candidates to be electors are nominated by their political parties. They pledge to support a certain candidate if they are elected to the electoral college. When you cast your vote for a presidential candidate, you are in fact voting for the slate of potential electors who support that candidate.
37%
100%
OF ELECTORAL VOTES GO TO WINNER
61%
WINNING A STATE
Most states give all of their electoral college votes to the candidate who wins the most votes from citizens in the state. So, even if a candidate only gets 51% of the vote in the state, his or her entire slate of electors is elected, and he or she gets all of the state's votes in the electoral college.

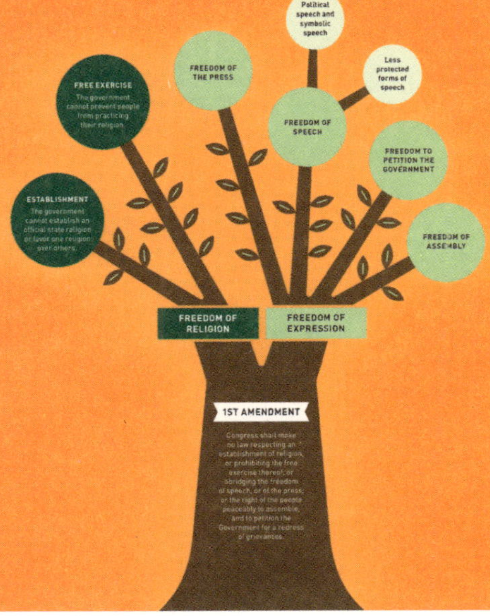
Political speech and symbolic speech
Less protected forms of speech
FREEDOM OF THE PRESS
FREE EXERCISE
The government cannot prevent people from practicing their religion.
FREEDOM OF SPEECH
FREEDOM TO PETITION THE GOVERNMENT
ESTABLISHMENT
The government cannot establish an official state religion or favor one religion over others.
FREEDOM OF ASSEMBLY
FREEDOM OF RELIGION
FREEDOM OF EXPRESSION
1ST AMENDMENT
Congress shall make no law respecting an establishment of religion, or prohibiting the free exercise thereof; or abridging the freedom of speech, or of the press; or the right of the people peaceably to assemble, and to petition the Government for a redress of grievances.

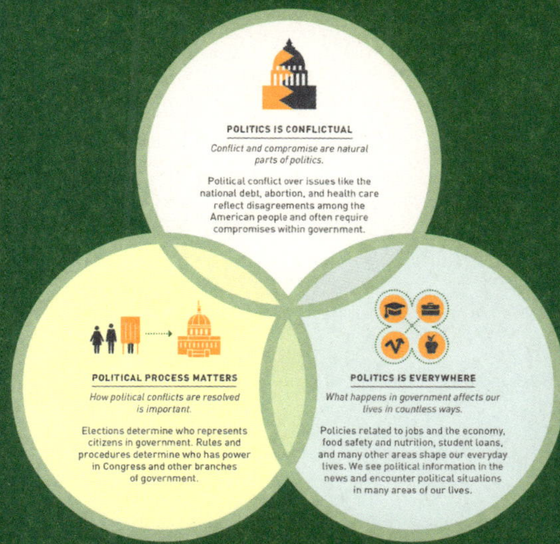
POLITICS IS CONFLICTUAL
Conflict and compromise are natural parts of politics.
Political conflict over issues like the national debt, abortion, and health care reflect disagreements among the American people and often require compromises within government.
POLITICAL PROCESS MATTERS
How political conflicts are resolved is important.
Elections determine who represents citizens in government. Rules and procedures determine who has power in Congress and other branches of government.
POLITICS IS EVERYWHERE
What happens in government affects our lives in countless ways.
Policies related to jobs and the economy, food safety and nutrition, student loans, and many other areas shape our everyday lives. We see political information in the news and encounter political situations in many areas of our lives.

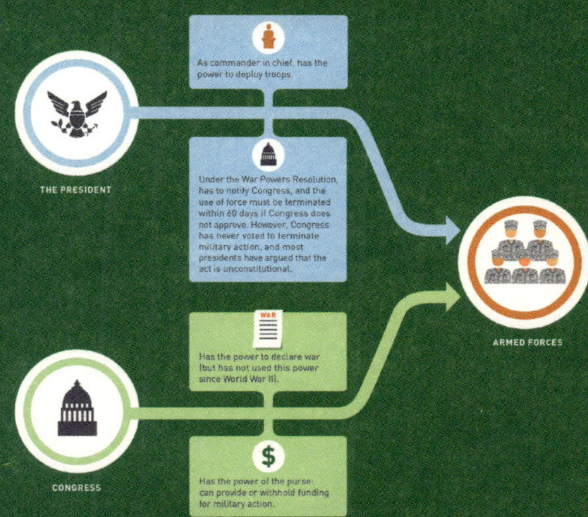
As commander in chief, has the power to deploy troops.
THE PRESIDENT
Under the War Powers Resolution, has to notify Congress, and the use of force must be terminated within 60 days if Congress does not approve. However, Congress has never voted to terminate military action, and most presidents have argued that the act is unconstitutional.
ARMED FORCES
WAR
Has the power to declare war (but has not used this power since World War II).
CONGRESS
Has the power of the purse: can provide or withhold funding for military action.

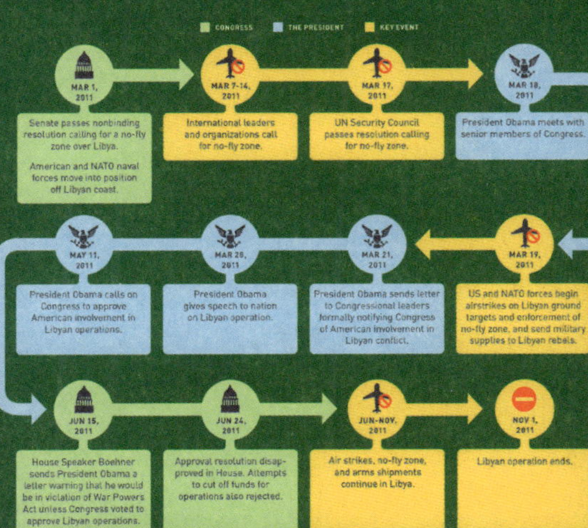
CONGRESS
THE PRESIDENT
KEY EVENT
MAR 1, 2011
Senate passes nonbinding resolution calling for a no-fly zone over Libya.
American and NATO naval forces move into position off Libyan coast.
MAR 7-14, 2011
International leaders and organizations call for no-fly zone.
MAR 17, 2011
UN Security Council passes resolution calling for no-fly zone.
MAR 18, 2011
President Obama meets with senior members of Congress.
MAR 19, 2011
US and NATO forces begin airstrikes on Libyan ground targets and enforcement of no-fly zone, and send military supplies to Libyan rebels.
MAR 21, 2011
President Obama sends letter to Congressional leaders formally notifying Congress of American involvement in Libyan conflict.
MAR 28, 2011
President Obama gives speech to nation on Libyan operation.
MAY 11, 2011
President Obama calls on Congress to approve American involvement in Libyan operations.
JUN 15, 2011
House Speaker Boehner sends President Obama a letter warning that he would be in violation of War Powers Act unless Congress voted to approve Libyan operations.
JUN 24, 2011
Approval resolution disapproved in House. Attempts to cut off funds for operations also rejected.
JUN-NOV, 2011
Air strikes, no-fly zone, and arms shipments continue in Libya.
NOV 1, 2011
Libyan operation ends.

NOMINATING PRESIDENTIAL CANDIDATES

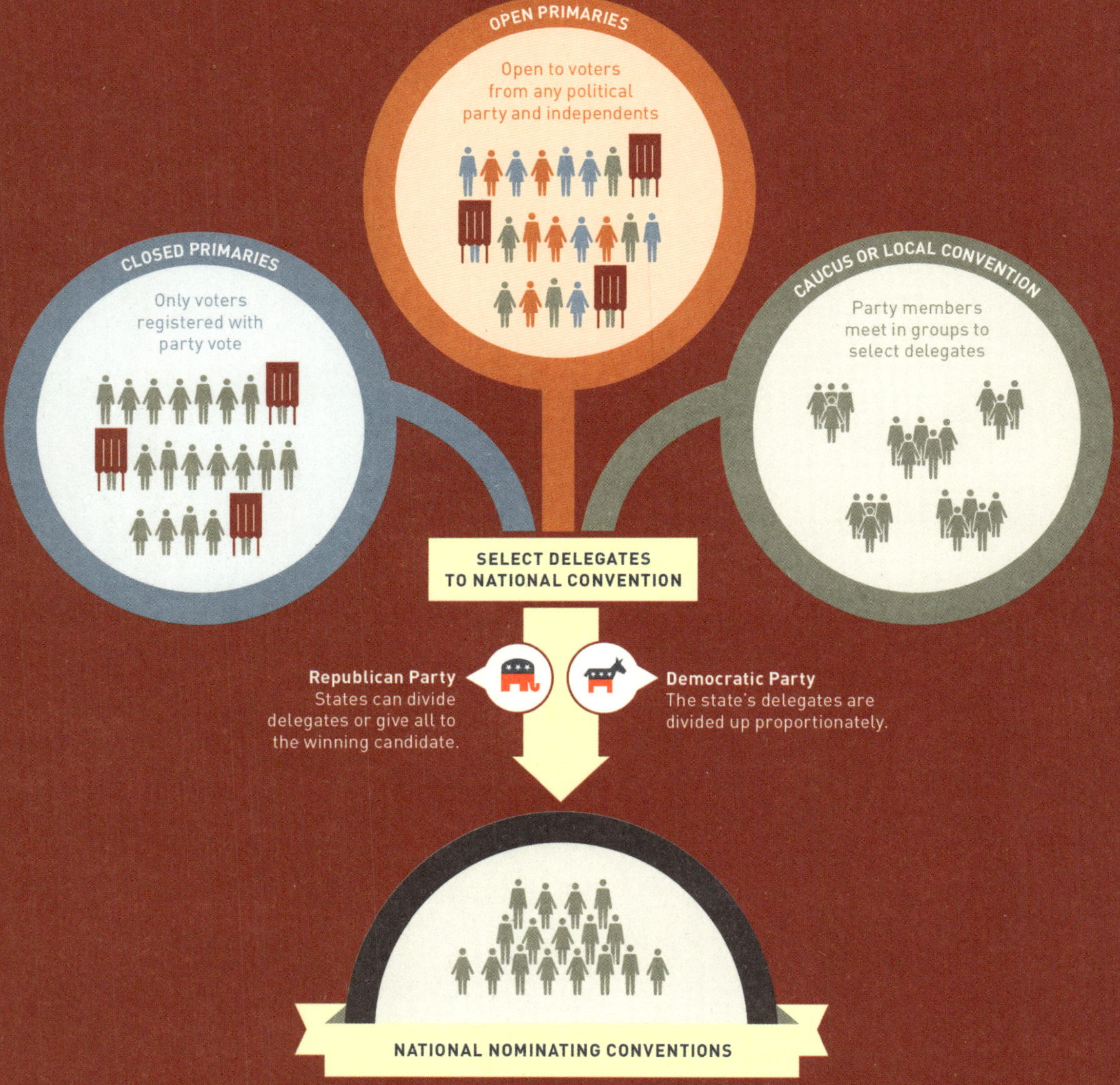

Delegates from all states attend the national convention, where they vote for the party's presidential and vice presidential nominees, based on the primary and caucus results. Superdelegates—important party leaders—also vote at the convention.

MEASURING WHAT A NATION OF 300 MILLION THINKS: A CHECKLIST
A RANDOM SAMPLE
Were the people who participated in the survey selected randomly, such that any member of the population had an equal chance of being selected?
SAMPLE SIZE
How many people do researchers need to survey to know what 300 million Americans think? Major national surveys usually use a sample of 1,000–2,000 respondants.
SAMPLE ERROR
As Nuts and Bolts 5.1 explains, for a group of any size (even 300 million), a survey of 1,000 randomly selected respondents will measure the average opinion in a population within 2%, 95% of the time. Reputable surveys will usually give the sampling error (sometimes also called "margin of error").
QUESTION WORDING
Did the way the question was worded influence the results? Scientific surveys try to phrase questions in a neutral way, but even in reputable polls, differences in question wording can influence answers.
RELIABLE RESPONDENTS
Respondents often give socially acceptable answers rather than truthful ones—or invent opinions on the spot. Is there a reason to think people may not have answered this survey honestly and thoughtfully?

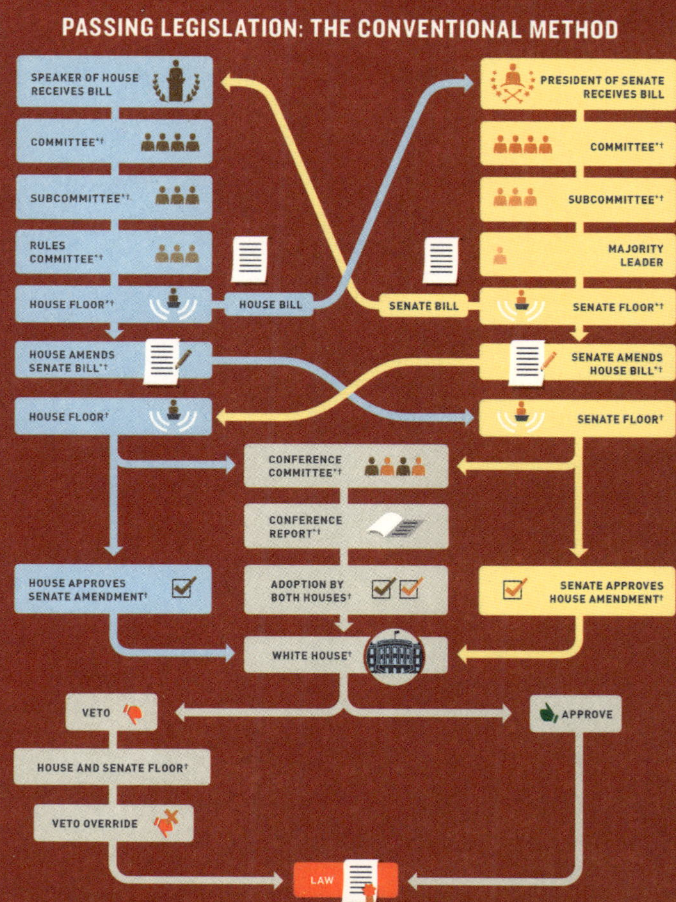
PASSING LEGISLATION: THE CONVENTIONAL METHOD
SPEAKER OF HOUSE RECEIVES BILL
COMMITTEE*†
SUBCOMMITTEE*†
RULES COMMITTEE*†
HOUSE FLOOR*†
HOUSE BILL
PRESIDENT OF SENATE RECEIVES BILL
COMMITTEE*†
SUBCOMMITTEE*†
MAJORITY LEADER
SENATE BILL
SENATE FLOOR*†
HOUSE AMENDS SENATE BILL*†
HOUSE FLOOR†
SENATE AMENDS HOUSE BILL*†
SENATE FLOOR†
CONFERENCE COMMITTEE*†
CONFERENCE REPORT*†
HOUSE APPROVES SENATE AMENDMENT†
ADOPTION BY BOTH HOUSES†
SENATE APPROVES HOUSE AMENDMENT†
WHITE HOUSE†
VETO
APPROVE
HOUSE AND SENATE FLOOR†
VETO OVERRIDE
LAW

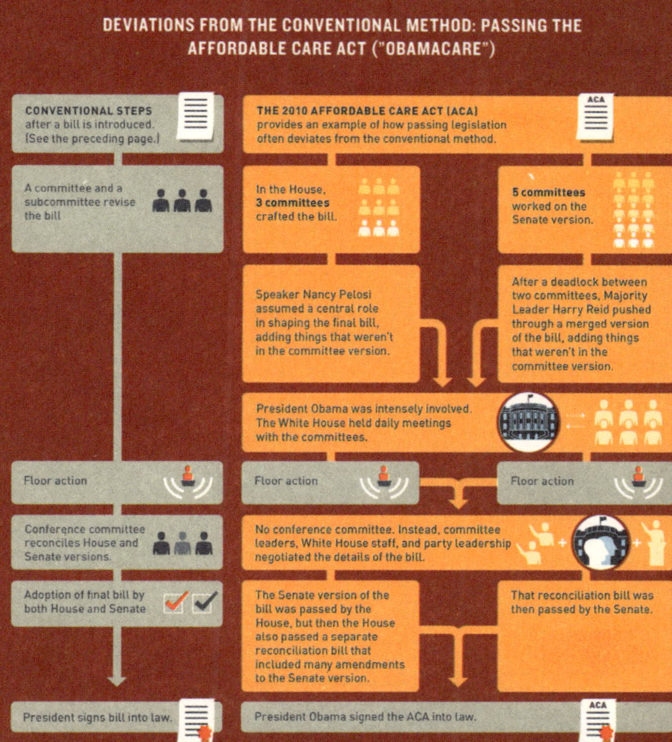
DEVIATIONS FROM THE CONVENTIONAL METHOD: PASSING THE AFFORDABLE CARE ACT ("OBAMACARE")
CONVENTIONAL STEPS after a bill is introduced. (See the preceding page.)
THE 2010 AFFORDABLE CARE ACT (ACA) provides an example of how passing legislation often deviates from the conventional method.
ACA
A committee and a subcommittee revise the bill
In the House, 3 committees crafted the bill.
5 committees worked on the Senate version.
Speaker Nancy Pelosi assumed a central role in shaping the final bill, adding things that weren't in the committee version.
After a deadlock between two committees, Majority Leader Harry Reid pushed through a merged version of the bill, adding things that weren't in the committee version.
President Obama was intensely involved. The White House held daily meetings with the committees.
Floor action
Floor action
Floor action
Conference committee reconciles House and Senate versions.
No conference committee. Instead, committee leaders, White House staff, and party leadership negotiated the details of the bill.
Adoption of final bill by both House and Senate
The Senate version of the bill was passed by the House, but then the House also passed a separate reconciliation bill that included many amendments to the Senate version.
That reconciliation bill was then passed by the Senate.
President signs bill into law.
President Obama signed the ACA into law.
ACA

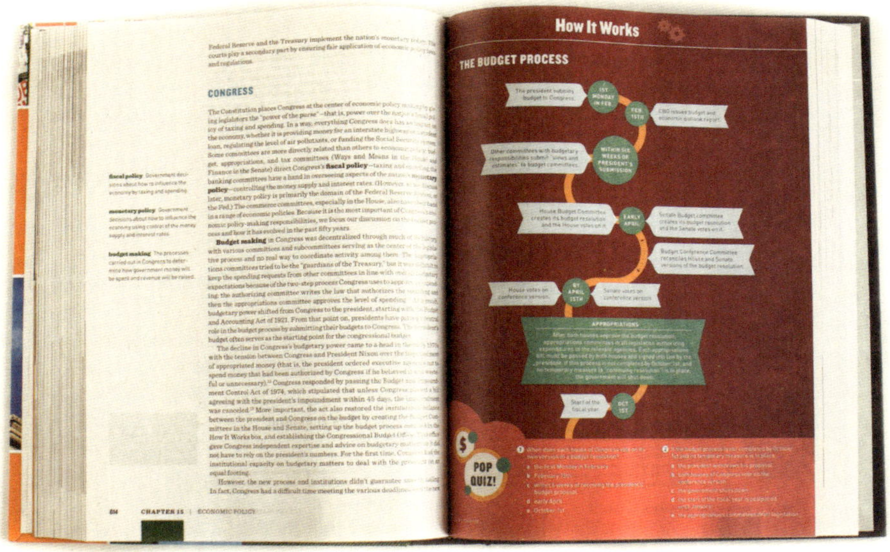
How It Works
THE BUDGET PROCESS
CONGRESS
POP QUIZ!

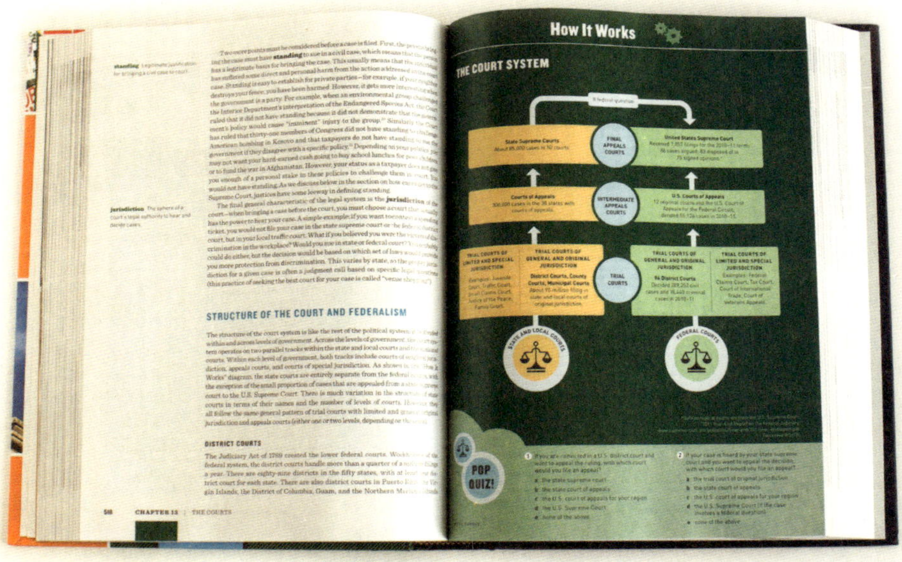
How It Works
THE COURT SYSTEM
STRUCTURE OF THE COURT AND FEDERALISM
DISTRICT COURTS
POP QUIZ!

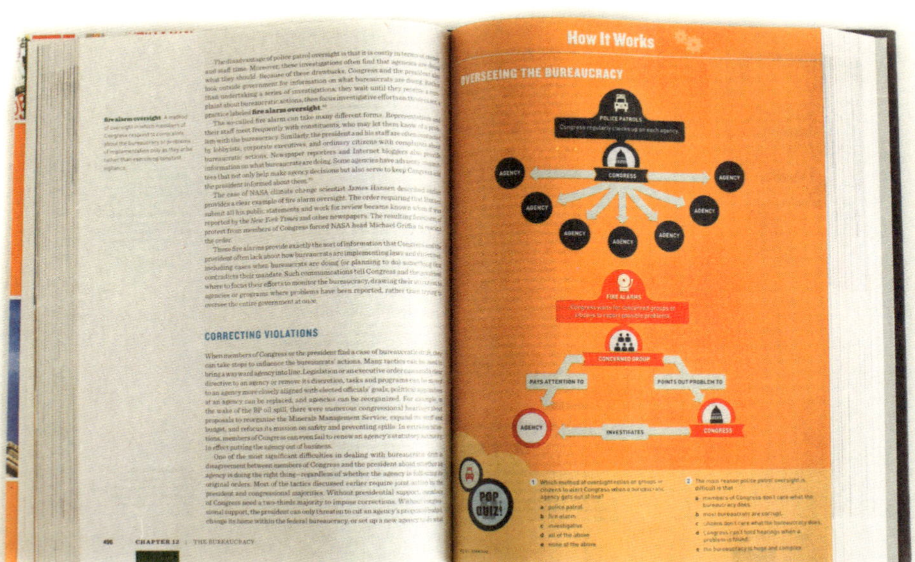
How It Works
OVERSEEING THE BUREAUCRACY
CORRECTING VIOLATIONS
POP QUIZ!

Il Tabacco

- Completion Year: 2013
- Designer: Luca Bonadei, Luca Mansi, Thomas Montorfano, Lorenzo Paolo Sdraffa

• Work Introduction

All submitted pages are regular news pages and double page spread opening pages for the main features. The idea of new design is to add more visual elements and make all pages more fluent and easy to read. The design draw the eyes to key elements highlighting essential informations. The result shows how the design came out following the story, not an infographic on purpose.

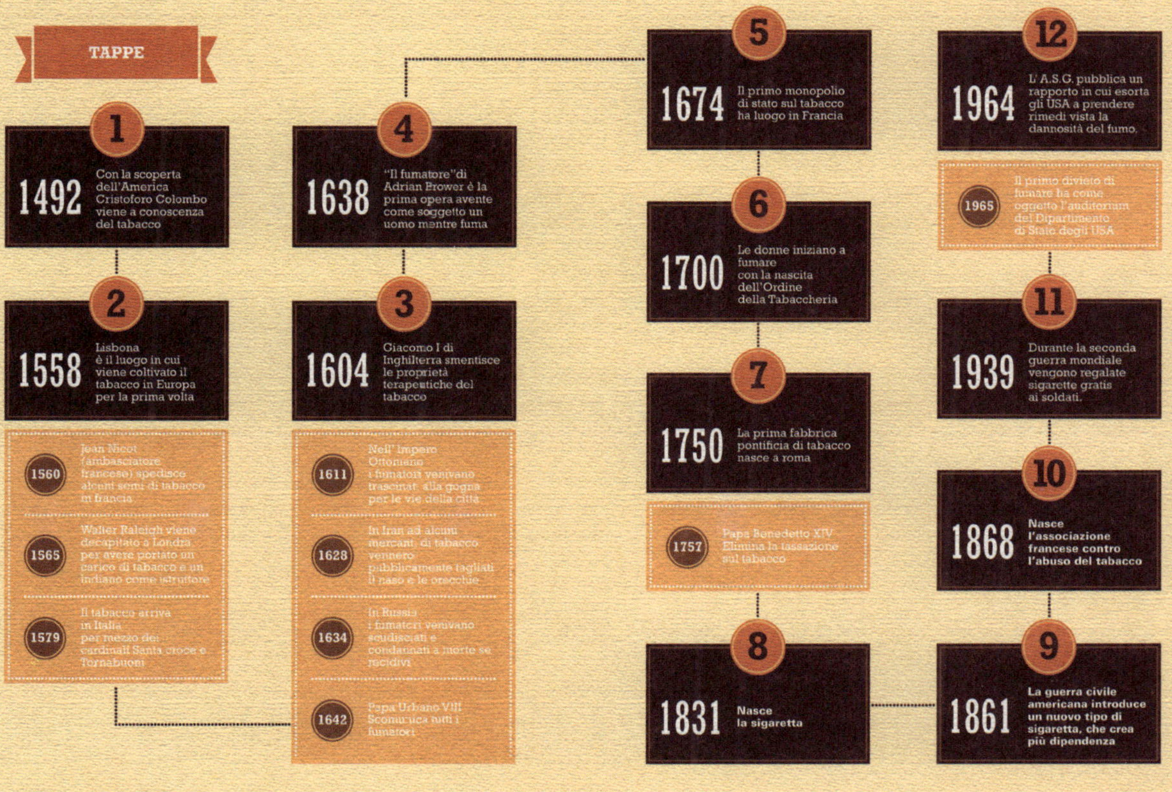

Dal Nido Alla Scuola Superiore 2013

- Completion Year: 2013
- Designer: Gianni Sinni, Silvia Basso, Lorella Chiavacci, Laurie Elie
- Client: Regione Toscana

- Work Introduction

From nursery to high school 2013 is the first attempt by the Region of Tuscany to make available to the general public, through infographics, the unique database of the most up to date information on the status of the school and education in Tuscany. The vivid and interesting infographic takes the colour of gentle grey as its background, which makes the overall design more harmonious.

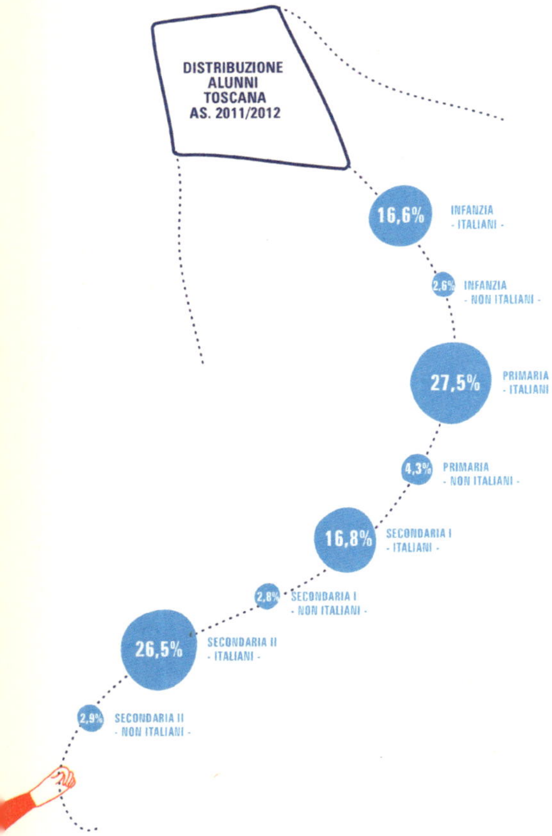

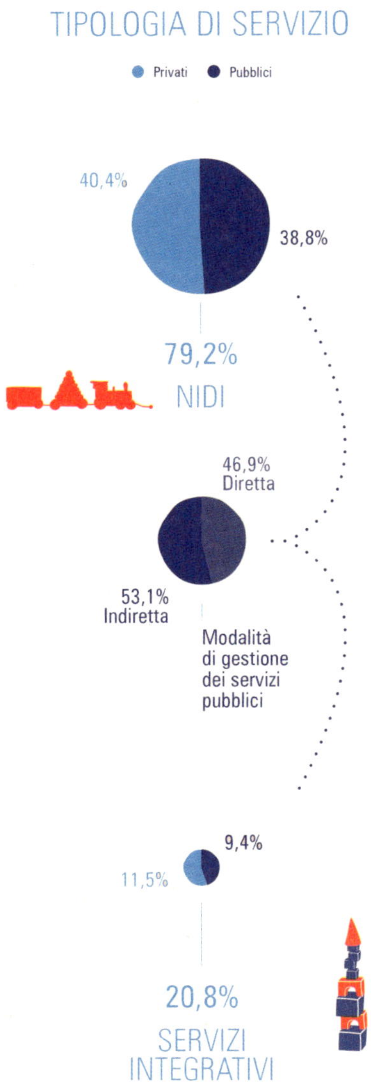

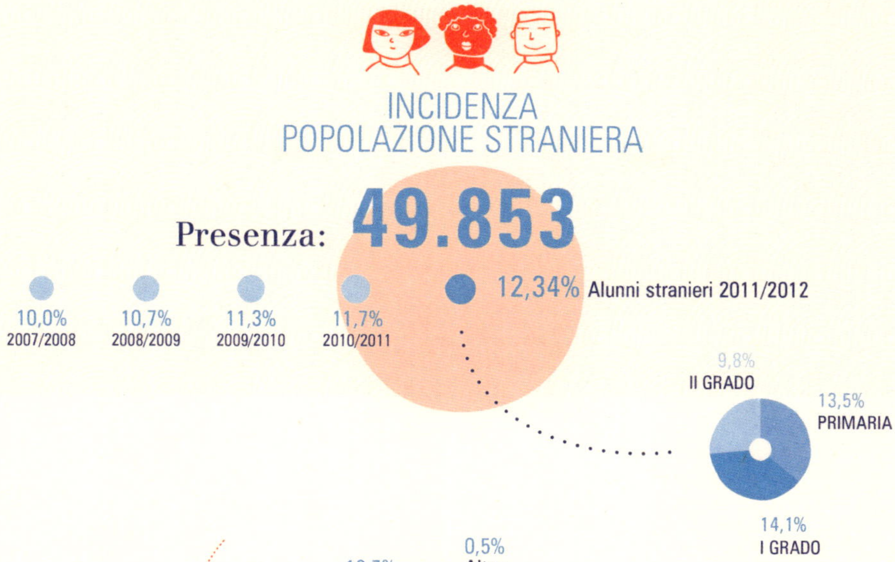
INCIDENZA
POPOLAZIONE STRANIERA
Presenza: 49.853
10,0%
2007/2008
10,7%
2008/2009
11,3%
2009/2010
11,7%
2010/2011
12,34% Alunni stranieri 2011/2012
9,8%
II GRADO
13,5%
PRIMARIA
14,1%
I GRADO

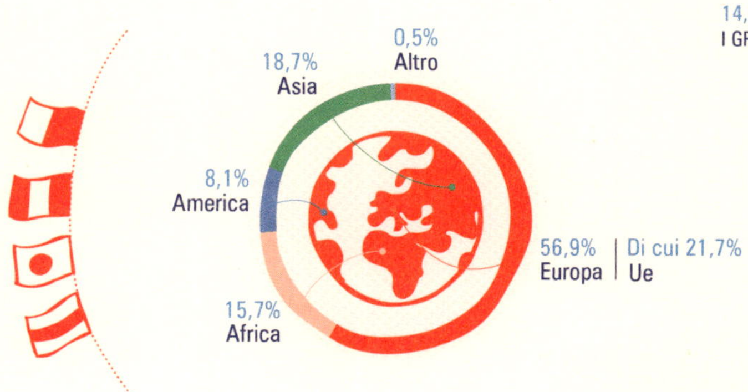
0,5%
Altro
18,7%
Asia
8,1%
America
56,9%
Europa
Di cui 21,7%
Ue
15,7%
Africa

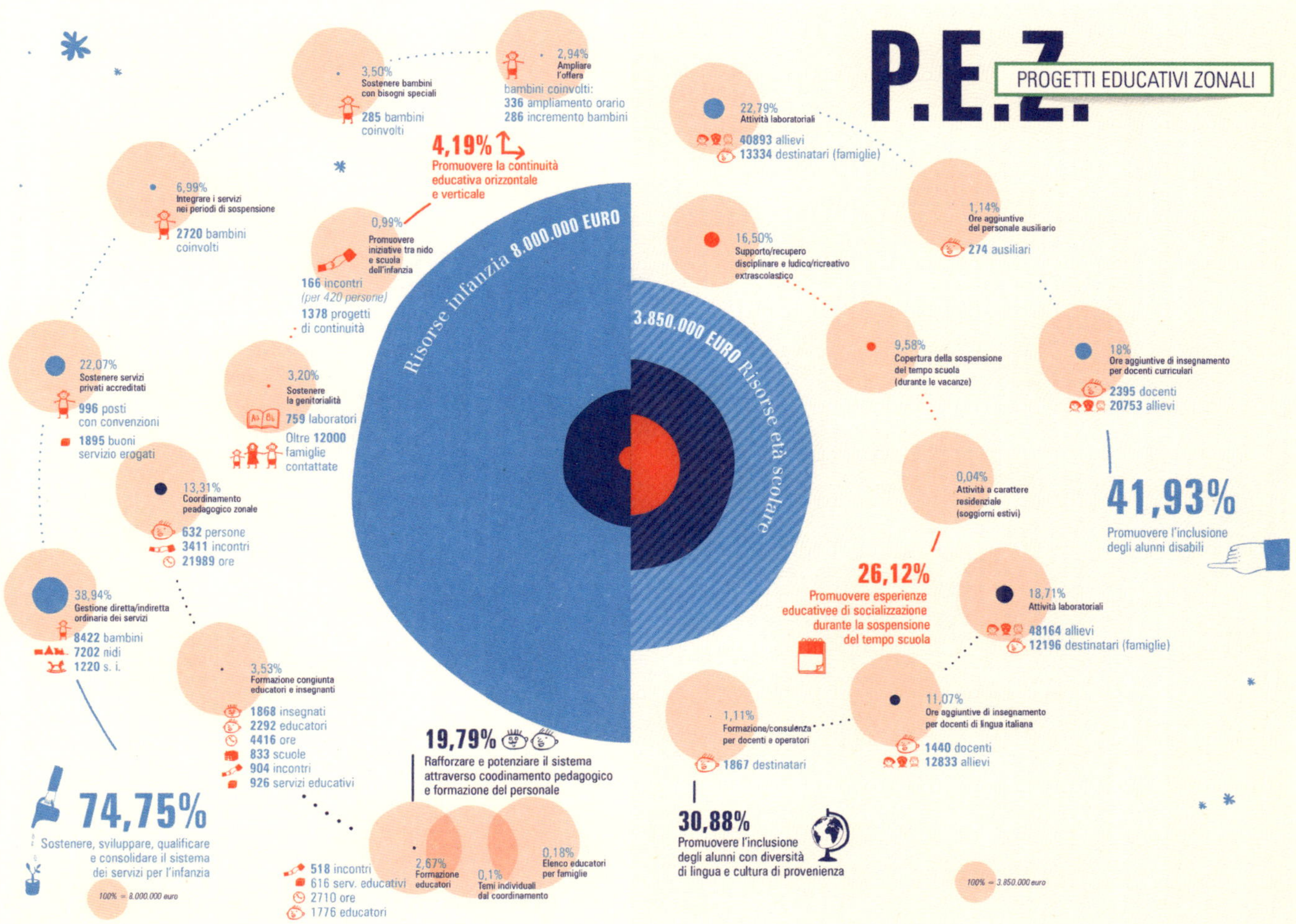
P.E.Z.
PROGETTI EDUCATIVI ZONALI
3,50%
Sostenere bambini con bisogni speciali
285 bambini coinvolti
2,94%
Ampliare l'offera
bambini coinvolti:
336 ampliamento orario
286 incremento bambini
4,19%
Promuovere la continuità educativa orizzontale e verticale
6,99%
Integrare i servizi nei periodi di sospensione
2720 bambini coinvolti
0,99%
Promuovere iniziative tra nido e scuola dell'infanzia
166 incontri
(per 420 persone)
1378 progetti di continuità
Risorse infanzia 8.000.000 EURO
3.850.000 EURO Risorse età scolare
22,07%
Sostenere servizi privati accreditati
996 posti con convenzioni
1895 buoni servizio erogati
3,20%
Sostenere la genitorialità
759 laboratori
Oltre 12000 famiglie contattate
13,31%
Coordinamento peadagogico zonale
632 persone
3411 incontri
21989 ore
38,94%
Gestione diretta/indiretta ordinaria dei servizi
8422 bambini
7202 nidi
1220 s. i.
3,53%
Formazione congiunta educatori e insegnanti
1868 insegnati
2292 educatori
4416 ore
833 scuole
904 incontri
926 servizi educativi
74,75%
Sostenere, sviluppare, qualificare e consolidare il sistema dei servizi per l'infanzia
100% = 8.000.000 euro
19,79%
Rafforzare e potenziare il sistema attraverso coodinamento pedagogico e formazione del personale
518 incontri
616 serv. educativi
2710 ore
1776 educatori
2,67%
Formazione educatori
0,1%
Temi individuali dal coordinamento
0,18%
Elenco educatori per famiglie
22,79%
Attività laboratoriali
40893 allievi
13334 destinatari (famiglie)
1,14%
Ore aggiuntive del personale ausiliario
274 ausiliari
16,50%
Supporto/recupero disciplinare e ludico/ricreativo extrascolastico
9,58%
Copertura della sospensione del tempo scuola (durante le vacanze)
18%
Ore aggiuntive di insegnamento per docenti curriculari
2395 docenti
20753 allievi
0,04%
Attività a carattere residenziale (soggiorni estivi)
41,93%
Promuovere l'inclusione degli alunni disabili
26,12%
Promuovere esperienze educativee di socializzazione durante la sospensione del tempo scuola
18,71%
Attività laboratoriali
48164 allievi
12196 destinatari (famiglie)
1,11%
Formazione/consulenza per docenti e operatori
1867 destinatari
11,07%
Ore aggiuntive di insegnamento per docenti di lingua italiana
1440 docenti
12833 allievi
30,88%
Promuovere l'inclusione degli alunni con diversità di lingua e cultura di provenienza
100% = 3.850.000 euro

ALUNNI CON DISABILITÀ IN TOSCANA COMPOSIZIONE %

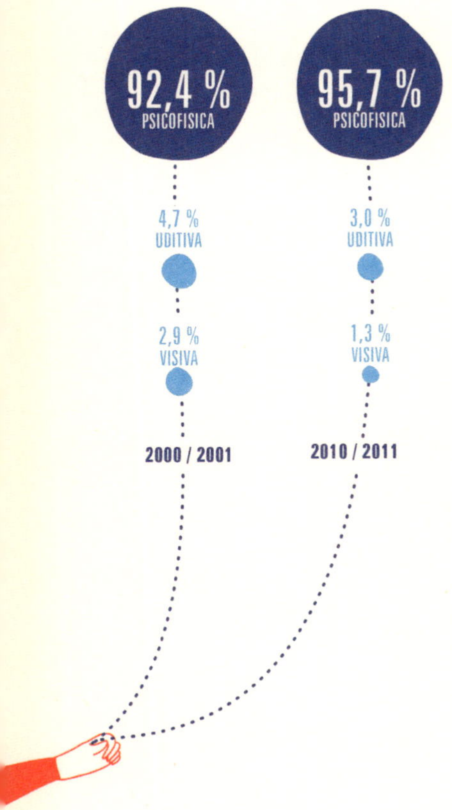

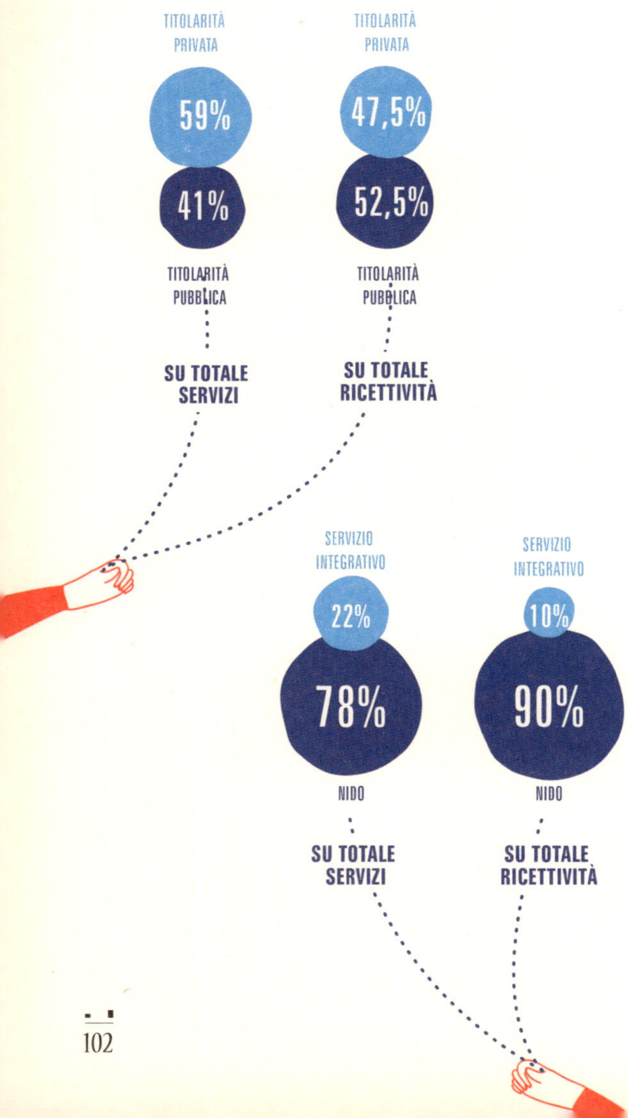

14_Giovani che abbandonano prematuramente gli studi

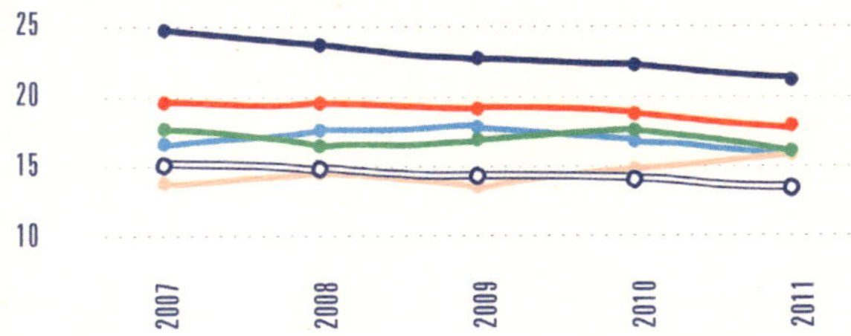

Nord | Centro | Italia
Mezzogiorno | Toscana | EU27

15_Giovani che abbandonano prematuramente gli studi

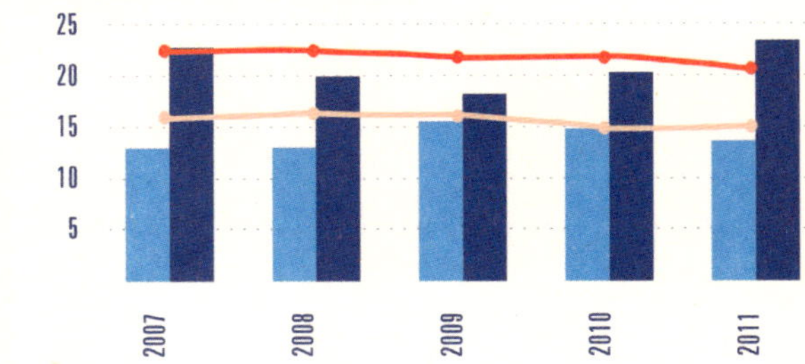

Toscana maschi | Italia maschi
Toscana femmine | Italia femmine

17_Giovani che abbandonano prematuramente gli studi

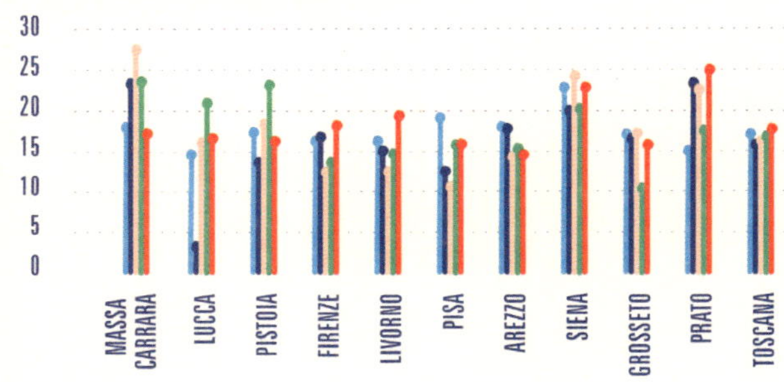

2007 | 2010
2008 | 2011
2009

39. Lista d'attesa per provincia

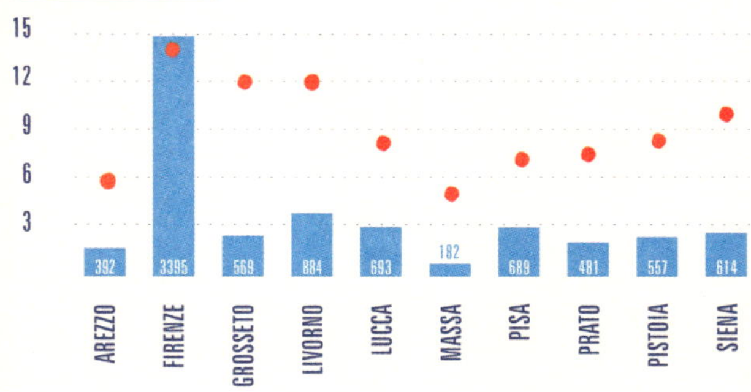

Liste d'attesa (valori assoluti) | Liste d'attesa su bambini 3-36 mesi (%)

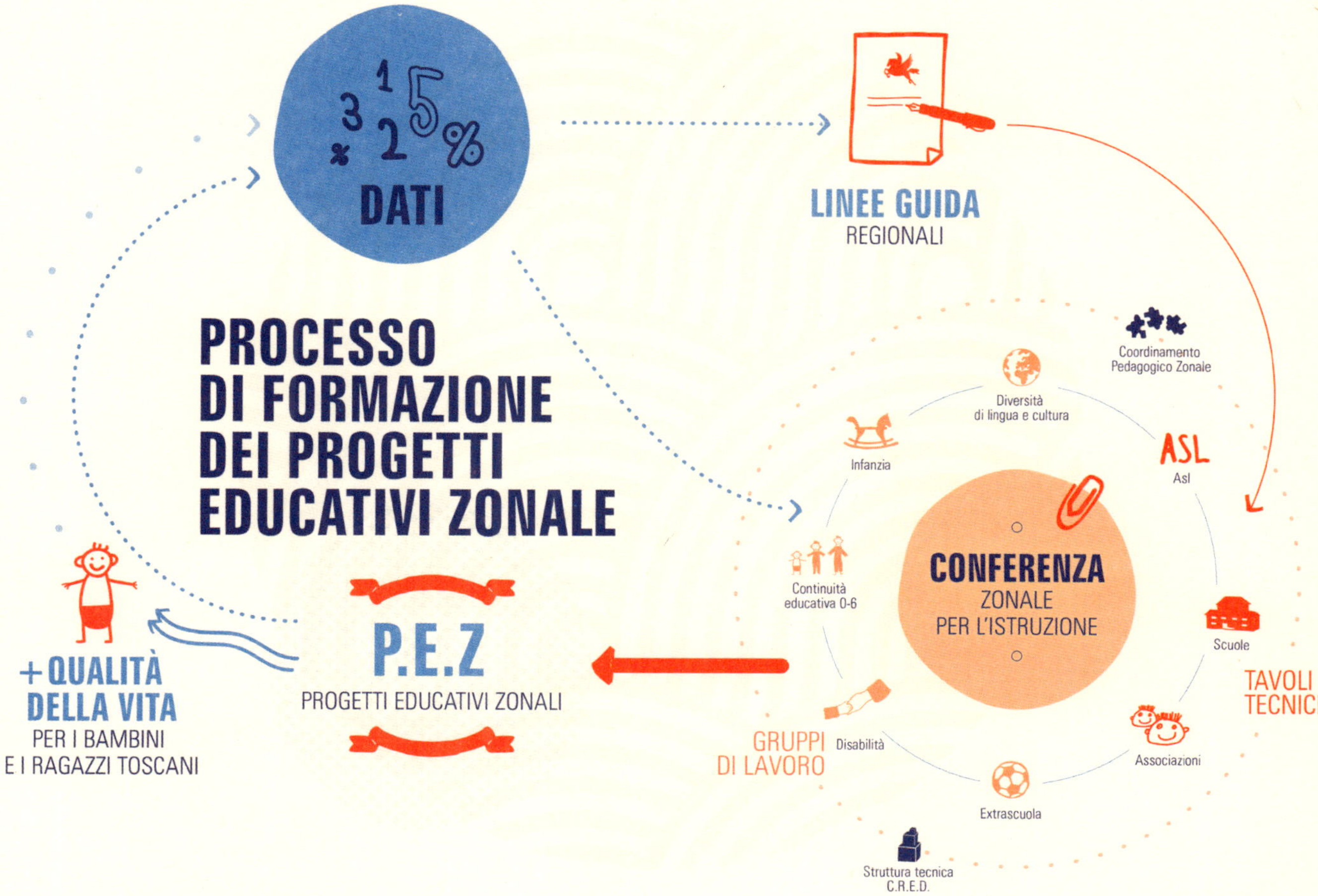

16_Composizione percentuale della ricettività

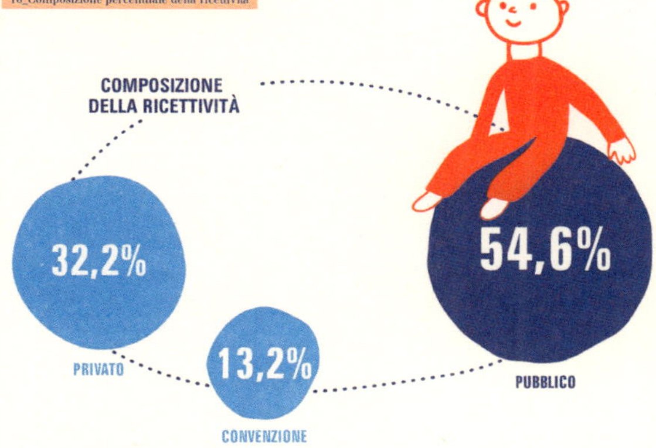

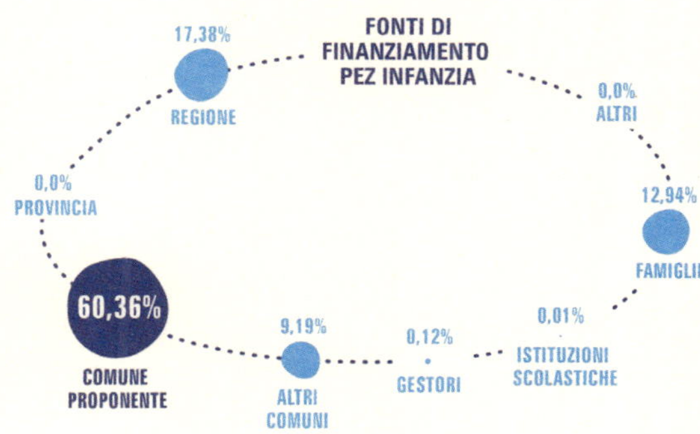

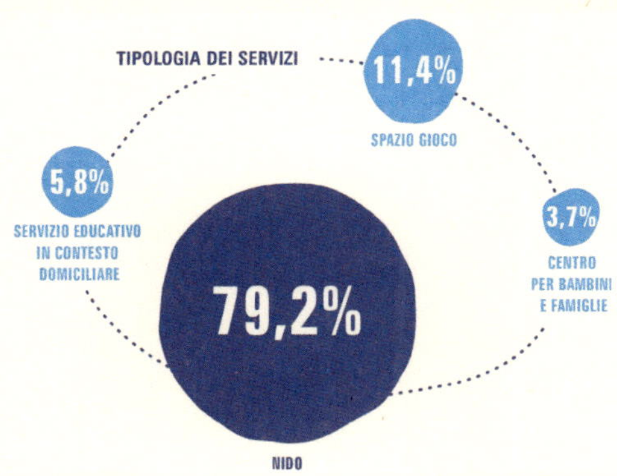

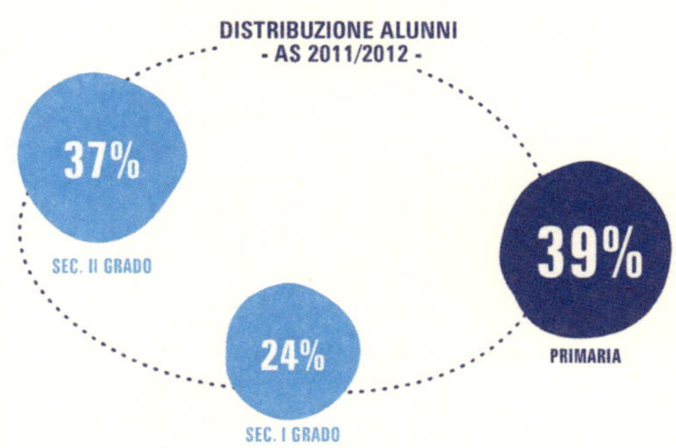

The Kent State Forum on the City: Madrid

- Completion Year: 2013
- Designer: Gianni Sinni, Silvia Basso
- Client: Kent State University

- Work Introduction

The Kent State Forum on the City: Madrid is a multi-platform project: Book + Web + App, all of them complementary and inter-connected, reflecting new trends in publishing practice through the acts of research, archive and exchange.

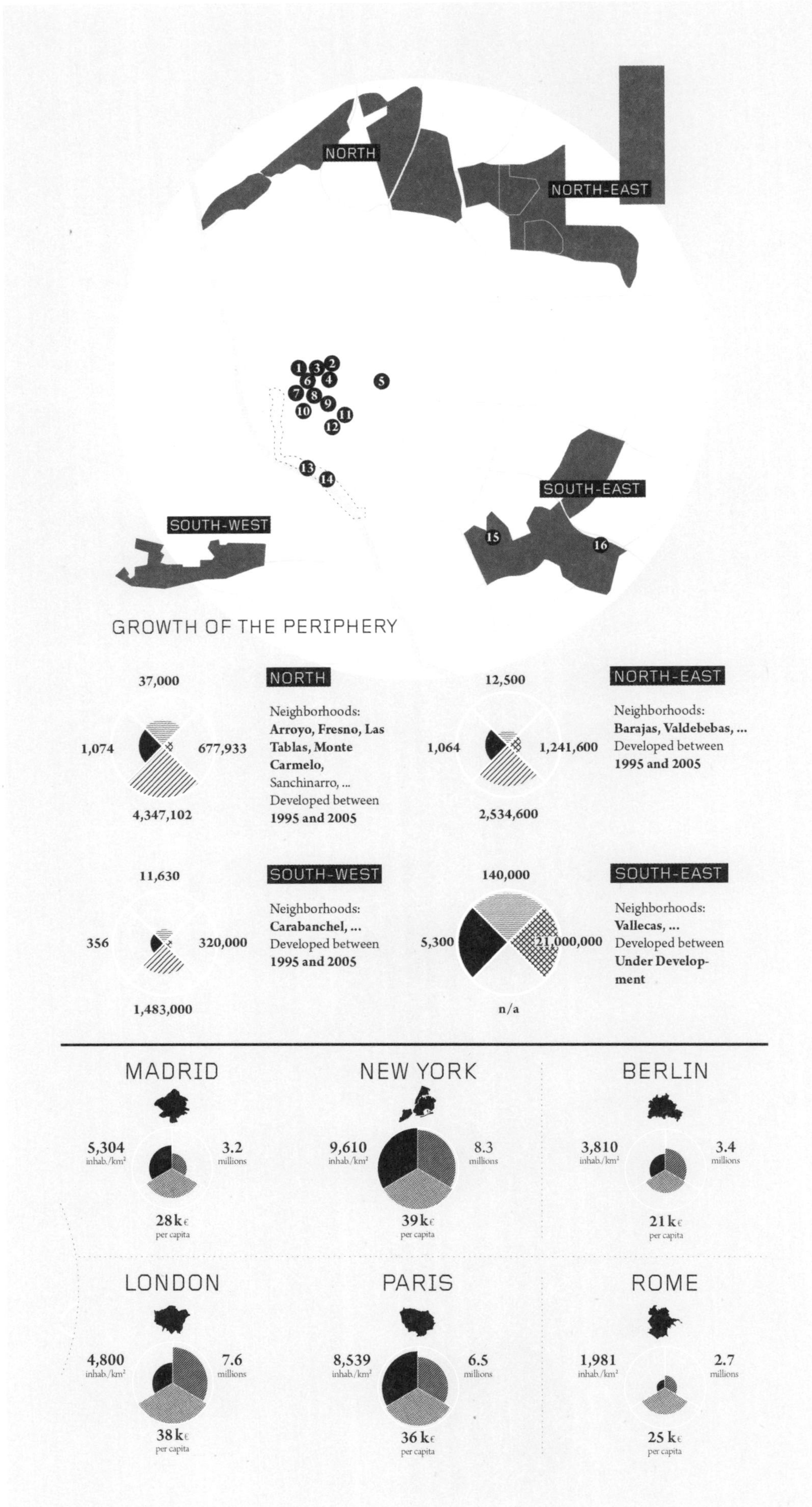

ITINERARY

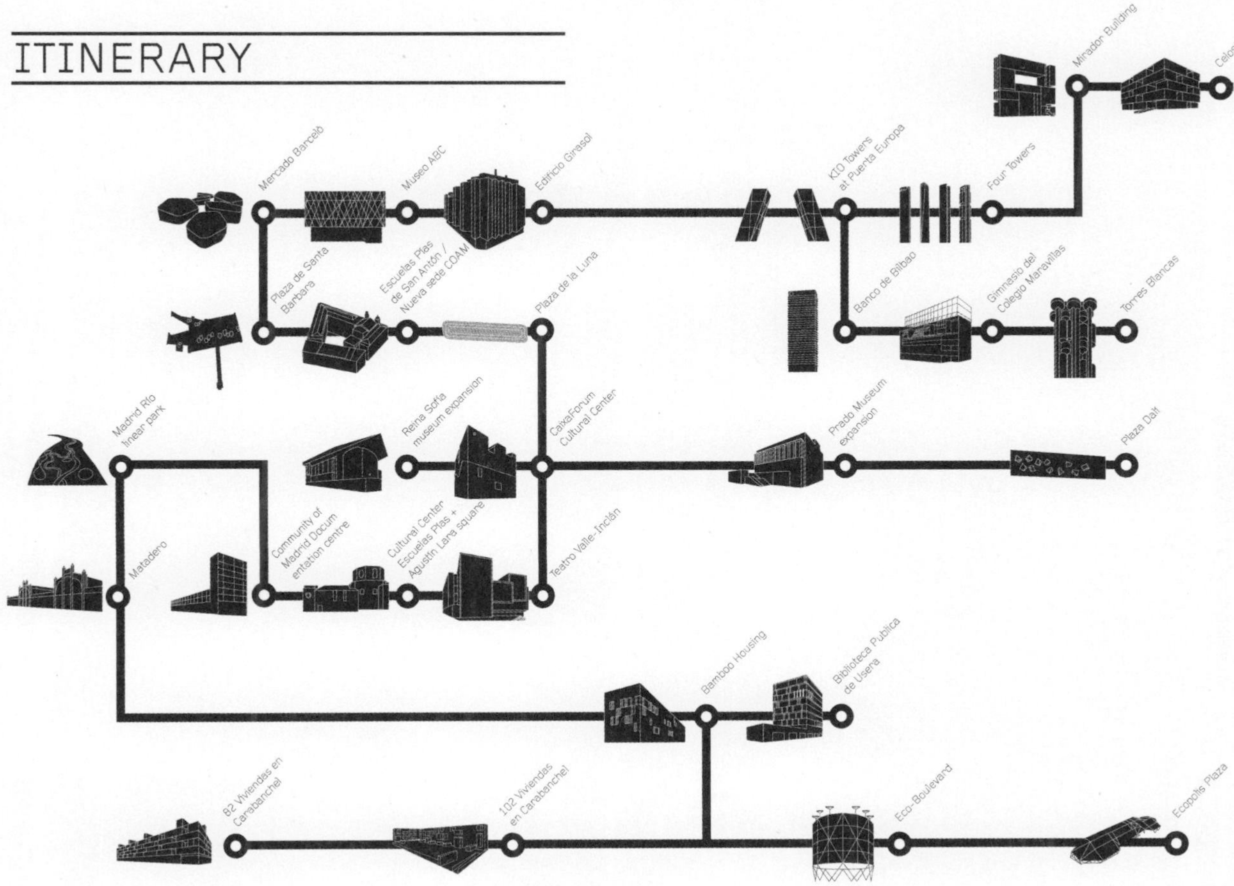

MAP #5 PARTECIPATORY MOOD

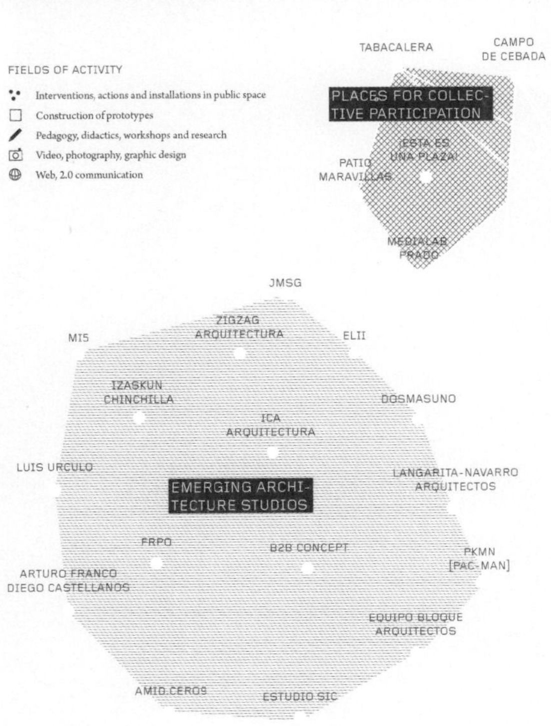

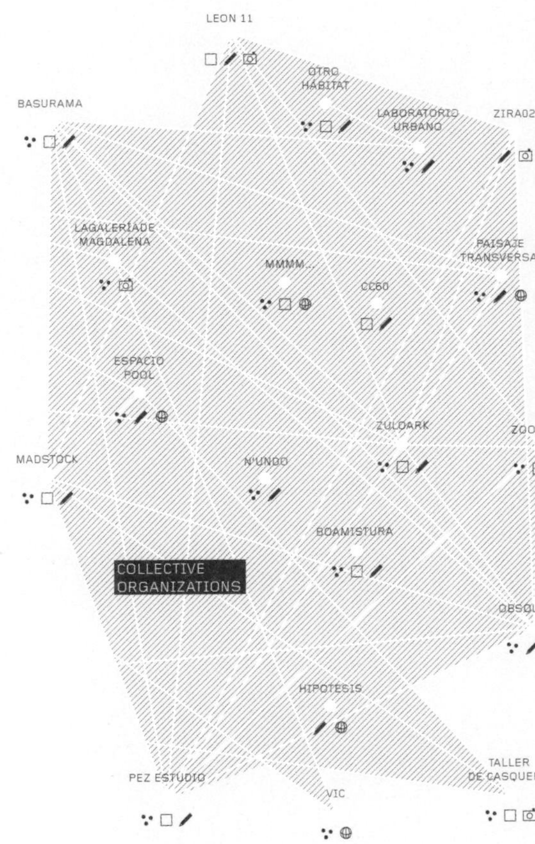

ARCHITECTURE SCHOOLS

PRIVATE
- Escuela de Arquitectura, Universidad Alfonso X El Sabio
- Escuela Politécnica Sup. y de Arquitectura, Universidad Nebrija
- Escuela de Arquitectura, Universidad Camilo José Cela
- Escuela de Arquitectura, Universidad Europea (UEM)
- Escuela de Arquitectura, Universidad Francisco de Vitoria
- Escuela de Arquitectura, Universidad San Pablo-CEU
- Grado en Arquitectura, Universidad Rey Juan Carlos

PUBLIC
- Escuela Técnica Sup. de Arquitectura ETSAM, (UPM)
- Escuela Técnica Sup. de Arquitectura y Geodesia, Un. de Alcalá

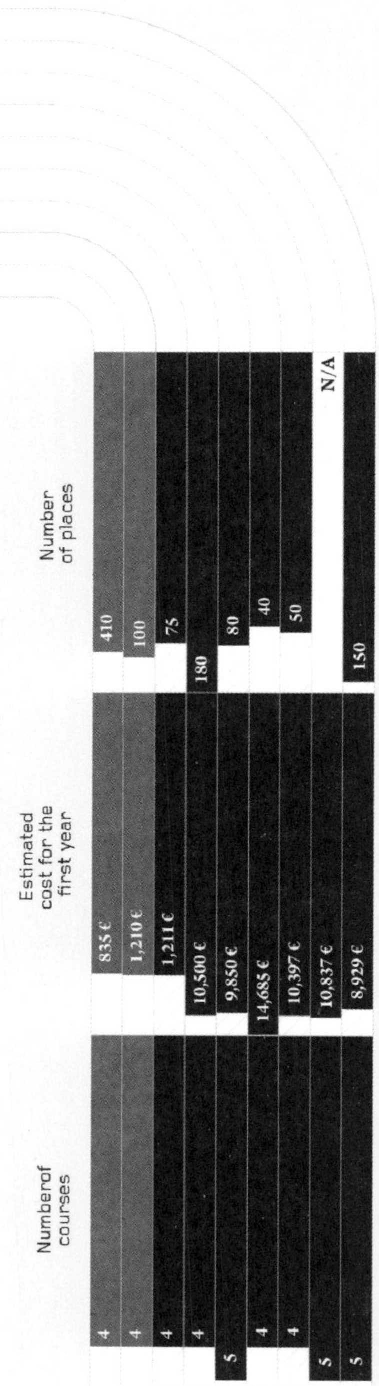

MUSEUMS

MUSEO NACIONAL CENTRO DE ARTE REINA SOFIA

Floor area
84,048
square meters

Collection
20,000
artworks

Yearly visitors
2,313,532
visitors

Displayed works
1,000
artworks

MUSEO THYSSEN-BORNEMISZA

Floor area
8,400
square meters

Collection
1,600
paintings

Yearly visitors
1,070,000
visitors

Displayed works
800
artworks

UNIVERSITIES

	Foundation year		Professors	Administrators and staff employees	Students	Students / professors ratio	Annual budget	Graduate programs
Universidad Alfonso X El Sabio	1993	PRIVATE	1,142	260	14,000	9.92	N/A	39
Universidad Antonio Nebrija	1995	PRIVATE	180	125	3,473	19.29	N/A	52
Universidad Camilo José Cela	1999	PRIVATE	302	62	4,906	16.25	12,000,000 €	41
Universidad Europea de Madrid	1995	PRIVATE	875	350	14,000	16.00	N/A	113
Universidad Francisco de Vitoria	2001	PRIVATE	285	240	3,215	11.28	32,000,000 €	22
Universidad Pontificia Comillas	1904	PRIVATE	993	342	10,011	10.08	64,460,662 €	17
Universidad San Pablo CEU	1994	PRIVATE	922	276	11,436	12.40	N/A	29
Universidad a distancia de Madrid	2008	PRIVATE	71	28	1,419	19.99	N/A	9
UAH [1]	1293	PUBLIC	1,762	787	28,909	16.41	164,486,989 €	46
UAM [2]	1968	PUBLIC	2,872	976	30,450	10.60	356,556,097 €	48
UC3M [3]	1989	PUBLIC	1,881	689	16,975	9.02	N/A	36
UCM [4]	1499	PUBLIC	6,206	4,625	85,000	13.70	595,577,038 €	68
UPM [5]	1971	PUBLIC	3,414	2,370	40,843	11.96	348,320,354 €	42
URJC [6]	1996	PUBLIC	1,667	532	30,524	18.31	N/A	75
UNED [7]	1973	PUBLIC	8,236	1,469	217,266	26.38	227,840,000 €	26

Foundation year axis: '2010, 2000, '1990, '1980, '1970, '1960, '1950, '1940, '1930, '1920, '1910, 1900, 1800, 1700, 1600, 1500, 1400, 1300, 1200

[1] UAH - Universidad de Alcalá
[2] UAM - Universidad Autónoma de Madrid
[3] UC3M - Universidad Carlos III de Madrid
[4] UCM - Universidad Complutense
[5] UPM - Universidad Politécnica de Madrid
[6] URJC - Universidad Rey Juan Carlos
[7] UNED - Universidad Nacional de Educación a Distancia

MUSEO NACIONAL DEL PRADO

Floor area
41,995
square meters

Collection
7,600
paintings

Yearly visitors
2,900,000
visitors

Displayed works
1,300
artworks

Restart, Italia!

- Completion Year: 2012
- Design Agency: Lcd
- Designer: Gianni Sinni, Donatello D'Angelo, Laurie Elie
- Client: Ministero dello Sviluppo Economico

• Work Introduction

Restart, Italia! is the book edited by the task force on start-up organized by the Italian Ministry of Economic Development to present a proposal of law to help start-up companies.

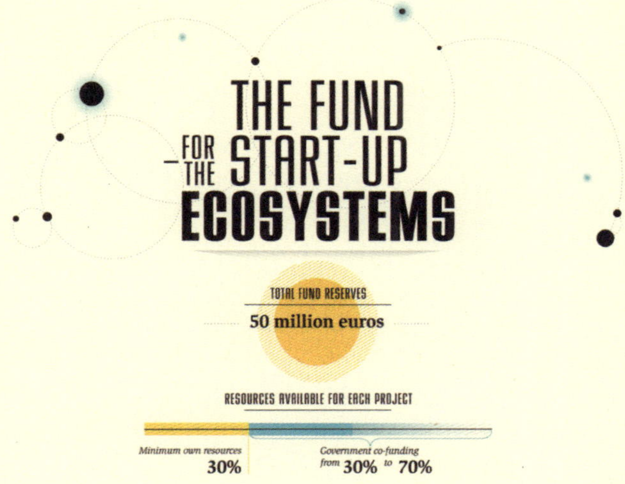

The reserve for start-ups with a social focus

The Fund of Funds will allocate up to 20% of its capital in support of funds specialised in start-ups with a social focus.

The fund for 'seed' investments

A 'Seed' fund funded by the Deposits and Loans fund and private fundraising (also by the management).
It provides financial support up to 500,000 euros, only as co-investment according to a Convertible Loan standard formula.

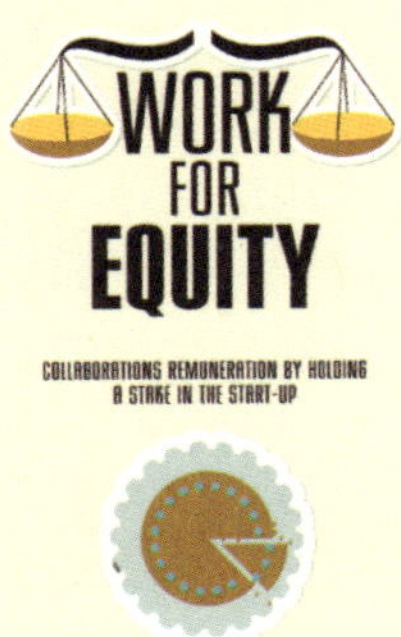

Work for equity

Remunerating an external collaboration by allowing the supplier to hold a stake in the start-up Sharing outlooks without worsening the financial position.

The fund of funds

An "anchor investor" that supports the fundraising process of private and institutional investors.
It supports the VC by investing in the fund and the informal investor by matching the single transactions

GARANTIRE IL CREDITO
DATO DALLE BANCHE ALLE STARTUP
Costituzione di una
SEZIONE SPECIALE
30 milioni di euro
0€
80%
INDICATORI
PER VALUTARE
IL TRACK RECORD
21
Indicatori per valutare
il track record
(e la performance)
di un incubatore
o acceleratore

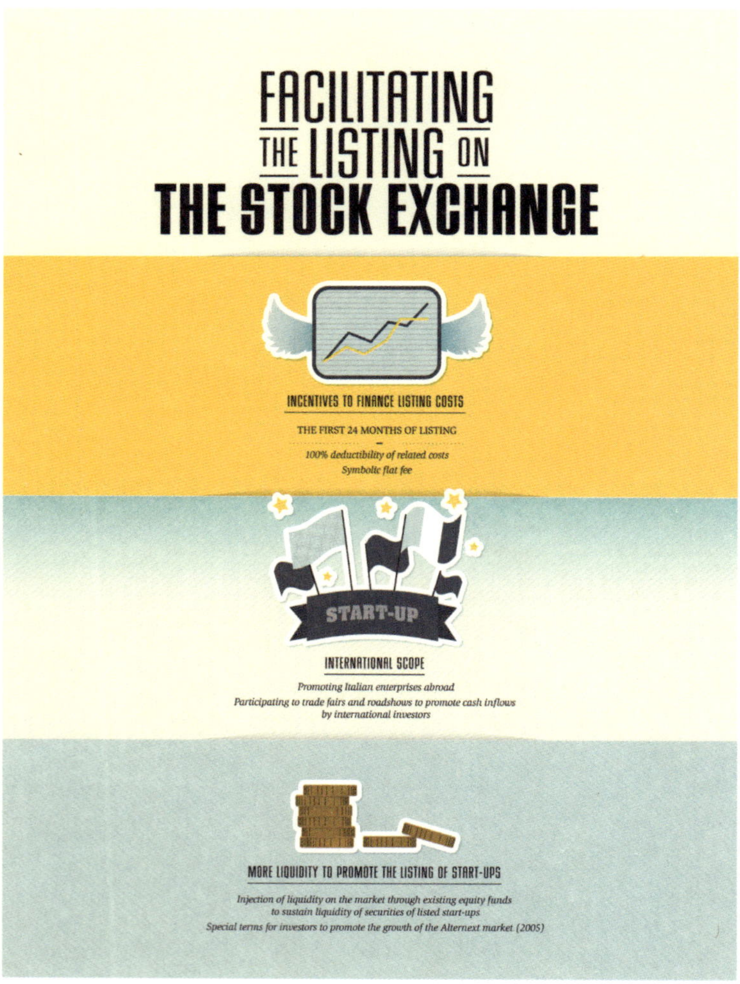
FACILITATING
THE LISTING ON
THE STOCK EXCHANGE
INCENTIVES TO FINANCE LISTING COSTS
THE FIRST 24 MONTHS OF LISTING
100% deductibility of related costs
Symbolic flat fee
START-UP
INTERNATIONAL SCOPE
Promoting Italian enterprises abroad
Participating to trade fairs and roadshows to promote cash inflows by international investors
MORE LIQUIDITY TO PROMOTE THE LISTING OF START-UPS
Injection of liquidity on the market through existing equity funds to sustain liquidity of securities of listed start-ups
Special terms for investors to promote the growth of the Alternext market (2005)

START-UPS
WITH A SOCIAL
FOCUS
Additional criteria
for social identification
THE SECTORS
SCIENTIFIC RESEARCH
TOOLS FOR ENTERPRISES WITH A SOCIAL FOCUS
EDUCATION, TEACHING AND TRAINING
INDUCTION
EXTRA-CURRICULAR TRAINING
CULTURAL SERVICES
SUPPORT TO YOUTH AND WOMEN EMPLOYMENT
SOCIAL TOURISM
UNIVERSITY EDUCATION
HEALTHCARE AND WELFARE
CULTURAL HERITAGE
ENVIRONMENT AND ECOSYSTEM PROTECTION

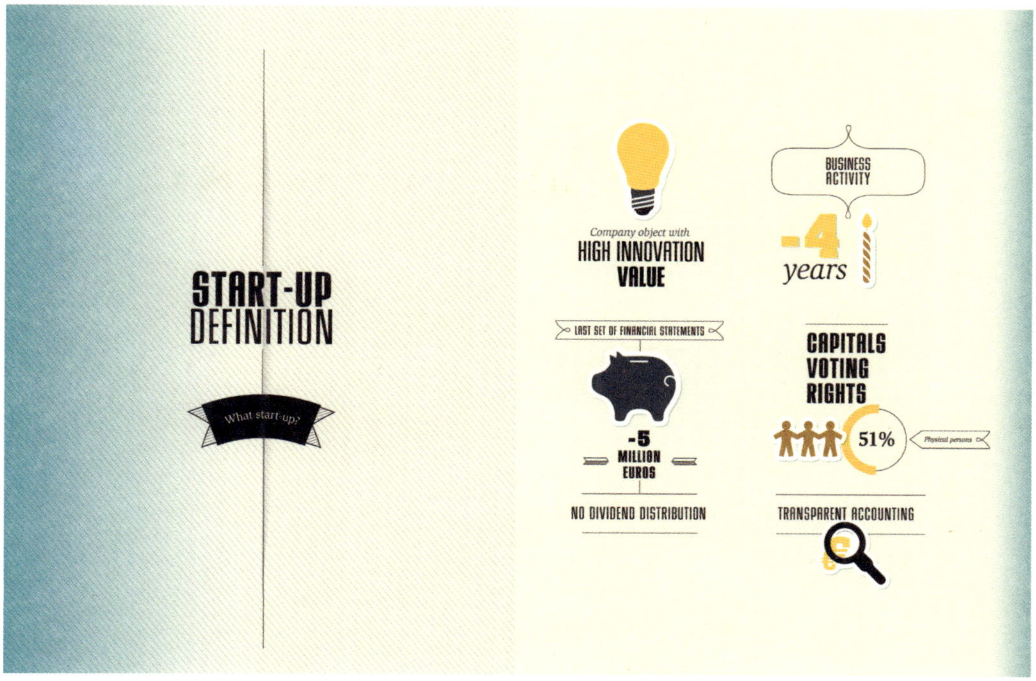
START-UP
DEFINITION
What start-up?
Company object with
HIGH INNOVATION
VALUE
BUSINESS
ACTIVITY
-4
years
LAST SET OF FINANCIAL STATEMENTS
-5
MILLION
EUROS
NO DIVIDEND DISTRIBUTION
CAPITALS
VOTING
RIGHTS
51%
Physical persons
TRANSPARENT ACCOUNTING

ONLINE
SET-UP
TOTAL COST
50 EURO
FAST
SET-UP
THE
i-LTD
AND
ZERO
STATUTE
NO AGE
CONSTRAINTS
NO ADDITIONAL
TAXES
REGISTRATION WITH THE COMPANIES' REGISTER
No stamp duty and registration fees
SIMPLIFIED BUREAUCRATIC PROCEDURE
Self-certification with Chamber of Commerce

9

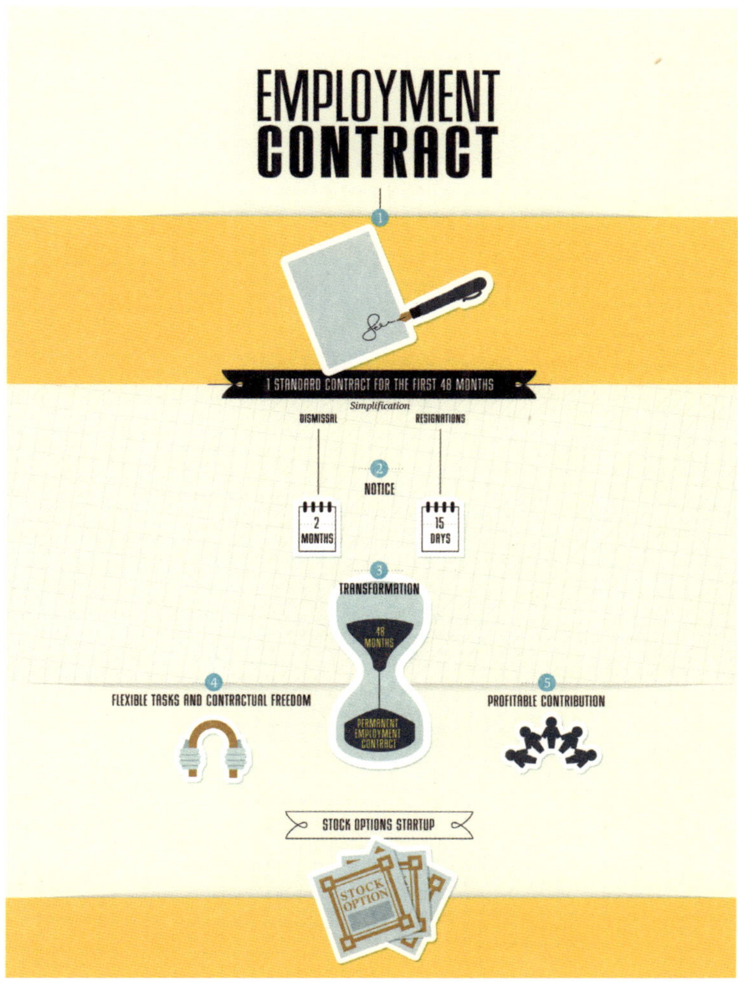
EMPLOYMENT
CONTRACT
1
1 STANDARD CONTRACT FOR THE FIRST 48 MONTHS
Simplification
DISMISSAL
RESIGNATIONS
2
NOTICE
2
MONTHS
15
DAYS
3
TRANSFORMATION
48
MONTHS
PERMANENT
EMPLOYMENT
CONTRACT
4
FLEXIBLE TASKS AND CONTRACTUAL FREEDOM
5
PROFITABLE CONTRIBUTION
STOCK OPTIONS STARTUP
STOCK
OPTION

Visualizing Controversies in Wikipedia

- Completion Year: 2014
- Designer: Martina Elisa Cecchi
- Client: Master's Degree Thesis, Communication Design, School of Design, Politecnico di Milano

- Work Introduction

In this thesis project is to analyze the article "Family planning" of the English version of Wikipedia as a case study for understanding the development of discussion on the web about controversial topic as this one. The designer produces the simple but not boring infographic by making advantage of attractive pie chart and lines in fresh colors, showing a simple designing style.

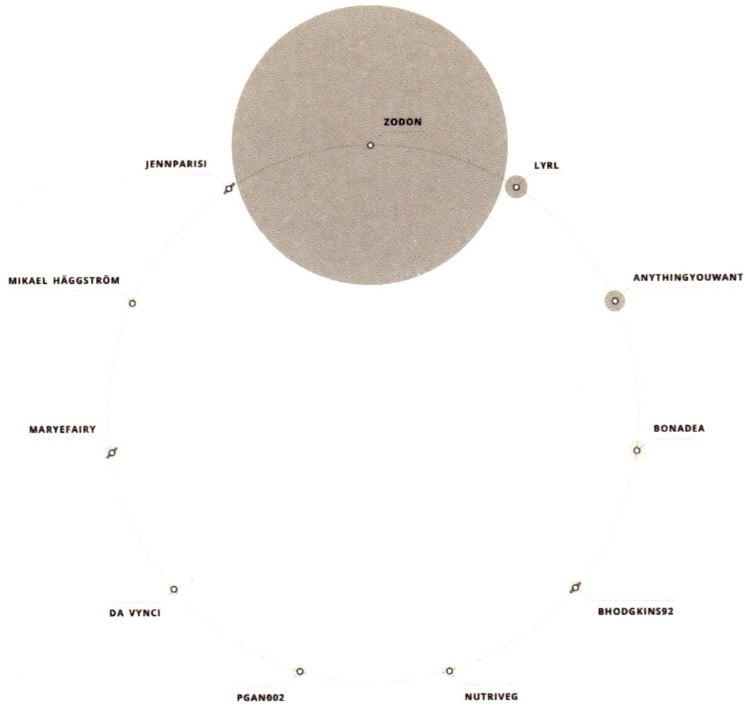

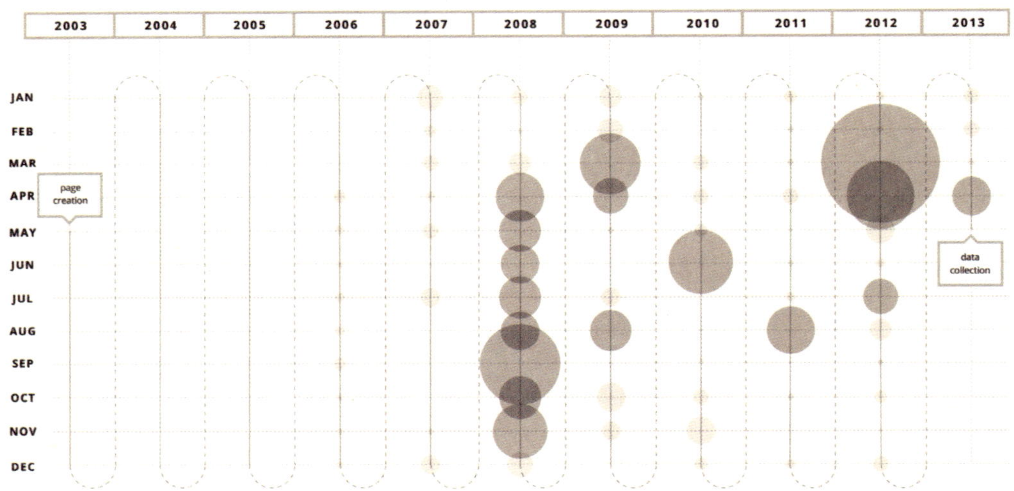

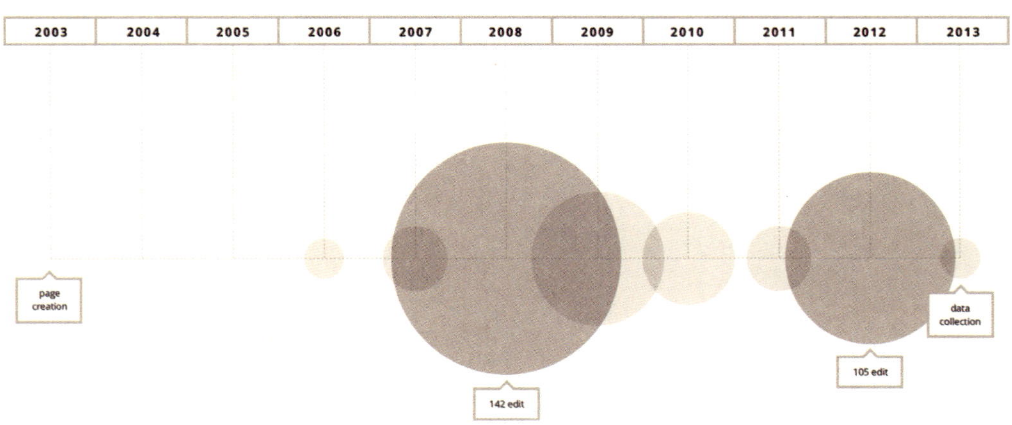

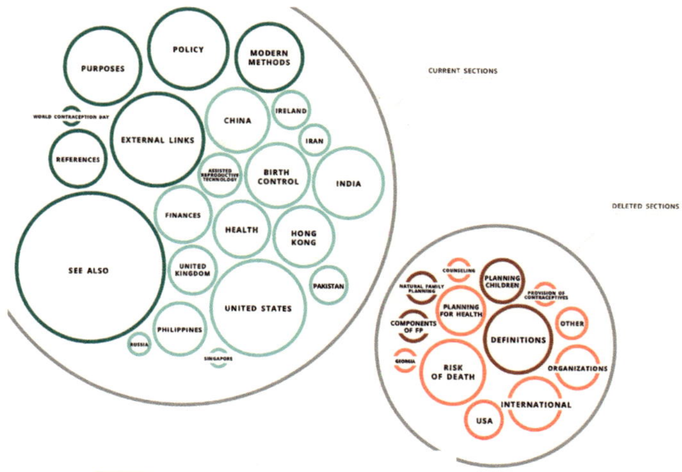

PURPOSES
POLICY
MODERN METHODS
CURRENT SECTIONS
WORLD CONTRACEPTION DAY
EXTERNAL LINKS
CHINA
IRELAND
IRAN
REFERENCES
ASSISTED REPRODUCTIVE TECHNOLOGY
BIRTH CONTROL
INDIA
FINANCES
HEALTH
HONG KONG
SEE ALSO
UNITED KINGDOM
UNITED STATES
PAKISTAN
PHILIPPINES
RUSSIA
SINGAPORE
DELETED SECTIONS
COUNSELING
NATURAL FAMILY PLANNING
PLANNING CHILDREN
PROVISION OF CONTRACEPTIVES
PLANNING FOR HEALTH
COMPONENTS OF FP
OTHER
DEFINITIONS
GEORGIA
RISK OF DEATH
ORGANIZATIONS
INTERNATIONAL
USA

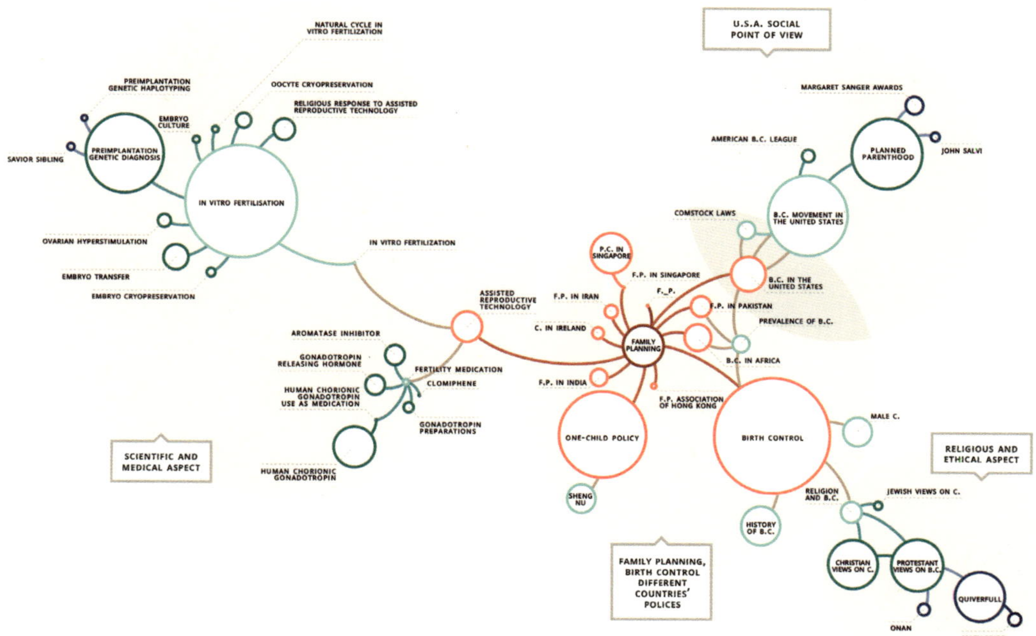

U.S.A. SOCIAL POINT OF VIEW
NATURAL CYCLE IN VITRO FERTILIZATION
PREIMPLANTATION GENETIC HAPLOTYPING
OOCYTE CRYOPRESERVATION
RELIGIOUS RESPONSE TO ASSISTED REPRODUCTIVE TECHNOLOGY
EMBRYO CULTURE
SAVIOR SIBLING
PREIMPLANTATION GENETIC DIAGNOSIS
IN VITRO FERTILISATION
OVARIAN HYPERSTIMULATION
EMBRYO TRANSFER
EMBRYO CRYOPRESERVATION
IN VITRO FERTILIZATION
MARGARET SANGER AWARDS
AMERICAN B.C. LEAGUE
PLANNED PARENTHOOD
JOHN SALVI
COMSTOCK LAWS
B.C. MOVEMENT IN THE UNITED STATES
P.C. IN SINGAPORE
F.P. IN SINGAPORE
F._P.
B.C. IN THE UNITED STATES
ASSISTED REPRODUCTIVE TECHNOLOGY
F.P. IN IRAN
F.P. IN PAKISTAN
PREVALENCE OF B.C.
C. IN IRELAND
FAMILY PLANNING
AROMATASE INHIBITOR
GONADOTROPIN RELEASING HORMONE
FERTILITY MEDICATION
CLOMIPHENE
B.C. IN AFRICA
HUMAN CHORIONIC GONADOTROPIN USE AS MEDICATION
F.P. IN INDIA
F.P. ASSOCIATION OF HONG KONG
GONADOTROPIN PREPARATIONS
MALE C.
ONE-CHILD POLICY
BIRTH CONTROL
RELIGIOUS AND ETHICAL ASPECT
SCIENTIFIC AND MEDICAL ASPECT
HUMAN CHORIONIC GONADOTROPIN
SHENG NU
RELIGION AND B.C.
JEWISH VIEWS ON C.
HISTORY OF B.C.
FAMILY PLANNING, BIRTH CONTROL DIFFERENT COUNTRIES' POLICES
CHRISTIAN VIEWS ON C.
PROTESTANT VIEWS ON B.C.
QUIVERFULL
ONAN
MARY PRIDE

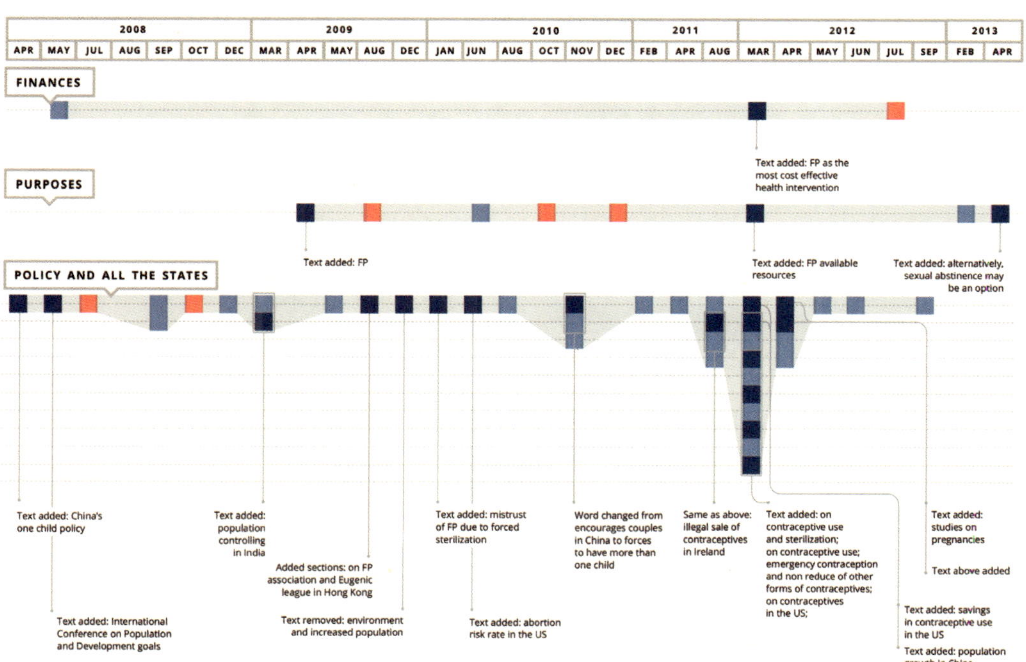

2008
2009
2010
2011
2012
2013
APR MAY JUL AUG SEP OCT DEC MAR APR MAY AUG DEC JAN JUN AUG OCT NOV DEC FEB APR AUG MAR APR MAY JUN JUL SEP FEB APR
FINANCES
Text added: FP as the most cost effective health intervention
PURPOSES
Text added: FP
Text added: FP available resources
Text added: alternatively, sexual abstinence may be an option
POLICY AND ALL THE STATES
Text added: China's one child policy
Text added: population controlling in India
Text added: mistrust of FP due to forced sterilization
Word changed from encourages couples in China to forces to have more than one child
Same as above: illegal sale of contraceptives in Ireland
Text added: on contraceptive use and sterilization; on contraceptive use; emergency contraception and non reduce of other forms of contraceptives; on contraceptives in the US;
Text added: studies on pregnancies
Text above added
Added sections: on FP association and Eugenic league in Hong Kong
Text added: International Conference on Population and Development goals
Text removed: environment and increased population
Text added: abortion risk rate in the US
Text added: savings in contraceptive use in the US
Text added: population growth in China

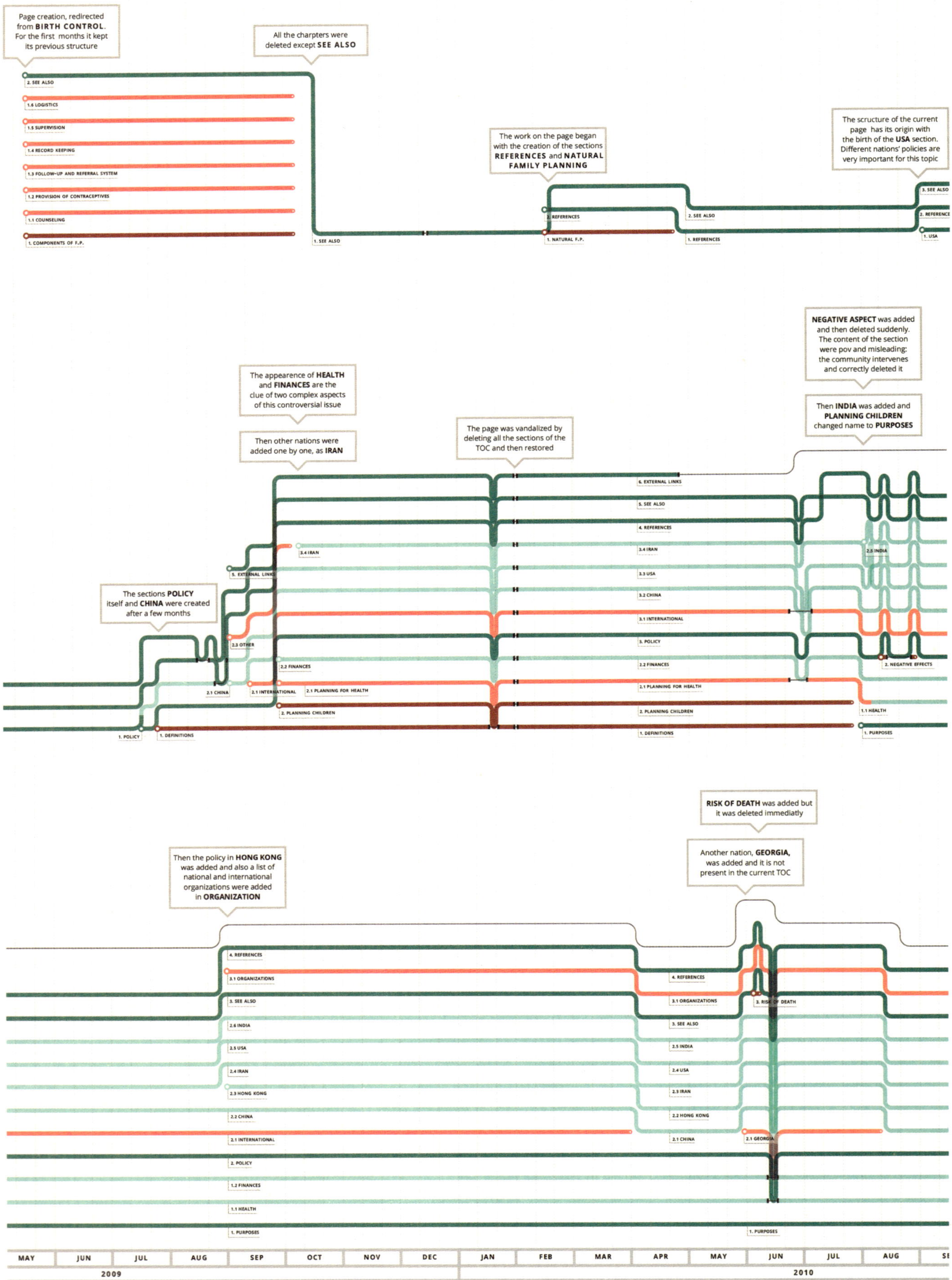

Page creation, redirected from BIRTH CONTROL. For the first months it kept its previous structure
All the charpters were deleted except SEE ALSO
2. SEE ALSO
1.6 LOGISTICS
1.5 SUPERVISION
1.4 RECORD KEEPING
1.3 FOLLOW-UP AND REFERRAL SYSTEM
1.2 PROVISION OF CONTRACEPTIVES
1.1 COUNSELING
1. COMPONENTS OF F.P.
1. SEE ALSO
The work on the page began with the creation of the sections REFERENCES and NATURAL FAMILY PLANNING
2. REFERENCES
1. NATURAL F.P.
2. SEE ALSO
1. REFERENCES
The scructure of the current page has its origin with the birth of the USA section. Different nations' policies are very important for this topic
3. SEE ALSO
2. REFERENCE
1. USA
NEGATIVE ASPECT was added and then deleted suddenly. The content of the section were pov and misleading: the community intervenes and correctly deleted it
Then INDIA was added and PLANNING CHILDREN changed name to PURPOSES
The appearence of HEALTH and FINANCES are the clue of two complex aspects of this controversial issue
Then other nations were added one by one, as IRAN
The page was vandalized by deleting all the sections of the TOC and then restored
The sections POLICY itself and CHINA were created after a few months
3.4 IRAN
5. EXTERNAL LINKS
2.3 OTHER
2.2 FINANCES
2.1 CHINA
2.1 INTERNATIONAL
2.1 PLANNING FOR HEALTH
2. PLANNING CHILDREN
1. POLICY
1. DEFINITIONS
6. EXTERNAL LINKS
5. SEE ALSO
4. REFERENCES
3.4 IRAN
3.3 USA
3.2 CHINA
3.1 INTERNATIONAL
3. POLICY
2.2 FINANCES
2.1 PLANNING FOR HEALTH
2. PLANNING CHILDREN
1. DEFINITIONS
2.5 INDIA
2. NEGATIVE EFFECTS
1.1 HEALTH
1. PURPOSES
RISK OF DEATH was added but it was deleted immediatly
Another nation, GEORGIA, was added and it is not present in the current TOC
Then the policy in HONG KONG was added and also a list of national and international organizations were added in ORGANIZATION
4. REFERENCES
3.1 ORGANIZATIONS
3. SEE ALSO
2.6 INDIA
2.5 USA
2.4 IRAN
2.3 HONG KONG
2.2 CHINA
2.1 INTERNATIONAL
2. POLICY
1.2 FINANCES
1.1 HEALTH
1. PURPOSES
4. REFERENCES
3.1 ORGANIZATIONS
3. SEE ALSO
2.5 INDIA
2.4 USA
2.3 IRAN
2.2 HONG KONG
2.1 CHINA
3. RISK OF DEATH
2.1 GEORGIA
1. PURPOSES
MAY
JUN
JUL
AUG
SEP
OCT
NOV
DEC
JAN
FEB
MAR
APR
MAY
JUN
JUL
AUG
2009
2010

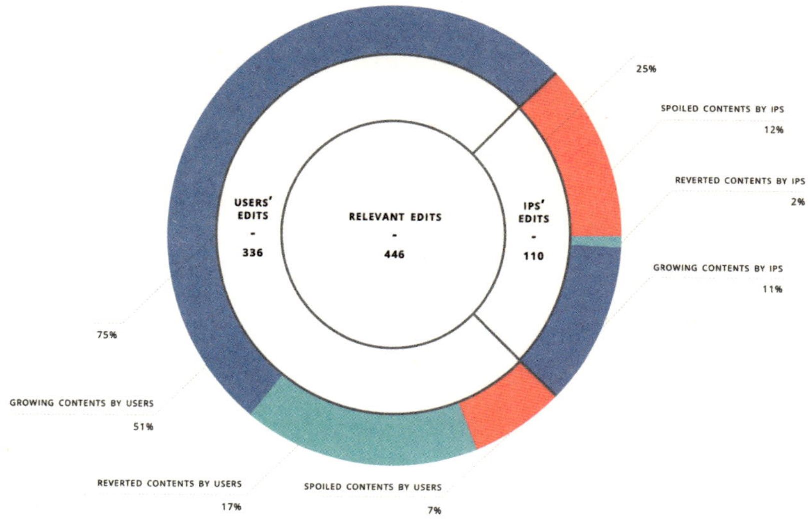
USERS' EDITS
-
336
RELEVANT EDITS
-
446
IPS' EDITS
-
110
25%
SPOILED CONTENTS BY IPS
12%
REVERTED CONTENTS BY IPS
2%
GROWING CONTENTS BY IPS
11%
75%
GROWING CONTENTS BY USERS
51%
REVERTED CONTENTS BY USERS
17%
SPOILED CONTENTS BY USERS
7%

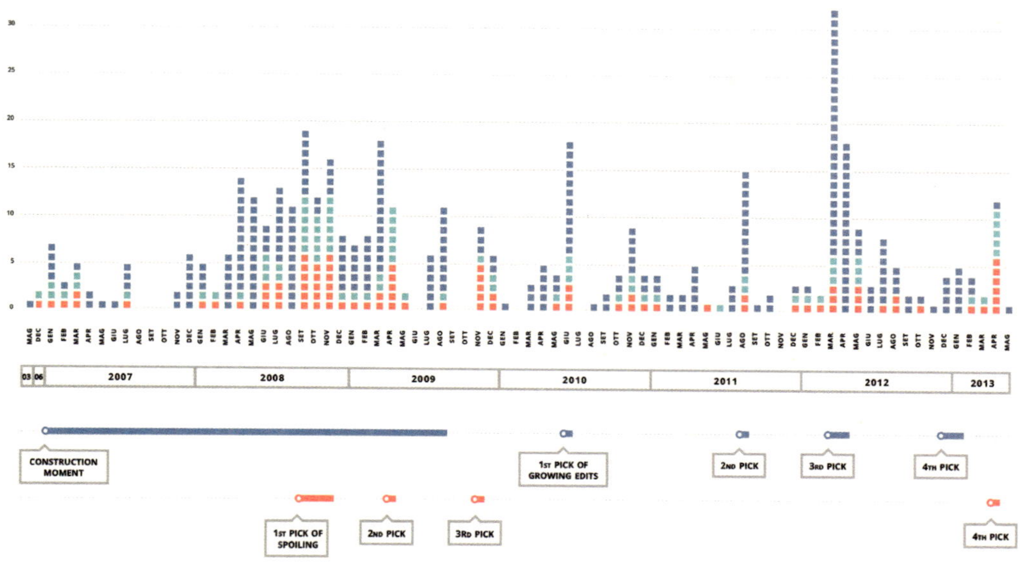
03
06
2007
2008
2009
2010
2011
2012
2013
CONSTRUCTION MOMENT
1ST PICK OF GROWING EDITS
2ND PICK
3RD PICK
4TH PICK
1ST PICK OF SPOILING
2ND PICK
3RD PICK
4TH PICK

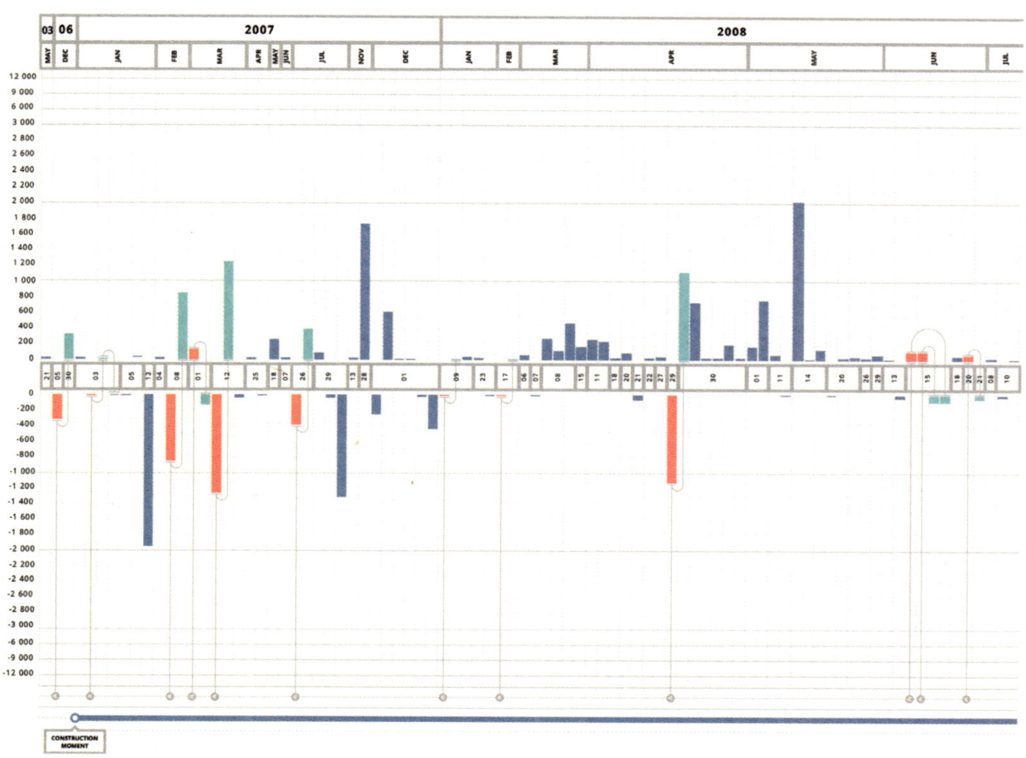
03
06
2007
2008

Immaculate Conception Available

- Completion Year: 2014
- Designer: Sofia Girelli, Eleonora Grotto, Pietro Lodi, Daniele Lupatini, Emilio Patuzzo

• Work Introduction

The controversial topic the book revolves around the surrogacy practice. Surrogacy is an arrangement in which a woman carries and delivers a child for another couple or person. Even if a lot of people don't know about this practice, after a first step of methodic web research we discovered that the topic was trending and generating many discussions throughout the web.

A biggest subtopic emerged from this preliminary research: surrogacy tourism in India. And this is what the designers decided to focus on. "How different countries look at surrogacy tourism in India?" They started from this question to develop their research, looking at four different domains: com (golbal/USA), co.in (India), co.uk (United Kingdom), it (Italy). The choice was related with the different law regulations of those countries.

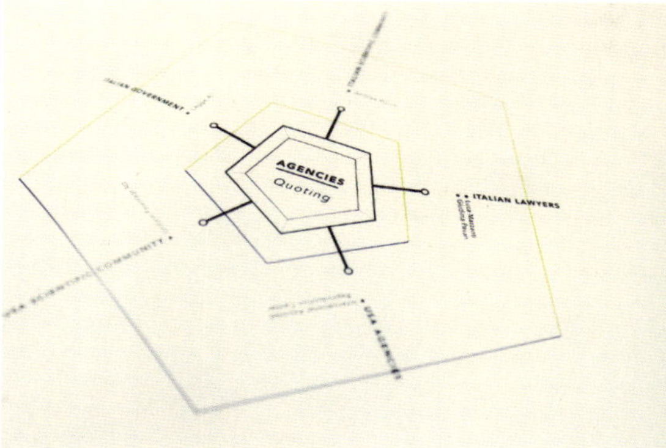
AGENCIES
Quoting
ITALIAN LAWYERS
ITALIAN GOVERNMENT

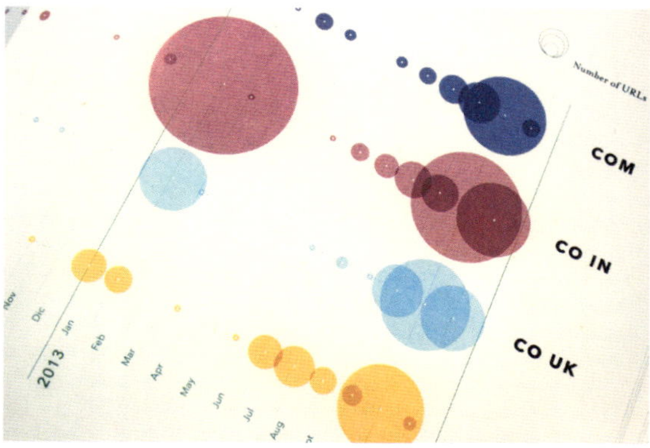
Number of URLs
COM
CO IN
CO UK
2013
Dec
Jan
Feb
Mar
Apr
May
Jun
Jul
Aug

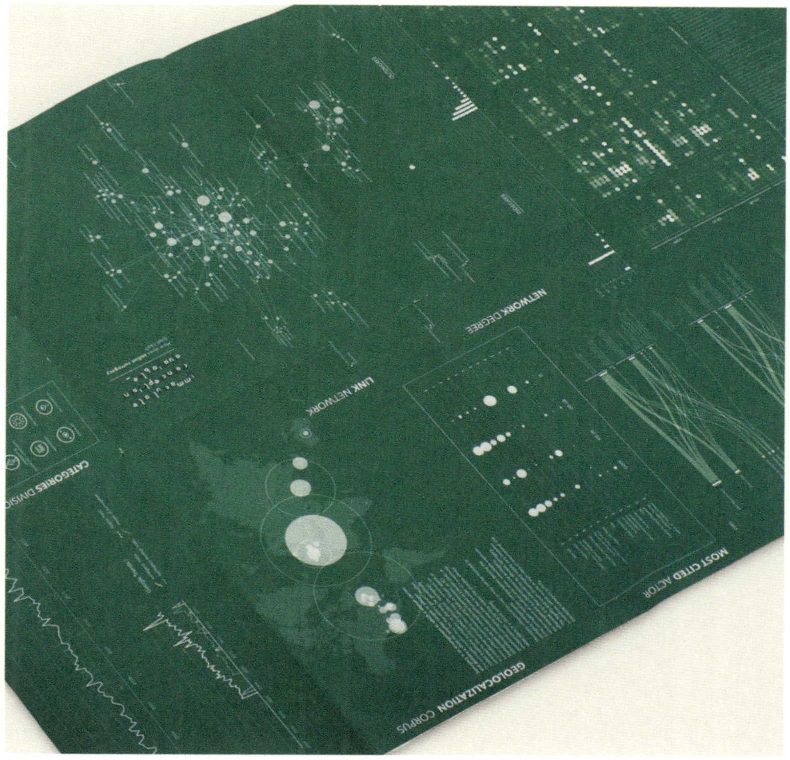
NETWORK DEGREE
LINK NETWORK
MOST CITED ACTOR
GEOLOCALIZATION CORPUS

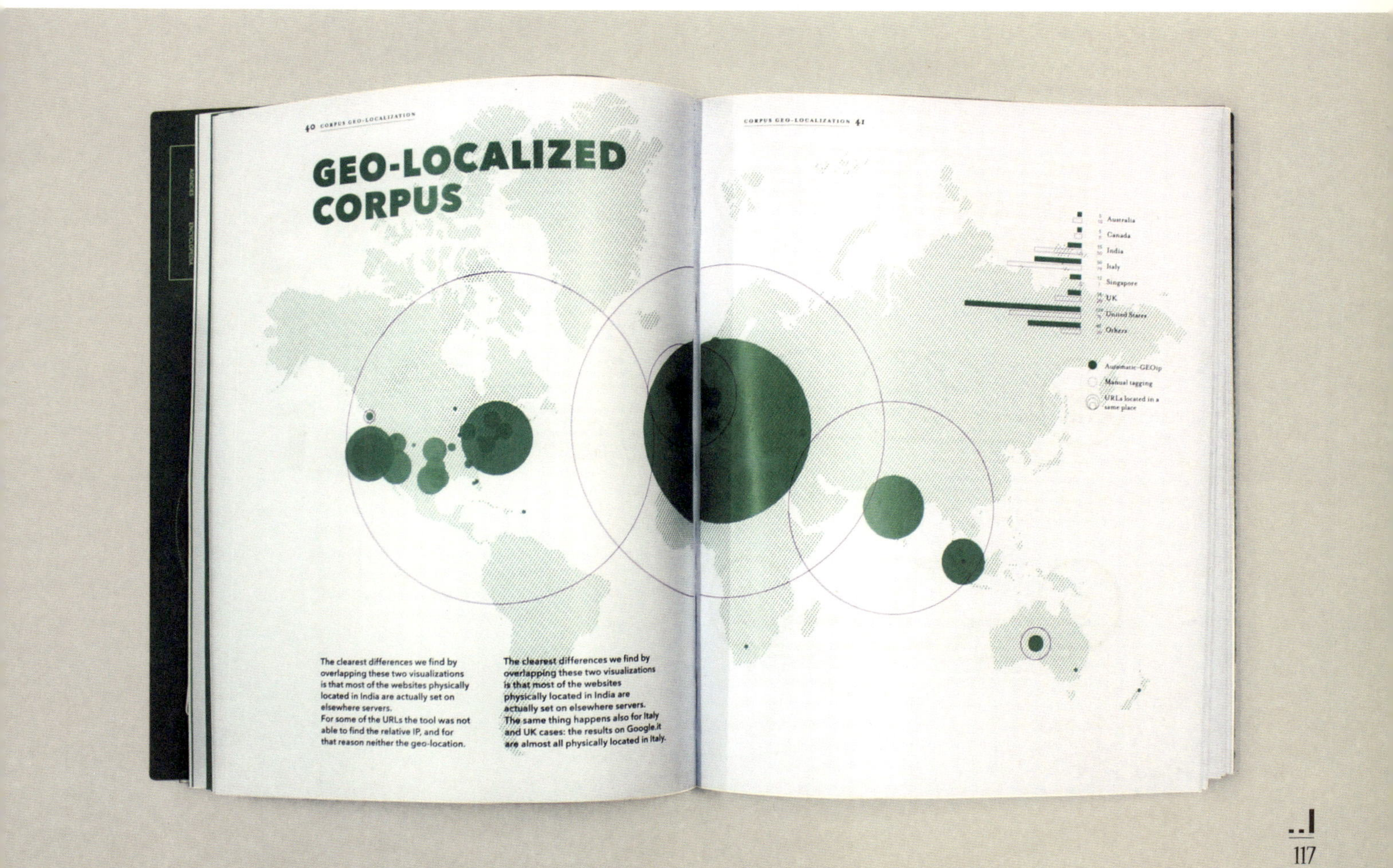
40 CORPUS GEO-LOCALIZATION
GEO-LOCALIZED CORPUS
CORPUS GEO-LOCALIZATION 41
Australia
Canada
India
Italy
Singapore
UK
United States
Others
Automatic-GEOip
Manual tagging
URLs located in a same place
The clearest differences we find by overlapping these two visualizations is that most of the websites physically located in India are actually set on elsewhere servers.
For some of the URLs the tool was not able to find the relative IP, and for that reason neither the geo-location.
The clearest differences we find by overlapping these two visualizations is that most of the websites physically located in India are actually set on elsewhere servers.
The same thing happens also for Italy and UK cases: the results on Google.it are almost all physically located in Italy.

Bernard Van Deik

- Completion Year: 2012
- Designer: Martin Panchaud
- Client: L'Octopode Associations

- Work Introduction

Bernard Van Deik is part of the art book project "Jardin" which aims to develop sequential narration. Telling a story through an abstract form and a codified visual language is this work's core concept. The narration is expressed through the codes of data graphics.

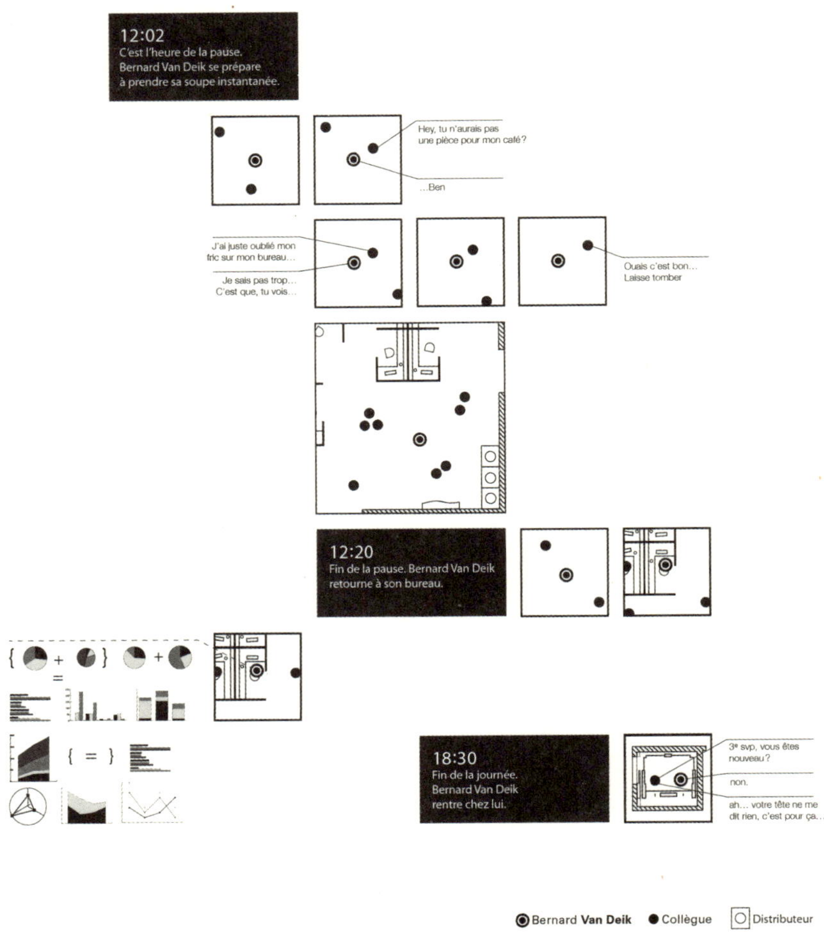

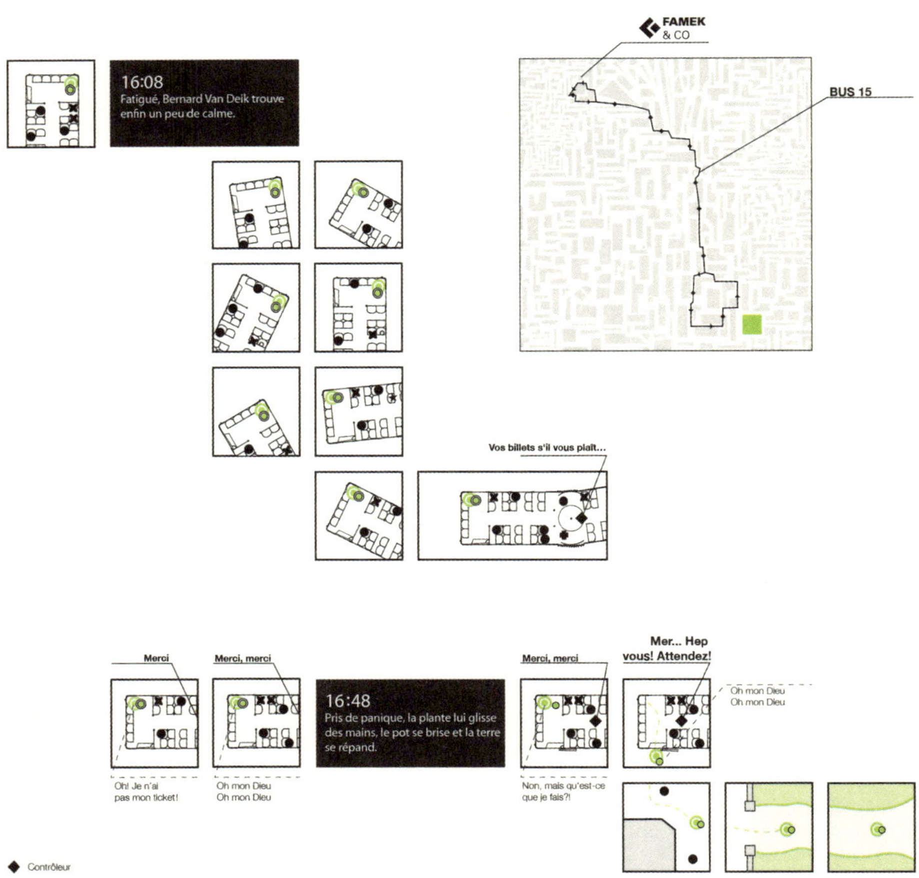

Qu'est-ce que vous avez tous? Et c'est qui lui d'abord?
Je ne sais pas, tout à coup il est devenu bizarre
Il faudrait l'amener chez le doc, il a vraiment pas l'air bien.
Qu'est-ce qui se passe?
Je ne sais pas, ce mec a commencé à pousser des cris et à dire des choses incompréhensibles… Et il veut pas lâcher sa plante.
Eh mais attends!
Oh doucement!
15:45
Bernard Van Deik court et fuit cet environnement qui lui semble désormais hostile.
Plus vite, plus vite, plus vite, plus vite, plus vite, plus vite…
17:04
Il tient à même ses mains un monticule de terre surmonté de la plante.
Elle va mourir si tu la laisses comme ça…
Je sais…
Tu ne veux pas qu'elle vive?
Je, je ne sais pas quoi faire, je ne sais pas comment faire.
Il faut juste la replanter… La remettre dans la terre.
Tu peux la mettre là-bas, près des fleurs, la terre est molle et les jardiniers pourront s'en occuper.
Pourquoi tu l'as déterrée cette plante?
Je ne l'ai pas déterrée… Elle est à moi, on me l'a donnée.
Joggeur
Cycliste

Bad Hire Survey Information Design

- Completion Year: 2013
- Designer: Rayz Ong
- Client: Recruitplus

• Work Introduction

Bad Hire Survey information design for RecruitPlus (Singapore). Whenever the focus is turns to improving companies' productivity, there are two solutions often touted. One is continuous training and the other automation. The selection of the human resource is always neglected. That is akin to having world class culinary training and kitchen equipment but using someone who don't even know how to handle a knife to begin with. That is why RecruitPlus Consulting decided to commission our first survey targeting exclusively on companies' hires that just couldn't deliver (or as we termed as a bad hire) and measuring them against the perceived contribution by the hires on the opposite end of the spectrum, the Super Performers or A Players.

BAD HIRE SURVEY 2013
THE DATA FOR THE SURVEY WAS COLLECTED THROUGH AN E-SURVEY THAT WAS SENT OUT TO OVER 4,000 HR PRACTITIONERS AND BUSINESS LEADERS.
The purpose of this survey is to get a better understanding of the least spoken about element in productivity. We are talking about the kind of performance gained from an engaged employee, an A Player, a Super Performer. The result shows us the average number of A Player across industry and what could be ways to bring up that figure.
84%
Will Be HIRING IN THE FIRST HALF OF 2013
SINGULARLY, THE CONNOTATION OF A BAD HIRE MEANS NEGATIVE Attitudes for 18%
A Whopping 71%
FEEL IT IS A COMBINATION OF NEGATIVITY, LACKLUSTRE WORK, ATTENDANCE ISSUE failure to work well with others, failure to meet deadlines.
URGENT
Consequence OF A BAD HIRE?
Lost time to recruit and train another worker
Cost to recruit and train another worker
LOST PRODUCTIVITY
64% believe they have 10% bad hires
18% believe they have 20%
13% have 30% and 4% have 50% bad hires.
62% of the participants feel their companies only have between 10% to 30% Super Performer
This shows the extreme imbalances these group of people's super effort is over-compensating the other 70% to 90% who are under performing.
Super Performers Usually come from Referral
2ND IS RECRUITMENT AGENCY
3rd is job board
All believe SUPER PERFORMERS CAN perform the job of 2 to 5 Bad Hires
They will Pay 10% to 30% MORE for Super Performers
93% are keen to review a tried-and-tested assessment tool that can guarantee them Super performers, or in other words, no bad hires.
64% plan to train their BAD HIRES TO MAKE GOOD
11% will live with it (gasp!)
EVEN THOUGH MOST KNOW OF THIS ISSUE, 38% of them DON'T HAVE TIME TO TURN THESE Bad Hires into super performers.
Assuming each of them is paid $2,000 the $2k super performer CAN DO THE JOB OF 5 X $2K OTHER HIRES. that is $2k vs $10k a savings of 400%
Granted a Super Performer will ask to be paid more. But even if you pay him $3K, you are still saving $7,000 a month (versus 5 x $2k other hires)
It is paramount that companies examine and exploit the channels they are getting their Super performers from. With a whopping 93 percents keen to look at an assessment tool to guarantee a good hire, this shows whatever is on the market now probably isn't really working out.
Much as there is a different opinion on what constitutes a bad hire, the bottom line is they drag the performance of any business. By ensuring the right fit via a stringent, structured interview process, companies can minimize the bad hires that come through the door of the office.
RECRUITPLUS
Your Talent Specialist
www.recruitplus.com

Visualize Food

• Completion Year: 2014
• Designer: Edoardo Moruzzi

• Work Introduction

Use of info-graphic technique to present a cooking recipe, this concept is developed for a cookbook. The designer, by taking the icons of edible oil, tomatoes, and garlic as designing elements, of plate as pie chart with plain numbers, presents a creative poster of menu.

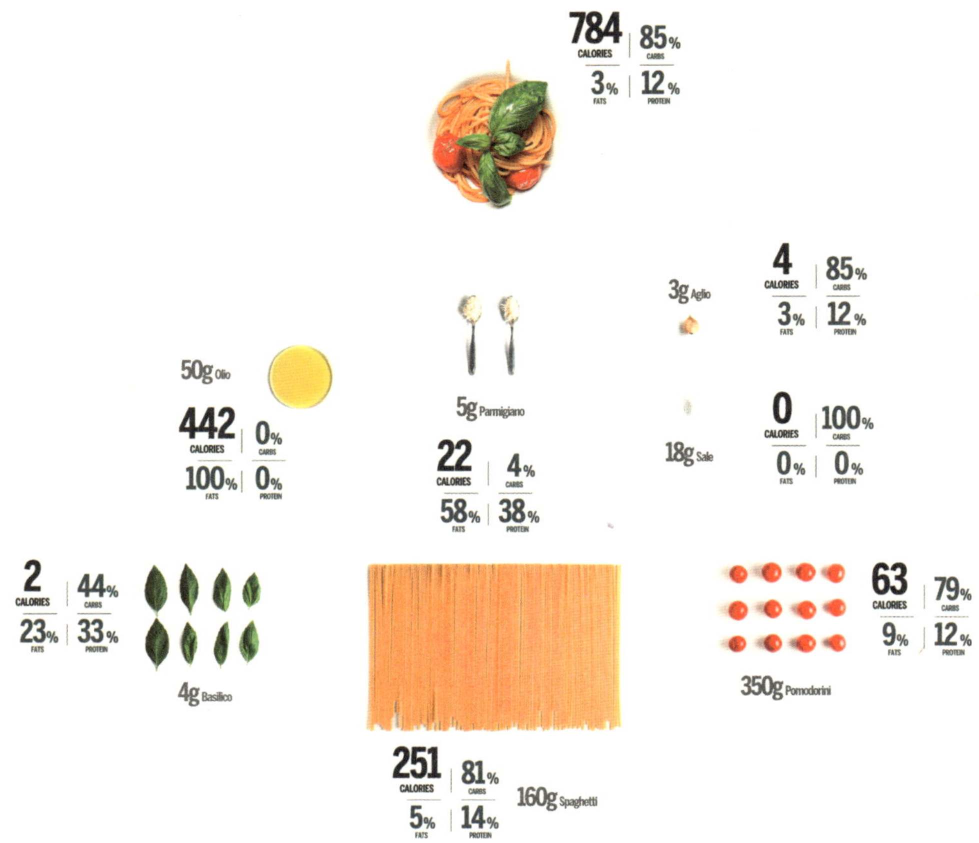

SPAGHETTI AI
POMODORINI
RICETTA PER 2 PERSONE
442
50g Olio
3g Aglio
22' TIMING
2 PORTIONS
50% DIFFICULTY
20$ COST

Engaging the Power of Visual Story Telling Infographic

- Completion Year: 2013
- Designer: Rayz Ong
- Client: Mindlite Studios

• Work Introduction

The Engaging the power of visual story telling Infographic design show why videos works better as a story telling media. As organizations increasing compete for slices of the decreasing attention spans of today's online audiences, videos are the format-of-choice for anyone wanting to broadcast their content as effectively as possible.

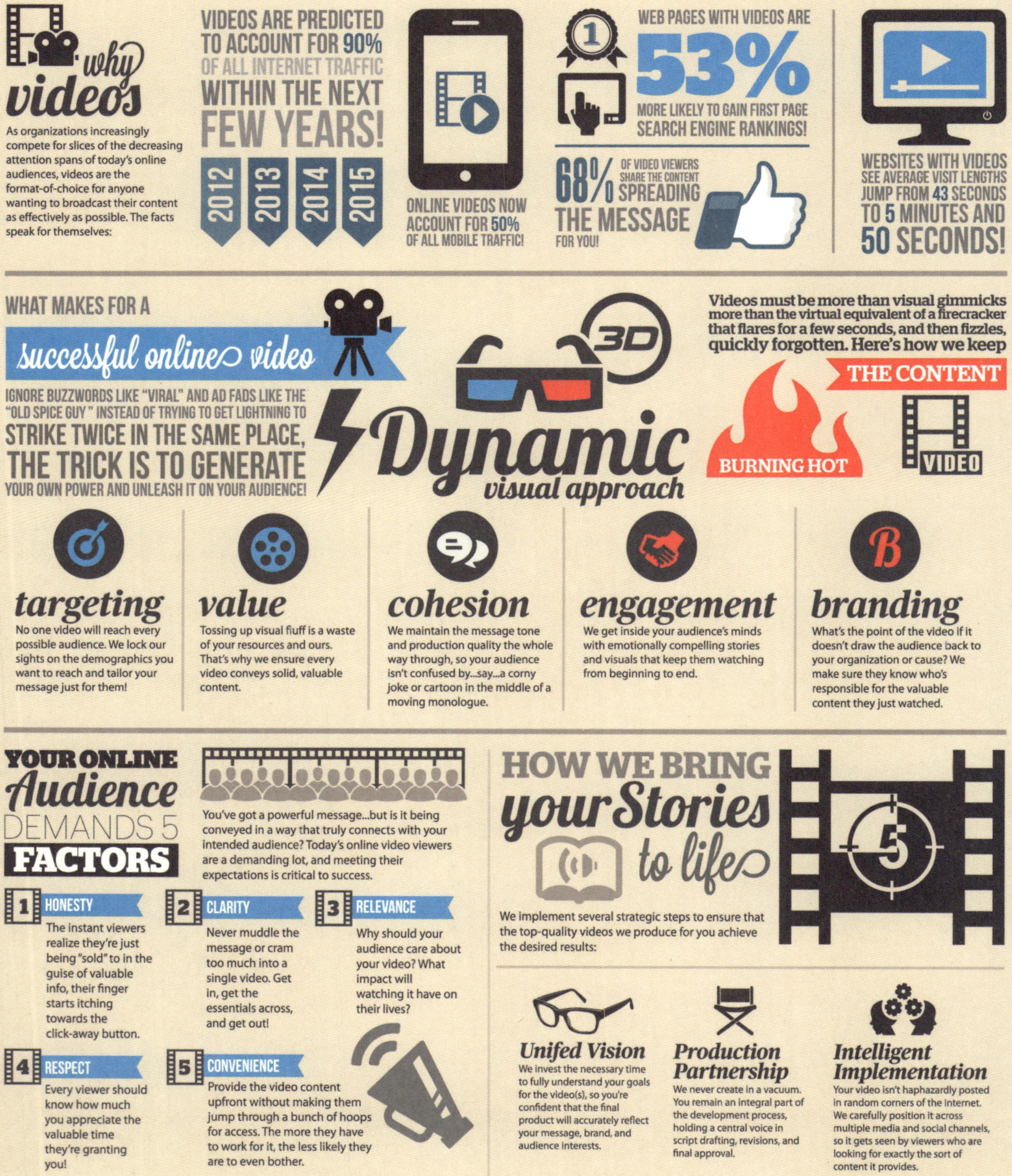

The Numbers of School Education

- Completion Year: 2012
- Designer: Sergio Piergallini
- Client: Province of Florence

• Work Introduction

This infographic shows the difference in instruction both in the Province and the City of Florence. Differences include mobility, qualifications, school attendance, school performance and other data.

The designer takes the black colour as under-painting, and the mint green & orange colours as dominant colour, producing an effect of visual impact.

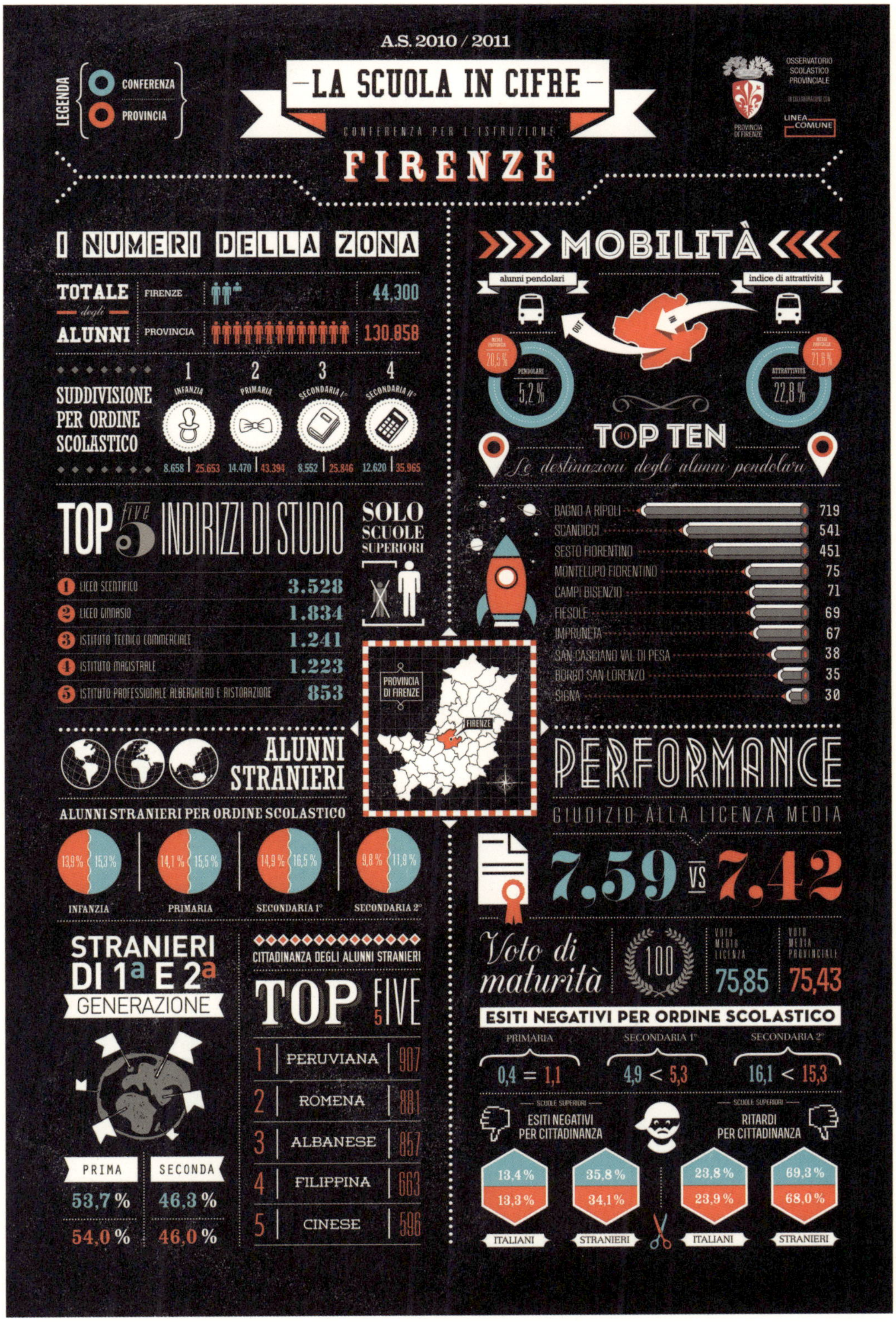

- Completion Year: 2013
- Designer: Elisa Bianchet, Manuel Bortoletti, Sara Aurora Pizzardo

- Work Introduction

Infodesign projectis about specialised crops of Veneto, aregion in the north-east of Italy. Their project consists of a Panel system for the enhancement and the popularization of the sweet potato from Zero Branco, a typical product from their territory, through the history, land, tools, methods of cultivation and eating. The challenge is to represent their subject in a concise way, easy to understand, by using an organic visual language stylistically well-defined. then you need to understand the issue that you are dealing with, identify the target audience and contextualize the project.

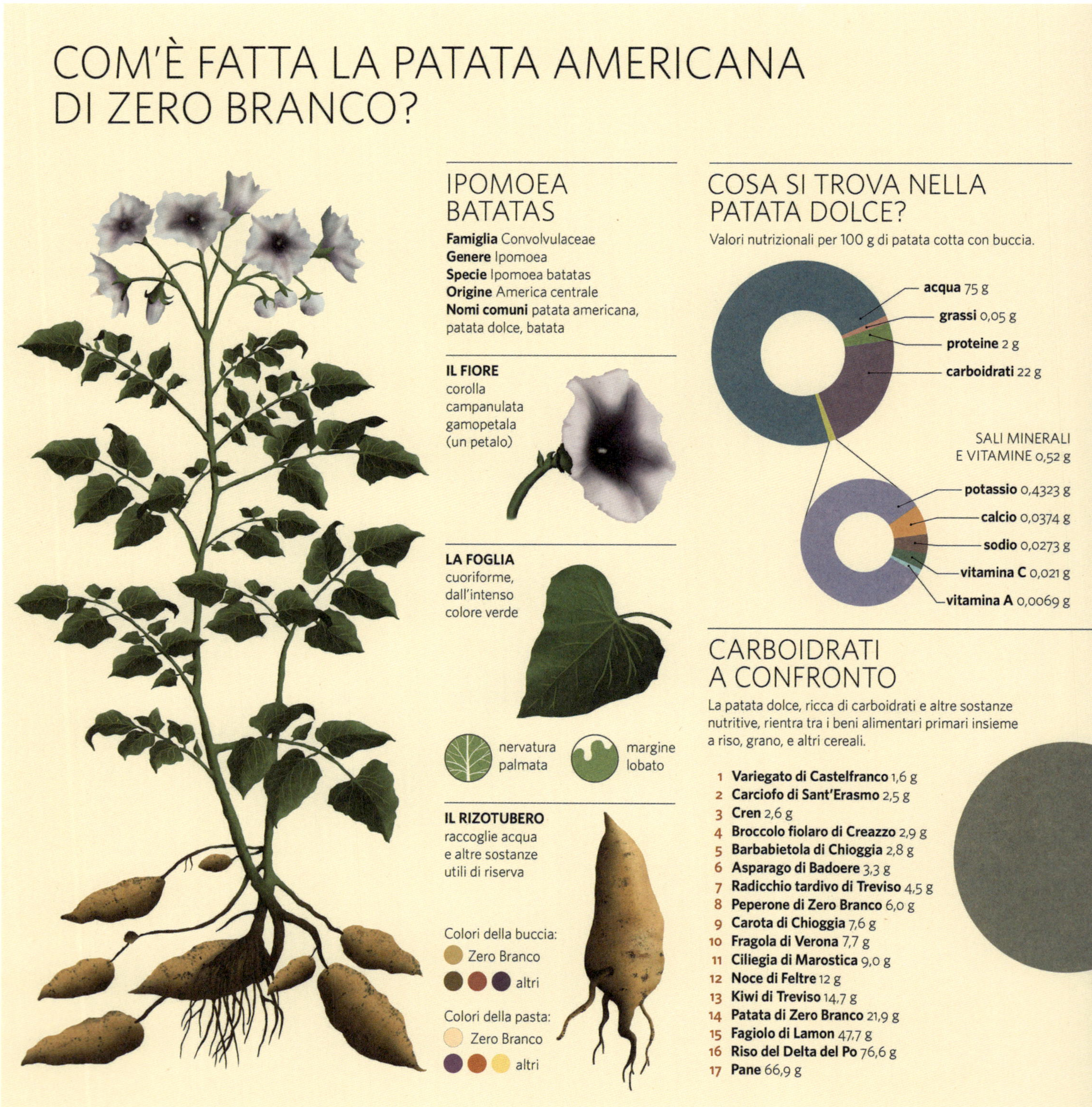

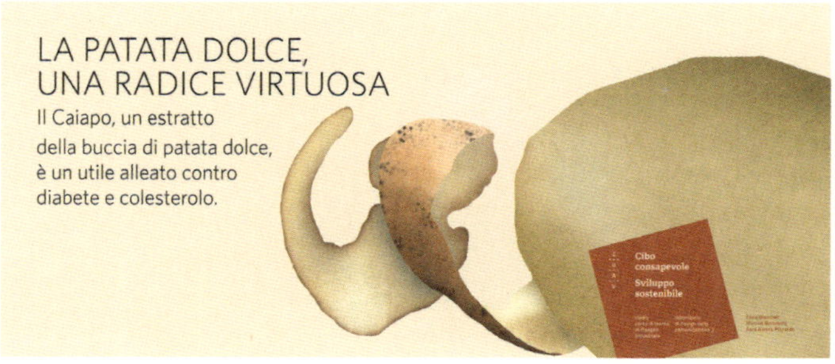
LA PATATA DOLCE,
UNA RADICE VIRTUOSA
Il Caiapo, un estratto
della buccia di patata dolce,
è un utile alleato contro
diabete e colesterolo.
Cibo
consapevole
Sviluppo
sostenibile

MANGIARE SECONDO STAGIONE
Dic
Gen
Feb
Mar
Apr
Mag
Giu
Lug
Ago
Set
Ott
Nov
Cibo
consapevole
Sviluppo
sostenibile

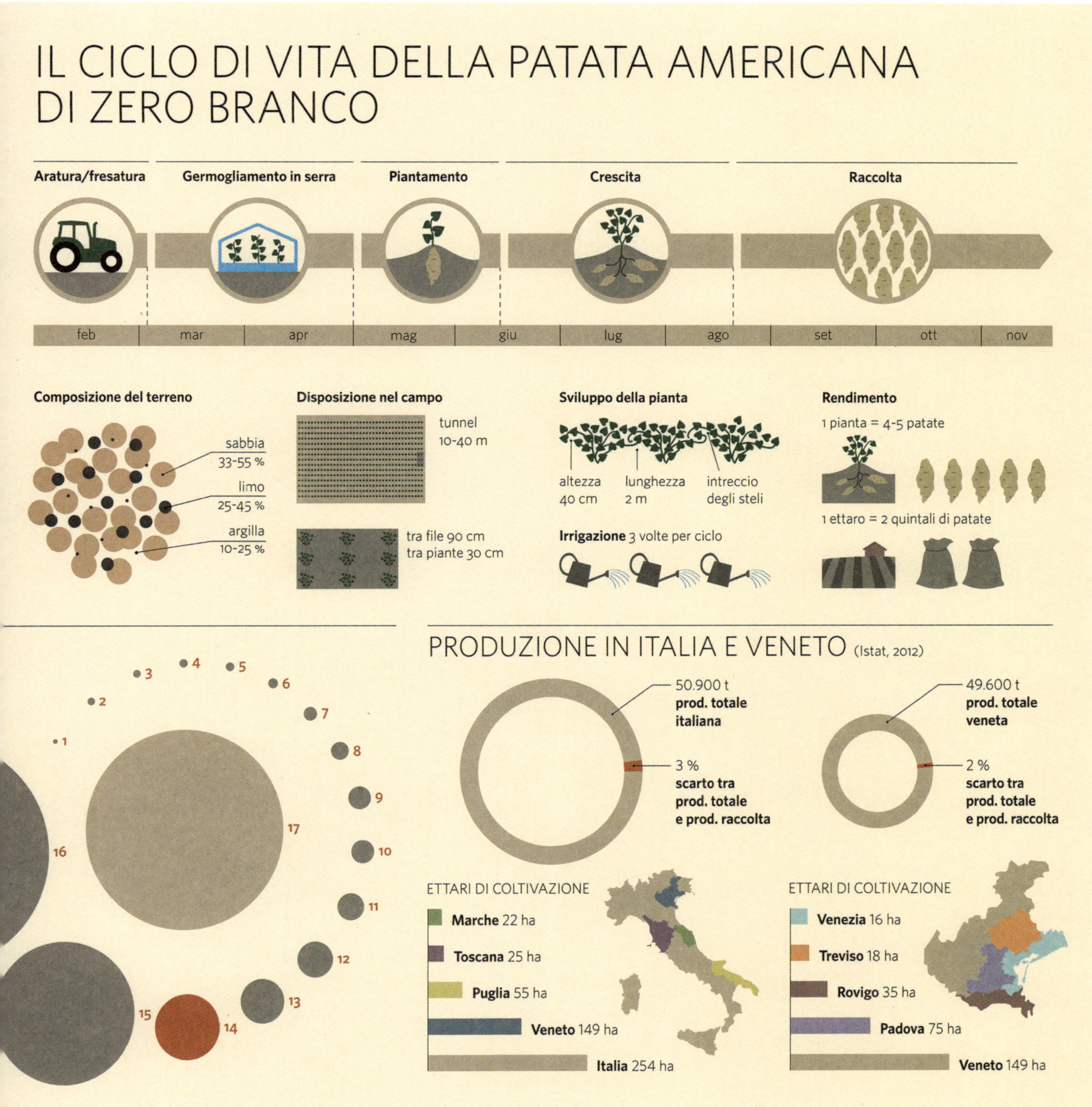
IL CICLO DI VITA DELLA PATATA AMERICANA
DI ZERO BRANCO
Aratura/fresatura
Germogliamento in serra
Piantamento
Crescita
Raccolta
feb
mar
apr
mag
giu
lug
ago
set
ott
nov
Composizione del terreno
sabbia
33-55 %
limo
25-45 %
argilla
10-25 %
Disposizione nel campo
tunnel
10-40 m
tra file 90 cm
tra piante 30 cm
Sviluppo della pianta
altezza
40 cm
lunghezza
2 m
intreccio
degli steli
Irrigazione 3 volte per ciclo
Rendimento
1 pianta = 4-5 patate
1 ettaro = 2 quintali di patate
1
2
3
4
5
6
7
8
9
10
11
12
13
14
15
16
17
PRODUZIONE IN ITALIA E VENETO (Istat, 2012)
50.900 t
prod. totale
italiana
3 %
scarto tra
prod. totale
e prod. raccolta
49.600 t
prod. totale
veneta
2 %
scarto tra
prod. totale
e prod. raccolta
ETTARI DI COLTIVAZIONE
Marche 22 ha
Toscana 25 ha
Puglia 55 ha
Veneto 149 ha
Italia 254 ha
ETTARI DI COLTIVAZIONE
Venezia 16 ha
Treviso 18 ha
Rovigo 35 ha
Padova 75 ha
Veneto 149 ha

TORTA DI CIOCCOLATO E PATATE AMERICANE DI ZERO BRANCO

Ingredienti

- zucchero a velo
- cacao in polvere
- zucchero di canna
- biscotti secchi 250 g
- burro 250 g
- patate dolci 250 g
- uova 2
- succo di limone 1/2

Strumenti

- mixer
- mestolo
- spatola
- pela-patate
- coltello
- schiaccia-patate
- colino
- padella
- pentola

Tempo di preparazione 1h 50m

Dosi per 5 persone

UNA PASSEGGIATA A ZERO BRANCO

SCANDOLARA, LA FRAZIONE DELLA PATATA DOLCE

L'ortolana
Azienda ortofrutticola che collega i produttori veneti ai mercati.

APO
Associazione Produttori Ortofrutticoli marca trevigiana

Chiesa
di S. Martino vescovo

OPO Veneto
Organizzazione Produttori Ortofrutticoli Veneto

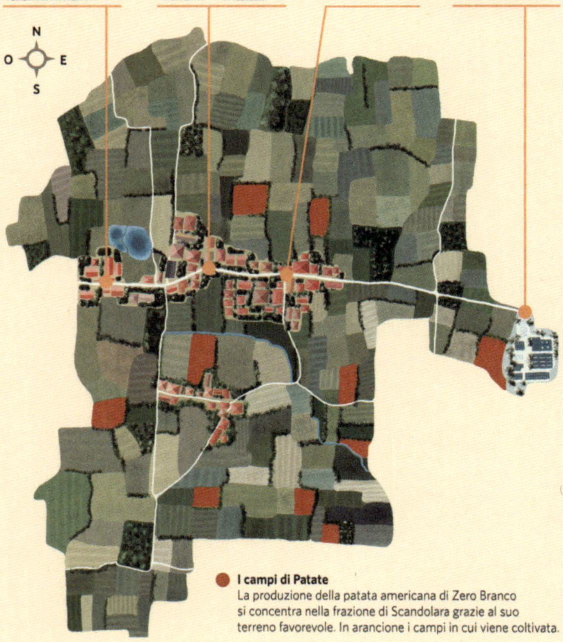

I campi di Patate
La produzione della patata americana di Zero Branco si concentra nella frazione di Scandolara grazie al suo terreno favorevole. In arancione i campi in cui viene coltivata.

Le tre frazioni

Luoghi d'interesse

1. Comune di Zero Branco
2. Villa Guidini
3. Chiesa di Zero Branco
4. Chiesa di Sant'Alberto
5. Chiesa di Scandolara
6. Fiume Zero
7. Ostiglia, vecchia ferrovia ora pista ciclabile

La permeabilità del terreno (Arpav, 2011)
I terreni che meglio si prestano alla coltivazione della patata dolce sono quelli sciolti, ad alta permeabilità, caratterizzati quindi da un buon drenaggio dell'acqua.

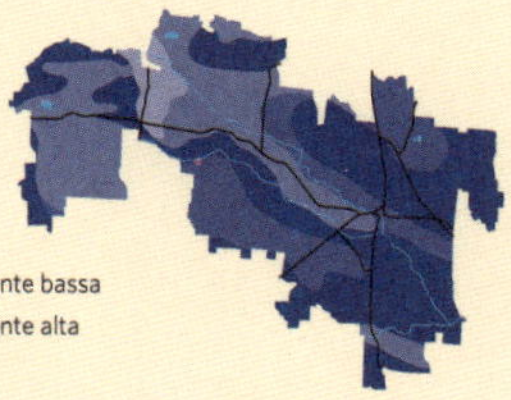

- bassa
- mediamente bassa
- mediamente alta
- alta

Sostanza organica (Arpav, 2011)
La patata dolce raccoglie le sostanze nutritive nei rizotuberi e necessita di terreni fertili, ricchi di materia organica.

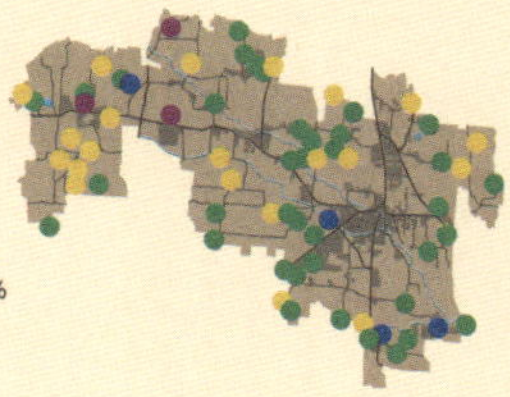

- 0 - 0,8 %
- 0,8 - 1,2 %
- 1,2 - 2 %
- 2 - 4 %

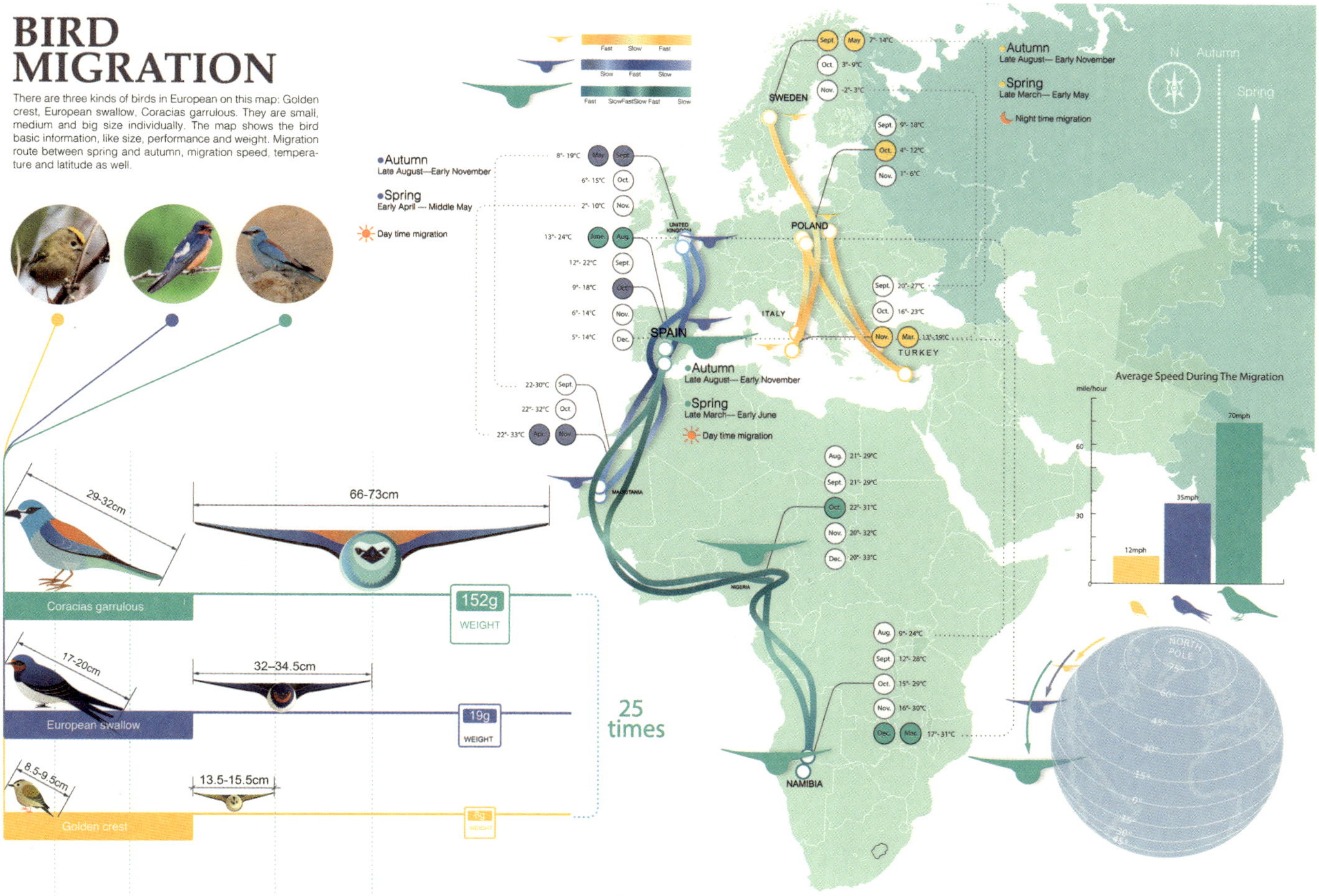

Bird Migration

- Completion Year: 2014
- Designer: Longjuan Liang, Todd Timney

• Work Introduction

For a class project, the designer used visualization as a method to present research data on a topic of her own interest. The class taught her how to effectively visualize information based on principles from graphic design, art, and cognitive science. This phase includes research topic, data collection, sketching, test people, redesign, review and final print. Her topic is about the migration of three kinds of bird which are all located in Europe. The information contains the length of body, weight, the migration routes, and temperature.

100 Meals with Rice

- Completion Year: 2014
- Designer: Karyll Catubig

• Work Introduction

They were assigned to choose a topic that could consist of 100 things that they had access to. they needed to back those up with data consisting of 7 attributes. They then had to design an infographic with the data collected.

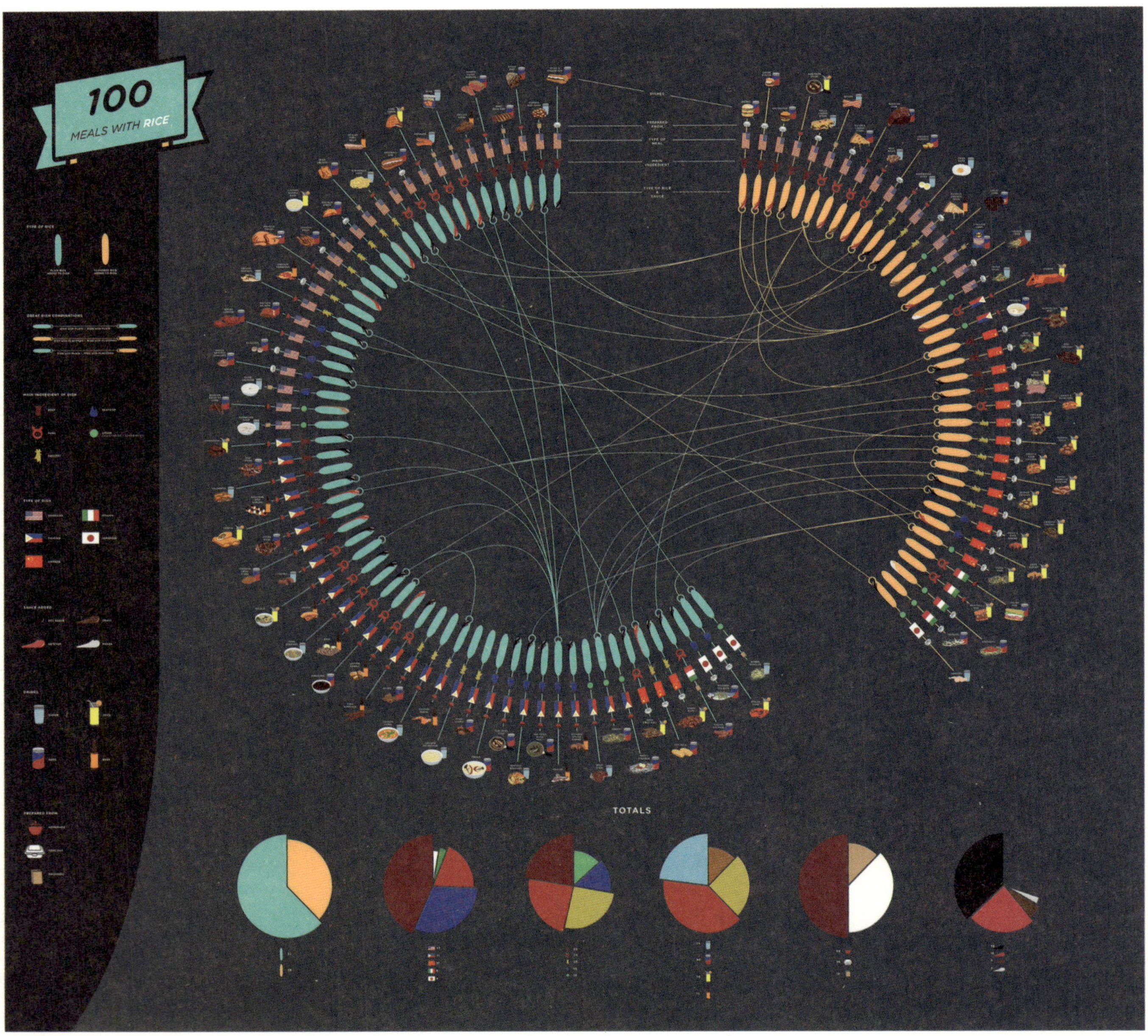

The Young Giants

- Completion Year: 2012
- Designer: Kavya Singh Barthwal
- Photographer: Kavya Singh Barthwal

- Work Introduction

The Young Giants is an infographic about the youngest and highest mountain range in the world, the Himalayas. This shows the 11 highest peaks of this range along with role this range plays in the countries it is presented in.

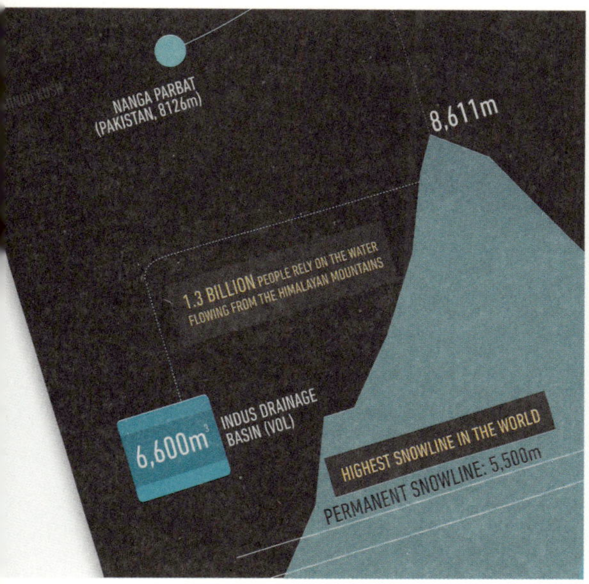

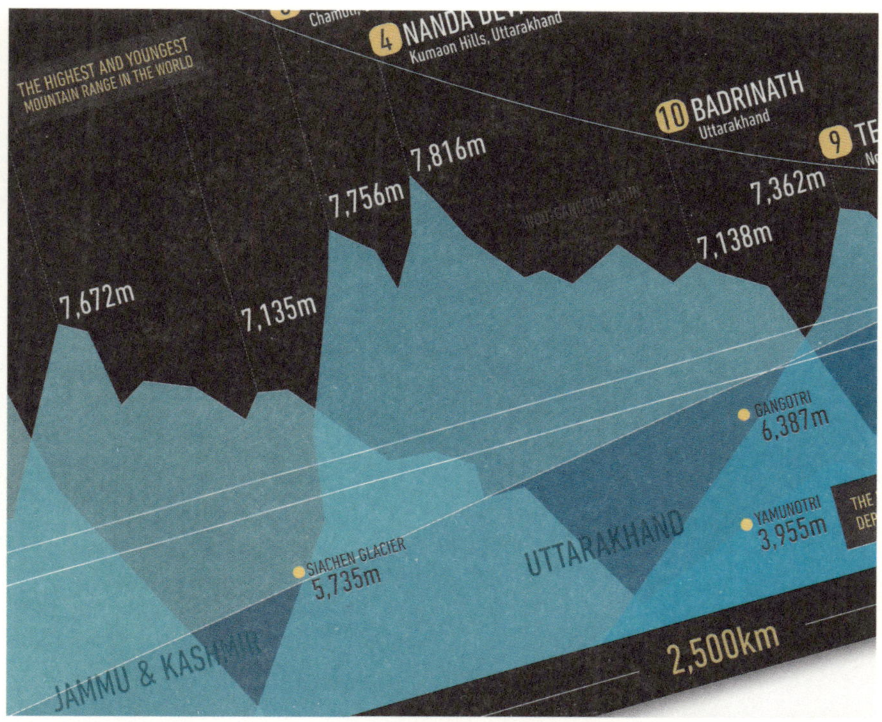

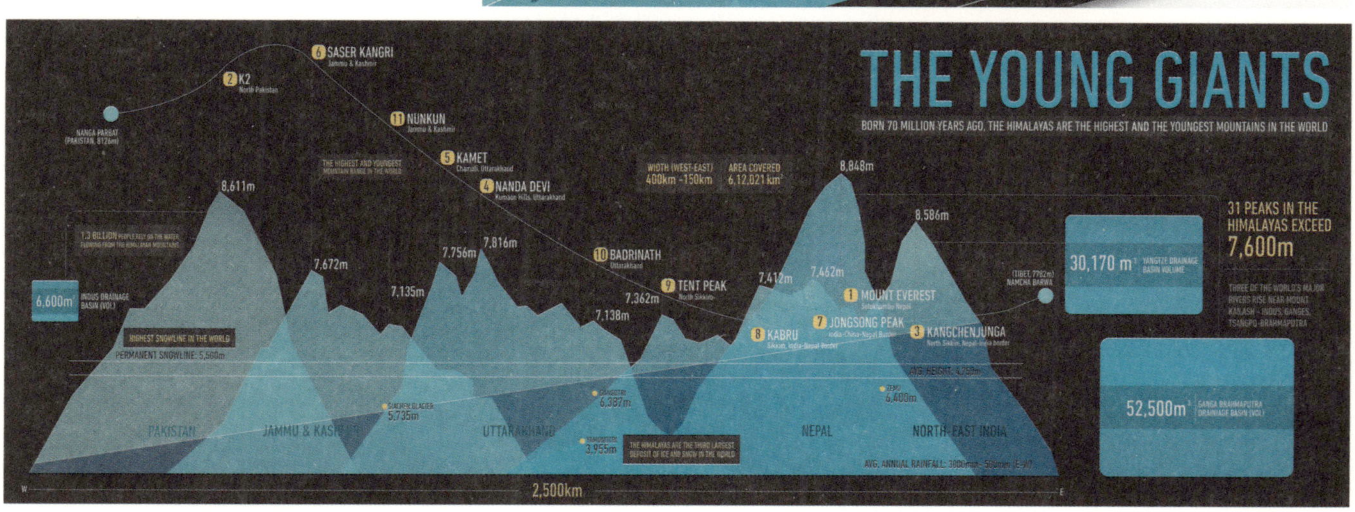

The Analytical Tourism Map of Piedmont

- Completion Year: 2014
- Designer: Marco Bernardi, Federica Fragapane, Francesco Majno
- Web: www.behance.net/gallery/15058221/The-Analytical-Tourism-Map-of-Piedmont

- Work Introduction

The Analytical Tourism Map of Piedmont is an information design project that analyzes the situation of tourism in Piedmont, Italy. The poster has been divided in two parts: attraction factors and tourism flows. On the left, the main attraction factors have been analyzed and geolocated: landscape assets, architectural Heritage and museums, sports facilities, food and wine. The right side shows the tourist flows compared with the accommodations (hotels, bed and breakfasts, hostels, campgrounds…). This project has been realized analyzing the open data made available by the Piedmont region.

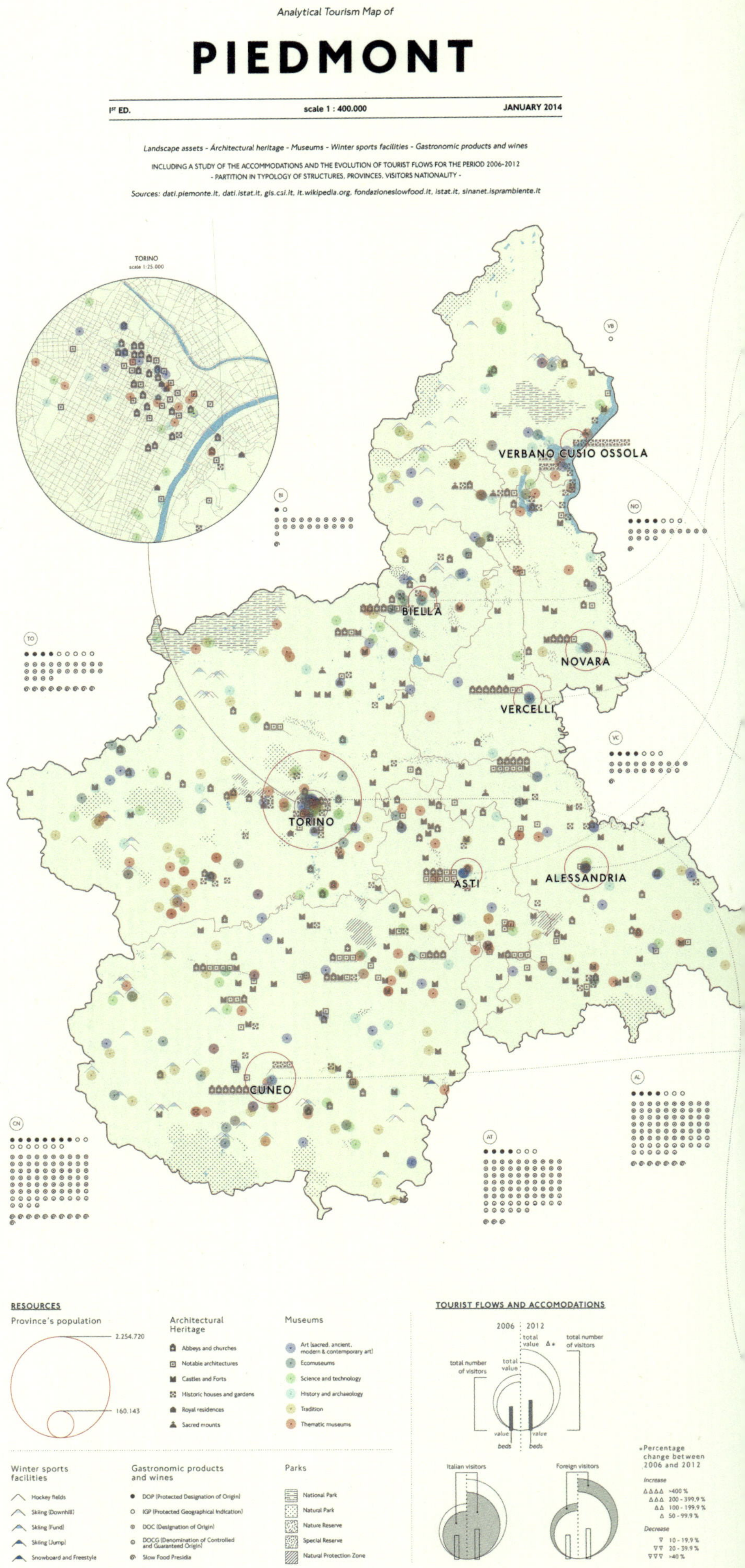

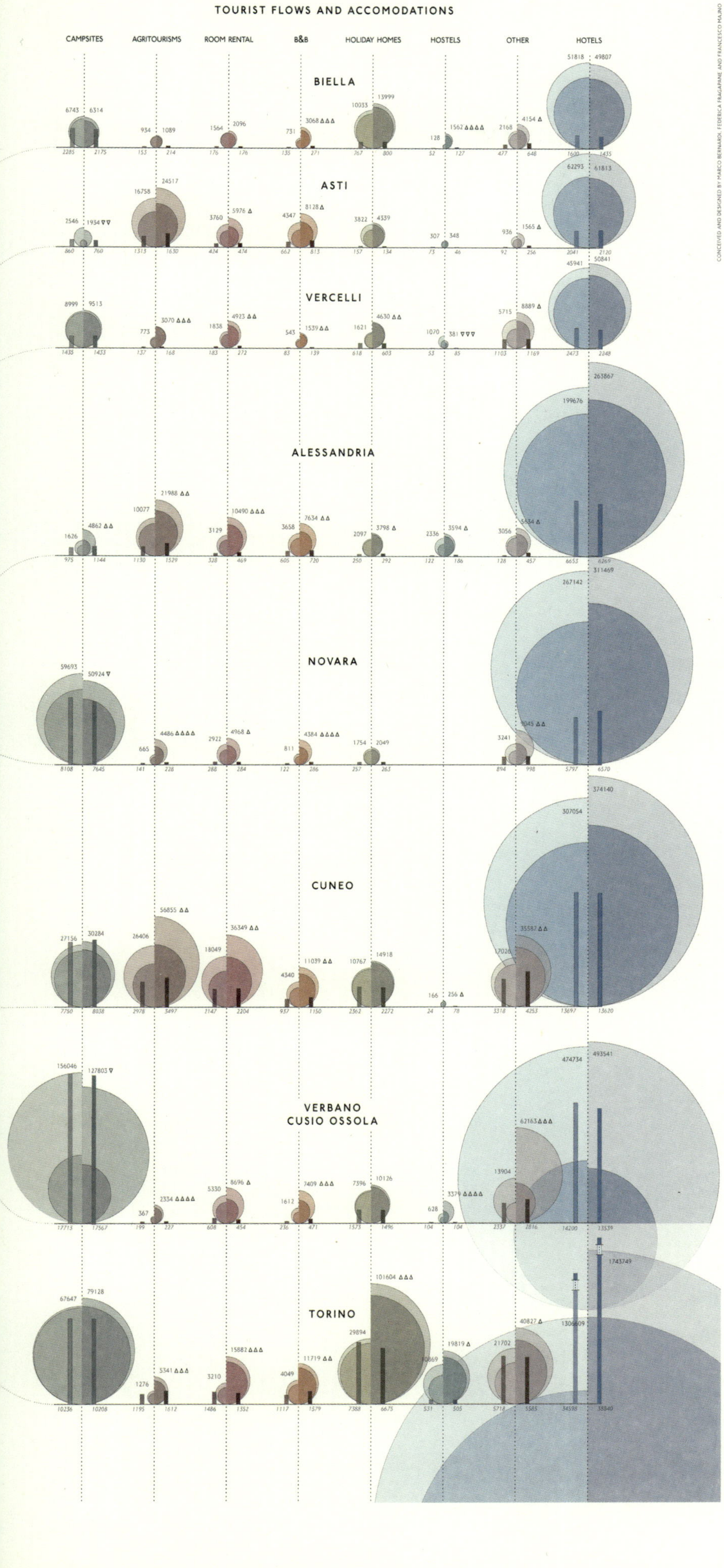

CONCEIVED AND DESIGNED BY MARCO BERNARDI, FEDERICA FRAGAPANE AND FRANCESCO MAJNO

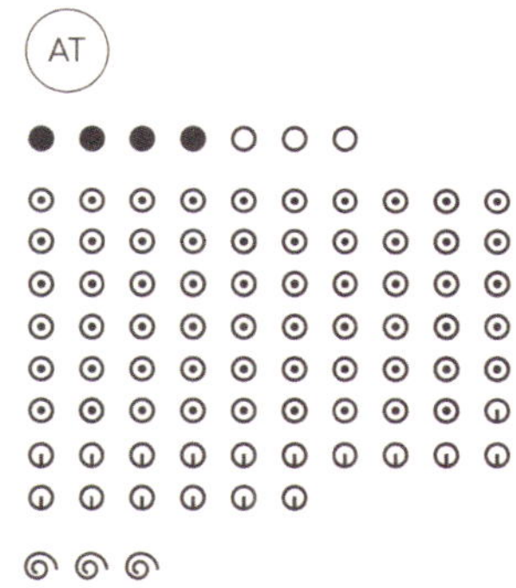

TOURIST FLOWS AND ACCOMODATIONS

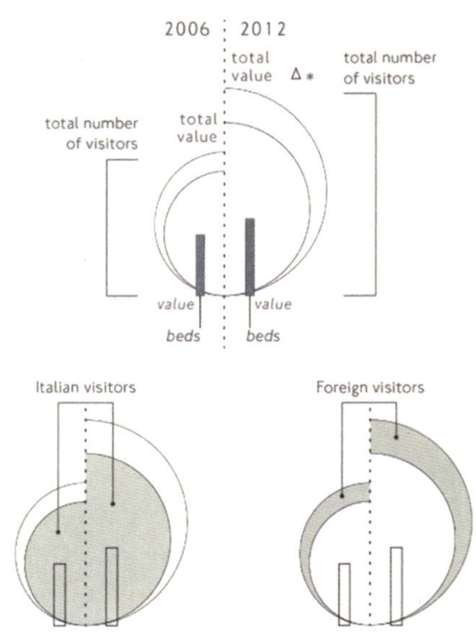

The End of the Fish

- Completion Year: 2013
- Designer: Jian Haake, Manuel Reitz

- Work Introduction

The overfishing of the oceans is one of the most serious problems in the ecological system. Since the beginning of industrial fisheries in the 1950s there is a dramatic decline of nearly 90% in fish stocks. Their Poster makes partial aspects like catch quotas, global consumption, by-catch, aquaculture and fishing zones visible hoping to increase consumer awareness.

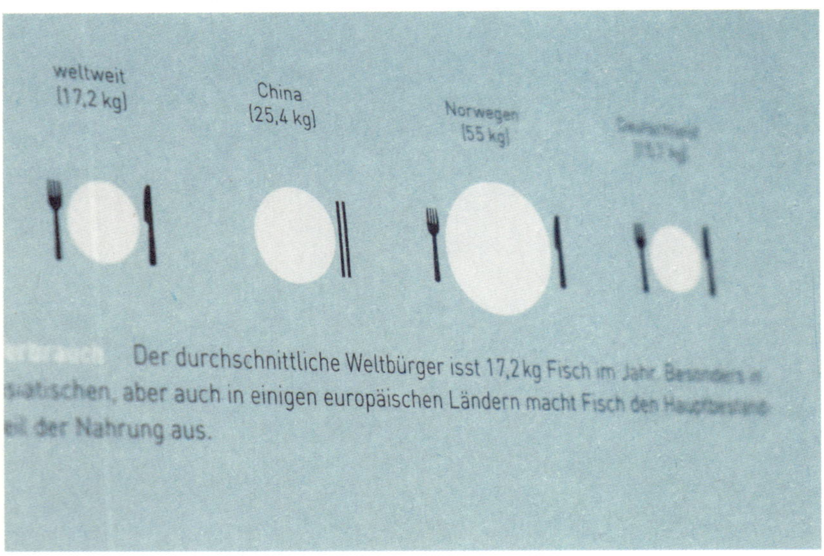

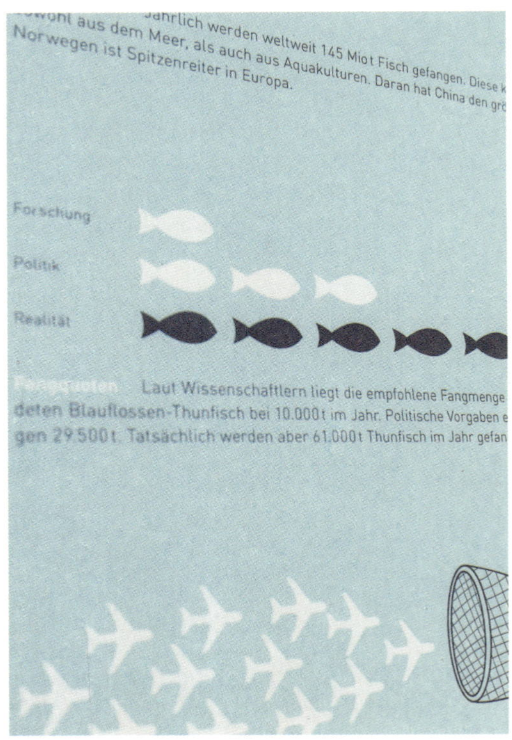

Das Ende des Fisches
Die Bestände der großen Fischarten sind in den letzten 60 Jahren um 90% gesunken. Hier zeigt sich deutlich das verheerende Ausmaß der industriellen Fischerei seit 1950
Viele Bestände weltweit sind überfischt. Es gibt aber immernoch einige Fische, die man bedenkenlos essen kann. Dazu gehören gezüchtete Regenbogenforelle aus Nordeuropa, Hering aus der westlichen und östlichen Ostsee und Pazifischer Lachs aus Alaska. Wichtig ist es, nicht nur auf die Art, sondern auch auf die Fangregion zu achten.

Saving Water Infographic Design

- Completion Year: 2013
- Designer: Rayz Ong
- Client: Lochness Gardens

• Work Introduction

How much water are you really using? Many of us have low flow shower heads and our toilets are using less water, but how does that compare to the water that goes into the things we use and consume every day? We created this infographic to help better understand what our daily impact really is. Some of the information might surprise you…

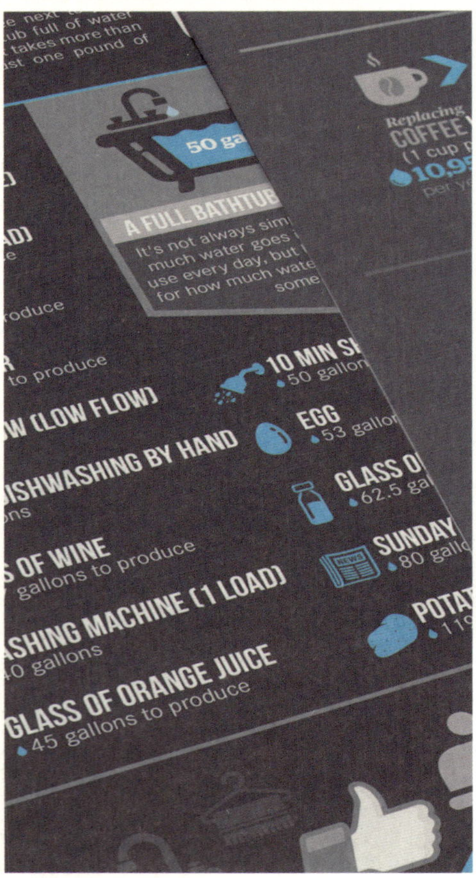

SO YOU WANT *to Save Water?*

How much water is in that cup of coffee next to your desk? Well, about a cup, plus the bathtub full of water that it took to produce the beans for it. It takes more than 2500 gallons of water to produce just one pound of roasted coffee beans.

2,500 gallons

one pound roasted Coffee

A FULL BATH TUB IS 100 GALLONS

100 gallons

It's not always simple to figure out how much water goes into making what we use every day, but here are some figures for how much water goes into producing some of them.

CUP OF TEA
8 gallons to produces

WHEAT BREAD (1 SLICE)
10.6 gallons to produces

DISHWASHER (1 LOAD)
15 gallons to produces

APPLE
18.5 gallons to produces

GLASS OF BEER
19.81 gallons to produces

10 MIN SHOW (LOW FLOW)
25 gallons to produces

10 MIN DISHWASHING BY HAND
30 gallons to produces

GLASS OF WINE
31.7 gallons to produces

WASHING MACHINE (1 LOAD)
40 gallons to produces

GLASS OF ORANGE JUICE
45 gallons to produces

EGG
53 gallons to produces

GLASS OF MILK
62.5 gallons to produces

10 MIN SHOWER (HIGH FLOW)
70 gallons to produces

SUNDAY NEWSPAPER
80 gallons to produces

POTATOES (1 LB)
119 gallons to produces

SUGAR (1LB)
180 gallons to produces

VEGETABLES (1LB)
188 gallons to produces

INSTANT POTATOES (1LB)
227 gallons to produces

COTTON SHIRT
700 gallons to produces

CEREAL GRAINS (1LB)
956 gallons to produces

SET OF NEW TIRES
2072 gallons to produces

CHICKEN MEAT (1LB)
2515 gallons to produces

BUTTER (1LB)
3228 gallons to produces

PORK (1LB)
3481 gallons to produces

BEEF (1LB)
8962 gallons to produces

What can you SAVE *by switching?*

Replacing
COFFEE WITH TEA
(1 cup per day)
10,950 gallons per year

Replacing
ORANGE JUICE WITH WATER
(1 glass per day)
16,717 gallons per year

Replacing
MILK WITH BEER
(1 glass per day)
15,582 gallons per year

Replacing
BEEF WITH CHICKEN
(1 pound per day)
335,244 gallons per year

Replacing
HIGH-FLOW SHOWER WITH A LOW-FLOW SHOWER
(10-minute shower a day)
16,425 gallons per year

Replacing
BEEF WITH VEGETABLES
(1 pound per day)
456,248 gallons per year

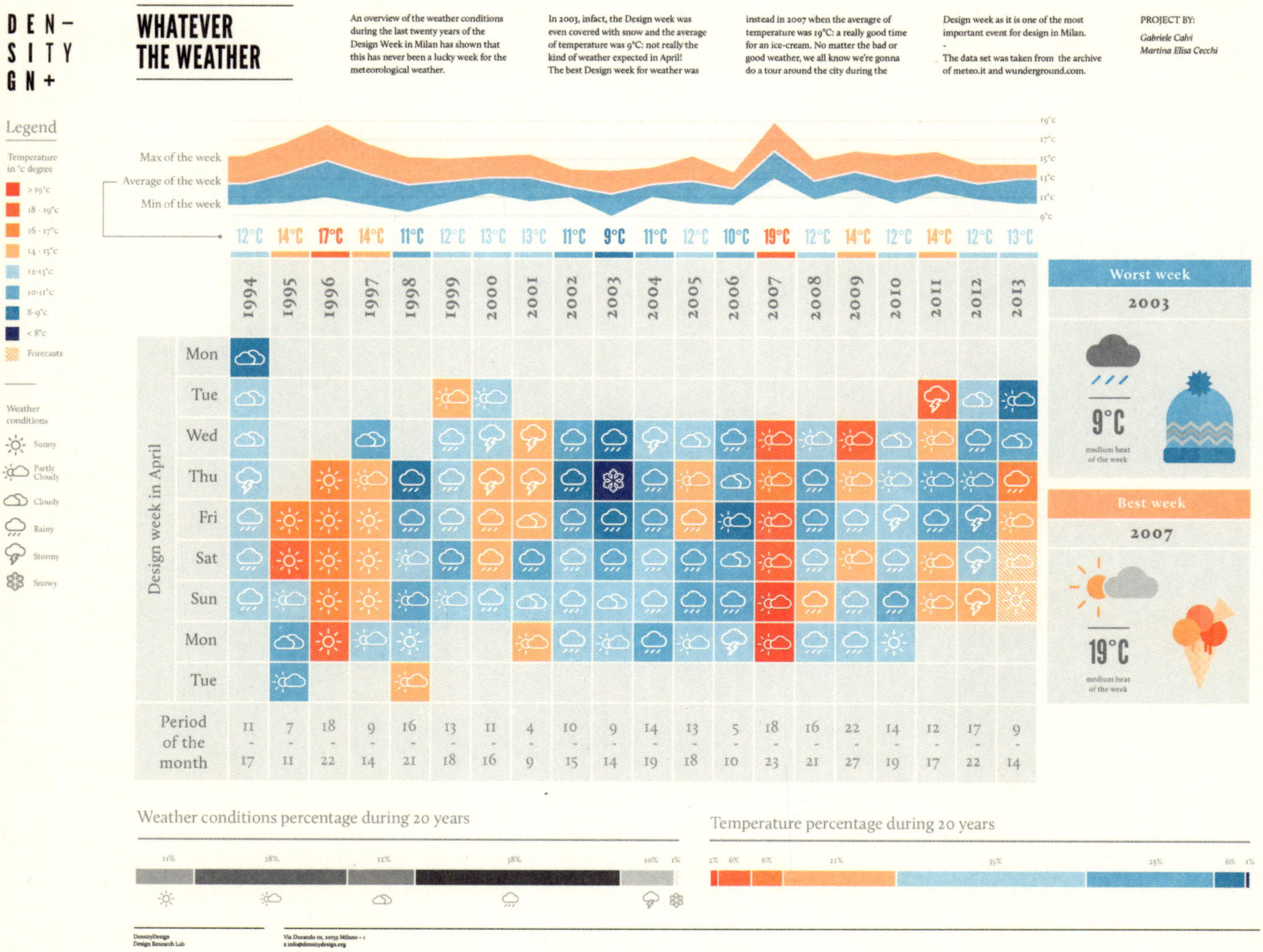

Whatever the Weather

- Completion Year: 2013
- Designer: Martina Elisa Cecchi and Gabriele Calvi
- Client: Research project realized within Density Design Research Lab

- Work Introduction

The infographic gives an overview of the weather conditions during the last twenty years of the Design Week in Milan and shows that this has never been a lucky week for the meteorological weather.

The infographic is ingenious by adopting simple lines and various icons involved with weather to show the changes of temperature in tabulation.

Wash Your Hands Before Eating

• Completion Year: 2014
• Designer: Olesya Tkach

• Work Introduction

The project was dedicated to Global Handwashing Day (15 october) and it contains information about how important to wash hands before eating, and how do it in right way. Presenting simple and interesting icons, this poster catches the attention of readers. There are a lot of children in the world who dying every day because of diarrhea. It could be changed by entering into the habit this simple rule.

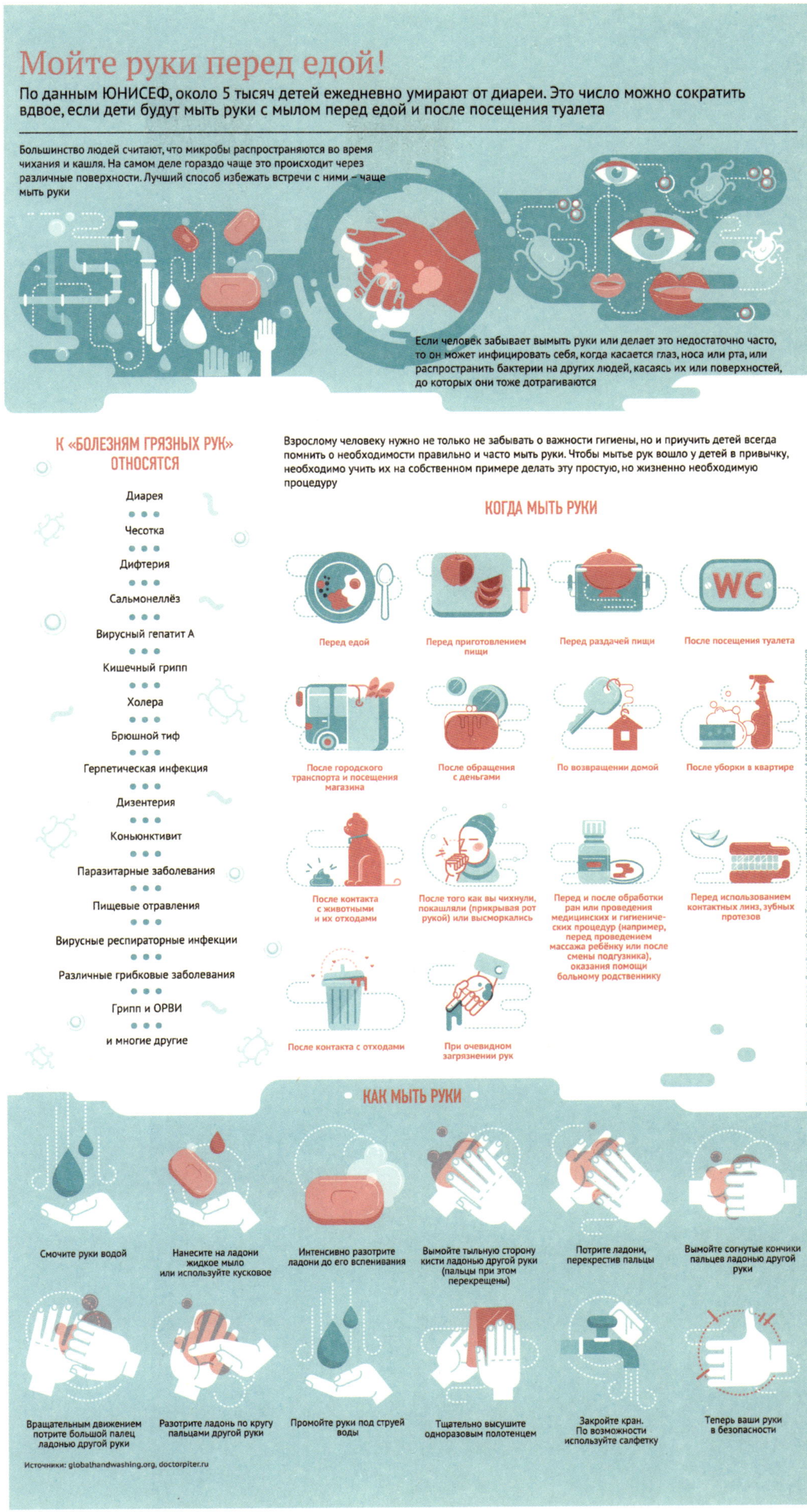

Personal Infographic

- Completion Year: 2013
- Designer: Jessica Hankinson

• Work Introduction

A promotional portfolio piece designed to demonstrate how, simple information can be displayed in a visually appealing and interesting way. This poster in edition to a resume was used as a mail out to design studios to advertise my skills as a designer in an attempt to get a job and a foot in the design industry.

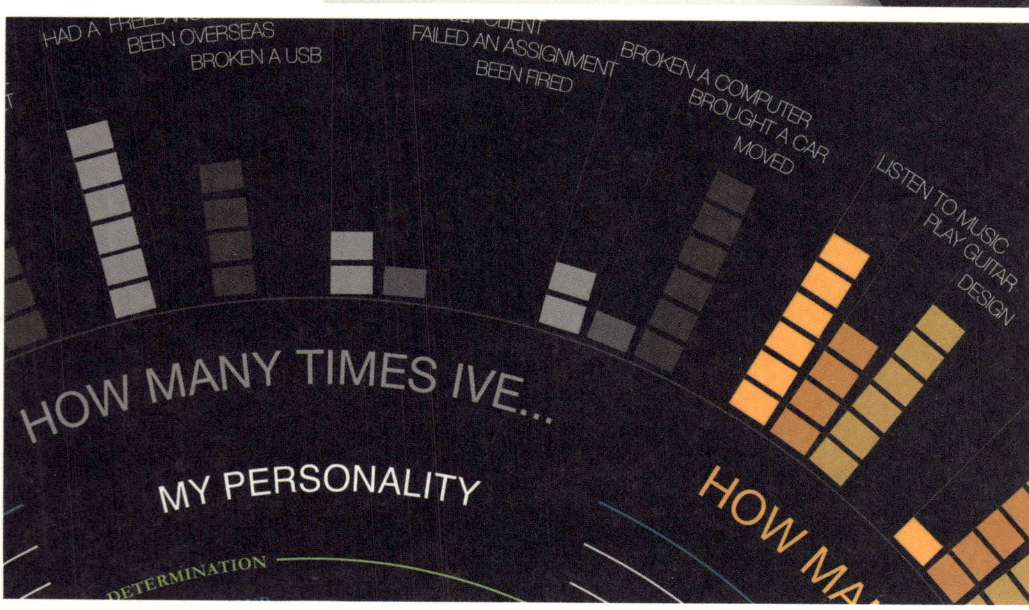

OPERATING SYSTEMS

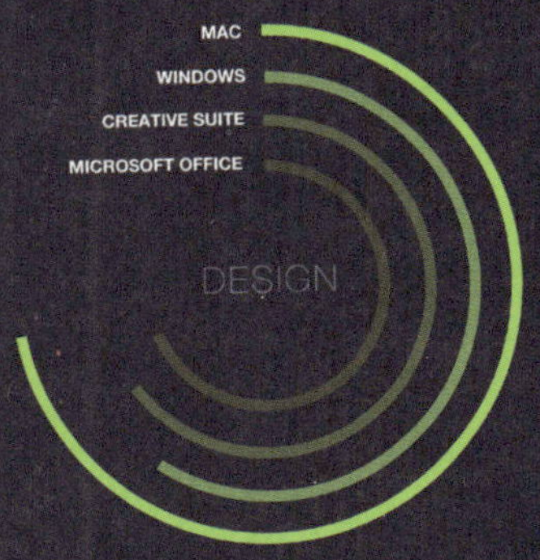

APPLICATION ABILITY

DESIGN INTERESTS

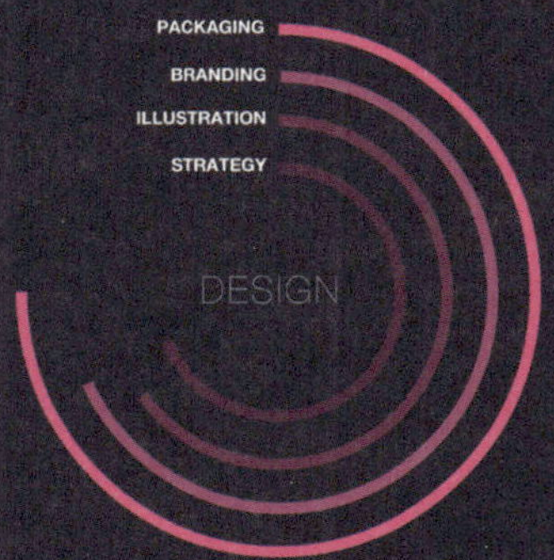

The Art of Motivation Infographic Design

- Completion Year: 2014
- Designer: Rayz Ong
- Client: Motivat
- Photographer: Rayz Ong

- Work Introduction

The Art of Motivation infographic design tells you about the productivity and motivation during daily working experience. A flowchart gives an idea of what personality your employees may have and tips to motivate them which we had classified them into four different categories: Social, Workaholic, insecure, power player.

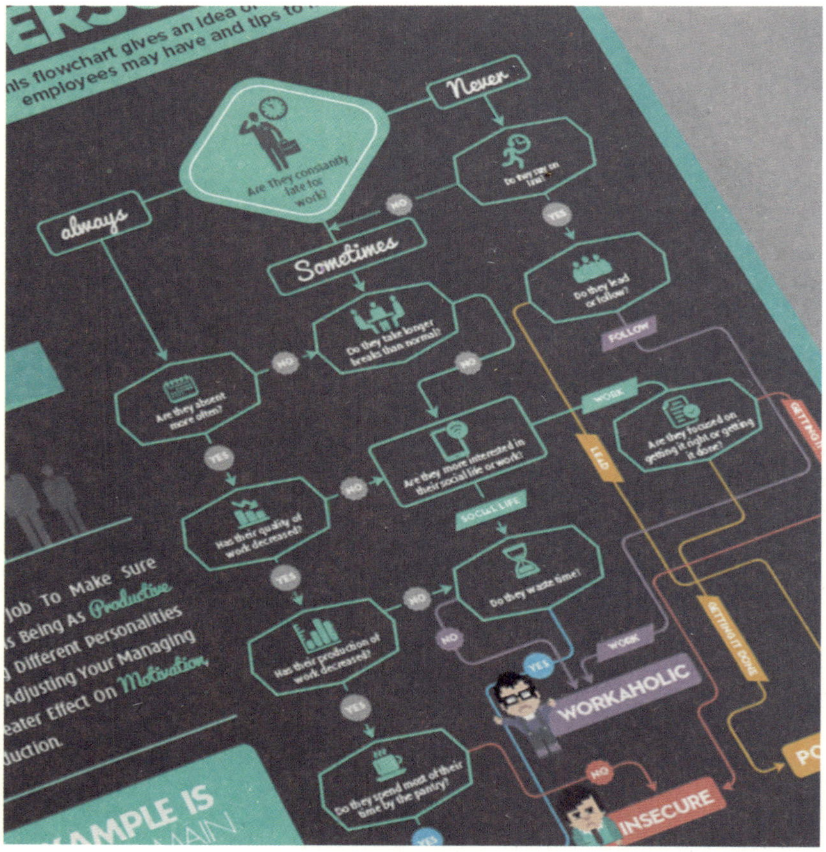

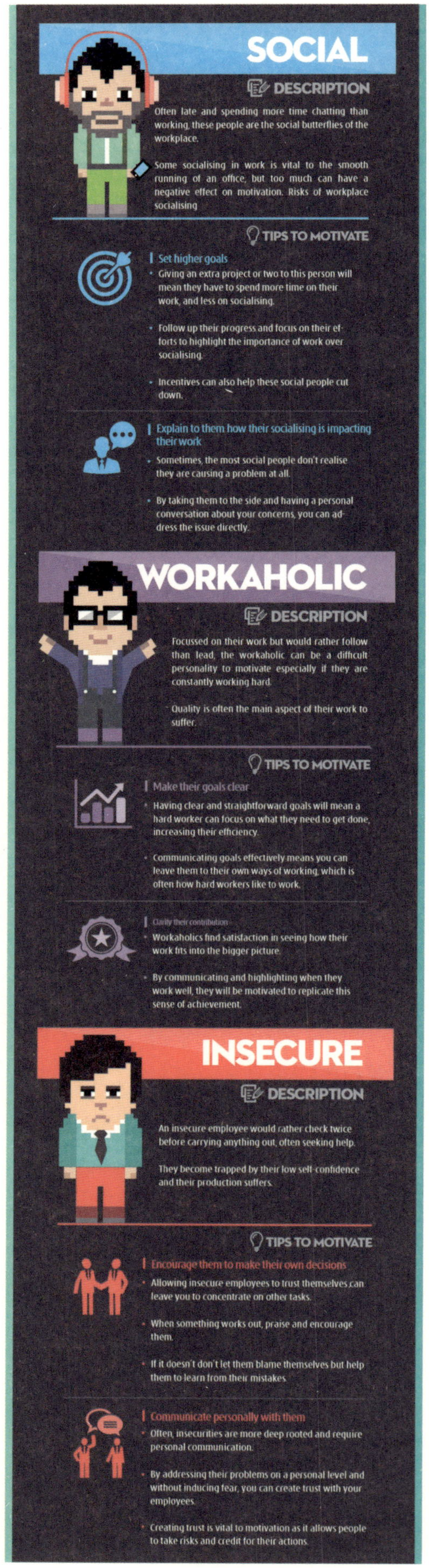

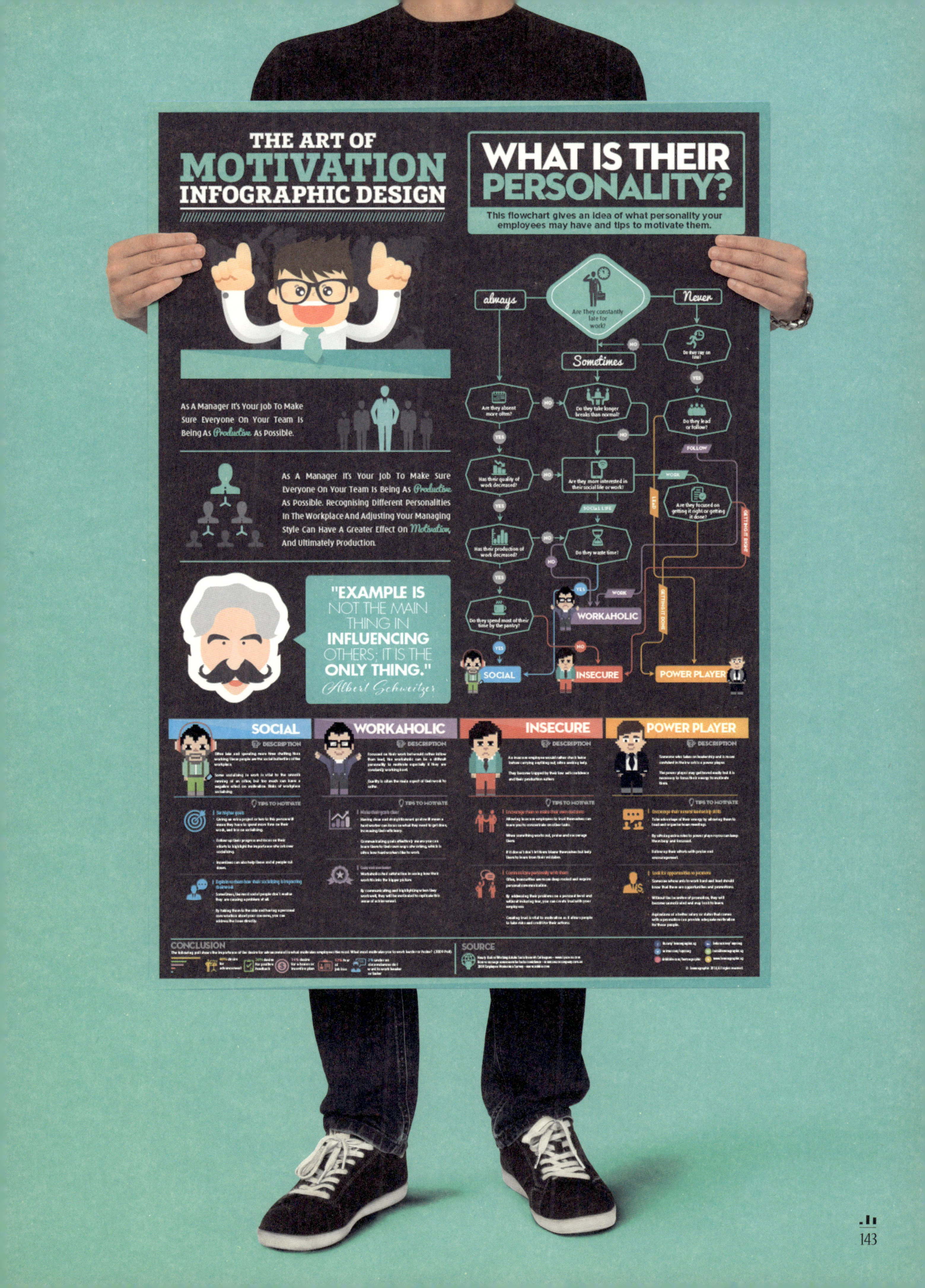
THE ART OF
MOTIVATION
INFOGRAPHIC DESIGN
WHAT IS THEIR
PERSONALITY?
This flowchart gives an idea of what personality your employees may have and tips to motivate them.
As A Manager It's Your Job To Make Sure Everyone On Your Team Is Being As Productive As Possible.
As A Manager It's Your Job To Make Sure Everyone On Your Team Is Being As Productive As Possible. Recognising Different Personalities In The Workplace And Adjusting Your Managing Style Can Have A Greater Effect On Motivation, And Ultimately Production.
"EXAMPLE IS NOT THE MAIN THING IN INFLUENCING OTHERS; IT IS THE ONLY THING."
Albert Schweitzer
always
Are They constantly late for work?
Never
Sometimes
Are they absent more often?
Do they take longer breaks than normal?
Do they lead or follow?
Has their quality of work decreased?
Are they more interested in their social life or work?
Are they focused on getting it right or getting it done?
Has their production of work decreased?
Do they waste time?
Do they spend most of their time by the pantry?
WORKAHOLIC
SOCIAL
INSECURE
POWER PLAYER
SOCIAL
WORKAHOLIC
INSECURE
POWER PLAYER
DESCRIPTION
TIPS TO MOTIVATE
CONCLUSION
SOURCE

Website Simplified Information Design

- Completion Year: 2014
- Designer: Rayz Ong
- Client: Internet initiatives

• Work Introduction

Website simplified infographic design is a process of website design in a more simplified way using 3 effective stages from planning, design layout to strategic implementation. A one piece A1 size infographic poster for you to understand and simplified your process in developing your website.

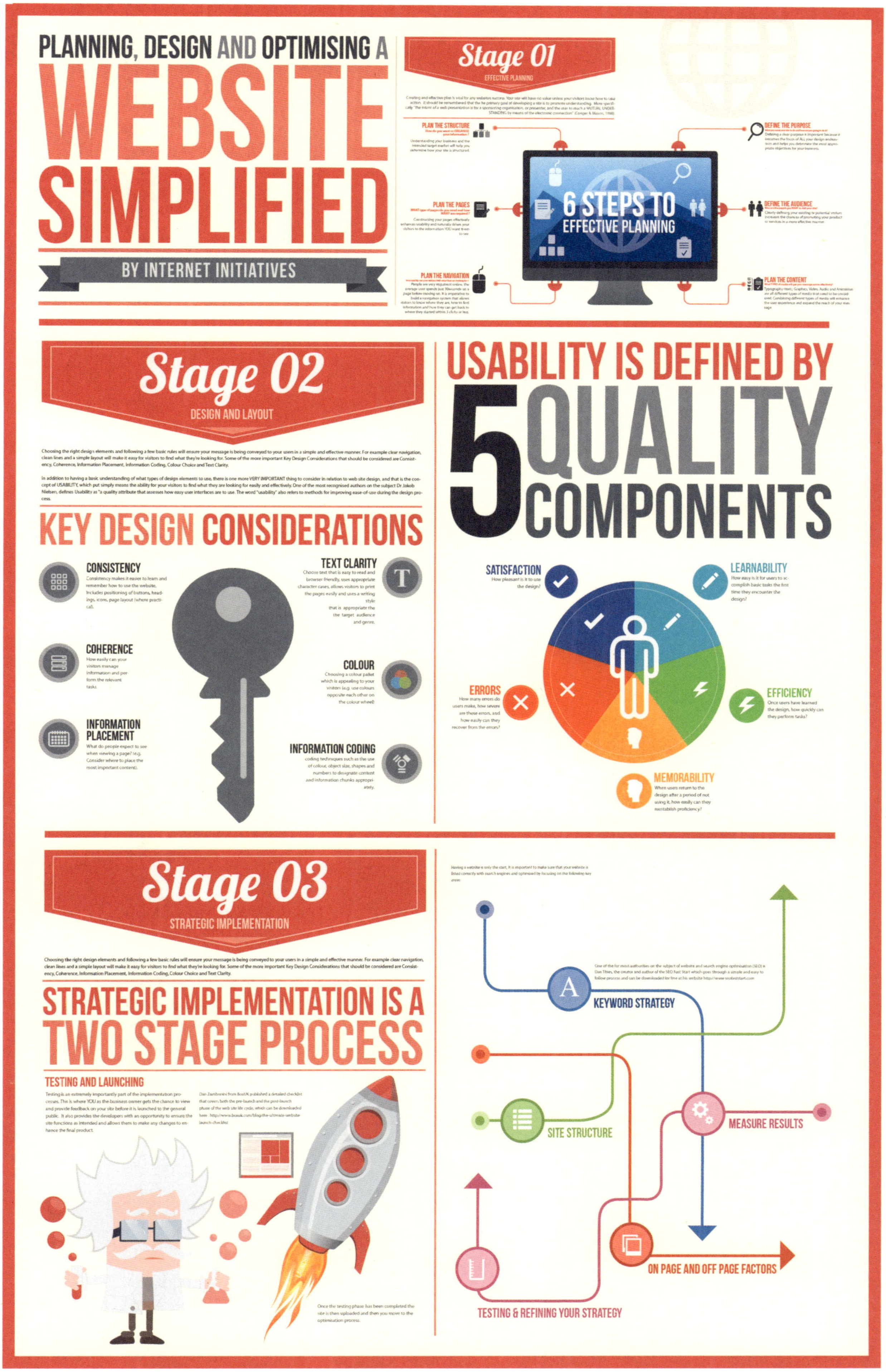
PLANNING, DESIGN AND OPTIMISING A
WEBSITE SIMPLIFIED
BY INTERNET INITIATIVES
Stage 01
EFFECTIVE PLANNING
Creating and effective plan is vital for any websites success. Your site will have no value unless your visitors know how to take action. It should be remembered that the he primary goal of developing a site is to promote understanding. More specifically "the intent of a web presentation is for a sponsoring organisation, or presenter, and the user to reach a MUTUAL UNDERSTANDING by means of the electronic connection" (Conger & Mason, 1998).
PLAN THE STRUCTURE
How do you want to ORGANISE your information?
Understanding your business and the intended target market will help you determine how your site is structured.
PLAN THE PAGES
Constructing your pages effectively enhances usability and naturally drives your visitors to the information YOU want them to see.
PLAN THE NAVIGATION
People are very impatient online, the average user spends just 30seconds on a page before moving on. It is imperative to build a navigation system that allows visitors to know where they are, how to find information and how they can get back to where they started within 3 clicks or less.
6 STEPS TO
EFFECTIVE PLANNING
DEFINE THE PURPOSE
Defining a clear purpose is important because it becomes the focus of ALL your design endeavours and helps you determine the most appropriate objectives for your business.
DEFINE THE AUDIENCE
Clearly defining your existing or potential visitors increases the chances of promoting your product or services in a more effective manner.
PLAN THE CONTENT
Typography (text), Graphics, Video, Audio and Animation are all different types of media that need to be considered. Combining different types of media will enhance the user experience and expand the reach of your message.
Stage 02
DESIGN AND LAYOUT
Choosing the right design elements and following a few basic rules will ensure your message is being conveyed to your users in a simple and effective manner. For example clear navigation, clean lines and a simple layout will make it easy for visitors to find what they're looking for. Some of the more important Key Design Considerations that should be considered are Consistency, Coherence, Information Placement, Information Coding, Colour Choice and Text Clarity.
In addition to having a basic understanding of what types of design elements to use, there is one more VERY IMPORTANT thing to consider in relation to web site design, and that is the concept of USABILITY, which put simply means the ability for your visitors to find what they are looking for easily and effectively. One of the most recognised authors on the subject Dr Jakob Nielsen, defines Usability as "a quality attribute that assesses how easy user interfaces are to use. The word "usability" also refers to methods for improving ease-of-use during the design process.
KEY DESIGN CONSIDERATIONS
CONSISTENCY
Consistency makes it easier to learn and remember how to use the website. Includes positioning of buttons, headings, icons, page layout (where practical).
COHERENCE
How easily can your visitors manage information and perform the relevant tasks.
INFORMATION PLACEMENT
What do people expect to see when viewing a page? (e.g. Consider where to place the most important content).
TEXT CLARITY
Choose text that is easy to read and browser friendly, uses appropriate character cases, allows visitors to print the pages easily and uses a writing style that is appropriate the the target audience and genre.
COLOUR
Choosing a colour pallet which is appealing to your visitors (e.g. use colours opposite each other on the colour wheel)
INFORMATION CODING
coding techniques such as the use of colour, object size, shapes and numbers to designate content and information chunks appropriately.
USABILITY IS DEFINED BY
5 QUALITY COMPONENTS
SATISFACTION
How pleasant is it to use the design?
LEARNABILITY
How easy is it for users to accomplish basic tasks the first time they encounter the design?
ERRORS
How many errors do users make, how severe are these errors, and how easily can they recover from the errors?
EFFICIENCY
Once users have learned the design, how quickly can they perform tasks?
MEMORABILITY
When users return to the design after a period of not using it, how easily can they reestablish proficiency?
Stage 03
STRATEGIC IMPLEMENTATION
Choosing the right design elements and following a few basic rules will ensure your message is being conveyed to your users in a simple and effective manner. For example clear navigation, clean lines and a simple layout will make it easy for visitors to find what they're looking for. Some of the more important Key Design Considerations that should be considered are Consistency, Coherence, Information Placement, Information Coding, Colour Choice and Text Clarity.
STRATEGIC IMPLEMENTATION IS A TWO STAGE PROCESS
TESTING AND LAUNCHING
Testing is an extremely importantly part of the implementation processes. This is where YOU as the business owner gets the chance to view and provide feedback on your site before it is launched to the general public. It also provides the developers with an opportunity to ensure the site functions as intended and allows them to make any changes to enhance the final product.
Dan Zambonini from BoxUK published a detailed checklist that covers both the pre-launch and the post-launch phase of the web site life cycle, which can be downloaded here : http://www.boxuk.com/blog/the-ultimate-website-launch-checklist
Once the testing phase has been completed the site is then uploaded and then you move to the optimisation process.
Having a website is only the start, It is important to make sure that your website is listed correctly with search engines and optimised by focusing on the following key areas
One of the for most authorities on the subject of website and search engine optimisation (SEO) is Dan Thies, the creator and author of the SEO Fast Start which goes through a simple and easy to follow process and can be downloaded for free at his website http://www.seofaststart.com
KEYWORD STRATEGY
SITE STRUCTURE
MEASURE RESULTS
ON PAGE AND OFF PAGE FACTORS
TESTING & REFINING YOUR STRATEGY

Low by Flo Rida

- Completion Year: 2014
- Designer: Yofany Susanto

• Work Introduction

This infographic's data is based on the basses and synthesizers found in the song. The infographic is created with gold scheme colors in circle to represent the iconic gold chain of hip-hop street style and Flo Rida's obsession with gold necklace. The gold colour itself represent gold necklace but in more elegant way to show it -as gold necklace often stereotyped as a low-class style for the street performer. Purpose of using gold nails and needles is to enhance the tough life of a black street performer in society that often looks down on them as results of stereotype.

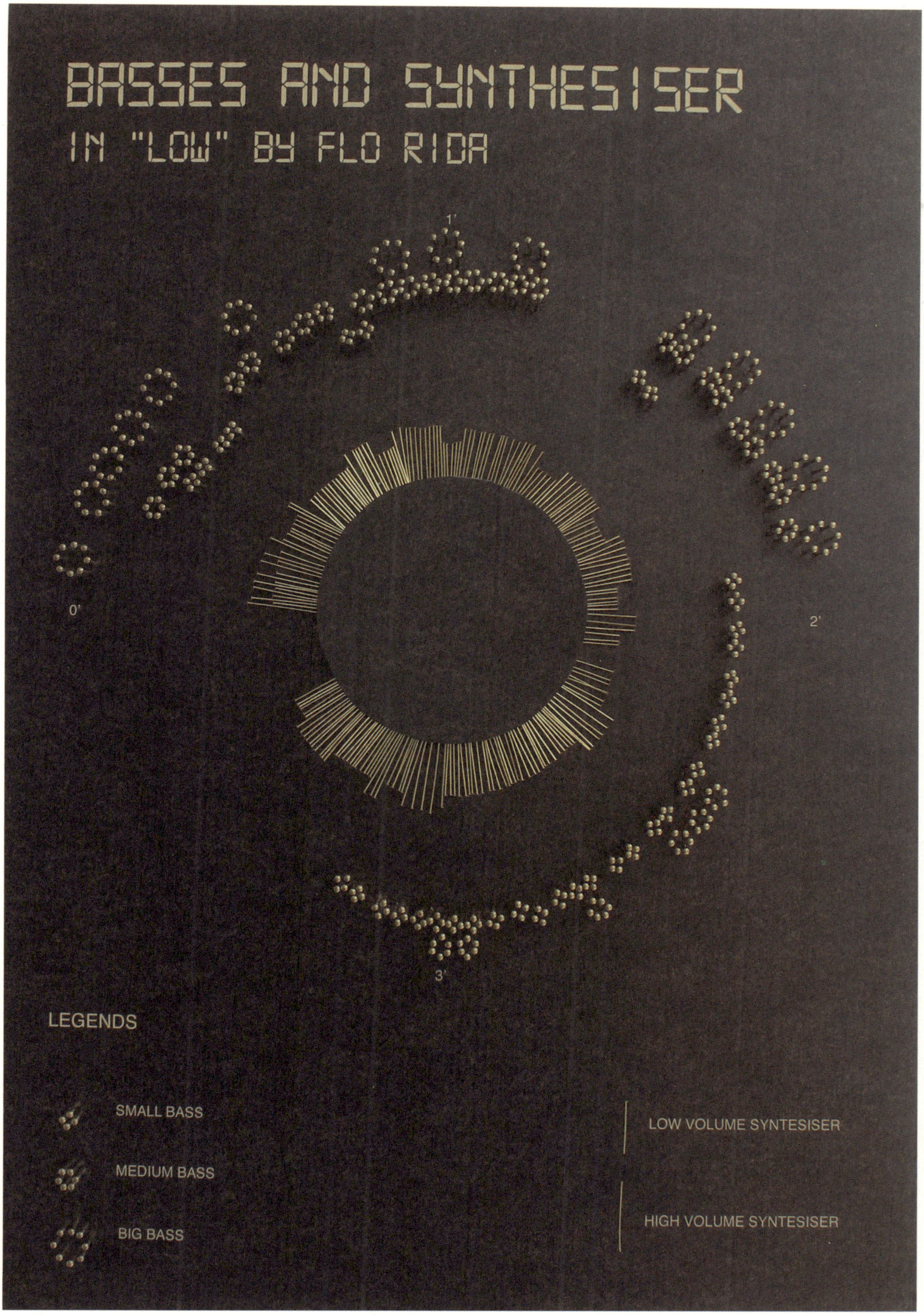
BASSES AND SYNTHESISER
IN "LOW" BY FLO RIDA
1'
0'
2'
3'
LEGENDS
SMALL BASS
MEDIUM BASS
BIG BASS
LOW VOLUME SYNTESISER
HIGH VOLUME SYNTESISER

Statistic Information About the Results of Checks on the Building Sites

- Completion Year: 2014
- Designer: Toma Gogolazde
- Client: stroi.mos.ru

• Work Introduction

This information graphic analyses the results of the amount of checks of the construction sites. It shows the recorded damages and the sums of the fine for the last 9 months of 2014. Designer decided to illustrate this information with the help of a round diagram. Each scale matches the certain stage of verification and a detailed explanation of each kind of mistake and the sums of the fines.

За нарушения на стройках Мосгосстройнадзор оштрафовал застройщиков **более чем на 360 млн руб.**

Итоги проверок

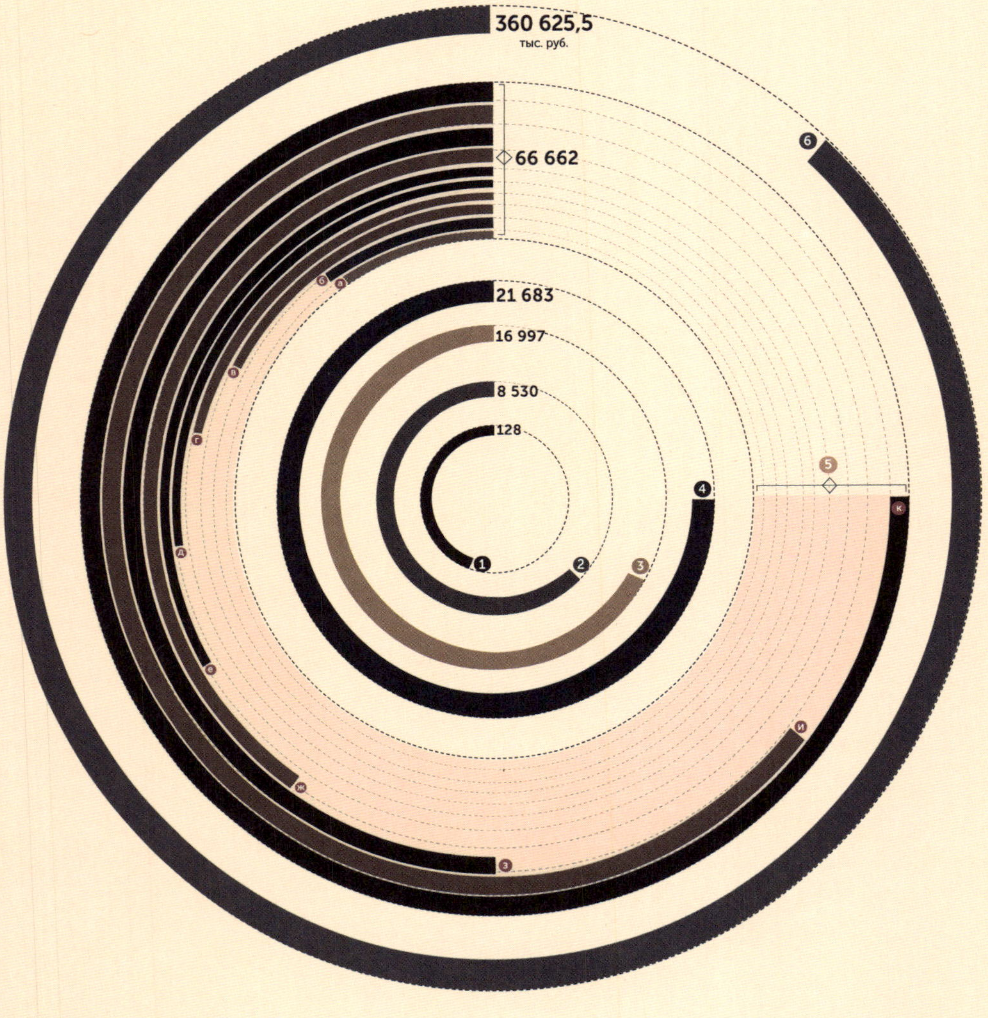

1. направлено обращений в СРО
2. проведено проверок
3. проведено обследований
4. выдано предписаний
5. выявлено нарушений, из них:*
6. сумма наложенных штрафов (тыс. руб.)

*

- а — ведение работ без разрешения на строительство (реконструкцию) и эксплуатация объекта без разрешения на ввод объекта в эксплуатацию 306
- б — нарушение порядка осуществления работ в соответствии с обязательными требованиями 495
- в — нарушение требований охраны окружающей среды 1 311
- г — нарушение санитарно-эпидемиологических требований 1 845
- д — нарушение порядка осуществления строительного контроля 3 570
- е — нарушение требований пожарной безопасности 4 917
- ж — отсутствие исполнительной, проектной, рабочей документации 5 024
- з — отступлений от проектных решений 7 545
- и — по содержанию строительных площадок 17 105
- к — по качеству строительных работ 24 544

Cost of Having a Baby in the Philippines

- Completion Year: 2014
- Design Agency: Alien Werewolf
- Designer: Alexis Angulo and Ruth Madrid
- Client: Moneymonkeys.net

- Work Introduction

The designers split the poster into showing the expenses before and after the baby is born, thus the split baby came into the design. Splitting the poster also made the work allocation easier for the designers.

9 Small Things More Expensive than Health Insurance

- Completion Year: 2014
- Designer: Alexis Angulo
- Client: moneymonkeys.net

- Work Introduction

The designer utilized a simple layout for the list, enabling her to highlight each item, enhanced with flat icon graphics.

CLUBBING/
DRINKING
₱ TWICE THE REGULAR PRICE
*Additional entrance fees
PARKING FEE
₱ 20-40/3 hrs.
*Depends on establishment
TAXI FARE
₱ 200/average per day
VS.
Public Transportation
₱ 8.50-25 +

PARKING FEE
₱ 20-40/3 hrs.
*Depends on establishment
TAXI FARE
₱ 200/average per day
VS.
Public Transportation
₱ 8.50-25 +
POSTPAID PLANS
₱ VARIES ON CONSUMER'S USAGE
*Some plans have hidden charges
MALL TRIPS
₱ VARIES ON SHOPS VISITED
*Simple window-shopping may get out of hand
EXPENSIVE CLOTHES
VS.
₱ 1000 +
*Varies in every brand
MONEY MONKEYS
The Basic Bananas of Financial Planning
www.moneymonkeys.net
SOURCE:

How to Build Portfolio of Mutual Funds

- Completion Year: 2014
- Designer: Alexis Angulo
- Client: Moneymonkeys.net

- Work Introduction

In this infographic, the designer used the comparison of building a home as thc visual representation of building a person's portfolio of mutual funds.

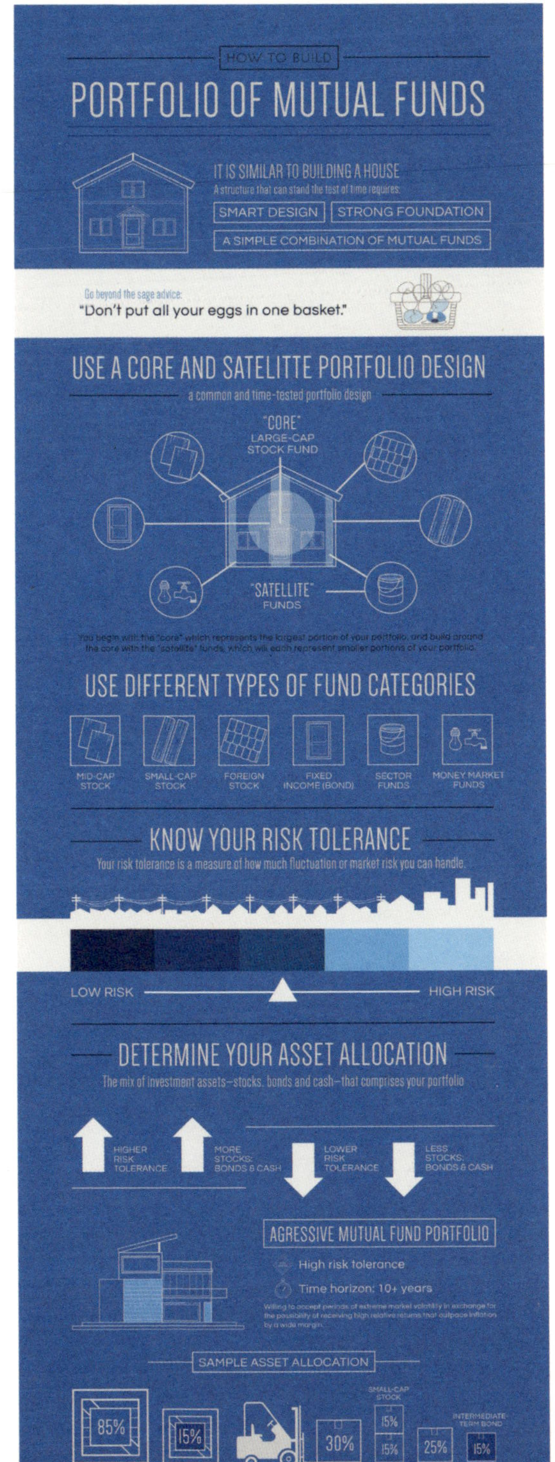

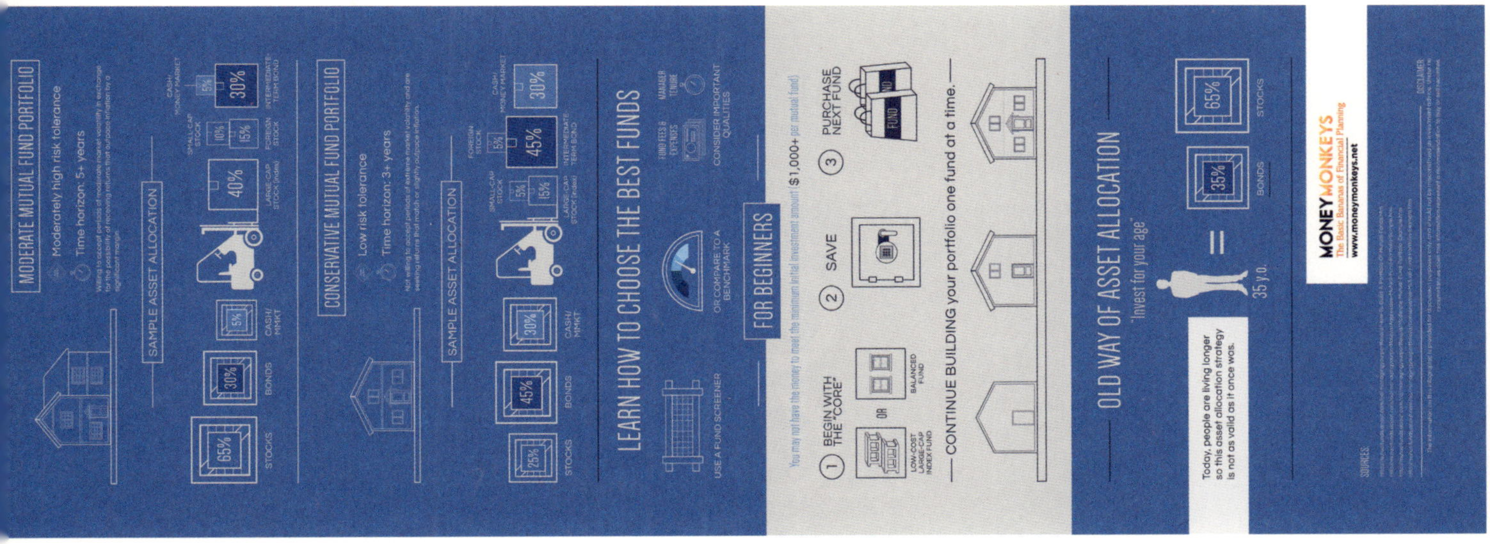
DETERMINE YOUR ASSET ALLOCATION
The mix of investment assets—stocks, bonds and cash—that comprises your portfolio
MODERATE MUTUAL FUND PORTFOLIO
Moderately high risk tolerance
Time horizon: 5+ years
SAMPLE ASSET ALLOCATION
65%
STOCKS
30%
BONDS
5%
CASH/MMKT
40%
LARGE-CAP STOCK (index)
10%
15%
30%
CONSERVATIVE MUTUAL FUND PORTFOLIO
Low risk tolerance
Time horizon: 3+ years
SAMPLE ASSET ALLOCATION
25%
STOCKS
45%
BONDS
30%
CASH/MMKT
5%
15%
45%
30%
LEARN HOW TO CHOOSE THE BEST FUNDS
USE A FUND SCREENER
OR COMPARE TO A BENCHMARK
FUND FEES & EXPENSES
MANAGER TENURE
CONSIDER IMPORTANT QUALITIES
FOR BEGINNERS
$1,000+
1 BEGIN WITH THE "CORE"
LOW-COST LARGE-CAP INDEX FUND
OR
BALANCED FUND
2 SAVE
3 PURCHASE NEXT FUND
FUND
— CONTINUE BUILDING your portfolio one fund at a time. —
OLD WAY OF ASSET ALLOCATION
"Invest for your age"
35 y.o.
=
35%
BONDS
65%
STOCKS
Today, people are living longer so this asset allocation strategy is not as valid as it once was.
MONEY MONKEYS
www.moneymonkeys.net
SOURCES
DISCLAIMER
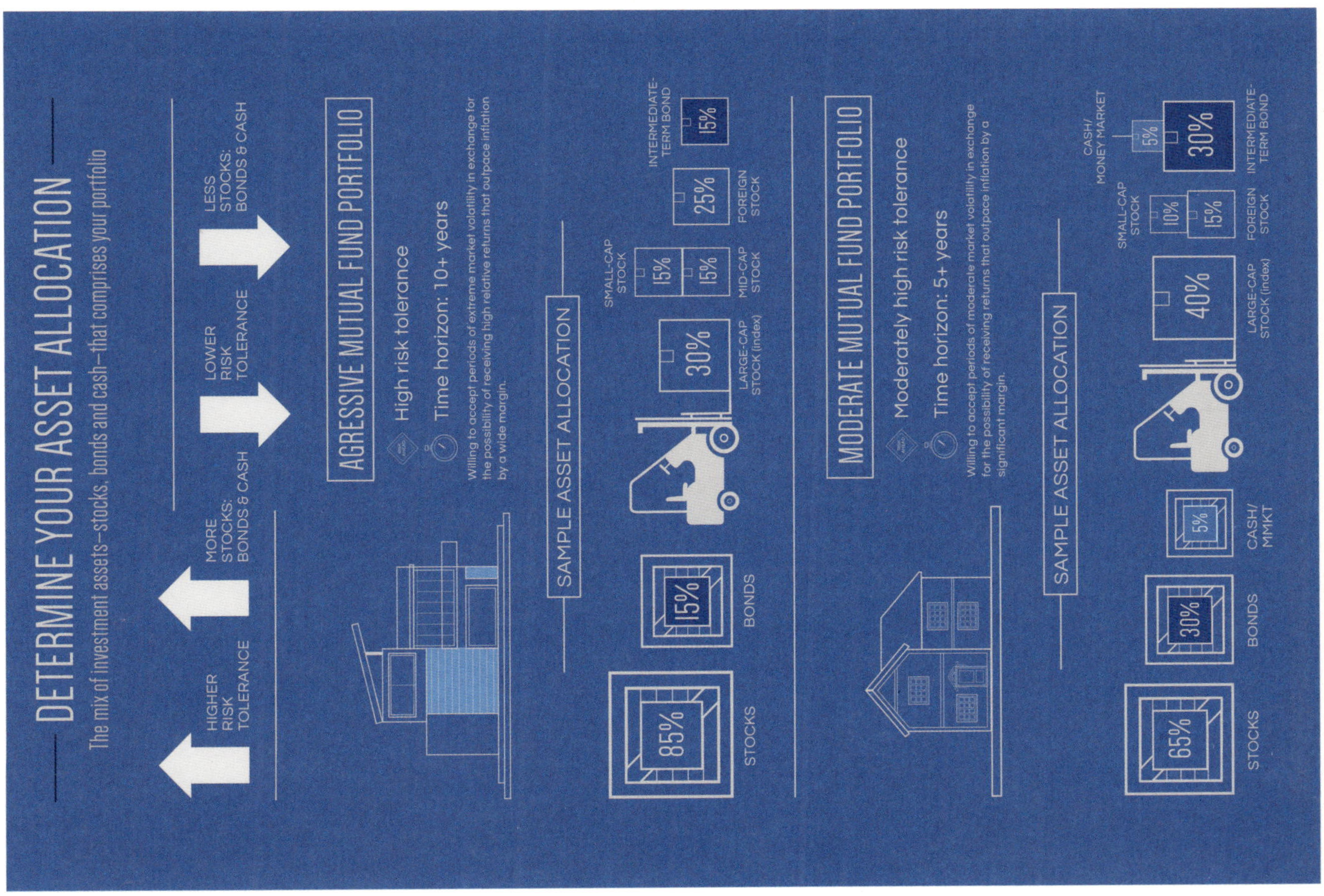
DETERMINE YOUR ASSET ALLOCATION
The mix of investment assets—stocks, bonds and cash—that comprises your portfolio
HIGHER RISK TOLERANCE
MORE STOCKS: BONDS & CASH
LOWER RISK TOLERANCE
LESS STOCKS: BONDS & CASH
AGRESSIVE MUTUAL FUND PORTFOLIO
High risk tolerance
Time horizon: 10+ years
Willing to accept periods of extreme market volatility in exchange for the possibility of receiving high relative returns that outpace inflation by a wide margin.
SAMPLE ASSET ALLOCATION
85%
STOCKS
15%
BONDS
30%
LARGE-CAP STOCK (index)
SMALL-CAP STOCK
15%
15%
MID-CAP STOCK
25%
FOREIGN STOCK
INTERMEDIATE-TERM BOND
15%
MODERATE MUTUAL FUND PORTFOLIO
Moderately high risk tolerance
Time horizon: 5+ years
Willing to accept periods of moderate market volatility in exchange for the possibility of receiving returns that outpace inflation by a significant margin.
SAMPLE ASSET ALLOCATION
65%
STOCKS
30%
BONDS
5%
CASH/ MMKT
40%
LARGE-CAP STOCK (index)
SMALL-CAP STOCK
10%
15%
FOREIGN STOCK
CASH/ MONEY MARKET
5%
30%
INTERMEDIATE-TERM BOND

Studio Culture

- Completion Year: 2013
- Designer: Shonali Ahooja

- Work Introduction

A visual representation of diverse and quirky studio practices and studio culture. The graphs created are based on data collected trom five different design studios.

(The Green Ivy Plant In A Bright Yellow Pot With A White Background was manufactured by Evermotion.)

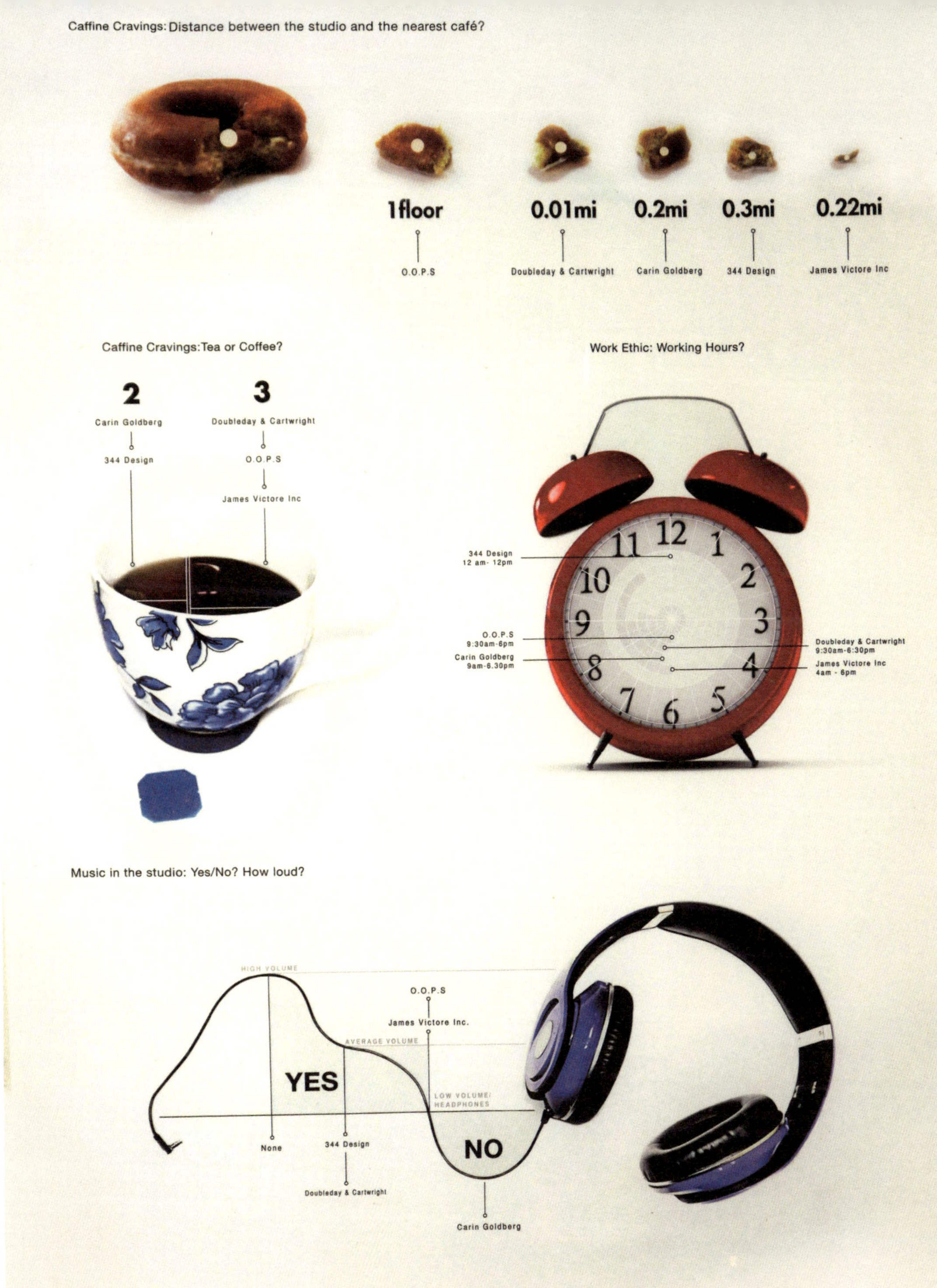
Caffine Cravings: Distance between the studio and the nearest café?
1floor
O.O.P.S
0.01mi
Doubleday & Cartwright
0.2mi
Carin Goldberg
0.3mi
344 Design
0.22mi
James Victore Inc
Caffine Cravings: Tea or Coffee?
2
Carin Goldberg
344 Design
3
Doubleday & Cartwright
O.O.P.S
James Victore Inc
Work Ethic: Working Hours?
344 Design
12 am- 12pm
O.O.P.S
9:30am-6pm
Carin Goldberg
9am-6.30pm
Doubleday & Cartwright
9:30am-6:30pm
James Victore Inc
4am - 6pm
Music in the studio: Yes/No? How loud?
HIGH VOLUME
AVERAGE VOLUME
LOW VOLUME/
HEADPHONES
YES
NO
None
344 Design
Doubleday & Cartwright
O.O.P.S
James Victore Inc.
Carin Goldberg

Tuesday Social #19: Social Video & Brand Engagement

- Completion Year: 2014
- Designer: Jo Lavie
- Client: IMAS

- Work Introduction

This is according to the lovelies at video content creation company Contented, who have collated these and many other interesting factoids in this infographic about social video and how this impacts brand engagement.

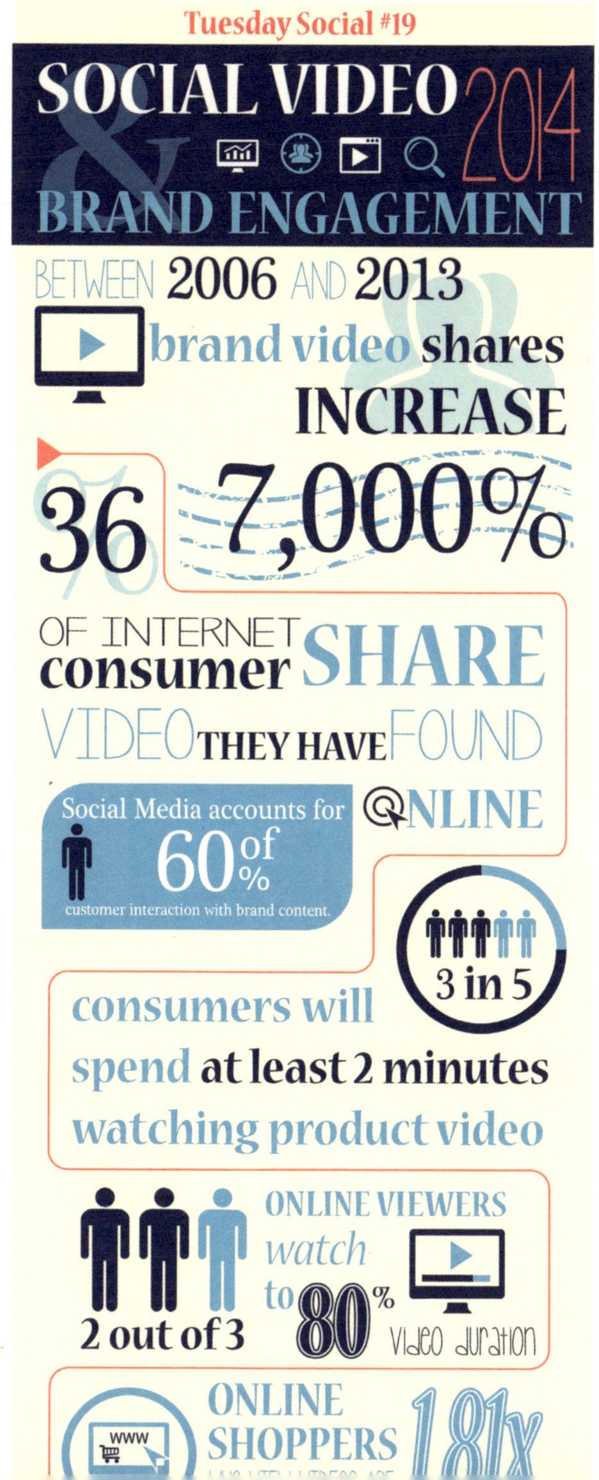

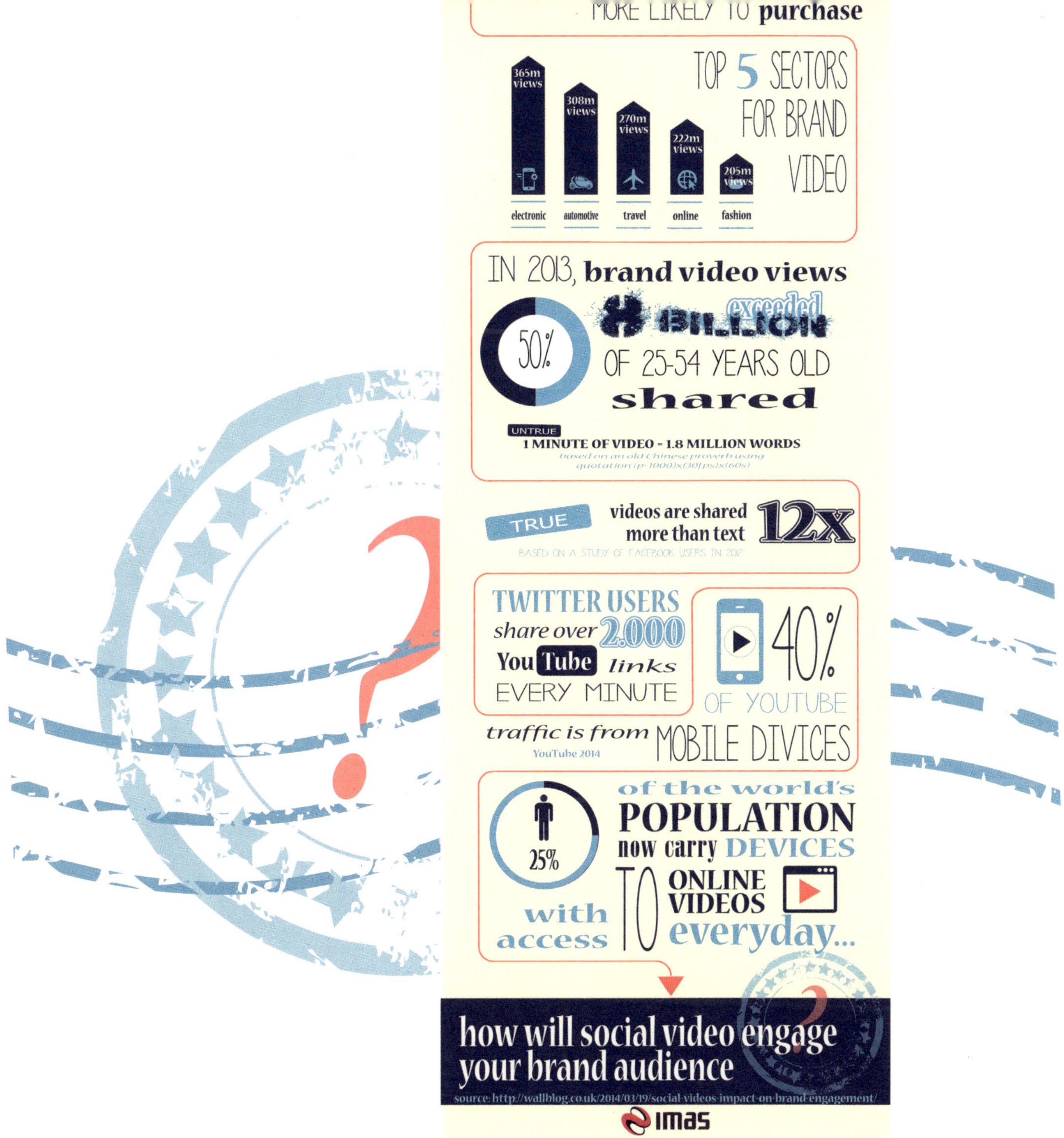
MORE LIKELY TO purchase
TOP 5 SECTORS FOR BRAND VIDEO
365m views
308m views
270m views
222m views
205m views
electronic
automotive
travel
online
fashion
IN 2013, brand video views
exceeded
50%
OF 25-54 YEARS OLD
shared
UNTRUE
1 MINUTE OF VIDEO - 1.8 MILLION WORDS
TRUE
videos are shared more than text
12x
BASED ON A STUDY OF FACEBOOK USERS IN 2012
TWITTER USERS
share over 2,000
YouTube links
EVERY MINUTE
40%
OF YOUTUBE
traffic is from MOBILE DIVICES
YouTube 2014
25%
of the world's
POPULATION
now carry DEVICES
with access
TO
ONLINE VIDEOS
everyday...
how will social video engage your brand audience
source: http://wallblog.co.uk/2014/03/19/social-videos-impact-on-brand-engagement/
imas

The Numbers of Estra

- Completion Year: 2014
- Designerr: Sergio Piergallini
- Client: Estra Spa

- Work Introduction

The customer needed to produce a vertical infographic that synthesizes all the numerical results of the company.

LE NOSTRE ATTIVITÀ
ENERGIA
Approvvigionamento, vendita e distribuzione gas energia elettrica e gpl.
IMPIANTI E SERVIZI ENERGETICI
Riqualificazione e gestione di impianti energetici e global service
TELECOMUNICAZIONI
Connessioni a banda larga in fibra ottica, ADSL, videosorveglianza, sicurezza
ENERGIE RINNOVABILI
Fotovoltaico, eolico, biomasse, idroelettrico

DATI
ECONOMICO
2013
COMMERCIALI
NUMERO CLIENTI
650.000
VOLUME VENDITA GAS IN MC
1.000.000.000
DATI FINANZIARI
2013
RICAVI TOTALI CONSOLIDATI
696 MILIONI €
CAPITALE INVESTITO
416 MILIONI €
PATRIMONIO NETTO
241 MILIONI €
ALTRI BUSINESS
PUNTI DI PRELIEVO ELETTRICITÀ
29.286
VOLUME VENDITA ELETTRICITÀ
576 GWh
FATTURATO VENDITA ELETTRICITÀ
96 MILIONI / €
FATTURATO SISTEMI ENERGETICI INNOVATIVI
5,7 MILIONI €
INTERVENTI DI RIQUALIFICAZIONE
1.500
IMPIANTI TERMICI GESTITI CON IL SERVIZIO ENERGIA
350
FATTURATO TELECOMUNICAZIONI
4,5 MILIONI €
CHILOMETRI DI INFRASTUTTURE
250
CHILOMETRI DI FIBRA OTTICA
18 MILA
WWW.ESTRASPA.IT

Chorizo Especial // Special Chorizo

- Completion Year: 2014
- Designer: Ayelén Vidal

- Work Introduction

The designer wanted to focus on the inappropriate bromatological conditions of the process of production and distribution of the chorizo. So the estructure of the poster is given by the representation of this process. Dispite the graphic system reinforce this idea, it also tries to be as simple as possible in the codification of the information, making a very careful use of the color.

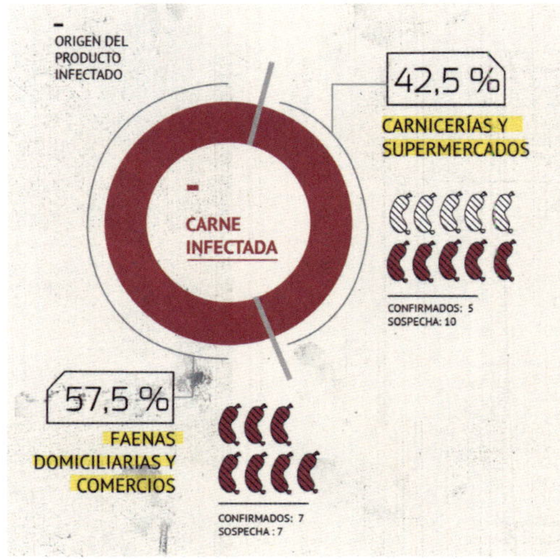

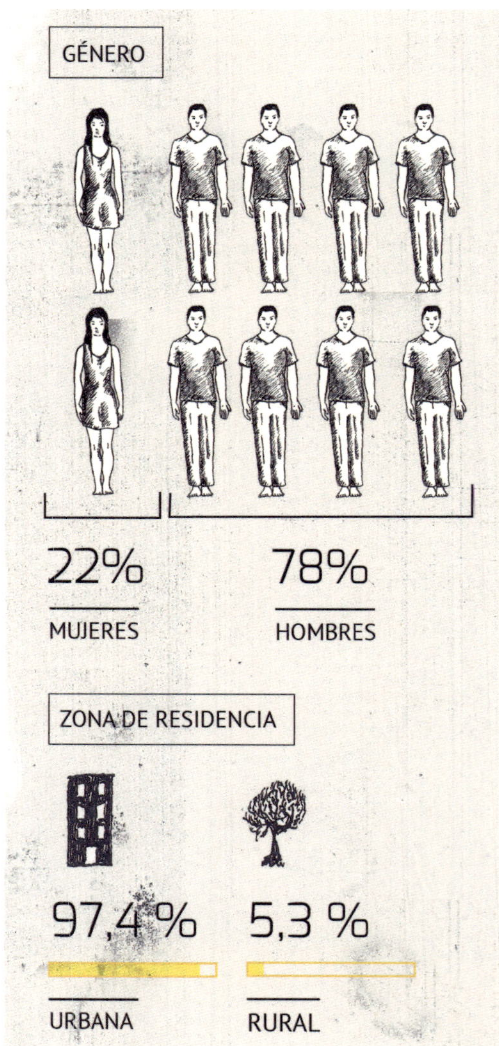

TRIQUINOSIS

ESTA PARASITOSIS REPRESENTA UN IMPORTANTE PROBLEMA DE SALUD PÚBLICA EN EL PAÍS. SE REGISTRAN ANUALMENTE AL MENOS 10 BROTES ENDÉMICOS.

El presente estudio tuvo como objetivo determinar la presencia de triquinosis humana en un área considerada históricamente libre de esta parasitosis en la Argentina. Los estudios realizados demuestran la existencia de triquinosis humana en un área considerada libre de esta parasitosis y sugieren su relación con la ingesta de carne porcina y/o sus subproductos, hábito alimenticio de riesgo. Estos resultados indican que la falta de denuncia de casos de la enfermedad no debe ser el único criterio a tener en cuenta para considerar a una región área libre de triquinosis. El conocimiento de la presencia del parásito en un área determinada favorece la instauración de medidas de control y prevención evitando la diseminación de la parasitosis.

Debe tenerse en cuenta que actualmente en el país se realizan campañas tendientes a promocionar la incorporación de carnes porcinas en la dieta habitual de la población. Para evitar la diseminación de la triquinosis, estas campañas deben ser realizadas teniendo en cuenta la real situación epidemiológica del país, formando personal específicamente capacitado para detectar la parasitosis y ser acompañadas de programas de control de inocuidad de las carnes.

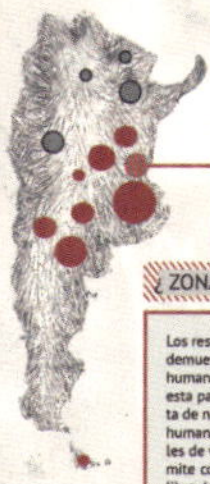

¿ ZONA LIBRE ?

Los resultados obtenidos en este estudio demuestran la existencia de triquinosis humana en un área considerada libre de esta parasitosis y demuestran que la falta de notificación de casos de triquinosis humana y porcina, en ausencia de controles de vigilancia epidemiológica, no permite considerar a una región como área libre de la infección parasitaria.

ZONAS ENDÉMICAS	ZONAS LIBRES
Tierra del Fuego	Chaco
Buenos Aires	Formosa
Santa Fe	Salta
Córdoba	San Juan
San Luis	Entre Ríos
La Pampa	
Río Negro	
Neuquén	
Santa Cruz	

CONSUMO

CARNICERÍA	SUPERMERCADO	FAENA
80,3 %	34 %	38,1 %

Los productos porcinos más incorporados a la alimentación habitual de los individuos fueron los chacinados

94,7 % CHORIZO PARRILLERO

83,3 % SALAMINES

DESCONTROL BROMATOLÓGICO

PREVENCIÓN

CORRECTA COCCIÓN — 70° en el centro por 1'

CORRECTO CONGELADO — -15° por 30 días

CONTROL BROMATOLÓGICO — Técnica de digestión artificial

Si bien se considera que la ingesta de carne de cerdo y/o sus derivados proveniente de faenas domiciliarias representa un importante factor de riesgo en el país en el área estudiada el riesgo de contraer la parasitosis fue independiente del origen del producto consumido, ya que los porcentajes de los productos sólo en comercios como en los que compraban tanto en comercios como en granjas. Esta observación sugiere que el control sanitario de las carnes no es el adecuado, hecho estrechamente relacionado con la falta de información sobre la presencia de esta parasitosis en el área

Siempre hay que saber el origen cuando se compra. Hay que hacerlo en lugares habilitados y conociendo que estén en condiciones. Es imposible que se den casos de esta manera. El contagio suele ocurrir cuando la gente compra en la ruta y sigue de largo, o cuando comerciantes adquieren los productos de una persona que por ahí los tiene más barato para poder sacarle ganancia sin pedir los controles aprobados. Hay que tomar conciencia desde la sociedad y el comercio. Los controles bromatológicos y de salud son muy importantes. Si se da un caso hay una cadena de responsables por desidia o ignorancia.

ORIGEN DEL PRODUCTO INFECTADO — CARNE INFECTADA

42,5 % CARNICERÍAS Y SUPERMERCADOS — CONFIRMADOS: 5, SOSPECHA: 10

57,5 % FAENAS DOMICILIARIAS Y COMERCIOS — CONFIRMADOS: 7, SOSPECHA: 7

FALTA INFORMACIÓN

FALTAN CONTROLES SANITARIOS

FALTAN MEDIDAS DE PREVENCIÓN

CHORIZO ESPECIAL

LA INGESTA DE CARNE PORCINA PARASITADA AFECTÓ EN LOS ÚLTIMOS 5 AÑOS A MÁS DE 2700 INDIVIDUOS

DIAGNÓSTICO: CONFIRMADO / SOSPECHA

8,0 % INFECTADO

EL CUADRO CLÍNICO EN EL SER HUMANO PUEDE IR DESDE UNA INFECCIÓN ASINTOMÁTICA HASTA UNA ENFERMEDAD FULMINANTE Y MORTAL.

Es muy variable, dependiendo del número de larvas ingeridas y del estatus inmunológico del huésped. Lamentablemente se terminan ocasionando problemas mayúsculos porque la triquinosis no se detecta rápido.

Los resultados obtenidos de los estudios inmunoserológicos demuestran nuevamente que el empleo de más de una técnica inmunoserológica permite diagnosticar la infección en un mayor número de individuos. Al emplear una sola metodología se pueden obtener resultados falsos negativos, impidiendo que se realice el diagnóstico de sospecha, que podría ser confirmado analizando otras determinaciones de laboratorio.(enzimas musculares, leucocitosis, IgE, eosinófilos, etc.), los datos clínicos del paciente y la epidemiología.

Síntomas
- Dolores musculares
- Edema de párpados
- Fiebre
- Síntomas abdominales
- Fotofobia

RESULTADOS DE LAS TÉCNICAS INMUNOSEROLÓGICAS

IET: inmunoelectrotransferencia
EIA: enzimoinmunoensáisis
IFI: inmunofluorescencia indirecta

	Individuos	%	
DIAGNÓSTICO NEGATIVO			
IFI, EIA E IET	121	80,7	80,7 % NEGATIVO
IFI	8	5,3	11,3% SOSPECHA
EIA	9	6,0	
DIAGNÓSTICO POSITIVO			
IFI Y EIA	1	0,7	8% CONFIRMADO
IFI E IET	5	3,3	
IFI, EIA E IET	6	4,0	

Las muestras que resultaron positivas por EIA y/o IFI fueron evaluadas por la técnica de IET.

A pesar de haberse incluido en el estudio sólo individuos que consumían productos cárnicos porcinos de producción local, se podría considerar que aquellos que presentaron serología positiva se hubieran infectado en otra región, pero el alto porcentaje de resultados de metodologías inmunoserológicas de diagnóstico positivo, los hábitos de consumo de los pobladores y los recientes resultados hallados por el grupo confirman la presencia de la parasitosis porcina.

Cuando se llega a un infectado se sabe que hay muchos más, incluso probablemente de una misma familia

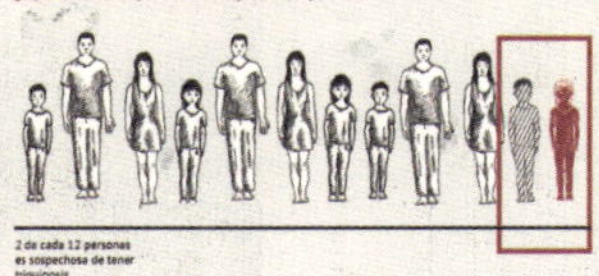

2 de cada 12 personas es sospechosa de tener triquinosis

DONANTES

Se analizaron, por técnicas inmunoserológicas, muestras de sangre de 150 donantes que concurrieron a un banco de sangre local. Las muestras fueron tomadas al azar entre individuos de ambos sexos, residentes de la ciudad y sus alrededores. Los estudios se realizaron con consentimiento escrito de los dadores de sangre para utilizar una alícuota del material biológico y la publicación de los datos. Los estudios se ajustaron a las condiciones establecidas por la Declaración Universal de los Derechos Humanos de 1948, las normas éticas instituidas por el Código de Nüremberg de 1947, la Declaración de Helsinki de 1964 y a lo normado por la Ley Nacional 25.326 de Protección de los Datos de las Personas.

NINGUNO RECORDABA HABER PRESENCIADO SÍNTOMAS DE TRIQUINOSIS DESPUÉS DE CONSUMIR CARNE DE CERDO

RELACIÓN CON EL PRODUCTO

150 DONANTES

98 % CONSUME CARNE DE CERDO

2 % NO CONSUME CARNE DE CERDO (por prácticas religiosas o por mantener una dieta ovolacteovegetariana)

11,3 % COMERCIANTES O ELABORADORES DE CHANCINADOS

GÉNERO

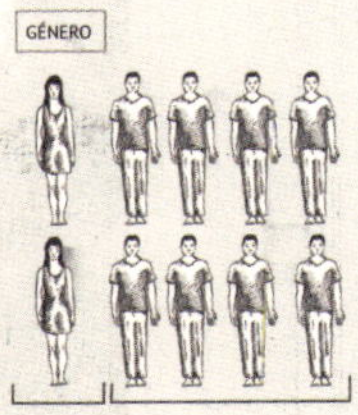

22% MUJERES — 78% HOMBRES

ZONA DE RESIDENCIA

97,4 % URBANA — 5,3 % RURAL

CRIADEROS BASURALES

INGIERE CARNE PARASITADA DE LOS ROEDORES, SUS DESECHOS Y DEL CANIBALISMO, COMIENDO OTROS CERDOS INFECTADOS.

CONTAGIO

Ciclo de contagio del parásito Trichinella

El rol de la rata toma importancia en el hábitat doméstico, estando ésta frecuentemente infectada con T. spiralis, manteniendo la infección y actuando como huésped reservorio y vector al transmitirla a los animales domésticos. Es por esto que es fundamental eliminar la presencia de roedores del hábitat donde se realice cría de cerdos.

EL PARÁSITO

La triquinosis o trichinellosis es una zoonosis alimentaria causada por parásitos metazoarios del género Trichinella. La enfermedad afecta tanto a animales silvestres como domésticos y puede ser transmitida al hombre por la ingestión de carne cruda o mal cocida que contenga larvas viables de Trichinella. Diferentes especies de este parásito se encuentran distribuidas por todo el mundo, siendo Trichinella spiralis la especie causante de triquinosis en la Argentina.

ZOONOSIS: Cualquier enfermedad propia de los animales que incidentalmente puede comunicarse a las personas.

INFRACCIONES MÁS FRECUENTES

A la Ley 10510 de Explotaciones Porcinas y al decreto reglamentario 4933:

- Cría de cerdos en basural, quema o deposito de basura, *Art. 5 de la Ley*
- Presencia de roedores y falta de higiene, *Art. 7 de la Ley*
- Falta de cerco que contenga a los animales, *Art. 2 del decreto*

Chemical Composition of the Human Body

- Completion Year: 2014
- Designer: Marcus Marritt

- Work Introduction

A minimal information graphic using block colours and shapes to communicate the chemical composition of the human body, available in digital and art print form. Creatively using Adobe Illustrator.

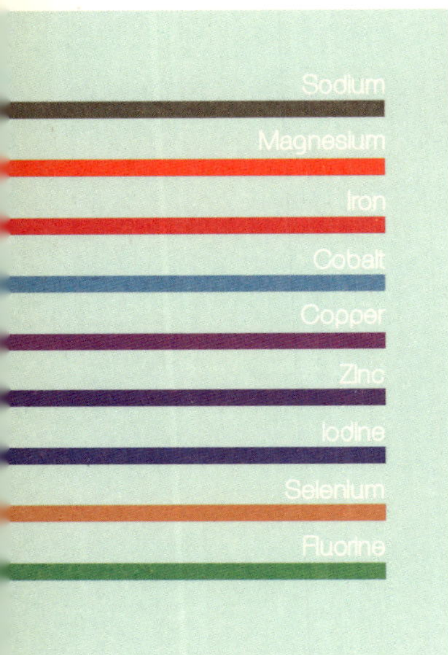

Chemical Composition of the Human Body
Oxygen
Carbon
Hydrogen
Nitrogen
Calcium
Phosphorus
Potassium
Sulfur
Chlorine
Sodium
Magnesium
Iron
Cobalt
Copper
Zinc
Iodine
Selenium
Fluorine

Climate Change: Twenty Years of Discussions

- Completion Year: 2014
- Designer: Martina Elisa Cecchi
- Client: Wired Italia

• Work Introduction

The map shows the debate around climate change, which took place during the ONU conferences, and the different nations' role in the discussion.

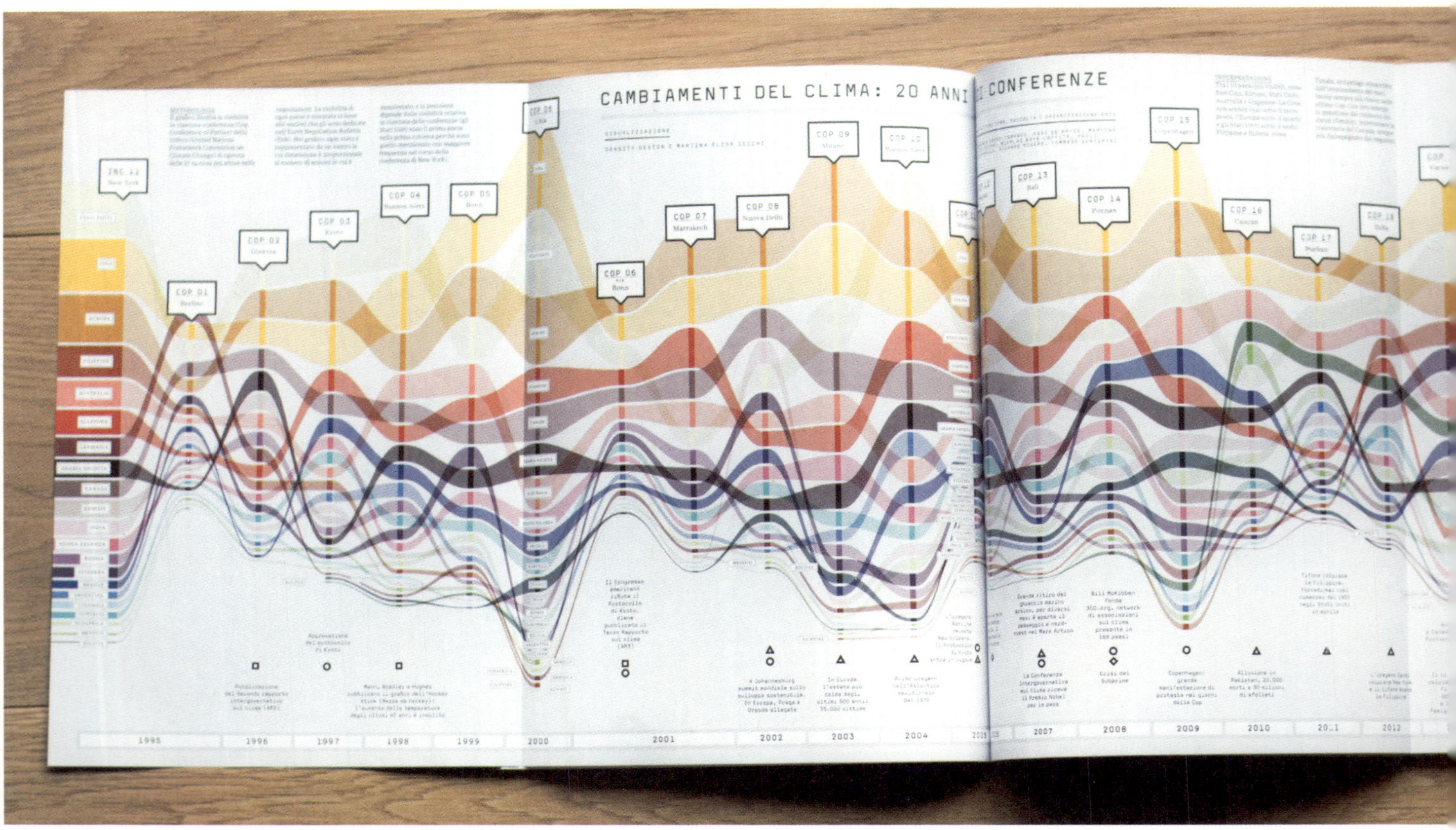

Grande ritiro del ghiaccio marino artico, per diversi mesi è aperto il passaggio a nord-ovest nel Mare Artico
Esce nelle sale Una scomoda verità, il documentario con Al Gore

ADATTAMENTO, DOPO TANTI DISCORSI ARRIVANO I SOLDI

COP 09 Milano
COP 10 Buenos Aires
COP 12 Nairobi
COP 13 Bali

Infographic of Sustainable Fishing

- Completion Year: 2014
- Designer: Mei Cheng Wang

- Work Introduction

An infographic poster highlighting the main points of overfishing and unsustainable catching. The chart is split into four basic tiers of the food chain stacked to demonstrate how much one group feeds another. The poster also doubles as a guide for choosing seafood that doesn't harm the environment.

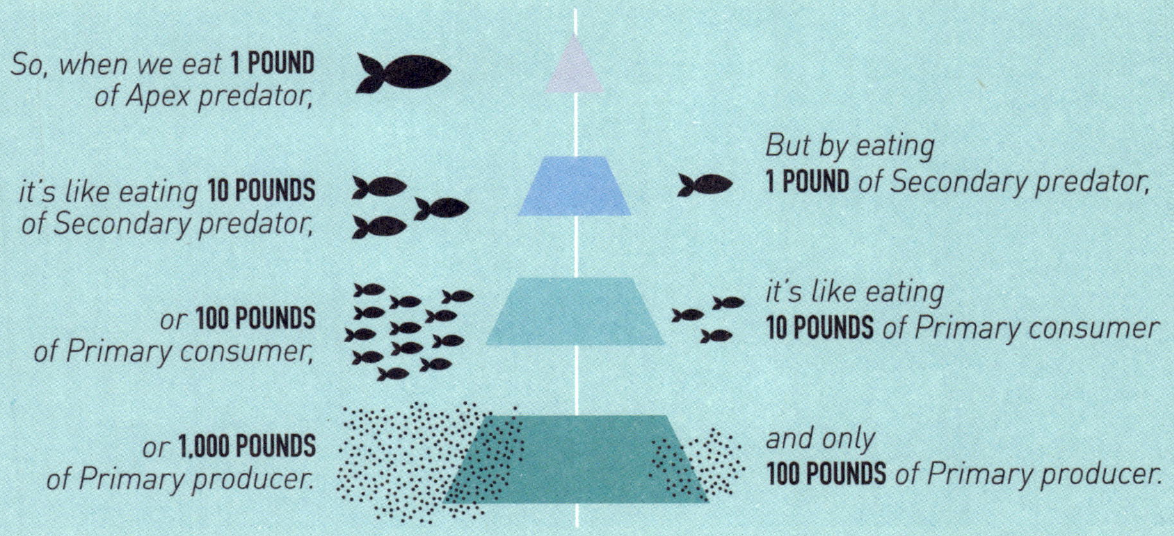

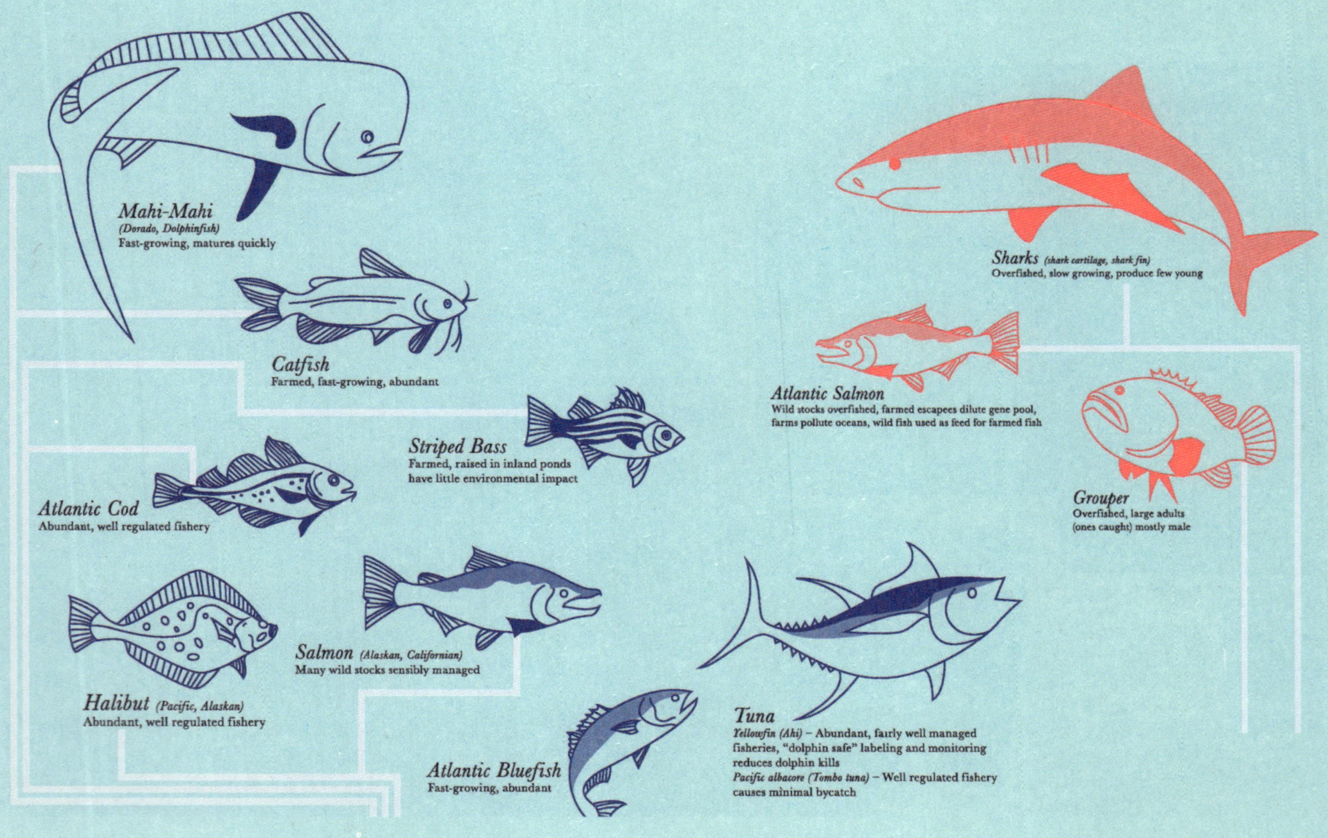

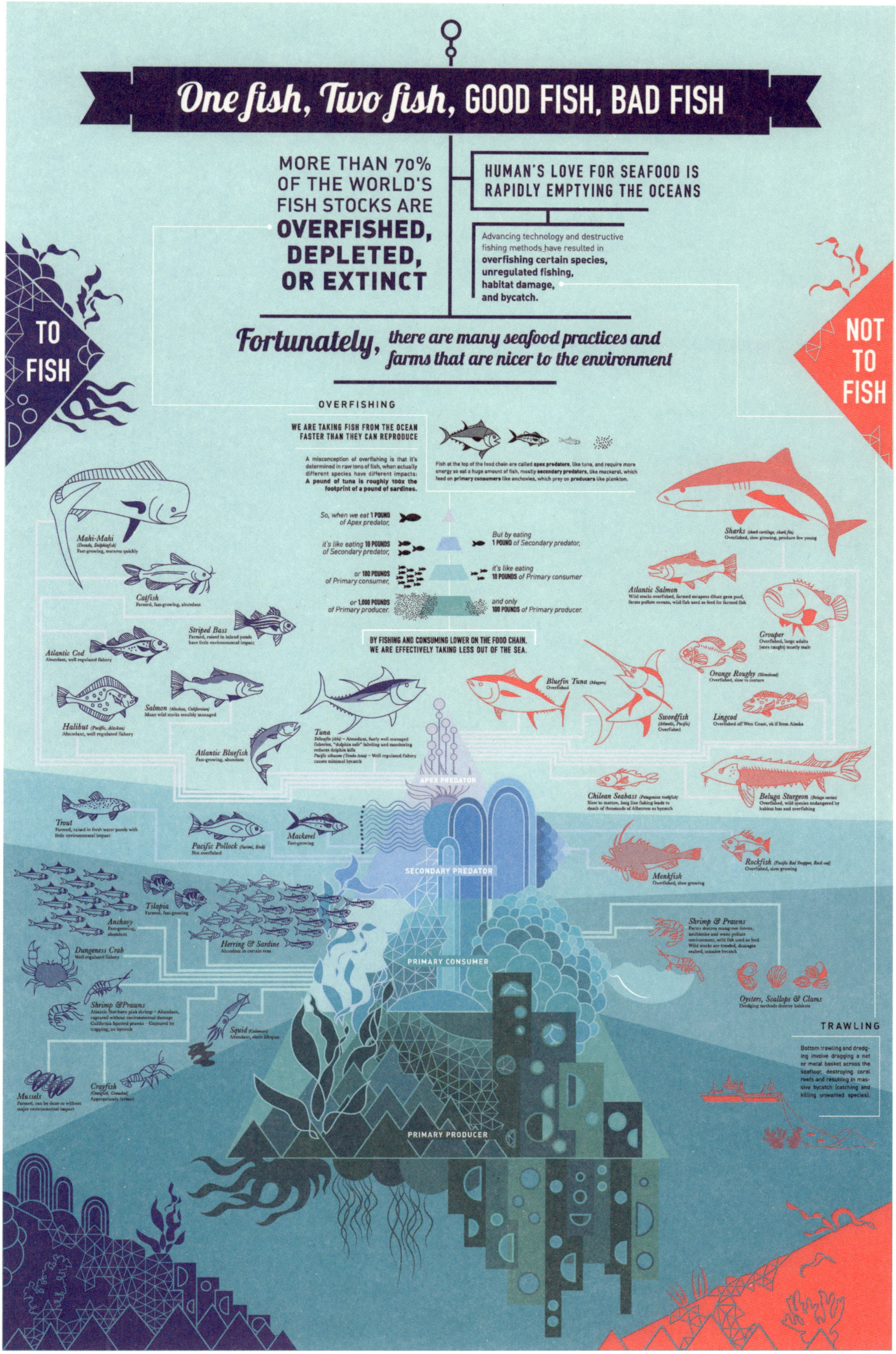

One fish, Two fish, GOOD FISH, BAD FISH
MORE THAN 70% OF THE WORLD'S FISH STOCKS ARE OVERFISHED, DEPLETED, OR EXTINCT
HUMAN'S LOVE FOR SEAFOOD IS RAPIDLY EMPTYING THE OCEANS
Advancing technology and destructive fishing methods have resulted in overfishing certain species, unregulated fishing, habitat damage, and bycatch.
Fortunately, there are many seafood practices and farms that are nicer to the environment
TO FISH
NOT TO FISH
OVERFISHING
WE ARE TAKING FISH FROM THE OCEAN FASTER THAN THEY CAN REPRODUCE
A misconception of overfishing is that it's determined in raw tons of fish, when actually different species have different impacts: A pound of tuna is roughly 100x the footprint of a pound of sardines.
Fish at the top of the food chain are called apex predators, like tuna, and require more energy so eat a huge amount of fish, mostly secondary predators, like mackerel, which feed on primary consumers like anchovies, which prey on producers like plankton.
So, when we eat 1 POUND of Apex predator,
it's like eating 10 POUNDS of Secondary predator,
or 100 POUNDS of Primary consumer,
or 1,000 POUNDS of Primary producer.
But by eating 1 POUND of Secondary predator,
it's like eating 10 POUNDS of Primary consumer
and only 100 POUNDS of Primary producer.
BY FISHING AND CONSUMING LOWER ON THE FOOD CHAIN, WE ARE EFFECTIVELY TAKING LESS OUT OF THE SEA.
Mahi-Mahi (Dorado, Dolphinfish) Fast-growing, matures quickly
Catfish Farmed, fast-growing, abundant
Striped Bass Farmed, raised in inland ponds have little environmental impact
Atlantic Cod Abundant, well regulated fishery
Halibut (Pacific, Alaskan) Abundant, well regulated fishery
Salmon (Alaskan, Californian) Many wild stocks sensibly managed
Tuna Yellowfin (Ahi) – Abundant, fairly well managed fisheries, "dolphin safe" labeling and monitoring reduces dolphin kills
Pacific albacore (Tombo tuna) – Well regulated fishery causes minimal bycatch
Atlantic Bluefish Fast-growing, abundant
Trout Farmed, raised in fresh water ponds with little environmental impact
Pacific Pollock (Surimi, Krab) Not overfished
Mackerel Fast-growing
Tilapia Farmed, fast-growing
Anchovy Fast-growing, abundant
Herring & Sardine Abundant in certain seas
Dungeness Crab Well regulated fishery
Shrimp & Prawns Atlantic Northern pink shrimp – Abundant, captured without environmental damage California Spotted prawns – Captured by trapping, no bycatch
Squid (Calamari) Abundant, short lifespan
Mussels Farmed, can be done so without major environmental impact
Crayfish (Crawfish, Crawdad) Appropriately farmed
Sharks (shark cartilage, shark fin) Overfished, slow growing, produce few young
Atlantic Salmon Wild stocks overfished, farmed escapees dilute gene pool, farms pollute oceans, wild fish used as feed for farmed fish
Grouper Overfished, large adults (ones caught) mostly male
Orange Roughy (Slimehead) Overfished, slow to mature
Bluefin Tuna (Maguro) Overfished
Swordfish (Atlantic, Pacific) Overfished
Lingcod Overfished off West Coast, ok if from Alaska
Chilean Seabass (Patagonian toothfish) Slow to mature, long line fishing leads to death of thousands of Albatross as bycatch
Beluga Sturgeon (Beluga caviar) Overfished, wild species endangered by habitat loss and overfishing
Monkfish Overfished, slow growing
Rockfish (Pacific Red Snapper, Rock cod) Overfished, slow growing
Shrimp & Prawns Farms destroy mangrove forests, antibiotics and waste pollute environment, wild fish used as feed Wild stocks are trawled, damages seabed, massive bycatch
Oysters, Scallops & Clams Dredging methods destroy habitats
TRAWLING
Bottom trawling and dredging involve dragging a net or metal basket across the seafloor, destroying coral reefs and resulting in massive bycatch (catching and killing unwanted species).
APEX PREDATOR
SECONDARY PREDATOR
PRIMARY CONSUMER
PRIMARY PRODUCER

Kerch Strait Bridge Project

- Completion Year: 2014
- Designer: Olesya Tkach

- Work Introduction

The project proposes solutions for crossing the Kerch Strait, where ferries currently provide transportation and a bridge is planned. The designer considers different sections of the strait and options for bridges: the differences in potential designs and their impact on cost of construction and efficiency. This infographic presents the planning scheme of a complex strait bridge with simple and striking illustrations.

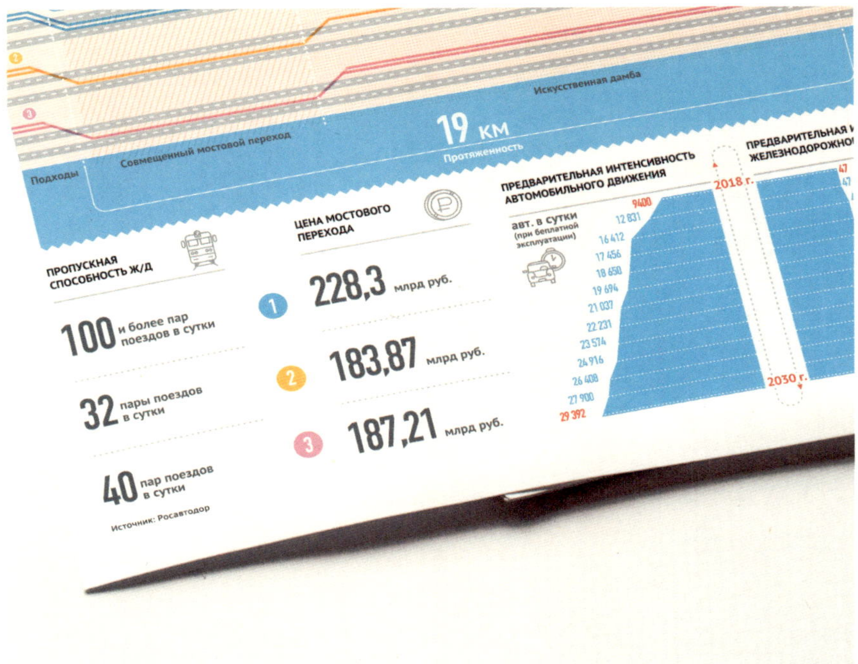

Проект Керченского моста

Тузлинская коса поможет связать полуостров с материком

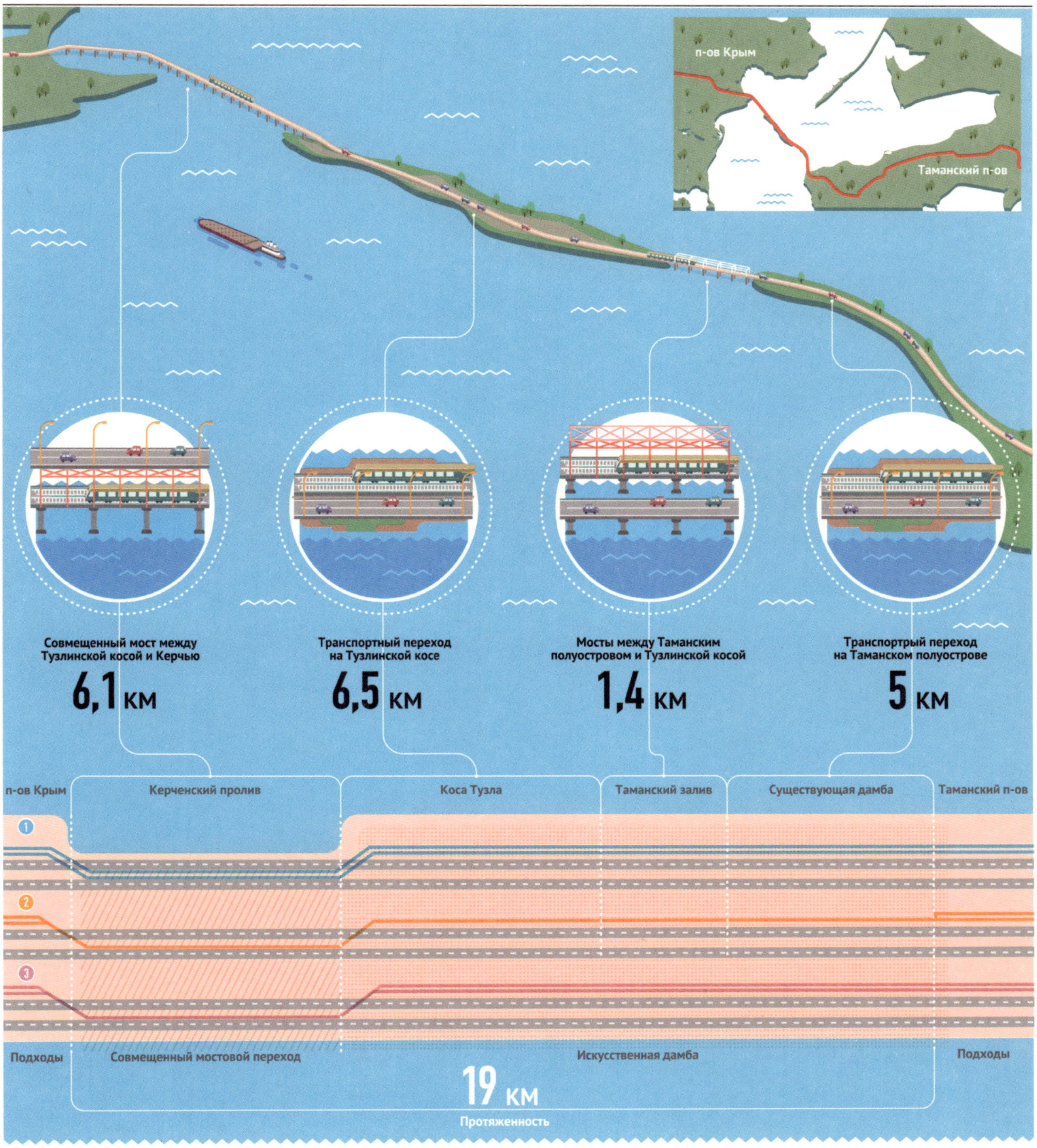

Редактор: Александр Вершинин. Дизайнер: Олеся Ткач. Руководитель: Михаил Симаков. Арт-директор: Антон Степанов

ПРОПУСКНАЯ СПОСОБНОСТЬ Ж/Д

100 и более пар поездов в сутки

32 пары поездов в сутки

40 пар поездов в сутки

ЦЕНА МОСТОВОГО ПЕРЕХОДА

1 **228,3** млрд руб.

2 **183,87** млрд руб.

3 **187,21** млрд руб.

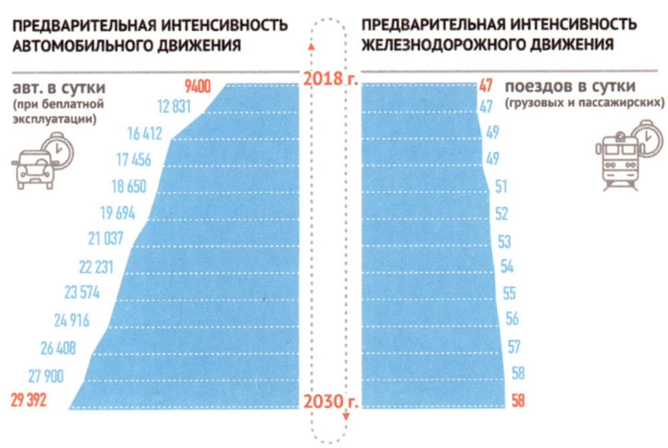

Источник: Росавтодор

Kerch Ferry Crossing

- Completion Year: 2014
- Designer: Olesya Tkach

- Work Introduction

The project addresses the difficult conditions at the Kercn ferry crossing during the high season in Crimea. Currently there is no road to the entrance of the Caucasus Port, which is always overloaded. The designer's goal was to demonstrate how best to address this trouble area and properly organize a trip. The designer marked facilities located at the ports on both sides of the bay – cafes, restaurants, ATMs and others – and provided ferry schedules, ticket prices, and a list of items that would be necessary for a trip.

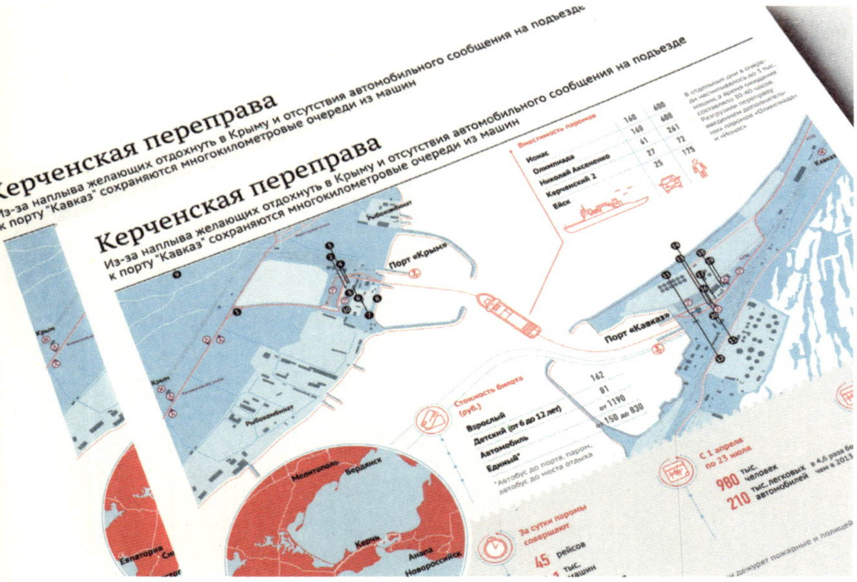

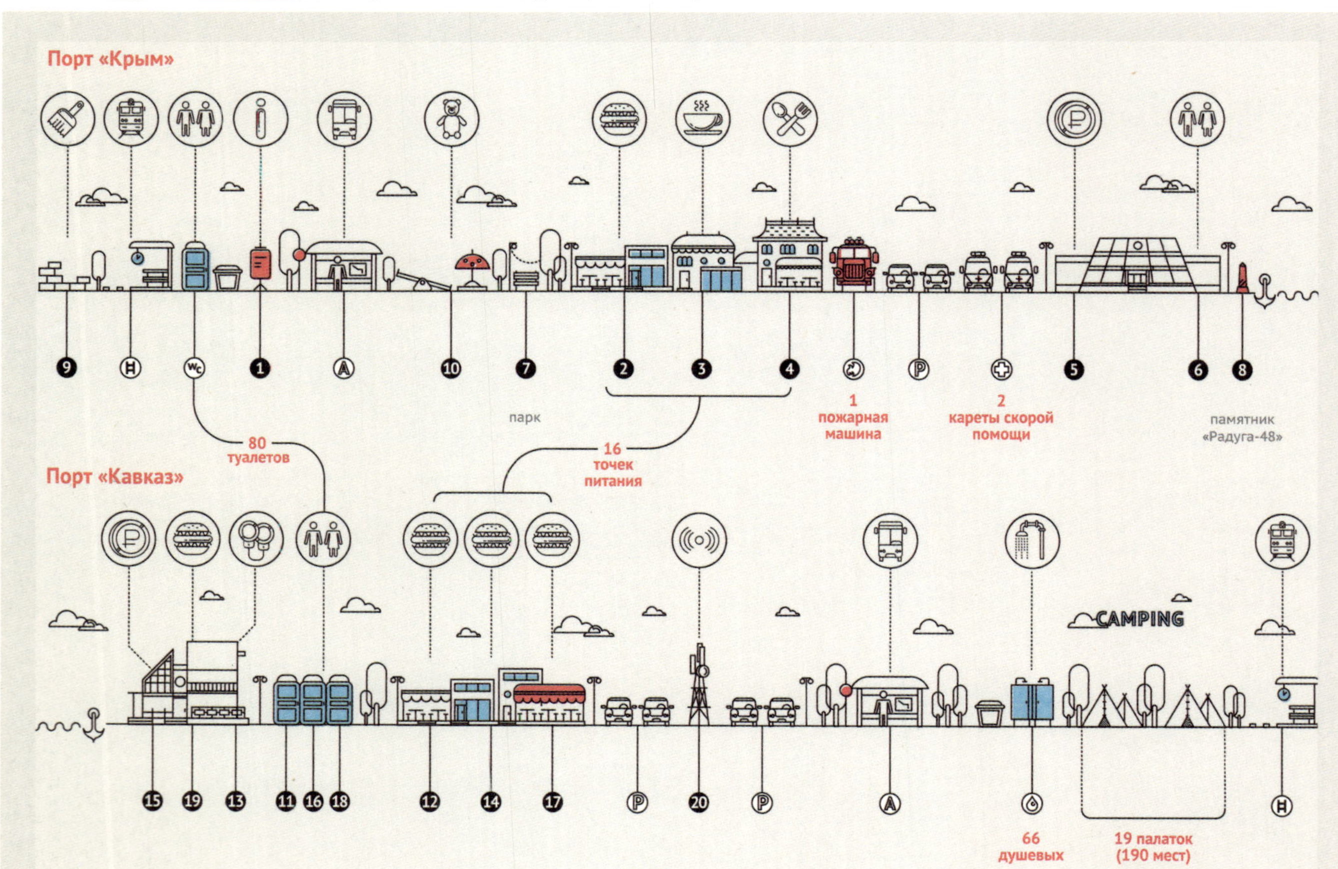

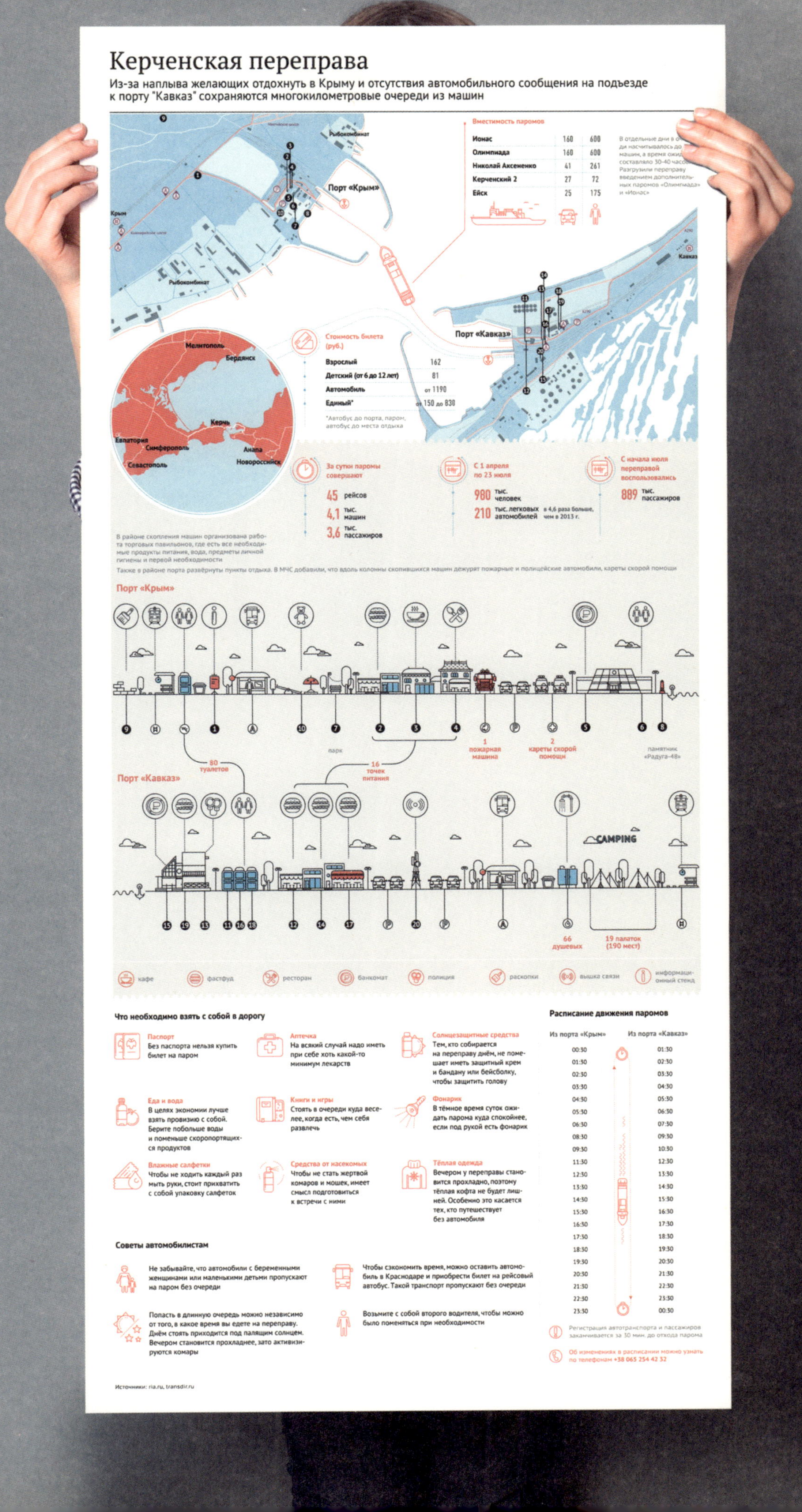
Керченская переправа
Из-за наплыва желающих отдохнуть в Крыму и отсутствия автомобильного сообщения на подъезде к порту "Кавказ" сохраняются многокилометровые очереди из машин
Рыбокомбинат
Порт «Крым»
Крым
Рыбокомбинат
Вместимость паромов
Ионас 160 600
Олимпиада 160 600
Николай Аксененко 41 261
Керченский 2 27 72
Ейск 25 175
Кавказ
Порт «Кавказ»
Мелитополь
Бердянск
Керчь
Евпатория
Симферополь
Анапа
Новороссийск
Севастополь
Стоимость билета (руб.)
Взрослый 162
Детский (от 6 до 12 лет) 81
Автомобиль от 1190
Единый* от 150 до 830
*Автобус до порта, паром, автобус до места отдыха
За сутки паромы совершают
45 рейсов
4,1 тыс. машин
3,6 тыс. пассажиров
С 1 апреля по 23 июля
980 тыс. человек
210 тыс. легковых автомобилей
в 4,6 раза больше, чем в 2013 г.
С начала июля переправой воспользовались
889 тыс. пассажиров
В районе скопления машин организована работа торговых павильонов, где есть все необходимые продукты питания, вода, предметы личной гигиены и первой необходимости
Также в районе порта развёрнуты пункты отдыха. В МЧС добавили, что вдоль колонны скопившихся машин дежурят пожарные и полицейские автомобили, кареты скорой помощи
Порт «Крым»
парк
1 пожарная машина
2 кареты скорой помощи
памятник «Радуга-48»
80 туалетов
16 точек питания
Порт «Кавказ»
CAMPING
66 душевых
19 палаток (190 мест)
кафе
фастфуд
ресторан
банкомат
полиция
раскопки
вышка связи
информационный стенд
Что необходимо взять с собой в дорогу
Паспорт
Без паспорта нельзя купить билет на паром
Аптечка
На всякий случай надо иметь при себе хоть какой-то минимум лекарств
Солнцезащитные средства
Тем, кто собирается на переправу днём, не помешает иметь защитный крем и бандану или бейсболку, чтобы защитить голову
Еда и вода
В целях экономии лучше взять провизию с собой. Берите побольше воды и поменьше скоропортящихся продуктов
Книги и игры
Стоять в очереди куда веселее, когда есть, чем себя развлечь
Фонарик
В тёмное время суток ожидать парома куда спокойнее, если под рукой есть фонарик
Влажные салфетки
Чтобы не ходить каждый раз мыть руки, стоит прихватить с собой упаковку салфеток
Средства от насекомых
Чтобы не стать жертвой комаров и мошек, имеет смысл подготовиться к встречи с ними
Тёплая одежда
Вечером у переправы становится прохладно, поэтому тёплая кофта не будет лишней. Особенно это касается тех, кто путешествует без автомобиля
Советы автомобилистам
Не забывайте, что автомобили с беременными женщинами или маленькими детьми пропускают на паром без очереди
Чтобы сэкономить время, можно оставить автомобиль в Краснодаре и приобрести билет на рейсовый автобус. Такой транспорт пропускают без очереди
Попасть в длинную очередь можно независимо от того, в какое время вы едете на переправу. Днём стоять приходится под палящим солнцем. Вечером становится прохладнее, зато активизируются комары
Возьмите с собой второго водителя, чтобы можно было поменяться при необходимости
Расписание движения паромов
Из порта «Крым»
00:30 01:30 02:30 03:30 04:30 05:30 06:30 08:30 09:30 11:30 12:30 13:30 14:30 15:30 16:30 17:30 18:30 19:30 20:30 21:30 22:30 23:30
Из порта «Кавказ»
01:30 02:30 03:30 04:30 05:30 06:30 07:30 09:30 10:30 12:30 13:30 14:30 15:30 16:30 17:30 18:30 19:30 20:30 21:30 22:30 23:30 00:30
Регистрация автотранспорта и пассажиров заканчивается за 30 мин. до отхода парома
Об изменениях в расписании можно узнать по телефонам +38 065 254 42 32
Источники: ria.ru, transdir.ru

Ebola Hemorrhagic Fever: Spread, Symptoms and Prevention

- Completion Year: 2014
- Designer: Olesya Tkach

- Work Introduction

Ebola is a serious infectious disease. The first outbreaks were first recorded in 1976. The project includes data as of October 25, 2014 on hotspots and the number of deaths. It also contains information on previous outbreaks (location, coefficient of deaths, virus subtype, etc.), sources of infection, symptoms, precautions and myths associated with the virus.

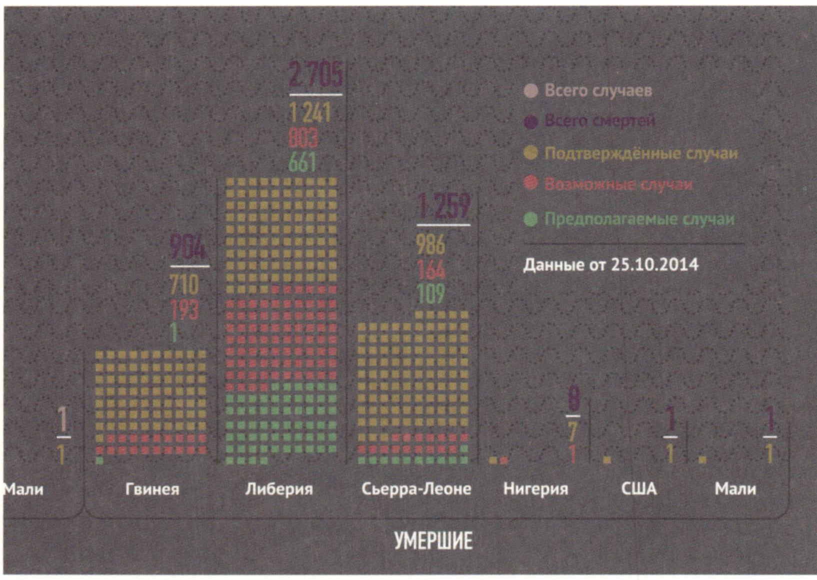

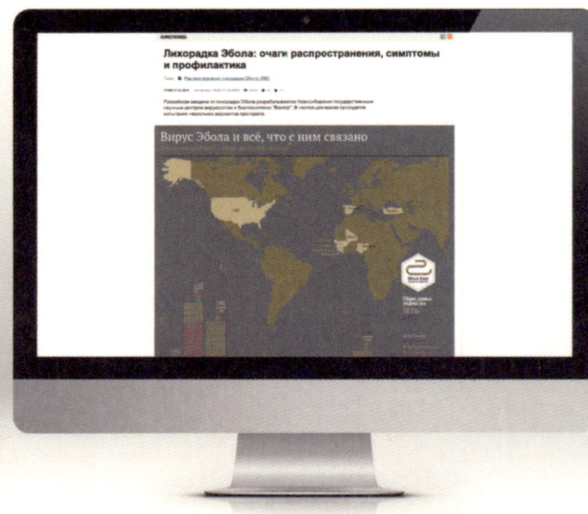

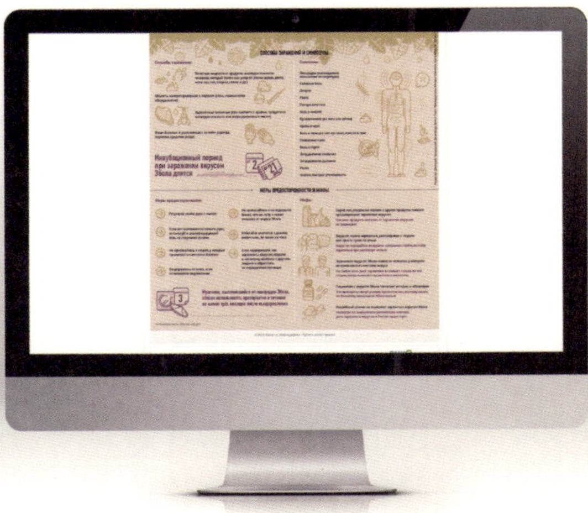

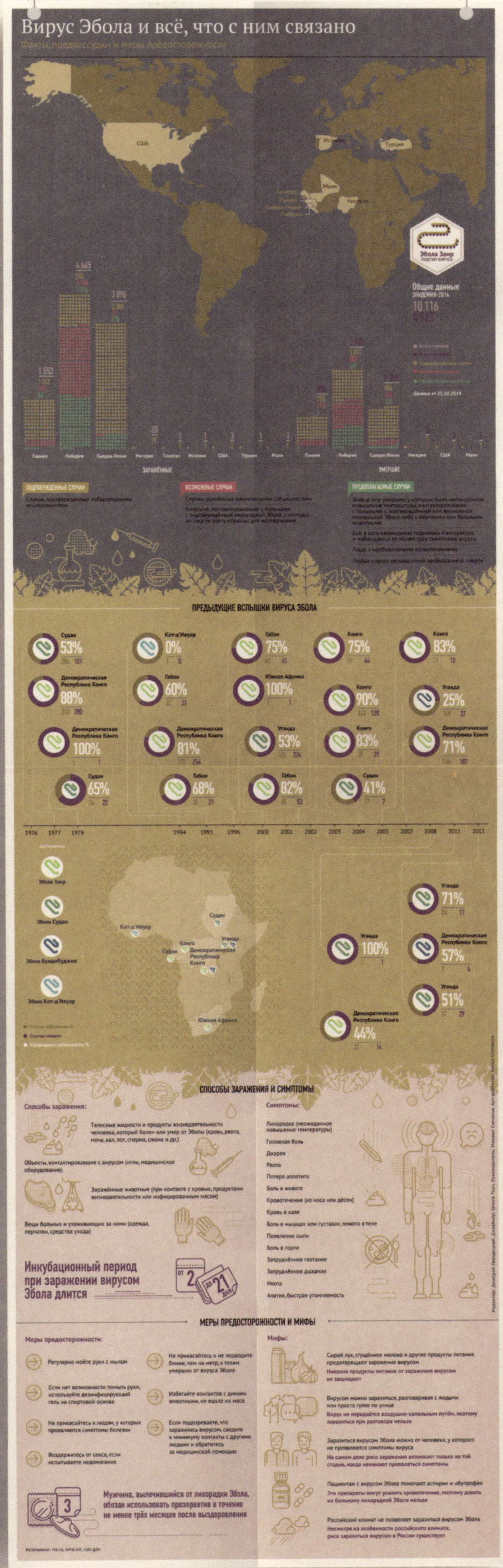

Вирус Эбола и всё, что с ним связано
Факты, предрассудки и меры предосторожности
США
Турция
Эбола Заир
Общие данные
Данные от 25.10.2014
Гвинея
Либерия
Сьерра-Леоне
Нигерия
Сенегал
Испания
США
Турция
Мали
ЗАРАЖЁННЫЕ
УМЕРШИЕ
ПОДТВЕРЖДЁННЫЕ СЛУЧАИ
ВОЗМОЖНЫЕ СЛУЧАИ
ПРЕДПОЛАГАЕМЫЕ СЛУЧАИ
ПРЕДЫДУЩИЕ ВСПЫШКИ ВИРУСА ЭБОЛА
Судан
53%
Кот-д'Ивуар
0%
Габон
75%
Конго
75%
Конго
83%
Демократическая Республика Конго
88%
Габон
60%
Южная Африка
100%
Конго
90%
Уганда
25%
Демократическая Республика Конго
100%
Демократическая Республика Конго
81%
Уганда
53%
Конго
83%
Демократическая Республика Конго
71%
Судан
65%
Габон
68%
Габон
82%
Судан
41%
1976
1977
1979
1994
1995
1996
2000
2001
2002
2003
2004
2005
2007
2008
2011
2012
Эбола Заир
Эбола Судан
Эбола Бундибуджио
Эбола Кот-д'Ивуар
Судан
Кот-д'Ивуар
Габон
Конго
Уганда
Демократическая Республика Конго
Южная Африка
Случаи смерти
Уганда
71%
Уганда
100%
Демократическая Республика Конго
57%
Уганда
51%
Демократическая Республика Конго
44%
СПОСОБЫ ЗАРАЖЕНИЯ И СИМПТОМЫ
Способы заражения:
Телесные жидкости и продукты жизнедеятельности человека, который болен или умер от Эболы (кровь, рвота, моча, кал, пот, сперма, слюна и др.)
Объекты, контактировавшие с вирусом (иглы, медицинское оборудование)
Заражённые животные (при контакте с кровью, продуктами жизнедеятельности или инфицированным мясом)
Вещи больных и ухаживающих за ними (одежда, перчатки, средства ухода)
Инкубационный период при заражении вирусом Эбола длится
от 2 до 21 дня
Симптомы:
Лихорадка (неожиданное повышение температуры)
Головная боль
Диарея
Рвота
Потеря аппетита
Боль в животе
Кровотечение (из носа или дёсен)
Кровь в кале
Боль в мышцах или суставах, ломота в теле
Появление сыпи
Боль в горле
Затруднённое глотание
Затруднённое дыхание
Икота
Апатия, быстрая утомляемость
МЕРЫ ПРЕДОСТОРОЖНОСТИ И МИФЫ
Меры предосторожности:
Регулярно мойте руки с мылом
Если нет возможности помыть руки, используйте дезинфицирующий гель на спиртовой основе
Не прикасайтесь к людям, у которых проявляются симптомы болезни
Воздержитесь от секса, если испытываете недомогание
Не прикасайтесь и не подходите ближе, чем на метр, к телам умерших от вируса Эбола
Избегайте контактов с дикими животными, не ешьте их мясо
Если подозреваете, что заразились вирусом, сведите к минимуму контакты с другими людьми и обратитесь за медицинской помощью
3
Мужчина, вылечившийся от лихорадки Эбола, обязан использовать презерватив в течение не менее трёх месяцев после выздоровления
Источники: ria.ru, who.int, cdc.gov
Мифы:
Сырой лук, сгущённое молоко и другие продукты питания предотвращают заражение вирусом
Никакие продукты питания от заражения вирусом не защищают
Вирусом можно заразиться, разговаривая с людьми или просто гуляя по улице
Вирус не передаётся воздушно-капельным путём, поэтому заразиться при разговоре нельзя
Заразиться вирусом Эбола можно от человека, у которого не проявляются симптомы вируса
На самом деле риск заражения возникает только на той стадии, когда начинают проявляться симптомы
Пациентам с вирусом Эбола помогают аспирин и ибупрофен
Эти препараты могут усилить кровотечение, поэтому давать их больному лихорадкой Эбола нельзя
Российский климат не позволяет заразиться вирусом Эбола
Несмотря на особенности российского климата, риск заразиться вирусом в России существует

Eco Training Machines

- Completion Year: 2014
- Designer: Ottavia Alieri

- Work Introduction

The Info-graphic is used to promote a company that sells eco-training machines. Using the 2D icons placed in the info-graphic, as a communication tool, the designer builds an easy and striking poster. This conveys the message that the eco-machines can help the users to stay healthy and save the world at the same time, producing clean energy while burning calories.

WORK OUT
SAVE YOURSELF
AND THE WORLD

WORK OUT
AND SAVE
THE WORLD

WORK OUT
SAVE YOURSELF
AND THE WORLD

WORK OUT
AND SAVE
THE WORLD

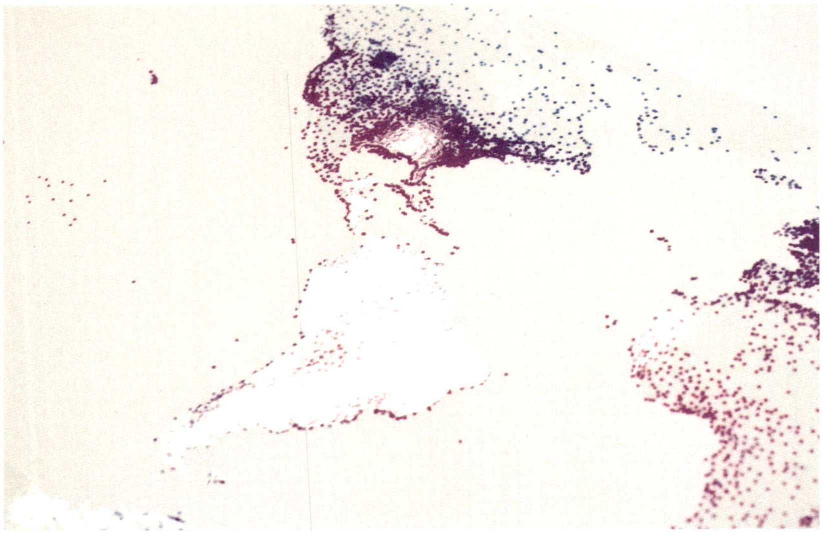

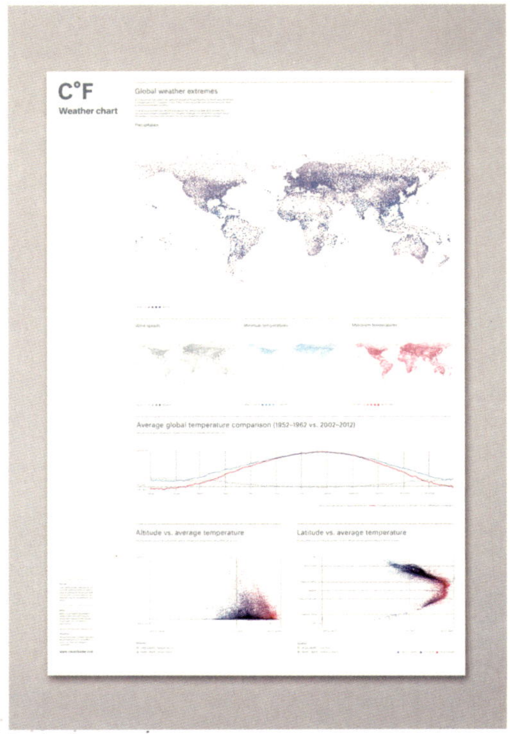

Weather Chart 2013

- Completion Year: 2013
- Designer: Gert Franke, Thomas Clever, Jonas Groot Kormelink, Wilco Tomassen

• Work Introduction

The weather chart of 2013 shows the global ranking of countries based on temperature, precipitation and wind. The hottest country in the world is Djibouti, where an average temperature of 30.4°C / 86.8°F is measured. The coldest area is Antarctica, where the average temperature reaches -15°C / -26.1°F .

Global ranking of countries based on average temperature (1962–2012)

Legend / Global averages

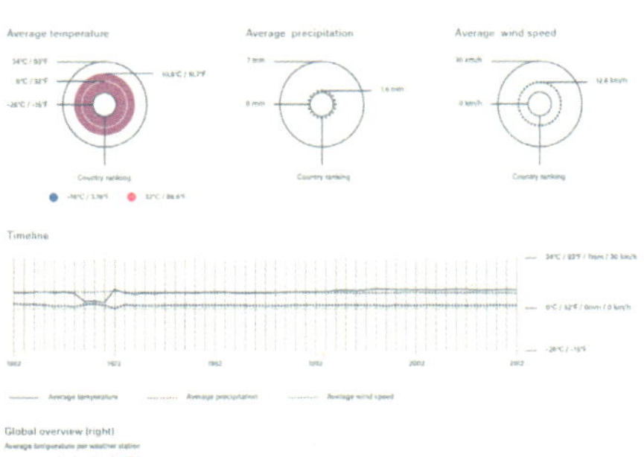

Global weather station overview

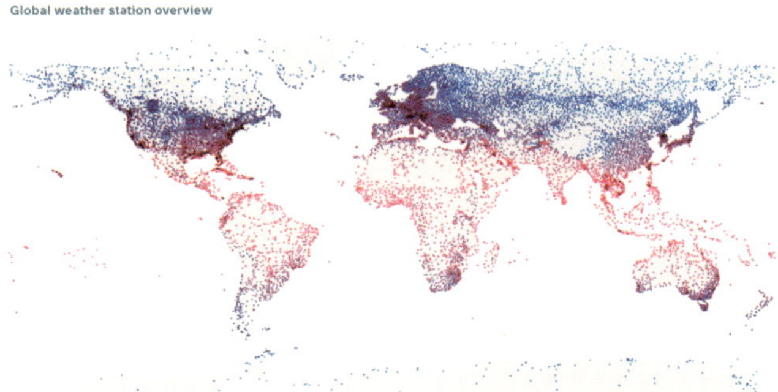

WEATHER CHART
CLEVER°FRANKE
DESIGN FOR COMPLEX
WWW.CLEVERFRANKE.COM

Irish Open Preview

- Completion Year: 2014
- Designer: Alan McNamara
- Client: Irish Examiner Newspaper

- Work Introduction

A huge event in the Irish sporting calendar is the Irish Open Golf Competition, taking place once a year on a chosen course. This infographic served as a preview to the 2014 competition taking place in Fota Island, Cork. The information in the piece ranges from the weekends events, to a course preview and a brief history breakdown providing readers with a more in depth knowledge going into the event.

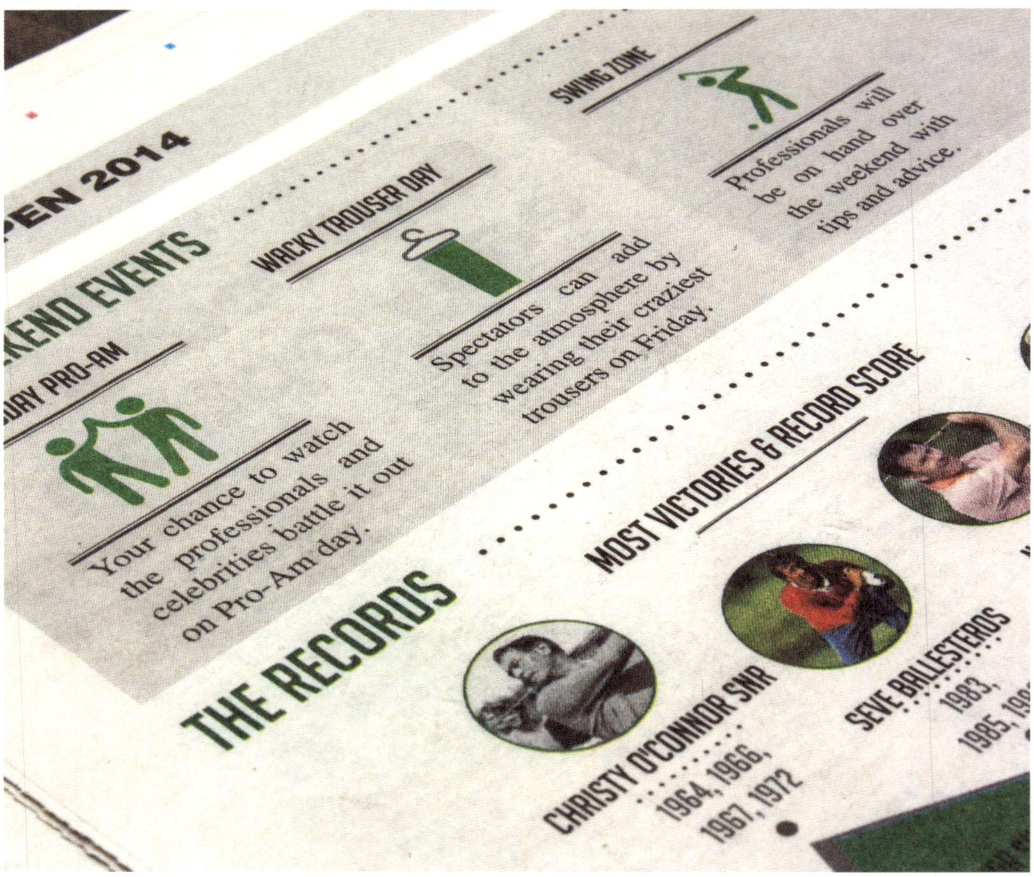

THE WEEKEND EVENTS

WEDNESDAY PRO-AM
Your chance to watch the professionals and celebrities battle it out on Pro-Am day.

WACKY TROUSER DAY
Spectators can add to the atmosphere by wearing their craziest trousers on Friday.

SWING ZONE
Professionals will be on hand over the weekend with tips and advice.

THE VENUE

DEERPARK COURSE
PAR 71

TOTAL YARDAGE 6927

LONGEST HOLE - 4TH
PAR 5

TOTAL YARDAGE 580

THE RECORDS

MOST VICTORIES & RECORD SCORE

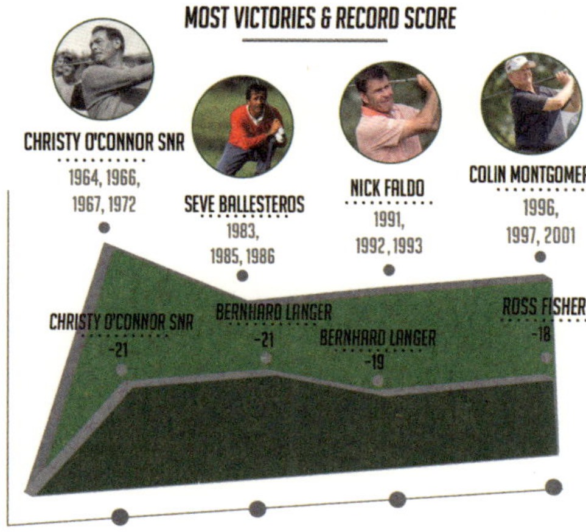

YOUNGEST WINNER
SERGIO GARCIA
19 YEARS 176 DAYS

19

OLDEST WINNER
SAM TORRANCE
41 YEARS 319 DAYS

41

TOP 10 FINISHES
NICK FALDO
WITH 10

10

THE OPEN WILL BE CONTESTED BY 156 PLAYERS **156**

COMPETING FOR A PRIZE OF **€2M**

IMPACT ON THE LOCAL ECONOMY

50 OVER 50 TELEVISION CAMERAS

70 EUROPEAN TOUR STAFF

120 TELEVISION & CAMERA CREW

100,000 SPECTATORS EXPECTED TO ATTEND

1,600 THE NUMBER OF STAFF & VOLUNTEERS

€202M WORTH OF THE GOLF INDUSTRY

THE IRISH CONTINGENT

DARREN CLARKE
WORLD RANKING #349
BEST FINISH 2ND (2001)

SHANE LOWRY
WORLD RANKING #71
BEST FINISH 1ST (2009)

GRAEME MCDOWELL
WORLD RANKING #22
BEST FINISH 11TH (2004)

RORY MCILROY
WORLD RANKING #6
BEST FINISH 7TH (2008)

PÁDRAIG HARRINGTON
WORLD RANKING #228
BEST FINISH 1ST (2007)

PAUL MCGINLEY
WORLD RANKING #478
BEST FINISH 3RD (2000)

Sochi 2014 – Winter Olympics

- Completion Year: 2014
- Designer: Alan McNamara
- Client: Irish Examiner Newspaper

• Work Introduction

The Sochi Winter Olympics were held from 7-23 February, 2014 in the city of Sochi near the Russian/ Georgian boarder. The lead up to the games were dominated by controversy, from allegations of corruption to high costs, this Winter Olympics certainly was one to remember. Through this infographic he has tried to capture both the basics to get people excited about the event while also trying to be as informative as possible.

• Newspaper Introduction

Major Irish newspaper founded on August 30, 1841. Largest and most circulated newspaper in Southern Ireland. Maintaining a core misson to inform, engage and entertain.

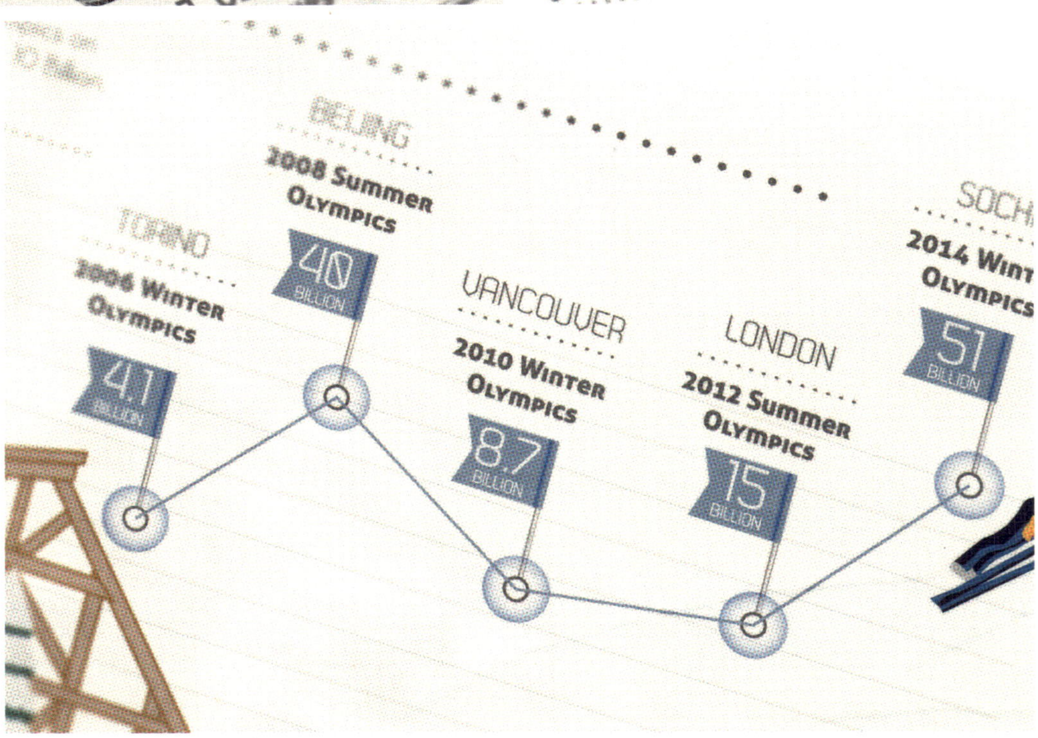

7 Sports across 16 Disciplines

85 Participating Nations

11 Olympic Venues

98 Medals up for grabs

The Sochi torch relay

14,000 Olympic Torch handlers

65,000 Over alomst 65,000 km

2,900 Through 2,900 towns & cities

123 Over a 123 day period

Olympic Spending

Sochi is the highest costing Olympics on record, eclipsing Beijing by over 10 Billion. So where did the money go?

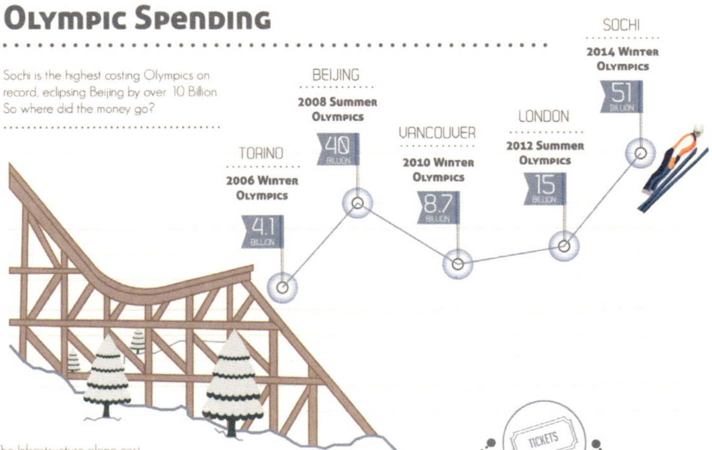

The Infrastructure alone cost more than the 2012 Winter Olympics did in total.

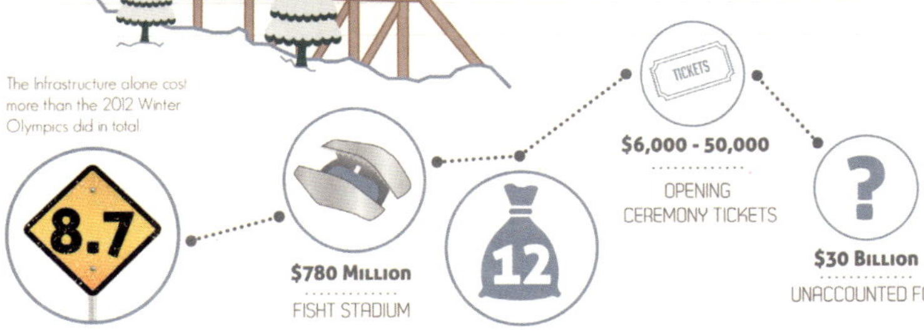

$8.7 Billion
INFRASTRUCTURE

$780 Million
FISHT STADIUM

$12 Billion
THE ORIGINAL BUDGET

$6,000 - 50,000
OPENING CEREMONY TICKETS

$30 Billion
UNACCOUNTED FOR

They're watching you!

100,000 Security Personnel

40,000 Police Officers

30,000 Armed Troops

Closing Ceremony
23rd February 4pm

Gdansk Stadium

- Completion Year: 2012
- Designer: Andras Dancsak
- Client: Nepszabadsag

• Work Introduction

The 2012 Football European Championship had eight venues, and they made each one as an infographic for their publications in *Népszabadság*. They downloaded many images from the web as a reference to construct the stadium and the section view of the grand stand.

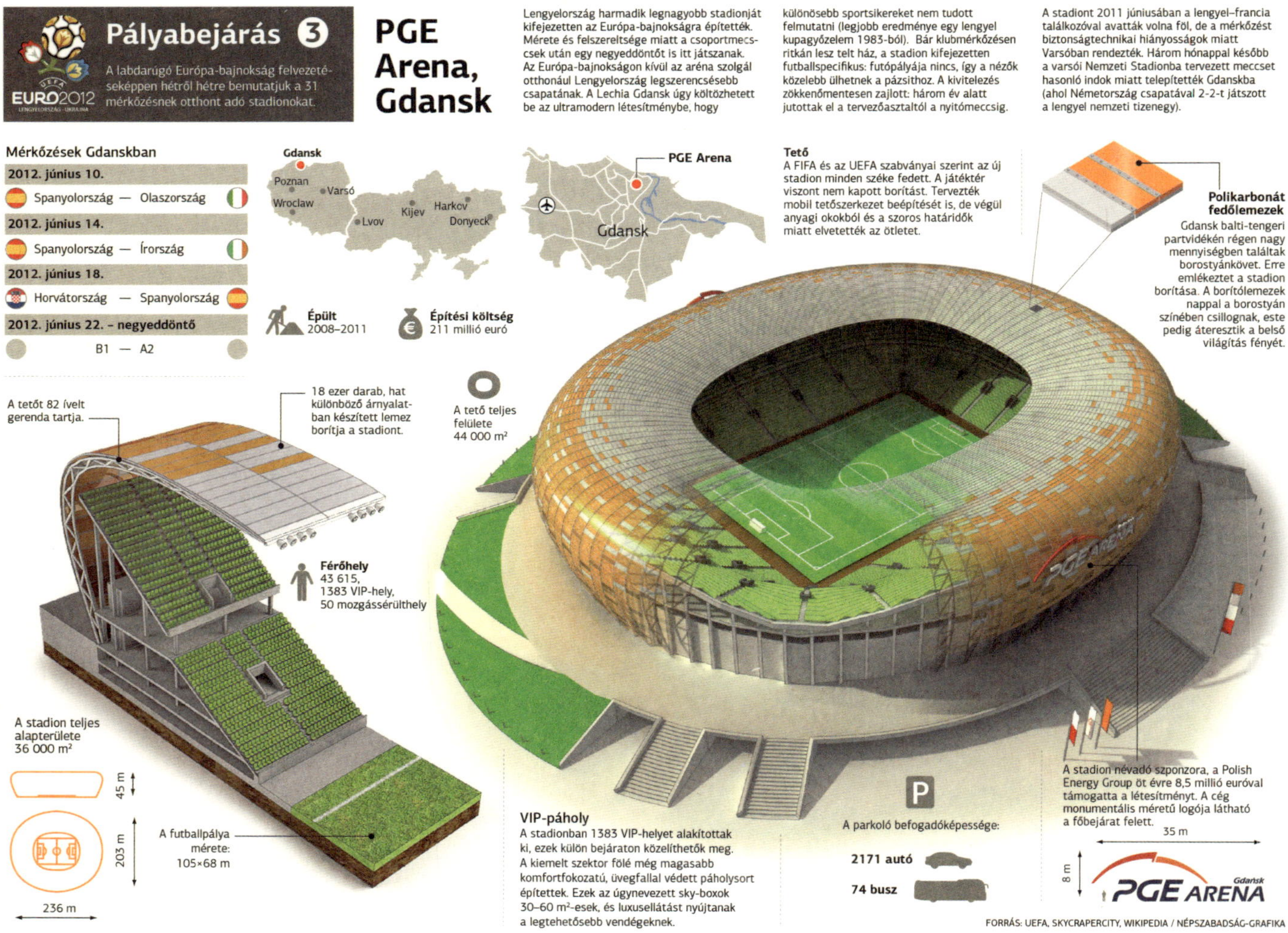

• Newspaper Introduction

Népszabadság is a major left-leaning Hungarian newspaper, founded in 1956 as successor of "Szabad Nép" (The Free People), the central organ of the dissolved Hungarian Working People's Party. "Népszabadság" literally means "People's Freedom", and is a reference to the paper's communist roots: it was the mouthpiece of the communist Hungarian Socialist Workers' Party until 1989 and is often considered as supportive to the present Hungarian Socialist Party (MSZP).

World Cup 2014 Final

- Completion Year: 2014
- Designer: Andras Dancsak
- Client: Nemzeti Sport

• Work Introduction

This is a spread page infographic in *Nemzeti Sport*, the Hungarian sports daily. There were so many statistics and other information available on the internet, so the most important thing was to organize the data to make it be understood easily and quickly when they made an infographic, and they had to decide which the most important information was. Nobody can read two pages with full text without any visual information, so they had to find the way to visualize the data.

• Newspaper Introduction

Nemzeti Sport (the title means "National Sport") is a Hungarian sports daily founded in 1903, owned by Ringier of Switzerland. This traditional newspaper has the third largest circulation in the country. It is frequently cited by quality English-language media.

The Power of Social Media in Sport

- Completion Year: 2014
- Designer: Alan McNamara
- Client: Irish Examiner Newspaper

- Work Introduction

Social media has played and continues to play an increasingly important role in modern day sport. From boosting fan player relations to keeping the fan base in the loop and keeping them involved, social media will continue to be a huge part of sport for many years to come.

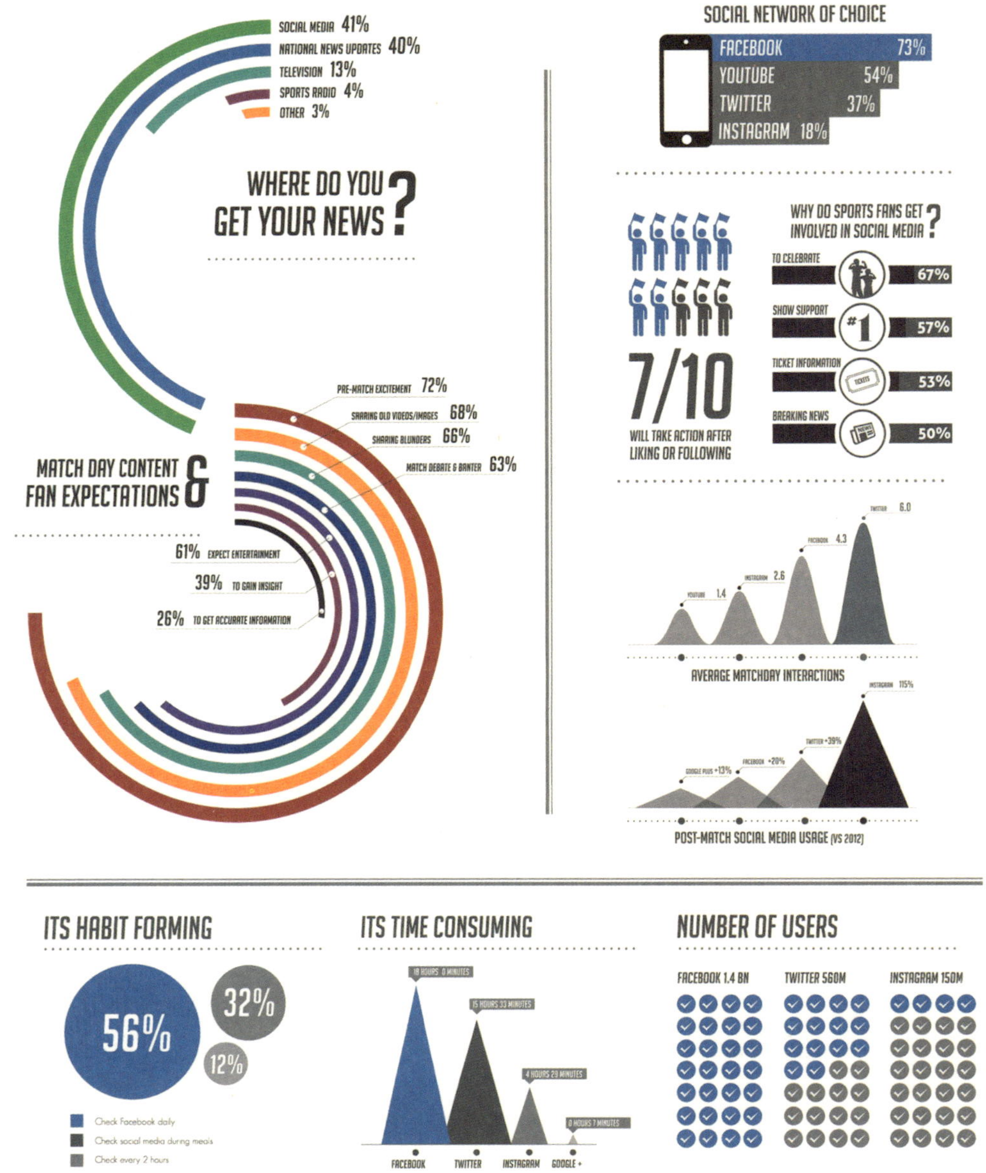

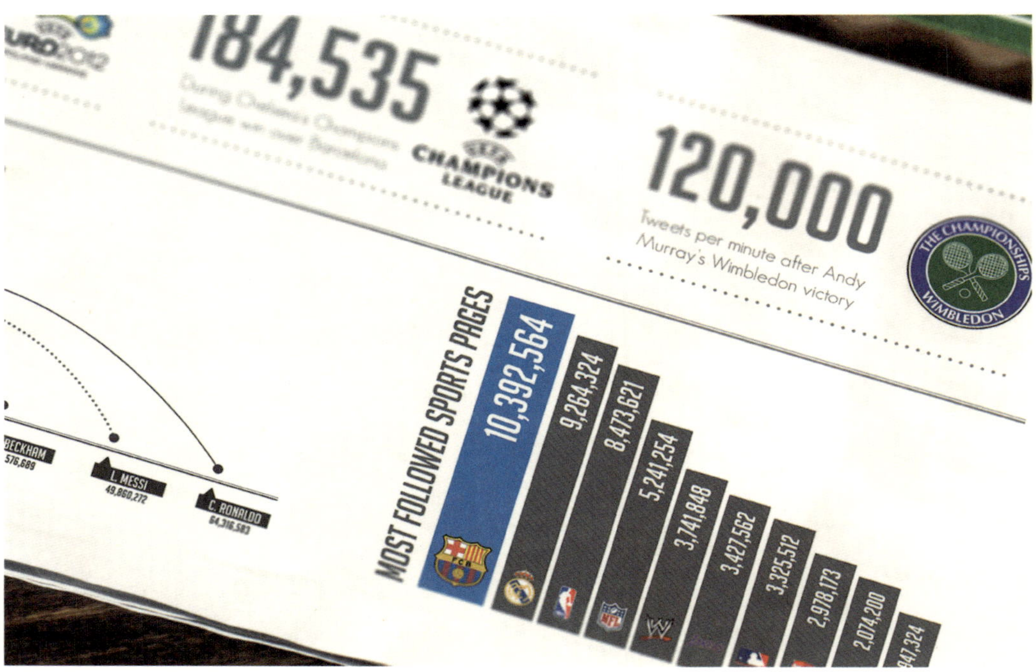

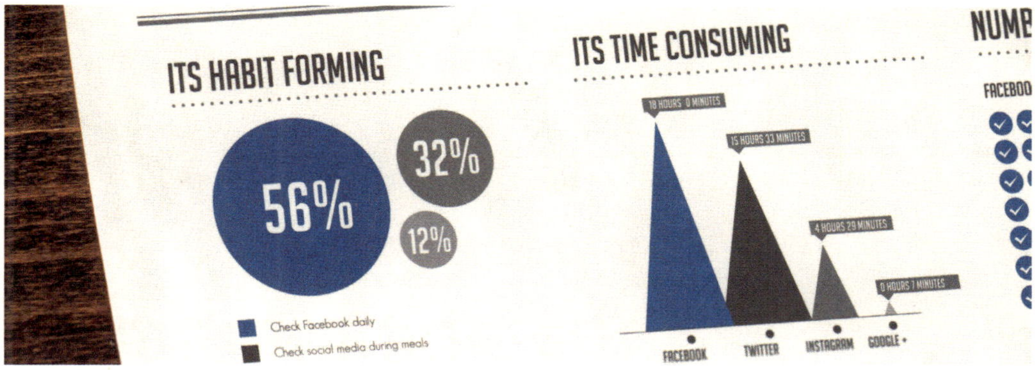

SOCIAL MEDIA EXTENDS TO THE GAME ITSELF

HIGHEST SOCIAL MEDIA RELATED FINES

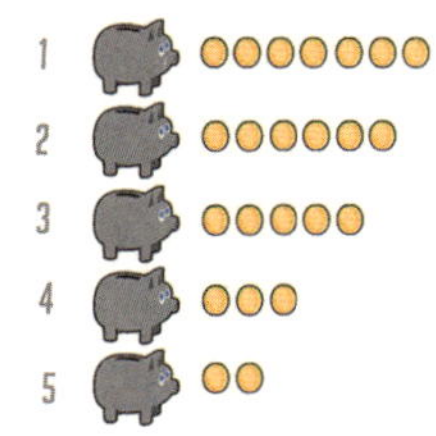

Joey Barton (Newcastle United) - £140,000 fine for criticising employer

Ashley Cole (Chelsea) - £90,000 fine for criticising FA

Darren Bent (Tottenham Hotspur) - £80,000 fine for criticising chairman

Rio Ferdinand (Manchester United) - £45,000 fine for racism-related tweet

Carlton Cole (West Ham) - £20,000 for racism-related tweet

MOST FOLLOWED FOOTBALLERS ON TWITTER

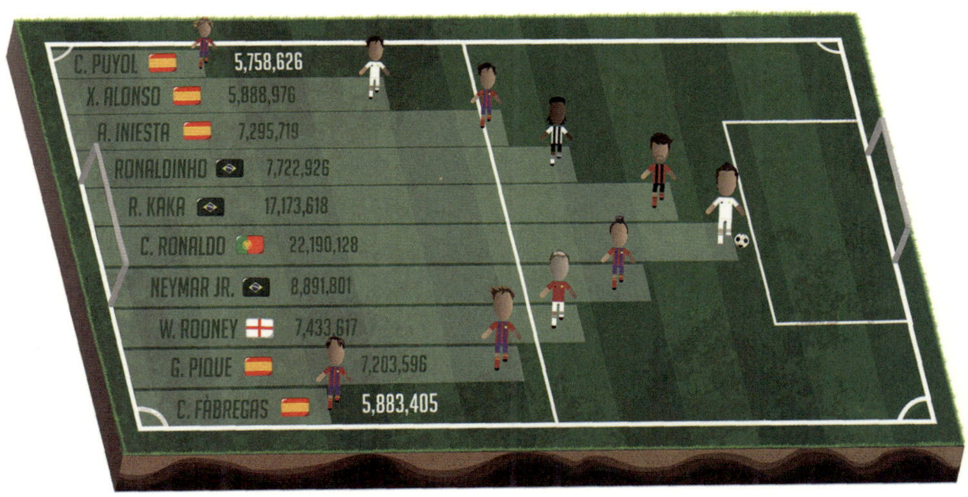

MOST TWEETED SPORTING EVENTS

267,000
Tweets per minute in Spain's victory to win Euro 2012

184,535
During Chelsea's Champions League win over Barcelona

120,000
Tweets per minute after Andy Murray's Wimbledon victory

MOST 'LIKED' FOOTBALLERS
ON FACEBOOK

Super Bowl XLVIII – More than a Game

- Completion Year: 2014
- Designer: Alan McNamara
- Client: Irish Examiner Newspaper

• Work Introduction

The Super Bowl is called 'The greatest show on earth'for a reason. From advertising to the half time show, the Super Bowl is a huge event attracting millions upon millions of viewers from roughly 198 countries and territories in more than 25 languages. This infographic is an attempt to show the scale of the Super Bowl through information which is easy for the reader to relate to.

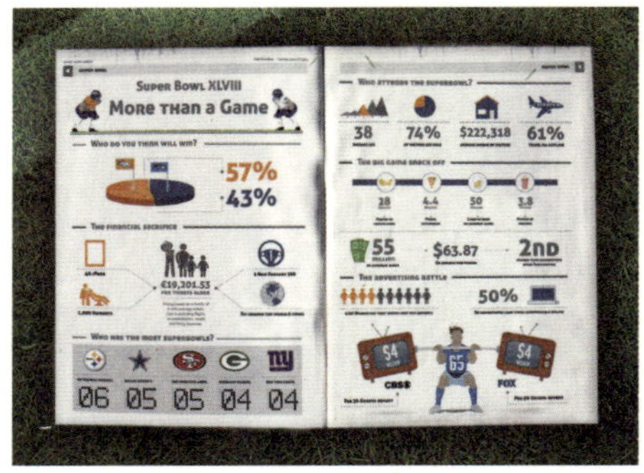

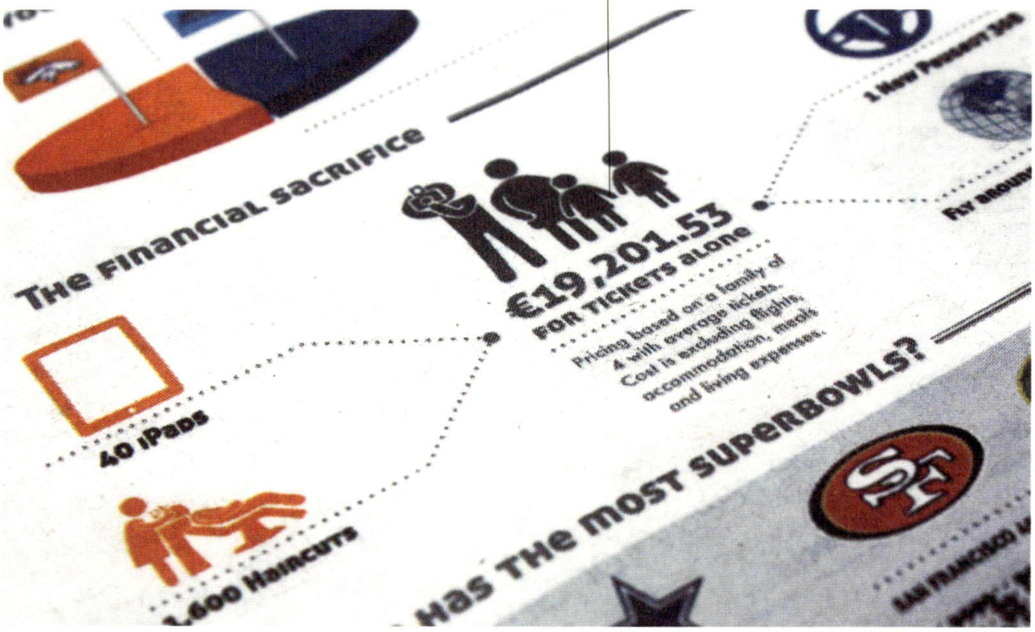

Super Bowl XLVIII
More than a Game
Who do you think will win?
57%
43%
The financial sacrifice
40 iPads
1,600 Haircuts
€19,201.53
for tickets alone
Pricing based on a family of 4 with average tickets. Cost is excluding flights, accommodation, meals and living expenses.
1 New Peugeot 308
Fly around the world 5 times
Who attends the superbowl?
38
AVERAGE AGE
74%
OF VISITORS ARE MALE
$222,318
AVERAGE INCOME OF VISITORS
61%
TRAVEL VIA AIRPLANE
The big game snack off
28
million
Pounds of potato chips
4.4
million
Pizzas nationwide
50
million
Cases of beer on gameday alone
3.8
million
Pounds of popcorn
55
million
on gameday alone
$63.87
On average per person
2nd
Highest food consumption after Thanksgiving
The advertising battle
4/10 Women say they watch just for adverts
50%
Of advertisers leak their commericals online
$4
MILLION
CBS
Per 30-Second advert
65
$4
MILLION
FOX
Per 30-Second advert

US Masters Infographic

- Completion Year: 2014
- Designer: Alan McNamara
- Client: Irish Examiner Newspaper

• Work Introduction

The main focus of this infographic is to deliver a clear and informative piece about the US Masters. Providing an in depth history about the event while also giving a preview of the events which were about to unfold was integral. Delivering information beyond the actual play such as course infomation and history was also important to put the tournament into perspective and give viewers a deeper understanding and interest.

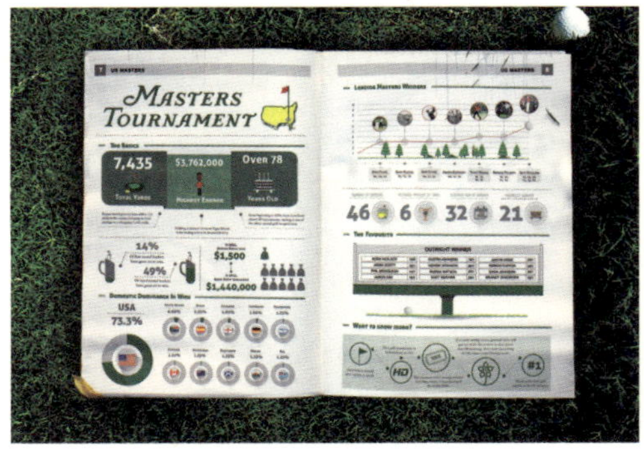

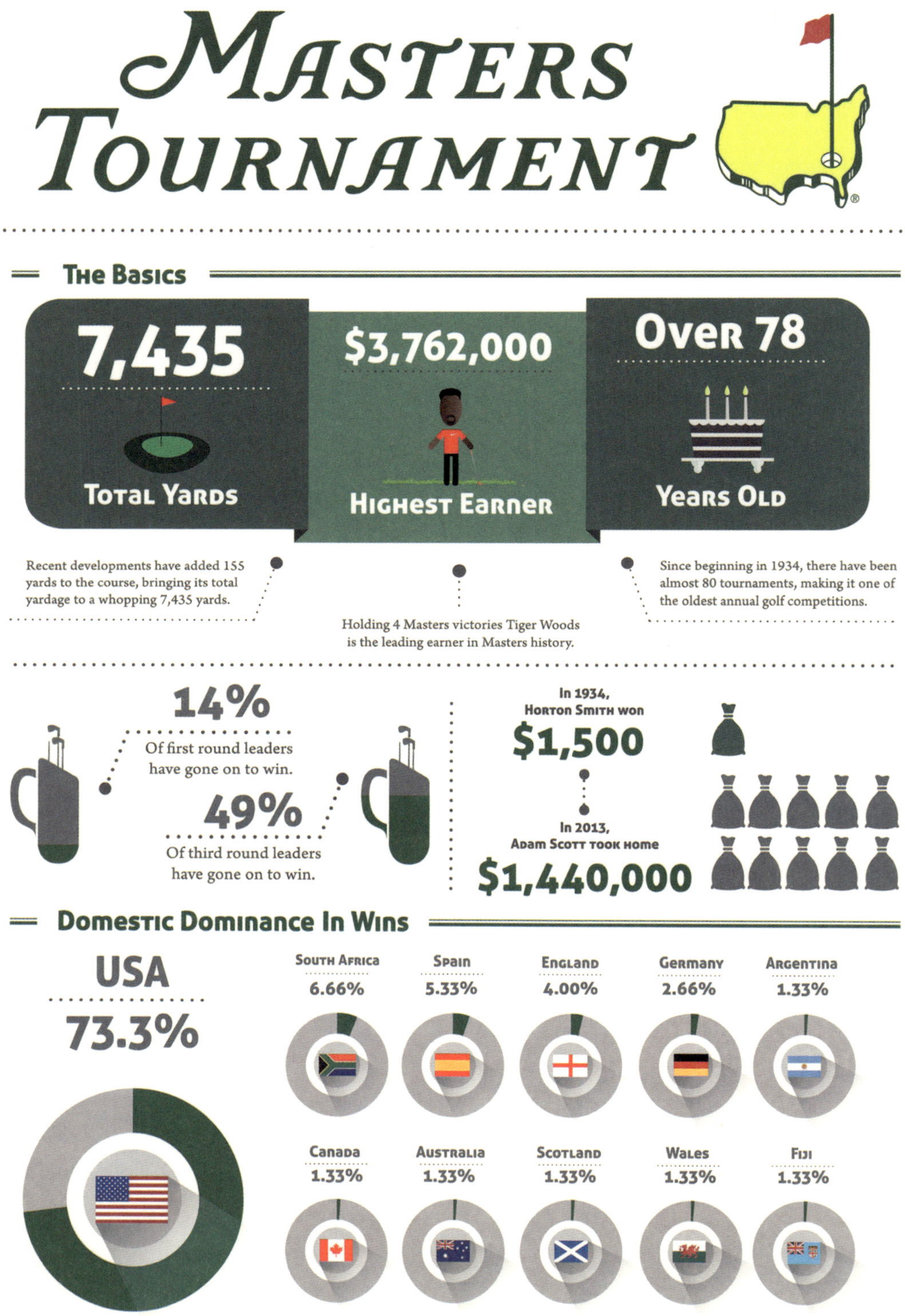

Leading Masters Winners

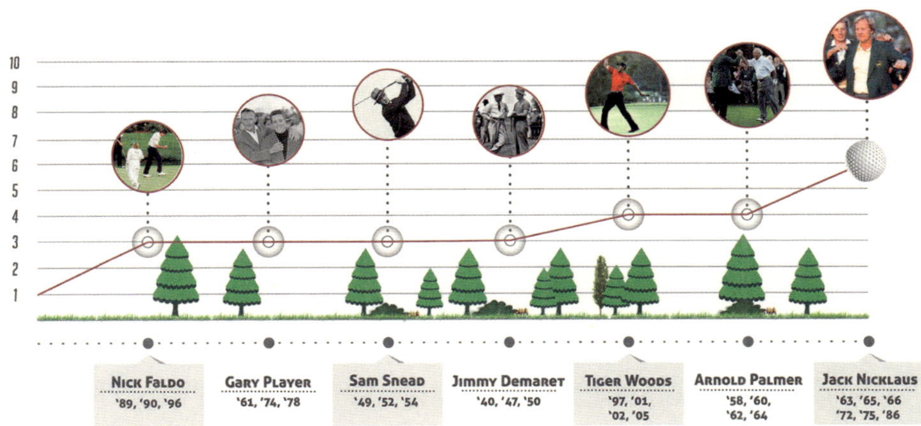

The Favourite

Want to know more?

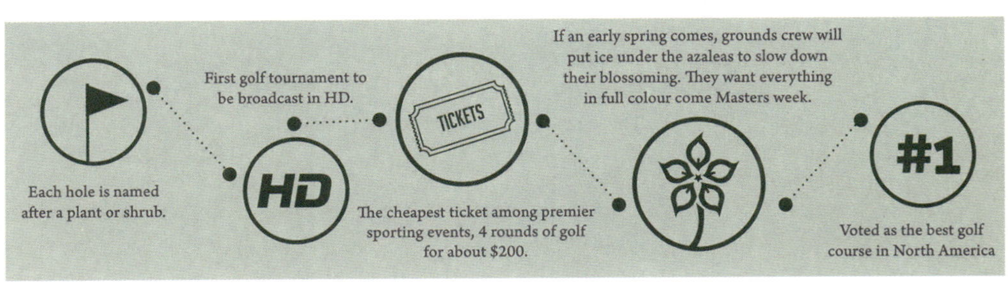

World Cup Preview

- Completion Year: 2014
- Designer: Alan McNamara
- Client: Irish Examiner Newspaper

- Work Introduction

The Brazil World Cup was one of the most anticipated sporting events of the 2014 calendar. Therefore, it was important to provide a detailed and informative preview to give readers a more in depth knowledge of the world cup. This was done by providing such information as a stadium preview, potential star player as well as history etc. about the tournament.

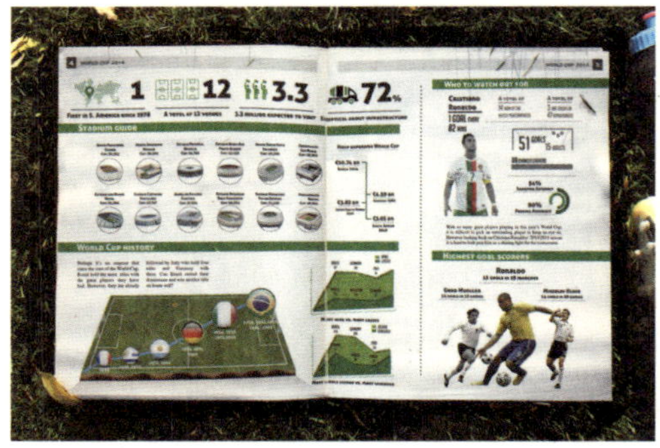

1 — First in S. America since 1978

12 — A total of 12 venues

3.3 — 3.3 million expected to visit

72% — Skeptical about infrastructure

Stadium guide

Arena Panatanal Cuiaba Cap: 39,553	Arena Amazonia Manaus Cap: 39,573	Estadio Nacional Brasilia Cap: 65,702	Estadio Beira-Rio Porto Alegre Cap: 42,153	Arena Fonte Nova Salvador Cap: 49,280	Corinthians Sao Paulo Cap: 59,955

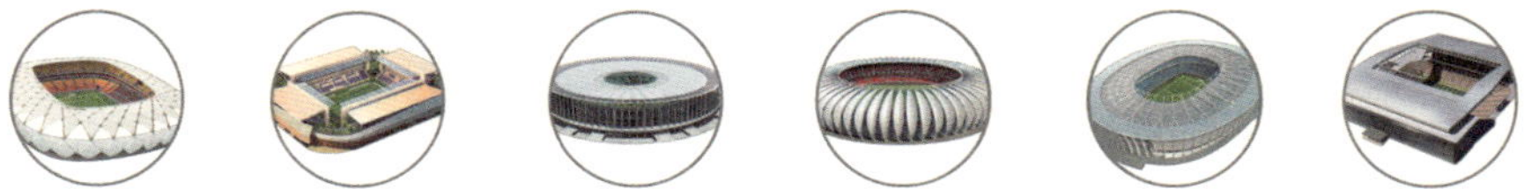

Estadio das Dunas Natal Cap: 39,304	Estadio Castelao Fortaleza Cap: 57,747	Arena da Baixada Curitiba Cap: 37,634	Estadio Mineirao Belo Horizonte Cap: 56,091	Estadio Maracana Rio de Janeiro Cap: 71,159	Pernambuco Recife Cap: 40,604

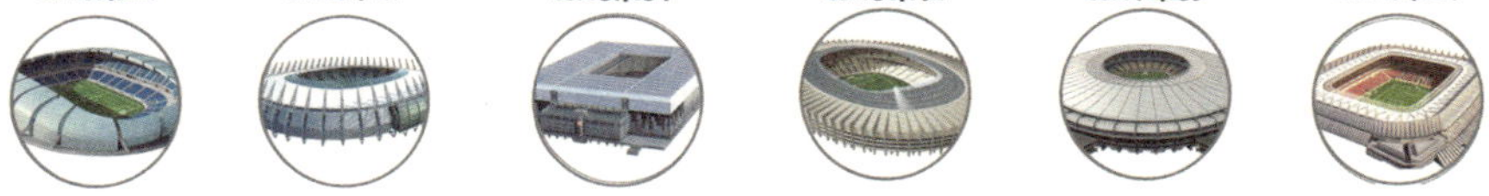

Most expensive World Cup

€10.74 bn — Brazil 2014

€4.59 bn — Germany 2006

€3.82 bn — Japan/South Korea 2002

€3.05 bn — South Africa 2010

World Cup history

Perhaps it's no surprise that since the start of the World Cup, Brazil hold the most titles with the great players they have had. However, they are closely followed by Italy who hold four titles and Germany with three. Can Brazil extend their dominance and win another title on home soil?

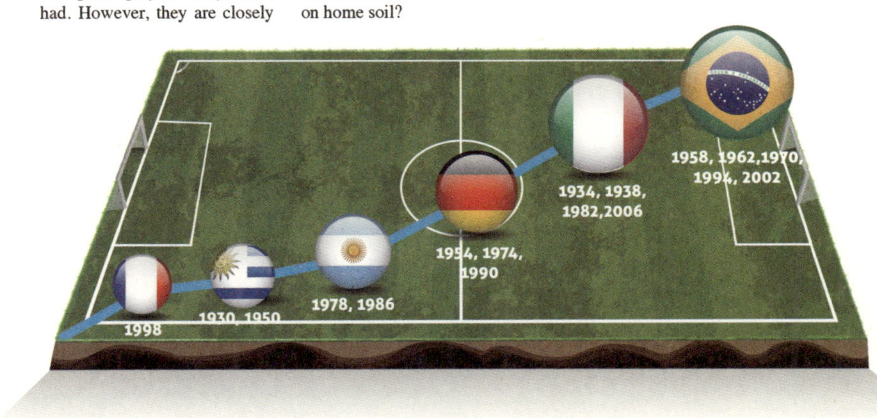

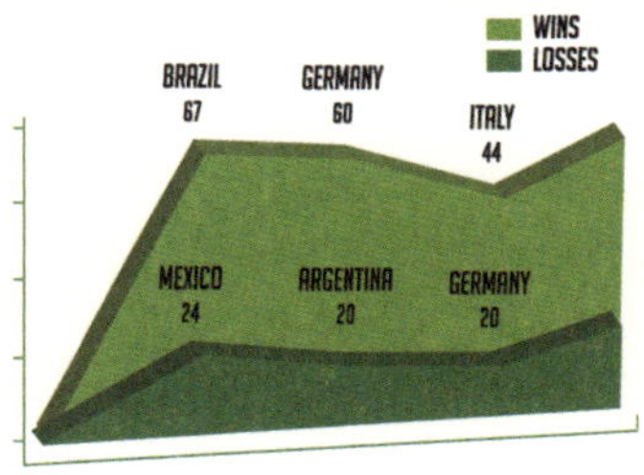

Most wins vs. most losses

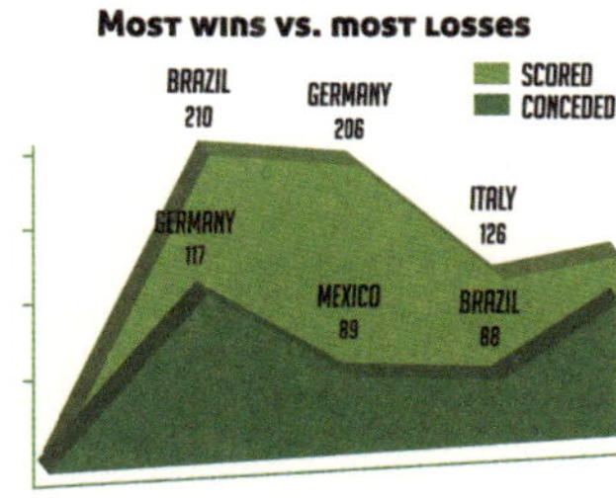

Most goals scored vs. most conceded

Who to watch out for

Cristiano Ronaldo

1 GOAL EVERY 82 MINS

A total of 14 MAN OF THE MATCH PERFORMANCES

A total of 3 HAT-TRICKS IN 47 APPEARANCES

51 GOALS 15 ASSISTS

69 CHANCES CREATED

54% Shooting Accuracy

80% Passing Accuracy

With so many great players playing in this year's World Cup, it is difficult to pick an outstanding player to keep an eye on. However looking back on Cristiano Ronaldos' 2013/2014 season it is hard to look past him as a shining light for the tournament.

Highest goal scorers

Ronaldo
15 goals in 19 matches

Gerd Mueller
14 goals in 13 games

Miroslav Klose
14 goals in 19 games

- Completion Year: 2014
- Designer: Ruth Fogden

- Work Introduction

442 is a weekly newspaper aimed at capturing the imagination of sports fans who want to catch up with the weekly football matches and news. 442 combines infographics and type to discuss and analyze in detail, player performances, match reports and the latest off-field antics.

Newcastle United vs Swansea

A deserved score by both sides on Sunday with neither team really looking the better. Swansea had a last minute chance to take all threee points but in the end left it too late.

Chelsea vs Hull

It was another dominating performace by Chelsea proving their worth at the top of the table. Hull played well creating some chances in the first half but were simply out classed.

Manchester City vs Everton

Manchester City dug deep to hold off Everton as they charged into action in the dying minutes of the game. However Kompany's defence stood strong showing there true strengh.

Tottenham vs Fulham

Yet another draw for Tim Sherwood and another poor performance full of mistakes. Fulham were unlucky not to win but played well considering their injury list.

Sunderland vs Cardiff

With both clubs fighting for survival this was set to be a real battle. Cardiff came out all guns blazing leaving Sunderland stranded and without a defence after two red cards.

Stoke.City vs Manchester United

With a 10th place finish in sight, Stoke put in a worthy performance against a struggling United, giving them the boost they needed for that crucial finishing spot.

Arsenal vs Norwich

After Arsenal's recent bad form they proved their worth at the top of the table with a comprehensive win against Norwich who have yet to make an impact on the league.

West Bromwich Albion vs Crystal Palace

Palace stormed a raging comeback on Saturday giving them the point they desperatly needed to stay in the top flight. However they owe everything the their star goal keeper.

Southampton vs Aston Villa

With the England manager looking on form the stands there was more than just points to play for and Ricky Lambert was certaining out to impress with two fantastic goals.

WORLD CUP 2014

Our Predictions for the Brazilian 2014 World Cup

GROUP A		GROUP B		GROUP C		GROUP D		GROUP E		GROUP F		GROUP G		GROUP H	
Brazil	3/1	Australia	750/1	Ivory Coast	150/1	Costa Rica	2500/1	Ecuador	150/1	Argentina	9/1	Germany	11/1	Algeria	1000/1
Cameroon	750/1	Chile	40/1	Columbia	22/1	England	33/1	France	20/1	Bosnia-Herzegovina	150/1	Ghana	200/1	Belgium	14/1
Mexico	150/1	Spain	7/1	Greece	250/1	Italy	25/1	Honduras	2500/1	Iran	750/1	Portugal	33/1	Korea Republic	250/1
Croatia	200/1	Netherlands	28/1	Japan	125/1	Uruguay	28/1	Switzerland	100/1	Nigeria	250/1	United States	150/1	Russia	66/1

Opinions are open on who will win this years World Cup in Brazil. With Brazil going in as one of the favourites will they be able to handle their own heat. We will be keeping a close eyeon group D as England face their toughest group in years. But as we predict the winners and losers of this years competition its time for you to place your bets.

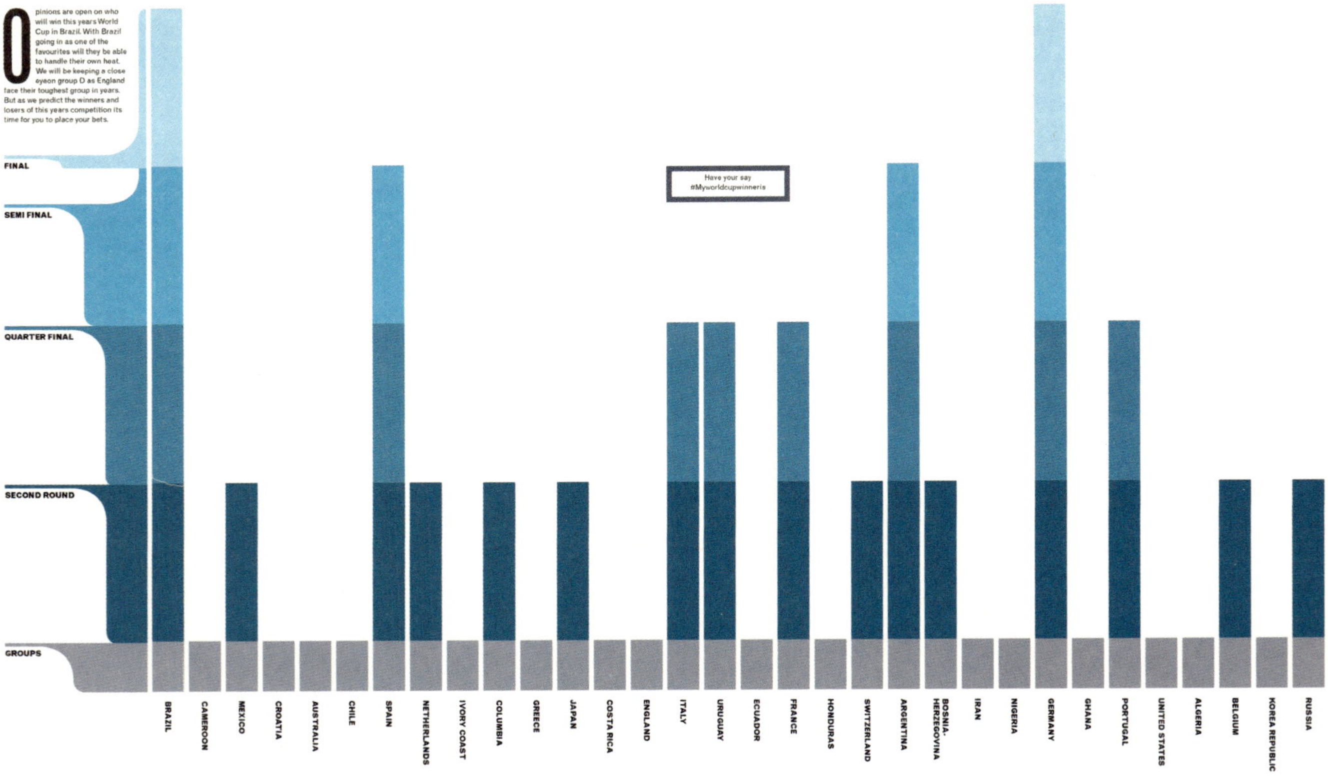

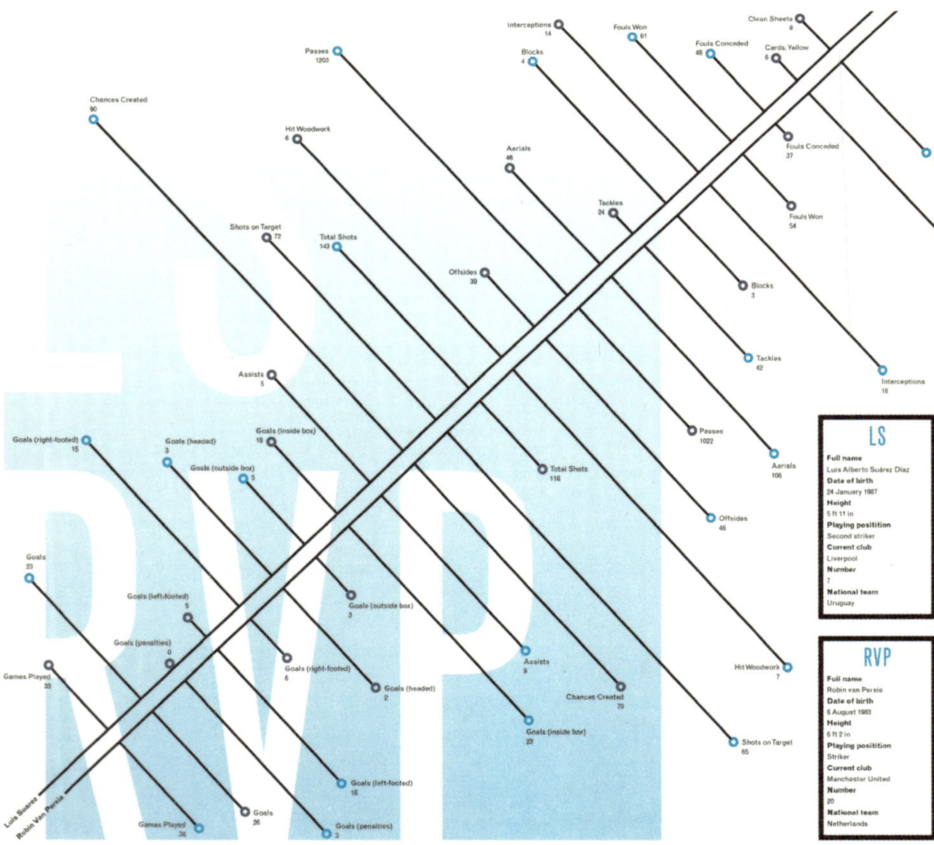

Key

Player with the highest stat

Player with the lowest stat

Suarez is having the season of his life. The only man equal to his scoring record is the Manchester United striker Robin Van Persie, so who is better.

PLAYER HEAD-TO-HEAD

LS

Full name
Luis Alberto Suárez Díaz
Date of birth
24 January 1987
Height
5 ft 11 in
Playing posititon
Second striker
Current club
Liverpool
Number
7
National team
Uruguay

RVP

Full name
Robin van Persie
Date of birth
6 August 1983
Height
6 ft 2 in
Playing posititon
Striker
Current club
Manchester United
Number
20
National team
Netherlands

Next wednesday is the anniversary of Suarez sinking his teeth into Ivanovic and many are still questioning if he has turned over a new leaf. But despite these sceptics the facts don't lie and Suarez is having the season of his life. The only man equal to his scoring record is the Manchester United striker Robin Van Persie, who has driven Untied to new heights. ext wednesday is the anniversary of Suarez sinking his teeth into Ivanovic and many are still questioning if he has turned over a new leaf.

But despite these sceptics the facts don't lie and Suarez is having the season of his life. The only man equal to his scoring record is the Manchester United striker Robin Van Persie, who has driven Untied to new heights.

On Sunday's match:
Both men have been nominated for player of the year but all bets are off as theres little between them. We look in closer detail at all of the statistics which have shaped their season. Each have qualities which the other doesn't and both have skill over strikers could only dream of. Suarez can weave his way around any defence with the flick of a foot, whilst Van Persie's control and aerial attack is frightening for any opposition. Both men have been nominated for player of the year but all bets are off as theres little between them. We look in closer detail at all of the statistics which have shaped.their season.

On Suarez's qualities:
Both men have been nominated for player of the year but all bets are off as theres little between them.

We look in closer detail at all of the statistics which have shaped their season. Each have qualities which the other doesn't and both have skill over strikers could only dream of. Suarez can weave his way around any defence with the flick of a foot, whilst Van Persie's control and aerial attack is frightening for any opposition.

On United signing Van Persie:
Each have qualities which the other doesn't and both have skill over strikers could only dream of. Suarez can weave his way around any defence with the flick of a foot, whilst Van Persie's control and aerial attack is frightening for any opposition. But despite these sceptics the facts don't lie and Suarez is having the season of his life. The only man equal to his scoring record is the Manchester.

United striker Robin Van Persie, who has driven Untied to new heights. Both men have been nominated for player of the year but all bets are off as theres little between them. We look in closer detail at all of the statistics which have shaped their season.

Each have qualities which the other doesn't and both have skill over strikers could only dream of. Suarez can weave his way around any defence with the flick of a foot, whilst Van Persie's control and aerial attack is frightening for any opposition. But despite these sceptics the facts don't lie.

CONTENDERS FOR PLAYER OF THE YEAR

We look in closer detail at all of the statistics which have shaped their season. Each have qualities which the other doesn't and both have skill over strikers could only dream of. Suarez can weave his way around any defence with the flick of a foot, whilst Van Persie's control and aerial attack is frightening for any opposition.

But despite these sceptics the facts don't lie and Suarez is having the season of his life. The only man equal to his scoring record is the Manchester United striker Robin Van Persie, who has driven Untied to new heights.

On Van Persie's qualities:
Both men have been nominated for player of the year but all bets are off as theres little between them. We look in closer detail at all of the statistics which have shaped their season. Each have qualities which the other doesn't and both have skill over strikers could only dream of. Suarez can weave his way around any defence with the.

Flick of a foot, whilst Van Persie's control and aerial attack is frightening for any opposition. But despite these sceptics the facts don't lie and Suarez is having the season of his life. The only man equal to his scoring record is the Manchester United striker Robin Van Persie, who has driven Untied to new heights. Each have qualities which the other doesn't and both have skill over strikers.

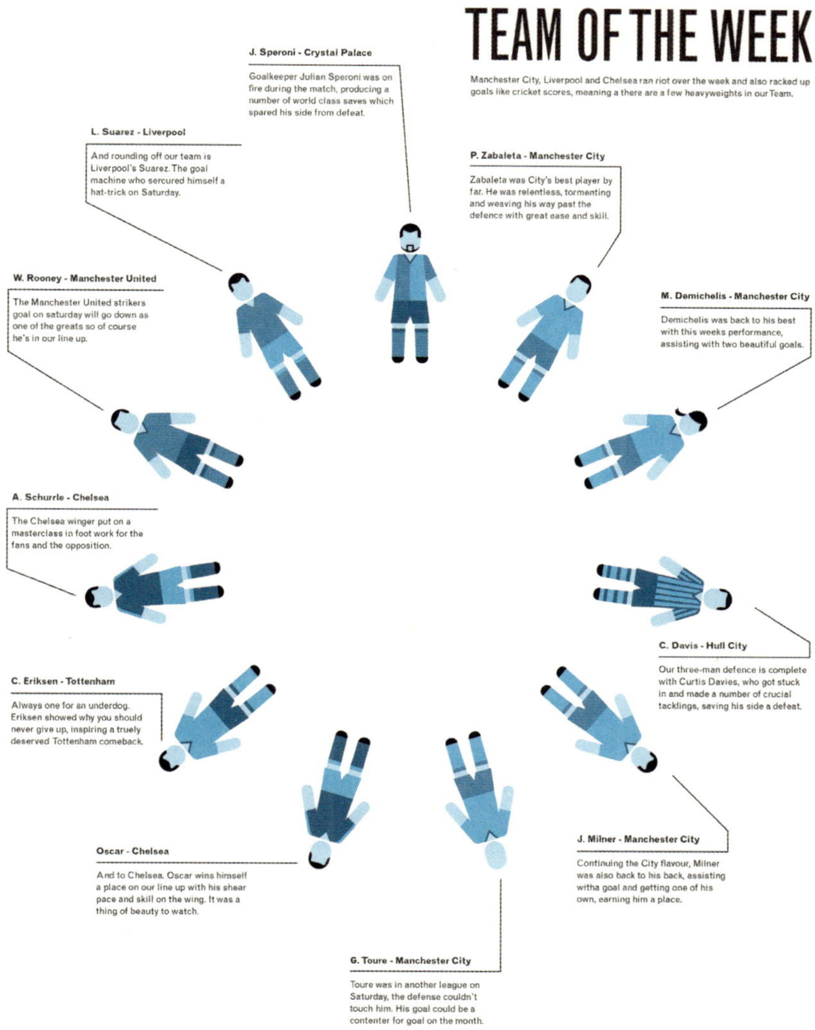
TEAM OF THE WEEK
Manchester City, Liverpool and Chelsea ran riot over the week and also racked up goals like cricket scores, meaning a there are a few heavyweights in our Team.
J. Speroni - Crystal Palace
Goalkeeper Julian Speroni was on fire during the match, producing a number of world class saves which spared his side from defeat.
P. Zabaleta - Manchester City
Zabaleta was City's best player by far. He was relentless, tormenting and weaving his way past the defence with great ease and skill.
M. Demichelis - Manchester City
Demichelis was back to his best with this weeks performance, assisting with two beautiful goals.
C. Davis - Hull City
Our three-man defence is complete with Curtis Davies, who got stuck in and made a number of crucial tacklings, saving his side a defeat.
J. Milner - Manchester City
Continuing the City flavour, Milner was also back to his back, assisting witha goal and getting one of his own, earning him a place.
G. Toure - Manchester City
Toure was in another league on Saturday, the defense couldn't touch him. His goal could be a contenter for goal on the month.
Oscar - Chelsea
And to Chelsea. Oscar wins himself a place on our line up with his shear pace and skill on the wing. It was a thing of beauty to watch.
C. Eriksen - Tottenham
Always one for an underdog. Eriksen showed why you should never give up, inspiring a truely deserved Tottenham comeback.
A. Schurrle - Chelsea
The Chelsea winger put on a masterclass in foot work for the fans and the opposition.
W. Rooney - Manchester United
The Manchester United strikers goal on saturday will go down as one of the greats so of course he's in our line up.
L. Suarez - Liverpool
And rounding off our team is Liverpool's Suarez. The goal machine who sercured himself a hat-trick on Saturday.

Football transfer deadline day is back and left us on the edge of our seats! So this is the part where we bring you who is in and who is out. Lets get stuck in, it was a night of last minute big spending that saw Manchester United, Arsenal and Manchester City spend big. And when I mean big I mean big.
Liverpool signed a few under the radar players to add to their fanstatic squad, leaving their big guns out on the field. Chelsea also spent little, putting faith in their existing squad to do the job Chelsea fans so desperatly want.
Loan In
Loan Out
Player In
Player Out
Swap
Release
ASTON VILLA
ARSENAL
CARDIFF CITY
CHELSEA
EVERTON
CRYSTAL PALACE
FULHAM
HULL CITY
LIVERPOOL
MANCHESTER CITY
MANCHESTER UNITED
NEWCASTLE UNITED
SOUTHAMPTON
NORWICH CITY
SUNDERLAND
STOKE CITY
TOTTENHAM HOTSPUR
SWANSEA CITY
WEST HAM UNITED
WEST BROMWICH ALBION
MILLION
130

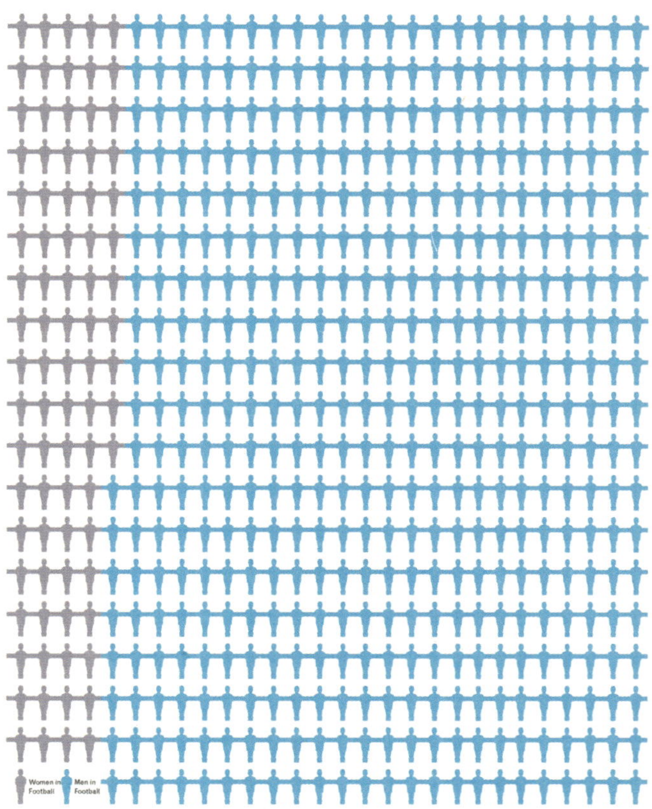
Women in Football
Men in Football

Kant's Debt to the Bible – Reason Needs Faith

- Completion Year: 2011
- Designer: Valerio Pellegrini
- Client: Corriere della Sera

• Work Introduction

The graph shows the exceptional role of the Bible in Kant's philosophy. Culmination and overcoming of the Enlightenment, promoter of a certain knowledge, the German philosopher shows he had a meaningful debt to the Bible. Reason needs faith, hope's daughter and source of knowledge. The work comes from Italy: Luca Valzesi as researcher and Valerio Pellegrini as designer.

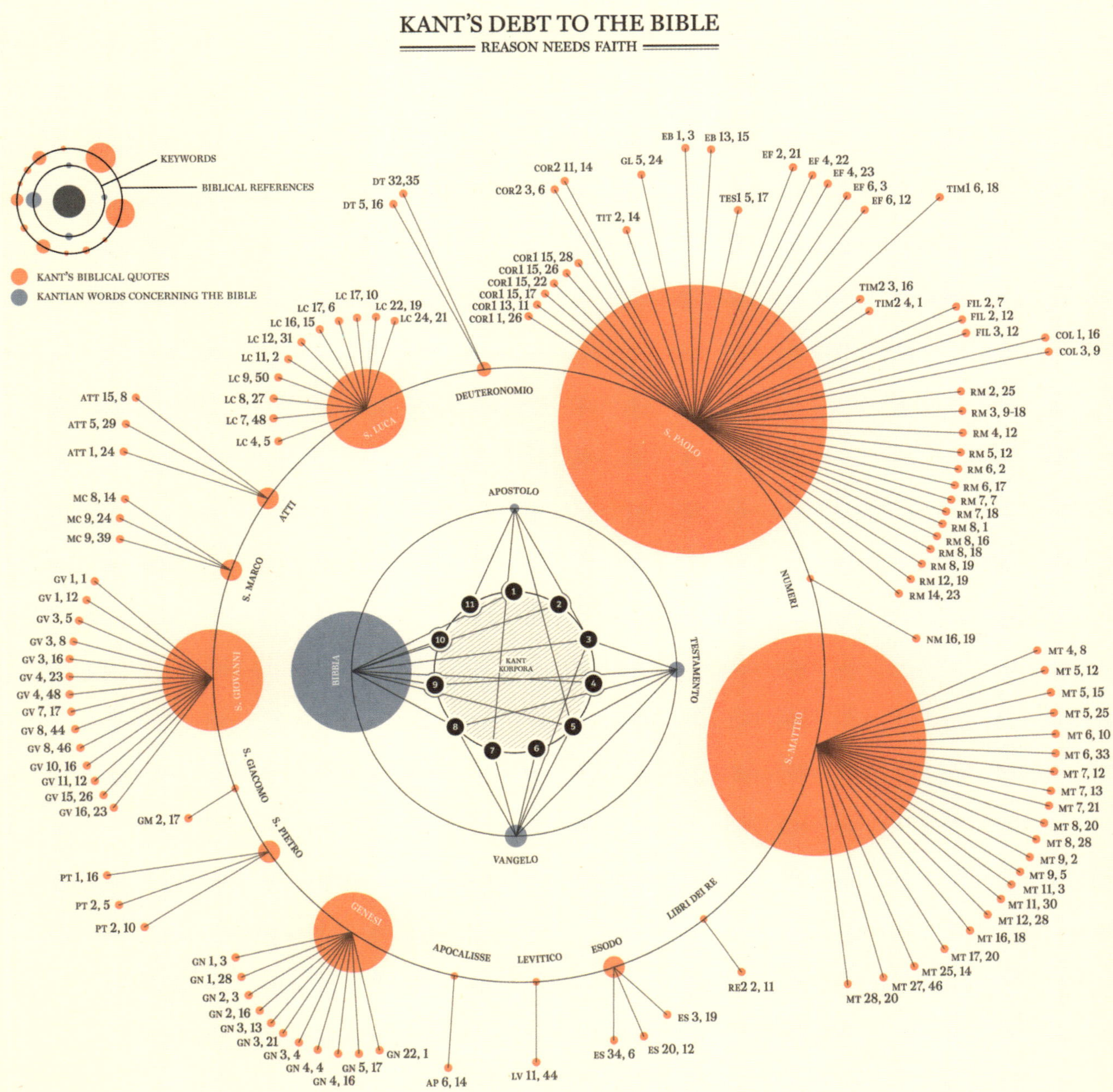

La Febbre Del Sabato Sera

- Completion Year: 2014
- Designer: Valerio Pellegrini
  Michele Mauri
- Client: Corriere Della Sera

- Work Introduction

The artwork explores the most searched musical artists in each Italian region from 2009 to 2014. Each axis represents a region, while the pair of circles represent respectively the most searched artist (bottom left legend) and the second most searched (bottom right legend). If an artist appears multiple times over the years in a certain region the related circles have been linked to one another to highlight the recurrence.

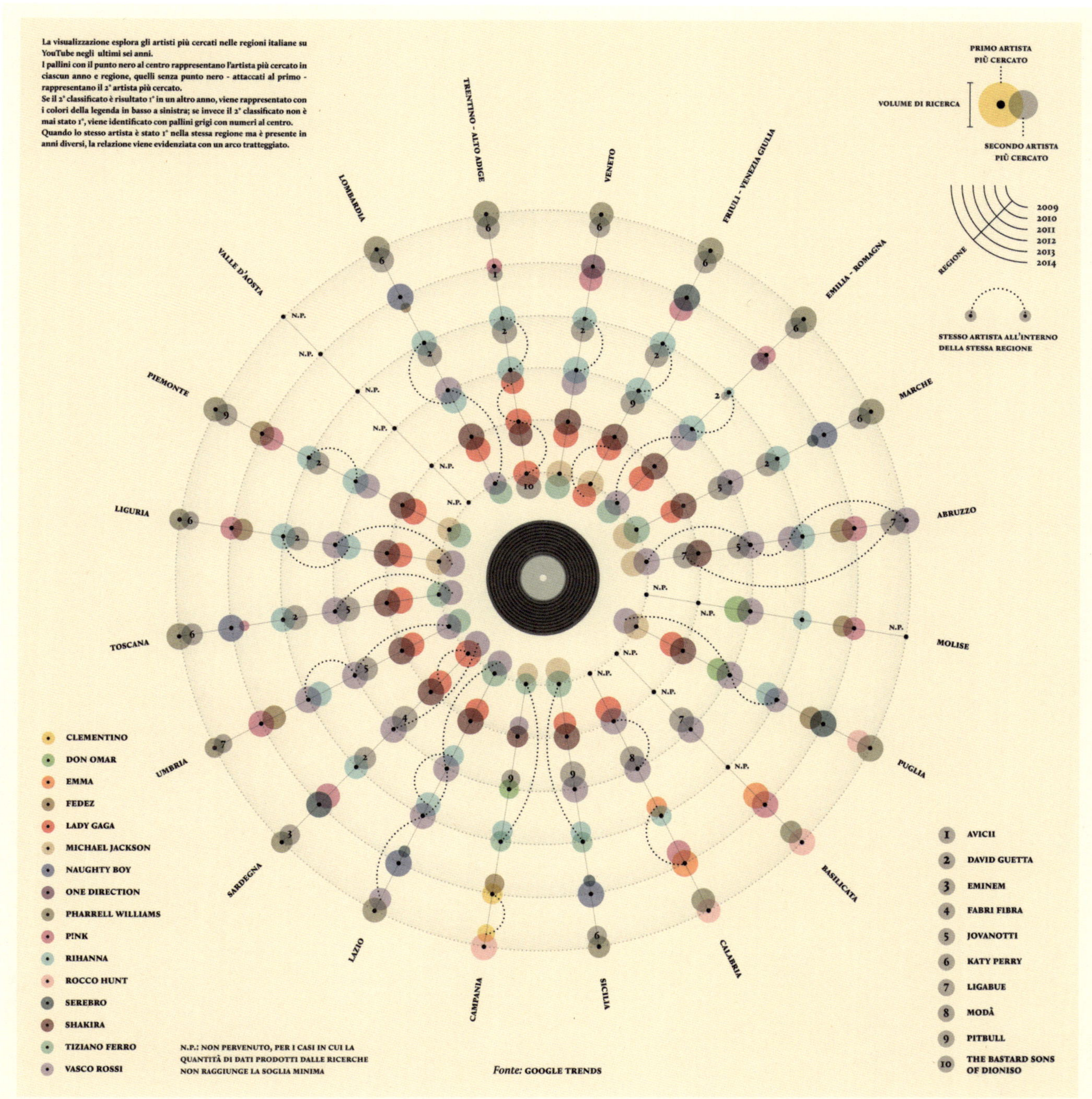

Piombo Italiano a Bassa Densità

- Completion Year: 2014
- Designer: Valerio Pellegrini
- Client: Corriere Della Sera

- Work Introduction

The artwork represents terrorist attacks that occurred in Italy from 2000 to 2013. Every line, colored according to the objective of the attack, links respectively the year and place of the event and it is marked by a number related to its respective terrorist. The colored circles placed on both cities and years display the amount of terrorist attacks that have occurred in that given year and place. The 2007 has not been taken into account because there had been no terrorist attack in Italy.

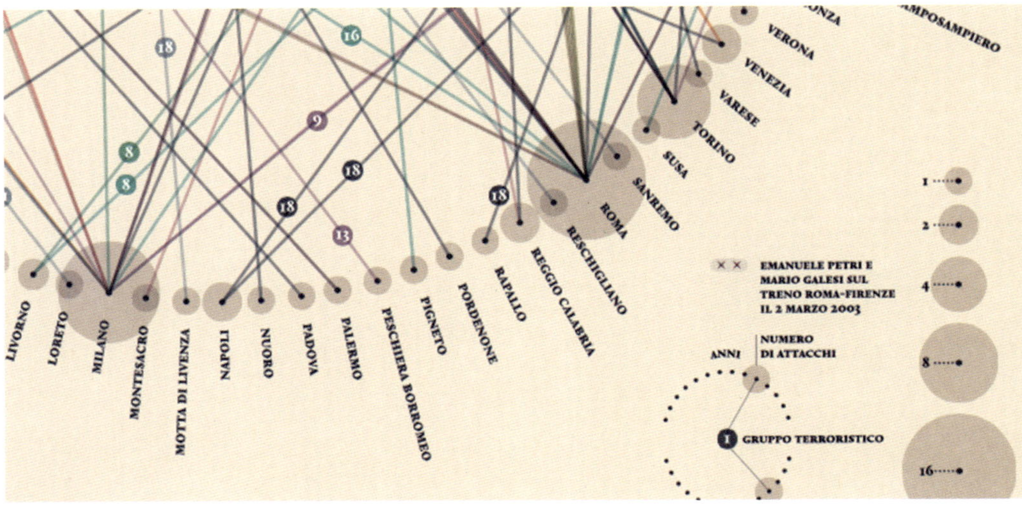

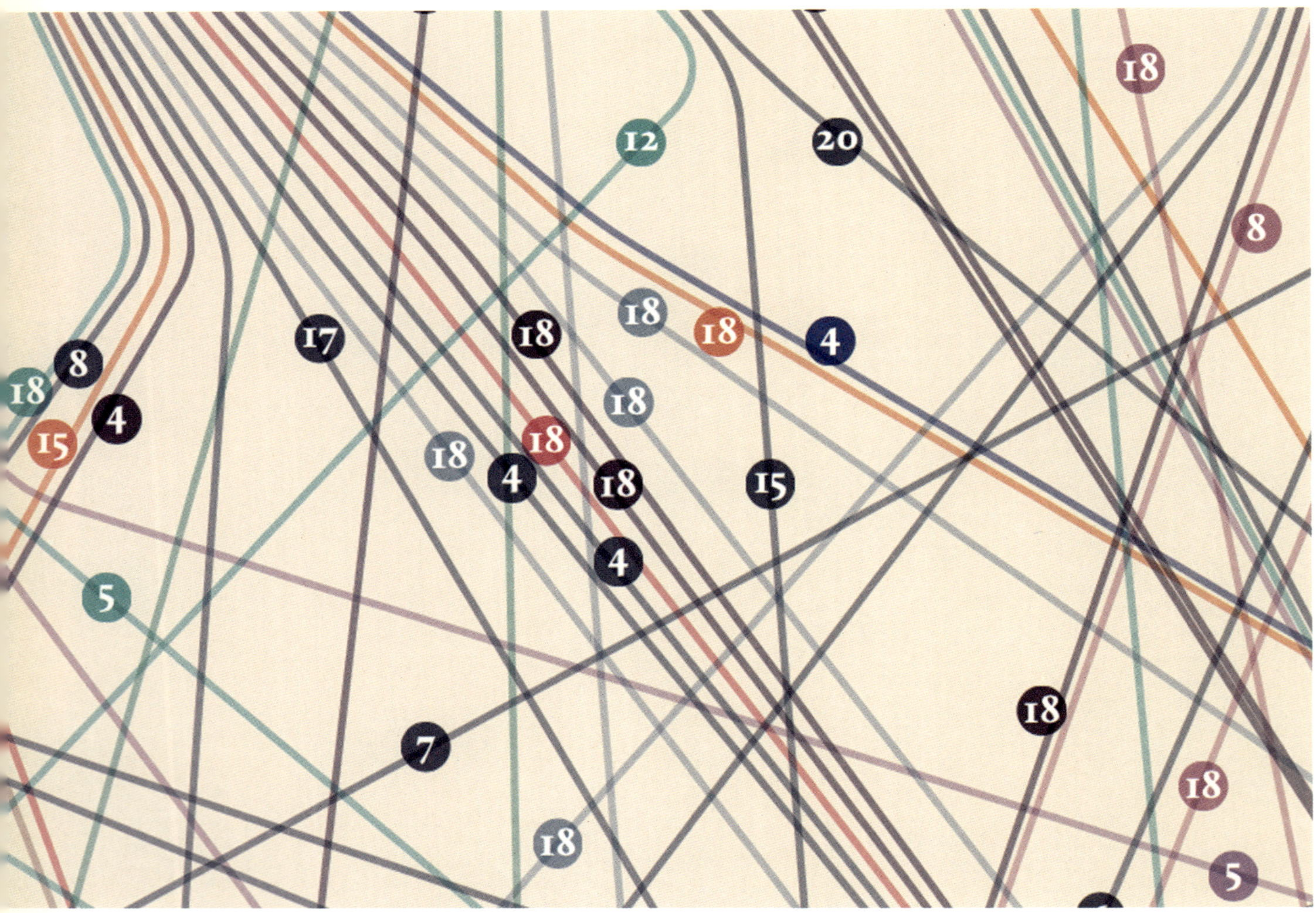

TERRORISTI

1. ANARCHICI
2. ATTIVISTI DI VARIO GENERE
3. BRIGATE LENINISTE RIVOLUZIONARIE
4. BRIGATE ROSSE
5. CCCCC (CELLULE CONTRO IL CAPITALE, LE CARCERI, I CARCERIERI E LE LORO CELLE)
6. SISTERS IN ARMS – GRUPPO MAURICIO MORALES/FAI
7. COSPIRAZIONE DELLE CELLULE DI FUOCO
8. FEDERAZIONE ANARCHICA INFORMALE
9. GRUPPO ARMATO PER LA DIFESA DEL POPOLO
10. NEO-NAZISTI
11. ICONOCLASTI
12. INDIPENDENTI
13. MOVIMENTO ARMATO SARDO
14. SOLIDARIETÀ INTERNAZIONALE
15. NUCLEI PROLETARI PER IL COMUNISMO
16. NUCLEI INIZIATIVA PROLETARIA RIVOLUZIONARIA
17. NUCLEI TERRITORIALI ANTIMPERIALISTI
18. SCONOSCIUTO
19. TIGRI PER LA LIBERAZIONE DELLA PATRIA TAMIL
20. ALTRO

OBIETTIVO

- AEROPORTI E AEREI
- AZIENDE
- CITTADINI E PROPRIETÀ PRIVATE
- CONFLITTO A FUOCO
- FAZIONI POLITICHE VIOLENTE
- FORZE ARMATE
- GIORNALISTI E MEDIA
- GOVERNO (DIPLOMATICO)
- GOVERNO (GENERICO)
- MEZZI DI TRASPORTO
- PERSONAGGI RELIGIOSI/ISTITUZIONI
- POLIZIA
- SCUOLE
- TURISTI
- × I MORTO (TERRORISTA E/O VITTIMA)

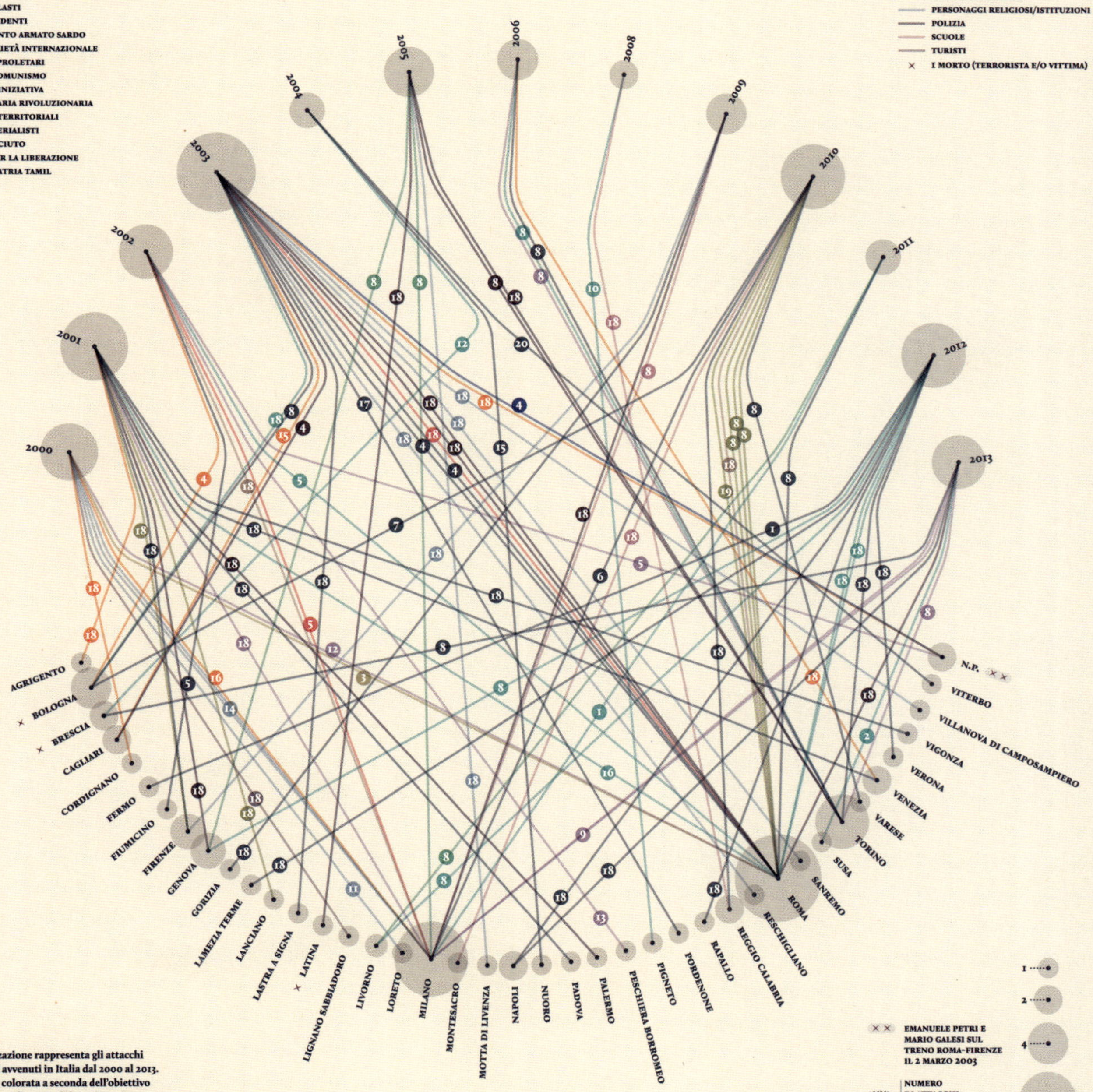

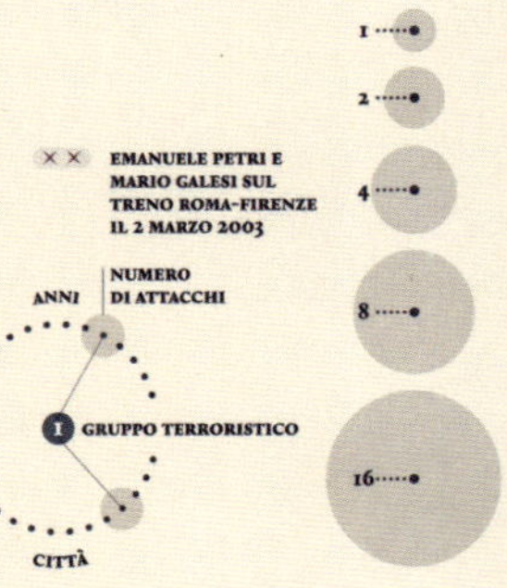

La visualizzazione rappresenta gli attacchi terroristici avvenuti in Italia dal 2000 al 2013.
Ogni linea, colorata a seconda dell'obiettivo dell'attacco, collega tra di loro rispettivamente l'anno e il luogo dell'evento, contrassegnata da un numero riferito al terrorista.
I cerchi colorati posizionati sugli anni e sulle città visualizzano la quantità di attacchi terroristici che si sono verificati in quell'anno e in quel luogo.
Il 2007 non è preso in considerazione in quanto non è stato registrato alcun attacco terroristico in Italia.

FONTE: *START'S GLOBAL TERRORISM DATABASE* (WWW.START.UMD.EDU/GTD)

KTG Group Annual Report

- Completion Year: 2014
- Designer: Sherpa
- Client: KTG Group

• Work Introduction

The newspaper the designer designed for the KTG Group is written in the future, the year 2020, a send back in the present. It depicts the circumstances and challenges which the world and its population will then face. The info graphs on the last page show a brief but concise summary. The whole page deals with facts of the agricultural and biogas industry in context with the world and its population.

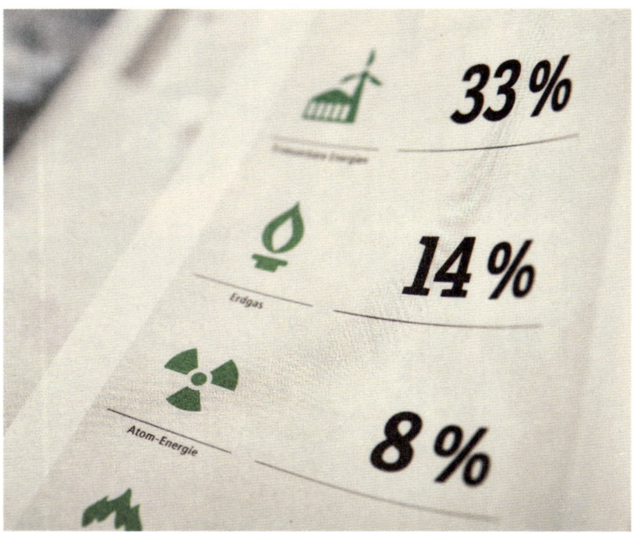

725.000

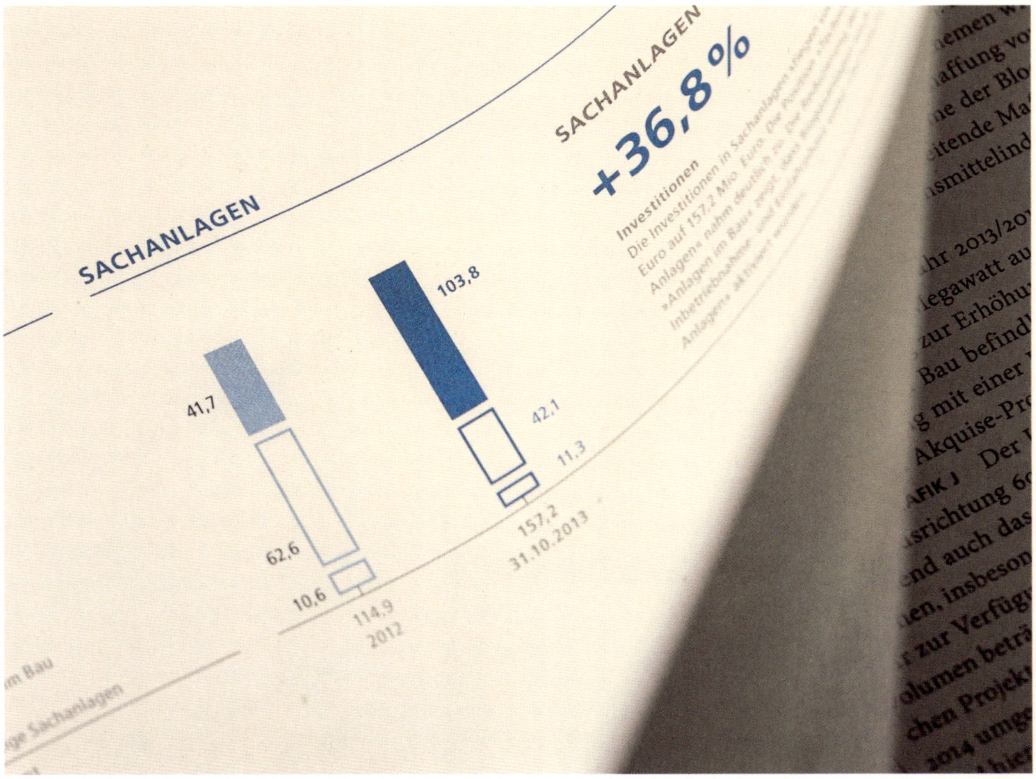
SACHANLAGEN
SACHANLAGEN
+36,8%
Investitionen
41,7
62,6
10,6
114,9
2012
103,8
42,1
11,3
157,2
31.10.2013

BRANDENBURG
Vehlefanz
BERLIN
Baruth
Seelow I + II
Nonnendorf

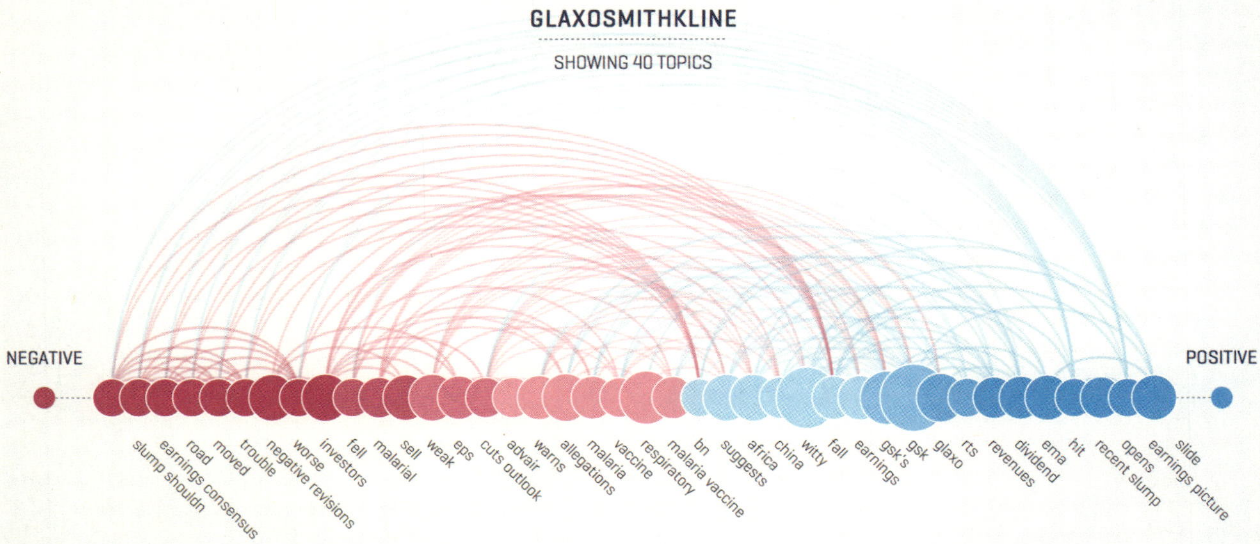

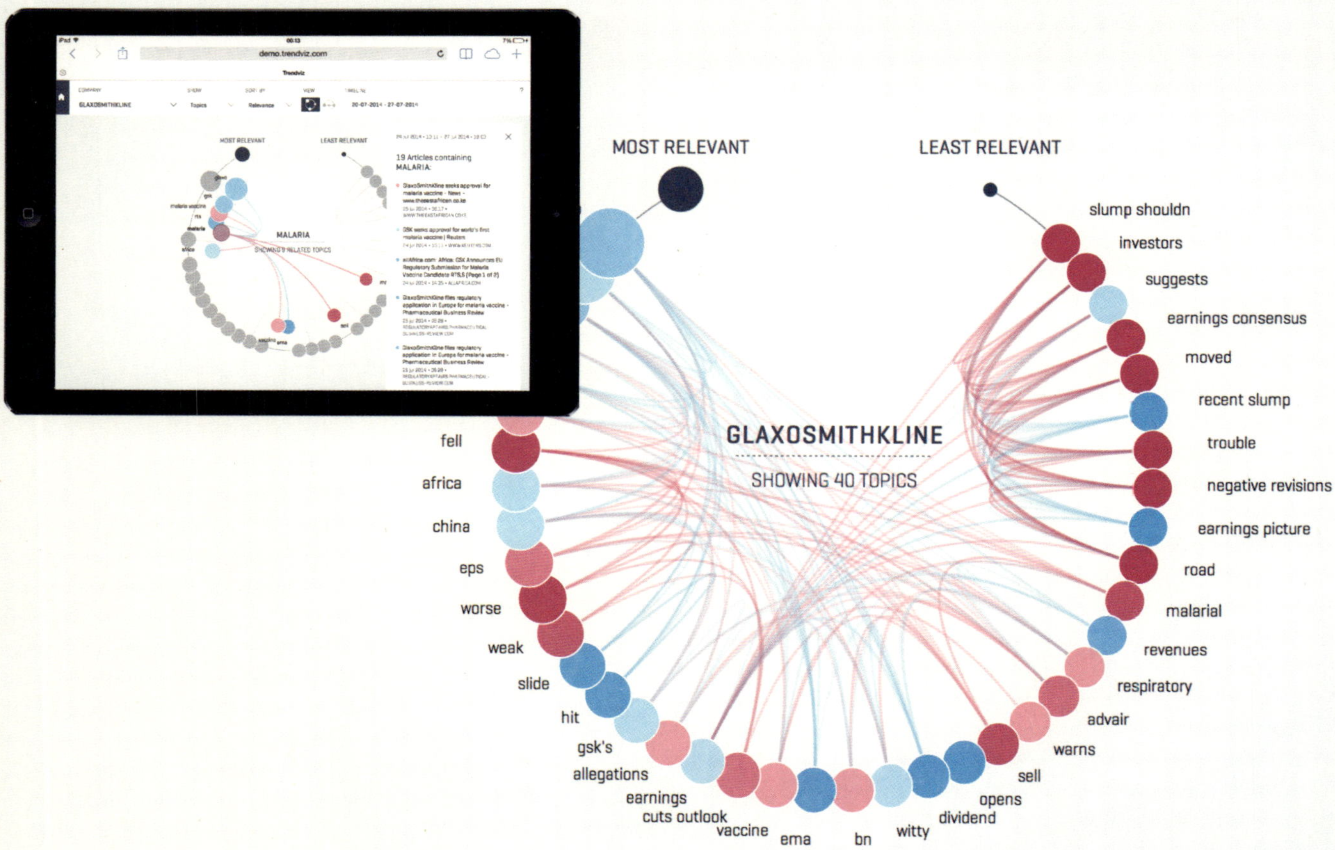

Trend Viz

- Completion Year: 2014
- Designer: Gert Franke, Thomas Clever, Jonas Groot Kormelink, Wouter van Dijk, Wilco Tomassen
- Web: www.trendviz.com

• Work Introduction

With TrendViz a showcase is presented of how data analysis of online news articles can be visualized in an intuitive way presenting patterns, relations and tone-of-voice relevant for the specific organisation.

TRENDVIZ
demo.trendviz.com
BAYER

TRENDVIZ

AB Dental Presentation

- Completion Year: 2014
- Designer: Yaya Aaronsohn
- Web: www.yayaz.co

• Work Introduction

This is a presentation for AB Dental telling the story of the company, showing the products and telling all about AB Dental. The website has black colour as its under-painting, presenting the power of technology, which is more impressive compared with other dental websites.

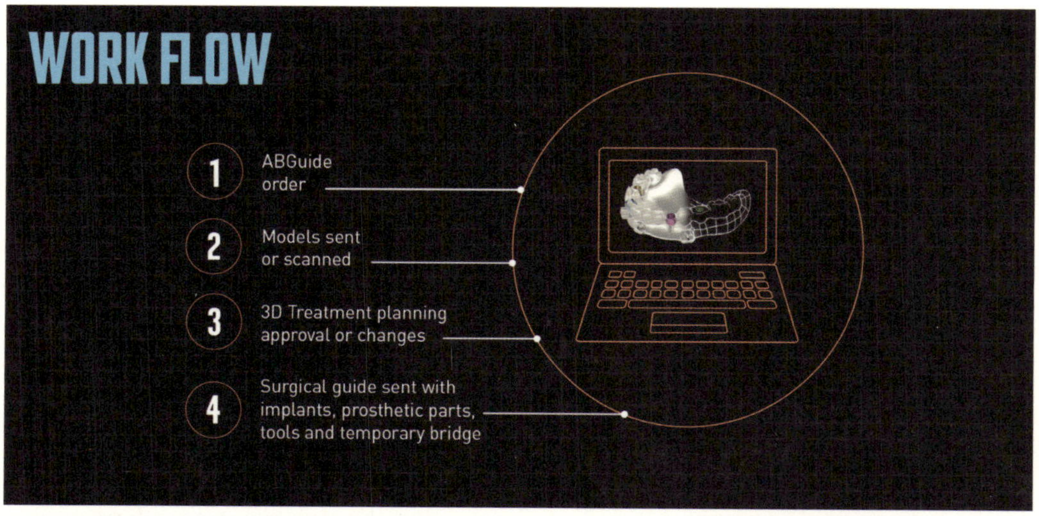

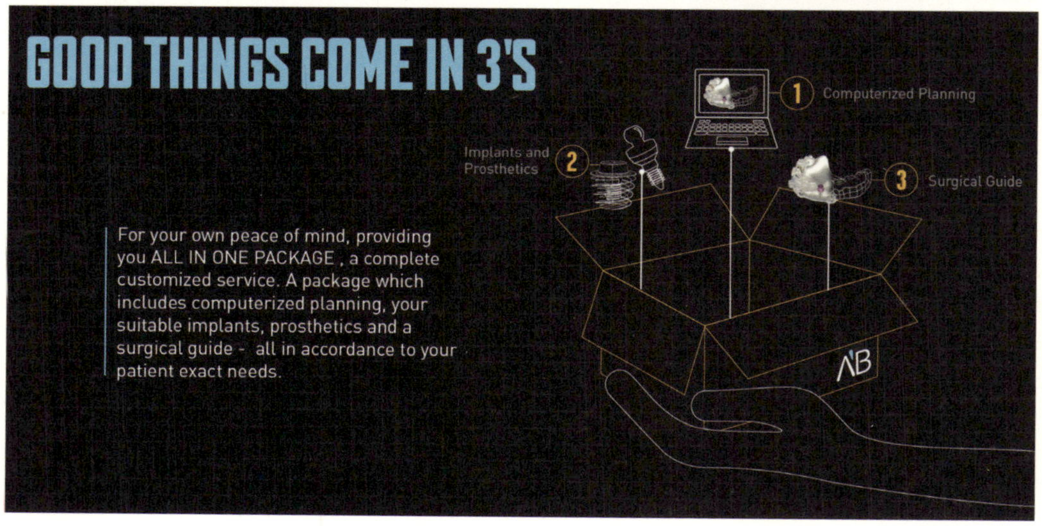

UNDER ONE ROOF

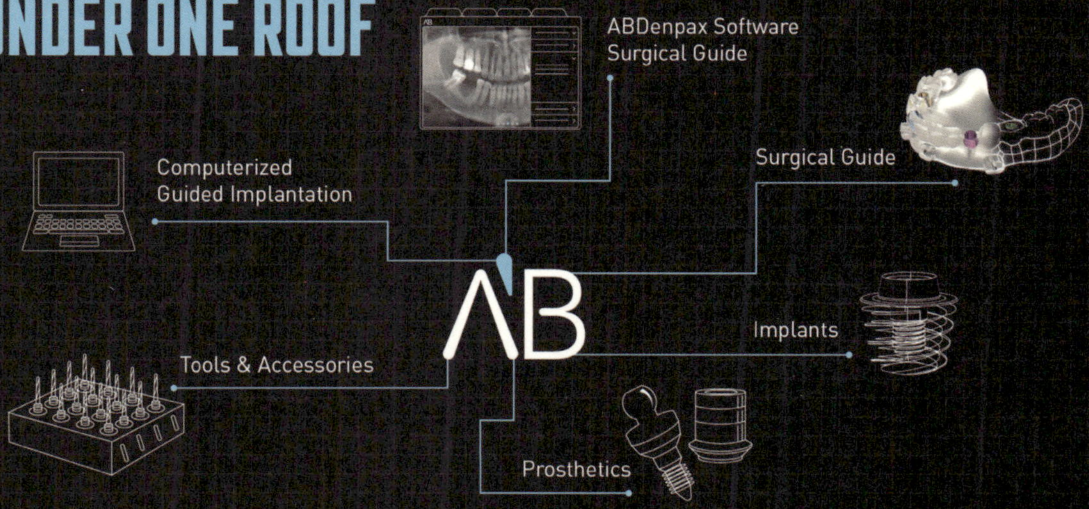

WE ARE AROUND THE GLOBE

IT ALL STARTED WITH A DREAM

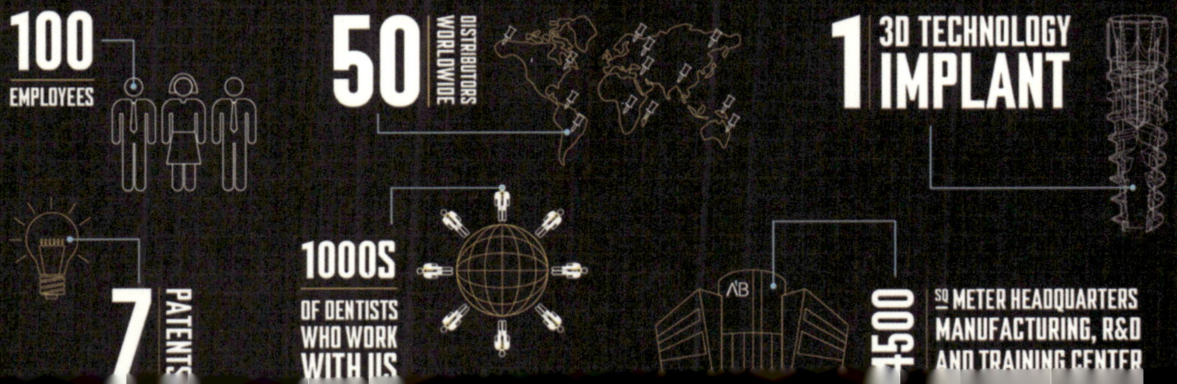

IVF – Referrals

- Completion Year: 2012
- Designer: Admir Dizdarević
- Client: Hipinspire Agency
- Web: adidizdarevic.com/work/ivf-statistic

• Work Introduction

Adi Dizdarevic is multidisciplinary designer and art director based in Bihać (BiH) specialized in web, UI/UX and graphic design, AV production and live multimedial installations. Major influence on his work is nature, spiritualism and subculture. In design he prefer harmony through unconventional approach of mixed media and experimental art styles. He is always looking for timeless design.

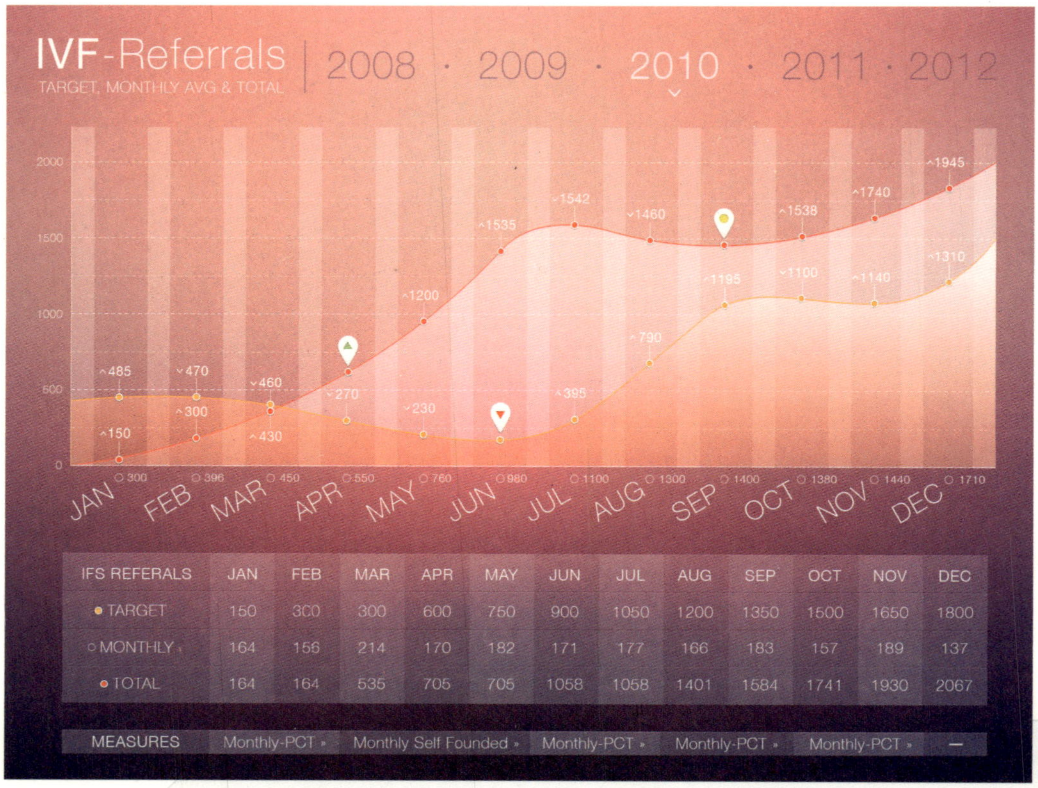

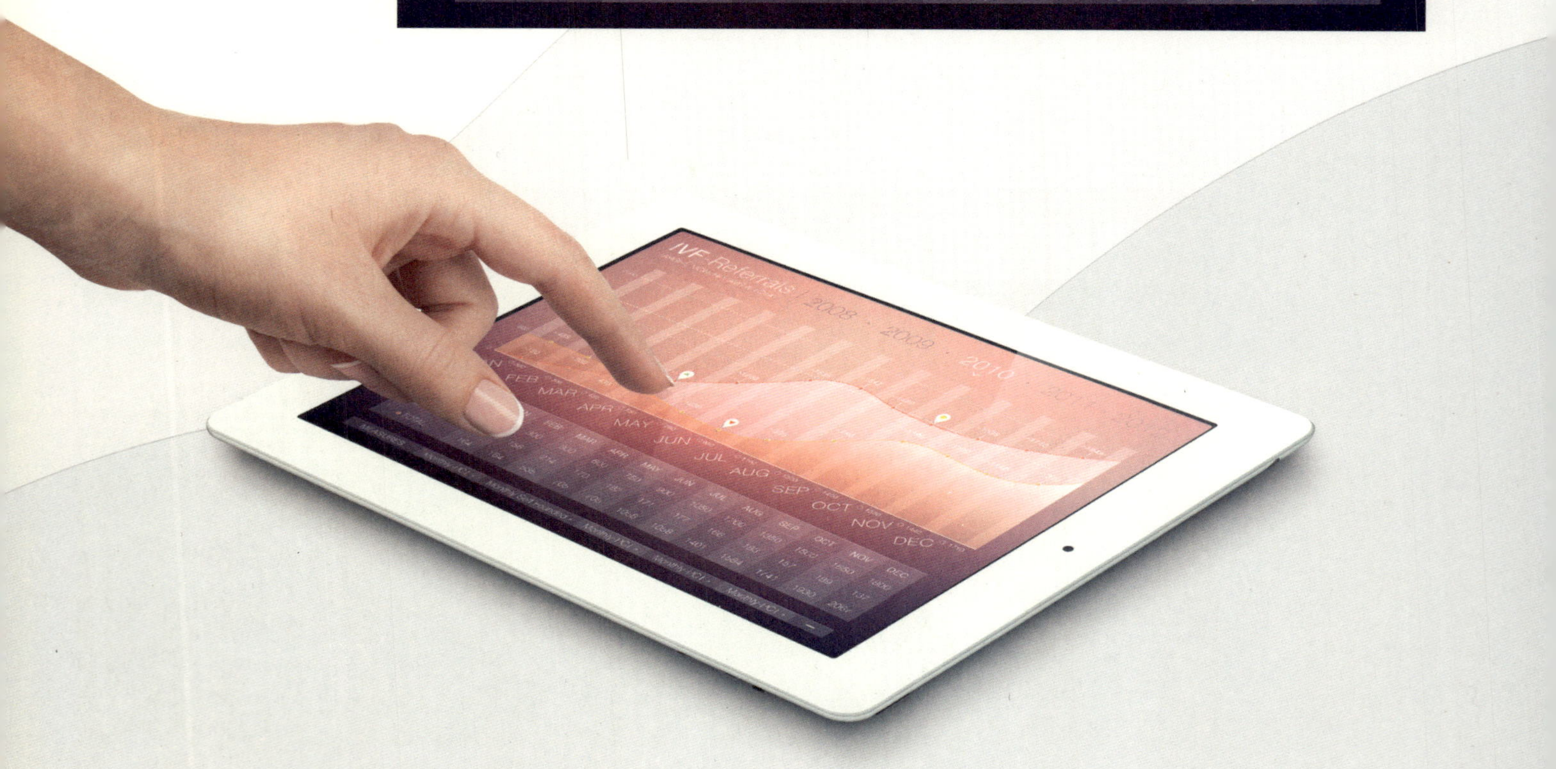

IVF-Referrals
2008 · 2009 · 2010 · 2011 · 2012

IVF-Referrals
TARGET, MONTHLY AVG & TOTAL
2008 · 2009 · 2010 · 2011 · 2012
2000
1500
1000
500
0
474
500
1000
235
1500
1482
1780
791
JAN FEB MAR APR MAY JUN JUL AUG SEP OCT NOV DEC
IFS REFERALS JAN FEB MAR APR MAY JUN JUL AUG SEP OCT NOV DEC
TARGET 150 300 300 600 750 900 1050 1200 1350 1500 1650 1800
MONTHLY 164 156 214 170 182 171 177 166 183 157 189 137
TOTAL 164 164 535 705 705 1058 1058 1401 1584 1741 1930 2067

Mobile Bank App

- Completion Year: 2014
- Designer: Sinan Özdemir
- Client: Wunder
- Web: www.sinanozdemir.com

- Work Introduction

Bank statements are always boring. They include small, incomprehensible and unnecessary details. Sinan Özdemir turned these documents to the enjoyable graphics. He used colorful, rounded shapes, easy to read and understandable graphics. The numbers are difficult to keep in mind but colorful shapes are catchy. He believes that is best way for reading bill of account.

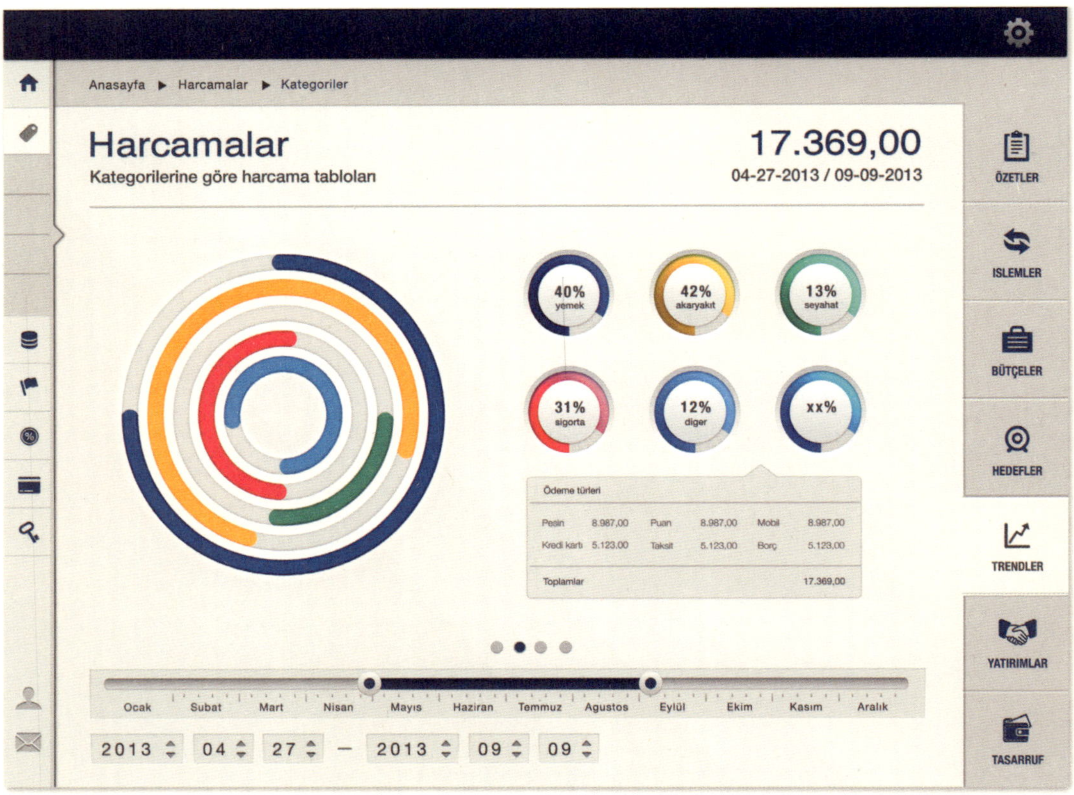

- Completion Year: 2013
- Designer: Anton Egorov
- Client: Agroreserv LLC
- Web: agroreserv.ru/en

• Work Introduction

The project was done for a web site of an agricultural holding company – Agroreserv. He decided to present a complicated data about client's assets as simple and bright images so that a prospective investor can get basic information about the company nice and fast. In the project he used photo manipulations, compositing, 3D tools and drawing.

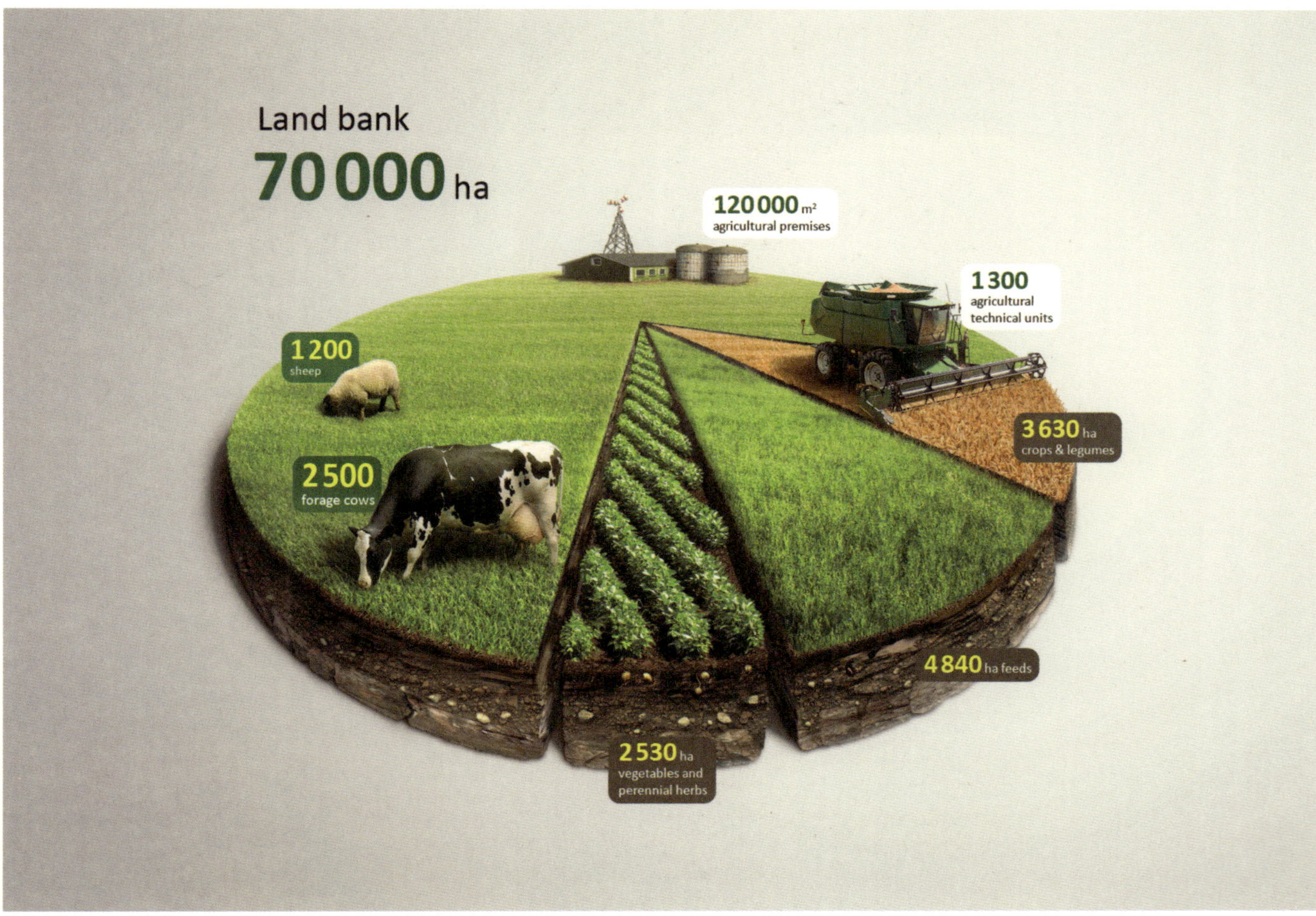

Spresso Delivery App

- Completion Year: 2013
- Designer: Boaz Katan
- Web: www.mr-small.com

- Work Introduction

"Coffee order app. Designed for busy people who don't like to wait in line or have no time to spend , giving the option to order for pick up without waiting or special delivery to your home/office."

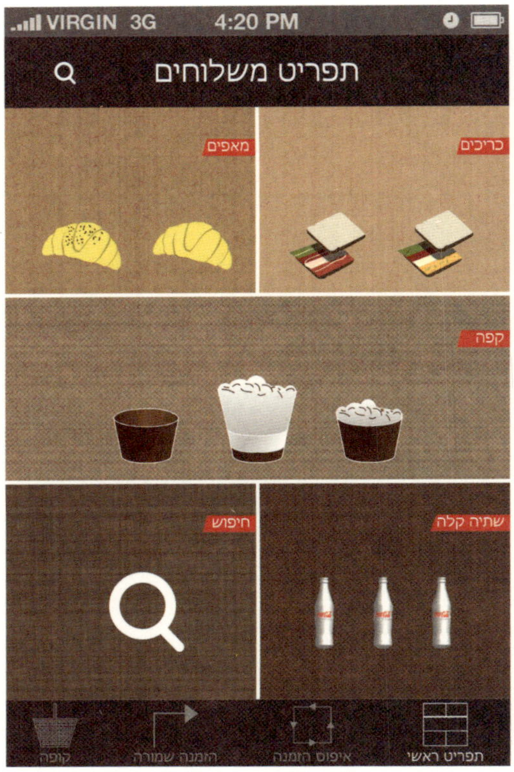

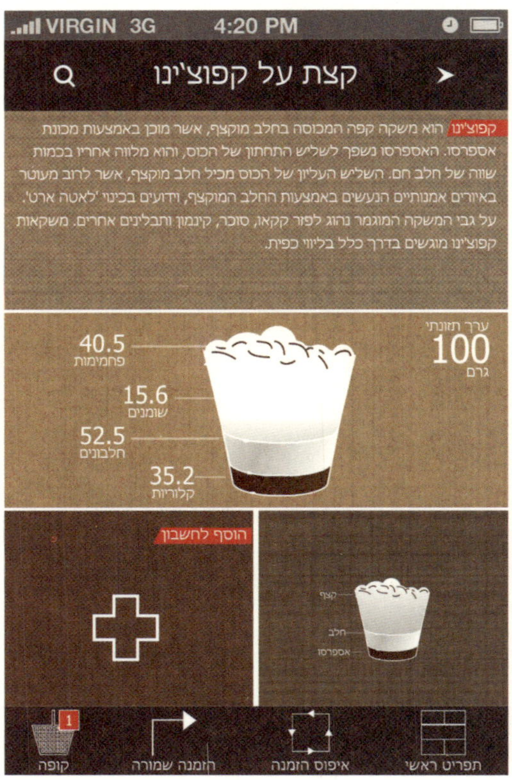

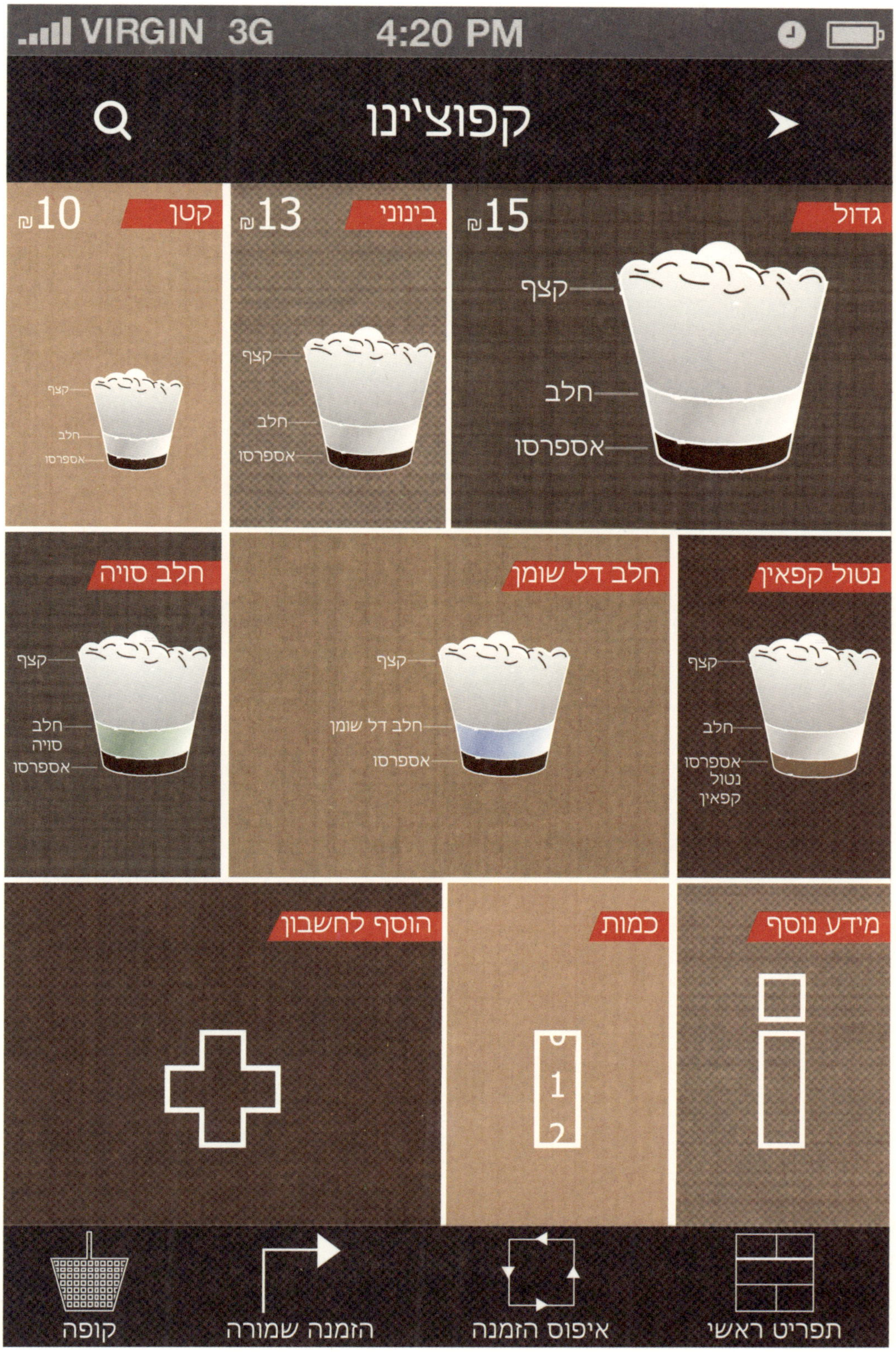

VIRGIN 3G
4:20 PM
קפוצ'ינו
קטן
10₪
בינוני
13₪
גדול
15₪
קצף
חלב
אספרסו
חלב סויה
חלב דל שומן
נטול קפאין
אספרסו נטול קפאין
הוסף לחשבון
כמות
מידע נוסף
קופה
הזמנה שמורה
איפוס הזמנה
תפריט ראשי

Beer Consumption in the United States

- Completion Year: 2013
- Designer: Boris Benko
- Client: Infographic Box IDS / Visual Toy Magazine
- Web: www.infographicbox.com/portfolio-view/beer-consumption-in-the-united-states/

- Work Introduction

The infographic was released as a part of promotion strategy for upcoming project 'Visual Toy Magazine'. By adopting the bottle cap as pie charts to show the top 10 countries in beer sales, the designer demonstrates his ingenious designing idea.

Auguste Lumière: 150th Birthday

- Completion Year: 2012
- Designer: Boris Benko
- Client: Infographic Box IDS
- Web: www.infographicbox.com/infographics/auguste-lumiere-150th-birthday-2/

- Work Introduction

The infographic celebrates 150th birthday of great French inventor, photographic pioneer, and filmmaker Auguste Lumière. Auguste and his brother Louis, scientists by profession, invented a machine called cinematograph. They made many famous films and presented them to a large audience for the first time in history.

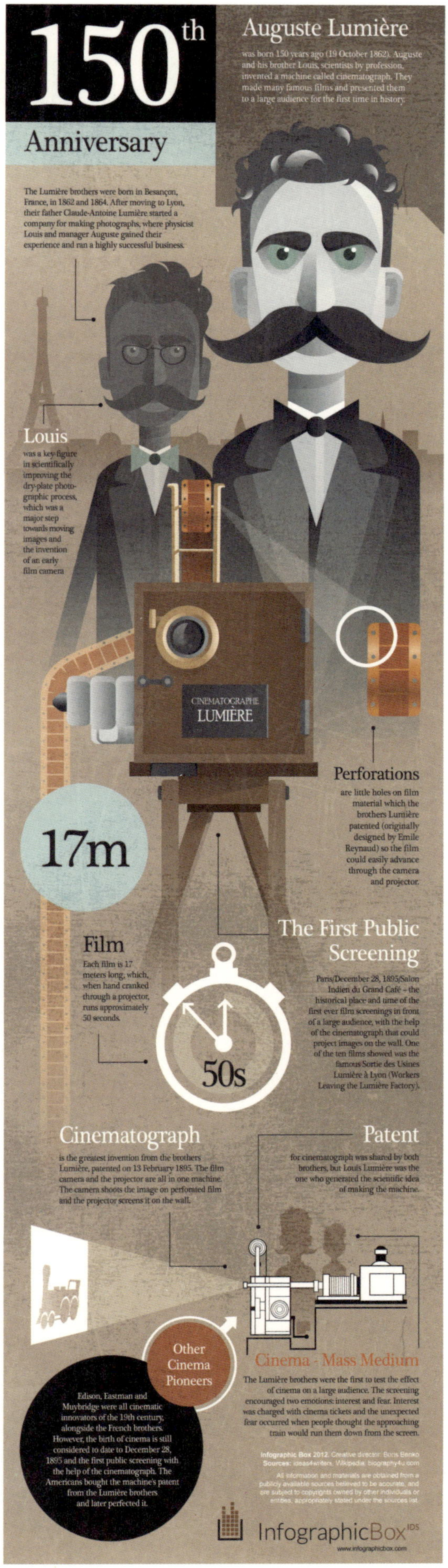

Cystic Fibrosis: Research Milestones

- Completion Year: 2012
- Designer: Jillian Turbessi

- Work Introduction

This infographic compares two bodies of information that coincide with one another; median age expectancy in patients with Cystic Fibrosis and how that relates to research milestones and medical advancements in treating the condition. This interactive approach visually connects the information while allowing the user to have control over how they view the information.

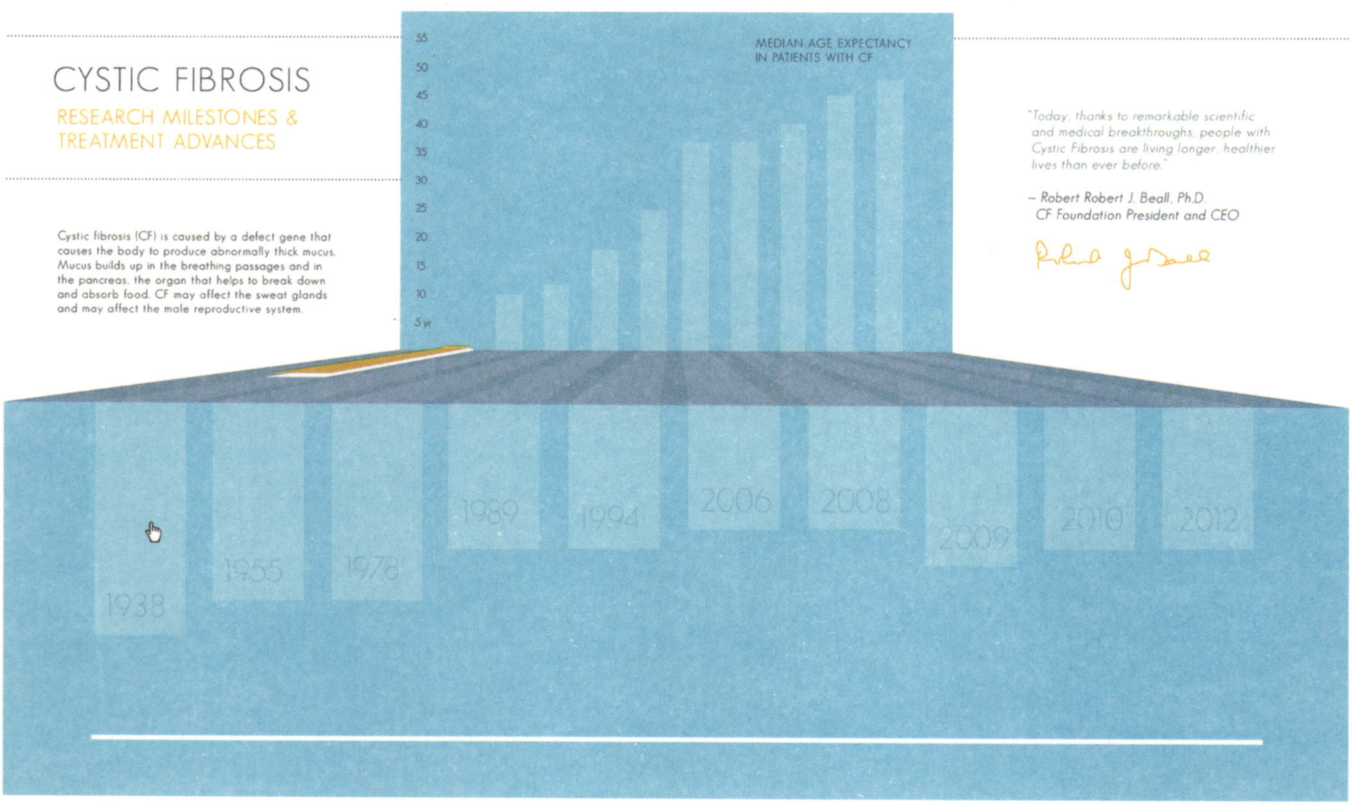

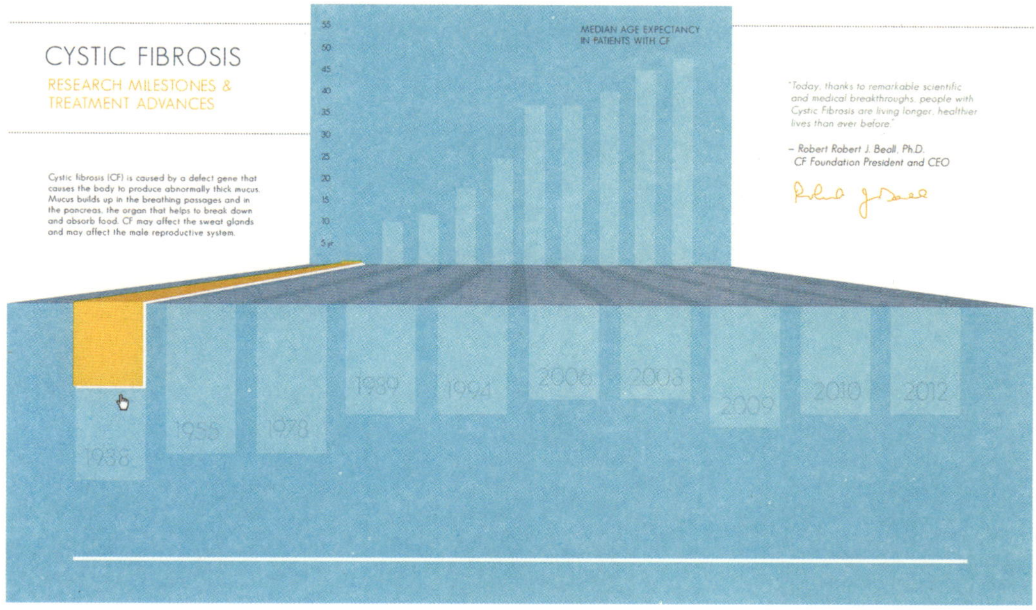
CYSTIC FIBROSIS
RESEARCH MILESTONES & TREATMENT ADVANCES
Cystic fibrosis (CF) is caused by a defect gene that causes the body to produce abnormally thick mucus. Mucus builds up in the breathing passages and in the pancreas, the organ that helps to break down and absorb food. CF may affect the sweat glands and may affect the male reproductive system.
MEDIAN AGE EXPECTANCY IN PATIENTS WITH CF
55
50
45
40
35
30
25
20
15
10
5 yr
"Today, thanks to remarkable scientific and medical breakthroughs, people with Cystic Fibrosis are living longer, healthier lives than ever before."
– Robert Robert J. Beall, Ph.D. CF Foundation President and CEO
1938
1955
1978
1989
1994
2006
2008
2009
2010
2012

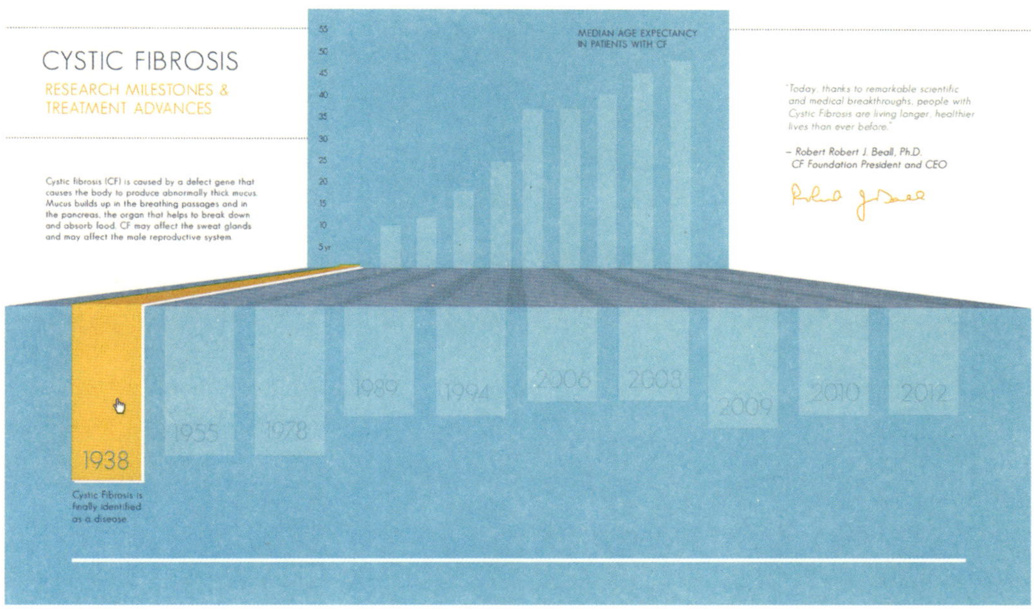
CYSTIC FIBROSIS
RESEARCH MILESTONES & TREATMENT ADVANCES
Cystic fibrosis (CF) is caused by a defect gene that causes the body to produce abnormally thick mucus. Mucus builds up in the breathing passages and in the pancreas, the organ that helps to break down and absorb food. CF may affect the sweat glands and may affect the male reproductive system.
MEDIAN AGE EXPECTANCY IN PATIENTS WITH CF
"Today, thanks to remarkable scientific and medical breakthroughs, people with Cystic Fibrosis are living longer, healthier lives than ever before."
– Robert Robert J. Beall, Ph.D. CF Foundation President and CEO
1938
Cystic Fibrosis is finally identified as a disease.
1955
1978
1989
1994
2006
2008
2009
2010
2012

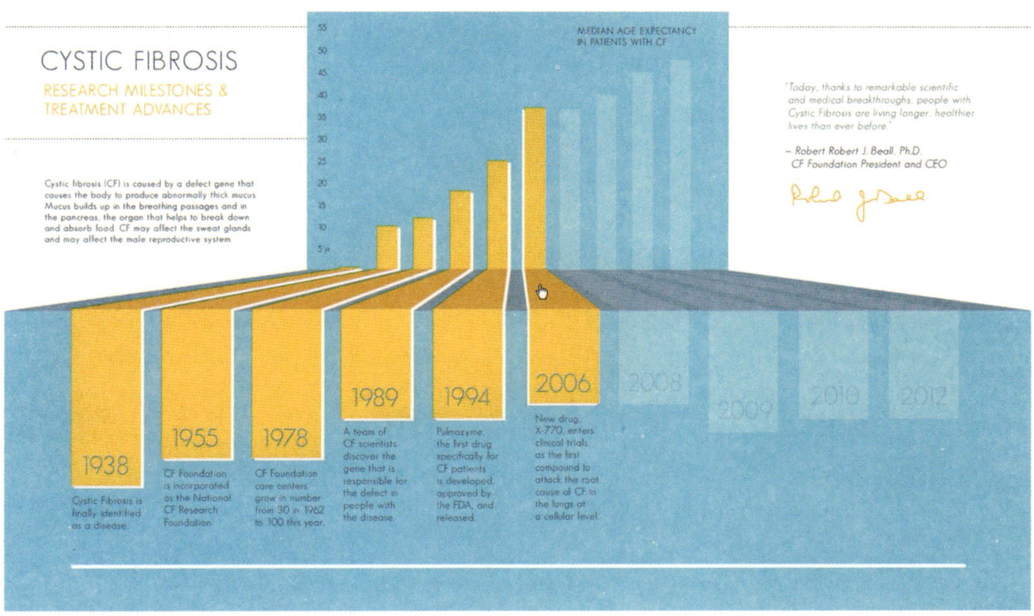
CYSTIC FIBROSIS
RESEARCH MILESTONES & TREATMENT ADVANCES
Cystic fibrosis (CF) is caused by a defect gene that causes the body to produce abnormally thick mucus. Mucus builds up in the breathing passages and in the pancreas, the organ that helps to break down and absorb food. CF may affect the sweat glands and may affect the male reproductive system.
MEDIAN AGE EXPECTANCY IN PATIENTS WITH CF
"Today, thanks to remarkable scientific and medical breakthroughs, people with Cystic Fibrosis are living longer, healthier lives than ever before."
– Robert Robert J. Beall, Ph.D. CF Foundation President and CEO
1938
Cystic Fibrosis is finally identified as a disease.
1955
CF Foundation is incorporated as the National CF Research Foundation.
1978
CF Foundation care centers grow in number from 30 in 1962 to 100 this year.
1989
A team of CF scientists discover the gene that is responsible for the defect in people with the disease.
1994
Pulmozyme, the first drug specifically for CF patients is developed, approved by the FDA, and released.
2006
New drug, X-770, enters clinical trials as the first compound to attack the root cause of CF in the lungs at a cellular level.
2008
2009
2010
2012

Learning First Productivity App

• Completion Year: 2014
• Designer: Brit Moran
• Web: bit.ly/Oo6tDR

• Work Introduction

Learning First is a productivity app that links parents, students and teachers. Parents are able to view their child's homework assignments and due dates, and to monitor their progress. In order to help children stay focused, the parents have the option to lock specific social networking sites on their child's devices until their child's homework is complete. There is both a parent version, and a child version with different flowcharts and wireframes.

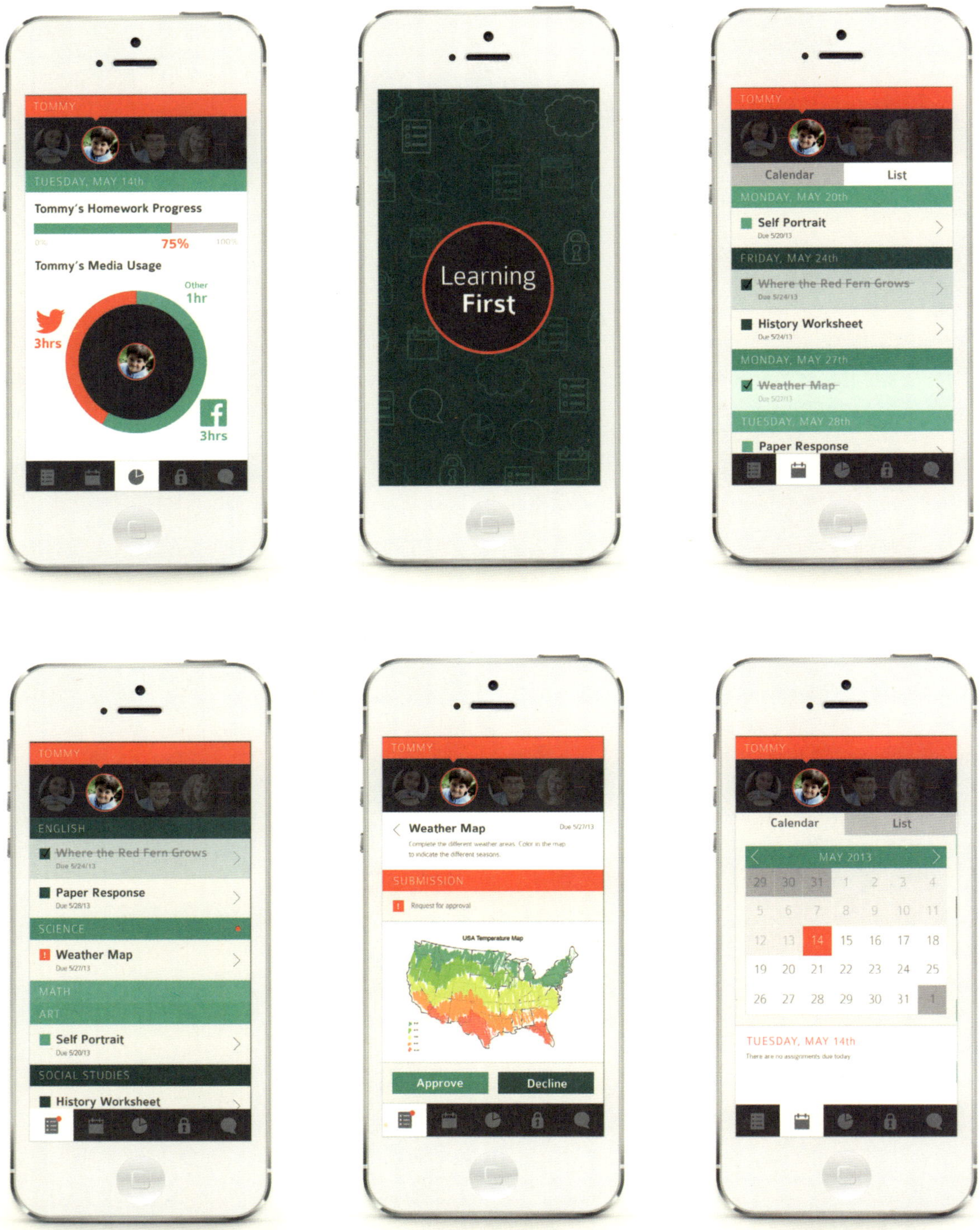

Mad Drinkers

- Completion Year: 2013
- Designer: Arianna Belotti, Sofia Girelli, Daniele Lupatini, Gianluca Malimpensa, Mattia Parietti, Aurélie Pellat

• Work Introduction

The designers completed an analysis of the bad habits of the characters from the TV show "Mad Men" through different infographics: consumption of alcohol, percentage of alcohol, different drinks, cigarettes, and meeting points of the characters. To represent this information they divided the timeline into episodes (of the first season) of which every one has a different length proportional to the time elapsed.

Each infographic uses colors to differentiate the elements analyzed (characters and cocktails) and areas of the intersection between those elements and the timeline to represent the quantity.

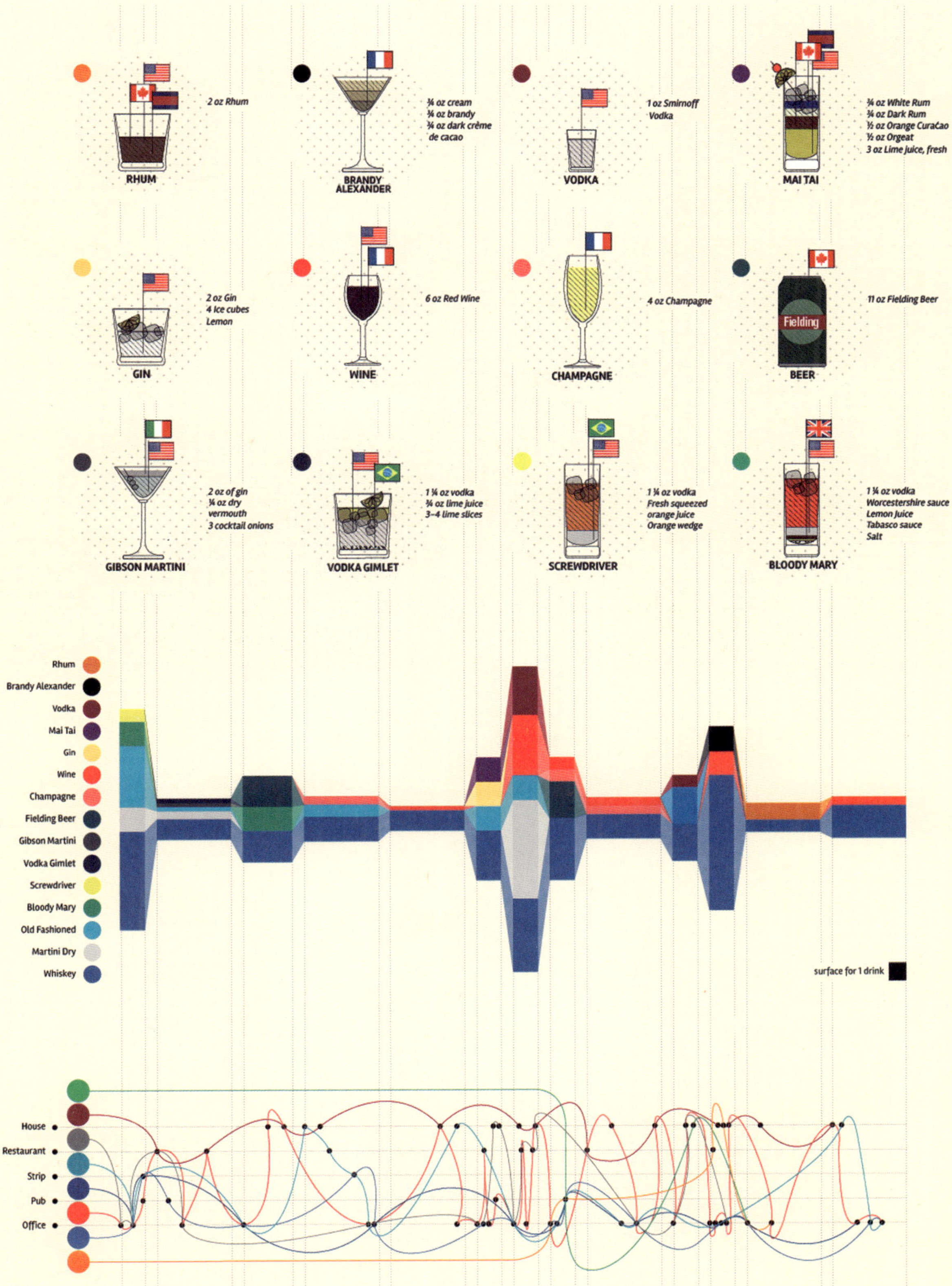

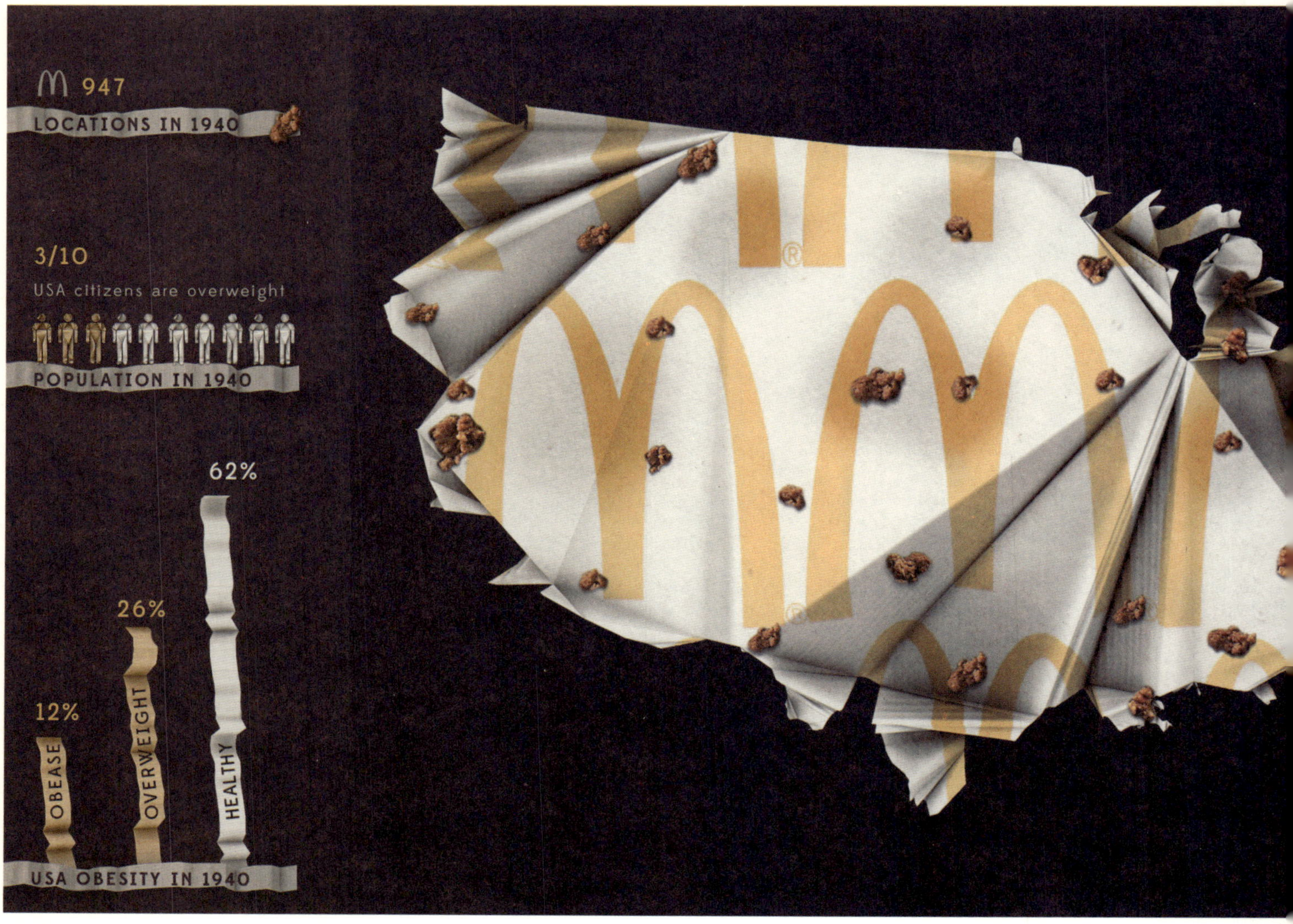

Fast Food Outbreak Interactive Infographic

- Completion Year: 2013
- Designer: Brit Moran
- Web: bit.ly/Yeaons

• Work Introduction

This is an infographic on the expansion of fast food over the years, and how it relates to obesity. The crinkled wrapper represents the map, and the food represents the areas that the locations are most prominent in. The user can click on a state, or view the full United States map, and from there the user can select a fast food restaurant, and see how the locations change over time as the user scrolls through the time line. The obesity information on the left updates accordingly.

NEW YORK

374
LOCATIONS IN 2012
6/10
NY citizens are overweight
POPULATION IN 2012
25%
37%
38%
OBEASE
OVERWEIGHT
HEALTHY
NY OBESITY IN 2012

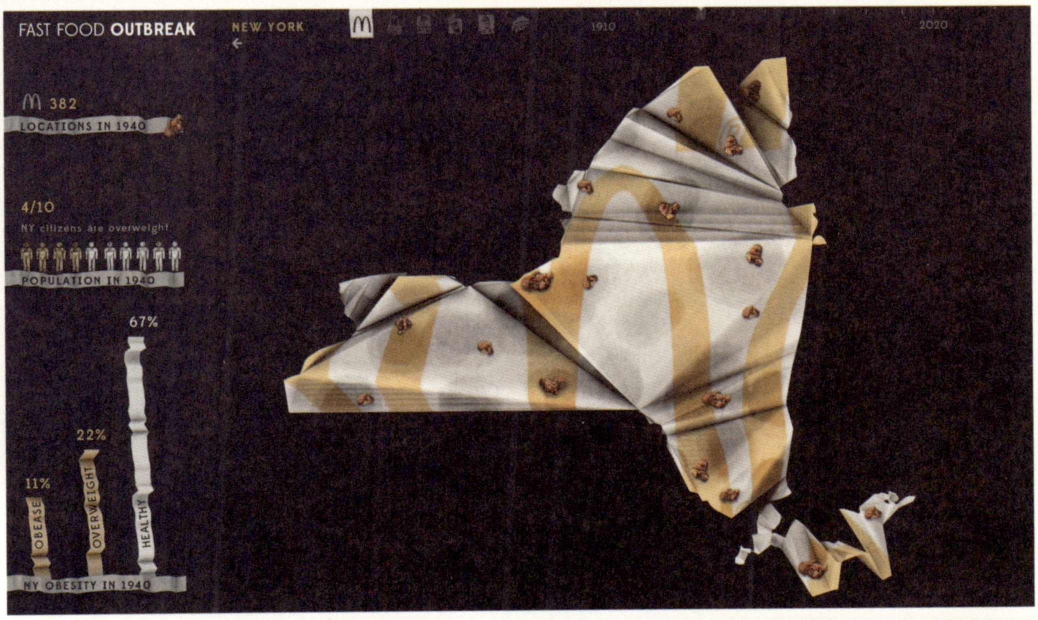
FAST FOOD OUTBREAK
NEW YORK
1910
2020
382
LOCATIONS IN 1940
4/10
NY citizens are overweight
POPULATION IN 1940
11%
22%
67%
OBEASE
OVERWEIGHT
HEALTHY
NY OBESITY IN 1940

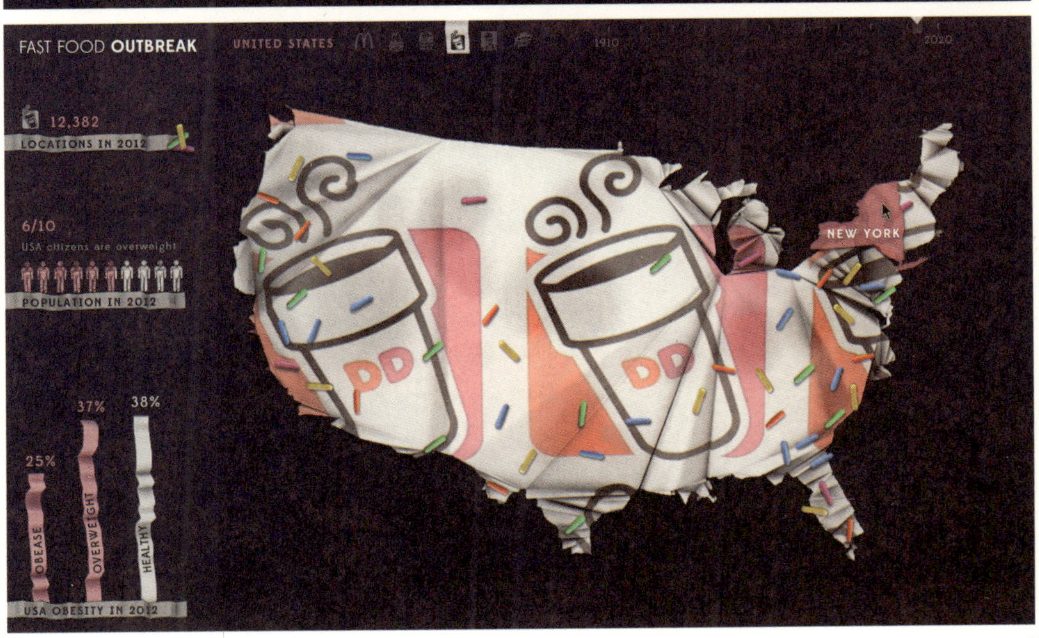
FAST FOOD OUTBREAK
UNITED STATES
1910
2020
12,382
LOCATIONS IN 2012
6/10
USA citizens are overweight
POPULATION IN 2012
25%
37%
38%
OBEASE
OVERWEIGHT
HEALTHY
USA OBESITY IN 2012
NEW YORK

Foco Design

- Completion Year: 2014
- Designer: Elis dos Anjos, Laís Pedroza
- Client: Foco Laser
- Web: www.focodesign.org

• Work Introduction

Criamia developed Foco's communication system and website. The aim problem was identifying their various services and process. The solution is an organized system created for each service performed by Foco Design leading to an effective communication.

1 IMAGEM
escolha o que deseja gravar
e onde deseja gravar
2 E-MAIL
envie-nos sua ideia,
especificando material*
e quantidade em que
serão produzidos.
*caso deseje que a gravação em um objeto, como por exemplo, uma taça ou troféu, será necessário que nos envie ou traga esse material aqui na Foco.
3 ANÁLISE
analisaremos a viabilidade
da gravação no objeto com
a imagem enviada.
4 ORÇAMENTO
dentro de 48 horas, enviaremos uma
proposta de orçamento e prazo.
Poderá ser marcada uma visita para
conferir o resultado da análise.
5 APROVAÇÃO
aprove por e-mail
o orçamento, os
resultados e a produção.
6 PRODUTO FINAL
7 PAGAMENTO
efetue o pagamento
e retire seu produto!
R$

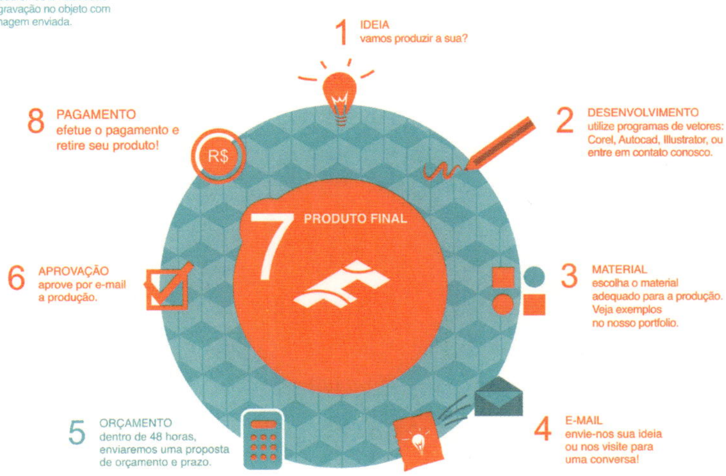

1 IDEIA
vamos produzir a sua?
2 DESENVOLVIMENTO
utilize programas de vetores:
Corel, Autocad, Illustrator, ou
entre em contato conosco.
3 MATERIAL
escolha o material
adequado para a produção.
Veja exemplos
no nosso portfolio.
4 E-MAIL
envie-nos sua ideia
ou nos visite para
uma conversa!
5 ORÇAMENTO
dentro de 48 horas,
enviaremos uma proposta
de orçamento e prazo.
6 APROVAÇÃO
aprove por e-mail
a produção.
7 PRODUTO FINAL
8 PAGAMENTO
efetue o pagamento e
retire seu produto!
R$

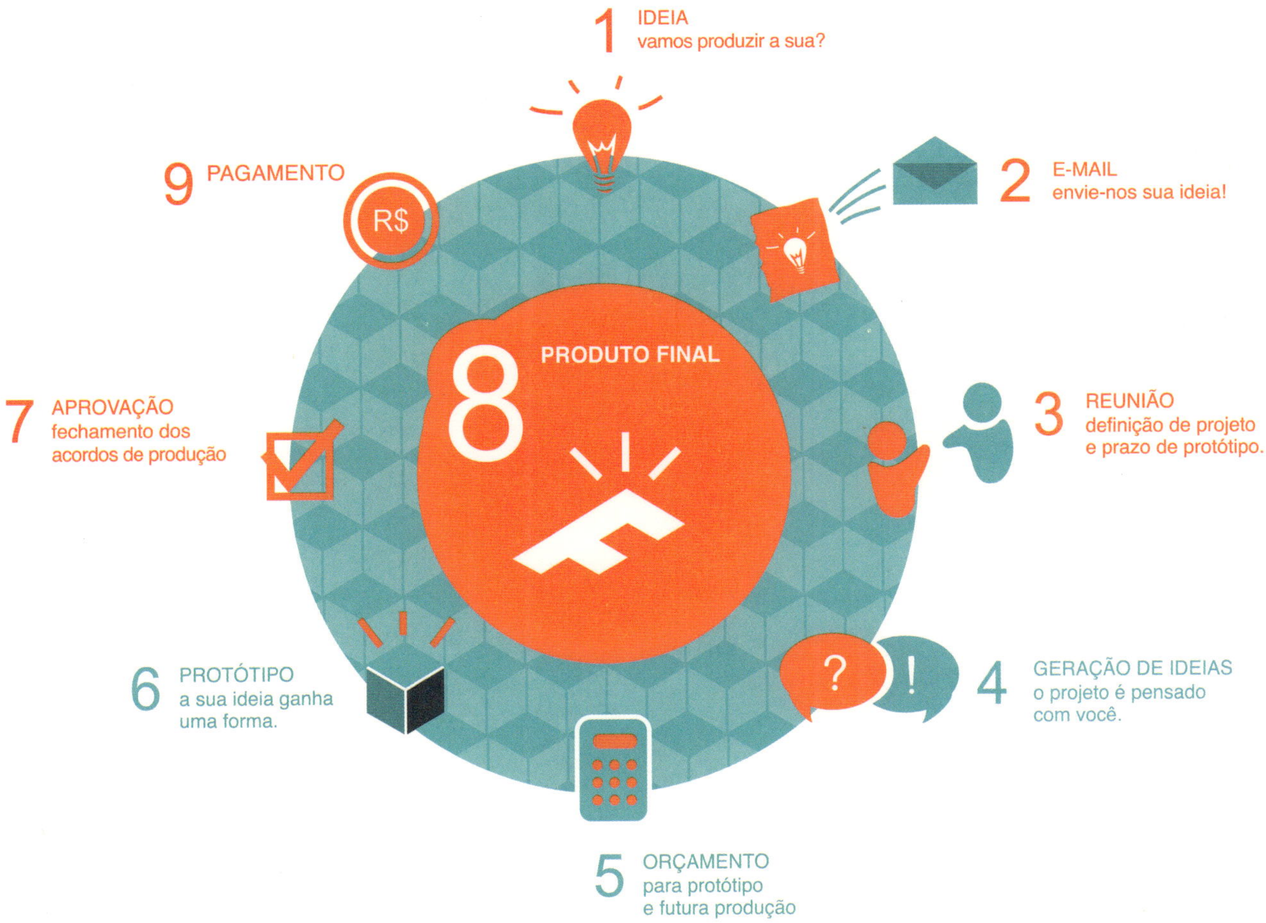

1 IDEIA
vamos produzir a sua?
2 E-MAIL
envie-nos sua ideia!
3 REUNIÃO
definição de projeto
e prazo de protótipo.
4 GERAÇÃO DE IDEIAS
o projeto é pensado
com você.
?
!
5 ORÇAMENTO
para protótipo
e futura produção
6 PROTÓTIPO
a sua ideia ganha
uma forma.
7 APROVAÇÃO
fechamento dos
acordos de produção
8 PRODUTO FINAL
9 PAGAMENTO
R$

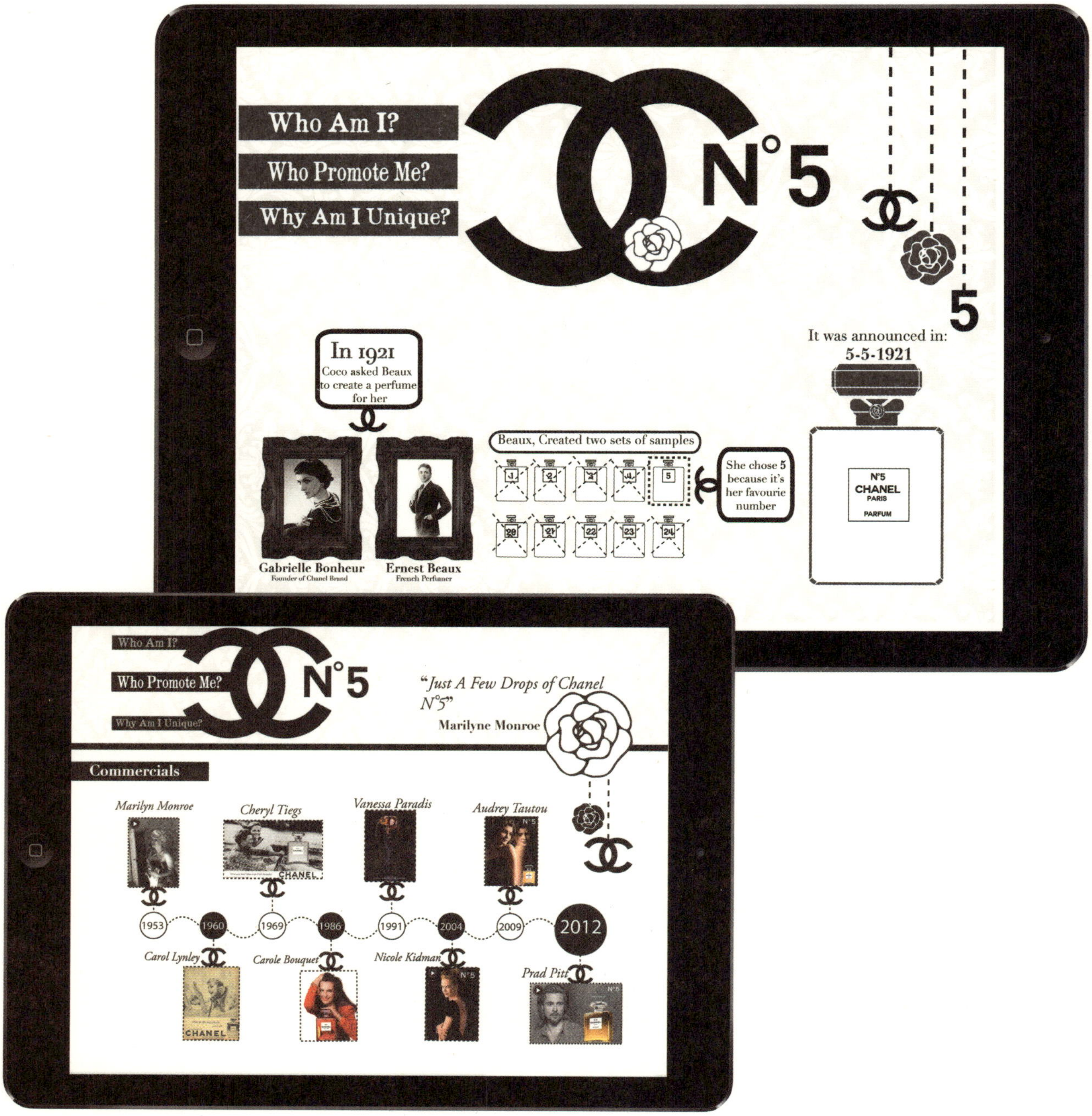

Infographic Website Coco Chanel N°5

- Completion Year: 2013
- Designer: Ghadeer Al-Oufi
- Web: galoufi.zxq.net/index.html

- Work Introduction

This infographic website is about Coco Chanel N°5, to make the readers learn about the process of creating the perfume and its history.

Who Am I?
Who Promote Me?
Why Am I Unique?
N°5
"A woman who doesn't wear perfume has no future."
Coco Chanel
Ingredients:
Bergamont
Lemon
Aldehydes
Iris
Lily of theVally
Vetiver
Neroli
Sandalwoods
N°5
CHANEL
PARIS
PARFUM
Ylang-Ylang
Rose
Jasmin
Patchouli
Vanilia
Amber
5
1921

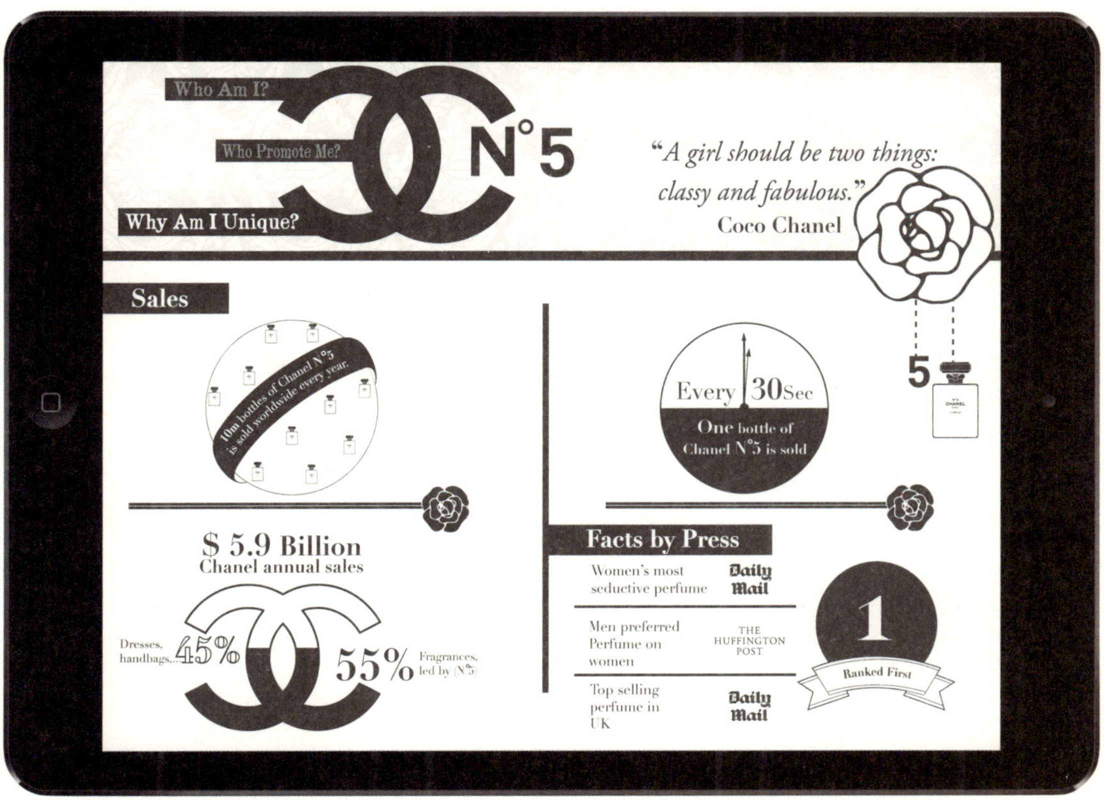
Who Am I?
Who Promote Me?
Why Am I Unique?
N°5
"A girl should be two things: classy and fabulous."
Coco Chanel
Sales
10m bottles of Chanel N°5 is sold worldwide every year.
Every 30Sec
One bottle of Chanel N°5 is sold
5
$ 5.9 Billion
Chanel annual sales
Dresses, handbags... 45%
55% Fragrances, led by N°5
Facts by Press
Women's most seductive perfume
Daily Mail
Men preferred Perfume on women
THE HUFFINGTON POST
Top selling perfume in UK
Daily Mail
1
Ranked First

Infographic Recipe

- Completion Year: 2014
- Designer: Yaya Aaronsohn
- Client: Yedioth Aharonot newspaper
- Web: www.yayaz.co

- Work Introduction

This is a section in a magazine that has a weekly recipe designed and illustrated that gives the reader the fun way of cooking with recipes.

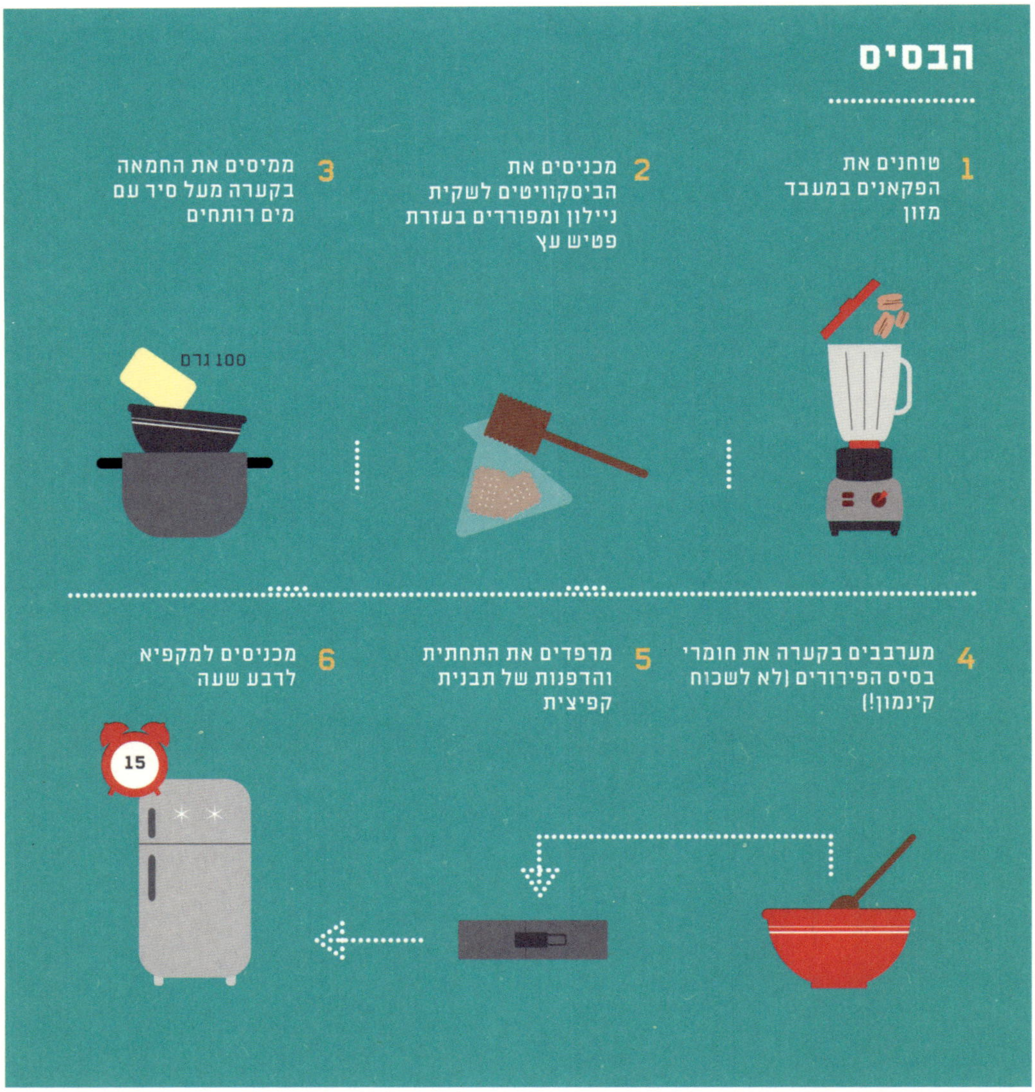

ידיעות אחרונות שישי
ניו יורק צ׳יז קייק
נירה רוסו
10 מנות
30 דקות אפייה
75 דקות הכנה
המתכון המלא
2. עוגה
סוכר
שני שליש
כוס סוכר
4 ביצים
750 גרם גבינת
שמנת "פילדלפיה"
אינסטנסט
פודינג
קורט
קינמון
2 כוסות פירורי
ביסקוויט בטעם שוקולד
100 גרם
חמאה מומסת
חצי כוס
פקאן סיני טחון
1. בסיס
3. ציפוי
כף גרידת לימון
תמצית
שקדים
2 מיכלי שמנת
חמוצה
3 כפות סוכר
כלים
מטרפה
כף עץ
פטיש עץ
כוס מדידה
תבנית קפיצית
24 ס"מ
3 קערות
סיר
שרלוט לימון ודובדבנים
אורן דגן כפיר
8 מנות
5 שעות קירור
המתכון המלא
2 ורבע כפיות
ג'לטין עם
4 כפות מים
6 חלמונים
אחד ושלושת
רבעי כוסות
שמנת מתוקה
85 גרם
חמאה חתוכה
לקוביות
קליפה
מגוררת ומיץ
מ-3 לימונים
שלושת רבעי
כוס סוכר
2. מלית מוס לימון
כף ליקר
דובדבנים
2 כפות
אבקת סוכר
כוס דובדבנים
מגולענים
1. בסיס
שני שליש
כוס סוכר
תפריט

Frame the Lab

- Completion Year: 2011
- Designer: Gianpaolo Tucci, Mauro D'alessandro, Caterina Fiorentino, Claudio Moderini

- Work Introduction

Using the metaphor of the "laboratory", where each project is visualized as a polygon and each face of that represents a project's team player, Frame aims to create and support online design communities by offering collaboration tools to three categories of users: Designers, Universities and Companies. Frame acts as an idea incubator platform where designers can trace the creative process, deposit documentation and resources and visualize each step of a project's progress.

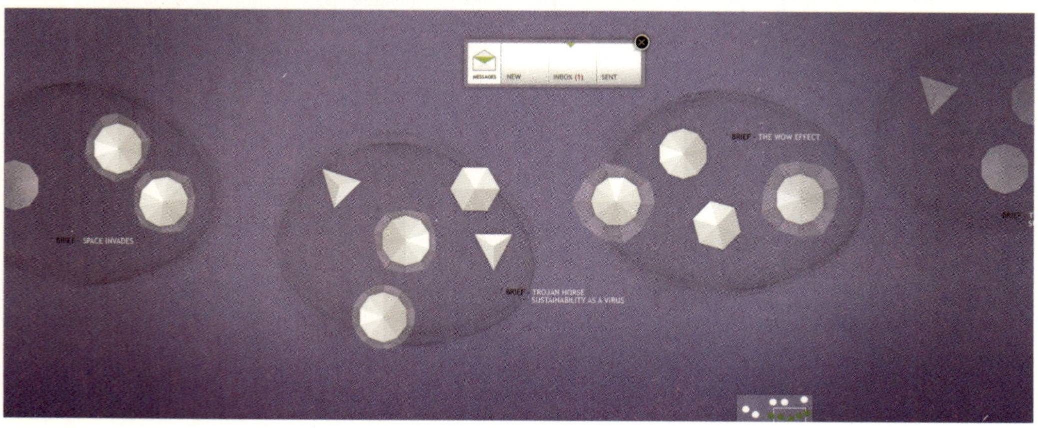

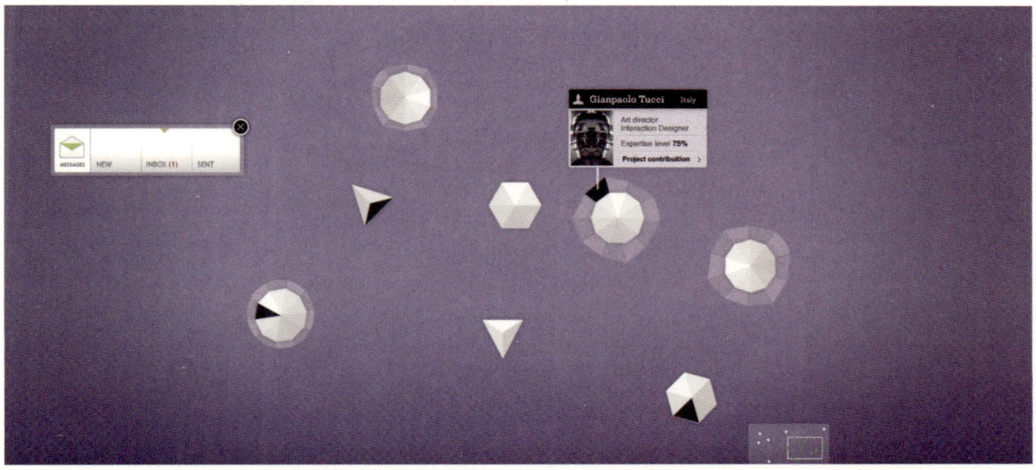
MESSAGES
NEW
INBOX (1)
SENT
Gianpaolo Tucci
Italy
Art director
Interaction Designer
Expertise level 75%
Project contribution

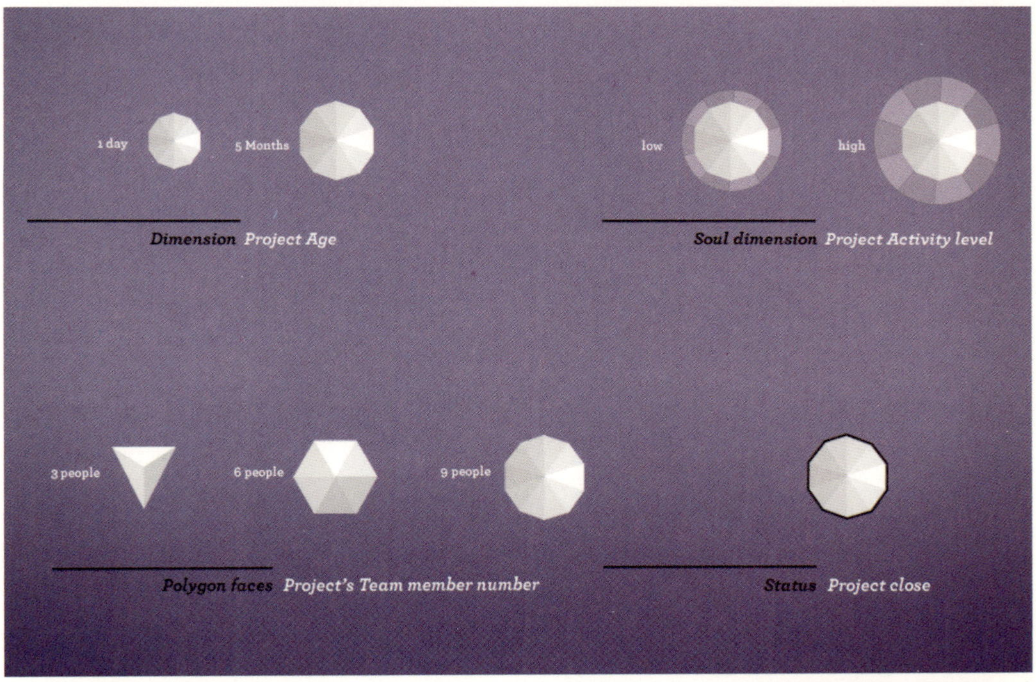
1 day
5 Months
Dimension Project Age
low
high
Soul dimension Project Activity level
3 people
6 people
9 people
Polygon faces Project's Team member number
Status Project close

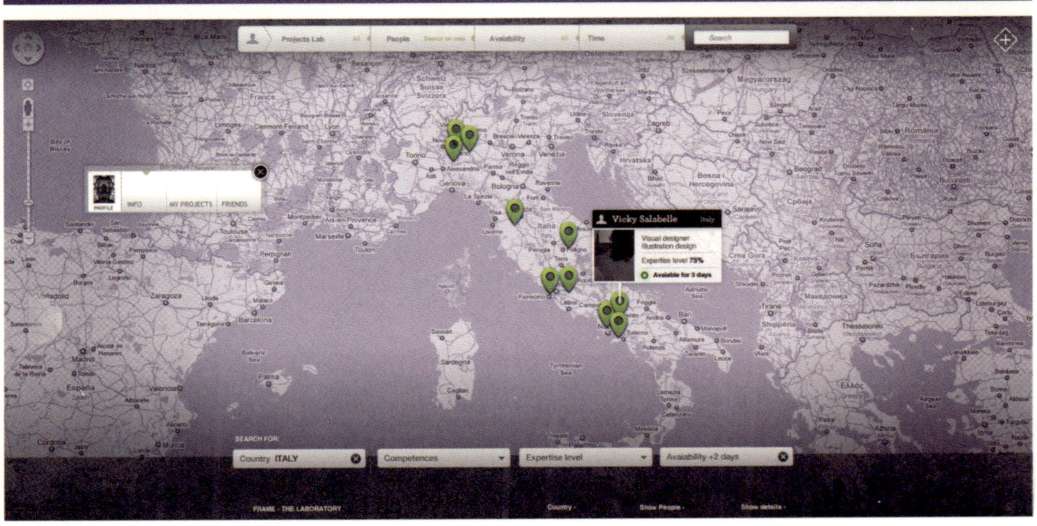
Projects Lab
People
Availability
Time
Search
PROFILE
INFO
MY PROJECTS
FRIENDS
Vicky Salabelle
Italy
Expertise level 75%
SEARCH FOR
Country ITALY
Competences
Expertise level
Availability +2 days
FRAME - THE LABORATORY

MIT ID Sky – Online Portal

- Completion Year: 2012
- Designer: Tushar Ghei

- Work Introduction

This was an attempt to build an internal system for our college where students can get inspired, stay motivated and be up to date about the occurrences and developments in their environment. The brief for this project was to select a physical space; identify the people involved; understand their tasks and problems within the system using detailed research methods. Next step was to introduce a solution available to all within the system. Initially the study was done separately for Students, Faculty and Parents—understanding their difficulties and concerns individually.

Tushar Ghei
Dashboard
Discussion Board
Blog
Portfolio
Live Feed
Current Course
Progress Analytics
Portfolio Archive
Student Showcase
iDid Store
Events
Navin Devnani
Harshit Desai
Eesha Keskar
Academic Calendar
26
November
Filter
Student Showcase
Want to get on the showcase?
Not Dinner Yet
Caava Design
Flourntа Theme Park
Been There Done That
City Games
The Redbull Music Academy

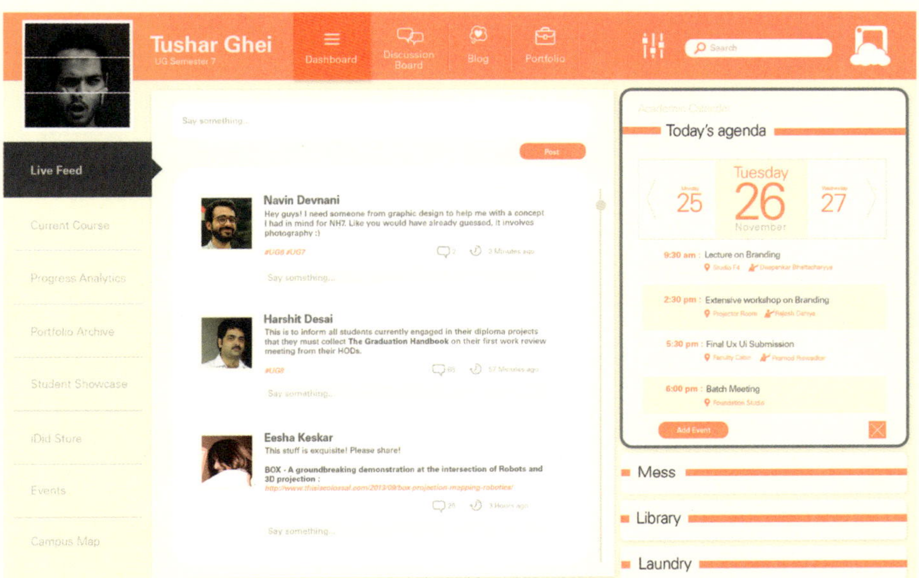
Tushar Ghei
UG Semester 7
Dashboard
Discussion Board
Blog
Portfolio
Live Feed
Current Course
Progress Analytics
Portfolio Archive
Student Showcase
iDid Store
Events
Campus Map
Navin Devnani
Hey guys! I need someone from graphic design to help me with a concept I had in mind for NH7. Like you would have already guessed, it involves photography :)
Harshit Desai
This is to inform all students currently engaged in their diploma projects that they must collect The Graduation Handbook on their first work review meeting from their HODs.
Eesha Keskar
This stuff is exquisite! Please share!
BOX - A groundbreaking demonstration at the intersection of Robots and 3D projection :
Today's agenda
Tuesday
25
26
27
November
9:30 am : Lecture on Branding
2:30 pm : Extensive workshop on Branding
5:30 pm : Final Ux Ui Submission
6:00 pm : Batch Meeting
Add Event
Mess
Library
Laundry

MIT ID
Sky

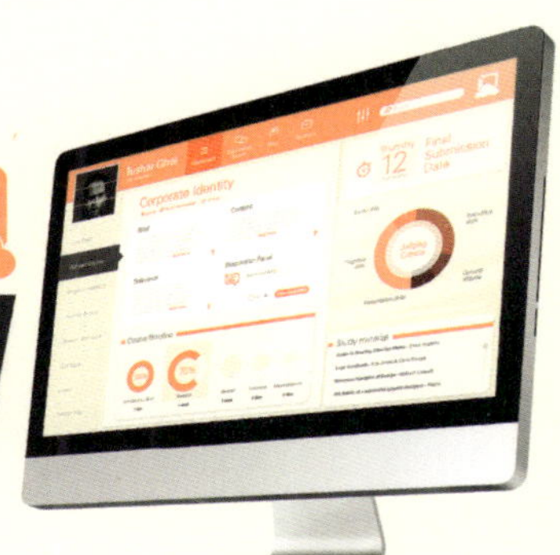

10,000 Gardens in Africa

- Completion Year: 2014
- Designer: Yaya Aaronsohn
- Client: "Slow food" Italy
- Web: www.yayaz.co

- Work Introduction

This infographics shows the growth of gardens in Africa between 2003 and 2013. within a click you could see online the change made by the program and the Slow Food Organization.

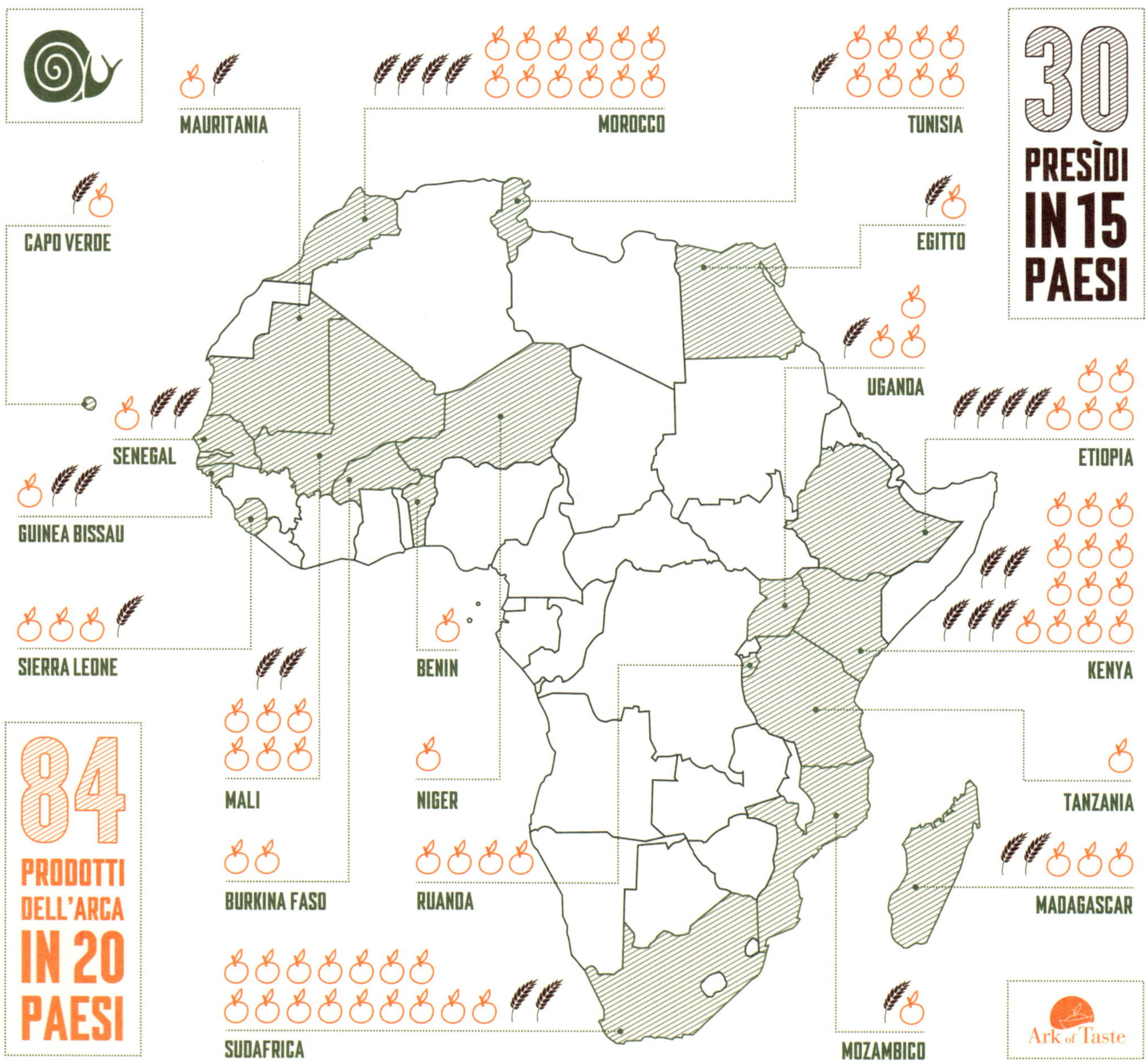

Ruby Pseudo – Network Management System

- Completion Year: 2013
- Designer: Adam Robbins
- Client: Ruby Pseudo Consulting

• Work Introduction

Ruby Pseudo Consulting is an agency which provide research for brands using a network of tastemaker kids around the world. Through this closed web-based tool they are able to query their network and view its size and spread by location, keywords, gender and age range in a visually engaging and interactive way.

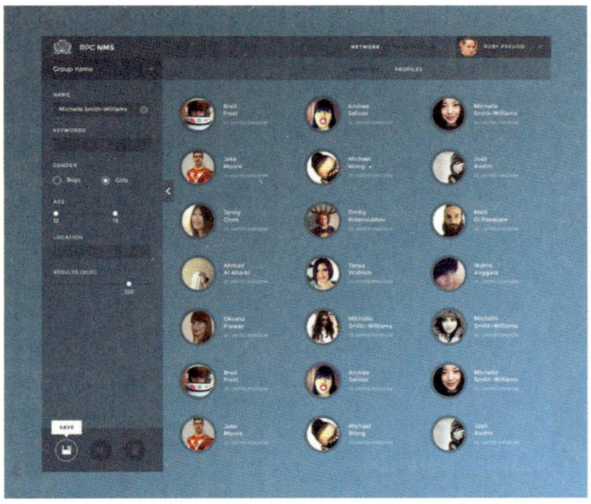

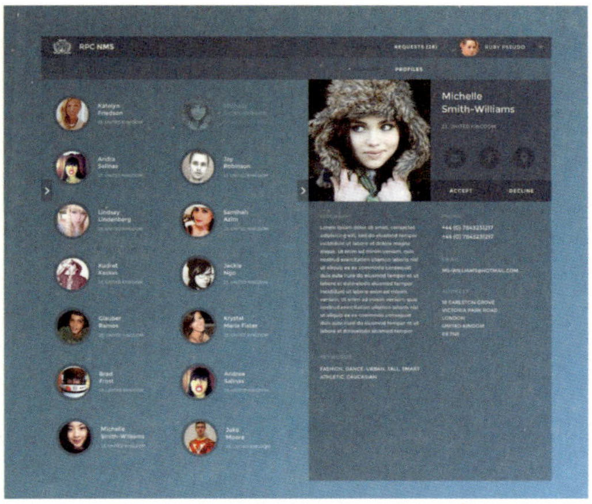

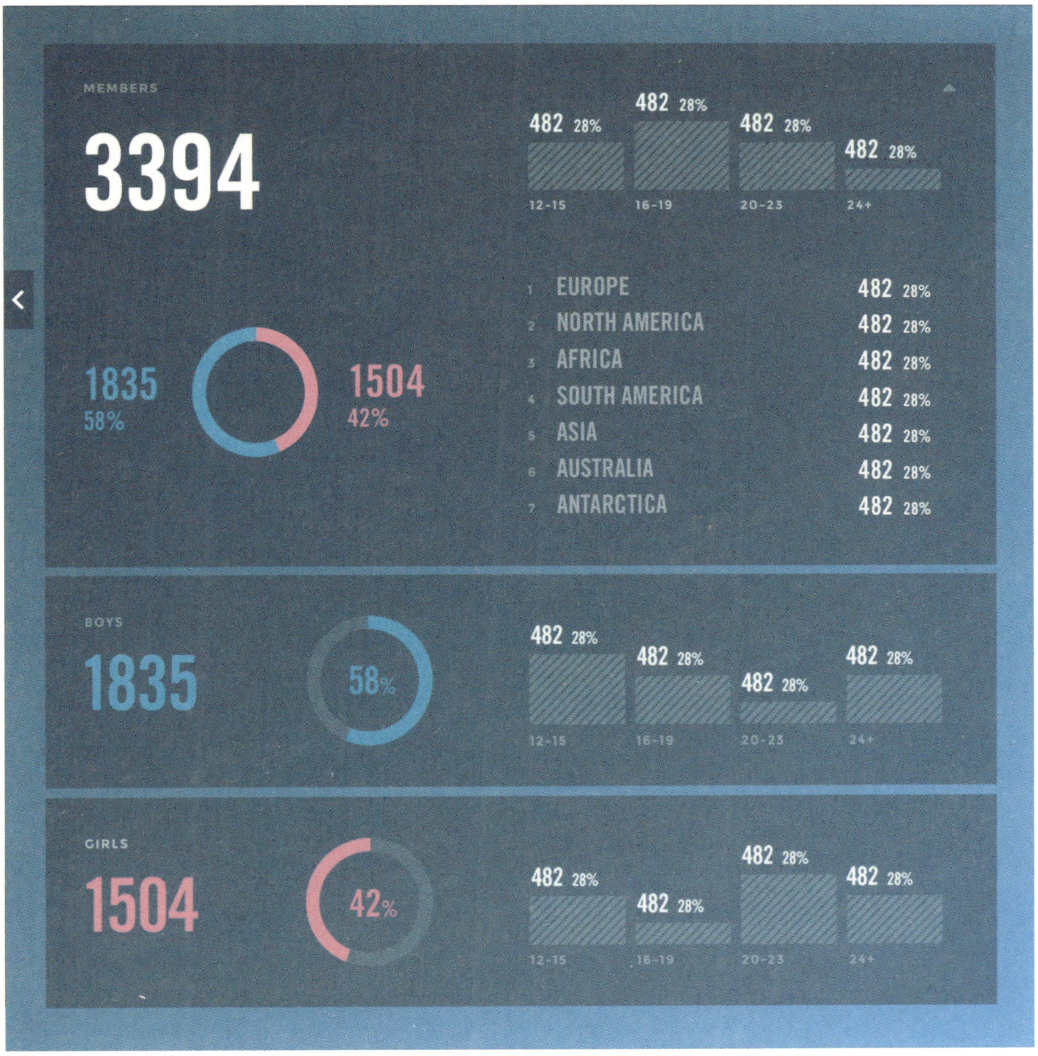

- Completion Year: 2014
- Designer: Yaya Aaronsohn
- Web: www.yayaz.co

• Work Introduction

They were instructed to design a double-spread for each of the entries, explaining it in an infographical way. She chose kids to be my target audience, and the values: Popcorn, Panda bear and Finland (In hebrew they all begin with the same letter...)

Her main objective in this project was to show that almost any subject or entry from the encyclopedia can be transformed in to an enticing visual object, which appeals both to children and adults.

פַּנְדָּה
מוצאם של דובי הפנדה הוא בסין הרחוקה
השם דב פנדה בשפה הסינית הוא
צבעם של דובי הפנדה הוא שחור ולבן
כמו בובת צעצוע בזכות פניהם המתוקות.
2
מנוחה
אוכל
3
פירות, דגים ועלים נוספים
8

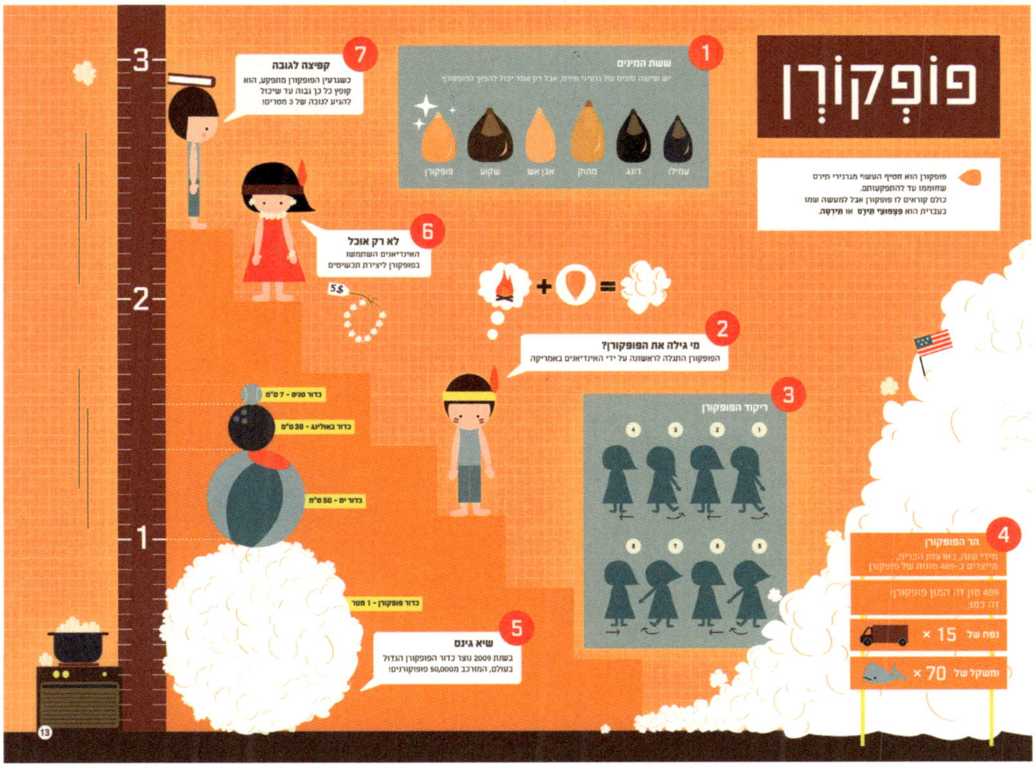

פּוֹפְּקוֹרְן
פופקורן הוא חטיף העשוי מגרגירי תירס שחוממו עד להתפקעותם.
כולם קוראים לו פופקורן אבל למעשה שמו בעברית הוא פצפוצי תירס או תירקה.
1
ששת המינים
יש שישה סוגים של גרעיני תירס, אבל רק אחד יכול להפוך לפופקורן
עמילן
דונג
מתוק
אבן אש
שקוע
פופקורן
7
קפיצה לגובה
כשגרעין הפופקורן מתפקע, הוא קופץ כל כך גבוה עד שיכול להגיע לגובה של 3 מטרים!
6
לא רק אוכל
האינדיאנים השתמשו בפופקורן ליצירת תכשיטים
5$
2
מי גילה את הפופקורן?
הפופקורן התגלה לראשונה על ידי האינדיאנים באמריקה
3
ריקוד הפופקורן
1 2 3 4
5 6 7 8
4
הר הפופקורן
מידי שנה, בארצות הברית, מייצרים כ-489 טונות של פופקורן
489 טון זה המון פופקורן! זה כמו:
נפח של × 15
ומשקל של × 70
3
2
1
כדור טניס - 7 ס"מ
כדור באולינג - 30 ס"מ
כדור ים - 50 ס"מ
כדור פופקורן - 1 מטר
5
שיא גינס
בשנת 2009 נוצר כדור הפופקורן הגדול בעולם, המורכב מ50,000 פופקורנים!
13

פִּינְלַנְד
פינלנד היא מדינה בצפון יבשת אירופה.
מקור שמה פינלנד הוא בשפה השבדית, ופרושו "ארץ משובחת".
בפינלנד מדברים בשפה הפינית ובשבדית
1
המומינים
בפינלנד המציאו את המומינים ב-1945. ומאז הם הצליחו בכל העולם, בטלוויזיה ובקולנוע!
2
חינוך פיני
השיגי התלמידים בפינלנד הם הגבוהים בעולם
פינלנד
הונג קונג
קנדה
טאיוואן
אסטוניה
יפן
3
בפינלנד כולם יודעים לקרוא ולכתוב
פינלנד 100%
צרפת 99%
ישראל 95%
מצרים 71%
הודו 60%
אתיופיה 42%
7
מדינה גדולה
פינלנד היא כה גדולה עד שיכולה להכיל בתוכה את ישראל כשישה-עשר פעמים
פינלנד
מדינת ישראל
= × 16
32%
אדמה ואגמים
68%
יערות
6
יערות פינלנד
68% מהמדינה זה יער. רוב עצי היערות הם אורן ואשוח
שתייה
דייג
רחצה
כבישים
5
מים בשפע
בפינלנד יש כ-180,000 אגמים ולהם שימושים רבים: מי שתייה, דייג, שחייה בחורף משמש האגם הקפוא ככביש נסיעה למכוניות
180,000
אגמים
קיץ
חורף
4
חושך ואור
החורף בפינלנד מאוד מושלג וכמעט כל היום חשוך, בקיץ לעומת זאת השמש שוקעת רק לשעתיים ושאר היום מואר ובהיר
11
10

Human Cost Data Challenge

- Completion Year: 2014
- Designer: Katie Coughlan
- Web: www.behance.net/gallery/21343935/Human-Cost-Data-Challenge

- Work Introduction

"Human Cost" was created in response to a data challenge given by the Kantar Information is Beautiful Awards in March 2014. They asked designers to create a visual that depicts the price of human life. Featuring information all the way from Ancient Egypt through present day, the data is organized to help the viewer realize current trafficking trends. The designer refrains from reducing people to mere data by utilizing the human silhouette. The shelves these silhouettes are resting on are representative of stock shelving in many retail stores today.

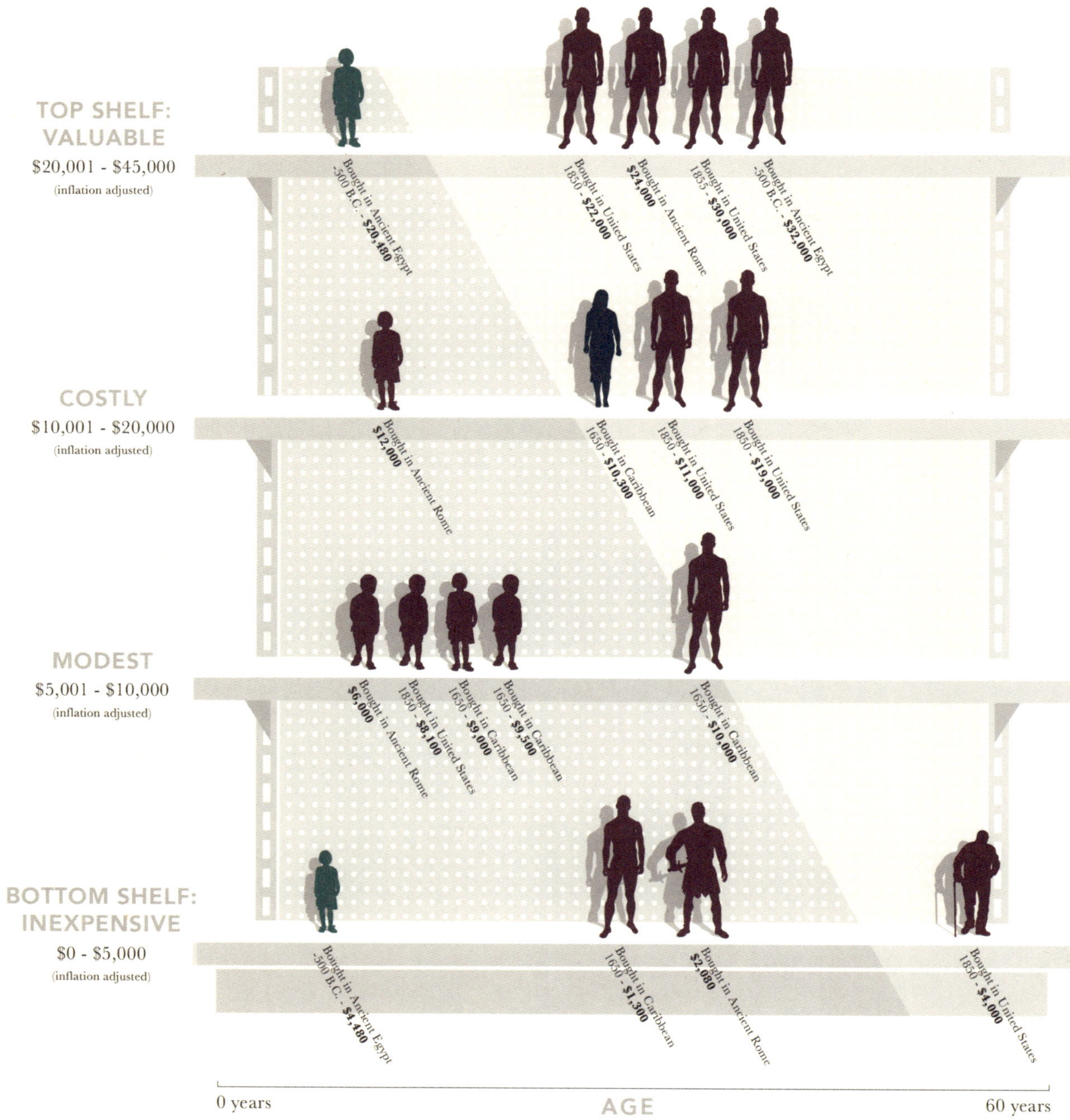

BETWEEN -500 B.C. AND 1855 A.D.

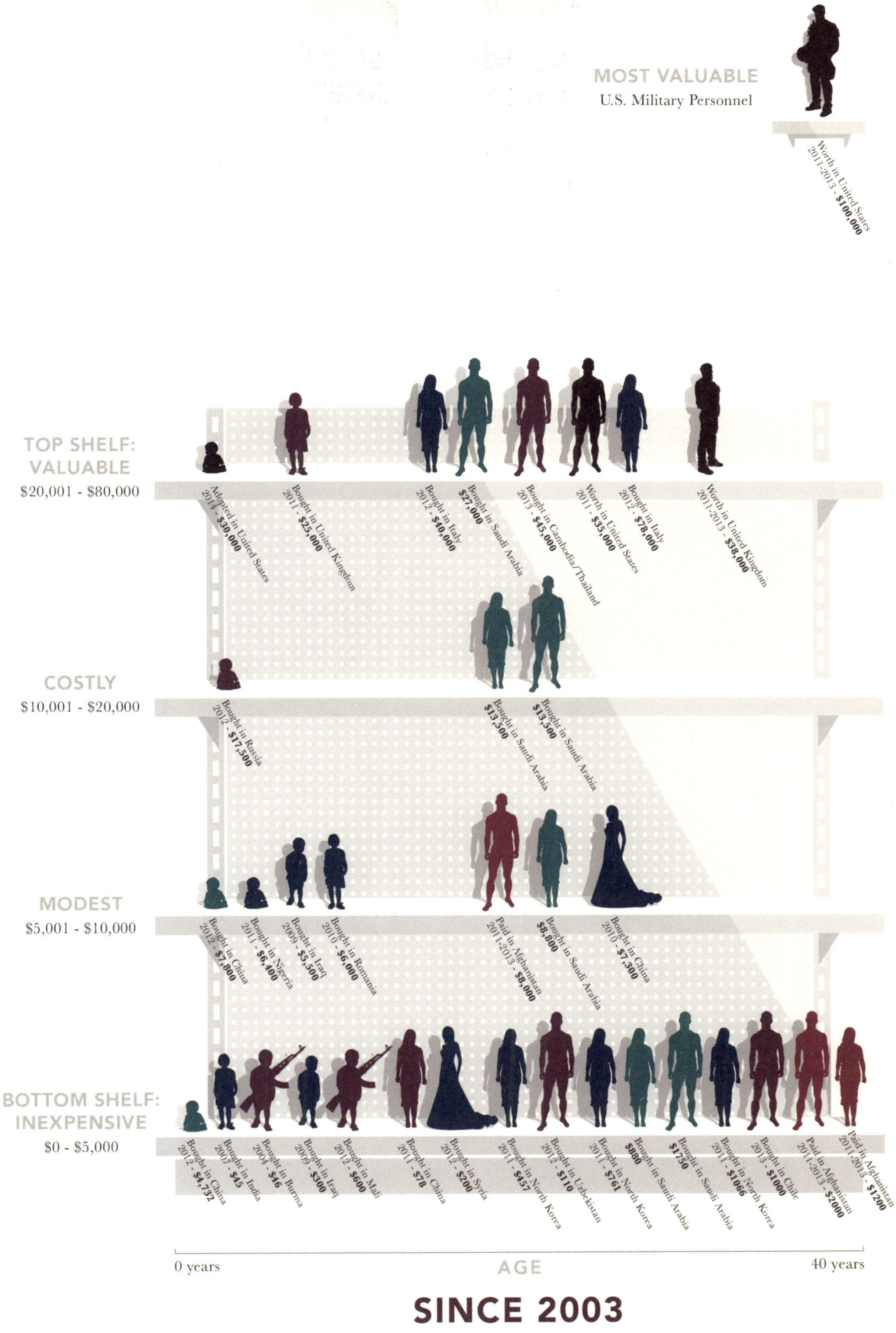
MOST VALUABLE
U.S. Military Personnel
Worth in United States 2011-2013 - $100,000
TOP SHELF: VALUABLE
$20,001 - $80,000
Adopted in United States 2014 - $30,000
Bought in United Kingdom 2011 - $25,000
Bought in Italy 2012 - $40,000
Bought in Saudi Arabia $27,000
Bought in Cambodia/Thailand 2013 - $45,000
Worth in United States 2011 - $35,000
Bought in Italy 2012 - $78,000
Worth in United Kingdom 2011-2013 - $38,000
COSTLY
$10,001 - $20,000
Bought in Russia 2012 - $17,500
Bought in Saudi Arabia $13,500
Bought in Saudi Arabia $13,500
MODEST
$5,001 - $10,000
Bought in China 2012 - $7,800
Bought in Nigeria 2011 - $6,400
Bought in Iraq 2009 - $5,500
Bought in Romania 2010 - $6,000
Paid in Afghanistan 2011-2013 - $8,000
Bought in Saudi Arabia $8,800
Bought in China 2010 - $7,300
BOTTOM SHELF: INEXPENSIVE
$0 - $5,000
Bought in China 2012 - $4,732
Bought in India 2007 - $45
Bought in Burma 2004 - $46
Bought in Iraq 2009 - $300
Bought in Mali 2012 - $600
Bought in China 2011 - $78
Bought in Syria 2012 - $200
Bought in North Korea 2011 - $457
Bought in Uzbekistan 2012 - $110
Bought in North Korea 2011 - $761
Bought in Saudi Arabia $880
Bought in Saudi Arabia $1750
Bought in North Korea 2011 - $1066
Bought in Chile 2013 - $1000
Paid in Afghanistan 2011-2013 - $2000
Paid in Afghanistan 2011-2013 - $1200
0 years
AGE
40 years
SINCE 2003

Saving the Great Barrier Reef

- Completion Year: 2013
- Designer: Kelly Loh
- Client : WWF

- Work Introduction

The aim of this project is to use information design principles and techniques to communicate facts and knowledge about a particular issue, on behalf of WWF Australia—a Non-Government Organisation (NGO)—for the purpose of providing public awareness, understanding, solutions and action (such as policy change) in Australia on that issue. The overall approach is to develop an app, based on an information design solution, which presents information via a digital touchscreen interface (iPad). The app will help the WWF in its campaigns. Here, the idea of a campaign is to coordinate publicity across different media over a defined period with the aim of achieving a defined outcome, such as behavioural or policy change. Or, to put it differently, "an organised course of action designed to arouse public opinion" (Oxford English Dictionary).

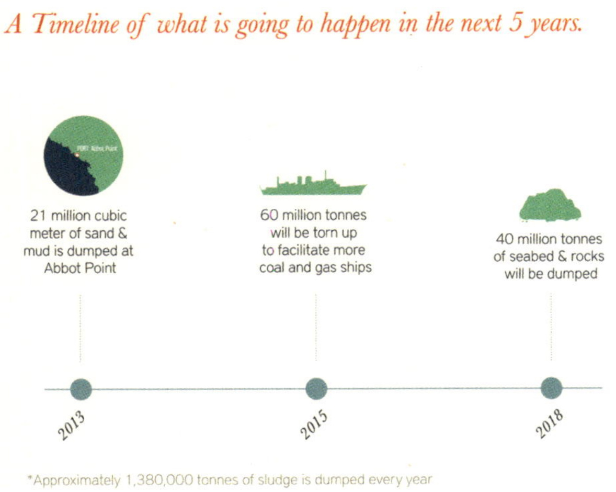

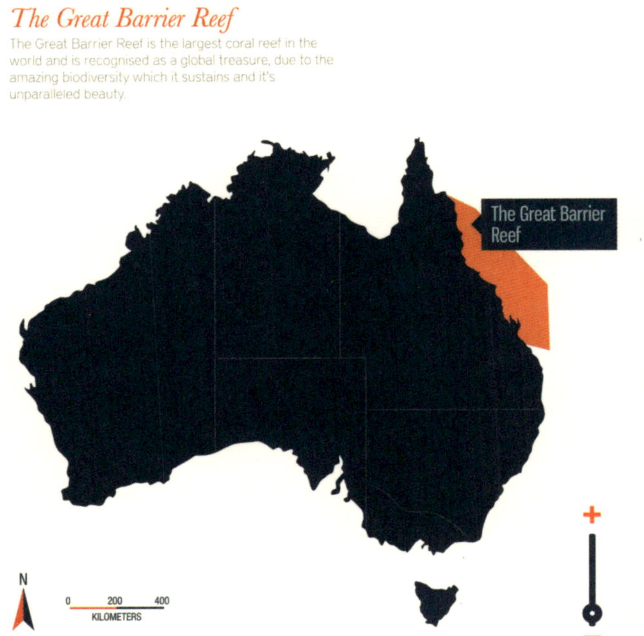

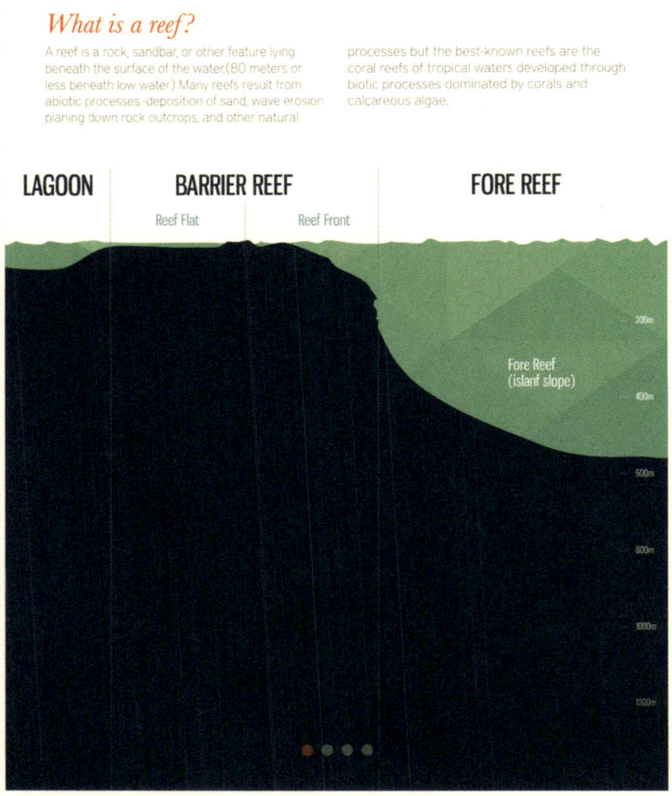

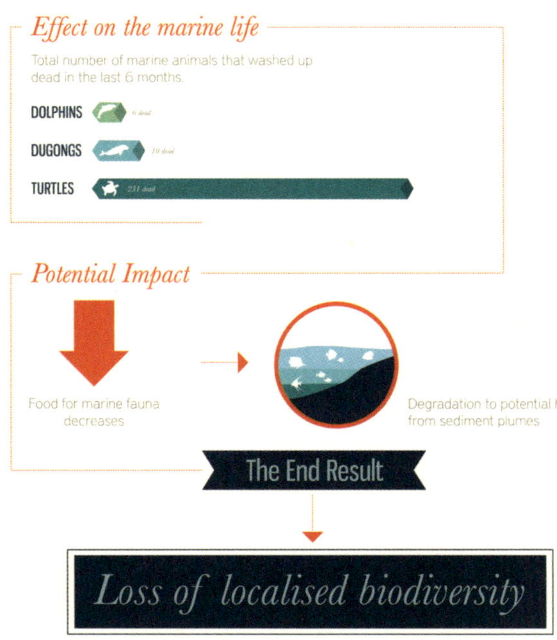

The designer's idea as to create the interface in a way that people from various ages would understand in a split second after interacting with the app. Meaning simple graphics and information that is summarised and easily understood by the layman. The main call to action for this particular app was to ensure that the public knew about the problems and act to fix them which in this case is to "Sign the petition". The designer designed the app in a way that the audience will have a fair share of interactive components and relative information.

Marine Life In The Reef

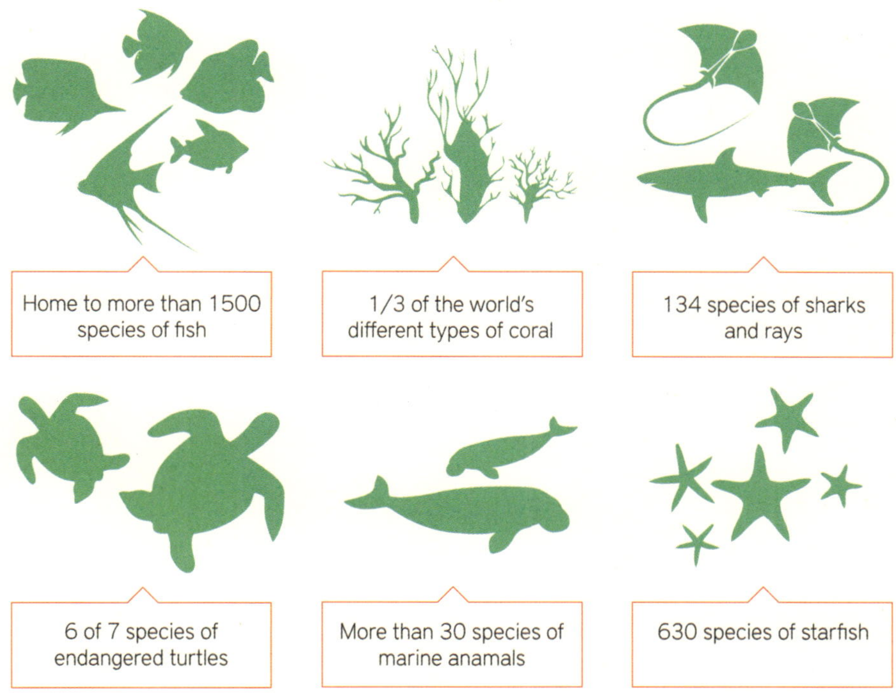

Sign the Petition

In August this year, the decision to dredge and dump 3 million cubic metres of seabed and rock off Abbot Point was delayed. But the clock is ticking again, and the Reef needs your help.

The new Environment Minister Greg Hunt is currently deciding whether to green light this dredging and dumping off Abbot Point – just 50 km from the Whitsunday Islands.

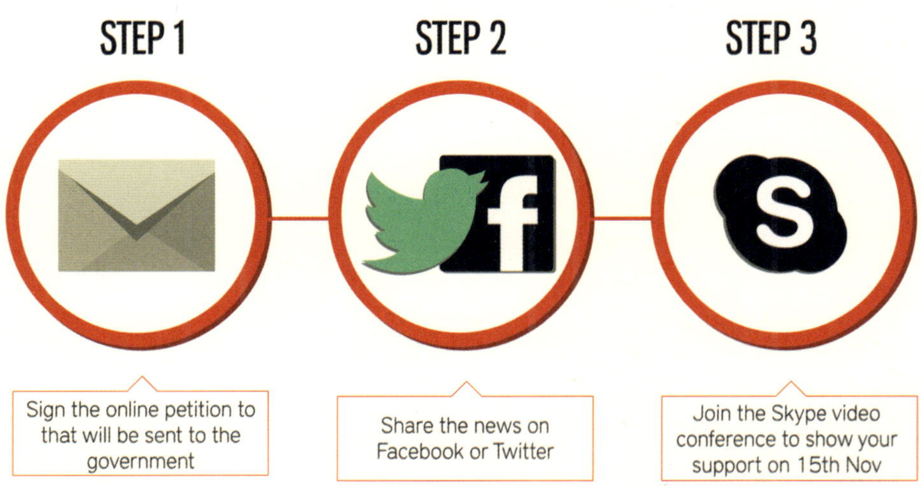

Graphic Interface Study for Exploring Datasets in Open Data Portals

- Completion Year: 2012
- Designer: Emanuela Giovannoni and Laura Pippinato
- Client: Polytechnic of Turin – Thesis project 2012
- Web: issuu.com/laurapippinato/docs/visual_exploration_of_open_data_ff3775ec9f734f/1

- Work Introduction

The project presents a Web interface to improve user experience in the exploration of information within Open Data Portals, likedati.piemonte.it. The interface, based on Data Visualization, allows a comprehensive view of all datasets contents in a simple and user-friendly way, while facilitating the comparison and the creation of links that improve dynamic navigation.

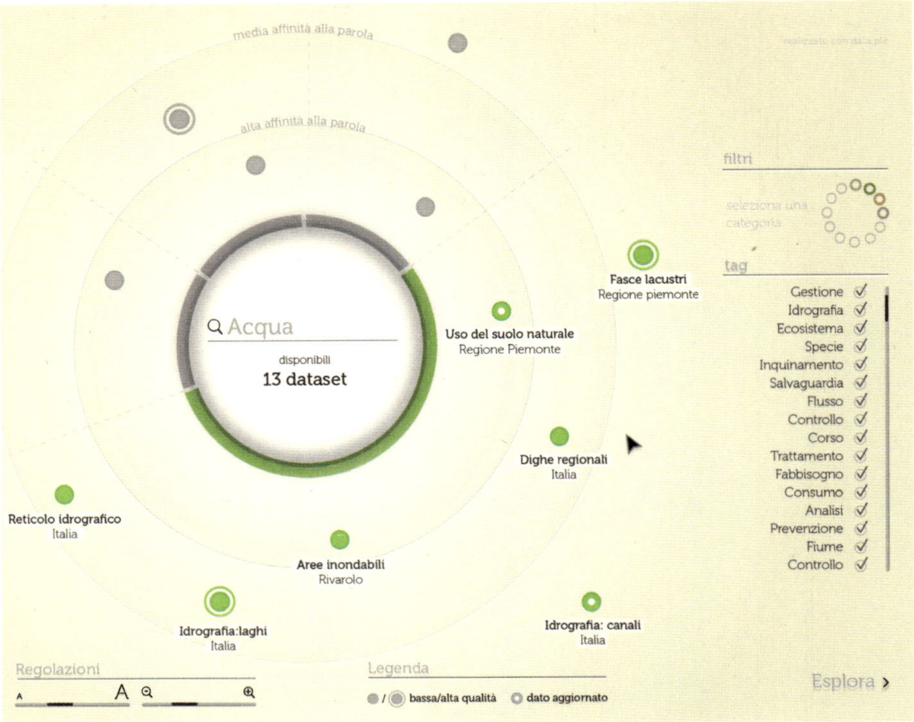

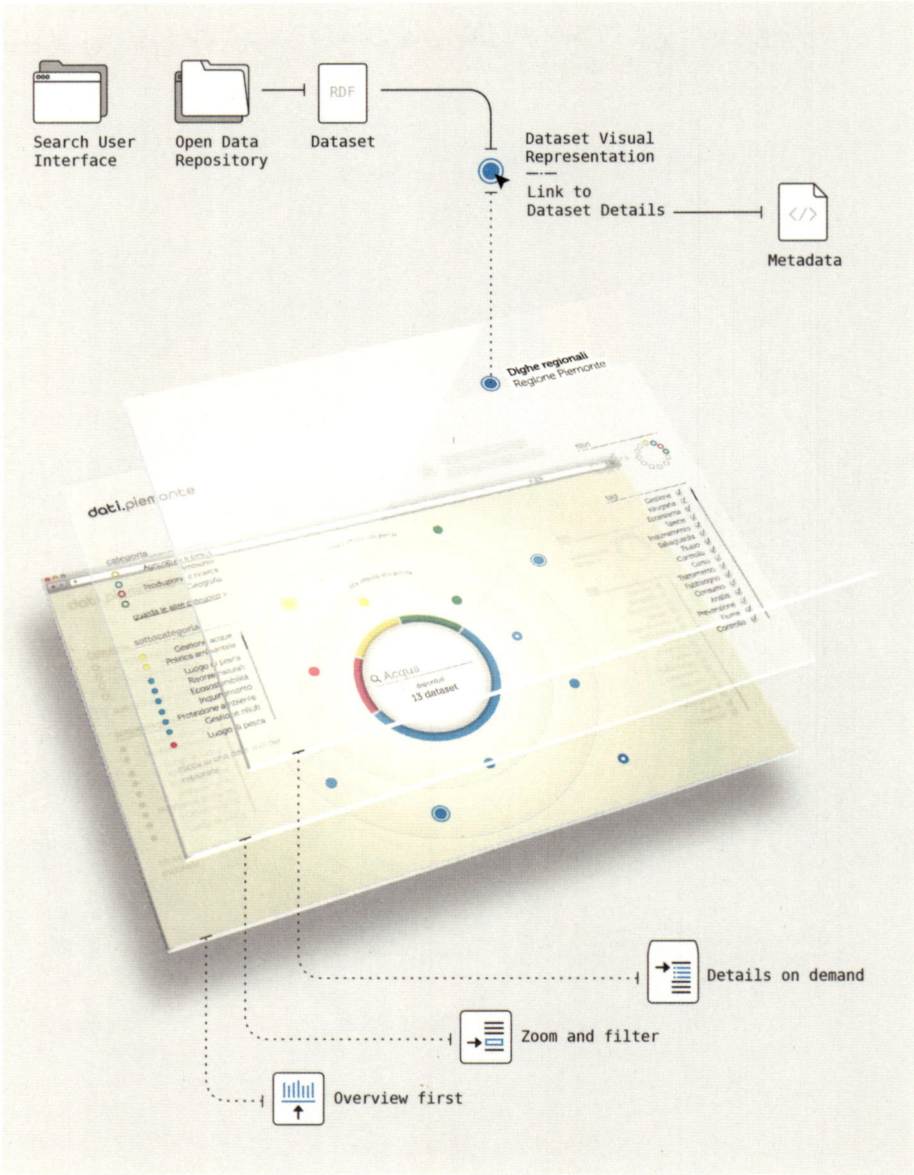

datapie
http://datapie.com/
dati.piemonte
media affinità alla parola
alta affinità alla parola
categoria
Agricoltura e pesca
Ambiente
Produzione e ricerca
Geografia
guarda le altre categorie >
sottocategoria
Gestione acque
Politica ambientale
Luogo di pesca
Risorse naturali
Ecosostenibilità
Inquinamento
Protezione ambiente
Gestione rifiuti
Luogo di pesca
Acqua
disponibili
13 dataset
filtri
tag
Gestione
Idrografia
Ecosistema
Specie
Inquinamento
Salvaguardia
Flusso
Controllo
Corso
Trattamento
Fabbisogno
Consumo
Analisi
Prevenzione
Fiume
Controllo

dati.piemonte
Avanzate
Effettua una ricerca mirata attraverso filtri come categoria, ente o qualità
Cerca
disponibili
301 dataset
Esplora
Naviga liberamente tra i dataset presenti e trova quelli a te più utili
Fasce fluviali e lacustri: fasce lacustri
Descrizione
Delimitazioni delle aree di rispetto fluviale e lacustre calcolate sui dati del dataset Idrografia SITA 100000 con una larghezza di 150 metri e 300 metri per corsi d'acqua e laghi. La selezione sugli elementi è stata fatta in base all'importanza per tutte le province, ad eccezione della provincia di Cuneo.
Categorizzazione
Ambiente >
Politica ambientale
Ente
Regione Piemonte
Licenza
CC BY
Data creazione
21/02/2008
aggiornato il 23/03/2010
Formato
Shapefile
Download
67
Views
105
Suggerimenti
Canali Cuneo
Fasce fluviali Regione Piemonte
Corsi d'acqua Settimo torinese
Idrografia Cuneo
DOWNLOAD

Foreign Exchange Responsive Infographics

- Completion Year: 2014
- Designer: Luciana Flora

- Work Introduction

In this project, the designer explores how to convey different emotions. Both infographics created have the exact same content, however, through design, one expresses a positive view towards "Foreign Exchange" while the other does the opposite. Both infographics are responsive.

Music Theory Visualized

- Completion Year: 2014
- Designer: Khyati Trehan

- Work Introduction

The infographic compresses and presents few key concepts of music theory. The artful use of piano keyboard shows the highlighted contents and the types of musical theory, attracting the immense attention from the audiences.

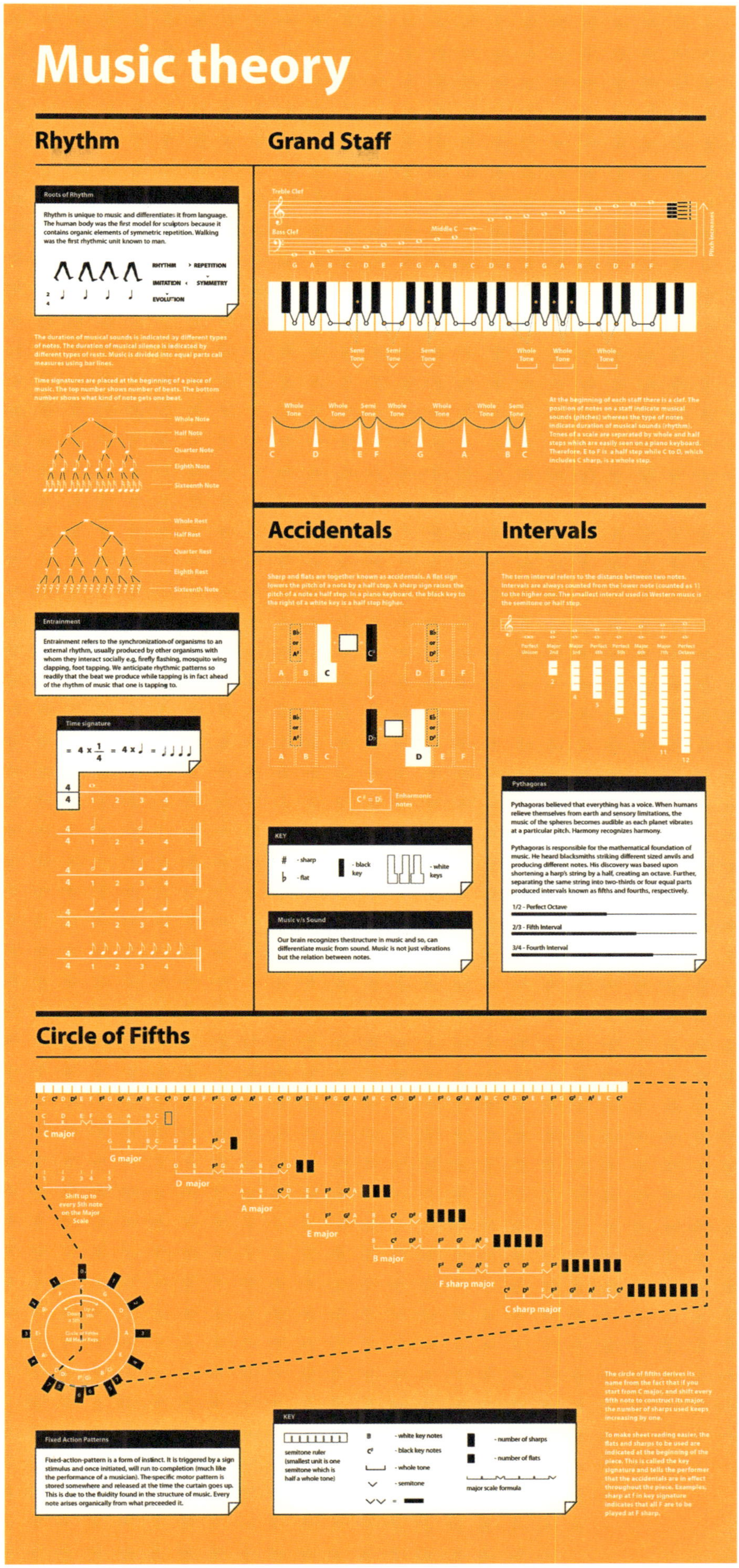

Inspiract

- Completion Year: 2013
- Designer: Ludovica Saccenti
- Client: H-FARM, 24-hour marathon, San Paolo Bank

• Work Introduction

This project is a concept made during the workshop of H-Farm last 24 hours, with the collaboration of developers, designer and economists. We have created an application that monitors with the debit card Inspire of Intesa S. Paolo bank. The app advice you with a community, about your interest and search the best offers.

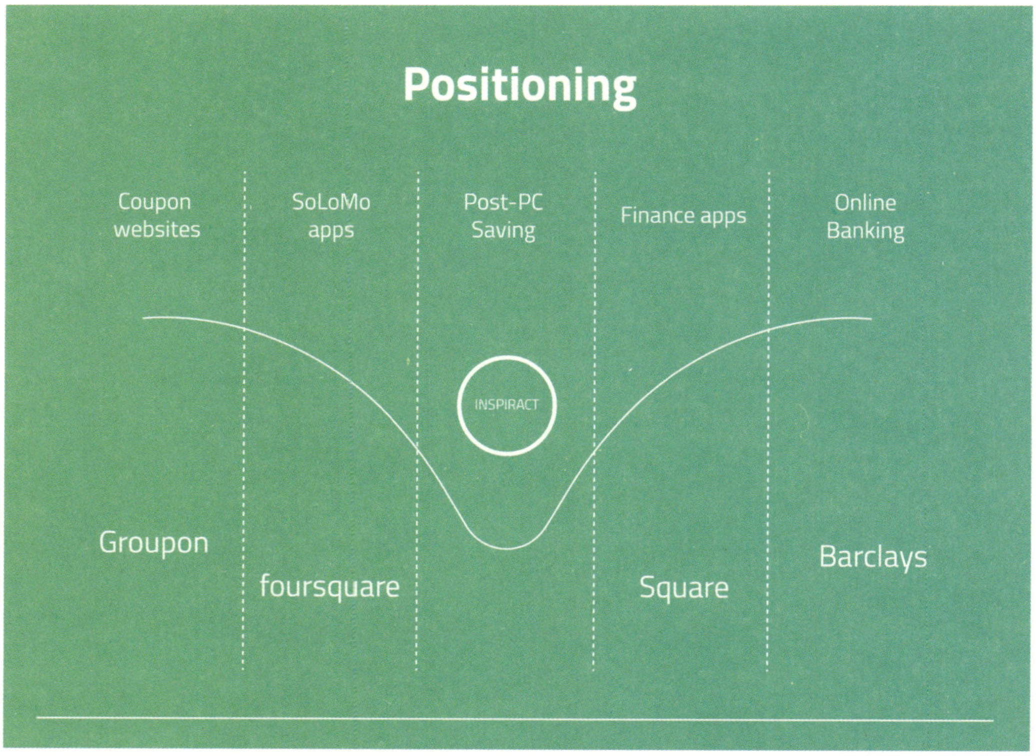

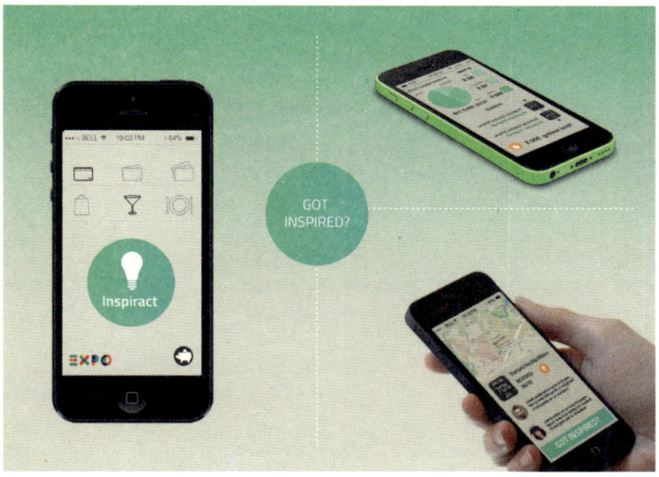

This project is a concept made during the workshop of H-Farm last 24 hours, with the collaboration of developers, designer and economists. We have created an application that monitors with the debit card Inspire of Intesa S. Paolo bank.
The app advice you with a comunity, about your interest and search the best offers.

TEAM
Graphic Project: Ludovica Saccenti
Marketing: Agostino Massaro, Angela Parrozzani, Alessandro Piccollo
Developer: Enrico Dall' Acqua, Diego Pizzocaro, Filippo Zannella

Mobile Bank App 1

- Completion Year: 2014
- Designer: Sinan Özdemir
- Web: www.sinanozdemir.com

- Work Introduction

He aimed responsive design for all digital device. This web page project can also be displayed in both desktop and mobile screens. Therefore, this design includes salient big graphics and detailed data for the information fancier. People can loan measurement in this page. Frankly, loan calculating is boring process for everyone but this design has imaginative and funny user experience.

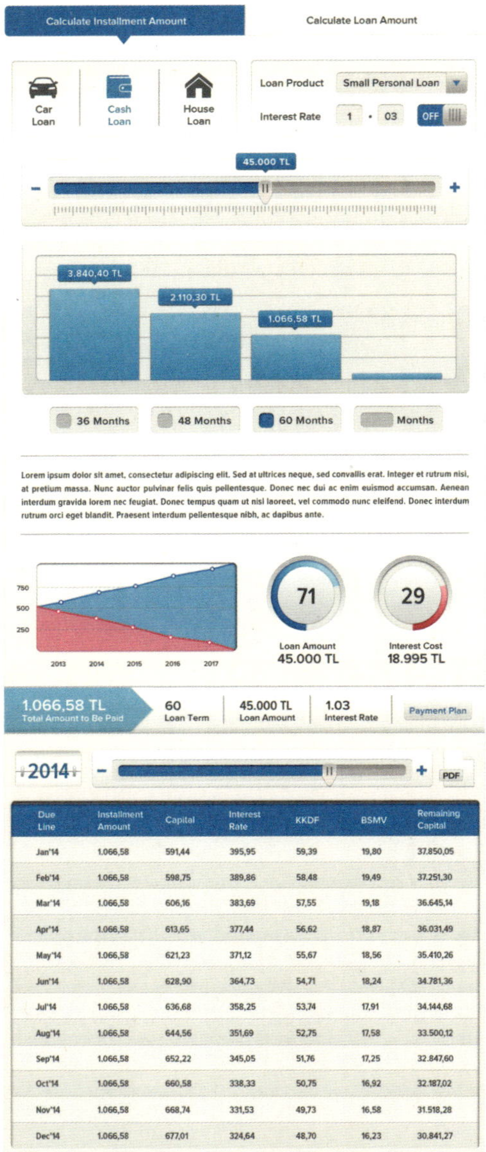

Mobile Bank App 2

- Completion Year: 2014
- Designer: Sinan Özdemir
- Web: www.sinanozdemir.com

- Work Introduction

Most people do not understand their bill of account. Financial statements are boring. The designer aim was to make understandable communication between the bank and people. Phone screens are small as is known to all and small screens. It is impractical to give detailed information. Therefore he translated writings to graphics. He used the advantages of visual memory and I aimed to create eye candy images in human mind.

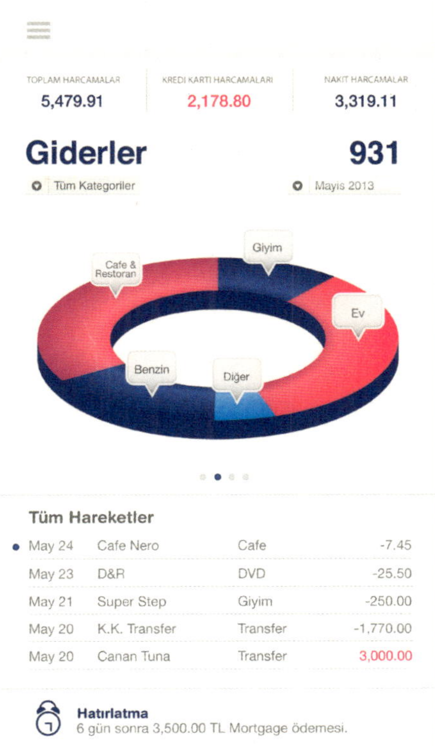

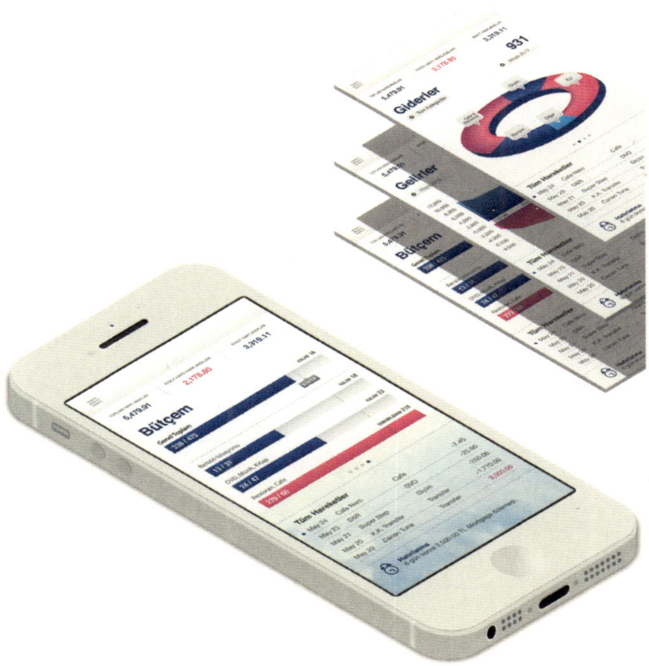

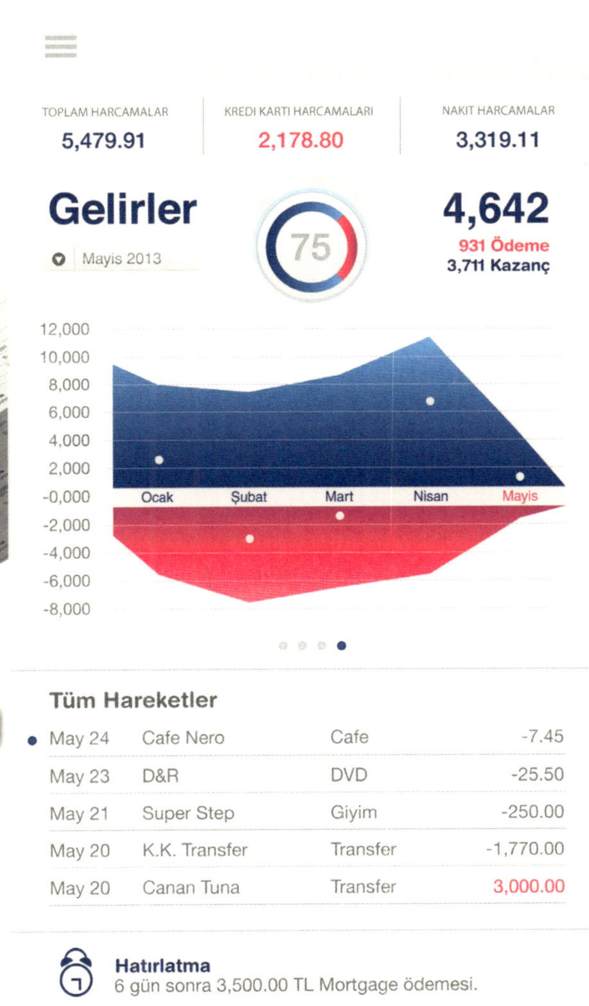

KYM Sahra Okullari

- Completion Year: 2014
- Designer: Musab BEN
- Client: Kimse Yok Mu
- Web: www.
  kymsahraokullari.com

The designer received several tasks like logo, concept, video, animation, posters, web design and presentation design. This way the charity that was going to be made for Africa have been presented with a single method. The designer also directed the animation to keep the clarity.

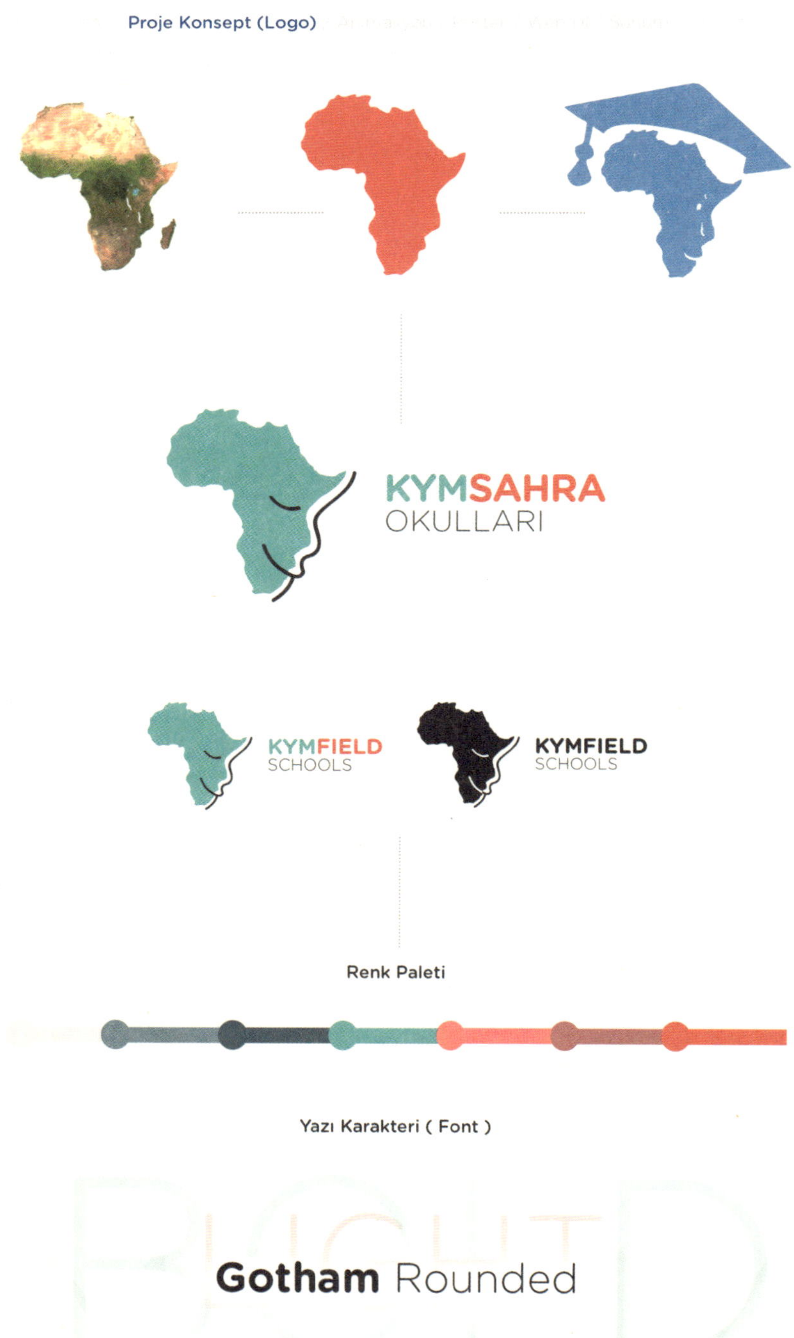

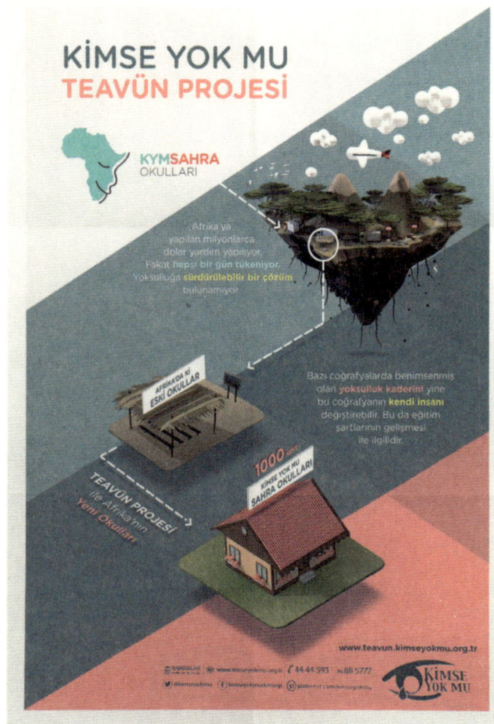

Poster

www.kymsahraokullari.com
KYMSAHRA OKULLARI
PROJE YARIŞMASI
S.S.S.
İSTATİSTİKLER
BAĞIŞ YAP
KYM KURUMSAL
KİMSE YOK MU SAHRA OKULLARI NEDİR?
AFRİKA
1,111,000,000 Nüfuslu, 54 Ülkeye sahip
dünyanın en büyük ve en fazla nüfus yoğunluğuna sahip ikinci büyük kıtasıdır.
Bir yer düşünün,
Doğal kaynaklar açısından dünyanın en zengin coğrafyalarından biri olmasına rağmen
Afrika dünyanın en gelişmemiş ve yoksul bölgelerinden biridir.
Salgın hastalıklar ve açlık ile mücadele eden,
Suya hasret kalan,
İç savaşların hüküm sürdüğü,
Çocukların okula gidemediği...
Kronik yoksulluğun yaşandığı Afrika ülkelerinde
okuma yazma oranı
%5-%23
arasında seyrediyor.
Birleşmiş Milletler Ekonomik ve Sosyal Konseyi (ECOSOC) danışman üyesi olan Kimse Yok Mu (KYM), sürdürebilir kalkınmanın eğitimli insanlar ile sağlanabileceğini savunmaktadır.
KYM
Eğitimli insanların yetişmesi için ise; temel eğitimin yaygınlaştırılması gerekliliğine inanmaktadır.
Sahra Okulları Projesi;
Çocukların temel haklarından biri olan eğitim hakkından yararlanmalarını sağlamak için ihtiyaç duydukları okulların Afrika'da inşa edilmesi ve yerel yönetimlere teslim edilmesi projesidir.
1.000 adet
okul inşası
100 m² kapalı alan
300 m² brüt alan

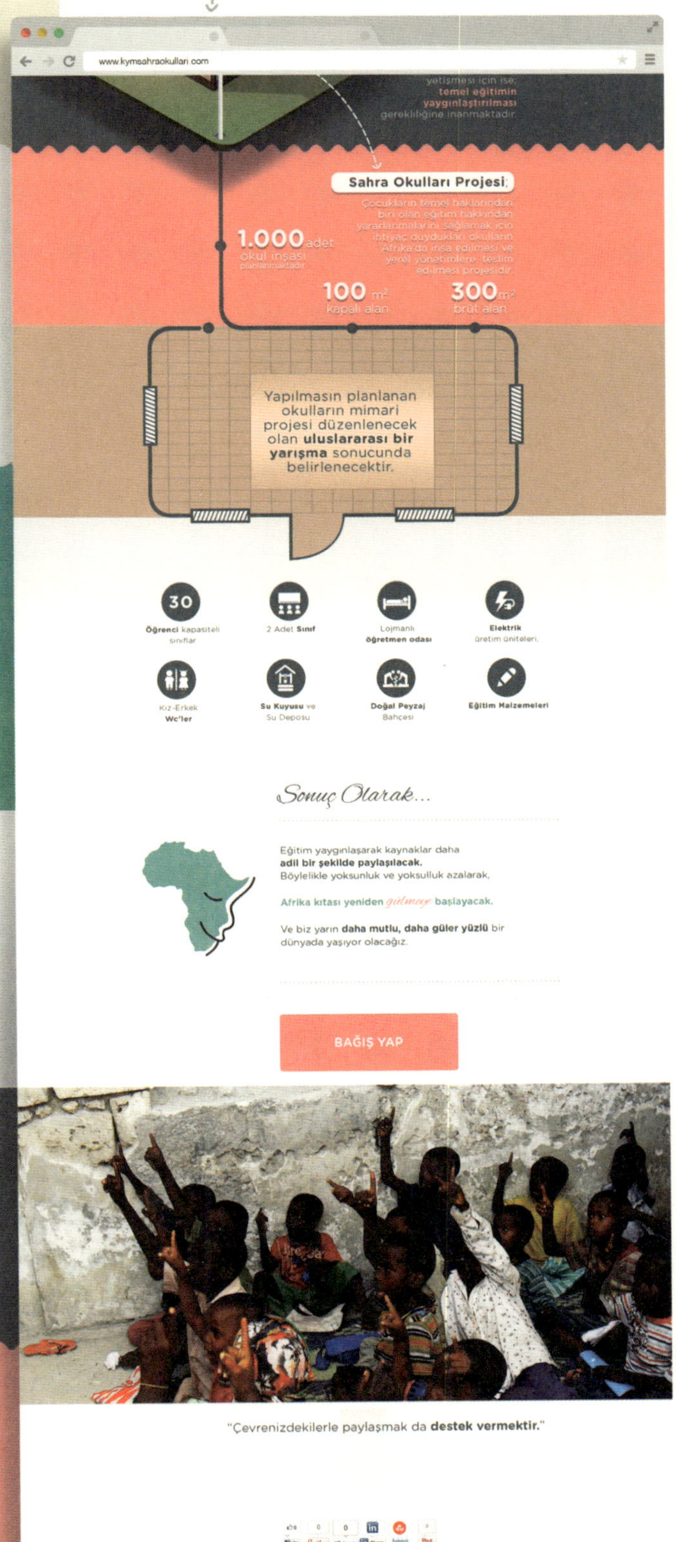
www.kymsahraokullari.com
Sahra Okulları Projesi;
1.000 adet
okul inşası
100 m² kapalı alan
300 m² brüt alan
Yapılması planlanan okulların mimari projesi düzenlenecek olan uluslararası bir yarışma sonucunda belirlenecektir.
30
Öğrenci kapasiteli sınıflar
2 Adet Sınıf
Lojmanlı öğretmen odası
Elektrik üretim üniteleri
Kız-Erkek We'ler
Su Kuyusu ve Su Deposu
Doğal Peyzaj Bahçesi
Eğitim Malzemeleri
Sonuç Olarak...
Eğitim yaygınlaşarak kaynaklar daha adil bir şekilde paylaşılacak.
Böylelikle yoksunluk ve yoksulluk azalarak,
Afrika kıtası yeniden gülmeye başlayacak.
Ve biz yarın daha mutlu, daha güler yüzlü bir dünyada yaşıyor olacağız.
BAĞIŞ YAP
"Çevrenizdekilerle paylaşmak da destek vermektir."

Keynote & Power Point

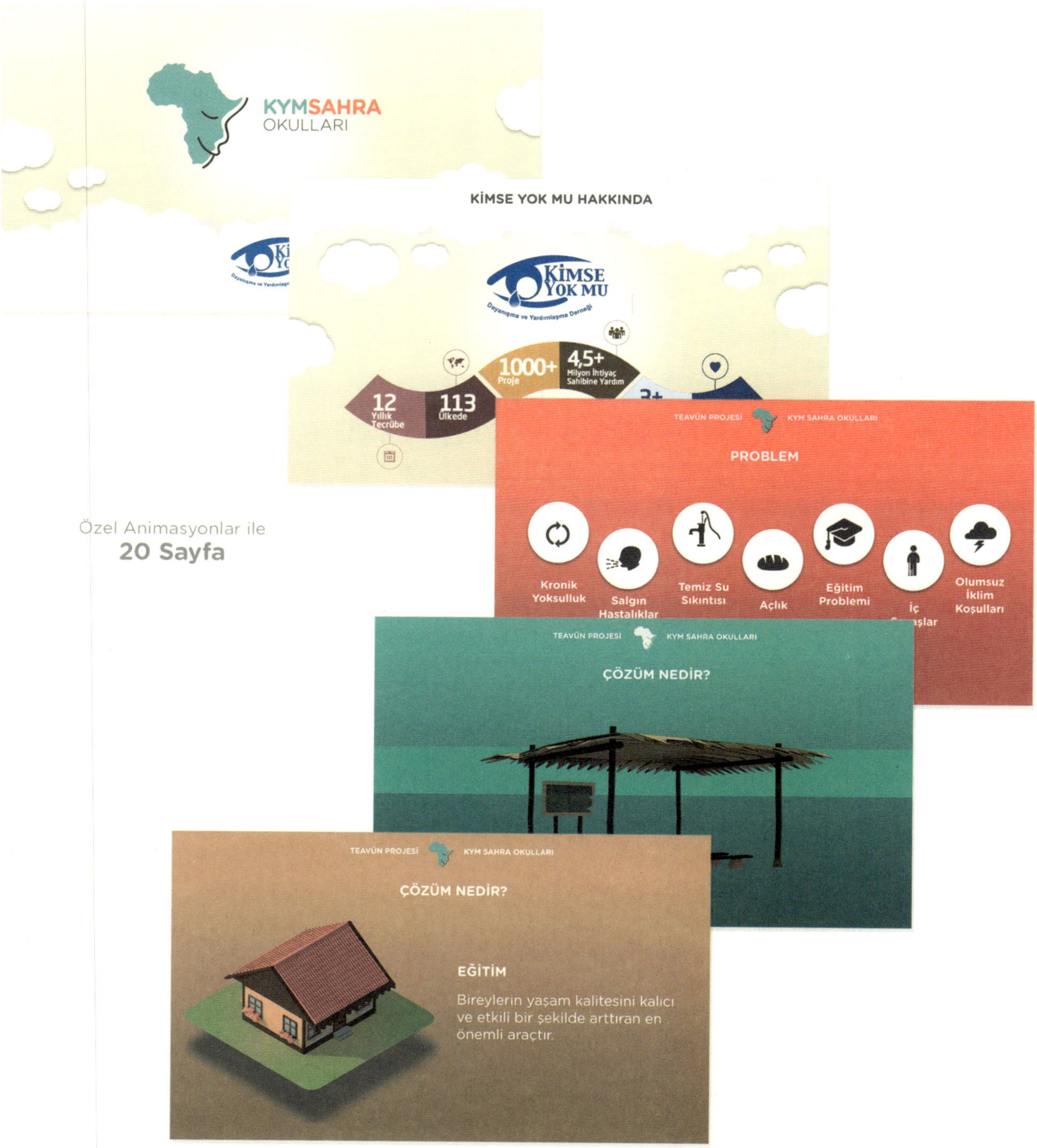

Özel Animasyonlar ile
20 Sayfa

Poppy Field

• Completion Year: 2014
• Designer: Valentina D'Efilippo
• Web: www.poppyfield.org

• Work Introduction

Poppy Field reflects on human life lost in war. To observe Remembrance Day and commemorate the Great War's Centenary, the project visualises the timing, involvement and death totals for individual wars since 1900.

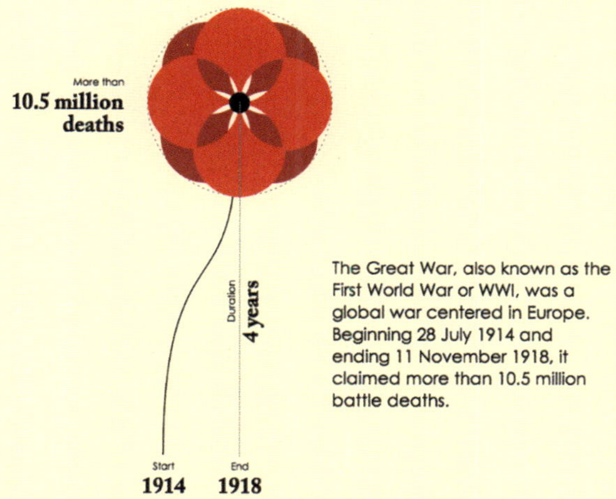

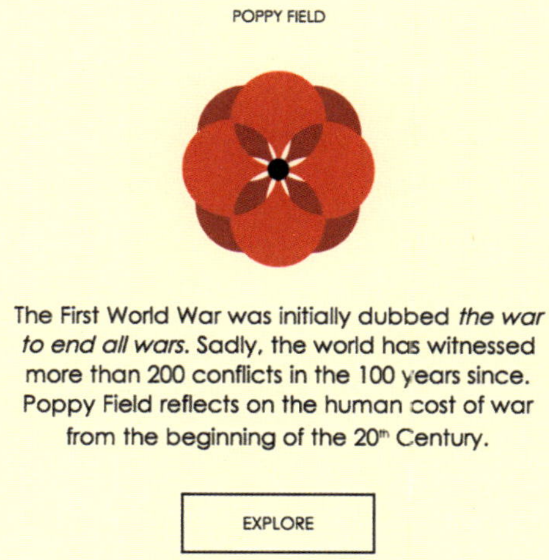

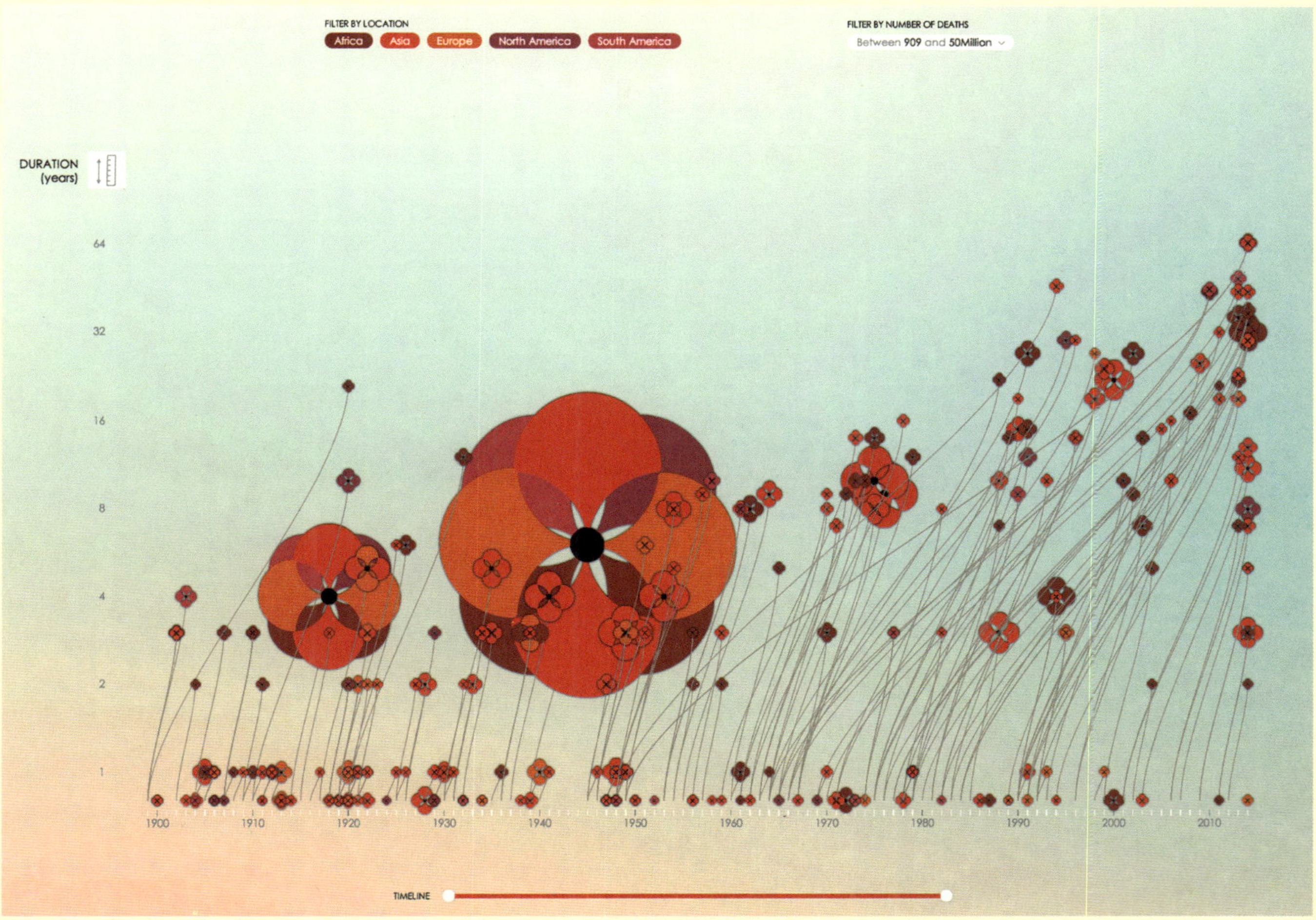

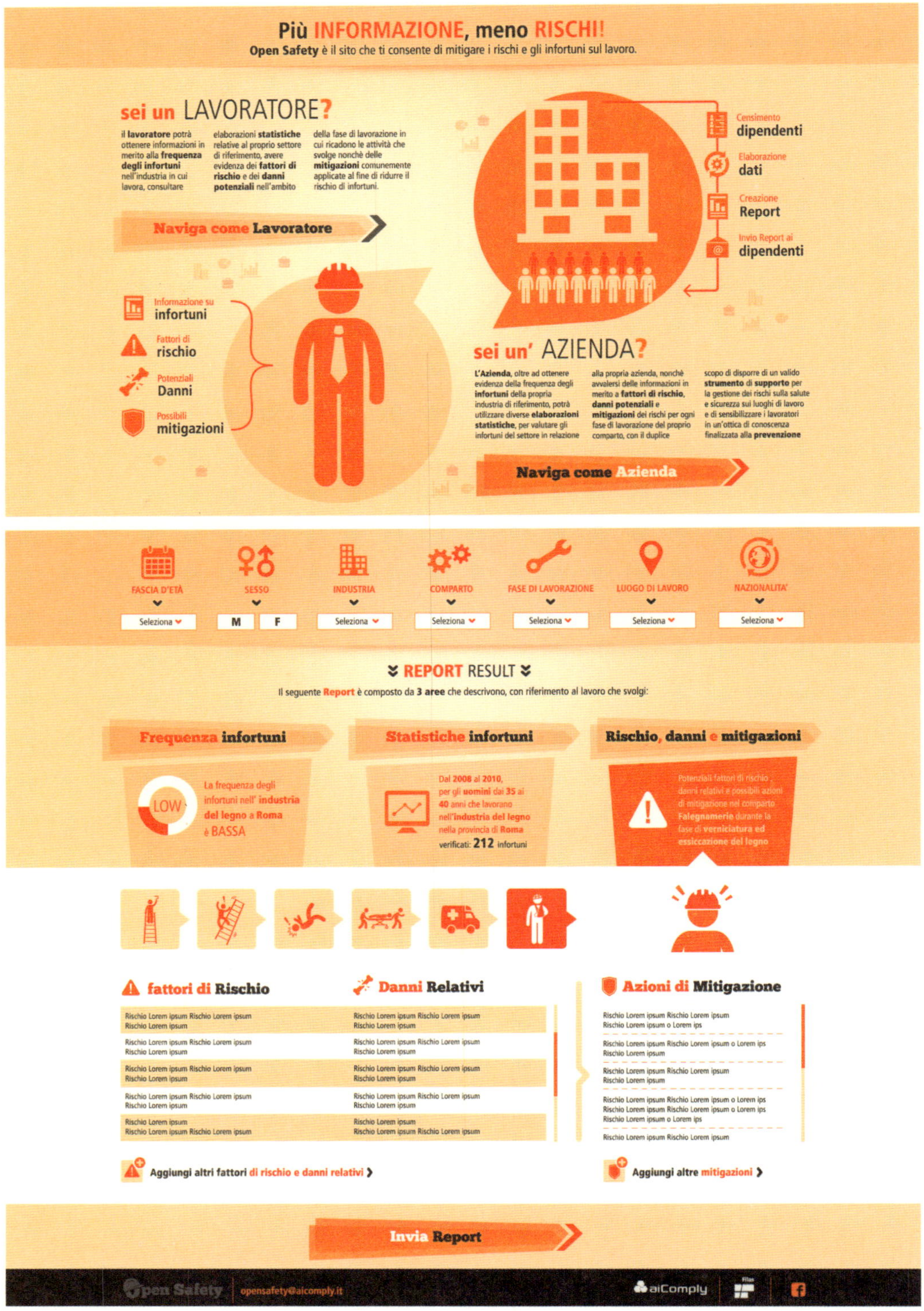

Open Safety

- Completion Year: 2014
- Designer: Sara Caruso
- Client: AiComply
- Web: www.opensafety.it

- Work Introduction

With OpenSafety you can obtain info on frequency of industrial accidents/accidents at work in any section and how to avoid them.

The Designer intended to guide the user through these important info with a graphic style based on intuitive and easy using infographic-system.

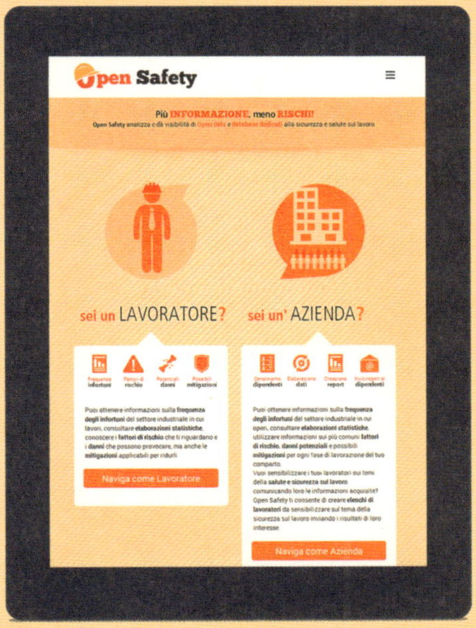
Open Safety
Più INFORMAZIONE, meno RISCHI!
sei un LAVORATORE?
sei un' AZIENDA?
Naviga come Lavoratore
Naviga come Azienda

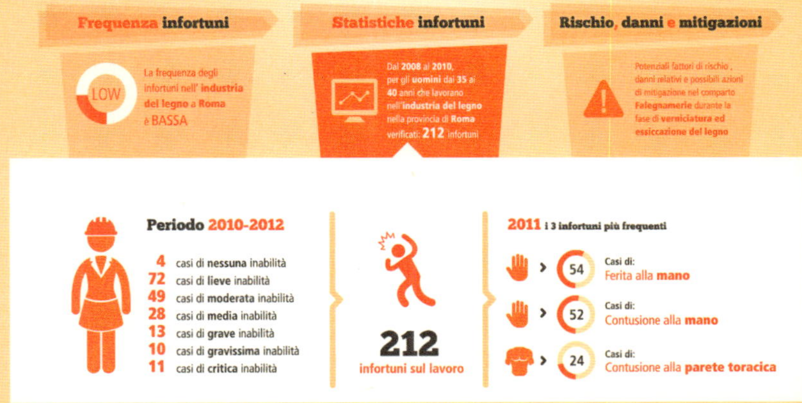
Frequenza infortuni
Statistiche infortuni
Rischio, danni e mitigazioni
LOW
La frequenza degli infortuni nell' industria del legno a Roma è BASSA
Dal 2008 al 2010, per gli uomini dai 35 ai 40 anni che lavorano nell'industria del legno nella provincia di Roma verificati: 212 infortuni
Potenziali fattori di rischio, danni relativi e possibili azioni di mitigazione nel comparto Falegnamerie durante la fase di verniciatura ed essiccazione del legno
Periodo 2010-2012
4 casi di nessuna inabilità
72 casi di lieve inabilità
49 casi di moderata inabilità
28 casi di media inabilità
13 casi di grave inabilità
10 casi di gravissima inabilità
11 casi di critica inabilità
212
infortuni sul lavoro
2011 i 3 infortuni più frequenti
54 Casi di: Ferita alla mano
52 Casi di: Contusione alla mano
24 Casi di: Contusione alla parete toracica

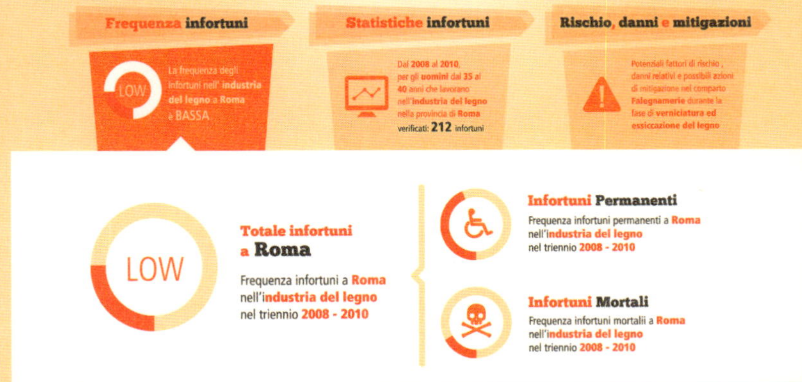
Frequenza infortuni
Statistiche infortuni
Rischio, danni e mitigazioni
LOW
Totale infortuni a Roma
Frequenza infortuni a Roma nell'industria del legno nel triennio 2008 - 2010
Infortuni Permanenti
Frequenza infortuni permanenti a Roma nell'industria del legno nel triennio 2008 - 2010
Infortuni Mortali
Frequenza infortuni mortali a Roma nell'industria del legno nel triennio 2008 - 2010

Open Safety
HOME
LAVORATORE
AZIENDA
aiComply
sei un Lavoratore?
sei un' Azienda?
Lorem ipsum...
Informazione su infortuni
Fattori di rischio
Potenziali Danni
Possibili mitigazioni
Naviga come LAVORATORE
Naviga come AZIENDA
Lorem Ipsum Lorem
Lorem ipsum dolor sit amet, consectetur adipiscing elit. Morbi non hendrerit urna, at lobortis lectus.
opensafety@aicomply.it

RISE: a Voluntourism Brand Identity Campaign

- Completion Year: 2013
- Designer: Andrea Cerrilla
- Web: http://www.andreacerrilla.com/#rise

- Work Introduction

This infographic is part of a broad-based identity campaign whose goal is to provide a fresh approach on how adventure service can achieve sustainable development in fair trade communities across the world, and bring about change through service. Working off a sustainable model, the volunteer's involvement is economically viable, environmentally conscientious, culturally respectful and politically acceptable.

Brazil World Cup 2014: Who's Your Pick?

- Completion Year: 2014
- Designer: Boris Benko
- Client: Infographic Box IDS
- Web: www.infographicbox.com/infographics/worldcup2014/

- Work Introduction

The infographic brings some predictions related to Brazil World Cup 2014 favorites. It was used as a promotional piece for Infographic Box IDS design service.

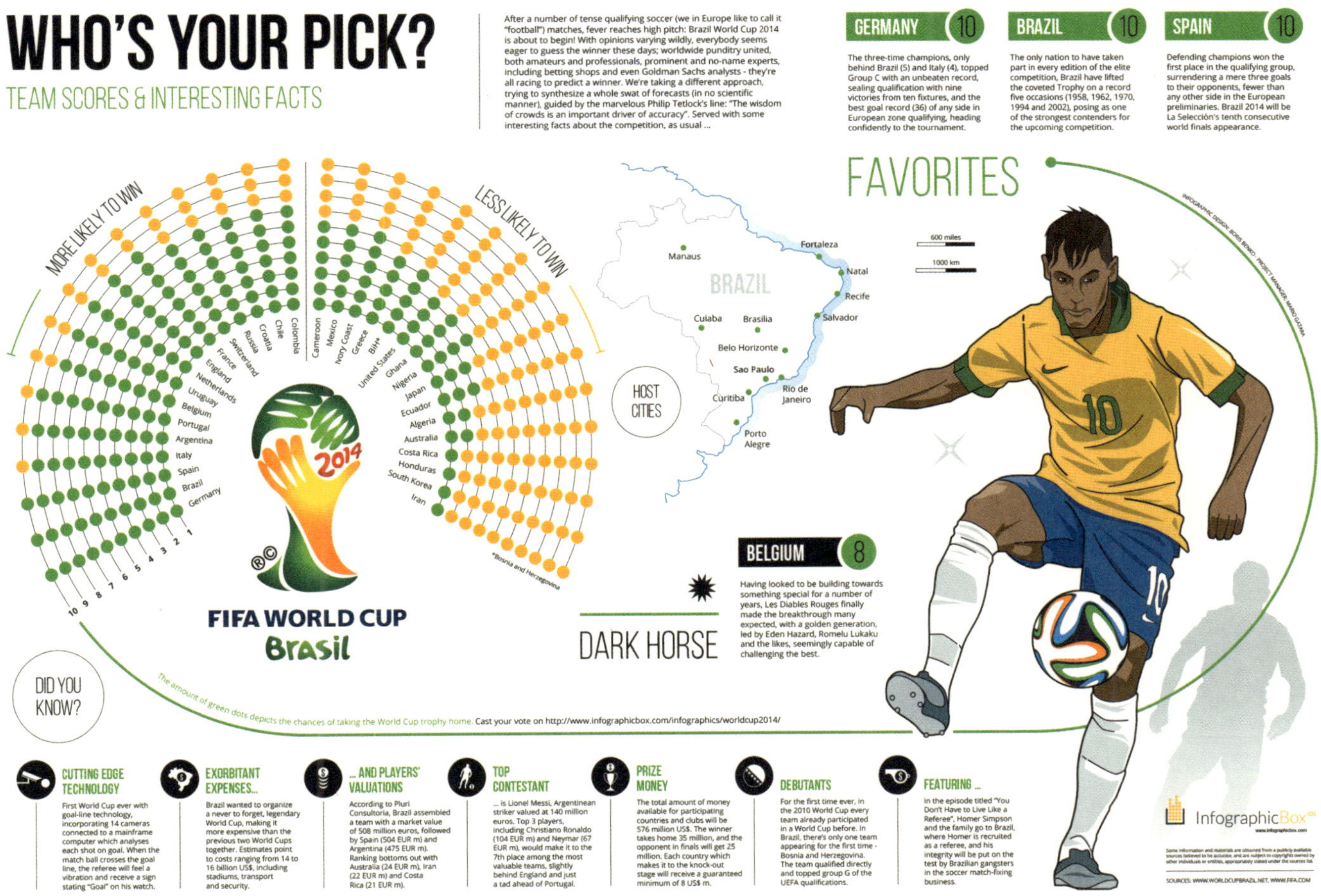

INDEX

Jessica Hankinson
hello@studiotwenty7design.com
P140

Jillian Turbessi
look@jillianplz.com
P214

Jo Lavie
jolavie1702@gmail.com
P156

KARTHIKEYAN R
Karthir2day@gmail.com
P36

Karyll Catubig
kjcatz@gmail.com
P130

Katie Coughlan
kcoughlan44@gmail.com
P234

Kavya Singh Barthwal
kavyasingh.973@gmail.com
P131

Kelly Loh
kelly.naru@gmail.com
P236

Khyati Trehan
Trehan.khyati@gmail.com
P241

Longjuan Liang
lianglu@mail.uc.edu
P129

Luciana Flora
lucianaflora7@gmail.com
P240

Ludovica Saccenti
ludovica.saccenti@gmail.com
P242

Manuel Bortoletti
manuel.bortoletti@gmail.com
P126

Manuel Reitz
reitzmanuel@googlemail.com
P134

Marcus Marritt
marcusmarritt@gmail.com
P162

Martin Panchaud
martin3gs@me.com
P118

Martina Elisa Cecchi
martinaelisa.cecchi@gmail.com
P112, P138, P164

Meicheng Wang
meichengwang3@gmail.com
P166

Musab BEN
musabben@gmail.com
P246

Nishad Nadeeke Rupasinghe
nishad.nadeeke@gmail.com
P68

Olesya Tkach
o.g.tkach@yandex.ru
P139, P168, P170, P172

Ottavia Alieri
ottaviaalieri@gmail.com
P174

Rayz Ong
info@lemongraphic.sg
P70, P120, P124, P136, P142, P144

Ruslan Valikhanov
barikdrum@gmail.com
P57, P58

Ruth Fogden
ruthfogden@gmail.com
P192

Sara Caruso
saracaruso@hotmail.com
P250

Sergio Piergallini
sergio@seltzer.it
P125, P158

Sherpa
info@sherpa-design.de
P200

Shonali Ahooja
sahooja@mica.edu
P154

Sinan Özdemir
sinanozdemir@gmail.com
P208, P244, P245,

Sofia Girelli
sofiasofter.girelli@gmail.com
P116, P217

Stefan Große Halbuer
info@geistreiz.com
P72

Stefan Weyer
schneller@buntebrause.de
P82

Stinne Marie Wilhelmsen
stinnewilhelmsen@gmail.com
P76

Thomas Montorfano
thomas.montorfano@gmail.com
P99

Toma Gogolazde
tomagogoladze@gmail.com
P148

Tushar Ghei
tushar.ghei@hotmail.com
P228

Uve Portillo
uveportillo@gmail.com
P46, P48

Valentina D'Efilippo
hello@valentinadefilippo.co.uk
P80, P249

Valerio Pellegrini
lapaiarda@hotmail.it
P196, P197, P198

Yaya Aaronsohn
yayanetter@gmail.com
P204, P224, P230, P232

Yofany Susanto
yofanysusanto@gmail.com
P146

Published in Australia in 2015 by
The Images Publishing Group Pty Ltd
ABN 89 059 734 431
6 Bastow Place, Mulgrave, Victoria 3170, Australia
Tel: +61 3 9561 5544 Fax: +61 3 9561 4860
books@imagespublishing.com
www.imagespublishing.com

The Images Publishing Group Reference Number: 1190

National Library of Australia Cataloguing-in-Publication entry:

Title: Infographic Design in Media / Wang Kai (ed.).
ISBN: 9781864706345 (hardback)
Subjects: Graphic arts.
Computer graphics.

Dewey Number: 006.6

Coordinated and edited by Images Publishing, Shanghai office.

Printed by Toppan Leefung Printing (Shenzhen) Co. Ltd